Psychological Research Methods

Psychological Research Methods

A CONCEPTUAL APPROACH

HAROLD O. KIESS
DOUGLAS W. BLOOMQUIST

Framingham State College

ALLYN AND BACON, INC.

Boston • London • Sydney • Toronto

Library of Congress Cataloging in Publication Data

Kiess, Harold O., 1940–
    Psychological research methods.

    Bibliography: p.
    Includes index.
    1. Psychology—Research.   I. Bloomquist, Douglas W.,
1941–   .   II. Title.
BF76.5.K45 1985   150'.72   84-24399
ISBN 0–205–08381–1

Managing Editor: Bill Barke
Production Coordinator: Helyn Pultz
Production Services: Bywater Production Services
Cover Coordinator: Christy Rosso
Cover Designer: Dorothy Cullinan

Printed in the United States of America

10 9 8 7 6 5 4 3 2 1   89 88 87 86 85

Dedicated with love to

Sandy, Kimberley, and Jeffrey

Paula and Kathryn

———————————————————————

Contents

Preface

We were prompted to write this text because, like other authors, we found available texts on research methodology in psychology did not quite meet our teaching needs. Specifically, we have observed that students studying research methodology often have difficulty integrating and using fundamental concepts of psychological research. We think the reason is that the concepts frequently are presented free of the context in which they are used. Therefore, we illustrate the major concepts within a framework in which we discuss, in some detail, actual examples of published research. We want students to appreciate that scientific research reflects the synthesis of myriad facts and skills. To this end, we reprint a journal report of an experiment in Chapter 1 and refer to this research repeatedly in the beginning chapters to illustrate many of the concepts discussed. For several reasons we deliberately choose to present an experiment that deals with a problem in counseling psychology, an area that is not typically regarded as within the scope of experimental psychology proper. We recognize, however, that many students major in psychology because they want to help people. Consequently, they are inclined to question the relevance of research methodology to achieving that goal. We think the article selected from the *Journal of Counseling Psychology* will help students appreciate that many psychologists who help people in applied settings also conduct research and that this area of psychology, too, stands upon a research foundation.

Similarly, all too often the principles of research design are taught independently of statistical analysis. In many instances statistics used for analyzing data are presented simply as a tool and are introduced in a text before their need and value can be appreciated by students. It is important for students to understand that experimental designs are not independent of the statistical analyses required for making decisions about research hypotheses and drawing conclusions; knowledge of statistical techniques, separate from the procedures used to obtain data, seems to limit understanding of research procedures. To aid the student in developing firm understanding of research methodology and statistical analysis, we emphasize how statistical techniques are related to the research designs with which they are used. Moreover, we present detailed conceptual explanations of descriptive and inferential statistical techniques so students will not be overwhelmed with formulas. Yet, where appropriate, we also present definitional formulas to promote understanding of the statistical concepts. Alternative computational formulas for the statistics are also presented and illustrated so students can more readily apply statistical analysis to their own research or homework problems.

We would appreciate any comments or suggestions that you have on this text. Please write to us at the Department of Psychology, Framingham State College, Box 2000, Framingham, Massachusetts 01701.

ACKNOWLEDGMENTS

Numerous individuals contributed in many ways to this text. First, we are most grateful to our editor, Bill Barke, whose confidence in two first-time authors since the beginning stages of this project provided us with sustaining encouragement; he also supported us most effectively through many delays and difficulties (usually by simply leaving us alone). The text could not have taken its present form without the willing and gracious cooperation of Professors Patricia R. McCarthy (Southern Illinois University) and Nancy E. Betz (Ohio State University). In the highest traditions of science they shared all of the facets of their research with both us, and you, the reader. Thanks to one-semester sabbatical leaves from Framingham State College, each of us was able to work on early drafts of the manuscript without the usual office, laboratory, and classroom distractions. Framingham State College also generously provided us with access to computer and word-processing facilities; we are especially thankful to Paul S. Ferguson and Susan Hovencamp for their cooperation and patience in assisting us in using these facilities. (How, we wonder, did people write books before word processors were invented?) Adele Downing, Donna Bassett, Maureen McGrath, Sandra Kiess, Mona Areano, Cheryl Houle, Sharon Rousseau, and Donald Hitchings cheerfully (more or less) typed many pages of various drafts of the manuscript.

The organization and content of this text were shaped considerably by constructive suggestions provided by reviewers. Lambert Deckers (Ball State University), who carefully reviewed all chapters of the manuscript, provided extensive comments and many helpful suggestions for clarifying and expanding our presentation of concepts. Robert M. Stern (The Pennsylvania State University), William F. McDaniel (Georgia College), and two anonymous reviewers also contributed many thoughtful suggestions. Our colleague, Barrie Westerman, used a draft of the manuscript as a text; he and his students were most vigilant in catching some typographical and computational errors we missed. A number of individuals at Allyn and Bacon also deserve our thanks. Eileen McNulty and Lauren Whittaker guided us caringly through the maze of manuscript development. Allan Workman helped to shape our writing and extricated us from many pitfalls awaiting novice authors. At the late stages of preparation our writing was carefully edited and refined by the staff at Bywater Production Services, especially David W. Lynch and Winifred Hodges. Jane Shulman, Judy Shaw, and Linda Knowles-Dickinson helped to put the finishing touches on the book and marketing materials. And CRC Press, Inc. has been very cooperative and gracious in granting permission for us to use many of the statistical tables found in the Appendix.

Finally, we are indebted to our families, who have been most tolerant and understanding of peculiar behaviors, such as apparent obsessions with paper, pens, and typewriters, which evidently afflict authors.

To the Student

We hope you will find this text a conceptually clear and intellectually stimulating introduction to psychological research methods. We believe that understanding research methodology will provide you with skills and attitudes that you will find useful in many aspects of your life. Specifically, after completing your study of this text you should:

- Be able to read many published reports of research with understanding of the methodology employed.
- Recognize that advances in the social sciences come not from isolated studies, but from research done with awareness of previous work on the problem area.
- Possess healthy skepticism, bring it to bear on established dogma, and realize that for most dogmatic explanations of behavior there are likely to be plausible rival explanations.
- Realize that your observations are directed by your conceptualizations of the world.
- Be able to employ quantitative thinking in dealing with psychological problems and thought.
- Be able to carry out careful and objective measurements of behavior.
- Realize that for all types of behavior many conflicting opinions and explanations may be offered, but data should be respected as a final arbiter on which of these are to be accepted or rejected.
- Understand that scientific knowledge of behavior is essentially probabilistic and uncertain.
- Understand that much of scientific explanation is a process of inference.
- Be able to communicate scientific information effectively.

Mastering the concepts presented in this text and acquiring methodological skills will not be easy. We believe you will better understand the concepts if you try to relate them to published articles of research. Moreover, we urge you to take advantage of opportunities to conduct your own experiments. Experience with evaluating research articles and doing experiments should make the concepts presented throughout the text more meaningful and, therefore, should help consolidate your understanding of research methodology in psychology.

Psychological Research Methods

1

In this chapter we discuss why it is important to understand the methodology of psychological research. Topics include:

- The skeptical and empirical bases of psychological knowledge
- The excitement of creative research and who contributes to psychological knowledge
- The importance of ethics in research and the ethical principles followed when conducting research
- An example of published research on the effects of two types of statements by counselors on ratings of the counselors' expertness, attractiveness, and trustworthiness

WHY YOU NEED TO KNOW THIS MATERIAL

The facts of psychology constantly change. A student of psychology should appreciate how important methodology is in producing psychological knowledge and how valuable it is to understand the methodology as a consumer of psychological research.

Why Understand Psychological Research Methods

To many, psychology is the scientific method applied to the area of behavior rather than the approximate findings that psychologists have so far produced. Rather than any substantive theory, psychology's methodology gives shape to the field.

James A. Kulik (1973, p. 39)

What is the most important contribution psychology has made to our understanding of behavior? Asked such a question, a fair number of professional psychologists would answer something similar to "its methodology; its methodology for asking questions and obtaining information about human behavior." Indeed, curricula in most undergraduate psychology departments implicitly reflect, at least to a modest extent, this valuation of the methodology of psychology. Students typically are required to take a statistics course and a research methods–experimental psychology course. For many students, however, the relevance of such courses to psychology or to career or life goals is often hazily or sporadically apparent. Professors are often told, "I want to work with people. Why do I have to learn about research methods?" This doubt is understandable, and the question is too important to dismiss cavalierly. In this chapter we provide some answers that demonstrate how important it is to understand the methodology of scientific psychology.

A SKEPTICAL VIEW OF KNOWLEDGE

Each day, newspapers, news magazines, weekly tabloids, and books for popular consumption report a variety of "facts" about human behavior. Most often, these reports convey the impression that the particular problem has been settled and then cite research at a university or some "expert" in the area to substantiate the conclusions drawn. For example:

> *True or False?*   The better opinion you have of yourself, the less you care about "what other people think."
>   *True.* Studies at Poland's Institute of Psychology, Mickiewicz University, show that people who are overly concerned with "what people think" (how others evaluate them) are characterized by "low levels of self-evaluation and self-acceptance, feelings of inadequacy and sensitivity and anxiety concerning the revelation of inadequacy." This is ascribed to a high, negative discrepancy between perceptions of the ideal self (the kind of person one feels one should be) and the actual or real self. (From *Family Weekly,* October 11, 1981. Copyright © 1981, *Family Weekly.* Used by permission.)

In various other popular sources recently, we have found articles in which "authorities" are cited as stating that teaching a child to read too early can harm his or her intellectual growth; the best way to raise children so that they won't be lured into so-called cult religious groups is by giving them both a strong dose of Christian teaching and a spanking for any wrongdoing; changing your handwriting or your clothing styles can change your personality; females with blonde hair are more fickle than brunettes; a man's preference for pets reveals the type of husband he will be; rock music leads to open sexual behavior among youths; astrology really works, and the "scientific" tests demonstrating this truth have had their "integrity and good faith" guaranteed by a psychologist; personality traits can be predicted from facial wrinkles; and the worst natural mother is considerably better for a child than is a day-care "mother."

Psychologists trained in research methodology approach such statements quite skeptically. One who is skeptical believes that knowledge in a discipline is uncertain, and in a positive sense exhibits a questioning or doubting attitude toward knowledge. A skeptical approach to knowledge of behavior is inherent in the study of psychological research methods. Psychologists realize that findings from their research are most often conflicting, tentative, and uncertain. As we will explain later, the scientific method applied to psychological research does not allow one to "prove" anything; conclusions from scientific research are always open to alternative explanations. There simply are no absolute right or wrong answers to questions of human behavior; there is always need to be tolerant of uncertainty in our explanations (Bronowski, 1973; Marx, 1976a). Anyone aspiring to understand psychological phenomena should not fail to notice this important characteristic of the nature of scientific explanations of behavior. As Selltiz, Wrightsman, and Cook (1976), have stated, "Scientific knowledge is knowledge under conditions of uncertainty. Other arenas of human experience should be investigated by those who desire knowledge with absolute certainty" (pp. 47–48).

Testimonials and "guarantees" of the validity of a finding by so-called experts are antithetical to the scientific approach. At one time in their advertisements, manufacturers demonstrated the efficacy of their products by listing prominent and presumably knowledgeable endorsers, as illustrated in Figure 1–1. But, as you

TRADE MARK.
Registered Nov. 24, 1896.

OXYDONOR APPLIED.

Absorb Oxygen and Live. . .

OXYDONOR builds up the system by natural means. It causes the absorption of oxygen through the pores of the skin and membranes, thus strengthening the entire system and making it naturally healthy. Oxydonor introduces the vital energy which supports the highest physical effort.

We appeal to those who have chronic sickness, to all who are pronounced incurable, and who are discouraged with drugs and threatened with operations. The record of cures made by Oxydonor is doubly wonderful when you consider that many of them were made after the cases had been given up to die by the best physicians in this country and Europe. It will cause the cure of any disease at any reasonable stage, and is invaluable in all summer complaints,

HAY FEVER,
ASTHMA,

Rheumatism, Sciatica, Neuralgia, Catarrh, La Grippe, Pneumonia, Constipation, Indigestion, Dyspepsia, Bright's Disease, all Nervous Troubles, Typhoid and all Fevers, and all Diseases of Children.

Our claims are reinforced by letters from all parts of the world.

Our 56-page book, containing prices and many grateful reports, will be mailed free.

OXYDONOR
is endorsed by

Mr. W. W. Manning, Marquette, Mich.; **Mr. Geo. Huntington**, of Huntington & Clark, Detroit, Mich.; **Mr. Geo. P. Goodale**, Vice-Pres't Detroit Free Press Co., Detroit, Mich.; **Mr. Franklin Hubbard**, Mgr. Toledo Board of Education, Toledo, Ohio; **Mr. Washington Midler**, Gen'l Agt. Pullman Palace Car Co., Chicago, Ill.; **Mr. A. F. Horst**, Tacoma, Wash.; **Rev. Henry A. Newell**, PastorBethany Presbyterian Church, Los Angeles, Cal.; **Hon. Lafe Young**, Des Moines, Iowa; **Mr. Geo. F. Nixon**, 106 Wall Street, New York; **Mrs. O. W. Ruggles**, 33 Rosslyn Place, Chicago, Ill.; **Mrs. James Leonard**, 162 Ash Street, Detroit, Mich.; **Mrs. Elfonzo Youngs**, Washington, D. C., and many others.

Ask your druggist for OXYDONOR,
or send direct to us.

DR. H. SANCHE & CO.
61 Fifth St., Detroit, Mich.
261 Fifth Avenue, New York City.
57 State St., Chicago, Ill.
CANADA:
2268 St. Catherine St., Montreal, Quebec.

Beware of Fraudulent Imitations.

An advertisement that appeared in The Cosmopolitan, *September 1901. Notice the listing of prominent endorsers of a product with dubious value.*

FIGURE 1–1

are aware, such practices are no longer an acceptable manner of demonstrating a product's effectiveness; rather, the evidence must come from well-done scientific research. In psychology, the product is knowledge of behavior, but the rules are the same: testimonials are unacceptable to the psychologist as a source of evidence for a belief.

AN EMPIRICAL BASE OF KNOWLEDGE

If testimonials are not an acceptable source for establishing knowledge about behavior, then what is? For the psychologist, the source is observable evidence relevant to the statement about behavior that is being made. The approach followed by psychologists is to pose testable questions and then to follow specific rules to obtain observable evidence, which scientists prefer to call empirical evidence, from which an answer to the question is derived. The methods of psychology demand that evidence be supplied from which the conclusions are to be drawn and that procedures for gaining that evidence be clearly and publicly stated.

Is it true that the worst natural mother is considerably better for a child than a day-care mother is? No doubt one could find presumed experts and perhaps nonexperts who would be willing to endorse either side of this statement. A psychologist's approach is to put the statement to empirical test, comparing children cared for by their natural mothers to children cared for in day-care settings. But the test will not generate absolute answers to questions about differences, if any, in the children. There are simply too many associated differences between the children to arrive at definitive answers about the effects of day care. In many instances, children in and out of day care will differ in such characteristics as socioeconomic status, ethnic and racial background, and cohesiveness and intactness of the family. Further, day-care facilities vary widely in quality. Therefore, a psychologist will arrive at very tentative conclusions, as illustrated by this statement:

> The absence of demonstrated consistent effects in the studies done so far does not warrant the sweeping conclusion that nonmaternal care is not harmful to young children. The *evidence* [italics added] does permit the more cautious conclusion that high-quality nonmaternal care has not been found to have negative effects on the development of preschool children. Further study of the variables that mediate the specific effects of various care arrangements clearly is called for. (Etaugh, 1980, p. 316.)

This view of psychological knowledge is perhaps unsettling, because it means that you should learn to view the so-called facts of behavior that are presented in textbooks and reported elsewhere for public consumption with a healthy dose of skepticism. It suggests that you should learn to develop tolerance for ambiguity and not look for cut-and-dried, black-and-white, definitive answers to questions. All but the most trivial questions about behavior, perhaps, usually invite answers in shades of gray.

At first, this qualification may seem to you to be a failure of psychological research methods rather than psychology's greatest achievement. But if you stop and think for a moment, you may see the virtues of an approach to knowledge which is skeptical, questioning, empirical, and which recognizes no absolute truths. With such an approach, one will challenge a dogmatic belief and put it to empirical test. Therefore, one will dispute absolute, simplistic, sometimes fanatical solutions to the complex problems of human life.

EXCITEMENT OF RESEARCH

One who understands research methodology possesses enduring skills useful in many settings and situations. But even more usefully, knowledge of research methodology opens the opportunity for conducting original research. It is difficult to convey in words the intellectual excitement of the research process. It is, in a sense, the supreme opportunity for creative work in psychology. To ask a question for which the answer is not known, to create a situation in which the answer may be obtained, to ascertain what the answer means for the understanding of human behavior, and to ask what new questions the answer provokes—these are imposing challenges to the intellect. As Dethier (1962) has stated, "A properly conducted experiment is a beautiful thing. It is an adventure, an expedition, a conquest" (p. 18). Frequently, students who initially approach research with trepidation discover that it opens a whole new intellectual vista for them. With good fortune your study of psychological research methods will lead you to success in this adventure.

A CONSUMER OF RESEARCH

Everyone who reads newspapers and magazines is a consumer of psychological research. Furthermore, as a student of psychology you will have occasion to read professional journals in psychology and related disciplines. It is evident, we think, that one must understand the basic concepts of research methodology in order to read, understand, and evaluate written reports of research using that methodology. One of the major goals in studying research methods, then, is to develop the *analytical thinking* skills that will enable you to *critically evaluate* research conducted by others. You will be able to make a careful, detailed evaluation of the research so that you understand its strengths and weaknesses. And, in making this critical evaluation, you will come to see the importance of data collected by the social scientist as the basis for arriving at conclusions about the nature of behavior.

A reader of psychological literature who does not have basic understanding of research methodology is, functionally at least, psychologically illiterate. He or she is likely to be intimidated by a report that appears in print in a journal or newspaper, and therefore is vulnerable to being intellectually seduced by the authors of inadequate research. We view an understanding of scientific methodology as a means of overcoming this kind of handicap. The ability to think clearly and critically, to approach problems analytically and skeptically, is a key to intellectual liberation.

WHO DOES PSYCHOLOGICAL RESEARCH?

Research in psychology is rarely conducted by psychologists who devote full time to their research activities. So-called academic psychologists are responsible for most of the published research. These psychologists are employed in colleges or universities, and they engage in teaching, counseling, testing, consulting, and other professional activities in addition to research. Although a few government laboratories and some large universities have full-time research scientists, the bulk of psychological research is not conducted by a cadre of scientists who devote all their professional activity to research.

One of the authors is acquainted with a well-known psychologist who argues that if the United States or any other government were truly interested in research, then it would release scientists from other responsibilities. They would be given adequate funds and provided with a cave somewhere in the woods where they could dwell after work and where all the needs of flesh and spirit would be met without the everyday obligations faced by most people. To the best of our knowledge, however, such facilities are not provided, and scientists must often squeeze in their research around other responsibilities.

Research is often a collaborative effort. You will find that many published research reports have two or more authors. Often the first author is a psychologist who may have conceived and planned the research, and who assumed a major role in writing the article. Frequently, however, the coauthors are graduate or undergraduate students working under the psychologist's supervision, who thereby receive practical training in research. Typically, the nitty-gritty research activity—the actual conduct of an experiment—is done by students who administer the experimental procedure and record the data obtained from the participants.

There are no professional restrictions specifying who is eligible to conduct or publish psychological research. Some of the research presented at conferences or published in journals represents work mainly conceived, conducted, and written by undergraduate students. Such research may have been performed in an experimental psychology course, pursued in an independent study, or undertaken as a project for an undergraduate honors thesis. Therefore, undergraduate students as well as graduate students, contribute to the research literature in psychology.

The research that is published varies widely in scope and quality. The articles may describe one experiment conducted for an undergraduate course, thesis work performed by graduate students in master's or doctoral degree programs, or the results of continuing and funded research for problems investigated by psychologists. There are many psychological journals, and therefore numerous publication outlets for the variety of research that is done.

ETHICAL PRINCIPLES FOR RESEARCH WITH HUMAN PARTICIPANTS

The fundamental aspect of all psychological research is awareness and understanding of the ethics for conducting research with our fellow human beings. The relationship between a psychological researcher and the individuals who participate in his or her research is unusual. Often a psychologist is in a position of power over the participants, similar to teacher-student, therapist-client, adult-child, therapist-prison inmate, and so on. A psychologist may be perceived as a person with unique knowledge and powers of control over human behaviors (Schultz, 1969). The research conducted by a psychologist may violate the privacy of the participant (that is, the subject)[1] and it may deal with issues of great sensitivity. On occasion, because psychological research deals with human issues, the need will arise to expose participants to deception, stress, or painful stimuli, or to induce powerful emotions such as fear or anger that may have either short- or long-term psychological effects. At the very least, a psychologist may ask that the participant spend some time performing a dull and meaningless task that he or she would not do otherwise. Sometimes research is ill-conceived, and the participant's time may be wasted (Steiner, 1972). The information collected may reveal intimate information and may even indicate that the individual is engaging in illegal activities (such as drug use or thievery), information that could conceivably be used to the participant's disadvantage at some later time. Certainly, these elements are not the makings of ideal human relationships.

It is important that research psychologists (and students who conduct psychological research) be cognizant of these issues and consider them whenever research is undertaken. The American Psychological Association has established ethical principles that prescribe guidelines for dealing with human participants in research. These principles are presented in Table 1–1. Be aware that these are merely the basic principles; the entire document detailing ethical conduct in research is a seventy-six-page book.

The ethical principles outline a code of acceptable professional conduct for a research psychologist.[2] They prescribe no absolute rights or wrongs in the conduct of research, but they focus upon the ethical issues that must be addressed whenever research is contemplated or conducted. As you can see from Principle A, the psychologist must entertain ethical considerations even when attempting to decide whether or not research is to be conducted. A psychologist is ethically obliged to do the best research that he or she can do; in deciding whether or not to do

---

[1]For many years, the people or animals employed in psychological research were referred to as *subjects*. In recent years, the term *participants* has been gaining greater acceptance (Gillis, 1976). And yet, the term *subjects* is strongly ingrained in psychological research methods in a variety of contexts. We use the terms interchangeably. We do, however, employ the term *subjects* in discussing research designs and statistical analyses that are often called *between-subjects* or *within-subjects* designs. The use of *participants* rather than *subjects* in these instances seems unnecessarily awkward to us at this time.

[2]There is a similar code for clinical and counseling psychologists on ethical behavior with clients seeking therapy or counseling.

TABLE 1-1   *The ethical principles for research with human participants*

The decision to undertake research rests upon a considered judgment by the individual psychologist about how best to contribute to psychological science and human welfare. Having made the decision to conduct research, the psychologist considers alternative directions in which research energies and resources might be invested. On the basis of this consideration, the psychologist carries out the investigation with respect and concern for the dignity and welfare of the people who participate and with cognizance of federal and state regulations and professional standards governing the conduct of research with human participants.

A. In planning a study, the investigator has the responsibility to make a careful evaluation of its ethical acceptability. To the extent that the weighing of scientific and human values suggests a compromise of any principle, the investigator incurs a correspondingly serious obligation to seek ethical advice and to observe stringent safeguards to protect the rights of human participants.

B. Considering whether a participant in a planned study will be a "subject at risk" or a "subject at minimal risk," according to recognized standards, is of primary ethical concern to the investigator.

C. The investigator always retains the responsibility for ensuring ethical practice in research. The investigator is also responsible for the ethical treatment of research participants by collaborators, assistants, students, and employees, all of whom, however, incur similar obligations.

D. Except in minimal-risk research, the investigator establishes a clear and fair agreement with research participants, prior to their participation, that clarifies the obligations and responsibilities of each. The investigator has the obligation to honor all promises and commitments included in that agreement. The investigator informs the participants of all aspects of the research that might reasonably be expected to influence willingness to participate and explains all other aspects of the research about which the participants inquire. Failure to make full disclosure prior to obtaining informed consent requires additional safeguards to protect the welfare and dignity of the research participants. Research with children or with participants who have impairments that would limit understanding and/or communication requires special safeguarding procedures.

E. Methodological requirements of a study may make the use of concealment or deception necessary. Before conducting such a study, the investigator has a special responsibility to (1) determine whether the use of such techniques is justified by the study's prospective scientific, educational, or applied value; (2) determine whether alternative procedures are available that do not use concealment or deception; and (3) ensure that the participants are provided with sufficient explanation as soon as possible.

F. The investigator respects the individual's freedom to decline to participate in or to withdraw from the research at any time. The obligation to protect this freedom requires careful thought and consideration when the investigator is in a position of authority or influence over the participant. Such positions of authority include, but are not limited to, situations in which research participation is required as part of employment or in which the participant is a student, client, or employee of the investigator.

G. The investigator protects the participant from physical and mental discomfort, harm, and danger that may arise from research procedures. If risks of such consequences exist, the investigator informs the participant of that fact. Research procedures likely to cause serious or lasting harm to a participant are not used unless the failure to use these procedures might expose the participant to risk of greater harm or unless the research has great potential benefit and fully informed and voluntary consent is obtained from each participant. The participant should be informed of procedures for contacting the investigator within a reasonable time period following participation should stress, potential harm, or related questions or concerns arise.

H. After the data are collected, the investigator provides the participant with information about the nature of the study and attempts to remove any misconceptions that may have arisen. Where scientific or humane values justify delaying or withholding this information, the investigator incurs a special responsibility to monitor the research and to ensure that there are no damaging consequences for the participant.

I. Where research procedures result in undesirable consequences for the individual participant, the investigator has the responsibility to detect and remove or correct these consequences, including long-term effects.

J. Information obtained about a research participant during the course of an investigation is confidential unless otherwise agreed upon in advance. When the possibility exists that others may obtain access to such information, this possibility, together with the plans for protecting confidentiality, is explained to the participant as part of the procedure for obtaining informed consent.

---

research, this obligation must always be weighed against potential harmful effects of the research on participants.

If the proposed research places a subject "at risk" of either long- or short-term psychological or physiological harm, then the researcher is obligated to consult with others and to consider alternative approaches to study of the problem (Principle B). Consultation with others provides an opportunity for individuals who are not associated with the research and who will not personally benefit from it to assess and evaluate the potential scientific value of the study, considering possible harm to the participants. Consultation also gives disinterested individuals a chance to review the appropriateness of the ethical safeguards proposed.

Once the decision to do the research has been made, then the ethical principles must be considered at each stage in development of the procedure. When a psychologist is planning research and the procedures to be followed in dealing with the participants, he or she must always keep their welfare in mind as the main priority. As the explanatory material that accompanies the ethical principles states:

The fundamental requirements are that the participants have made a fully informed and competent decision to participate and that they emerge from their research experience unharmed—or, at least, that the risks are minimal, understood by the participants, and accepted as reasonable. If possible, participants should enjoy some benefit. In general, after research participation, the participants' feelings about the experience should be such that the participant would willingly take part in further research. (American Psychological Association, 1982, p. 18)

Principles C through J ensure that these requirements are met. The intent of these principles is to provide clear delineation for the investigator's responsibility for maintaining ethical practice in the conduct of the research. They ensure that subjects will be treated ethically from the time they are recruited for participation to the time they leave the experimental setting.

For the most part, research that may be done in the context of a college course will usually involve procedures of minimal risk to participants. The subjects will be individuals who can freely and competently make a decision about participation when appropriate information is provided them. To the extent that these considerations are true, then application of the ethical principles in the research is quite straightforward. Where the research poses risk to the participant, however, requires deception, or involves individuals who may not be competent to give a freely formed decision about participation (for example, children, prisoners, or psychologically impaired patients), then the ethical principles require that utmost attention be given by all involved in the research. We cannot, however, deal with the myriad of ethical issues here. The student interested in pursuing the issue more fully should consult the *Ethical Principles in the Conduct of Research with Human Participants* (American Psychological Association, 1982) and an excellent chapter by Cook (1981).

ETHICAL PRINCIPLES FOR THE CARE AND USE OF ANIMALS

Ethical awareness is no less important when animals are used in research. Indeed, animals cannot give free and informed consent about their participation in research. Their participation is, in a sense, always involuntary. To ensure that ethical principles are followed in dealing with animals, the American Psychological Association has developed *Principles for the Care and Use of Animals,* and these principles are reprinted in Table 1–2. Additionally, both federal and state regulations cover research with animals, and all researchers must also adhere to any such applicable regulations.

From *Principles for the Care and Use of Animals.* Committee on Animal Research and Experimentation, Board of Scientific Affairs, American Psychological Association, Washington, D.C., 1979.

An investigator of animal behavior strives to advance our understanding of basic behavioral principles and to contribute to the improvement of human health and welfare. In seeking these ends, the investigator should ensure the welfare of the animals and should treat them humanely. Laws and regulations notwithstanding, the animal's immediate protection depends upon the scientist's own conscience. For this reason, the American Psychological Association has adopted the following Principles to guide individuals in their use of animals in research, teaching, and practical applications. All research conducted by members of the American Psychological Association or published in its journals must conform to these Principles.

1. The acquisition, care, use, and disposal of all animals shall be in compliance with current federal, state or provincial, and local laws and regulations.

2. A scientist trained in research methods and experienced in the care of laboratory animals shall closely supervise all procedures involving animals and be responsible for insuring appropriate consideration of their comfort, health, and humane treatment.

3. Scientists shall insure that all individuals using animals under their supervision have received explicit instruction in experimental methods and in the care, maintenance, and handling of the species being used. Responsibilities and activities of individuals shall be consistent with their respective competencies.

4. Scientists shall make every effort to minimize discomfort, illness, and pain to the animals. A procedure subjecting animals to pain, stress, or privation shall be used only when an alternative procedure is unavailable and the goal is justified by its prospective scientific, educational, or applied value. Surgical procedures shall be performed under appropriate anesthesia; techniques to avoid infection and minimize pain must be followed during and after surgery. Euthanasia shall be prompt and humane.

5. Investigators are strongly urged to consult with the Committee on Animal Research and Experimentation at any stage preparatory to or during a research project for advice about the appropriateness of research procedures or ethical issues related to experiments involving animals. Concerned individuals with any questions concerning adherence to the *Principles* should consult with the Committee.

6. Apparent violations of these *Principles* shall be reported immediately to the facility supervisor whose signature appears below:

   Name: _____

   Position: _____ Phone: _____

   If a satisfactory resolution is not achieved, a report should be made to the responsible institutional authority designated below:

   Name: _____

   Position: _____ Phone: _____

   Unresolved allegations of serious or repeated violations should be referred to the APA Committee on Animal Research and Experimentation.

7. These *Principles* shall be conspicuously posted in every laboratory, teaching facility, and applied setting where animals are being used. All persons in each laboratory, classroom, or applied facility shall indicate by signature and date on the attached sheet that they have read these *Principles*.

EXAMPLE OF PSYCHOLOGICAL RESEARCH

The most obvious way to become acquainted with the issues and problems of psychological research is to begin to read research articles. As an example of a psychological experiment, we reprint an article written by Patricia R. McCarthy and Nancy E. Betz, which was published in the *Journal of Counseling Psychology* in 1978. We chose this article because it deals with a topic in counseling psychology that will interest many students who are being introduced to the research methods of psychology. The article also illustrates a number of the concepts that are presented throughout this text, and we frequently refer to it. Although some aspects of the article probably will not be clear to you at present, particularly in the Method and Results sections, we feel that the article requires no advanced knowledge of psychology to understand the purpose of the experiment as described in the introduction.

Notice that this article, like most research articles in psychological journals, is organized in four major sections: *Introduction* (which is not identified with a heading because it is understood that the beginning of an article is the introduction), *Method, Results,* and *Discussion.* In the introduction, McCarthy and Betz review relevant research, which leads to the purpose of their experiment and provides the basis for their predictions of results. Therefore, in this section the authors tell why they conducted the experiment. In the Method section, they tell how they did the research. Here they describe in detail who the participants in the experiment were, what materials were used to test the individuals, and what measures of behavior were obtained from each, how the experimental situation was manipulated, and the procedures employed in testing each subject. Next, the statistical analysis of the data is presented in the Results section, which tells what they found. In the Discussion section, the authors tell what their results mean; they draw conclusions, provide interpretations, discuss the implications of their findings, and relate their results to previous research in the problem area.

Throughout the text we use the research done by McCarthy and Betz to illustrate and clarify concepts involved in psychological research. Our presentation of the methods of research will mostly parallel the order in which they are presented in research articles. For example, in Chapter 2, we discuss development of problems, hypotheses, and theoretical explanations of behavior. In Chapter 3 we introduce the fundamentals of experimental design, including the research design used by McCarthy and Betz, a basic design employed in many psychological experiments. In Chapter 4 we present the strategy of experimental design. Basic concepts necessary for understanding how to analyze data, interpret results, and reach conclusions from results are presented in later chapters.

Differential Effects of Self-disclosing Versus Self-involving Counselor Statements

Patricia R. McCarthy and Nancy E. Betz
Ohio State University

One hundred and seven female undergraduates listened to one of two audio-taped recordings of a counseling interview between an experienced male counselor and a female client. One half of the subjects heard a tape containing counselor self-disclosure statements; the other half heard a tape containing counselor self-involving statements. Subjects rated the counselor's expertness, attractiveness, and trustworthiness and generated written responses to each self-disclosing or self-involving counselor statement. The self-involving counselor was rated as significantly more expert and trustworthy than was the self-disclosing counselor. Further, client responses to the self-disclosing counselor statements contained significantly more questions about and references to the counselor, whereas responses to self-involving counselor statements contained significantly more self-referents. Finally, client responses to the self-involving counselor were significantly more likely to be phrased in the present, rather than the past or future, tense. Implications for the practice of counseling and for further research on self-disclosure are discussed.

In a recent article in this journal, Goodstein and Russell (1977) stress the need for greater attention to definitional issues in research on self-disclosure. This need is particularly evident in the body of research concerning the effects of counselor use of self-disclosure on the process and outcome of counseling. Studies of self-disclosure have frequently utilized definitions that are too vague to permit replication of the study or to communicate clearly how the response is to be accomplished. For example, Jourard and Jaffee (1970) considered self-disclosure to be the way one person willingly makes himself known to others, and Luft (1969) said that self-disclosure concerns what is going on between persons in the present.

Not only are such definitions vague, but in many cases there is lack of agreement among investigators as to the kinds of responses that should be labeled as self-disclosing. For example, Cozby (1973) indicated that self-disclosure is any information about oneself that a person verbally communicates to another, while Shapiro, Krauss, and Truax (1969) indicated that self-disclosure may be accomplished through nonverbal, as well as verbal, behaviors.

Most importantly, however, definitions of self-disclosure have failed to distinguish self-disclosing responses from another potentially important type of counselor response, that is, a self-involving response. Al-

The authors gratefully acknowledge the advice of Dr. Steven J. Danish of Pennsylvania State University.

Requests for reprints should be sent to Nancy E. Betz, Department of Psychology, Ohio State University, 1945 North High Street, Columbus, Ohio 43210.

McCarthy and Betz Experiment *continued*

though both self-disclosing and self-involving responses may be classified as self-referent responses, differences between them suggest that they may have very different effects on clients. According to Danish, D'Augelli, and Brock (1976), a self-disclosing response is "a statement of factual information on the part of the helper about himself or herself" (p. 261). In contrast, a self-involving response is "a statement of the helper's personal response to statements made by the helpee" (p. 261). Thus, self-disclosing responses are statements referring to the past history or personal experiences of the counselor, while self-involving responses are direct present expressions of the counselor's feelings about or reactions to the statements or behaviors of the client.

Failure to distinguish self-disclosing and self-involving responses is demonstrated in definitions of self-disclosure provided by Culbert (1968), Dies (1973), and Johnson and Noonan (1972); in their definitions, self-disclosure is a response in which an individual gives information about himself, his concerns, and his conflicts, or is one in which he talks about his here-and-now reactions and feelings to persons or situations. According to Danish et al. (1976), the first part of the definition would refer to self-disclosing responses, but the second part would refer to self-involving responses.

Differences in the definitions of these two types of counselor responses suggest the possibility that they have rather different effects on the client. The use of self-disclosing versus self-involving responses may lead, first, to differences in the way the client perceives the counselor. Further, the differences in focus of self-disclosing versus self-involving counselor statements may be expected to influence the nature and focus of subsequent client responses. Self-disclosure, since it is oriented toward past experiences of the counselor, may elicit client responses that continue to emphasize the

counselor's past experience. Thus, these responses may often be phrased in the past tense and refer primarily to the counselor's rather than the client's experience. Self-involving responses, on the other hand, are present centered and refer to the counselor's affective responses to the client. Such responses may demand from the client a present-centered response focused on himself or herself and responsive to the affect verbalized by the counselor. Thus, self-involving responses would appear to enhance the process of client self-exploration in the present to a greater extent than would self-disclosing responses.

The major purpose of this study was to investigate the differential effects of counselor use of self-disclosing versus self-involving responses. It was hypothesized that the two types of counselor responses would lead to differences in client perceptions of the counselor and to qualitative differences in client responses to counselor statements.

The design of the study involved the presentation of counseling interview stimulus material containing either counselor self-disclosure or counselor self-involving responses. Subjects rated the counselors on the dimensions of expertness, attractiveness, and trustworthiness and provided a *client response* to each self-disclosing or self-involving statement made by the counselor.

Method

Construction of Audiotaped Stimulus Materials

Tape recordings of two simulated counseling sessions involving a male counselor and a female client were developed. On one tape, the counselor made 10 self-disclosing statements but no self-involving statements. On the other tape, the counselor made 10 self-involving statements but no self-disclosing statements.

The counselor, played by an experienced counseling psychologist, and the client, played by a graduate student in a counseling-related field, role played the two interviews using prepared scripts.[1] The scripts, adapted from counselor–client interchanges utilized in the *Helping Skills Verbal Response Rating Tape* (Danish, D'Augelli & Brock, Note 1), were identical except for the insertion of self-disclosing versus self-involving counselor statements. Both scripts involved discussions of the client's dissatisfaction with herself, her lack of friends, and her problems relating to her parents. This discussion was divided into 10 segments; the first segment was 2 minutes in length to provide initial interview content, and the 9 subsequent segments were each 1 minute in length. With the exception of the last response in each segment (made by the counselor), all counselor responses were either open-ended questions, reflections of content, or reflections of feeling.

The last response in each segment was either a self-disclosing or a self-involving statement made by the counselor. Self-disclosing and self-involving counselor statements were written to be positive rather than negative in nature. That is, a positive self-disclosing statement was one expressing similarity, rather than dissimilarity, of personal experiences, and a positive self-involving statement was an expression of positive, rather than negative, feelings about or reactions to the client. On one tape, all segments ended with a positive self-disclosing statement, and on the other tape, all segments ended with a positive self-involving statement.

Subjects

Subjects were 107 female undergraduates enrolled in an introductory psychology course at Ohio State University. Subjects were randomly assigned to one of the two experimental conditions, with 54 subjects assigned to the self-disclosure condition and 53 assigned to the self-involving condition.

Dependent Measures

Perceptions of the counselor. The Counselor Rating Form (CRF; Barak & LaCrosse, 1975) was used to assess subjects' perceptions of the expertness, attractiveness, and trustworthiness of the self-disclosing or the self-involving counselor. The CRF consists of 36 7-point bipolar items, 12 on each of the three dimensions. Scores on each dimension may range from 12 to 84. Studies using the CRF have demonstrated reliable differences in perceived expertness, attractiveness, and trustworthiness as a function of appropriate experimental manipulations (Barak & Dell, 1977; Barak & LaCrosse, 1975; LaCrosse & Barak, 1976).

[1] Scripts are available upon request from the second author.

Client responses. Client responses were obtained by asking subjects to write a response to the last counselor statement (either self-disclosing or self-involving) in each segment of the interview. These responses were analyzed in terms of eight relevant dimensions: (a) total number of words; (b) number of questions about the counselor, for example, "So what did you do after you flunked math in high school?"; (c) proportion of counselor referents to total number of words; (d) proportion of self (i.e., client) referents to total number of words; (e) proportion of affective words to total words; (f) proportion of past tense verbs to total number of verbs; (g) proportion of present tense verbs to total number of verbs; and (h) proportion of future tense verbs to total number of verbs.[2]

Content analyses of the written client responses were done by three raters carefully trained to identify the presence or absence of each response category and without knowledge of the condition (i.e., self-disclosing versus self-involving) under which the client response was obtained.

Procedure

The experiment was conducted in a laboratory with a central tape system and 20 individual carrels equipped with headphones. Subjects, tested in groups of 20, were told that they would hear a tape of several segments of an initial counseling session. Instructions for writing client responses and for completing the CRF were given. For each subject group, either the tape using counselor self-disclosing responses or that using counselor self-involving responses was played. After hearing each of the 10 segments of the tape, subjects were given 1 minute to respond in writing to the counselor in the way they thought the client would respond. After the completion of the entire taped interview, subjects were given the CRF and asked to rate the counselor as they believed the client on the tape would rate him.

Analysis

Means and standard deviations of scores on the three dimensions of perceptions of the counselor and on the eight client response dimensions were obtained for the counselor self-disclosure and counselor self-involving conditions. Statistical comparisons of the two conditions were made using *t* tests for independent groups. Although the nature of self-disclosing versus self-involving responses suggested directional hypotheses on some of the client response dimensions, two-tailed tests were

[2] Definitions of client response dimensions and specific instructions for rating each dimension are available upon request from the second author.

McCarthy and Betz Experiment *continued*

Table 1
Means, Standard Deviations, and t-test Comparisons of Perceived Expertness, Attractiveness, and Trustworthiness of Self-disclosing Versus Self-involving Counselor

Dimension	Self-disclosing[a]		Self-involving[b]		t[c]	p
	M	SD	M	SD		
Expertness	63.1	14.6	68.5	11.1	−2.17	.03
Attractiveness	63.6	9.6	67.0	9.3	−1.88	.06
Trustworthiness	63.6	14.0	70.9	11.5	−2.95	.004

Note. Scores on each dimension may range from a minimum of 12 to a maximum of 84.
[a] $n = 54$.
[b] $n = 53$.
[c] $df = 105$.

used in all comparisons to control for the increased probability of Type I error inherent when several separate comparisons are made.

Results

Perceptions of the Counselor

Means and standard deviations of subjects' ratings of the expertness, attractiveness, and trustworthiness of the self-disclosing and the self-involving counselor are presented in Table 1; for each dimension the results of t tests for the significance of the difference between the two counselors are also shown.

Table 1 shows that in the condition where counselor self-involving responses were utilized, the counselor was rated as significantly more expert ($p = .03$) and significantly more trustworthy ($p = .004$) than he was in the condition where counselor self-disclosing responses were utilized. In addition, ratings of counselor attractiveness were somewhat higher in the self-involving condition than in the self-disclosing condition.

Client Responses

Scores on each of the eight client responses dimensions were calculated by adding the number of times a given response occurred over all 10 responses provided by each subject. Thus, the *total number of words* score represents the total words utilized in 10 responses to either a self-disclosing or self-involving counselor, while *number of questions about counselor* refers to the frequency of this response over 10 client responses. Scores on use of counselor or self-referents, affective words, and verb tenses are expressed in proportions to control for intersubject differences in number of words or number of verbs used in responses.

Means and standard deviations of the eight dimensions of client responses are presented in Table 2; again, results of t-test comparisons of the self-disclosing versus the self-involving counselor are indicated.

Results indicated significant differences on four of the eight dimensions of client response to a self-disclosing versus self-involving counselor. As shown in the table, responses to the self-disclosing counselor contained significantly more questions about the counselor ($p = .001$) and a significantly larger proportion of counselor referents relative to the total number of words used ($p = .005$) than did responses to the self-involving counselor. On the other hand, responses to the self-involving counselor contained significantly more self (i.e., client) referents relative to total number of words ($p = .001$) and were significantly more likely to be

Table 2

Means, Standard Deviations, and t-test Comparisons of Eight Dimensions of Client Responses to Self-disclosing Versus Self-involving Counselor Statements

Dimension	Self-disclosing[a]		Self-involving[b]		t^c	p
	M	SD	M	SD		
Total number of words	212.0	74.8	203.0	58.7	.69	.49
Number of questions about counselor	2.8	3.5	.1	.5	5.43	.001
Proportion of counselor referents	.03	.03	.02	.01	2.88	.005
Proportion of self-referents	.12	.04	.15	.02	−3.93	.001
Proportion of affective words to total words	.02	.01	.02	.01	−.62	.53
Proportionate use of verb tenses						
Past	.06	.07	.04	.04	1.50	.14
Present	.78	.14	.83	.13	−2.08	.04
Future	.16	.12	.13	.12	1.62	.11

Note. Scores on each dimension represent the sum over the 10 responses made by each subject.
[a] $n = 54$.
[b] $n = 53$.
[c] $df = 105$.

phrased in the present tense ($p = .04$) than were responses to the self-disclosing counselor. No significant differences were found in the total number of words used, the proportion of affective words to total words, or in proportionate use of past and future tense verbs.

Discussion

Generally, the results of this study suggest that counselor self-disclosing versus self-involving responses have differential effects on client perceptions of the counselor and on the nature of the client responses they elicit. The counselor who used self-involving statements was rated as significantly more expert and significantly more trustworthy than was the counselor who used self-disclosing responses. In addition, counselor self-disclosing responses elicited from the client significantly more questions about the counselor and significantly more counselor referents, while counselor self-involving responses elicited significantly more self-referents. Finally, while most verb usage in client responses was in the present tense, counselor self-involving responses elicited a

significantly larger proportion of present tense verbs relative to total number of verbs used than did counselor self-disclosing responses. Self-disclosing and self-involving responses did not differ significantly in the total number of words elicited in client responses or in the tendency of these responses to contain affective words and past or future tense verbs.

The results of this study have important implications both for the practice of counseling and for continued research on counselor self-referent responses, in particular, self-disclosure. For the practice of counseling, these results suggest that counselor use of self-involving responses enhances his or her expertness and trustworthiness to a greater extent than does counselor use of self-disclosing responses. Since a self-involving response requires the counselor to express his or her immediate feelings about or reactions to the client, it involves a greater degree of personal risk than does a self-disclosing response, which is often focused in the past and does not refer directly to the client. Willingness to risk oneself may be viewed as a quality of experts and, in necessitating that the counselor trust the client

McCarthy and Betz Experiment *continued*

with his or her personal feelings, may enhance the trust the client has in the counselor.

Further, these results suggest that counselor self-involving responses may be more likely to enhance the process of client self-exploration in the present and to maintain the focus of the counseling relationship on the client rather than on the counselor. Because the counselor is revealing his or her feelings toward the client, the client and his or her behavior remain the focus of conversation; client responses tend to be present tense "I" statements rather than questions about or references to the counselor. Counselor self-disclosure statements, on the other hand, may detract from the process of client self-exploration when their effect is to shift the focus of counseling to the counselor and his or her past experiences and problems. Counselors using self-disclosure need to be aware of this potential effect of their statements.

The findings of significant differences in the effects of two previously undifferentiated types of counselor self-referent responses suggest the need for more specific definition and careful differentiation of response types in further research on the use of self-disclosure and other self-referent responses and behaviors. From both the definitional problems pointed out in the introductory section and the results of this study, it is clear that studies of the effects of self-disclosure and related responses on the process and outcome of counseling will not be maximally useful, either theoretically or practically, until there is greater specificity in and agreement on the kinds of responses that do and do not constitute self-disclosure.

A possible limitation of this study derives from its analogue nature. Subjects listened to an interview and were asked to both rate the counselor on several dimensions and to generate responses that they thought the

client in that situation would make. Generalization of these findings to real counseling situations will necessitate studies of the perceptions and responses of clients whose counselors are utilizing some combination of self-disclosing and self-involving responses. Further, only female subjects were utilized in this study; additional research is needed to determine the effects of self-disclosing and self-involving counselor statements on male subjects or clients. Finally, the simulated interview portrayed a male counselor and a female client; thus, studies employing systematic variation in the sex of counselor, client, and subjects are necessary to establish the generalizability of these findings.

In conclusion, it is hoped that the results of this study will stimulate further research on the effects of specific counselor behaviors on counseling process and outcome. Attention to definitional issues should enhance the utility of research findings both for other investigators and for practicing counselors.

Reference Note

1. Danish, S. J., D'Augelli, A. R., & Brock, G. W. *Helping Skills Verbal Response Rating Tape.* Unpublished transcript, Pennsylvania State University, 1976.

References

Barak, A., & Dell, D. M. Differential perceptions of counselor behavior: Replication and extension. *Journal of Counseling Psychology*, 1977, *24*, 288–292.

Barak, A., & LaCrosse, M. B. Multidimensional perception of counselor behavior. *Journal of Counseling Psychology*, 1975, *22*, 471–476.

Cozby, P. C. Self-disclosure: A literature review. *Psychological Bulletin*, 1973, *79*, 73–91.

Culbert, S. A. Trainer self-disclosure and member growth in two T-groups. *Journal of Applied Behavioral Science*, 1968, *4*, 47–73.

Danish, S. J., D'Augelli, A. R., & Brock, G. W. An evaluation of helping skills training: Effects on helpers' verbal responses. *Journal of Counseling Psychology,* 1976, *23,* 259–266.

Dies, R. R. Group therapist self-disclosure: An evaluation by clients. *Journal of Counseling Psychology,* 1973, *20,* 344–348.

Goodstein, L. D., & Russell, S. W. Self-disclosure: A comparative study of reports by self and others. *Journal of Counseling Psychology,* 1977, *24,* 365–369.

Johnson, D. W., & Noonan, M. P. Effects of acceptance and reciprocation of self-disclosures on the development of trust. *Journal of Counseling Psychology,* 1972, *19,* 411–416.

Jourard, S. M., & Jaffee, P. E. Influence of an interviewer's disclosure on the self-disclosing behavior of interviewees. *Journal of Counseling Psychology,* 1970, *17,* 252–257.

LaCrosse, M. B., & Barak, A. Differential perception of counselor behavior. *Journal of Counseling Psychology,* 1976, *23,* 170–172.

Luft, J. *Of human interaction.* Palo Alto, Calif.: National Press, 1969.

Shapiro, J. G., Krauss, H. H., & Truax, C. B. Therapeutic conditions and disclosure beyond the therapeutic encounter. *Journal of Counseling Psychology,* 1969, *16,* 290–294.

Received July 22, 1977 ■

Journal of Counseling Psychology 1978, Vol. 25, No. 4, 251–256. Copyright © 1978, American Psychological Association. Used by permission of the publisher and authors.

SUMMARY

- Many psychologists consider research methodology to be the most important contribution to the discipline. Current methods of research produce empirical knowledge that must be accepted skeptically.
- Conducting original and creative research is both challenging and exciting.
- The contributors to psychological knowledge are typically psychologists who do research as only one of many activities.
- The ethical treatment of subjects, either human or animal, is always paramount in any research project.
- The published article by McCarthy and Betz on the effects of counselors' self-disclosure and self-involvement on subjects' ratings of the expertness, attractiveness, and trustworthiness of the counselor provides an example of contemporary research in psychology.

2

PREVIEW

In this chapter we introduce the importance of approaching a research problem with a "prepared mind" and a knowledge of the principles of scientific research. Topics include:

- The characteristics of scientific research
- The role of theory and research hypotheses in psychological research
- The empirical testing of research hypotheses through a process of falsification
- Why research in parapsychology does not meet the criteria of science

WHY YOU NEED TO KNOW THIS MATERIAL

As a student of psychology you should be aware of how psychologists approach the study of behavior scientifically. You should also understand that the scientific method applied to the study of behavior does not provide proof of any explanation of behavior. All scientific findings with respect to behavior are tentative and open to falsification. To know why requires an understanding of the philosophical basis of scientific methodology in psychology.

The Basis of Psychological Research

Well, now, I should think that perhaps there might be a fair amount
of evidence in favor of that theory, but then you know there are some
things against it. In fact, you might say that the evidence against it is
just as strong—perhaps.

Robert Sessions Woodworth,[1] 1869–1962

CHOOSING A RESEARCH PROBLEM

All psychological research starts with the choice of a research problem. Most
psychology students are required at some time in their course work to conduct an
original experiment that has not been constructed for them. When faced with such
a task, students may draw upon their own experience and informal observations
of people's behavior to come up with a proposed study that is of interest. Often, it
seems, the first inclination is to ask, "I wonder what would happen if. . . ." "If
people are given caffeine, do their reaction times decrease?" "Does the presence of
popular music interfere with performance on some task?" "What is the effect of
color on a person's mood?"

Students may regard such problems as important and interesting to investigate. Moreover, conducting research on any problem can prove to be a valuable
learning experience. Very often, however, the difficulty with selecting a research
problem off the top of the head is that it leads to research that a professional
psychologist would consider relatively trite. It is likely that such problems have
been extensively researched and that the proposed research potentially contributes
nothing new to an understanding of behavior.

[1]The quotation is from a eulogy in an obituary of Woodworth written by Gardner Murphy
(1963, p. 132).

If the research is to be worthwhile in the sense that it potentially contributes to understanding behavior, then there should be a **rationale**—an underlying reason or logical basis—for the research. A psychologist does not formulate a problem and select the variables that he or she plans to vary and measure merely on the basis of uninformed hunches. The psychologist does not enter into research with his or her mind a *tabula rasa*. Instead, formulating a sound rationale for one's research requires a prepared mind; one must be familiar with the published research in the problem area and understand the process of explanation in science.

Scientific and psychological research is a historical process. Research is not ahistorical (without history); almost all current problems in psychology have a historical context of development, as Boring (1957) states:

> The experimental psychologist, so it has always seemed to me, needs historical sophistication within his own sphere of expertness. Without such knowledge he sees the present in distorted perspective, he mistakes old facts and old views for new, and he remains unable to evaluate the significance of new movements and methods. In this matter I can hardly state my faith too strongly. A psychological sophistication that contains no component of historical orientation seems to me to be no sophistication at all. (p. ix)

Research on a problem without awareness of its historical development is likely to result in findings of little or no interest to anyone. Only if research in the behavioral sciences is developed in the context of a historical body of knowledge will it be meaningful and contribute to that body of knowledge. Webb (1961), a major contributor to our knowledge of sleep, argues:

> I think that there is a very general agreement that one can only work effectively in an area when he has a thorough understanding of this general area of concern. It is quite often that the significant finding comes from a fusion of quite a number of simple studies or a perception of gaps in the detailed findings or the methodologies and procedures of others. I am quite sure that the vaunted, creative insight of the scientist occurs more frequently within a thorough knowlege of one's area than as a bolt from the blue. (p. 226.)

You can clearly see this historical development of research in the work of McCarthy and Betz. It is evident that they were quite aware of the research that preceded their own; they carefully and critically reviewed the previous relevant research on the effects of type of counselor response. This review is indicated by their criticisms of previous research: The definitions of self-disclosure have been "vague"; there is a lack of agreement among investigators as to what types of responses should be labeled "self-disclosing"; and these responses have not been distinguished from "self-involving" responses. Thus, McCarthy and Betz's research becomes potentially important to psychology because it is based upon a firm knowledge of the problem, and they attempt to clarify some of the ambiguities in previous research.

CHARACTERISTICS OF SCIENTIFIC RESEARCH

Historically, psychology has embraced the method of inquiry used successfully by the natural and physical sciences—the scientific method. In using the scientific method to study behavioral phenomena, psychologists are tacitly adopting the two major assumptions underlying the method:

1. **Order.** Behaviors, like other natural phenomena, do not occur capriciously or willy nilly. There is an orderliness to their occurrence, with lawful relationships to be discovered. The implication, then, is that the behavior of organisms is potentially explainable and predictable, and ultimately controllable, if we identify the events and circumstances under which it occurs.
2. **Determinism.** It follows that scientific psychology is a quest for the cause-and-effect relationships in behavior. It is assumed that behavioral events are determined; that is, behavior is preceded by identifiable or potentially knowable causal events (antecedents) that make it occur.

Not all psychologists agree that people are "knowable" scientifically and that behavior is determined, but scientific psychological research progresses on these assumptions. Those who conduct psychological research implicitly adopt these assumptions, for their research is characterized by their varying some situation to see what effect the experimental manipulation has on the behavior that is of interest.

Causality

The assumptions of order and determinism explicitly convey a belief in an ability to establish causal relations in the study of behavior. The common conception of **causality** is of some event which can be manipulated and which is followed by a certain effect (Cook and Campbell, 1979). We believe that establishing causal relations between antecedent events and subsequent behavior is a major goal of psychological research. Some psychologists would probably disagree with us (e.g., Lindman, 1981), arguing tht most events have multiple causes and that it is better to merely establish reliable relationships among antecedent events and behaviors, than to speak of causes. But we believe this position denies what psychologists actually do in their research. Although psychologists often avoid using the word *cause*, causal thinking is clearly implied when they use such words as *determine, influence, reason why, effect,* or *evoke* to describe relationships between antecedent variables and behavior (Kerlinger and Pedhazur, 1973). In applied psychological research designed to produce or evaluate programs with social effects, assumptions typically are made about the causes of the social problem being addressed by the program (Rutman, 1977). Clearly, then, psychologists often seek answers to causal questions in their research.

Philosophers of science have long discussed the conditions necessary to arrive at causal relations and a variety of requirements have been suggested. For our purposes, we believe that three conditions discussed by Nagel (1961) will suffice.

1. The relation between the antecedent event and the behavioral change is a consistent and invariable relationship. Whenever the antecedent event occurs, it is followed by the behavioral change.
2. The antecedent event and the behavioral change must be spatially contiguous. That is, the antecedent event cannot occur at a distance so remote from the behavior that it would have little possibility of affecting that behavior.
3. The antecedent event must be temporally contiguous with the behavior change. That is, the antecedent event cannot occur at a time so much before the behavior that it would have little possibility of affecting that behavior.

These conditions for concluding causality carry with them an implication of manipulating antecedent events to ascertain their consequent effects. The experimental method has, indeed, built upon this manipulation of antecedent events. The true experiment, in which one actively varies antecedent events, allows psychologists to reach tentative causal relations much more easily than do some other approaches that do not allow a direct manipulation of the antecedent events. These approaches are discussed in much greater detail in Chapter 3.

Causal statements, however, will always be tentative and never absolute. As we discussed in Chapter 1, and for reasons explained in this and later chapters, a researcher can never "prove" knowledge of causes from research, for it is impossible to rule out all other possible and plausible causes for the changes in behavior that may have been observed.

Empirical Knowledge

Our conception of causality—manipulating an antecedent condition and then observing any behavioral changes—implies that scientific knowledge and understanding of human behavior is built upon a foundation of observation. More technically, psychologists say that knowledge is empirical, that is, based upon observation or experience.

Empirical knowledge implies that scientists are able to measure that which they are able to observe. The measurements should provide a quantitative indication of the observations, should be consistent from one measurement to the next, and should measure what the scientist thinks they are measuring. There are several scales of measurement that reflect various degrees of precision, and we discuss measurement more fully in Chapter 5.

Replicability

Scientific knowledge must be replicable and subject to agreement among different observers. In later chapters, you shall discover that the outcome of a single experiment usually provides only a very limited knowledge of and confidence in the existence of a phenomenon. Scientific knowledge of a phenomenon gains strength and generality when others can replicate the phenomenon in different settings and locations with different participants.

These characteristics of scientific research are clearly demonstrated in the work of McCarthy and Betz. Their frequent use of words such as *effect, elicit,* and *influence* indicate that they believe behavior is ordered and determined, and that there are antecedent events that are causally related to subsequent behaviors. Their approach was to manipulate an event—the counselor's response—and to measure its effect on the client's perception of the counselor. By publishing the study, they have made their results public and open to testing and replication by others.

ROLE OF THEORY AND RESEARCH HYPOTHESES

The goal of scientific psychology is to describe and explain behavior. The form of scientific explanation is theory. Theories are the psychologist's explanations of behavior. And, indeed, the ultimate purpose of all scientific psychological research is to provide explanations of behavior. Although psychologists may conduct research studies for a variety of reasons, we believe that the ultimate purpose of scientific research in psychology is the formulation of theory to explain behavior (Dixon, 1980; Kerlinger, 1969, 1973, 1979).

What Is Psychological Theory?

Popper (1959) said that "Theories are nets cast to catch what we call 'the world': to rationalize, to explain, and to master it. We endeavour to make the mesh ever finer and finer" (p. 59). Despite the metaphorical beauty of this statement, it provides little insight into the nature of psychological theory. More specifically, a theory is a set of propositions, that is, related statements that describe the relationships among antecedent conditions and behavior in an attempt to explain that behavior. Let us illustrate with an example of a proposition from a current theory in psychology.

Walster, Walster, and Berscheid (1978) have formulated a theory of social behavior that they call **equity theory.** Their purpose is to explain a broad range of behaviors that may occur in human relationships. This theory is presented in four propositions, but we will discuss only Proposition III.[2]

> When individuals find themselves participating in inequitable relationships, they will become distressed. The more inequitable the relationship, the more distress individuals will feel. (Walster et al., 1978, p. 6)

[2]You may expect that a theory will be stated in only a few sentences. Walster et al. present their four theoretical propositions in half a page. Often, however, theoretical formulations may require considerable explanation and their presentation will require more than a half a page or so.

First, notice that this proposition involves antecedent conditions—inequitable relationships, and potential behavioral consequences—distress. The statement of how these are related is at a very general or conceptual level. A variety of observable relationships can be subsumed under the concept of inequitable relations. Similarly, a number of observable behaviors can be subsumed under the concept of distress. The concepts are used in this proposition to represent all those possible relationships which may be inequitable and those possible behaviors which could be conceived of as representing distress.

Theories typically state relations between concepts or constructs (we use these terms synonymously), such as inequitable relationships and distress. When used in a theory, **concepts** or **constructs** are broad and abstract terms that possess no physical existence (Levitt, 1967). Many theoretical constructs are simply assumed attributes or characteristics of individuals such as anxiety, distress, fear, aggressiveness, depression, intelligence, expertness, or honesty. These terms are either borrowed from our everyday language or invented by the psychologist to help explain the behavior that is of interest. Moreover, the theoretical proposition may clearly imply that the constructs can assume different possible values or levels. That is, the constructs are often thought to be variable. For example, Proposition III of the Walster et al. theory implies that there may be varying amounts or types of an inequitable relationship, or of distress.

Proposition III is a universal statement; it is not limited to some individuals, or to certain individuals, or to people who live in Chicago. It is about all organisms that one could normally call "individuals." Theoretical statements are universal statements limited in generality only by restrictions contained within other propositions in the theory itself. A theoretical proposition may be either true or false; for equity theory, people either do or do not act as Proposition III states they will. Obviously, a psychologist attempting to explain behavior will attempt to formulate a theory of true propositions. One will never have complete assurance, however, that any of the propositions of a theory are true. It is a function of scientific research to bring as much evidence as possible to bear on theory, but the research will never "prove" the truth of the theory (Ellsworth, 1977; Mahoney, 1978).

BOX 2-1

Theory is, of course, the energy cell of science. Facts, even elegant ones, isolated from relevant assumptions are lovely but unappreciated flowers. But facts have a refereeing function; they prevent presuppositions from becoming dogma. That is why Karl Popper (1962) insists that the primary function of mature empirical science is to refute, not to affirm, hypotheses—a directive that is occasionally annoying to psychologists who have many young candidates vying for affirmation but very few hardy enough to withstand rigorous examination and possible failure.

Jerome Kagan, "Emergent themes in human development," *American Scientist,* 1976, p. 186. Copyright © 1976 by Sigma Xi, The Scientific Research Society, Incorporated. Used by permission.

In order to gain confidence that a theory is of any value in explaining behavior, it must be empirically tested. A scientist cannot, however, directly test a theory, because the theory is composed of universal statements. It is impossible to test all individuals in all situations to see if they exhibit distress in inequitable relationships. How, then, can a theory be tested? The answer lies in research hypotheses.

Research Hypotheses

Certain logical conclusions flow from a theory. These conclusions are known as research hypotheses. A **research hypothesis** is a statement of a tentative relationship between an antecedent condition and a consequent behavior. Research hypotheses are arrived at by using either deductive or inductive reasoning.

Deductive Formulation of Research Hypotheses

A research hypothesis is often developed by deductive reasoning from the propositions of a theory. **Deduction** is a process of reasoning from the general to the specific, where the specific conclusions must necessarily follow from the general premise. In deductive reasoning from theory, research hypotheses must necessarily be true if the theoretical propositions are true. For example, if Proposition III in equity theory is true, then certain conclusions must logically follow from that proposition. These research hypotheses are simply more specific statements and predictions relating to certain individuals, situations, and behaviors.

To illustrate research hypotheses deduced from a theory, we use an example from the research of Austin and Walster (1974). Their work is based on equity theory, and the part of it that interests us is the following research hypothesis derived from Proposition III of equity theory:

> Persons who are given an equitable reward will be less distressed than persons who receive an inequitable reward (i.e., persons who are equitably rewarded will be less distressed than persons who are *either* underrewarded or overrewarded).[3] (p. 209)

If Proposition III is true, then this research hypothesis logically follows from that proposition. The research hypothesis is also a more specific and limited statement about relations among constructs than is the proposition of the theory.

[3]You may have noticed that the work by Austin and Walster (1974) preceded publication of the theory of Walster et al. (1978). How could they deduce a research hypothesis from a theory not yet published? The answer is straightforward: Components of equity theory had been published in a variety of articles prior to the 1978 book by Walster et al. The book was a more complete exposition of equity theory and the research it has generated, but certainly equity theory was well known to researchers on the subject prior to publication of the book. The actual beginnings of equity theory lie in the work of Adams (1963).

Where Proposition III states inequitable relationships, the research hypothesis states inequitable rewards. Inequitable rewards are one instance, but only one instance, of inequitable relationships.

Inductive Formulation of Research Hypotheses

When research is led by theory, research hypotheses are derived deductively. Not all research hypotheses, however, are developed in this way. In many areas of psychology, theory is either quite weak or nonexistent. When theoretical formulations are absent, research hypotheses are often closely tied to the empirical knowledge gained from other studies. In this sense, these research hypotheses may be inductively formed. **Induction** is the process of reasoning from the specific to the general. One may observe a particular instance of behavior in an individual under certain antecedent conditions and induce or infer that it would hold more generally. Such research hypotheses often summarize established empirical relationships and are an attempt to apply these relationships in different settings or under different circumstances.

Characteristics of Research Hypotheses

To be scientifically useful, research hypotheses must possess three important characteristics. They must: (1) state an explicit relationship between variables, (2) be empirically testable, and (3) be formulated in advance.

The hypothesis must be an explicit statement of the relationship   All research hypotheses state a relationship between variables—antecedent conditions and consequent behaviors. This relationship should be stated explicitly and should, if possible, indicate the direction of the relation. An example of such a statement is: "An increase in the antecedent condition will produce a decrease in the consequent behavior." In early stages of research on a problem, however, often called **exploratory research,** there may be little basis for making a specific prediction. With further understanding of the important antecedent variables, research hypotheses in the problem area usually become more explicit in stating the direction of the relationship.

The work of McCarthy and Betz provides an illustration. Their research hypothesis was formulated as follows:

> It was hypothesized that the two types of counselor responses would lead to differences in client perceptions of the counselor and to qualitative differences in client responses to counselor statements. (p. 252)

This research hypothesis relates an antecedent condition (type of counselor response) to two potential behaviors (client's perceptions of the counselor and client's responses to counselor's statements). The definition of a research hypothesis requires only one consequent behavior, not the two that McCarthy and Betz employed. The direction of current psychologocial research, however, is to employ more than one measure of the behavior whenever possible.

McCarthy and Betz did not indicate the direction of the predicted relationship in their research hypothesis. Based upon the knowledge of the effects of counselor responses at the time the research was conducted, McCarthy and Betz apparently were reluctant to more specifically predict the effects of the type of counselor response. With further research and replicated findings in this problem area, it would be expected that future research hypotheses would be more specific about the direction of the relationship between the antecedent event and behavior. And, indeed, this change occurs in a follow-up study by McCarthy (1982), in which she varied the intimacy of the self-disclosure: "It was generally expected that self-involving and high-intimacy self-disclosing statements would be more effective than low-intimacy self-disclosing statements" (p. 126).

The hypothesis must be empirically testable   If research hypotheses are to be scientifically useful, then they must lend themselves to empirical testing. That is, one must be able to make some measurable observations that will either agree or disagree with the prediction. The constructs of the research hypothesis must eventually be defined or anchored in terms of observable events and behaviors. If they cannot, then the research hypothesis is untestable and scientifically useless.

The hypothesis must be formulated prior to empirical testing   A third characteristic is less frequently cited formally, but it is equally important. Research hypotheses must be formulated *prior to* being put to empirical test. This characteristic should seem evident; however, all too often students, and perhaps research psychologists themselves, seem to formulate research hypotheses to suit the outcome of their empirical tests, rather than design the tests to evaluate the research hypotheses (Schulman, Kupst, and Suran, 1976). The difference here is somewhat analogous to the difference between a person who can tell you the outcome of a horse race after the race has been run, and the person who can correctly predict the outcome of the race before it is run. Clearly, you would consider the latter person to have more knowledge about horses and horse races than the former. It is likewise with the formulation of scientific theory and research hypotheses. For almost any behavior a theory or a hypothesis can be formulated that will "post-dict" or account for the behavior after it has occurred. This statement would not be considered an acceptable scientific explanation.[4]

---

[4]Do you know someone who can always account for others' behavior after it has occurred? "I could have told you that she was not going to go shopping today." Is this person able to predict behavior as accurately as he or she post-dicts it?

Conceptual and Empirical Research Hypotheses

A research hypothesis may be stated at either a conceptual or an empirical level with respect to how closely it is related to observable manipulations or measurements. At a conceptual level the variables in the hypothesis need further definition for an empirical test to be conducted. As an example, the research hypothesis of Austin and Walster (1974) is stated at a conceptual level. Both inequitable rewards and distress are open to many possible manipulations and measurements, and the specific manipulations and measurements need to be identified before an experiment can be conducted. The research hypothesis of McCarthy and Betz is also stated at a conceptual level.

Some psychologists prefer to state research hypotheses at a more empirical level, indicating in the hypothesis itself the observable manipulations or measurements to be used. For example, at an empirical level, the research hypothesis of Austin and Walster could, on the basis of their manipulation of equity of reward and measurement of distress, be stated:

> Persons who expect to receive $2.00 for performing a task and receive the $2.00 will show greater positive moods on the Mood Adjective Checklist than persons who expect to receive $2.00 but receive only $1.00.

The term *research hypothesis* is also not universal nomenclature in psychology. As you read the psychological literature, you will find what we have called research hypotheses referred to sometimes as mere *hypotheses,* or as *conceptual, experimental, scientific, substantive, test, working, theoretical,* or *psychological hypotheses.* Under this variety of names you are likely to find the hypothesis expressed at either a conceptual or an empirical level.

Empirical Evaluation of Theories and Research Hypotheses

Psychologists propose theories and research hypotheses to explain behavior. The relationships expressed in these explanations must be either true or false. The scientist hopes that they are true, but how is he or she to know this? The resolution of the question is to put the relationship to empirical test. We give only an overview of this process here. Part of the process we have already discussed; part of it will be our subject in much of the remainder of this text.

We present the approach advocated by Popper (1959); however, we temper our discussion by reflecting what we see as the approach actually followed by many psychologists. In addition, although we couch our discussion mainly in terms of research hypotheses deduced from psychological theory, the approach is equally applicable to inductively formulated research hypotheses.

Central to Popper's approach is the concept of falsification. Popper argues that a theory may only be shown to be false, or not true (i.e., falsified). It cannot be shown to be true (i.e., verified). The basis for his argument is that one can never be sure of the generality of inductively reasoned conclusions from the outcome of a specific empirical test of a research hypothesis. As we have discussed, inductive inference is a process of reasoning from a particular instance to a general situation. As an example, suppose a psychologist testing Austin and Walster's empirical research hypothesis finds that individuals expecting and receiving $2.00 show greater positive moods than individuals expecting $2.00 but receiving only $1.00. If the psychologist applies inductive inference from this instance of support for a specific research hypothesis to the theoretical proposition, then he or she will conclude that all individuals, whether observed or not, become distressed when given an inequitable reward. In this case, the psychologist has reasoned from a singular occurrence (his or her own observations of a limited number of individuals in a certain situation) to a universal occurrence (the behavior of all individuals in many different situations).

Although each of us perhaps often engages in inductive reasoning, from a scientific view such reasoning must always be suspect. The reason is simple: If only one individual does not become distressed when given inequitable rewards, then the universal statement that individuals become distressed when given inequitable rewards is false. But, because an individual can never observe all people, he or she cannot be sure that there are not some people (or even one person) who do not become distressed when given inequitable rewards. Hence, one can never be sure of the accuracy of the induction from one's own observations of a phenomenon to all possible observations of that phenomenon. For this reason, Popper argues that observations can only show the proposed relationships of theories and research hypotheses to be false (Greenwald and Ronis, 1981; Mahoney, 1978; Popper, 1970; Rakover, 1981).

With this understanding of what Popper means by falsification, let us examine Figure 2–1, which outlines the steps in the empirical evaluation of a scientific explanation of behavior. The first step is to formulate a *research hypothesis*. Then a situation is arranged in which the research hypothesis is put to test. This situation is often generically called an *experiment,* although a research hypothesis may be tested in other ways. Then, a program or set of steps called a *research design* is developed to guide the observations and collection of evidence. The observations from the experiment are then compared against the predictions of the research hypothesis. If the observations and predictions do not agree, then, in principle, the theory and research hypothesis are falsified. For example, in a test of equity theory, falsification may occur if individuals do not become distressed after receiving an inequitable reward. If they do not, then the universal statement that individuals do become distressed in an equitable relationship cannot be true;

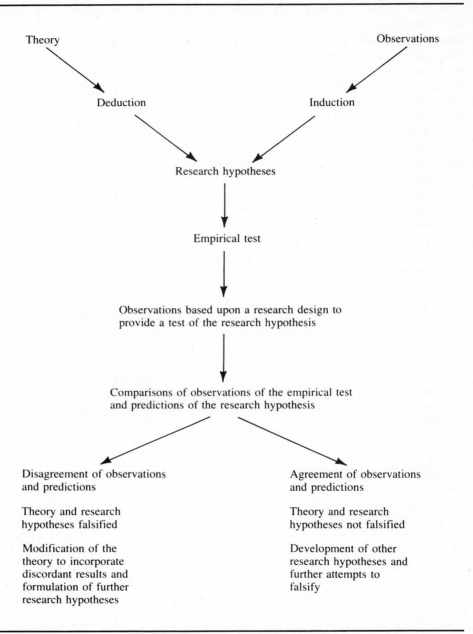

FIGURE 2-1   *A schematic representation of the process for empirically testing psychological theory and research hypotheses.*

it must be false. Presumably, then, the theory has been shown to be false and should be discarded or modified. In practice, however, deciding whether observations and predictions disagree is not always easily done. It may well be that the empirical test was simply not an adequate test of the research hypothesis, or that the research hypothesis was not correctly derived from the theory (such possibilities are more fully developed in later chapters). Thus, more realistically, a theory is modified to incorporate discordant findings, new predictions are developed, and further empirical tests are conducted.

What if the observations agree with the predictions in the research hypothesis? In this instance, Popper (1959) would argue that a scientist has given the theory an opportunity to be falsified and it was not. This failure to falsify does *not* verify, prove, or demonstrate the truth of the relationship. It provides, at best, only temporary support, and a scientist would develop further research hypotheses and once again attempt to falsify them.

This brief discussion suggests that theory must be *refutable*. That is, it must make predictions that can be falsified by observations; otherwise the theory is not scientifically useful; Popper (1963) summarized this condition: Whenever a scientist suggests that he or she has an empirical scientific theory, Popper proposes that one ask these questions:

> Can you describe any possible observations which, if they are actually made, would refute your theory? If you cannot, then your theory has clearly not the character of an empirical theory; for if all conceivable observations agree with your theory, then you are not entitled to claim of any particular observation that it gives empirical support to your theory.
>
> Or to put it more briefly: only if you can tell me how your theory might be refuted, or falsified, can we accept your claim that your theory has the character of an empirical theory. (p. 963. Copyright © 1963, Federation of American Societies for Experimental Biology. Used by permission.)

Beyond possessing the characteristic of refutability, a good theory has one further characteristic—*parsimony*. A good scientific explanation is as simple as possible. Scientists prefer simple explanations over complex explanations if both explain a phenomenon equally well. Simple explanations are much more easily put to empirical test than are complex explanations. This parsimony principle is often referred to as Occam's razor or Lloyd Morgan's canon (Marx, 1976a).

Current Theorizing in Psychology

Scientific psychology has a relatively short history compared to that of other scientific disciplines, and only modest success has been achieved in developing theories of behavior. In the mid-twentieth century, psychology passed through a period of grand theory building with the ambitious work of learning theorists such as Hull, Tolman, Guthrie, Lewin, and Spence (see Marx and Hillix, 1973).

BOX 2-2

So what does one do with "positive results," that is, an experimental outcome that is consistent with the hypothesis in question? How are these to be interpreted? In a word, cautiously. One can legitimately note their consistency with the hypothesis or state that they *corroborate* the hypothesis. Loosely speaking, corroboration refers to the act of having survived falsification (Popper, 1972). To say that a hypothesis has been "corroborated" is simply to state that it has been tested and has (tentatively) survived. This is very different, of course, from implying that it has been strengthened. No matter how many times a hypothesis survives falsification, it can never be legitimately said to have been "confirmed" or "supported." As corroborative instances accumulate, most of us experience a *psychological* increase in our confidence regarding the hypothesis in question. This subjective phenomenon should not, however, be confused with the logical warrant of the situation. As much as we scientists may like to view ourselves as rational creatures, there is a clear and significant difference between our rare use of logic and more common use of psycho-logic.

Michael J. Mahoney, Experimental methods and outcome evaluation. *Journal of Consulting and Clinical Psychology,* 46, 1978, pp. 670–671.

Most current theory building, however, is much more limited in scope. In fact, Marx (1976a, b) would call much of current psychological theory "theorizing" rather than "formal theory." He means that the propositions of current psychological theory are often not clearly conceptualized, and the development of research hypotheses from those propositions is often less rigorous than logic would demand. There is probably little disagreement with this position among social scientists. Selltiz et al. (1976) argue that "Social science *theories* are rarely elegant or sophisticated. In fact, social science theories usually assume the form of a series of assumptions that are loosely tied together and seem to lead to hypotheses" (p. 17).

When you begin to read reports of research published in the journals of psychology, you will quickly discover this shortcoming for yourself. You will have to tease out the propositions and theoretical guidelines that directed the research. The work of McCarthy and Betz is an example of theorizing. The theoretical propositions of their research have not been formally articulated, but an underlying proposition is that counselors' responses affect the client's perception of the counselor. A further underlying proposition is that self-disclosing responses by the counselor lead to different client perceptions than do self-involving responses by the counselor. Self-disclosing responses, self-involving responses, and clients' perceptions are all constructs that require further definition for empirical testing. Notice that McCarthy and Betz argue that these constructs have not been clearly conceptualized and differentiated in previous research.

The empirical testing of theory also often differs from the falsification approach we have presented. Many psychologists place more confidence in induction than Popper (1959) or other philosophers of science would find defensible.

Both Marx (1976a) and McGuigan (1978) argue that although a scientist can never be sure of the truth of a universal proposition of a theory, he or she can always provide some estimate of the probability of the truth of such a proposition. You will find this inference occurring in the literature of psychology, but there is certainly controversy over the appropriateness of such an inference.

The falsification concept also indicates that an instance of disagreement between the predictions of the research hypothesis and the results of the empirical test should lead to discarding a theory. But, as we have pointed out, this rejection rarely, if ever, happens on the basis of one apparent instance of disagreement. Cook and Campbell (1979) argue that discordant observations alone are not sufficient to lead a scientist to discard a theory. They propose that to falsify a theory, the discordant observations must be accompanied by an alternative explanation or theoretical formulation of the observed phenomenon. Indeed, the falsification approach advocated by Popper assumes that a theory that has not been falsified in an empirical test is only one of the many theories that may explain the behavior in question.

In practice, a psychologist may be quite fortunate to have even so much as one theory to explain the behavior in question (Cook and Campbell, 1979). Thus, a scientist will be quite reluctant to discard a theory merely on the basis of one set of observations that do not agree with the theory. Only if another viable explanation is available will the falsified theory be discarded. More realistically, as indicated in Figure 2–1, observations that falsify the propositions of the theory will lead to revisions and changes so that the discordant observations can be accommodated by the theory. In fact, it is quite likely that it will take a considerable number of empirical discomfirmations and the formulation of a more adequate new theory before an old theory will be considered falsified by the scientific community (see Kuhn, 1970)

Publishing theories in scientific journals and books is not akin to carving them in stone. They are not static, unchanging; scientists continually weave a kaleidoscopic tapestry of theory. Theories are ever-changing so that they will provide better and more precise explanations of the observations they generate.

Finally, we do not want to leave you with the impression that research always proceeds in the systematic straight-line path suggested in Figure 2–1. It often does not! "In point of fact, science is an extremely messy and untidy business, with errors and false starts much more common than successes" (Marx, 1976b, p. 262). In the early stage of investigating a problem, psychologists will often have little more than informed hunches to direct their investigations.

Usefulness of Theories in Psychological Research: Pro and Con

We have placed considerable emphasis on formulation of theories because it is the explanatory process of science. For the psychologist, theory provides a summary and explanation of behavior as well as guidance for new research. The value of

BOX 2-3

Issues in the philosophy of science seldom lead readers to write letters to the editor of a newspaper. However, a court test of the constitutionality of an Arkansas law requiring the teaching of "creation science" whenever evolutionary theory is taught in public schools and a letter to the editor supporting creation science prompted three readers of *The Boston Globe* to write letters discussing the scientific use of theory. We think these letters provide three different, but eloquent, statements about the importance of theory in research. Some of what the writers say is a reiteration of what we have already said; some is an elaboration of points which we have only briefly alluded to. For these reasons, we have reprinted excerpts from the letters here.

Theory is not the opposite of fact. To say that something is just theory is not to say that it is not based on fact. On the contrary, a theory is an explanation of facts.

A fact is a phenomenon about which all observers agree. The interpretation of facts may be open to question, but the facts themselves are not; a fact is not true or false—it simply is. Facts, then, are the raw material for theory.

One of the criteria for adequacy of scientific theories is that a theory must explain all the available facts. Only when an explanatory scheme does this is it a "theory." But, in principle, theories must also be falsifiable—that is, it must be possible to discover facts which contradict and thus falsify the theory. Only as long as such facts are not discovered is the theory valid.

A scientific theory is not a belief. It is an explanatory scheme which may be generated inductively from facts and which may be tested deductively with rules of evidence. "Scientific method" refers to the systematic examination of facts and testing of theories according to those rules of evidence. (Paula Swilling, Department of Sociology, Boston University)

To say that something is "only" a theory and "not yet" a fact is to fundamentally misconstrue the scientific method and its results.

The implication in such talk is that there are eternal "facts," a view which may be good religion but is surely bad science.

. . . A scientific theory must be tentative and always subject to revision or abandonment in light of facts that are inconsistent with or falsify a theory.

. . . To advance any old hypothesis without empirical verifiable data which supports it just is not science. It may be persuasive or psychologically useful or comforting . . . but it is not good science—any more than advancing the theory that the earth is flat is good science. (Grant Wiggins)

No scientific "law" or "theory" is fact—they're all only models that are reasonable approximations of nature that fit all known scientific observations, and (most importantly) are found to predict any future experimental observations. (David J. Glass, Ph.D. Biotechnica International, Inc.)

theory cannot be overemphasized; theory guides a scientist in his or her observations of the world. Indeed, the observations all of us make are based on some theoretical formulations, whether or not we are explicitly aware of them (Kaplan, 1964; Popper, 1963). Our observations of behavior are always interpreted in the context of our own theoretical formulations of human behavior.[5] Indeed, it is doubtful that "pure" observation, i.e., observation without a theoretical interpretation, exists.

Dixon (1980) argues that theory is also important in understanding and directing the search for causal relationships in psychology. As he states in quoting from Hanson (1958), "The conclusion is that causes are connected with effects 'because our theories connect them, not because the world is held together by cosmic glue'" (p. 273). Clearly, then, whether a scientist thinks the causes of a phenomenon have been adequately identified and explained will depend upon that scientist's theoretical conceptualizations of the phenomenon (Deese, 1972). Wolman (1965) summarized these points emphatically:

> A mere description is incomplete knowledge; it is necessary to *explain* and to form hypotheses and inferences. When some scientists and philosophers suggest limiting scientific inquiry to description, they may be reducing the adequacy of scientific systems below that of simple commonsense inquiry. "Pure" empiricism does not make science more rigorous; rather it makes it less adequate. A mere collection of facts is no more a science than a pile of bricks is a house. (p. 11)

Not all psychologists agree with the conceptualization of the science of psychology that we have described. Bachrach (1981) is quite wary of the "formal theoretical method" we have presented. He fears that theories may become rigid, that people often use the same observations to support several theories, and that theories are often developed on the basis of too little observation of behavior and meager data. It is difficult to disagree with these points. Bachrach favors an "informal theoretical method," wherein the goal of research is not formulation of theory, but an ordering of data to seek laws of behavior. Skinner (1975) argues strongly for careful observation of the organism in its environment without formulating scientific theory as the road to developing a science of psychology. Cook and Campbell (1979) assert that psychologists should achieve the "stubborn facts" before yielding to the temptation to develop elaborate theories of the behavior that interests them. Once again, we find it difficult to disagree with these points and, indeed, there is no doubt that the atheoretical approach espoused by Skinner has led to an important understanding of the nature of behavior.

---

[5]If you are inclined to respond to this point with some skepticism, as you might, consider the issue of prejudice in our society. Do you think that perhaps some of the discrimination problems of society may be related to individuals holding some universal propositions such as "All _____ [substitute your own example of an ethnic group] are _____ [substitute your own characterization, such as "lazy," "frugal," "arrogant," "dirty," etc.]"? Do you think that such beliefs might influence both your observations and interpretations of behavior?

Applying the Criteria of Science: Parapsychology

We have discussed a number of criteria typically imposed on the scientific study of behavior. In practice, published research in psychology meets these criteria more or less well. Research in the area of *parapsychology,* however, often falls considerably short of satisfying these requirements. Parapsychology includes the study of postulated phenomena such as extrasensory perception (ESP), which is the conjectured ability to have knowledge of objects and events without using normal sensory channels (vision, audition, taste, touch, smell) and psychokinesis (PK), which is the presumed ability to move or influence the movement of objects by thought or mental effort alone. In ESP studies, individuals frequently try to identify unseen cards, often at great distances (e.g., Osis, Turner, and Carlson, 1971), and at other times merely in different rooms (e.g., Roll and Klein, 1972). In PK studies, the task may involve an attempt to move a small object by mental powers alone (e.g., Pratt and Keil, 1973); to raise the temperature of a probe at a distance (e.g., Schmeidler, 1973); or to change the characteristics of an electronic random-event generator (Jahn, 1982). On occasion, the source of the PK may even be a recording of the voice of a person who supposedly has powers of PK (e.g., Pratt and Stevenson, 1976).

Postulated paranormal phenomena, such as ESP and PK, are given wide credence in the popular magazines and newspapers of today. But how well does parapsychological research meet the criteria of science that we have discussed?

Parapsychological phenomena have been investigated for hundreds of years; as yet, there are no coherent theories in the area, simply because theories explain reliable and replicable phenomena, the "stubborn facts." But stubborn facts are difficult to arrive at in parapsychology. So-called paranormal phenomena such as ESP and PK are erratic and unpredictable, and public replicability of the phenomena is nonexistent (Kurtz, 1978). From the point of view of the scientist, then, parapsychological phenomena do not meet the criteria of an orderly and determined world.

We have stressed the concept of falsification as an important component of the scientific study of a problem. To be useful, a theory or hypothesis must be testable and there must be potential observations that will refute the hypothesized relationship. Whatever the outcome of an empirical test of a putative parapsychological phenomenon, however, the parapsychologist is able to explain it. Even a friendly critic of parapsychology acknowledges as much: "When a high-scoring ESP subject scores at the chance level whenever he is tested by a skeptical investigator, the parapsychologist explains that the phenomenon does not operate in a hostile atmosphere. If the atmosphere is friendly and the high scorer still scores at chance level, the parapsychologist explains that boredom or fatigue (of the subject or experimenter) inhibits the phenomenon from operating" (Ransom, 1971, p. 292).

Finally, scientists stress parsimonious explanations—explanations that involve as few complex constructs as possible. Explanations of parapsychological phenomena, however, are usually quite complex. As Zusne and Jones (1982) state,

"It is simpler to conclude that extrachance [i.e., above chance] performance at ESP tasks is due to some combination of expected probabilities, fraud, poor controls, conjuring, and so on, that [*sic*] it is to assume a mysterious, unknown, and indescribable force exists that invalidates many of the central principles of several areas of science, including physics, physiology, and psychology" (p. 432).

The Empirical Test

In this chapter we have stressed the development of scientific explanations of behavior and empirically testable research hypotheses. The next step in research is to develop a research strategy or design to provide an appropriate empirical test of the research hypothesis. The information obtained from this empirical test will then be used to assess whether the research hypothesis is true or false. In the following chapters we turn to the procedures used to test research hypotheses.

SUMMARY

- Psychologists begin research on a problem with a "prepared mind" by being informed of the previous research in the problem area.
- Scientific research is characterized by assumptions of order and determinism, a search for causal relations, an empirical approach to inquiry, and obtaining results that are replicable.
- Theories are the explanations of phenomena offered by scientists.
- Research hypotheses are statements of tentative relations between antecedent conditions and consequent events (e.g., behavior). They are formulated either deductively from theories or inductively from observation of behavior.
- A research hypothesis provides an explicit statement of a relationship that is empirically testable, and it is formulated prior to testing.
- Theories and research hypotheses are empirically evaluated by establishing situations in which the theory or research hypothesis may be falsified.
- Some psychologists argue against the use of theory in research, contending that psychologists should first establish the "stubborn facts" of behavior before attempting to explain them.
- The field of parapsychology is viewed skeptically by many psychologists because purported parapsychological phenomena do not conform to scientific criteria.

3

In this chapter we introduce the fundamental concepts of the experimental method that are applicable to a wide variety of research problems. Topics include:

- The types of variables involved in psychological research
- Variables as constructs and the development of empirical referents for these constructs
- The basic design of an experiment and the problem of confounding
- Between-subjects and within-subjects experimental designs
- Two types of one-factor between-subjects designs—the true experiment and ex post facto studies

WHY YOU NEED TO KNOW THIS MATERIAL

Certain basic principles pervade much of psychological research. The design of experiments to provide answers for the questions asked builds upon these principles.

Fundamentals of Experimental Design

Several major approaches are used by psychologists to study behavior scientifically. They are usually identified as the experimental method, the ex post facto study, the correlational method, naturalistic observation, and the case-study approach. All these methods have some common features. For example, all involve observation and measurement of behavior. All methods are attempts to identify some events, variables, or circumstances that are related to the occurrence of the behaviors that are of interest. Only one of these methods, however — the experimental method—enables investigators to demonstrate the effect of a specific antecedent event on behavior and thus to establish cause-and-effect relationships. The key to demonstrating cause-and-effect relationships is the direct manipulation and control over the variables that influence the behavior that is of interest. Manipulation and control of variables are the essential features that distinguish the experimental method from the other approaches to psychological research. This chapter provides an introduction to the experimental and ex post facto methods of research. Correlational, naturalistic observation, and case-study approaches are discussed in Chapter 14.

VARIABLES OF PSYCHOLOGICAL RESEARCH

We have thus far frequently used the word *variable,* but we have not explicitly defined it. Quite simply, in psychology a **variable** is any environmental condition or event, stimulus, personal characteristic or attribute, or behavior that can take on different values at different times or with different people. Essentially, three major types of variables are of interest in psychological research—independent, dependent, and extraneous variables.

Independent Variables

The antecedent event that a psychologist may systematically vary to determine its effect on behavior is called an **independent variable.** Virtually anything that may affect behavior is potentially an independent variable. Psychologists typically distinguish between two types of independent variables—active and attribute variables.

Active Independent Variables

When a psychologist has direct control over and can manipulate the amount of the variable presented to participants in an experiment, then he or she is using an **active independent variable.** Active variables are often called **experimental** or **non-subject variables.**

As an example, the independent variable that is manipulated by McCarthy and Betz, type of counselor response, is an active independent variable. They had direct control over which participants received self-involving or self-disclosing statements.

Attribute Independent Variables

Attribute independent variables are characteristics or attributes of a participant such as sex,[1] age, handedness, anxiety, intelligence, or amount of schooling. An experimenter can select participants who possess the characteristic, but he or she cannot assign, administer, or present the characteristic to a person. Attribute variables are also often referred to as **subject, levels, organismic,** or **categorical variables.**

As an example of an attribute-independent variable, a psychologist may be interested in gender differences in behavior. Gender of the participant is an attribute variable. The experimenter may select individuals on the characteristic of sex, but cannot actively vary gender by designating whether a participant will be a male or a female.

Active independent variables characterize true experiments, but attribute independent variables are used in ex post facto research. The distinction between active and attribute independent variables is critical because it represents a difference in the ease with which cause-and-effect relations can be reached from research.

Dependent Variables

A psychologist engaged in the scientific study of behavior believes that this behavior is determined in an orderly way by the independent variable being manipu-

---

[1]The word *sex* designating an attribute-independent variable will always refer to the word in its noun form—that is, to designate the two commonly recognized divisions of living organisms, male and female. In some recent research the word *gender* is often used instead of sex.

lated. For this reason, the behavior of a participant that a psychologist studies is called the **dependent variable,** for changes in behavior depend upon variation of the independent variable. For example, McCarthy and Betz expected several different client perceptions of the counselor and the client's responses to the counselor to vary depending upon the type of counselor statement the participant was exposed to. The client's perceptions and client's responses are their dependent variables.

Independent Variables, Dependent Variables, and Research Hypotheses

In Chapter 2, we defined a research hypothesis as a statement of an expected relationship between an antecedent event and a consequent behavior. We have now pointed out that in psychological research antecedent events are called independent variables and consequent behaviors are called dependent variables. Using this terminology, we may recast the definition of a **research hypothesis** as a statement of a relationship between an independent variable and a dependent variable.

Extraneous Variables

All behaviors are multiply determined; that is, a variety of variables may influence a particular behavior. In an experiment, a scientist is concerned with determining the effect of only one (or at the most a few) independent variables. All the other variables which can affect behavior and which are not of direct interest in a particular study are called **extraneous variables.** In a sense, extraneous variables (sometimes called *nuisance variables*) are potential independent variables. That is, they are known to affect behavior, and they could be varied in an experiment. But, in an experiment in which they are extraneous to the independent variable that is of interest, a psychologist does not want to let them vary in any systematic way. Failure to control for their effects may result in an experiment that does not adequately test the research hypothesis of interest.

Extraneous variables are aptly named, for they literally are "extra" variables that are of no relevance to the purpose of the experiment. They are not included in the research hypothesis that specifies the relationship between the independent and dependent variables. They are also extratheoretical in that they lie outside the theoretical framework from which the research hypothesis was derived. In a real sense, they are a nuisance to the experimenter.

Sources of Extraneous Variables

In any type of psychological research, several sources of extraneous variables are possible.

Physical environment variables   A variety of variables that may affect behavior are always present in the physical environment in which the research is conducted. For example, the behavior exhibited in a task may depend upon environmental variation in ambient temperature, time of day, background noise, or lighting.

Attributes of the participants   People or animals have a variety of attributes or characteristics that may be related to the behavior in a research study. For example, differences in behaviors may be associated with age, intelligence, sex, weight, motivation, or anxiety of participants.

Procedural variations   If all aspects in the procedure of the experiment, except for the administration of the independent variable, are not held constant for each treatment group, then extraneous variables may be introduced into the experiment. For example, the experimenter may vary the instructions slightly from subject to subject. The instructions to subjects then become an extraneous variable in the research. Or perhaps the experimenter gives some participants more time to complete the experimental task, which introduces time as an extraneous variable into the experiment.

Extraneous variables can be quite subtly introduced into research. A psychology experiment is fundamentally a social situation in which the experimenter and participant interact. Whenever an individual knows that he or she is in an experiment, the experiment becomes reactive; the person may react to many aspects of the experimental situation that may not be actively manipulated by the experimenter. The subject may respond as he or she thinks the experiment demands based upon a variety of cues present in the experimental setting. On the other hand, the experimenter also enters the situation with certain expectancies about how the participants will behave and what the results will be. These potential effects of experimenter bias offer the possibility that the experimenter may behave differently toward the groups of participants in the experiment or may unintentionally record behaviors to favor the expected outcome. Certainly, the experimenter bias effects offer the possibility of introducing extraneous variables that may undermine the experiment. Thus, the potential extraneous variables stemming from the social nature of psychological research must be controlled in research situations. We discuss these potential problems more fully in Chapter 13.

Control of Extraneous Variables

The control of extraneous variables is a distinguishing feature of the experimental method. Indeed, the strategy of designing experiments is mainly one of controlling extraneous variables. If they are uncontrolled in an experiment, they will introduce unwanted variation in the behavior being measured. This unwanted variation in the dependent variable can lead the experimenter to the wrong conclusion about whether the independent variable has an effect or not. Controlling the effects of extraneous variables is thus a major challenge to the experimenter. Later in this chapter, we more fully discuss the effects of extraneous variables, how they affect the "integrity" of an experiment, and how they may be controlled.

VARIABLES AS CONSTRUCTS

In discussing psychological theory in Chapter 2, we stated that the terms used in a theory were often employed at a conceptual level. We referred to these terms as either *constructs* or *concepts* and gave examples such as *inequitable relationships* or *distress.* Most frequently when psychologists refer to variables they do so at a conceptual level. Theories and research hypotheses are often stated in terms of conceptual variables. Indeed, they were so stated in the example of Proposition III of equity theory and in the research hypothesis that was deduced from it. Because many of the independent and dependent variables of research hypotheses are stated at a conceptual level, we must more fully discuss them.

Concepts and Constructs

A **concept** is defined as "something conceived in the mind" or "an abstract or generic idea generalized from particular instances" (*Webster's Ninth New Collegiate Dictionary,* 1983, p. 272). Likewise, a **construct** is "something constructed, especially by mental synthesis" (*Webster's Ninth New Collegiate Dictionary,* 1983, p. 281).

These definitions indicate that constructs or concepts are merely invented terms that can be used to represent or symbolize categories of observations of the world. We stress that these constructs or concepts are ideational: they are neither tangible nor directly observable; rather, they are remote and unobservable. To emphasize that their origin lies in thought processes, Vandervert (1980) suggests that they be called *ideational constructs.* We, however, will usually call them simply *concepts* or *constructs.*

The constructs used in psychology are often borrowed from everyday language and then utilized in psychological research in a more limited way than ordinary language allows. You deal with such potential theoretical constructs each day when you discuss such things as anxiety, intelligence, distress, reward, aggression, hunger, motivation, fear, forgetting, attitude, grief, attractiveness, level of aspiration, and self-esteem. McCarthy and Betz employed constructs such as self-disclosing responses, expertness, and trustworthiness. Each of these terms is a construct which has been inferred from observations of behavior and which represents or summarizes those observations.

As another example we point out that a variety of behaviors can be subsumed under the construct of hunger: seeking out food, preparing it, sitting down at a table preparing to eat, ingesting food, and so on. The ideational construct of "hunger" is used to symbolize and summarize these behaviors rather than referring to the specific behaviors that led to development of the concept of hunger. These constructs are often used to represent behavioral or environmental variables that can vary in either quality or quantity. A person can be more or less hungry, highly anxious or not at all anxious, or in various states of distress.

Empirical Referents

The construct of "expertness" (or self-referent responses, distress, anxiety, motivation, intelligence, and others) cannot be directly observed. Rather, constructs are inferred from and measured by their empirical referents. As we stated in Chapter 2, the word *empirical* refers to observation; thus, the **empirical referents of a construct** are those observable objects, events, and behaviors from which the construct is inferred. For example, the referents of distress are behaviors and events that can be observed: crying, certain oral expressions, responses on a paper-and-pencil inventory, nonverbal behaviors, and others. Notice that no single empirical referent—no one event, object, or behavior—fully represents an ideational construct. Therefore, no one empirical referent fully represents the construct of distress.

Operational Definitions

The constructs or conceptual variables used by psychologists may have a variety of meanings for different people, or they may be vague or ambiguous. If someone tells you that she did not do well in a course because she was "not motivated," you may well wonder "what does she mean by 'not motivated'?" As we have stated, if a construct such as motivation is to be scientifically useful, then empirical referents must be provided for it. In research the empirical referents for conceptual variables are provided by operational definitions. An **operational definition** specifies and describes the empirical referents for a conceptual variable—the observable events that may be manipulated or measured in an experiment. Kerlinger (1973) refers to an operational definition as a "manual of instructions" (p. 31), and he distinguishes between experimental and measured operational definitions.

Experimental Operational Definition

An **experimental operational definition** specifies the operations used to manipulate a conceptual independent variable. Such a definition thus "explains" the specific use of the independent variable in the experiment. Because experimental operational definitions specify how the conceptual independent variable is to be manipulated, they can be used only when dealing with an active independent variable.

Let us use McCarthy and Betz's experiment to illustrate an operational definition. In the Method section of their report they describe the empirical referents for the self-disclosing and self-involving counselor responses: "A positive self-disclosing statement was one expressing similarity, rather than dissimilarity, of personal experiences, and a positive self-involving statement was an expression of positive, rather than negative, feelings about or reactions to the client" (p. 252). These statements indicate how the conceptual independent variable of type of counselor response was varied in the experiment. The exact words of the counselor in each condition that provide the specific operations used to manipulate the independent variable are provided by a script, however.[2] So that you may see this script, we have presented part of it in Table 3–1. The last two sentences, which we have labeled "self-disclosing" and "self-involving," thus provide McCarthy and Betz's experimental operation definition of the independent variable.

Measured Operational Definition

A **measured operational definition** specifies the procedures used to measure a conceptual variable. Two different uses of measured operational definitions occur in psychological research. One use specifies the procedures used to measure the dependent variable in an experiment. For example, McCarthy and Betz identified two conceptual dependent variables, client perceptions of the counselor and client responses, in their research hypothesis. The operational definitions that provide empirical referents for these conceptual dependent variables are also found in the Method section of their report. Because these operational definitions specify the empirical measurement of the conceptual dependent variables, they are measured operational definitions of the constructs of client perceptions and client responses.

The operational definition for measurement of the perceptions of the client was given by stating that the Counselor Rating Form (CRF) was used and by a reference to Barak and LaCrosse (1975). Barak and LaCrosse devised the CRF; their 1975 article presents the details of the items on the form and explains how the separate scales for expertness, attractiveness, and trustworthiness were derived and scored. So that you may see what the CRF looks like, we have reproduced it in Table 3–2.

---

[2]For the reader who is interested in this level of detail for the experiment, a footnote to the article indicates that a copy of the complete script can be had by writing to Dr. Betz. Any readers of this textbook who would like the complete script, however, should write not to Dr. Betz, but to Dr. Patricia R. McCarthy, Department of Psychology, Southern Illinois University at Carbondale, Carbondale, Illinois 62901.

TABLE 3-1   *A portion of the script used by McCarthy and Betz for simulated interview using counselor self-disclosure or counselor self-involving responses (Co = Counselor, Cl = Client)*[a]

Segment 1

Co: Hello, Miss Adams. Tell me what is bothering you.

Cl: Well, I don't know exactly. I just seem to be tired and irritable.

Co: What do you mean by tired and irritable?

Cl: You know, tired, not up to snuff. I seem to mope around a lot.

Co: What do you mean you mope around?

Cl: Well, I mostly eat and watch T.V. I just hate myself when I do that. I hate to watch T.V. when I'd really like to be doing something else.

Co: You hate yourself when you're not doing what you want to do?

Cl: Right.

Co: What would you like to do?

Cl: I'd really like to get out of here. Sort of start all over again. A lot of times I feel as though I've missed the boat somewhere along the road.

Co: You really don't like it here.

Cl: Yes. I want to be someone else. Someone at peace with themselves. I want a sort of quiet approach to life. Away from all this noise and hassle. I'm all closed-in.

Co: Tell me, when you start to feel closed-in with everything, what do you do to get yourself back together?

Cl: I don't know, just listen to records or something. I like to take walks in the woods. You know, withdraw from the maddening crowd.

Co: You like to be alone with yourself.

Cl: Right. I really get off on just separating myself from the whole mess. Spacing out, shaking off the dust.

Co: You just said you like to be alone; you've also said that you usually eat and waste your time when you're alone.

Cl: No, I like to be alone. I just eat when I'm not doing what I want to do.

Co: What stops you from doing what you want to do?

Cl: I'm not sure; that's why I'm coming to you. I want to get some insight into what is stopping me.

Co: It seems that you're pretty irritated with how you stop yourself.

Cl: Yeah! I *really* get mad at myself. I get angry and then nervous and then start to bite my fingernails. Look at my nails. They are all bitten down. I hate them, too.

Co: When you feel frustrated you sort of attack yourself.

Cl: Yeah. I think about all the things I don't like about myself.

*Tape 1—Co SD [self-disclosing]: I do that, too, at times, get down on myself.

*Tape 2—Co SI [self-involving]: Well, I like the good things I've seen about you.

"Write your response now."

---

[a]Used by permission of Dr. Patricia R. McCarthy and Dr. Nancy E. Betz.

The Counselor Rating Form. [a] ***The instructions below are those used by McCarthy and Betz***   **TABLE 3-2**

Listed below are several scales which contain word pairs at either end of the scale and seven spaces between the pairs. Please rate the counselor you just heard on each end of the scales. Please rate the counselor as you believe *the client* on the tape would rate him.

If the client feels that the counselor *very closely* resembles the word at one end of the scale, place a check mark as follows:

fair ___ : ___ : ___ : ___ : ___ : ___ : _X_ unfair

OR

fair _X_ : ___ : ___ : ___ : ___ : ___ : ___ unfair

If the client thinks that one end of the scale *quite closely* describes the counselor then make your check mark as follows:

rough ___ : _X_ : ___ : ___ : ___ : ___ : ___ smooth

OR

rough ___ : ___ : ___ : ___ : ___ : _X_ : ___ smooth

If the client feels that one end of the scale *only slightly* describes the counselor, then check the scale as follows:

active ___ : _X_ : ___ : ___ : ___ : ___ : ___ passive

OR

active ___ : ___ : ___ : ___ : _X_ : ___ : ___ passive

If both sides of the scale seem equally associated with the client's impression of the counselor or if the scale is irrelevant, then place a check mark in the middle space:

hard ___ : ___ : ___ : _X_ : ___ : ___ : ___ soft

Your first impression is the best answer.

PLEASE NOTE: PLACE CHECK MARKS IN THE MIDDLE OF THE SPACES

agreeable ___ : ___ : ___ : ___ : ___ : ___ : ___ disagreeable
unalert ___ : ___ : ___ : ___ : ___ : ___ : ___ alert
analytic ___ : ___ : ___ : ___ : ___ : ___ : ___ diffuse
unappreciative ___ : ___ : ___ : ___ : ___ : ___ : ___ appreciative
attractive ___ : ___ : ___ : ___ : ___ : ___ : ___ unattractive
casual ___ : ___ : ___ : ___ : ___ : ___ : ___ formal
cheerful ___ : ___ : ___ : ___ : ___ : ___ : ___ depressed
vague ___ : ___ : ___ : ___ : ___ : ___ : ___ clear
distant ___ : ___ : ___ : ___ : ___ : ___ : ___ close
compatible ___ : ___ : ___ : ___ : ___ : ___ : ___ incompatible
unsure ___ : ___ : ___ : ___ : ___ : ___ : ___ confident
suspicious ___ : ___ : ___ : ___ : ___ : ___ : ___ believable

(continued)

TABLE 3-2   *continued*

undependable	___ :	___ :	___ :	___ :	___ :	___ :	___ dependable
indifferent	___ :	___ :	___ :	___ :	___ :	___ :	___ enthusiastic
inexperienced	___ :	___ :	___ :	___ :	___ :	___ :	___ experienced
inexpert	___ :	___ :	___ :	___ :	___ :	___ :	___ expert
unfriendly	___ :	___ :	___ :	___ :	___ :	___ :	___ friendly
honest	___ :	___ :	___ :	___ :	___ :	___ :	___ dishonest
informed	___ :	___ :	___ :	___ :	___ :	___ :	___ ignorant
insightful	___ :	___ :	___ :	___ :	___ :	___ :	___ insightless
stupid	___ :	___ :	___ :	___ :	___ :	___ :	___ intelligent
unlikeable	___ :	___ :	___ :	___ :	___ :	___ :	___ likeable
logical	___ :	___ :	___ :	___ :	___ :	___ :	___ illogical
open	___ :	___ :	___ :	___ :	___ :	___ :	___ closed
prepared	___ :	___ :	___ :	___ :	___ :	___ :	___ unprepared
unreliable	___ :	___ :	___ :	___ :	___ :	___ :	___ reliable
disrespectful	___ :	___ :	___ :	___ :	___ :	___ :	___ respectful
irresponsible	___ :	___ :	___ :	___ :	___ :	___ :	___ responsible
selfless	___ :	___ :	___ :	___ :	___ :	___ :	___ selfish
sincere	___ :	___ :	___ :	___ :	___ :	___ :	___ insincere
skillful	___ :	___ :	___ :	___ :	___ :	___ :	___ unskillful
sociable	___ :	___ :	___ :	___ :	___ :	___ :	___ unsociable
deceitful	___ :	___ :	___ :	___ :	___ :	___ :	___ straightforward
trustworthy	___ :	___ :	___ :	___ :	___ :	___ :	___ untrustworthy
genuine	___ :	___ :	___ :	___ :	___ :	___ :	___ phony
warm	___ :	___ :	___ :	___ :	___ :	___ :	___ cold

As with all of the information obtained in this experiment, the contents of this questionnaire are strictly confidential.

[a]Copyright by M. B. LaCrosse and A. Barak, 1974, 1975. Used by permission.

The measured operational definition for client responses reveals that subjects were asked to provide a written response to the last counselor statement and that the content of these responses was analyzed. Notice that the authors indicate in a footnote that even more detailed information on how the responses were scored is available by writing to one of the authors. (We present this information in Table 4.1.)

A second use of measured operational definitions occurs when an attribute variable is employed as an independent variable. In this instance, participants must first be measured on some attribute and then categorized according to that measurement. A measured operational definition provides the specific procedures used for that process. For example, Smith, Snyder, and Handelsman (1982) compared high and low test-anxious individuals (an attribute variable) on symptom expression in a threatening situation. Their operational definition of high and low test anxiety was:

> Subjects were preselected on the basis of their scores on the Test Anxiety Questionnaire (Sarason, 1972), administered in a previous group-testing session. Fifty-eight females from the top fifth of a distribution of test-anxiety scores and 59 females from the lowest fifth of this distribution were selected. . . . Mean scores on this measure for the high and low test-anxious group were 27.2 and 8.6, respectively. (p. 317)

Difference Between Conceptual Variables and Operationally Defined Variables

Psychological theory and research hypotheses typically express relations among constructs or conceptual variables. Conceptual variables are usually identified in a theory or hypothesis in a few words at most. Operational definitions of these variables are typically described in the Method section of a research article and rarely are so briefly summarized.

The operational definition of a construct does not provide the full meaning of that construct, however. The meaning of a construct is *open* and therefore it is never fully defined (Meehl, 1970b); its meaning comes from its use in psychology, the theory in which it is embedded, and the various empirical referents that have been used with the construct. Because scientific research is a continuous process, theories and research hypotheses are never static; they are constantly undergoing test and emendation to more accurately reflect the accumulated information. Consequently, conceptual variables may gain new and different meanings as well as new empirical referents as theories and hypotheses become more fully developed.

Variables as Either Independent or Dependent

From a research point of view psychological variables often have no autonomous status as either independent or dependent variables. Whether the variable is independent or dependent in a study depends upon the relationship the experimenter is attempting to investigate. Something that is an independent variable in one study may be a dependent variable in another. In one study the psychologist may employ anxiety as an active independent variable and attempt to manipulate it in the participants. Spielberger and Smith (1966) manipulated anxiety by shock-threat instructions and measured learning performance. In this research, anxiety was the independent variable and learning performance the dependent variable. In another study anxiety may be the dependent variable. Bowman, Roberts, and Giesen (1978) measured anxiety in counselor trainees either during a counseling session or in a neutral session with a client. Here anxiety was the dependent variable and the type of training session was the independent variable.

Recall that the independent variable in the McCarthy and Betz experiment was the counselor's response. Other investigators may be interested in manipulating variables that affect the type of response the counselor makes. In this instance, the type of response by the counselor would become the conceptual dependent variable in the research.

THE EXPERIMENT

Although we have used the term "experiment," we have not explicitly defined it and have been content to let you apply a variety of interpretations to it. An **experiment** is a procedure in which an active independent variable is systematically manipulated, and changes in the dependent variable are measured, under controlled conditions. In an experiment, a psychologist manipulates an independent variable by establishing two or more levels (or values) of the independent variable. McCarthy and Betz established two levels of their independent variable of type of counselor responses—self-disclosing and self-involving responses. The effect of the independent variable can then be assessed by comparing the performance of participants who receive different treatments or levels of the independent variable.[3]

To determine the effect of an independent variable, it is necessary to compare the behavior of participants under at least two conditions. If there is an effect of the independent variable, then the behavior of participants exposed to different levels of the independent variable, that is, to different treatment conditions, should differ. Subjects assigned to different levels of the independent variable should be treated in exactly the same way in every aspect except one—the level of the independent variable administered. Thus, if a change of behavior occurs between the two levels of the independent variable, then—everything else being equal—it is reasonable to attribute the differences in behavior to the different treatments the participants received.

Control and Experimental Conditions

Any experiment employs at least two conditions, that is, two levels of the independent variable. In many instances, the conditions are called *control* and *experimental conditions*. Participants in an experimental condition receive some particular treatment. In a control condition, participants are not exposed to a particular treatment; the condition corresponds to an absence of a treatment or to a zero level of the independent variable. Thus, these participants are tested in a so-called normal condition.

---

[3]We use the terms *levels of the independent variable, experimental treatment, experimental condition,* and *treatment condition* synonymously.

It is not necessary to employ a control condition in which no specific treatment is administered in order to establish that an independent variable affects behavior. The important requirement is that there be at least two different conditions corresponding to two levels of the independent variable so that behavior can be compared. Suppose an experimenter wanted to determine whether or not hunger has an effect on rats running a straight alley for food. Hunger as an independent variable could be manipulated in a simple experiment by arranging a control condition (e.g., no hours of food deprivation) and an experimental condition (e.g., twelve hours of food deprivation). The experiment could be conducted too, however, by employing low and high levels of hunger (eight and twenty-four hours of food deprivation). In either experiment, if a difference between the two groups in the measure of running is obtained, then similar conclusions are warranted. In each instance, the two conditions represent two levels of an independent variable (zero versus twelve hours or eight versus twenty-four hours of food deprivation).

Confounding

To demonstrate that an independent variable affects a behavior, it is also necessary to rule out the influence of any other variable on that behavior. All other factors that can affect the behavior among individuals must be controlled. We used the cliché "everything else being equal" in stating the basis for establishing a causal relationship between an independent variable and a dependent variable. By that phrase we mean that all other variables which influence the behavior that is of interest are controlled so that they do not systematically affect the behavior being measured.

An experiment is **confounded** when an extraneous variable is unintentionally but systematically manipulated so that its levels *covary* (i.e., vary in conjunction) with the independent variable. In a confounded experiment the effect of the independent variable cannot be separated from the effects of the confounding extraneous variable. The confounding then offers a plausible alternative explanation for the results. Avoiding confounding is one of the major goals of an investigator in designing and conducting any experiment. Let us look at a few simple examples of confounding.

Suppose a psychologist who is interested in the effect of hunger on aggression in laboratory rats decides to investigate the problem using two levels of the independent variable, hunger. Suppose also that in the control condition aggression is measured in ten female white rats after zero hours of food deprivation, and in the experimental condition aggression is measured in ten white male rats after sixteen hours of food deprivation. If more aggression is found in the experimental group, is it due to hunger or to the sex of the rats? The psychologist does not know, and cannot tell, because the experiment was confounded. The sex of the animals covaried with the levels of the independent variable of hunger. The effects of hunger cannot be separated in this instance from the effects of the confounding extraneous variable of the animals' sex. It may be that male rats are more aggressive than female rats when not deprived of food.

Confounded "experiments" are also often encountered in everyday life. For example, television commercials and newspaper reports of so-called experiments provide numerous examples of confounding. Television commercials often present demonstrations that purport to show superiority of one product over another. Although a mere sixty seconds is not enough time to adequately describe or demonstrate a well-designed experiment, some of the examples of confounding are quite apparent to the perceptive and skeptical viewer.

A few years ago one shaving-cream manufacturer wanted to show that its product (let's call it "Beard Breaker") would give closer shaves than other shaving creams. The roughness of an unshaven man's beard was measured by the sound produced by scraping the beard with a credit card. Then the right side of his face was lathered with Beard Breaker and the left side with a "regular" shaving cream (i.e., the independent variable was type of shaving cream). As the viewer watched the man shaving his face, the announcer explained, "We used more pressure on the Beard Breaker side because its special lubricant permits us to." After shaving, the man's face was scraped again with the credit card. There was an audible difference in the resulting sound with less "scratching" from the right side of the face that had been lathered with Beard Buster. From this "experiment," can you conclude that the promoted shaving cream with the "special lubricant" was responsible for the closer shave? Or did the man get a closer shave with Beard Buster because he used more pressure while shaving on that side? Clearly, the demonstration was confounded. The pressure applied to the razor is obviously a potential independent variable which affects closeness of shave and which was not controlled in this demonstration.

In other commercials, the viewer is invited to perform his or her own test that is designed to show a product's effectiveness. One deodorant manufacturer asked viewers to "let the left side convince the right side" that a product (let's call it "Arm Sentry") was more effective than another popular deodorant. Viewers were asked to use Arm Sentry under their left arm and another popular deodorant under their right arm. (What is the independent variable?) Suppose people who went to the effort to conduct the test did find that the side with the manufacturer's deodorant was drier than the other side. Does this difference mean that Arm Sentry was more effective? Is there some other explanation for the result? For example, because most people are right-handed and therefore use their right arm more actively, is it surprising that there would be less "wetness" on the left side where Arm Sentry was used?

The research that you will encounter published in psychological journals is rarely so blatantly confounded; rather, the sources of confounding in an experiment may be quite subtle. As an example of possible confounding, consider an experiment by Hart (1973). The purpose of the experiment was to see if open-mindedness could be increased among counselor trainees through a written self-teaching program. The participants were sixty students in a first-year graduate counseling course. The procedure, as described in the article, was:

Half of the subjects were selected randomly into an experimental group that completed one exercise per week for eight weeks. Each subject completed an exercise and mailed his answers to the experimenter, who made comments and returned them to the subject along with the next exercise in the sequence. The experimenter's comments served to reinforce evidence of open-mindedness through praise. Lack of open-mindedness was corrected and more appropriate responses were suggested. The other half of the subjects served as a control group and had no contact with the experimenter during the eight-week period. (Hart, 1973, p. 569)

The results showed that the experimental group exhibited more "open-mindedness" on three simulated counseling measures than the control group. Although it was not stated explicitly, it is clear that the author attributes the difference in the amount of open-mindedness to the effect of the self-teaching program using the written exercises. We do not necessarily agree with that conclusion. We argue that the experiment was confounded because the treatments administered to the experimental and control participants differed in more than one way. The experimental participants not only completed a written exercise each week, but they also received written comments from the experimenter praising evidence of open-mindedness and suggesting appropriate responses where errors were made. The control group had no contact at all with the experimenter during the eight weeks. Therefore, it is not possible to ascertain whether it was the praise given to participants for open-mindedness responses, the mere experience in doing the written exercises regardless of praise received, or the weekly attention given to the experimental participants that was responsible for the differences. We shall describe a variety of techniques for controlling the effects of extraneous variables to avoid confounding in Chapter 4.[4]

THE BASICS OF EXPERIMENTAL DESIGN

As we have pointed out, control is the essential feature of the experimental method that ultimately aims to demonstrate a cause-and-effect relationship between an independent variable and a dependent variable. Over the years, approaches called experimental designs have been developed to guide construction of an experiment. An **experimental design** is an outline or general plan of an experiment that includes the number of independent variables, the number of levels of each independent variable, and how participants are to be assigned to conditions (Yaremko, Harari, Harrison and Lynn, 1982). An experimental design provides a framework within which a psychologist can establish controlled conditions for making observations to test the research hypothesis.

Several well-established experimental designs—identified by names—are used when one or more independent variables are manipulated or employed in an

[4]A book by Schuyler W. Huck and Howard M. Sandler, *Rival Hypotheses* (Harper & Row, 1979), provides a variety of other examples of confounding, many selected from reports in newspapers and magazines.

experiment. The type and name of an experimental design depends upon the number of independent variables manipulated or employed and upon how participants are assigned to levels of the independent variable.

Number of Independent Variables Employed

Experimental designs are described as one-factor, two-factor, three-factor, and so on, designs. The word *factor* is used in the context of experimental design synonymously with the words *independent variable*. Thus, a one-factor design has one independent variable with two or more levels of that independent variable. McCarthy and Betz's experiment is an example of a one-factor experimental design. A two-factor design has two independent variables and each of the two independent variables may have two or more levels. Two-factor designs are discussed in Chapter 10.

Between-Subjects and Within-Subjects Designs

Experimental designs are also identified as between-subjects or within-subjects, depending upon how participants are assigned to levels of the independent variable. If different groups of individuals receive different treatments, and therefore all subjects in a group receive just one level of an independent variable, then a **between-subjects design** is employed.[5] With this type of design, differences between groups of different subjects are used to assess the effect of the independent variable on the dependent variable. There are as many groups of different subjects as there are levels of the independent variable.

    The simplest type of experimental design is a *one-factor between-subjects design* with only two levels or values of the independent variable. This is the type of design used by McCarthy and Betz. They manipulated one independent variable (type of counselor response), which had only two levels (self-disclosing or self-involving statement). Moreover, it is clear from the Method section of their article that they used a between-subjects design: "Subjects were randomly *assigned to one* of the two experimental conditions. . . . For *each subject group,* either the tape using counselor self-disclosing responses or that using counselor self-involving responses was played" (pp. 252–253, italics added). This type of design is discussed more fully in the next section.

    In **within-subjects designs**, one group of subjects is exposed to all levels of each independent variable. That is, the participants first receive one experimental treatment or level of the independent variable and then their responses are measured. Then, each individual is administered a second experimental condition

---

[5]Between-subjects designs are sometimes called *separate-group designs, independent-group designs, random-group designs, completely randomized one-factor designs, single-factor designs,* or *post-test-only control designs.*

corresponding to another level of the independent variable and their responses are recorded again. If there is another experimental condition or a third level of the independent variable, the subjects are tested again. In a within-subjects design, each participant is exposed to *all* levels of the independent variable or independent variables. Individuals receive one experimental treatment or condition at a time and therefore are measured repeatedly.[6] With this type of design, the effect of the independent variable is assessed by examining differences within individuals responding to different treatment conditions.

If McCarthy and Betz had used a within-subjects design, they would have had one group of participants who would have been given both self-disclosing and self-involving responses. For their problem, however, such a design would not have adequately tested their research hypothesis. Within-subjects designs are discussed in Chapter 11.

ONE-FACTOR BETWEEN-SUBJECTS DESIGNS

In this section we introduce two forms of between-subjects designs—the true experiment with an active independent variable, and the ex post facto study with an attribute independent variable. Both of these designs are widely used in psychological research; the two share many characteristics, but also have fundamental differences that affect the ease with which we can arrive at cause-and-effect conclusions. We begin our discussion with the so-called true experiment.

The True Experiment

The two interdependent criteria for the design of a true experiment employing a between-subjects design are: (1) The independent variable is an active variable, and (2) equivalent groups of subjects are created before the independent variable is manipulated. In a **true experiment,** the experimenter controls which subjects receive a particular experimental treatment and when it is administered or given to the individuals (Campbell and Stanley, 1963). Because of these characteristics, true experiments provide the prototype for arriving at causal relationships from empirical research.

The basis for drawing conclusions about the effect of an independent variable from a true experiment is supplied by creating equivalent groups of participants prior to manipulating the independent variable and therefore prior to administering treatment conditions to individuals. Conclusions about the effects of the independent variable are then based upon differences observed between the equivalent groups of participants after the independent variable has been manipulated.

---

[6]Within-subjects designs are thus sometimes called *repeated-measures* or *single-group* designs.

Equivalent Groups

Equivalent groups (notice that we do not say equal groups) means that the groups of subjects that are created are not expected to differ in any systematic way prior to presenting the treatment conditions. This similarity does not imply that participants in each group will be exactly alike prior to receiving the experimental treatments, obviously an impossible requirement. When equivalent groups are formed, however, a psychologist expects that the overall differences between the groups on the dependent variable that is of interest would be minimal before subjects are exposed to different treatments. Any differences between the groups should be so-called chance differences, and, as we explain in Chapter 7, a psychologist can assess the probability of their occurrence.

The key to forming equivalent groups is to use an *unbiased* assignment procedure in allocating individuals to levels of the independent variable. As an example of a *biased* assignment procedure, consider an experiment with two levels of the independent variable in which the experimenter wants to determine the effect of duration of counseling sessions on a counselor's perceived effectiveness. Suppose the experimenter, a male counselor, arbitrarily assigns mostly females to the group that receives most time with the counselor and a majority of males to the condition that requires least time. To the extent that males and females may respond to male counselors differently—regardless of the duration of sessions on which the participants' evaluations of effectiveness are presumably based—the experiment has obviously been confounded with sex of the participant. By failure to form equivalent groups prior to introduction of the independent variable, the groups may differ on the dependent measure before the intended treatment is introduced. Females may tend to evaluate male counselors differently than males even before an independent variable is manipulated.

Random assignment   Equivalent groups in a true experiment are created by randomly assigning subjects to the experimental treatments or levels of the independent variable. Essentially, **random assignment** means that any individual selected for the experiment has an equal chance of being assigned to any one of the experimental conditions. More specifically, random assignment satisfies two criteria: (1) The probability of assignment to any of the treatment conditions is equal for every subject, and (2) the assignment of each individual is independent of the assignment of every other individual (i.e., the assignment of one participant to a condition does not affect the assignment of any other individual to that same condition). Random assignment of participants to levels of the independent variable is the *sine qua non* of the true experiment. To have a true experiment, subjects must be randomly assigned to treatment conditions.

The purpose of random assignment, then, is to form equivalent groups by effectively ensuring, though not guaranteeing, that the effects of extraneous attribute variables, such as motivation, sex, anxiety, intelligence, and age are distributed without bias among the groups. The treatment groups should not differ in any systematic way before the treatments are given.

The research of McCarthy and Betz is an example of a true experiment. The independent variable is an active independent variable, a between-subjects design was employed, and equivalent groups of participants were created by random assignment. Because these criteria were met, and because apparently no extraneous variables confounded the experiment, McCarthy and Betz felt it was appropriate to arrive at causal conclusions from their research. This intent is clearly seen from their discussion: "Generally, the results of this study suggest that counselor self-disclosing versus self-involving responses have differential *effects* on client perceptions of the counselor and on the nature of the client responses they *elicit*" (p. 254, italics added). Clearly, McCarthy and Betz conclude that the overall differences between their two groups of participants on perceptions of the counselor and clients' responses were caused by their manipulation of the independent variable. If they ruled out confounding by any extraneous variable, then their conclusions are appropriate.

Ex Post Facto Studies

Many so-called experiments in psychology appear to be true experiments because they utilize between-subjects research designs. They differ from true experiments, however, in a very important way: The independent variable is an attribute rather than an active variable. These studies, known as ex post facto studies[7] pose problems to the researcher that true experiments do not; let us see what these problems are.

Ex post facto studies employ attribute independent variables such as gender of participants, anxiety levels, intelligence, birth order, age, smoking habits, personality characteristics (e.g., introverted or extroverted), or handedness. When a psychologist "manipulates" such independent variables, subjects cannot be randomly assigned to a particular treatment condition to create equivalent groups. Instead, participants are "assigned" to a group or level of the independent variable because they possess a particular attribute that is of interest to an experimenter. So that it is clear that the attribute variables cannot be directly manipulated by the experimenter, we will say ex post facto studies *employ* rather than manipulate an attribute independent variable. We use the word *manipulate* only when discussing active independent variables that can be directly manipulated by the experimenter.

In studies employing attribute independent variables, subjects essentially *select* themselves into the levels of the independent variable. Suppose a psychologist is interested in comparing people who are high and low on test anxiety (an attribute independent variable) on their performance on a difficult intellectual

---

[7]As with some of the terminology in psychological research, the term *ex post facto* is not used consistently among authors. Cook and Campbell (1979) do not use the term in their discussion of quasi-experimental designs. Kerlinger (1979) uses the designations *nonexperimental research* and *ex post facto research* synonymously. Farrant (1977) calls them *after-the-fact* designs.

task. In this study people would be measured on test anxiety prior to their selection to participate in the study. Those people who represent the highest and the lowest 20 percent of the scores on the test-anxiety measure would then be selected to form high- and low-anxiety groups. Subsequently, their performance on the intellectual task would be measured. Notice that the individuals who participate in this study are *self-selected* into a level of test anxiety. Essentially then, the "manipulation" of the independent variable of test anxiety took place before the individual was selected as a participant in the research.

The term *ex post facto* is of Latin origin and refers to something "done, made, or formulated after the fact" (*Webster's Ninth New Collegiate Dictionary*, 1983, p. 438). Thus, in the sense that the subjects assign themselves into treatment conditions (by birth, choice, or by choice of others) prior to the study the experimenter's employment of the attribute variable occurs after the fact; that is, after the attribute variable has already been "manipulated." For example, if you were to participate in the test-anxiety study, the factors determining whether you are high or low in test anxiety would have occurred before you participated in the study.

The McCarthy and Betz True Experiment as an Ex Post Facto Study

To aid in discussing some of the difficulties in arriving at causal relations from an ex post facto study, we present a hypothetical study that McCarthy and Betz might have used to test their research hypothesis in lieu of the true experiment they did conduct.

Suppose McCarthy and Betz identified counselors who use either self-disclosing or self-involving statements routinely in their counseling practice. Then suppose they were able to anonymously identify clients of these counselors (the ethical issue of confidentiality aside for the moment) and administer the Counselor Rating Form (CRF) to 100 of these clients—50 undergraduates who received counseling by psychologists who used self-disclosing statements during counseling sessions, and 50 who were counseled by psychologists who invoked self-involving statements with their clients. Suppose further that McCarthy and Betz obtained ratings identical to those presented in their Table 1, and counselors using self-involving statements in their counseling were rated higher in expertness and trustworthiness than counselors who used self-disclosing statements. That is, suppose the same relationship between type of self-referent statement used by counselors and the client's rating of the counselor's expertness and trustworthiness is found in this ex post facto study as was found in their true experiment.

This brief description of a hypothetical ex post facto study suggests one approach that could be used to test the research hypothesis of McCarthy and Betz. This research study, however, would not permit the authors to conclude that differences in client ratings of the counselors are due to the types of self-referent statements used by the counselor. Why? The answer to this question resides in the difficulty of obtaining equivalent groups in ex post facto studies.

Nonequivalent Groups in Ex Post Facto Studies

Whenever an attribute variable is employed as an independent variable, nothing can ensure that the groups differing on the attribute are equivalent in all respects except for the attribute that is of interest. In fact, one can be quite certain that they are not equivalent. That is, the groups will systematically differ on many characteristics other than the attribute that is of interest (Meehl, 1970a). It may be that one of these characteristics is the variable that leads to the differences in behavior and not the attribute on which participants were selected. Unfortunately, there are so many related characteristics that a psychologist is unlikely to ever know and be able to control for all of them in one study. Therefore, *ex post facto studies are inherently confounded,* and one cannot establish cause-and-effect relationships between the independent and dependent variables.

Consider our hypothetical experiment. The independent variable, type of counselor selected, was employed as an attribute variable; the two groups of participants were formed by self-selection. Clients of psychologists who typically used self-disclosing statements formed one group, and clients of counselors who routinely used self-involving statements formed the other group. Participants were not randomly assigned to groups before the independent variable was introduced; rather, they were selected because they had received counseling with counselors who used either self-disclosing or self-involving statements. By choosing a counselor with a particular style of counseling, the participants self-selected into one of the two levels of the independent variable of type of counselor response. A psychologist would not be confident that the two groups of individuals would be equivalent before they received their counseling with either type of counselor; it is easily possible that different types of individuals would seek out or continue counseling with a particular type of counselor. Thus, clients who sought counseling with counselors who reveal personal feelings through self-involving statements may have a tendency to generally evaluate counselors more favorably than clients who seek counselors using self-disclosing statements. Or perhaps the two groups systematically differed on the types of problem for which they sought counseling, or on the amount of time they had spent in counseling. Further, perhaps the two types of counselors who were sought out differed on a variety of characteristics such as age or sex in addition to type of response given to clients' statements.

Perhaps it has occurred to you that it might be possible to try to match the participants as closely as possible on attributes other than the one that is of interest; for example, match clients who sought self-disclosing and self-involving counselors on type of problem for which they sought counseling. If one could do so, then one could rule out any differences in ratings of the counselors between the two groups as due to the type of problem for which counseling was sought.

The advisability of attempting to match participants who have been selected on the basis of one attribute (e.g., type of counselor selected) on another attribute that may be related to the dependent variable (e.g., the type of problem for which counseling is sought) is, however, in doubt. Meehl (1970a) cautions against trying to equate groups created by the selection on the attribute of interest with another characteristic known to be related to the dependent variable. His argument is that whenever groups are matched on one attribute (e.g., matching the participants on the type of problem for which counseling was sought), then they are "systematically unmatched" on another characteristic that also may be related to performance on the dependent variable (e.g., amount of time spent in counseling). Meehl provides no solution to this problem, but he implies it may be better not to attempt to match subjects on a second attribute variable (e.g., type of problem) when they already differ on one (e.g., the type of counselor sought out). Farrant (1977), however, is less pessimistic on this issue and provides an example of matching deaf and normal-hearing children on intelligence, possible brain damage, and type of schooling.

Conclusions from Ex Post Facto Studies

Inferences from ex post facto research must always be more cautious than inferences from true experiments. Because participants in a true experiment are randomly assigned to treatment conditions, there should be no systematic differences in the attributes of the participants in the resulting groups. Ex post facto studies permit the investigator to observe a relationship between two variables (e.g., between type of counselor selected and ratings of the counselor); but, because the groups studied are not equivalent, causal relations are not easily reached. Only a true experiment that employs an active independent variable and equivalent groups permits reaching cause-and-effect conclusions from a study.

Smoking and health   The enormous difficulty of coming to firm conclusions by ex post facto research is shown by one of the major social-scientific debates of the century—the question of how cigarette smoking affects health. As early as 1927 and in published research of 1938 (see Brown, 1972), it was observed that high rates of lung cancer were associated with heavy cigarette smoking. Yet there is still debate about the causal relation of cigarette smoking and health.

Why has it taken so long to reach this conclusion on the effects of cigarette smoking and physical health? Although many social and economic factors impinge upon the answer to this question, a major reason is that research on the effects of smoking in human beings has been ex post facto. That is, people have been categorized on the attribute of smoking or nonsmoking and then the various aspects of their health have been observed. But notice that smokers and nonsmokers are likely to differ on a host of attributes—diet, amount of alcoholic beverages consumed, exercise taken, sleep obtained, anxiety levels, and so on. There even may be hereditary differences between smokers and nonsmokers (Brown, 1972). If differences in health are found between smokers and nonsmokers in ex post facto research, then each of the related attributes (such as diet or exercise) must be ruled out as the causal agent for the health differences before the research can be confident that the reason for the differences is the smoking behavior. If you follow your newspaper or magazines, you will discover that the debate is not over, as illustrated in Figure 3–1.

Can we have an open debate about smoking?

The issues that surround smoking are so complex, and so emotional, it's hard to debate them objectively.

In fact, many of you probably believe there is nothing to debate.

Over the years, you've heard so many negative reports about smoking and health—and so little to challenge these reports—that you may assume the case against smoking is closed.

But this is far from the truth.

Studies which conclude that smoking causes disease have regularly ignored significant evidence to the contrary. These scientific findings come from research completely independent of the tobacco industry.

We at R.J. Reynolds think you will find such evidence very interesting. Because we think reasonable people who analyze it may come to see this issue not as a closed case, but as an open controversy.

We know some of you may be suspicious of what we'll say, simply because we're a cigarette company.

We know some of you may question our motives.

But we also know that by keeping silent, we've contributed to this climate of doubt and distrust. We may also have created the mistaken impression that we have nothing to say on these issues.

That is why we've decided to speak out now, and why we intend to continue speaking out in the future.

During the coming months we will discuss a number of key questions relating to smoking and health. We will also explore other important issues including relations between smokers and non-smokers, smoking among our youth, and "passive smoking."

Some of the things we say may surprise you. Even the fact that we say them may prove controversial.

But we won't shy away from the controversy because, quite frankly, that's our whole point.

We don't say there are no questions about smoking. Just the opposite. We say there are lots of questions—but, as yet, no simple answers.

Like any controversy, this one has more than one side. We hope the debate will be an open one.

R.J. Reynolds Tobacco Company

A full-page advertisement that appeared in many national magazines. Copyright © 1984 by R. J. Reynolds Tobacco Company. Used by permission.

FIGURE 3–1

65

Do you suspect the issue could be resolved if scientists were able to conduct true experiments on smoking? Suppose a scientist could randomly assign individuals to a smoking condition and a nonsmoking condition and then follow their health for a long time. If the experiment found the massive differences in health between smokers and nonsmokers that have typically been found in ex post facto studies of smoking, do you suppose that scientists as well as lay people would remain unconvinced about the effects of smoking? Of course, ethical considerations preclude such an experiment, and the only way information can be obtained with people on this problem is by some form of ex post facto research.

On the other hand, the only way in which many of the potential independent variables that interest psychologists may be studied is by some type of ex post facto research. In fact, Kerlinger (1973) suggests that ex post facto studies outnumber true experimental studies in the social and behavioral sciences. Most attribute variables can be studied only as attribute independent variables either for pragmatic reasons (e.g., it is not easy to change the sex of a participant) or ethical reasons (even if it were easy to change the sex of participants, would it be ethical?).[8] Ex post facto designs are also particularly useful when dealing with problems involving physical disorders such as deafness or other sensory defects, or in problems dealing with "everyday-life" situations such as social drinking or drug use (Farrant, 1977).

In this chapter we have introduced the basic concepts needed to design a research study, the types of variables important in psychological research, the operational definition of variables, the nature of an experiment and the distinction between a true experiment and an ex post facto study. In Chapter 4, the principles of designing a sensitive experiment are introduced. These principles are aimed at detecting the effect of an independent variable when one exists, and in large part, are applicable to both true experimental and ex post facto designs.

SUMMARY

- The variables in psychological research include the independent variables manipulated by the experimenter, the dependent variable measured in the experiment, and extraneous variables, which, if not controlled, may confound an experiment.
- Variables are often used at a conceptual level. To be useful in research, however, empirical referents must be provided for these conceptual variables by using operational definitions.
- An experiment is a situation in which an active independent variable is systematically varied, a dependent variable is measured, and extraneous variables are controlled.

[8]There are some exceptions. One could study effects of smoking on performance by studying smokers who then quit smoking; or a psychologist could study the relationship of body weight to measures of self-esteem by repeatedly measuring individuals who are on a diet.

- Experimental designs are identified by the number of independent variables employed and by whether the design is a between-subjects or a within-subjects design.
- One-factor between-subjects designs include the true experiment and the ex post facto study. A true experiment requires an active independent variable and equivalent groups of subjects created by random assignment.
- Ex post facto studies involve nonequivalent groups of subjects created by selecting subjects who possess the desired level of an attribute independent variable.
- True experiments permit researchers to reach cause-and-effect conclusions from the experiment. Ex post facto studies lead to conclusions of relationships between the attribute independent variable and the dependent variable.

4

PREVIEW

In this chapter we focus on the techniques used to control extraneous variables in designing a sensitive experiment which will detect the effect of an independent variable and which is not confounded. Topics include:

- The effects of extraneous variables in an experiment
- The design of a sensitive experiment by maximizing variation due to the independent variable and minimizing variation due to extraneous variables
- Factors that determine the number of participants to be used and the importance of running a pilot study before the experiment is conducted

WHY YOU NEED TO KNOW THIS MATERIAL

Extraneous variables are the bane of all experimenters. Much of the effort in designing an experiment is directed at controlling them, for extraneous variables that are not adequately controlled may lead to results that cannot be interpreted.

Designing and Conducting
an Experiment

EFFECTS OF EXTRANEOUS VARIABLES

A major aim in any true experiment is to detect the possible effect of an independent variable. The road to testing a research hypothesis with an experiment is not smoothly paved, however. Good intentions such as actively manipulating the independent variable and selecting the appropriate experimental design are not enough. As we indicated in Chapter 3, an inadequately controlled experiment can lead the experimenter to wrongly conclude that the independent variable has no effect when it actually does, or, conversely, to conclude that it has an effect when it does not. Either way, failure to adequately control for the effects of extraneous variables would jeopardize the conclusions reached in the research. For this reason, much of the strategy of experimental design is directed at controlling extraneous variables. Although our discussion is about an experiment, control of extraneous variables is equally important for ex post facto studies. The discussion in this chapter, then, is applicable to both true experiments and ex post facto studies.

Extraneous variables can undermine an experiment and lead the experimenter to a wrong decision about the research hypothesis in two ways. They can (1) confound an experiment or (2) contribute unwanted "error variation."

Confounding

As we stated in Chapter 3, an experiment is confounded when the values of one or more extraneous variables are systematically varied with the levels of the independent variable. In a confounded experiment, the psychologist can never be certain whether the extraneous variable(s) or the independent variable is responsible for any observed differences in behavior of participants who received different levels of the independent variable. It is imperative that the treatments administered to subjects receiving different levels of the independent variable systematically differ in only one respect; otherwise the experiment is confounded, no matter how

69

little the treatments differ in these other respects. Confounding offers a plausible alternative explanation for the outcome of the experiment.

Confounding in true experiments can almost always be avoided by employing a variety of techniques that we describe later in the chapter. A psychologist can be certain, however, that ex post facto studies will be confounded in spite of his or her best efforts to avoid it. Participants in an ex post facto study are selected because the characteristic they possess corresponds to the appropriate level of the attribute being employed as an independent variable. But, as we discussed in Chapter 3, other characteristics inevitably covary with the designated attribute. Hence, we feel it quite appropriate to issue the caution that an ex post facto study is always inherently confounded.

Error Variation

If a scientist could design a perfect experiment, he or she would identify and control all variables that measurably affect the behavior that is of interest. If this could be done, then the only variation in the dependent variable among participants would be due to the different treatments they received; all subjects who received the same treatment would have the same scores. There would be no differences in scores among individuals within a treatment condition.

Unfortunately, such an ultimately controlled experiment never occurs in practice; it is strictly a figment of a researcher's imagination. The fact is that in any experiment there will be differences among individuals in the behavior measured that *cannot* be attributed to the experimental treatments the participants received. People will differ from one another on whatever behavior is measured, even when they all receive the same treatment condition. In research terminology, there will be *variability* or *variation* among the scores obtained. Some of the total variability in an experiment will be due to the systematic effects of the independent variable; but unsystematic variability will also occur among participants who received the same treatment or who possess the same attribute. This unsystematic variation in scores among individuals who receive the same treatment is called **error variation.**

Error variation is evident in the expertness ratings on the CRF in McCarthy and Betz's experiment. For example, the scores of the first five subjects who received the self-disclosing treatment were 59, 74, 65, 57, and 26, respectively.[1] Although all these individuals received the same treatment, their scores reflect considerable error variation.

Two major factors are responsible for error variation—extraneous variables and errors of measurement. We discuss each of these sources of error variation separately.

_____

[1]The meaning of these scores is explained in Chapter 5.

Error BOX 4-1

Using the word *error* to characterize the variability among participants' scores that is due to factors other than the independent variable is often confusing for beginning students of psychological research. Common usage of the word *error* carries the connotation that a mistake has been made and that the error can be recognized, if not during its occurrence, then at least after it has been made. Certainly, this is the connotation of error in sports. When a baseball player makes an error, it means that the player makes a mistake in playing that can be clearly identified. Further, there is an implication that the error could have been avoided if the player had done something differently.

In psychological research, however, the use of the term *error* carries a different connotation. Its only implication is that there is some variability in scores which is due to a variety of factors which cannot be specifically isolated and controlled. It does not necessarily mean that an identifiable mistake or blunder has been made in the research (although such a mistake may indeed have occurred). If we say that McCarthy and Betz have error variation in the scores of their experiment, it means only that the scores within a treatment condition are not identical; they differ from each other due to the variety of extraneous variables that are functioning in every experiment. At a later point, we quantify error variation into a quantity know as *error variance*. Error variance deals with nothing more than providing a measure of the error variation in the experiment.

If you clearly understand the use of the word *error* in this context of psychological research, then you will not be led to believe that it reflects an overt error by the experimenter, or that a more astute experimenter may have avoided making such an error. Error variation and error variance exist in every instance of psychological research. Psychologists do all they can to minimize and eliminate such error variation in research, but they cannot completely avoid it.

Extraneous Variables

In Chapter 3 we identified the kinds of extraneous variables in an experiment: Differences in the physical environment that occur from time to time, attributes or characteristics of the individuals who participate in the experiment, and procedural variations that may occur in the experiment. Each of these kinds of extraneous variables may lead to differences in subjects' performances in the experiment. Some variation in the measure of the dependent variable can be expected from changes in the physical environment in which the experiment is conducted—noise levels, illumination conditions, ambient temperature, and so forth. Similarly, some variation in scores can be expected from differences in attribute variables. It is nearly impossible to keep all subject characteristics in an experiment exactly the same for all participants. Preexisting or acquired individual differences in attributes such as motivation, manual dexterity, sensory acuity, anxiety, or intelligence can contribute to differences in scores among individuals depending upon the type of task employed in the experiment.

Procedural variations, such as the way in which participants are instructed by the experimenter, can also affect performance on the dependent variable. In some experiments, more than one experimenter conducts the experiment, which may add to procedural variations from subject to subject. As we have also indicated, the behavior of the experimenter toward different participants may vary, and this, too, can have an effect on the individuals' behavior in the experiment. Facial expressions, tone of voice, gestures, and other mannerisms of the experimenter may differ from one person to another.

An example: extraneous variables in counseling experiments　To illustrate the potential problems associated with extraneous variables, let us consider a variety of factors that have been shown to be related to a client's perception of a counselor. Krumboltz, Becker-Haven, and Burnett (1979), who reviewed the psychological research in this area, identify a number of features of the counseling situation (environmental variables) and characteristics of the client (attribute variables) that have been shown to influence the perceived competence of the counselor. For instance, they report that physical attractiveness of the counselor may influence clients' perceptions; physically attractive counselors have been shown to be rated as more expert than less attractive counselors. Moreover, cues in the counseling situation that provide evidence of experience, prestige, and self-confidence in the counselor's skills may affect clients' perceptions. Studies have shown that a doctoral diploma on the wall, a prestigious introduction to the client, and various counselor behaviors such as relaxed posture, appropriate voice modulation, fitting gestures, and addressing the client by first name have produced more positive judgments of a counselor's competence.

The perceived effectiveness of a counselor may also depend upon characteristics of the client. Krumboltz et al. point out that counselors typically want clients to "self-disclose" when discussing a problem. To get them going, counselors often model self-disclosure by disclosing aspects of their own background. (Notice that counselor self-disclosure was one level of the independent variable of interest to McCarthy and Betz.) Research indicates, however, that if the client is either much older or younger than the counselor, then the client may judge such counselor behavior to be quite inappropriate. Further, the client's reaction to such self-disclosing statements may also depend upon the client's cultural background.

Each of these variables has been investigated as an independent variable in the studies reviewed by Krumboltz et al. But in the McCarthy and Betz experiment, each of these is an extraneous variable. If they allowed one of these, or any other extraneous variable, to covary systematically with the independent variable of type of counselor statement, then their experiment would be confounded. On the other hand, however, any extraneous variable allowed to vary unsystematically would contribute only to the error variation in the scores. The presence of error variation in an experiment makes it more difficult to detect the effect of the independent variable, but it does not confound the experiment. We will clarify this important point shortly.

Measurements of the dependent variable often reflect more than the specific behavior that an investigator is attempting to measure. It is difficult to measure the behavior of all participants in the experiment with equal precision or accuracy. Consequently, so-called errors of measurement are an additional source of unsystematic variation in subjects' scores. These errors are due to problems that arise in the measurement process and can occur in numerous ways. For example, recording the latency or duration of a behavior with a hand-operated stopwatch will often lead to variability in scores because observers who operate the stopwatch will have different reaction times to events. Experimenters can also make perceptual errors in reading dials, meters, or instruments used in the experiment. Sometimes the criteria for identifying a kind of response may be ambiguous or subject to interpretation; in such cases an experimenter may not be consistent in scoring the behavior from one occurrence to another, or from one participant to another.

Some errors of measurement may arise from within the participants themselves. Individuals may guess at answers in certain tasks, or their attention to the task they are performing may momentarily lapse. In perceptual tasks where stimuli are often presented for less than a second, even an eyeblink may lead to erroneous measurement. And, if individuals are filling out a rating scale or performing some other paper-and-pencil task, they may accidentally mark an incorrect answer. Such errors of measurement, because they usually do not occur in a systematic fashion, are often called *random errors.*

Errors of measurement can be minimized in some instances. For example, to measure an individual's response time, instrumentation can be used that automatically starts a timer with the onset of a stimulus and stops it at the moment the individual responds either orally or manually. Where subjects' responses may be ambiguous or unclear, several raters or judges can be used to independently score such responses; scoring a participant's free recall or narrative prose may be an example of such an instance.

The errors of measurement that we have described can be minimized, but usually cannot be eliminated in an experiment. One source of measurement error, however, careless recording of scores by the experimenter, can be eliminated. For example, we found the following statement in the Method section of a published experimental report.

> Records were scored blind by an independent judge and also (non-blind) by myself. Where there was a discrepancy of a half-unit between our scores, the blind judge's score was used. The few larger discrepancies were evaluated by me, and in every case it was immediately clear that one of the scores had been a gross error (e.g., carelessly writing "5" instead of "35"). The other score was then used. (Schmeidler, 1973, p. 330)

We would argue that such "gross" measurement errors are inexcusable in careful experimental research.

Importance of Error Variation in an Experiment

Error variation, also called *nuisance variation* and *chance variation,* is a nemesis for the experimenter. Ideally, all variation due to "error" in an experiment will be eliminated so that only the independent variable will affect a score. But, in reality, whatever effect an independent variable has must rise above the already existing chance variation in order to be observed. If error variation in an experiment is extensive, then it will be more difficult for the effect of an independent variable to reveal itself. Systematic variation in scores among participants receiving different levels of the independent variable may be overwhelmed or "swamped" by the extensive error variation. Perhaps you see now why error variation is also called nuisance variation; it is literally annoying or unpleasant to experimenters because its presence may obscure the effect of an independent variable. This swamping is especially a problem when the independent variable has a weak effect.

To clarify this important point, let's use an analogy. You know that it is easier to detect a weak sound in a quiet setting than in a noisy one. One can hear a whisper in a quiet room, but perhaps not hear it if a stereo is playing at moderate volume. On the other hand, even if there is a fairly high level of extraneous noise in a room when music is playing, you would probably hear someone who shouted to you. Similarly, in an experiment, the effect of an independent variable must rise above extraneous "noise," that is, error variation, to be revealed or detected. Sometimes error variation is even referred to as *experimental noise.*

As we have stated, error variation cannot be completely eliminated. If the independent variable does influence behavior, however, then the overall differences in scores *between* groups of subjects receiving different treatments should be relatively greater than the differences in scores among subjects *within* treatment groups. In following chapters we shall see how the variability in scores is quantified. Statistical tests then use these measures to compare the amount of systematic variation in scores (presumably caused by the independent variable) to the error variation in scores. This approach enables a psychologist to determine whether or not the independent variable has an effect on the dependent variable. As you will discover, it is difficult to demonstrate the effect of an independent variable when error variation is extensive, that is, when extraneous variables and measurement errors have large measureable effects on the behavior that is observed.

In summary, extraneous variables and errors of measurement are a major headache for an experimenter. Extraneous variables can confound an experiment and lead the experimenter to wrongly conclude that an independent variable has an effect when it does not; an extraneous variable may be responsible for observed differences in scores of subjects receiving different treatments. On the other hand, extraneous variables and errors in measurement also produce error variation in participants' scores that, if too extensive, will obscure the effect of an independent variable and may lead an experimenter to wrongly conclude that an independent variable has no effect when it really does.

STRATEGY OF EXPERIMENTAL DESIGN

The strategy involved in designing an experiment—how the independent variable is to be manipulated and the extraneous variables are to be controlled—is dictated by two major goals that the experimenter seeks to accomplish: (1) Detect the effect of an independent variable if it has an effect, and (2) avoid confounding the experiment. Therefore, an experimenter wants to employ a *sensitive design* in which the effect of an independent variable has a chance to reveal itself. In addition, if overall differences in behavior are found among different treatment groups, an experimenter wants to be confident that the differences can be attributed to the manipulation of the independent variable and not to the effect of an unintended manipulation of an extraneous variable.

The strategies of experimental design for achieving these aims utilize procedures for maximizing the effect of the independent variable while minimizing the effects of extraneous variables.[2] As we will see, techniques that help minimize the effects of extraneous variables often serve a dual role, for they also prevent confounding by the extraneous variable.

Maximizing Variation due to the Independent Variable

One strategy for achieving a sensitive design; that is, a design in which the effect of the independent variable will be detected if it has an effect, is to maximize the variation in scores caused by the effects of the experimental manipulation. We have pointed out that if an independent variable has an effect, then on the average, scores among participants receiving different treatments will differ. Variation in behavioral measures due to the influence of the independent variable (or, if confounded, to an extraneous variable that is unintentionally manipulated), is called systematic variation. With a sensitive design, the systematic variation will be greater than the error variation. Two strategies of maximizing systematic variation will be discussed.

Using Extreme Values of the Independent Variable

To maximize systematic variation, an experimenter selects levels of the independent variable that differ as much as reasonably possible. The strategy simply is to "stack the cards in our favor" by manipulating the experimental conditions so that relatively extreme levels of the independent variable are used. For instance, hunger as a conceptual variable can be manipulated by hours of food deprivation.

[2]These strategies of experimental design have been formulated by Kerlinger (1973) as the MAXMINCON principle. To be compatible with our terminology, Kerlinger's principle is modified to read as follows: *Max*imize systematic variation, and *min*imize error variation through the *con*trol of extraneous variables.

In this example a control group receiving zero level of hunger would be deprived of food for zero hours; the subjects would be satiated when the behavior that is of interest is measured. An experimental group obviously would be deprived of food for some time greater than zero hours. If hunger does have an effect on behavior, then surely one would expect that the influence would be more apparent in individuals deprived of food for twenty-four hours rather than for a mere fifteen minutes.

Sometimes it may be difficult to ascertain how widely the levels of the independent variable differ. The difficulty appeared in the McCarthy and Betz experiment, for no one had previously manipulated the type of counselor response in the same way. From the script presented in Table 3–1, however, you can see that McCarthy and Betz had the counselor give clearly different responses for the self-disclosing and self-involving conditions. Although it is not possible to be sure that these are the maximum variations that can be attained with this independent variable, they are quite different responses by the counselor.

One strategy of experimental design, then, is to select a wide range of values of the independent variable in order to maximize systematic variation. But a caution is in order here: If only two levels of an independent variable are used, the strategy of selecting extreme values can sometimes backfire. For example, extreme levels of food deprivation, e.g., zero hours vs. seventy-two hours, may result in subjects in the two conditions exhibiting the same amount of aggressive behavior. The experimenter may then wrongly conclude that hunger has no effect on aggression, when it may be that three days of food deprivation was so severe that subjects were too weak to exhibit aggressive behavior.[3] Similarly, suppose an investigator employing an ex post facto design studies task performance as a function of anxiety by selecting individuals who have extremely high and low levels of anxiety. Again, differences between these groups may not be observed; poor performance may be due to a lack of arousal or motivation in the low-anxious group, and high levels of anxiety may incapacitate participants in the other group.

The problem with using extreme values of the independent variable in two-group experiments is that instead of maximizing systematic variation, the strategy may minimize the apparent effects of the independent variable; it may minimize systematic variation. This result can occur when a so-called *inverted-U relationship* exists between the independent and dependent variables, as shown in Figure 4–1. A moderate level of the independent variable may produce behaviors that differ from extremely low or high levels. For example, perhaps moderate levels of food deprivation would produce aggression where little is found between the satiated and severely deprived participants. Or, moderate levels of anxiety may facilitate performance on a task in which low performance is found in both extremely low and high anxious individuals.

[3]Would this experiment contain severe ethical considerations with either animals or humans? Under what circumstances do you think such an experiment could be carried out?

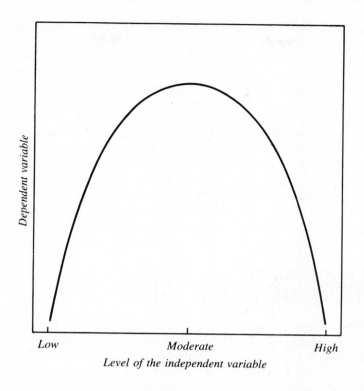

Low   *Moderate*   *High*

Level of the independent variable

An inverted U-shaped relationship between the level of the independent variable and the dependent variable.   **FIGURE 4-1**

Using More Than Two Levels of the Independent Variable

A second strategy for maximizing systematic variation avoids the problems just described when extreme levels of the independent variable are employed. The strategy is to select three or more levels of the independent variable that embrace a reasonably broad range. By taking this precaution, we will increase the probability of detecting the effect of an independent variable. If the independent variable does not have a simple, direct effect on the behavior that is of interest, then an investigator is more likely to find differences when multiple levels of the independent variable are employed. We might say that not only will the cards be stacked in our favor, but we will have covered more bets on the outcome.

Minimizing Variation due to Extraneous Variables

The "flip side" of the strategy for designing a sensitive experiment is reduction of unwanted error variation. If the independent variable has a relatively weak effect, then the effect of the treatments may be detected only if the variation due to relevant extraneous variables has been sufficiently minimized. The importance of reducing error variation due to extraneous variables is inversely related to the effect of the independent variable. More extraneous variation can be tolerated if the independent variable has a strong effect upon the dependent variable. Because the magnitude of the effect of an independent variable typically is not known in a particular experiment, however, techniques for minimizing error variation as much as possible need to be utilized in experiments.

Although the unsystematic variation of extraneous variables is responsible for error variation, systematic variation of an extraneous variable is the source of confounding in an experiment. Various techniques for controlling extraneous variables are routinely employed in experiments to reduce error variation and also to prevent confounding.[4] We shall next consider some of the major techniques for controlling extraneous variables.

Techniques for Controlling Effects of Extraneous Variables

Basically, two broad strategies are employed for controlling extraneous variables. One strategy is to merely *hold the variable constant;* if it is not allowed to vary, then its influence in the experiment is virtually removed. Second, if the extraneous variable cannot be held constant, then a variety of procedures can be employed to *hold the effects of the variable constant* so that it produces no systematic influence on behavior across treatment conditions. All the techniques described below are designed to prevent confounding in the experiment. Some of the methods are also used to reduce error variation. Although our discussion focuses on experiments, in most instances these techniques may be utilized in ex post facto studies as well as in true experiments. We will indicate the exceptions to this rule as we encounter them.

[4]Students sometimes seem to be confused about the different influences of an extraneous variable in their own experiments. For example, they will say that their experiment was "confounded" by an extraneous variable when they actually mean that they allowed an extraneous variable to increase error variation. The mere presence of an extraneous variable allowed to vary in an experiment does not necessarily confound an experiment. Confounding refers only to the unintentional but *systematic* manipulation of an extraneous variable along with an independent variable so that the values of each variable covary. An experiment with two groups would be confounded by the extraneous variable of ambient temperature if all individuals in one group were tested in a room early in the morning when it was cool and all individuals in the other group were tested later in the day when the room was hot. If participants had been randomly assigned to the groups, however, and if approximately equal numbers of participants in each group were tested in the room when it was cool as when it was hot, then the experiment would not be confounded; the temperature variable might increase the variation within groups, but it would not confound the experiment.

We have emphasized that in an experiment a researcher strives to allow only the independent variable to systematically influence the dependent variable. This plan implies that all other variables in the experiment are held constant, i.e., are not allowed to vary. In fact, constancy is the most fundamental control technique routinely applied in virtually all experiments. Wherever possible all conditions other than the treatment conditions should be maintained as nearly constant as possible for all participants. Holding the extraneous variables constant is one of the reasons many experiments in psychology utilize controlled laboratory conditions. Psychology laboratories are often constructed so that variables in the physical environment may be held constant.

Constancy removes the influence of extraneous variables on systematic and error variation in behavioral measures. Obviously, if a variable in the experimental environment or an attribute of participants is held constant, then its effects on the dependent variable will be removed. It is therefore eliminated as an extraneous variable in the experiment. The variable cannot produce any systematic influence on the behavior of participants across different treatment groups. But also, if the variable is held constant, then it cannot exert an influence on the performance of individuals within a treatment group; that is, it cannot contribute to error variation. Therefore, when any extraneous variable is held constant, it can neither confound the experiment nor contribute to error variation.

All types of extraneous variables can be controlled through constancy. For example, physical and environmental factors in the experimental setting such as room illumination, ambient temperature, and noise could be held constant. In interacting with participants, the experimenter can attempt to keep procedural variables constant by reading the same instructions to the participants, in the same tone of voice, using the same gestures. Attribute variables can be controlled through constancy by selecting individuals who possess the same level or degree of some characteristic such as age, sex, or birth order. Thus, for example, experimenters may employ only males to exclude variation in the experiment that could be due to differences between males and females.

McCarthy and Betz used the technique of constancy to control many of the extraneous variables in their experiment. Recall from the Krumboltz et al. (1979) review that numerous factors may affect clients' perceptions of counselors. McCarthy and Betz controlled these extraneous variables by holding them constant and thus effectively eliminating their influence. They did so by tape recording the simulated counseling sessions using the *same* simulated client and counselor in both treatment conditions. Thus, because a participant only heard a simulated counseling interview, any extraneous variables that depend upon actually seeing a counseling session were eliminated from their experiment. Any other extraneous variables that may depend upon the voice of the counselor or client were held constant from participant to participant by using a tape-recorded counseling session.

Extraneous variables arising from the social-reactive nature of an experiment were also controlled by constancy in McCarthy and Betz' research. Unless instructions are an independent variable, all participants in an experiment should receive identical instructions, delivered in an identical fashion. Participants in a self-involving group should not be told to "try harder" either explicitly in the instructions or implicitly by the tone of voice in which the instructions are delivered or by some other cues given by the experimenter. To ensure that both groups received identical instructions, McCarthy and Betz prepared written instructions that were read to each group of participants. Their written instructions are presented in Table 4–1.

McCarthy and Betz did not give their participants any practice on the task required of them, presumably because they felt the task was sufficiently easy and the instructions clear enough so that practice was not required. But we should

TABLE 4–1   *Instructions given to participants in the McCarthy and Betz experiment*[a]

This is an experiment in psychotherapy. In a couple of minutes you will be asked to put on the headphones in front of you. All of the carrels are turned on and ready. You may adjust the volume once the tape is in progress by turning the knob in front of you.

What you will listen to are various segments of a counseling session between an experienced male counselor and a female client who is a freshman at Ohio State. This is the first counseling session they have had together. The client will be discussing feelings of dissatisfaction with herself, her lack of friends, and problems interacting with her parents in the various segments of the tape.

There will be ten segments of conversation between the counselor and the client. Each segment will be announced, e.g., "Segment number one." The last response you will hear at the end of each segment will be made by the counselor. At the end of each segment you will be asked to write a written response that you believe the *client* might make at that point. There are no right or wrong answers. Just write the first response that occurs to you. It is important to answer every segment and answer them just as if you were the client (put yourself in her place). You will be given one minute to write each response.

The segments of the tape are from different points in the counseling session; one segment will not necessarily follow from the previous one. But each new segment you will hear *will* be from some progressively later time in the session.

After listening and responding to the entire tape you will be asked to complete a brief questionnaire as you believe the client would. The questionnaire will be handed out and explained at that time.

You have a packet of papers on your desk. Use each paper in the order in which you find them to write your responses to each segment. Each piece of paper should have the same subject number on it and should be numbered Segments 1 through 10. Turn over each piece of paper after you have made your response.

The experiment will be explained to you in more detail at the end. Do you have any questions?

[a]Used by permission of Dr. Patricia R. McCarthy and Dr. Nancy E. Betz.

notice that it appears McCarthy and Betz "lost" one participant in the self-involving condition. Although we do not know why, it may be that this individual failed to follow instructions or was confused about the nature of the task.

McCarthy and Betz surely had expectations about the outcome of the experiment, and they had to be sure that any tasks that required judgmental decisions by them were not influenced by their expectations. Such a possibility does arise in their research. Recall that participants were asked to write open-ended responses at the end of each segment of the simulated interview. Categorization of these responses required judgments to be made by some individual. In some instances, it is likely that ambiguity might arise about the appropriate categorization for a response (For example, was it an affective word? A self-referent? A question about the counselor?). If McCarthy and Betz had scored these responses and had known what condition a participant was in, it is possible that they might, quite unintentionally, have resolved any ambiguities in classifying a response in favor of their research hypothesis. To avoid this possibility, three raters judged and categorized the responses of the participants. The raters were not aware of which condition the participants were in. In addition, McCarthy and Betz developed a *protocol* or guideline for the raters to follow. This protocol is presented in Table 4–2. Notice the detail in which the protocol is spelled out. This thoroughness ensures that all people who rate the clients' responses are more likely to agree in scoring responses. Therefore, the categorization of a response is not likely to depend upon the particular person who scores it.

Not all extraneous variables that influence behavior can be eliminated or held constant, of course. The effects of such variables can be controlled, however, so that they exert no systematic influence on the dependent variable. The remaining techniques describe how this control can be accomplished.

Balancing: Balance the Effects of Extraneous Variables

If an extraneous variable cannot be held constant, or if the experimenter chooses not to hold it constant, then the *effects* of the variable can be held constant by balancing. This balance is accomplished by having different levels of an extraneous variable equally represented in the treatment conditions so that its effects are evenly distributed or balanced across treatments. This technique is used for both physical variables in the experimental setting and attribute variables.

To illustrate balancing, Hartnett, Rosen, and Shumate (1981) studied what traits individuals would attribute to age-discrepant couples (e.g., an older man dating a younger woman or an older woman dating a younger man). Assuming that males and females might react differently to an age-discrepant couple, Hartnett et al. randomly assigned an equal number of male and female participants to each of their treatment conditions. If the sex of the participants is related to the traits that they attribute to an age-discrepant couple, then the influence of this extraneous variable should be evenly distributed or balanced among the treatment

TABLE 4–2   *Procedures used by McCarthy and Betz for content analysis of client responses*[a]

I.   Number of Words:
  1.   Count every word.
  2.   A hypenated word counts as one word.
  3.   Contractions of two words count as two words.
  4.   Count only words that are there—do not count omitted words.

II. Number of Affective Words:
  1.   They are one-word direct statements of feelings. They are usually adjectives.
  2.   Count every affective word as long as it describes a *person's* state or feeling, sensation, awareness.
  3.   Usually if "I feel . . ." can be written in front of the word, then it is affective.
  4.   Good and bad are affective words; like, hate, love, are not.

III. Number of Verbs:
  1.   Count all verbs, verb phrases (1 verb), and gerunds (e.g., to be, in going, being, etc.).
  2.   Helping verbs are part of a verb phrase and count as one verb, e.g., is going, had done, would have felt.
  3.   Present-tense verbs are action now; at the present time; a habitual action (begun in the past but still happening); to express a general truth.
  4.   Past-tense verbs are action in the past that did not continue into the present.
  5.   Future-tense verbs are action in the future. They always include "shall" or "will"; also, "am going to" and "am about to."
  6.   Gerunds should be rated the same tense as the tense of the predicate in the sentence, e.g. "I want to know" = 2 verbs; both are present tense.

IV. Referents: Personal Pronouns
  1.   Client referents—I, me, mine, my, myself.
  2.   Counselor referents—you, your, you're (only if referring to the counselor).
  3.   Plural referents—we, our, ours, us (refer to counselor and client only).
  4.   Count every pronoun of these types.

V.   Question/Other
  1.   First decide how many complete sentences there are. Use the subjects' punctuation as a guide, e.g., 2 periods = 2 sentences (even if they are sentence fragments). If punctuation is omitted, then count only complete sentences.
  2.   Rate each individual sentence as either "question" or "other."
  3.   Questions are client responses that seek information about the counselor. They are asking him to talk more about himself, his ideas, feelings, etc. They may not be grammatical questions, e.g., "Tell me more about that" would be considered a question.
  4.   All sentences that are not counselor-directed questions, rate as "other."
  5.   One response may contain both types of sentences.

VI. Some general rules:
  1.   Read through a response first to get an understanding of it.
  2.   When counting verbs, circle them in pen.
  3.   Consistency is crucial! Be consistent from subject to subject in how you rate a certain word, sentence, etc.

---

[a]Used by permission of Dr. Patricia R. McCarthy and Dr. Nancy E. Betz.

conditions. No systematic variation related to the sex of the participant will be introduced, and therefore the experiment will not be confounded. If the subjects' gender is related to the dependent variable, however, then this extraneous variable will add to the variation in scores within a group, i.e., to error variation. Balancing, then, does not reduce error variation.

For balancing gender of the participants, it is not necessary to have an equal number of males and females in each group as Hartnett et al. did; but the same number of males or females should be assigned to each group so that the percentage of males (e.g., 60 percent) and the percentage of females (e.g., 40 percent) is the same. Moreover, the males and females should be assigned randomly to the treatment groups with the constraint that the proportion of the males and females be held constant in each treatment group.

When equal numbers of subjects are assigned to treatment groups on the basis of the amount or type of some characteristic they possess, then this balancing procedure is sometimes referred to as **blocking.** That is, individuals are grouped or "blocked" within a group on the basis of an attribute such as gender (male or female), weight (e.g., underweight, normal, or overweight), age (e.g., young adult, middle aged, or elderly) or some measured personality characteristics. Again, participants within a block would be randomly assigned to levels of the independent variable. Controlling the influence of attribute variables by balancing will prevent confounding, but it does not reduce error variation. If the blocked variable is treated as a second independent variable, however, then it becomes possible to statistically analyze for the variation contributed by the variable. We discuss this approach more fully in a later section of this chapter and in Chapter 10.

Randomization: Randomize Extraneous Variables

The easiest and perhaps the most widely used techniques for controlling the influence of extraneous variables that cannot be held constant is randomization. Randomization controls extraneous variables by distributing their effects among treatment conditions by chance. This technique prevents confounding by all known and unknown effects of any kind of extraneous variable. Therefore, a major virtue of randomization is that the relevant extraneous variables do not even have to be identified in order to be controlled!

We have already discussed one randomization procedure. In Chapter 3 we described how attribute variables are controlled by randomly assigning subjects to groups. Recall that *random assignment* is used to form equivalent groups *before* the independent variable is manipulated. To illustrate the scope of control by randomization, suppose an investigator was worried that anxiety level could confound his or her experiment. By randomly assigning participants to groups, any systematic effects of anxiety on the behavior are controlled; but, at the same time, the influences of all other attributes such as intelligence, emotional responsiveness, extroversion, and so forth—all other individual characteristics—are also distributed by chance.

Random assignment can also control for the influence of all physical or environmental variables in the experimental setting. Variations in ambient temperature, humidity, outside noise, daylight illumination, time of day, and other factors typically will differ from one participant to another if the participants are tested individually and at different times. By randomly assigning individuals to treatment conditions, a particular environmental condition (e.g., a specific temperature or noise level) has an equally likely chance of being assigned to any one of the treatment levels. As Keppel (1982) points out, "once we have controlled *one* environmental feature by randomization, we have controlled *all* other environmental differences as well" (p. 14).

The technique of randomization is also used to control for stimulus presentation effects in experiments. Often an experimental treatment involves presenting a number of stimuli to each participant. For example, individuals may be presented with series of words, pictures, or other stimuli to learn for later recall in a retention task. These stimuli should, if possible, be presented to participants randomly, with each participant receiving the stimuli in a different random order. By doing so, any unique characteristics of the stimuli will be equivalent over the treatment conditions. Kerlinger (1973) advises, *"Whenever it is possible to do so, randomly assign subjects to experimental groups and conditions, and randomly assign conditions and other factors to experimental groups"* (p. 310).

It should be clear that randomization is an excellent control for potential confounding by extraneous variables, but it does not reduce error variation due to extraneous variables. Randomization is merely an attempt to ensure that extraneous variables do not systematically vary across the treatment conditions of the experiment. Further, random assignment of participants can occur only when a psychologist manipulates an active independent variable. In an ex post facto design in which an attribute independent variable is employed, participants cannot be randomly assigned to different levels. This, of course, is one of the reasons why causal relationships are not easily reached from ex post facto research designs. Because participants cannot be randomly assigned to treatment groups, there can be no assurance that the groups are equivalent on all extraneous variables.

Matching: Match Participants on an Extraneous Attribute Variable

Randomization is always a desirable control procedure and is regarded as the best method for forming equivalent groups. Moreover, it has the advantage that a psychologist does not have to identify the extraneous variables to be controlled by randomization. On occasion, however, a psychologist may know or assume that a particular extraneous attribute variable is highly related to performance on the dependent variable. For example, it may be known that an individual's performance on a task is related to how anxious that individual is. If so, then a *matching* procedure can be used to try to equate the groups on that variable and thus make the groups more equivalent than they would be through random assignment of participants to groups alone.

As an example of matching, let us consider a hypothetical experiment similar to that of McCarthy and Betz that investigates the effect of two levels of counselor response on ratings of trustworthiness. Suppose that anxiety level is related to a client's perception of the trustworthiness of a counselor; highly anxious individuals perceive counselors as less trustworthy than do low-anxiety individuals. (There is evidence for such a relationship; see McCarthy, 1982.) To ensure that the two treatment groups are equivalent on anxiety, a psychologist may decide to match the participants in the two groups on anxiety level. To do so, it is necessary to obtain a measure of the subjects' anxiety levels by using an instrument such as the State-Trait Anxiety Inventory (Spielberger, Gorsuch, and Lushene, 1970). Then pairs of individuals will be formed on the basis of possessing similar anxiety levels. One pair of participants may be formed by selecting individuals who have the two highest anxiety scores; a second pair may consist of individuals with the third and fourth highest anxiety scores, and so forth. Therefore, with this matching procedure, a psychologist attempts to form pairs of individuals who are as alike or identical as possible on the attribute variable, in this case anxiety. After the pairs of participants have been selected, groups are formed by *randomly assigning* members of each pair to one of the two levels of the independent variable, type of counselor response.

This type of matching procedure can be extended to form three or more matched groups. For example, if there are three levels of an independent variable in an experiment, then matched groups would be created by forming triplets of individuals who are alike on the attribute that is of interest and then randomly assigning one member of each triplet to each group. The matching procedure for forming four or more matched groups would require a similar approach.

Matched-groups designs Experiments that form matched groups by obtaining pairs of subjects matched on an attribute variable and then randomly assigning members of the pairs to treatment groups employ **matched-groups designs.** As we have stated, the purpose of such designs is to provide more assurance that the groups of participants are equivalent on the matched attribute variable before the independent variable is introduced. Therefore, matching serves to prevent confounding by the attribute variable on which individuals are matched. In addition, the matching technique we have described may also reduce error variation. Because variation in scores from matched individuals should be less than would occur among unmatched individuals, the unsystematic error variation should be less in matched-groups designs than in random-groups designs. Thus, matching participants can increase the sensitivity of the experiment by reducing error variation.

Disadvantages of matched-groups designs Random-groups designs, in which groups are formed by random assignment, are used much more frequently in psychological research than matched-groups designs. Both types of designs are between-subjects designs, and generally a matched-groups design should be more sensitive than a random-groups design for detecting the effect of an independent variable. Several disadvantages associated with matched-groups designs account for their lesser use in psychological research, however. First, more effort is required to match individuals on an attribute variable than to randomly assign subjects to groups. It is necessary to measure the participants on the attribute variable before they can be matched and assigned to groups. For some attribute variables, such as gender or eye color, the measurement may require little effort or time. If participants are to be matched on variables such as intelligence or anxiety, however, then the effort required to obtain measures of the attribute variable may be substantial. Second, it is absolutely essential that the attribute variable on which the participants are to be matched be highly related to performance on the dependent variable and that it therefore can be expected to influence variation in the behavioral measures. If not, then the matching procedure is a waste of time; the potential benefits of matching will not be realized.

Although it is a between-subjects design, a matched-groups design is somewhat related to a within-subjects design. In a matched-groups design, participants who receive different treatments have been matched on one attribute variable that may influence the dependent variable. The experiment cannot be confounded by that attribute variable, for there should be no systematic influence of the variable across treatment conditions. Recall that in a within-subjects design, every individual in the experiment is tested under all treatment conditions. A given participant who may be female, moderately anxious, above average in intelligence, right-handed, a smoker, and extroverted in one treatment condition will have those same characteristics in each of the other treatment conditions. Therefore, a within-subjects design utilizes the ultimate matching procedure for controlling the influence of attribute variables! An experiment using a within-subjects design cannot be confounded by any attribute variable. Although matched-groups designs are rarely used in psychological research, within-subjects designs are frequently used. We will discuss other advantages, as well as limitations, of within-subjects designs in Chapter 11.

As we discussed in Chapter 3, matching may not be a particularly useful technique in an ex post facto study. Attempting to match participants on a second attribute who have already been selected on the basis of one attribute may lead to "unmatching" on a variety of other attributes. Anyone attempting to match individuals in an ex post facto study should certainly read the work of Meehl (1970a) and Farrant (1977) before proceeding.

Like some other terms in psychology, matching is not used identically by all psychologists. We have previously discussed the techniques of constancy and balancing for the control of extraneous variables. Some psychologists consider these techniques to be matching procedures also. By holding an attribute variable constant, separate groups are essentially matched on that variable. For example, by using only male participants, the dependent variable cannot systematically vary with gender of the participant; moreover, as we have pointed out, this technique serves to reduce error variation. Similarly, if equal numbers of male and female participants are assigned to each treatment condition, then the resulting groups are essentially matched on gender; this balancing procedure contributes to the formation of equivalent groups, but it does not reduce error variation.

Incorporating Extraneous Variables as Independent Variables

In Chapter 3 we defined an extraneous variable as a potential independent variable. If an extraneous variable has an influence on behavior, then a psychologist can arrange for it to systematically influence the dependent variable without confounding the experiment. This arrangement is accomplished by building the extraneous variable into the experiment as a second independent variable so that each level of that variable is combined with each level of the other independent variable. A particular treatment condition, then, consists of a combination of levels of the independent variables; in a between-subjects design, each participant is given one level of one independent variable and one level of the other at the same time. Such designs are called *factorial* because more than one factor or independent variable is manipulated in the experiment. These designs permit the experimenter to isolate the influence of each independent variable or factor on the dependent variable separately. By making an extraneous variable an independent variable, the psychologist is essentially converting that variable as a source of unsystematic variation into a source of systematic variation that can be statistically analyzed. The experiment cannot be confounded by that variation and error variation is reduced.

As an example of a factorial design, consider a test of the research hypothesis of Austin and Walster on the relation of inequitable reward and distress (see page 29). Assume there are two treatment groups, one that is equitably rewarded and one that is underrewarded, and the amount of distress is measured. If both male and female participants are randomly assigned to each group, then some variation in amount of distress within treatment groups that cannot be attributed to reward conditions, i.e., error variation, may be due in part to any differences in distress exhibited by males and females. If, however, gender is systematically varied by assigning equal numbers of males and females to each reward condition, thus employing a balancing or blocking procedure, and the difference in distress between males and females is subsequently analyzed, then the extraneous attribute variable of gender is employed as an independent variable. Notice, therefore, that an extraneous variable is employed as an independent variable only if its influence on the dependent variable is statistically analyzed. If equal numbers of males and females are placed in each reward condition, but differences between them are not analyzed, then an experimenter has merely used a balancing or blocking procedure, as described previously.

Research designs involving two independent variables are discussed in detail and this technique is more fully explained in Chapter 10. The various techniques used for controlling for the effects of extraneous variables are summarized in Table 4–3. We suggest that you review this table carefully to ensure that you are fully familiar with each of the techniques.

TABLE 4-3 *Techniques for controlling extraneous variables*

Technique	Use in		Purpose		Comments
	True experiments	Ex post studies	Eliminates confounding	Reduces error	
Constancy Holding the extraneous variable constant	Yes	Yes	Yes	Yes	By holding an extraneous variable constant at a single level, it is essentially eliminated as a variable.
Balancing Balancing the extraneous variable	Yes	Yes	Yes	No	The effects of the extraneous variable are equally distributed across treatment conditions.
Randomization Random assignment of participants	Yes	No	Yes	No	Random assignment of participants to levels of the independent variable is a requirement of a true experiment. In an ex post study, an attribute independent variable is employed. Participants self-select into levels of this independent variable; they cannot be randomly assigned.
Random assignment of stimuli, etc.	Yes	Yes	Yes	No	
Matching by pairs Matching participants on the extraneous variable	Yes	?	Yes	Yes	Matching participants on a second attribute may be done in an ex post facto study; however, the advisability of doing so is uncertain. The matching may lead to a systematic unmatching on other attributes.
Second independent variable Treating the extraneous variable as a second independent variable	Yes	Yes	Yes	Yes	Error variation is reduced by statistically analyzing for the influence of the extraneous variable as a second independent variable.

CONDUCTING THE EXPERIMENT

Once the experiment has been designed, the next step is to actually conduct the study. Now a decision has to be made about the number of subjects to be employed, and the procedure should be tested to ensure that the experiment can actually be run as planned.

How Many Participants Should Be Used?

A common problem facing all researchers is how many participants to use in an experiment; there is no simple answer. Numerous considerations enter into the decision. Two of these are the strength of the effect of the independent variable and the variability in measures on the dependent variable.

In general, the stronger or more powerful the effect of the independent variable, the fewer participants necessary to detect the effects of the variable. Conversely, the weaker the effect, the more subjects necessary for the effect of the manipulation to be seen. A few moments of thought will lead you to see the basis for the relationship between strength of the independent variable and the number of participants needed to detect the effect. A very powerful variable that could overwhelm all other determinants of behavior would require perhaps only one person to demonstrate its effect. As a gruesome but perhaps pedagogically useful example, consider determining the effect of a blow to the head on learning. Suppose in one treatment condition a strong blow with a sixteen-pound hammer is administered before a list of words is presented. We doubt if you would demand more than one individual to be sure that this condition is effective. On the other hand, suppose another condition was a very gentle tap on the head by a feather. We expect this to be a very weak treatment having very little effect on the capability of learning a list of words. Here you might need a large number of individuals to detect an effect of the feather tap, if one existed at all.

If the dependent variable is a behavior on which people or animals differ considerably among themselves or is quite variable from time to time in an individual, then a large number of subjects will be required to detect the effect of an independent variable. If, however, people differ little from individual to individual on that behavior, or vary little from time to time within themselves, then fewer participants are required to detect the effect of the independent variable.

Cowles (1974) suggests as a rule of thumb for between-subjects designs that one use about eighteen individuals per treatment condition when there are two levels of the independent variable, about sixteen participants per treatment condition when there are three levels, and about fourteen participants per group for four levels. In all cases, he recommends a minimum of at least ten participants per treatment group. A survey by Holmes (1979) of the number of participants used in psychological experiments indicated that the most frequently used number was either ten or twelve individuals in each treatment condition.

We recommend that Cowles's rule of thumb be tempered by a careful review of the recent literature to ascertain the number of participants previous researchers have used in their experimentation on the problem. One can make the judgment of the expected size of effects and the expected variability on the measures only from experience gained by careful reading of the literature and actual research in the problem area.

McCarthy and Betz used 107 participants, 54 in the self-disclosure condition and 53 in the self-involving condition.[5] Based upon this sample size, which is quite large compared to Cowles's recommendations and Holmes's survey results, we suspect that McCarthy and Betz either expected the independent variable of type of counselor response to be a relatively weak variable, or that scores on the CRF would be quite variable from person to person.[6]

Pilot Studies: Ensuring That the Experiment Can Be Run

In most instances, before plunging into full-scale conduct of the experiment, an experimenter will run several "pilot" subjects through the experiment. The purpose of testing these participants is to ensure that all procedures of the experiment are workable. Are the instructions clearly stated? Is sufficient time given for individuals to perform the requested task? Is the task required in the experiment too hard or too easy? Are there apparent cues that may lead participants to form expectations about the purpose of the experiment? Is the experimenter able to do all that is required during the procedure? These are all questions for which answers are sought when running pilot subjects through the experiment. If any changes are needed in the procedure of the experiment, then they should be made before conduct of the actual experiment begins.

Although almost all experimenters run pilot subjects before they conduct full-scale research, this practice is usually not apparent to readers of psychological literature. Journal articles seldom refer to pilot work on the experiment.

We must consider the issue of thoroughly instructing participants in the experiment and providing practice when necessary. Somewhere, somehow, the notion of having "naive subjects" has crept into the thinking of many students introduced to psychological research. Certainly in most instances a psychologist does not want participants to be familiar with the research hypotheses; to this

---

[5]The use of unequal numbers of participants in the two conditions is atypical and not a recommended procedure. The statistical analyses we present in later chapters are most easily and appropriately employed when the number of scores in each group is equal. We suspect that McCarthy and Betz had intended to use 108 participants, 54 in each condition, but that the data from one person in the self-involving condition were rejected because she failed to follow instructions or improperly completed the CRF.

[6]The raw data of scores on the CRF presented in Chapter 5 lend some credence to this latter supposition.

extent, participants should be naive. Of course, they should know what they are to do in the experiment! Too often, students engaged in their first research project develop reasonably complicated instructions for a rather unusual task and then expect that a rapid reading of the instructions to the participant is sufficient. If individuals do not understand the instructions or the tasks required of them, then another source of error variability has been created in the experiment. In many instances, participants should be given practice on the experimental tasks, so that the experimenter can be sure that the subject is performing the task according to the instructions. Most tasks used by psychologists are unfamiliar tasks for individuals. Thus, it is the experimenter's responsibility to ensure that participants know what is expected of them in the experiment. There should be no reason for having to discard subjects' scores because they failed to follow instructions.

When the experimenter is assured that the procedures are clear and workable, then he or she conducts the experiment with the planned number of participants. The measures obtained on the dependent variable become the raw data of the experiment. These data are compared to the predictions of the research hypothesis. Although such a comparison may appear quite simple, there is more to it than meets the eye. In the next several chapters we will develop the concepts of data analysis necessary to make this comparison.

SUMMARY

- Extraneous variables can confound an experiment or contribute to error variation in the scores obtained in the experiment.
- Confounding occurs when an extraneous variable is unintentionally but systematically manipulated with the independent variable, thereby possibly producing differences between treatment groups.
- Error variation occurs when extraneous variables vary unsystematically and add to the variability in the dependent variable within treatment groups. Error variation makes it hard to detect the effect of an independent variable.
- The strategy of experimental design is to maximize the variation due to the independent variable and to minimize both systematic and unsystematic variation due to extraneous variables.
- The effects of independent variables are maximized by employing extreme values of the independent variable and using more than two levels of the independent variable.
- Several techniques for controlling the effects of extraneous variables are used. All techniques (constancy, balancing, randomization, matching, and using the extraneous variable as a second independent variable) will prevent confounding, but only constancy, matching, and employing a second independent variable will reduce error variation.
- Before conducting the experiment, the number of subjects to be used should be decided on the basis of previous research, and a "pilot study" should be conducted to ensure that the procedure can be run as planned.

5

PREVIEW

In this chapter we discuss measurement and the procedures used to summarize raw data from an experiment. Topics include:

- The characteristics of measurement
- Organizing raw data by use of frequency distributions
- Describing typical or "average" performance with a measure of central tendency

WHY YOU NEED TO KNOW THIS MATERIAL

Psychological research often involves measuring the behavior of a large number of individuals. To find out "what happened" in the experiment, these data need to be organized and then summarized by statistics.

Measurement and Descriptive Analysis of Data

There is no excuse for failing to plot and look.

John W. Tukey (1977, p. 43)

Psychologists assume that behaviors or characteristics possessed by individuals may be measured and quantified. **Measurement** is simply the assigning of numbers to properties of objects, events, or behaviors according to a set of rules (Glass and Stanley, 1970; Stevens, 1951). In measuring, it is assumed that whatever is measured (e.g., perceived expertness, anxiety, intelligence) exists in some "true" amount. The actual empirical measurements, however, will only imperfectly measure this true amount. In Chapter 3 we indicated that *measured operational definitions* specify the procedures used to measure a conceptual variable. In most instances, the conceptual variables of psychology are not open to direct observation; rather, a psychologist must specify the empirical referent assumed to measure the construct.

An experiment by Smith, Snyder, and Handelsman (1982) provides an example of this approach to measurement in psychological research. They were interested in the problem of how people use anxiety to explain failure in situations in which they are evaluated. Smith et al. assumed that the construct of anxiety reflects a characteristic possessed by an individual and that the amount of anxiety possessed at any one time will depend upon past and current situational factors. A psychologist has no magical procedure, however, for tapping the actual amount of anxiety an individual experiences at a particular moment. Instead, certain observable behaviors must be used as indicants of the characteristic. Thus, Smith et al. employed a paper-and-pencil self-report measure of anxiety, the state form of the State-Trait Anxiety Inventory (Spielberger et al., 1970). This empirical referent is, at best, a somewhat fallible measure of the true level of anxiety. In spite of the limitations, though, a psychologist works with such instruments and from them infers the amount of the true characteristic possessed (Kerlinger, 1973).

This conceptualization of measurement is illustrated in Figure 5–1. A true amount of a variable, an object, or event being measured exists. An operational definition specifies the measurement procedure and provides an empirical referent of the measured variable. Various empirical referents may then differ on how well they measure the "true" dimension depending upon (1) their reliability, (2) their validity, and (3) the level of measurement achieved.

Reliability

If a construct does not change over time, then the empirical referents obtained from repeated measurements of that variable should also not change. A measure of a construct has reliability if consistent measurements are obtained from one time to another. Measures of a construct that are not stable when the variable itself does not change cannot be reliable. In practice, measures will not be perfectly reliable, but psychologists attempt to make their measurements as reliable as possible. One way of increasing reliability is to reduce random errors that may be associated with measurements. Such errors that result from misreading a stopwatch or incorrectly recording a response will decrease the reliability of the measurements.

Validity

Measurements may be very stable or reliable, but they might not represent the construct a psychologist is attempting to measure. That is, they may not be valid measures of the construct because they do not, in fact, measure what they

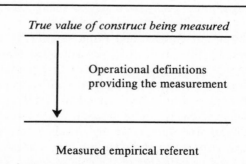

FIGURE 5–1   *Schematic illustration of the concept of measurement.*

are presumed to measure. Suppose, for example, that a psychologist measured anxiety by recording the waist circumference of individuals. It is likely that these measures would be reliable; barring unusual gains and losses in weight, we would expect the waist measurements to be quite stable from one time to another. Surely no one would argue, however, that waist size, though reliable, is a valid measure of the construct of anxiety. This example illustrates that reliability of a measure does not ensure the validity of that measure. Validity of a measure cannot, however, be achieved unless the measure is reliable. Validity assumes reliability, but reliability does not assume validity. Determining the validity of a measure is often an involved process. We discuss this process more fully in Chapter 13 when we consider the validity of experiments.

Levels of Measurement

The nature of the measurement rule used determines the level of measurement and therefore the precision with which variables can be measured. Further, as you shall see, the choice of statistics used to summarize the data is determined, in part, by the measurement level represented by the data. Most typically, measurements are classified into one of four levels: nominal, ordinal, interval, or ratio.

In each experiment you can expect that the rules used to measure the behavior that is of interest will be specified. In most published articles, however, the level of measurement represented by the empirical referent is not identified explicitly. Thus, the reader of research reports should be able to identify the types of measurement scales used from the information provided by operational definitions.

Nominal Measurement

Nominal measurement is essentially a classification of individuals or behaviors into *different categories*. As an example, people may be categorized as either anxious or not anxious. People may vary on the amount of a characteristic they possess (e.g., anxiety), but the rule of nominal measurement places individuals possessing varying amounts of the characteristic in the same category. That is, once people have been assigned to a category by a nominal measurement rule, all people in the same category (e.g., those exhibiting "helping" behavior, those expressing approval on an issue, liberals, conservatives) are equated on the empirical referent of the characteristic or behavior, even though they may not possess the characteristic or exhibit the behavior to the same degree. If numbers are assigned to describe the categories, the numbers are used only to "name" (hence the term "nominal") the category; each participant assigned to the same category will be assigned the same number. A schematic illustration of nominal measurement is shown in Figure 5–2a.

a. *Nominal level of measurement*

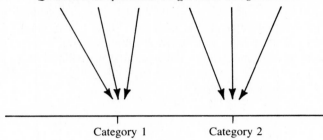

Construct being measured

Qualitative or quantitative differences being measured

Category 1   Category 2

Category or label

Measured empirical referent

b. *Ordinal level of measurement*

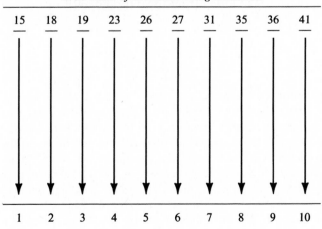

True value of construct being measured

| 15 | 18 | 19 | 23 | 26 | 27 | 31 | 35 | 36 | 41 |

| 1 | 2 | 3 | 4 | 5 | 6 | 7 | 8 | 9 | 10 |

Rank

Measured empirical referent (no 0 point)

FIGURE 5–2   *Schematic illustration of the levels of measurement.*

c. *Interval level of measurement*

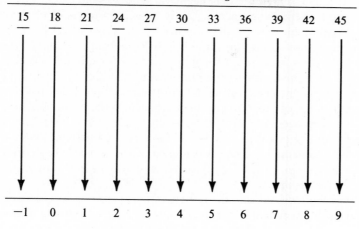

d. *Ratio level of measurement*

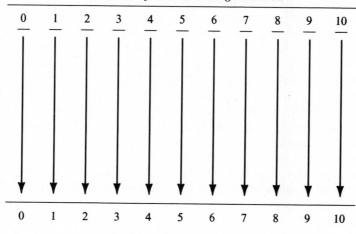

FIGURE 5–2

A study by Roberts, Hoffman, and Johnson (1978) illustrates the use of nominal measurement in psychology. As part of their research, they examined the effects of the severity of the potential punishment on a juror's decision of guilty or not guilty. In this research the dependent variable was the decision by each juror (the participant in the experiment). The level of measurement of the dependent variable was nominal, because the response of the juror could be placed in only one of two categories—guilty or not guilty. If Roberts et al. assigned a number to each juror's decision, such as a 1 for guilty and a 2 for not guilty (but notice that they did not), then the number would have been used only to identify the category of the participant's response. One could not perform any mathematical operations on the numbers except to tabulate how frequently the responses occurred and then derive percentages. For such measurement purposes, it would have been just as reasonable to assign a 0 to a guilty decision by a participant and a 1 for a not guilty. In fact, numbers need not be assigned to the response categories at all for such measurement purposes. The researcher could simply tabulate the juror's response as a yes or no.

Perhaps you can see why many psychologists do not regard nominal scales as actual measurement scales, for they convey no quantitative information. It is argued that such numbers serve only for identification and have no real measurement properties. However nominal scales are viewed, such numbers represent the crudest level of measurement.

Ordinal Measurement

When objects, individuals, or behaviors can be differentiated and *rank ordered* along some dimension, then an **ordinal scale** is employed. Participants may be asked to order a series of cartoons from most funny to least funny. Or, the pecking order for a flock of hens may be determined by identifying the birds along the dimension of most dominant to least dominant. Typically a rank of 1 is assigned to the stimulus or individual possessing the greatest amount of the characteristic being measured, a rank of 2 to that which exhibits the next greatest amount, and so forth. If, for example, anxiety is measured by means of an ordinal scale, then the person exhibiting the most anxiety is assigned a 1, the person showing the next largest amount of anxiety a 2, the next a 3, and so on. Although there may be a true zero amount of the variable being measured, this will not appear in the ranking. The value of 0 is not used in ordinal measurement.

An ordinal scale permits one to differentiate among objects, individuals, or behaviors and to determine the direction of the differences, for someone or something assigned a rank of 1 possesses more of the characteristic than one given a rank of 2. Ordinal measures do not, however, permit determination of how much of a real difference exists in the measured characteristic between ranks; it may be that a large difference in the true characteristic being measured exists between ranks 1 and 2, but only a small difference between ranks 2 and 3. Therefore, even though numerically there is an equal difference between rank values of 1 and 2 and between the values 2 and 3, one cannot determine how much of a real difference in the measured variable exists between adjacent ranks. This condition is illustrated in the rankings and their relation to the conceptual variable shown in Figure 5–2b.

An example of ordinal measurement in psychological research is provided in the research of Henry and Jacobs (1978) who attempted to determine if a person's preference for colors was related to that individual's perception of the colors as "sexually stimulating." Participants in the study were asked first to rank eight color samples by how sexually stimulating they were and then rank them again by preference for the colors. An example of a person's ranking of colors as sexually stimulating might have occurred as follows:

Rank	*Color*
1	Red-orange
2	Dark blue
3	Violet
4	Black
5	Yellow
6	Green
7	Brown
8	Gray

In this instance, the person ranked red-orange as the most sexually stimulating and gray as the least sexually stimulating of the eight colors. We know that for this individual red-orange is thought to be more sexually stimulating than dark blue and dark blue more stimulating than violet. From these ordinal measurements we cannot tell, however, how much more sexually stimulating red-orange is perceived to be than dark blue, or whether the difference in stimulation between red-orange and dark blue is the same as that between dark blue and violet. From the rank-order values a psychologist can be confident that one color is perceived as being more sexually stimulating than another, but he or she cannot know if the differences between adjacent ranks correspond to equal differences in amount of sexual stimulation.

Another limitation of ordinal scales is that rank ordering is merely a procedure in which the stimuli, individuals, or behaviors are measured along a continuum from most to least and *must* be assigned a rank. Thus, one cannot assume from the rankings that a rank of 1 necessarily corresponds to a large amount of the characteristic being measured. Nor can one assume that the lowest-ranked object or person possesses little of the property being measured. A person who is asked to rank order cartoons from most to least funny may find no humor in any of them. Yet, a rank of 1 assigned by this individual conveys the same information as a rank of 1 by another person who may regard all the cartoons as very funny.

Here, the same measured numerical value (e.g., a 1) from both individuals represents true characteristics which actually differ considerably in magnitude. Ordinal scales do *not* measure how much of the measured characteristic exists; they only provide information about relative differences among individuals or objects on the characteristic being measured.

Interval Measurement

If the requirements for an ordinal scale are met, and in addition the differences between the assigned numbers represent *equal increments* in the magnitude of the measured variable, then an **interval scale** (often called equal-interval scale) is created. An interval scale has no true zero point for which a value of zero represents the complete absence of the characteristic being measured. A zero value on an interval scale is merely an arbitrary starting point that could be replaced by any other value as a starting point.

The most familiar example of an interval scale is a thermometer used to measure temperature. Both the Fahrenheit and Celsius scales, which measure temperature in degrees, are interval scales. With neither of these scales, though, does 0° represent an absence of temperature; neither contains a true zero point because measured temperatures may fall below 0°. With such scales it is appropriate to state that the difference in temperature between 20° and 40° is equivalent to the difference in temperature between 40° and 60°, but it is not appropriate to say that 40° is twice as high a temperature as 20°. Interval level of measurement is illustrated in Figure 5–2c.

Examples of psychological scales that achieve true interval measurement are quite rare. Although some psychologists argue that scores on well-standardized tests such as intelligence tests represent interval measurement (e.g., Jensen, 1974), others clearly take issue with such a view (e.g., Thomas, 1982). If intelligence-test scores do represent an interval level of measurement (but notice that we are not arguing that they do), then it would be correct to state that the difference in intelligence between individuals who have intelligence scores of 100 and 105 is equal to the difference in intelligence between persons with scores of 75 and 80. It would not be correct, however, to say that a person with an intelligence-test score of 100 is twice as intelligent as a person with a score of 50, because scales of intelligence tests do not have a true zero that represents complete absence of intelligence.

Ratio Measurement

A **ratio scale** replaces the arbitrary zero point of the interval scale with a *true-zero starting point* that corresponds to the absence of the characteristics being measured. Thus, with a ratio scale it is possible to state that one thing (e.g., a stimulus, event, or individual) has twice or half or three times as much of the characteristic being measured as another. Ratio scales are frequently used in psychological research when the empirical referent requires measurement in physical units such as time (e.g., reaction time in milliseconds), length (e.g., in millimeters) or weight (e.g., in grams). Figure 5–2d illustrates the characteristics of ratio scales.

As an example, the magnitude of perceptual illusions may be measured with a ratio scale. An illusion occurs when the perceived characteristics of a stimulus do not correspond to the physical characteristics of the stimulus; that is, when one misperceives what actually exists. A familiar example in psychology is the Müller-Lyer illusion, which is illustrated in Figure 5–3. Here you perceive (or are most likely to perceive) line A to be longer than line B. In fact, however, both lines are physically equal in length. Your perception is in error. The magnitude of this illusion can be measured by determining how much the perceived length of the stimulus differs from the actual length of the stimulus (e.g., 3 millimeters). An individual's perceptual error measured in millimeters represents ratio level of measurement. It is possible for a person to have an error of 0 mm (i.e., no error) when the perceived length of the stimulus does not differ from the actual length. The difference between an error of 5 mm and an error of 8 mm is the same as the difference between errors of 10 mm and 13 mm; in each case the difference is 3 mm. Moreover, an error of 10 mm represents an illusion magnitude that is twice as great as an error of 5 mm. One example of an ex post facto study with this illusion using ratio measurement was conducted by LeTourneau (1976), who found that the magnitude of the illusion was smaller for architectural-design students than it was for optometry students.

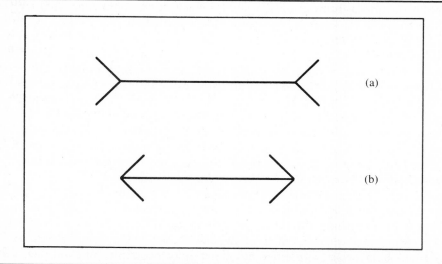

(a)

(b)

The Müller-Lyer illusion.   **FIGURE 5–3**

Measurements of behavior at the ratio level using psychological sales rather than physical sales are rare. One interesting example of a psychological scale that arguably achieves ratio measurement, however, has been developed by Stevens (1957) using the method of **magnitude estimation.** This is a procedure used to measure the subjective magnitudes of sensations that are produced by physical stimuli. For instance, one may ask the question, "How much sweeter is a solution with 2 teaspoons of sugar than one with 1 teaspoon?" Sweetness is a subjective experience; it is not a physical property of sugar. With the method of magnitude estimation, individuals are asked to assign numbers to represent the magnitude of their subjective responses to stimuli in proportion to one another. Thus, a participant attending to the perceived sweetness of a 4 percent sucrose solution (approximately equivalent to 1 teaspoon of table sugar dissolved in 6 ounces of water) may assign the number 10 to represent the amount of sweetness experienced. If a second solution is perceived as being twice as sweet, then the individual would assign the number 20; if half as sweet, a 5; and so forth. Stevens argues that people are capable of making such ratio judgments of subjective experiences quite reliably. A wide variety of sensory experiences have been measured using this ratio-scaling procedure, including brightness of lights, loudness of tones, pain from electric shock, and perceived length of lines (see Stevens, 1957, 1962).

Rating Scales and Level of Measurement

Rating scales, such as the Counselor Rating Form (CRF) used by McCarthy and Betz, are frequently used in psychological research to measure psychological constructs. Personality characteristics, attitudes, and other attributes are often measured with various forms of rating scales. It is not so clear, however, what level of measurement is represented, and thus what information is provided, by rating scales. We will therefore briefly discuss the nature of rating scales and use the CRF as an example.

A rating scale consists of a set of categories arranged along a continuum that represent varying degrees of intensity for some dimension (e.g., expert-inexpert, sincere-insincere). The sales may have any number of categories between the extremes, and the scales may be referred to as 5-point, 7-point, or 9-point scales, depending upon the number of categories provided. In many instances, a series of scales are presented and the scores on the separate sales are added or averaged to yield a score for a subject. Such scales are called **summated rating scales** (Isaac and Michael, 1971).

The CRF used by McCarthy and Betz is a summated rating scale. Recall that the CRF is designed to measure a client's perception of a counselor on three dimensions—expertness, attractiveness, and trustworthiness (Barak and LaCrosse, 1975). Scores for each of the three dimensions are based upon ratings on 12 separate 7-point scales with different bipolar adjectives represented on each scale (see Table 3–2). Notice that in the CRF the first of the 36 rating scales is anchored with the adjectives "agreeable" and "disagreeable." The participant's task is to check one of the seven categories that best describe his or her perception of the counselor on that characteristic. Which bipolar adjective pairs are related to which dimensions being measured (e.g., expertness, attractiveness, or trustworthiness) are not disclosed to the participant on the CRF, and the various adjective pairs associated with the three dimensions are randomly distributed on the form. In addition, the position of the positive (e.g., agreeable) and negative (e.g., disagreeable) adjective pairs is randomly arranged so that participants will not adopt a tendency to respond to all pairs by checking the same category. For example, in Table 3–2 observe that the first adjective pair is agreeable-disagreeable, but the second pair is unalert-alert. The seven points or categories on each scale are later appropriately numbered from 1 to 7 for purposes of deriving a participant's score. For each dimension the numerical values assigned to the 12 subscales are then summed to derive a score on that dimension.

What level of measurement is represented by scores on the CRF and similar rating scales? It should be clear that the values obtained from the scale for each adjective pair represent at least an ordinal level of measurement. A rating of 6 indicates more of a particular characteristic described by the adjectives than does a 5, and a 5 reflects more than a 4; however, one cannot be certain that the difference between a 6 and 5 represents the same difference in a participant's perception as that between a 5 and 4. In other words, one cannot assume that equal increments in numerical values along the scale correspond to equal increments in the underlying characteristic (e.g., alertness) being measured.

Although it is difficult to defend the values 1 to 7 on a 7-point scale as representing interval level of measurement, such rating scores do seem to provide more than merely ordinal information. We might expect that the participant, in selecting one of the seven categories to respond to, somehow subjectively divides the categories into roughly equal intervals between the extremes described by the adjectives. Moreover, if the values obtained from an individual on a number of separate scales are totaled or averaged, then it would seem reasonable to assume that the resulting scores provide more than just rank-order information. Indeed, Gardner (1975) argues that scores from such summated scales are elevated to a level of measurement in a gray region between ordinal and interval. Gardner adds that this category of measurement "obviously includes a large proportion of all the instruments used in educational and psychological research. The category occupies an intermediate position on the ordinal/interval continuum" (p. 53). Consequently, many psychologists treat summated rating scales as representing interval level of measurement.

We have devoted attention to scores derived from rating sales for several reasons. They are widely used in psychological research, and we think it is useful for students of psychology to gain some understanding of them.[1] In addition, we

---

[1]The standard reference for information on the construction and use of various types of rating scales is Guilford's (1954) text. In addition, Black and Champion (1976) provide an excellent discussion on rating scales (pp. 182–209). Marks (1982) used rating scales to measure cross-modality metaphors such as the "sound of sunset," the "color of thunder," or a "bright piano note."

do not wish to convey the impression that any measure of behavior necessarily fits neatly into one of the four major categories of measurement scales. Many measurements employed in psychological research, including rating scales and standardized test scores, probably represent a level of measurement between ordinal and interval. Finally, as we will briefly discuss in Chapter 6, the statistical treatment of rating-scale data is an issue of some dispute.

TREATMENT OF RAW DATA FROM AN EXPERIMENT

A measurement obtained from a participant in an experiment is often described as a **score.** The scores obtained from all the participants provide the **raw data** for the experiment.[2] The researcher's eventual task is to determine whether these data support or do not support the research hypothesis. This decision is based upon the results from analysis of the raw data. The analyzing of data involves a number of steps, and it will take us several chapters to describe the fundamental concepts and quantitative measures involved.

To illustrate the steps involved in analyzing data we will use the actual raw data obtained in the experiment by McCarthy and Betz. The scores they obtained from all 107 subjects on each of the three dimensions on the Counselor Rating Form are presented in Table 5–1. Recall that ratings of perceived expertness, attractiveness, and trustworthiness were obtained from each individual. The ratings for the 54 subjects in the self-disclosing condition are presented in the first three columns on the left side of the table, and the ratings for the 53 subjects in the self-involving condition appear in the remaining three columns. The scores are arranged in the order in which they were obtained for each experimental condition. The three scores in a single row were obtained from one participant.

TABLE 5–1   *CRF scores for individual participants from McCarthy and Betz's experiment*[a]

Self-disclosing (n = 54)			Self-involving (n = 53)		
Expertness	*Attractiveness*	*Trustworthiness*	*Expertness*	*Attractiveness*	*Trustworthiness*
59	69	68	77	71	78
74	71	73	77	73	73
65	54	75	73	67	73
57	56	64	70	63	76
26	45	35	75	76	82
56	64	52	69	68	72
81	75	80	64	71	82
78	77	70	67	75	77

[2]The word *data* is the plural form of the word *datum.* Thus, we say "these data are" or, if we refer to a single measurement value, "this datum is."

57	48	52	30	52	37
70	66	69	51	41	57
64	68	62	67	55	60
78	75	69	71	67	71
77	64	65	75	74	77
66	66	74	48	49	48
57	58	72	73	70	75
66	64	67	54	56	63
83	74	76	63	70	75
76	70	76	75	71	79
64	71	76	68	69	58
65	72	64	72	72	75
32	66	51	64	70	70
69	68	74	83	77	79
77	54	60	56	53	49
71	69	75	70	67	78
58	61	47	74	70	80
60	52	54	76	70	72
82	75	80	64	55	59
52	62	48	61	78	74
78	73	80	78	70	81
62	63	56	60	71	70
72	66	76	40	50	33
73	72	78	71	63	74
49	56	52	83	82	83
60	56	65	79	75	78
68	59	52	60	49	44
63	61	62	72	76	77
63	63	71	77	77	75
68	73	68	80	77	78
26	31	22	77	72	74
16	31	27	68	52	72
68	67	66	81	77	70
69	63	70	68	69	78
81	68	84	77	73	81
61	71	68	66	68	80
58	66	63	81	70	79
41	72	60	64	63	70
76	72	77	82	68	82
78	61	75	55	50	63
57	62	75	73	74	77
80	68	78	77	72	79
62	60	41	78	72	77
49	56	39	68	69	67
48	59	50	49	62	65
60	69	50			

[a]Used by permission of Dr. Patricia R. McCarthy and Dr. Nancy E. Betz.

We pointed out previously that McCarthy and Betz employed a summated rating scale. Recall that a participant checked off one of seven categories for each of twelve different bipolar adjective items on three dimensions (expertness, attractiveness, and trustworthiness). For scoring purposes numerical values from 1 to 7 were assigned to the categories. Therefore, a score for an individual was derived by adding up the numerical values of the ratings on the twelve items associated with each dimension. Accordingly, if an individual assigned ratings of 7 to all twelve items of a dimension, then the maximum score for that dimension would be 84. Similarly, a rating of 1 assigned to each of the twelve items would lead to a minimum score of 12. For the expertness dimension, then, a score of 84 indicates that a participant perceived the counselor as very expert, and a 12 would indicate that the individual regarded the counselor as not at all expert. A score of 48 occurs at the midpoint of the scale and represents a neutral perception of the counselor on a particular dimension. Essentially, then, any score above 48 is a favorable perception, and a score below 48 reflects a negative rating.

What Do the Raw Data Tell Us?

Suppose you met Patricia McCarthy or Nancy Betz at a psychology conference. In conversation you might find yourselves discussing their research on the effects of types of statements in counseling interviews on perceptions of counselors. After they describe what they did you might ask "How did the results turn out?" Although it would not occur, suppose she responded by showing you a copy of their raw data (i.e., Table 5–1) and said, "Oh, the results were interesting. Take a look." If you were then to inspect the scores in the table, you would quickly discover the difficulties a researcher encounters when attempting to make sense of raw data.

Consider the expertness ratings only that appear in Table 5–1.[3] You will notice considerable variation in the ratings scores given by the participants in both treatment conditions. In scanning the scores in the two columns you will probably observe that many of the ratings are in the 60s and 70s for both groups. Perhaps it appears that scores in the 60s are listed more often than scores in the 40s and 80s. Perhaps also, you will detect that there seems to be considerable overlap of scores; many participants in the two groups gave similar scores.

What sense are we to make of these data? It surely appears that there is considerable variation among scores in each treatment condition; that is, there seems to be extensive error variation, which may be attributed largely to extraneous variables. The effect of the independent variable, though, would be revealed by overall differences or systematic variation between the two treatments. Here, it

---

[3]Although we have presented the raw data for the three ratings obtained by McCarthy and Betz, we analyze and discuss only the expertness rating in the text. You will profit if you follow our discussion by conducting analyses on the attractiveness and trustworthiness scores as well.

may seem that self-involving statements yielded higher expertness ratings than self-disclosing statements by counselors; we notice, at least, that the three lowest ratings were given by participants who listened to self-disclosing statements. But, then again, many subjects in each group also have similar ratings and thus have similar scores. It is not readily apparent just from visual inspection of the raw data that the systematic variation due to the effects of the independent variable is relatively greater than the error variation. Therefore, it is not clear whether the data are or are not in agreement with the research hypothesis.

Rarely in psychological research are the effects of the independent variable so evident that overall differences in scores from participants in different experimental conditions virtually jump out at the investigator. Certainly, trying to use Table 5–1 to come to a conclusion about differences in expertness ratings in the two experimental groups by merely examining the scores is rather difficult. This inability to readily see the forest for the trees in raw data is especially a problem when there are many observations to deal with. Consider how much more complicated the task of comprehending the raw data would become if there were not just two levels of the independent variable, but four, and up to 75 scores in each condition. One would have a total of 300 scores to sort out visually! It would be virtually an impossible task to come to an appropriate conclusion about the research hypothesis merely by visually inspecting the raw data.

Organizing the Raw Data

A much clearer picture of the effect of the independent variable on the scores appears if the raw data are organized into a frequency distribution. A **frequency distribution** is a table showing each score for a particular group of participants and how often each score occurred. A simple ungrouped frequency distribution may be constructed by listing all the score values from highest to lowest and then placing an X beside each score every time it occurs. Table 5–2 illustrates an ungrouped frequency distribution for the expertness scores presented in Table 5–1.

If there is a wide range of score values, the simple, ungrouped frequency distribution can become quite spread out, making it difficult to see clear patterns in the data. Therefore, often it is useful to construct a grouped frequency distribution in which scores are grouped in class intervals. The class intervals are then arranged from highest to lowest, and the frequency of scores occurring within each class is tallied as described above. For the data in Table 5–1 a frequency distribution using grouped data and class intervals is probably more informative than one constructed on the ungrouped data such as that shown in Table 5–2. By collapsing the scores into class intervals a more compact distribution appears, providing a clearer picture of the subjects' ratings in the experiment.

Grouped frequency distributions of the scores for the expertness dimension are shown in Table 5–3. A class interval of 5 was used, and each X represents one

TABLE 5–2   *Ungrouped frequency distributions for self-disclosing and self-involving treatment conditions.*

	Self-disclosing	Self-involving		Self-disclosing	Self-involving
84			48	X	X
83	X	XX	47		
82	X	X	46		
81	XX	XX	45		
80	X	X	44		
79		X	43		
78	XXXX	XX	42		
77	XX	XXXXX	41	X	
76	XX	X	40		X
75		XXX	39		
74	X	X	38		
73	X	XXX	37		
72	X	XX	36		
71	X	XX	35		
70	X	XX	34		
69	XX	X	33		
68	XXX	XXXX	32	X	
67		XX	31		
66	XX	X	30		X
65	XX		29		
64	XX	XXXX	28		
63	XX	X	27		
62	XX		26	XX	
61	X	X	25		
60	XXX	XX	24		
59	X		23		
58	XX		22		
57	XXXX		21		
56	X	X	20		
55		X	19		
54		X	18		
53			17		
52	X		16	X	
51		X	15		
50			14		
49	XX	X	13		
			12		

score that fell within that class interval. Thus, for the self-disclosing condition five expertness scores fall in the class interval 80 to 84 (scores of 81, 83, 82, 81, and 80). In Table 5–3 these five scores have been represented by five Xs next to the interval of 80–84 for the self-disclosing condition.

Grouped frequency distributions for self-disclosing and self-involving treatment conditions.   **TABLE 5–3**

	Self-disclosing	Self-involving
80–84	XXXXX	XXXXXX
75–79	XXXXXXXX	XXXXXXXXXXXXX
70–74	XXXXX	XXXXXXXXXX
65–69	XXXXXXXXX	XXXXXXXX
60–64	XXXXXXXXXX	XXXXXXXX
55–59	XXXXXXXX	XX
50–54	X	XX
45–49	XXX	XX
40–44	X	X
35–39		
30–34	X	X
25–29	XX	
20–24		
15–19	X	
10–14		

At a glance, Tables 5–2 and 5–3 produce several impressions of the expertness ratings given by both groups of participants that are not so readily apparent from the unorganized raw data of Table 5–1. First, you can see a considerable amount of error variation among the scores within each group. But second, overall it appears that there may also be some systematic variation between the two groups; it seems that the ratings are somewhat higher for the self-involving group, because more scores seem to be clustered around the higher ratings (70 and above) and fewer around the lower ratings (below 60). And although we can easily see considerable overlap among ratings given by individuals in the self-disclosing and self-involving groups, we can also observe that no one in the self-involving group gave a rating lower than 30, but three subjects in the self-disclosing group did. Third, the ratings that the subjects in the self-involving group gave most frequently (75–79) were higher than those which occurred most often for the self-disclosing group (60–64). Therefore, it appears overall that the expertness ratings for the two groups may have differed.

As our opening quotation indicates, organizing the raw data in a frequency distribution makes it easier to "see" the data. It is still premature to draw conclusions, however, about the effect of the independent variable (type of counselor statements) on the dependent variable (perceived expertness of the counselor) by examining the frequency distributions alone. The data have merely been organized to facilitate visual judgments. But visual judgments alone are not sufficient. Before drawing conclusions and evaluating whether the research hypothesis is supported, the data must be quantified and subjected to statistical testing procedures.

Frequency distributions such as we have illustrated are rarely presented in published articles of research.[4] Instead, numbers called descriptive and inferential statistics are used to convey quantitatively what we have attempted to extract subjectively by examining both the raw data and simple frequency distributions. It is important, however, to look at the data in the form of frequency distributions before performing a statistical analysis on the scores. One reason for doing so is that the shape of the frequency distribution is, as we shall see, a major consideration in deciding which descriptive statistics should be calculated to summarize the data.

Shapes of Frequency Distributions

The distribution of a set of scores may take on any one of an endless variety of shapes. Thus, there is usually no simple way to precisely describe the shape of a frequency distribution in a word or two. There are, however, some general descriptive terms which apply to the shape of a distribution and which help to describe a distribution in words. Figure 5–4 presents examples of idealized or hypothetical frequency distributions in graphic form.

Symmetrical Distributions

A **symmetrical distribution** is one that, if it were to be folded in half about a midpoint, would produce two halves identical in shape. One side of the distribution is a mirror image of the other. The distributions a, b, and c in Figure 5–4 are symmetrical distributions, but distributions d, and e are not symmetrical; they are asymmetrical. One symmetrical distribution of particular importance in psychological research is bell-shaped or *normal distribution* (Figure 5–4a). As we will point out in Chapter 6, researchers often hope that their data conform closely to a normal distribution because the normal distribution has properties that permit use of some important techniques for analyzing data. We discuss the normal distribution more fully in Chapter 6.

[4]When they are presented, frequency distributions most typically are graphically depicted. In a graph of a frequency distribution, the values of the scores are presented on the horizontal axis (called the *abscissa* or x axis; remember it by saying "ab-sis-ah"; your lips will purse together and stretch laterally; i.e., horizontally), and frequencies of occurrence of the scores are listed on the vertical axis (called the *ordinate* or y axis; remember it by saying "or-din-it"; the mouth distinctly opens up and down, i.e., vertically, on the first syllable). The scores are arranged from low to high, left to right, along the abscissa. Similarly, frequencies start from zero at the bottom of the ordinate, where the two axes intersect at a right angle. The graphs can be constructed as a histogram, a form of bar graph, or as a frequency polygon, a curve formed with connecting straight lines. Most introductory-level statistics books provide detailed descriptions for constructing graphs of frequency distributions. For example, see McCall (1980), Chapter 2; Runyon and Haber (1980), Chapter 3; or Shavelson (1981), Chapter 3.

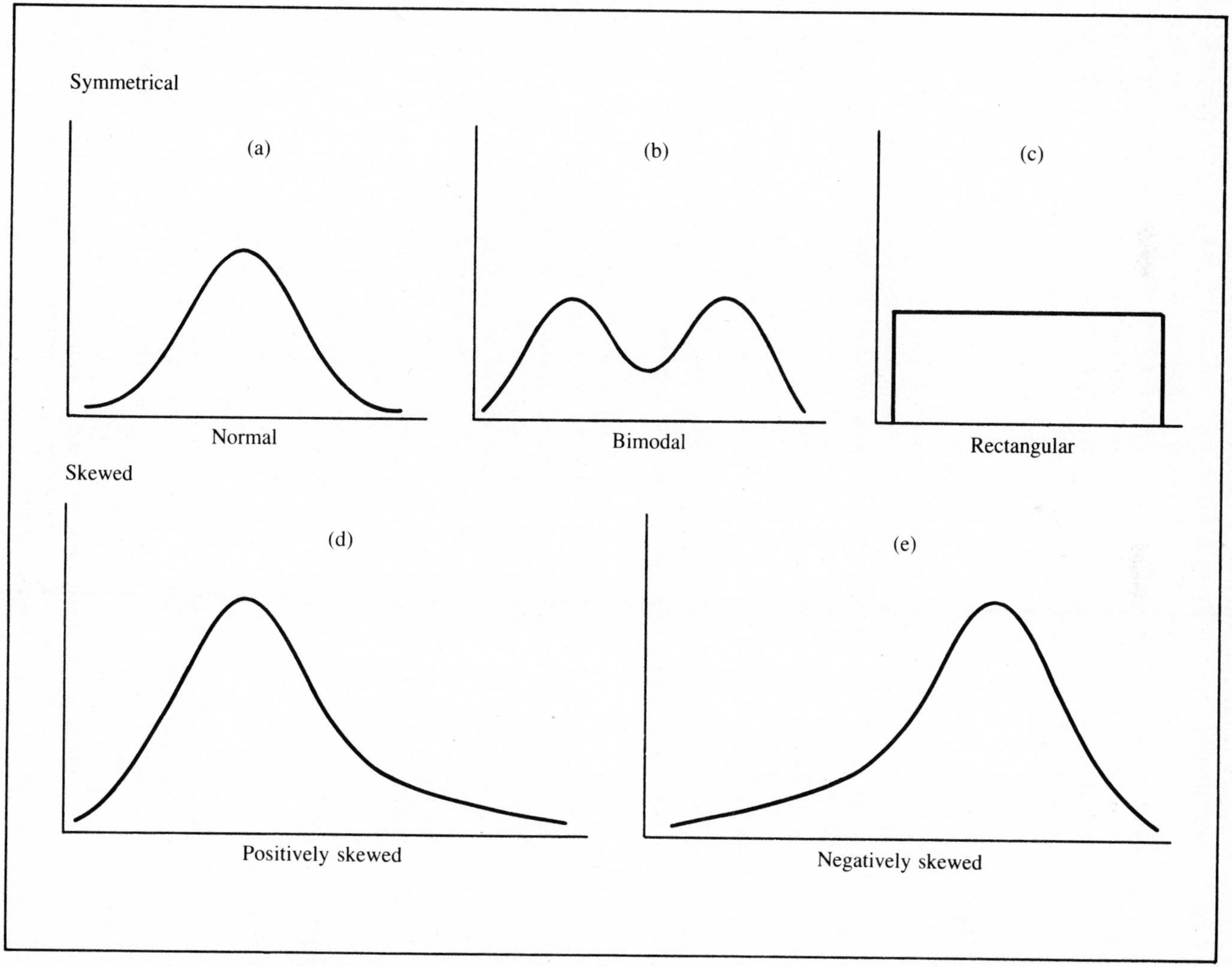

(a) Symmetrical — Normal

(b) Bimodal

(c) Rectangular

(d) Skewed — Positively skewed

(e) Negatively skewed

FIGURE 5–4   *Shapes of theoretical frequency distributions.*

A normal distribution is also described as being unimodal. A *unimodal* distribution (such as those in Figures 5–4a, d, and e) has just one peak or hump corresponding to the most frequently occurring score. Frequency distributions may also be *bimodal* (as illustrated in Figure 5–4b) or *multimodal,* depending upon how many peaks occur in the distribution. There is no mode in the flat rectangular distribution illustrated in Figure 5–4c; in such distributions each score occurs an equal number of times or nearly so.

Skewed Distributions

In practice, it is rare to obtain a distribution that is perfectly symmetrical. Instead, frequency distributions are likely to be somewhat asymmetrical; that is, they have some skewness. In a **skewed distribution** most scores are clustered at one end of the distribution, with scores occurring infrequently at the other end (or tail) of the distribution. A distribution is described as *positively skewed* if the tail occurs for the high scores at the right of the distribution (Figure 5–4d) or *negatively skewed* if the tail occurs for the low scores at the left of the distribution (Figure 5–4e).

Shape of Frequency Distributions in the McCarthy and Betz Experiment

If you were to construct a graph of the grouped frequency distributions for the data shown in Table 5–3, you would find that the distributions of the expertness scores for both treatment conditions are negatively skewed. In fact, even in Table 5–3 you may notice that most of the scores are grouped around the higher values (indicating that participants generally viewed the counselor favorably on the expertness dimension). Frequencies tail off for lower scores. Moreover, you can see that the frequencies for the scores in the self-involving condition peak at higher values (75–79) than the scores for the self-disclosing condition (60–64).[5]

DESCRIPTIVE STATISTICS

Need for Statistics

Reliable scientific conclusions cannot be based upon an investigator's judgment from visual examination of raw data alone. Although frequency distributions help one to gain a better feel for the data, merely inspecting the data in frequency

---

[5]We think it would be instructive for you to construct frequency distributions for the data on the perceived attractiveness and trustworthiness dimensions presented in Table 5–1. How would you describe the shapes of those distributions?

distributions does not allow us to decide whether two sets of scores are or are not different, and therefore, whether the independent variable had an effect on behavior. Clearly, what is needed is a procedure for simplifying and quantifying the decision process so that different researchers can reach the same objective decision about the data in an experiment. There are such quantitative procedures—*statistics*.

Descriptive and Inferential Statistics

Mere mention of the word *statistics* frequently induces a great deal of anxiety in students. But, **statistics** are merely numbers that transform raw data into a more usable form for describing the results and for making decisions about the outcome of the experiment. Two types of statistics are usually computed and reported in psychological research—descriptive and inferential statistics.

Descriptive statistics are simply numbers that are used to summarize and describe the raw data obtained from a sample of participants in an experiment. Descriptive statistics reduce the raw data into one or two numbers that summarize the scores for all of the individuals in each group of an experiment. Some statistics, called measures of central tendency, describe the "typical" score for a treatment condition, and others, called measures of variability, indicate the amount of dispersion or variation around the typical score.

Inferential statistics are used to infer characteristics or parameters of a population from the descriptive statistics obtained from the samples of participants in an experiment. A **population** is simply some set of organisms (people or animals), objects, or events that, in principle, can be identified. A **sample** of participants in an experiment, therefore, is made up of members obtained from a larger population. Rarely, if ever, are measurements made on all members of a population of interest. But researchers often assume that the measurements made on members of the sample are representative of measurements that could be made on the larger population to which the participants in the sample belong. For example, a sample mean, $\overline{X}$, is often used to estimate the parameter μ (pronounced "mu"), the mean of the population from which the sample was selected.

Inferential statistics include the use of tests of statistical significance on sample data in order to help determine whether or not the independent variable affected the behavior measured. This determination is done by evaluating the probability that observed differences in the descriptive statistics from the samples of participants represent "real" differences in the populations from which the samples were selected.

The remainder of this chapter is about the descriptive use of measures of central tendency. The descriptive uses of measures of variability and the use of descriptive statistics for inferring population characteristics are introduced in Chapter 6.

Measures of Central Tendency

Measures of central tendency are numbers (i.e., descriptive statistics) that describe or represent the "average" or typical score of participants within a treatment condition. We shall discuss the three most familiar measures of central tendency: the mode, median, and arithmetic mean.

The Mode

The **mode** is simply the most frequently occurring score in the set of scores in a treatment condition. The mode is readily determined by inspecting a simple un-grouped frequency distribution and observing which score was tabulated most often. As an example, we use the ungrouped frequency distributions of the McCarthy and Betz expertness scores in Table 5–2. For subjects in the self-disclosing condition two scores occur most frequently. Scores of 57 and 78 were both obtained from four individuals in that group; no other score was tabulated more than three times. Here, then, the distribution of expertness scores is bimodal (i.e., having two modes) with modes of 57 and 78; both values are used to describe the "average" score in the self-disclosing condition. In the self-involving condition, however, only one score (77) occurred most frequently (six times); accordingly, the mode is 77 for this group.

Although the mode is readily computed, it is rarely used or reported as a measure of central tendency in psychological research. We have already encountered one reason for this rarity: A distribution may have more than one or even more than two modes. Which is a more typical score for the participants in the self-disclosing condition, 57 or 78? What would you decide if there were three or more modes; that is, if the distribution were multimodal? Thus, the mode may not provide a unique typical or average score. Moreover, the mode is not as well suited for further statistical analysis as are the median and the mean.

The Median

The **median** (often abbreviated *Mdn* or *Md*) corresponds to a score in the middle of a frequency distribution such that in principle, one-half of the scores have values above the median and one-half of them have values below the median. The median is thus a value that corresponds to the *50th percentile point* in a distribution. A percentile point represents the value below which a certain percentage of scores in a distribution lie; for a median, then, 50 percent of the scores fall below its value.

With an even number of scores, the median is taken as the value that lies midway between the two middle scores in the frequency distribution. For example, there are 54 expertness scores in the self-disclosing condition shown in the fre-

Two Situations in Which the Mode Is Useful   BOX 5-1

We have dismissed the mode as a measure of central tendency rather perfunctorily. For the most part, the mode is not widely used to characterize behavioral science data. But Senders (1958) provides examples of two instances in which the mode provides the best measure of central tendency. Her first instance is a distribution of scores that is distinctively bimodal (or multimodal). She gives an example of measurements of political attitudes on the eve of an important political election. People would be very likely to lean firmly toward the Republican or Democratic candidate but would not be neutral at this time. The distribution of their attitudes would be quite bimodal, but a median or a mean as a measure of central tendency would characterize the typical political attitude as "neutral," a quite inappropriate characterization of all but perhaps a few people.

   Senders's second example is the instance when a score is needed that *exactly* characterizes or "fits" most people. "If a shoe salesman can take only one demonstration pair with him, he will do better to take a pair of the modal size than a pair of the median or mean size. Nobody may have feet that are fitted by either of the latter, and a shoe that *almost* fits is not much better than a shoe that is much too big or too small. What the salesman wants is the shoe that will fit perfectly the largest number of people, and a shoe of the modal size is just what he needs" (Senders, 1958, p. 161).

quency distribution of Table 5–2. The median for these scores is 64.5, a value that falls halfway between 64 (the 27th score) and 65 (the 28th score); therefore, one-half of the 54 scores lie below a value of 64.5 and one-half lie above it. With an odd number of scores, the median is usually determined by finding the middle score in a frequency distribution. For the 53 expertness scores in the self-involving condition in Table 5–2 the median is 71. This value is the 27th score and falls in the middle of the distribution. Notice, essentially, that a counting procedure is used to determine a median. The numerical values of the scores that go into the "count" are not utilized in determining the value of the median.

   You will observe in Table 5–2, however, that two of the 53 subjects in the self-involving condition had scores of 71. In this case 50 percent of the scores were lower than the median value of 71, but not exactly one-half of the remaining scores were higher than 71. Especially with large samples, it is not uncommon to find that the score in the middle of a frequency distribution occurs more than once. In such cases a more precise theoretical median value can be obtained by using a formula that is presented in most statistics texts.[6] Applied to the 53 expertness scores for the self-involving condition, the formula produces a median value of 70.75, which agrees closely with the median value of 71 that is the 27th score in the frequency distribution. But for most purposes, the median can be derived quickly by counting scores in the frequency distribution.

[6]See, for example, Hays (1973), p. 218; McCall (1980), pp. 64–66; Runyon and Haber (1980), p. 79; or Shavelson (1981), p. 118. The formula is used with either an equal or an odd number of scores in the frequency distribution.

The Arithmetic Mean

The most familiar measure of central tendency, the one most people think of as an average score, is the **arithmetic mean.** For data obtained from a sample the arithmetic mean is often called the sample mean, or simply the mean, and is abbreviated by the symbol $\bar{X}$ (pronounced "X bar" or "bar X"). It is defined as the sum of a set of scores divided by the number of scores that were summed. In statistical notation, the mean is defined as:

$$\bar{X} = \sum X_i/n.$$

The letter X_i represents a score for any individual. The symbol Σ (the Greek capital letter *sigma*) is a summation sign; it indicates summing or adding up a set of numbers. The letter n represents the number of scores that were summed; hence, it corresponds to the number of participants in the sample.[7]

To illustrate the calculation and use of a sample mean, we refer again to the data in Table 5–1. We use the subscripts A_1 and A_2 to identify the means for particular samples. The mean for the expertness score for the 54 participants in the self-disclosing group ($\bar{X}_{A_1}$) is obtained as follows:

$$\bar{X}_{A_1} = (59 + 74 + 65 + \cdots + 49 + 48 + 60)/54$$
$$= 3406/54$$
$$= 63.07 \text{ or } 63.1.[8]$$

Similarly, for the 53 participants in the self-involving condition, the sample mean ($\bar{X}_{A_2}$) is found by,

$$\bar{X}_{A_2} = (77 + 77 + 73 + \cdots + 78 + 68 + 49)/53$$
$$= 3631/53$$
$$= 68.51 \text{ or } 68.5.$$

These means agree with those presented in Table 1 in the McCarthy and Betz article (see Chapter 1). Incidentally, in McCarthy and Betz's table the sample mean is abbreviated by M instead of by $\bar{X}$. This style is consistent with the practice

---

[7]The letter n is typically used to indicate the number of subjects in a treatment condition or a sample. The letter N is used to represent the total number of subject in an experiment. For the McCarthy and Betz experiment, n for the self-disclosing group = 54, n for the self-involving group = 53, and $N = 107$.

[8]The number of places to which computations should be carried out is often confusing to students. A simple rule is that the final value of any computation should be rounded to one decimal place beyond the accuracy or value to which the dependent variable was measured. For McCarthy and Betz's experiment, participants' scores were measured to the nearest whole rating value; for example, 73 or 62. Thus, we round the end product of any computations involving these scores to one decimal place. Values that will be involved in additional computations, however, should be carried to at least two or three decimal places and not rounded until all computations are complete.

followed by many psychological journals, including all journals published by the American Psychological Association.[9]

Notice one important characteristic of the sample mean: Unlike the mode or the median, *all the participants' scores are used in obtaining the mean.* Therefore, although a change in the value of a score may not affect the mode or median, it will always change the value of the sample mean. Suppose the first expertness score in the self-disclosing condition (Table 5–1) was a 37 instead of a 59. A score of 37 still would not be the most frequently occurring, and it would not fall in the middle of the frequency distribution of scores. Therefore, neither the mode(s) nor the median of the 54 scores would be affected, but the sample mean would change from 63.1 to 62.7.

Comparing Measures of Central Tendency

A summary of the three principal measures of central tendency for the CRF expertness scores is provided in Table 5–4. It is obvious that the measures do not provide the same "average" values for the data in either experimental condition. This is not unusual, for only when the frequency distributions are truly symmetrical and unimodal will all three measures of central tendency have the same numerical values.

The question of which measure is the "best" average score quite naturally arises now. Most typically, because the mode is often not a single value for a set of scores or may not exist at all if one score does not occur most frequently, the answer to the question is resolved by deciding between the median and the mean.

Comparison of Measures of Central Tendency for the CRF Expertness Scores in Table 5–1.   **TABLE 5–4**

Measure of central tendency	Experimental condition	
	Self-disclosing	*Self-involving*
Mode	57, 78	77
Median	64.5	71.0[a]
Mean	63.1	68.5

[a] The precise value for the median, computed with a statistical formula, is 70.75. This value is slightly less than the middle score in the distribution (71), and represents a score that no participant could actually obtain. The median values differ because the formula takes into account that the middle score was not unique to one participant, but was obtained by two individuals in the sample. The difference in values is negligible.

[9] In statistical texts, though, the sample mean is usually given by $\bar{X}$ because the letter X is often used to symbolize scores. For this reason, we use $\bar{X}$ instead of M.

From a descriptive point of view, we notice that both the medians and the means presented in Table 5-4 lead to similar characterizations of average scores. Each of these measures of central tendency represents a typical score as a rating of from slightly to moderately expert. And for both measures the value for the self-involving condition is slightly larger than the value for the self-disclosing condition. Hence, in describing the typical score, both the mean and the median led to about the same conclusions.

These would not always be parallel, particularly if the data were more seriously skewed. When data are considerably skewed, then the median is more likely to be the appropriate descriptive measure of central tendency because the median is not influenced by extreme scores as is the sample mean.

To a large extent then, how adequately any measure of central tendency describes the typical performance of participants within a treatment condition depends upon both the shape of the frequency distribution of the scores and how much the individual scores vary from one another and from the measure of central tendency. Measures of variability about a central tendency and their descriptive and inferential uses are the topics of Chapter 6.

When a Mean Is Not *the* Mean: The Geometric Mean

When one describes the mean of a set of data it is generally understood that one is referring to the arithmetic mean. The arithmetic mean is most appropriate only when the scores represent interval or ratio level of measurement and the data are approximately normally distributed. Occasionally, however, you will find reported in the literature other kinds of means that are used instead of the median when the scores are skewed. One of these is the geometric mean, which may be used to transform a skewed distribution of scores into a more approximately normal distribution.

Earlier in this chapter we described the method of magnitude estimation, in which individuals assign numbers to quantify their subjective sensory experiences (e.g., how sweet a sugar solution tastes). Typically, the average magnitude estimates given to a stimulus by a sample of subjects will be reported as a geometric mean (e.g., see Moskowitz, 1971). Magnitude estimates tend to be positively skewed, but the logarithms[10] of the magnitude estimates will be more normally distributed. When a distribution is log-normal, i.e., the logarithms are normally distributed, the geometric mean is a better measure of central tendency than the arithmetic mean (Senders, 1958).

[10]A common logarithm of a given number is the exponent that indicates the power to which the base number 10 is raised to produce the given number. For example, the logarithm of 100 is 2, because 10^2 (10 raised to the second power) equals 100. Accordingly, the logarithm of 10 is 1, the log of 1000 is 3, and so forth. Notice that although numbers in a geometric progression (e.g., 10, 100, 1000) increase in equal ratio steps (i.e., 1 to 10), the logarithms of these numbers increase in equal arithmetic steps (e.g., 1, 2, 3). Therefore, a distribution of logarithms of scores will be less positively skewed than a distribution of scores that contain extremely high scores.

An Observation About Measures of Central Tendency to Chew on   BOX 5-2

For a recent year the Department of Agriculture reported that the per capita consumption of chewing tobacco in the United States was 1.33 pounds per person. When first brought to our attention, we viewed this statistic with incredulity. As far as we are aware, none of our colleagues or friends chews tobacco (which reveals that we don't know any professional baseball players). Neither of us can recall meeting a female tobacco chewer. Who, if anyone, does this mean of 1.33 pounds characterize? We think it is reasonable to assume that the distribution of use of chewing tobacco is severely skewed and not symmetrical. It is quite likely that a minority of the population uses chewing tobacco and their consumption is considerably in excess of 1.33 pounds per year, and the majority of the population does not chew tobacco at all.[a] The modal and median chewing-tobacco consumption probably is exactly 0 pounds per year, and it is likely that the mean of 1.33 pounds characterizes neither the tobacco chewer nor the nonuser. Glass and Stanley (1970) point out that "some groups of scores simply do not 'tend centrally' in any meaningful way, and it is often misleading to calculate one measure of central tendency" (p. 68). We think their point is clearly illustrated by the statistics spit out by the Department of Agriculture.

[a]A letter to newspaper columnist Ann Landers lends some support to this supposition. In the letter, a woman reports that her husband chews between one and two pouches of tobacco each day. Assuming a typical pouch of tobacco is 3 ounces, this works out to about 100 pounds of chewing tobacco per year for her husband.

The geometric mean can be defined in several ways. One definition is that the geometric mean is the antilogarithm[11] of the arithmetic mean of the logarithms of a set of scores. In notation, the geometric mean (GM) is defined as:

$$GM = \text{antilogarithm of } \frac{\sum \log X}{n}$$

where n is the number of scores, X_i. If logarithms are normally distributed, then the arithmetic mean of the logarithms is the center of the distribution. The antilogarithm merely converts the arithmetic mean of the logarithms back into the original units of measurement. A clear illustration of how this definition of the geometric mean is used to summarize magnitude estimation data is presented in Engen (1971, p. 77).

The geometric mean is also defined as the nth root of the product of all n scores in a distribution or,

$$GM = \sqrt[n]{(X_1)(X_2) \cdots (X_n)}.$$

Both this formula and the logarithmic formula provide the same numerical value of the geometric mean for a set of data.

[11]The antilogarithm is a number corresponding to the logarithm of that number. Thus, 100 is the antilogarithm of 2, 1000 the antilog of 3, and so forth.

For a better conceptual understanding of the geometric mean, it may be helpful to know that it is the central value of a geometric series of numbers. In a geometric series, all successive numbers in a sequence after the first number are in a constant ratio to one another. For example, the numbers 2, 4, 8, 16, and 32 form a geometric series, for each number is twice as large as the one that precedes it. The geometric mean of these numbers is 8 (in contrast to an arithmetic mean of 12.4). You can see from this example that the geometric mean gives less weight to large deviant scores than does the arithmetic mean.

SUMMARY

- Measurements of a dependent variable must be reliable and valid in order to be useful. Four levels of measurement—nominal, ordinal, interval, and ratio—typically are recognized.
- The raw data—the scores obtained from all the individuals in the experiment—must be organized and summarized. Frequency distributions are used to organize raw data. Descriptive statistics summarize the data. Two commonly used types of descriptive statistics are measures of central tendency and measures of variability.
- Measures of central tendency provide a value that represents a typical or "average" score in the experiment. The mode, median, and mean are the most familiar measures of central tendency.
- Measures of variability indicate the amount of dispersion or variability in scores around the typical score. These statistics are discussed in Chapter 6.

6

In this chapter we describe the use of measures of variability for describing data and discuss how sample statistics are used to estimate population values. Topics include:

- Several measures of variability, emphasizing the standard deviation and the variance
- Using the standard deviation to obtain information about the shape of a distribution of scores
- Choosing which descriptive statistics to use in an experiment
- Estimating population parameters from sample statistics.

WHY YOU NEED TO KNOW THIS MATERIAL

Measures of average performance alone do not adequately represent performance by subjects in an experiment, for individuals' scores may vary extensively around the typical score. Measures of variability indicate how much the scores vary. Moreover, measures of variability set the stage for understanding how accurately statistics computed on sample data estimate the parameters of a population of scores.

Measures of Variability and Estimation of Population Parameters

A measure of central tendency tells only part of the story about the scores obtained from a sample of participants. From the measure of central tendency alone one cannot tell whether the scores are widely dispersed about that "typical" score or clustered closely around it. Neither the median nor the mean itself gives any indication of how much dispersion or variability there is among the scores used to calculate that statistic. Thus, in order to know how well the measure of central tendency represents a typical score, a measure of the variability in scores must be associated with the measure of central tendency. Moreover, measures of variability are also important to the use of descriptive statistics as estimates of population parameters. The purpose of this chapter, then, is to introduce several measures of variability and introduce the concept of statistical inference.

To illustrate the concept of variability and its relevance to describing a set of scores, consider the two hypothetical sets of scores presented in Table 6–1. Suppose that these are CRF expertness scores for subjects who were exposed to a self-disclosing treatment. (The scores in both columns A_1 and A_2 were selected from actual scores, which appear in Table 5–1.) The mean for each set of scores is 64.0, but in examining the two sets of scores it is apparent that the mean of 64.0 is not equally representative of the subjects' ratings in both columns A_1 and A_2. In column A_1 the ten scores are clustered closely around the mean; no score deviates more than 2 rating points from the mean. In this case, then, the mean appears quite representative of all the ratings, for there is little variability among the individual scores. The situation is sharply different in column A_2. Here you can see considerable variability or dispersion in the ratings. No two individuals had the same score, and only three scores fall within 2 rating points of the mean; the remaining scores are considerably lower or higher than the mean (as low as 32 and as high as 82).

Variability refers to how much scores are spread out or dispersed in a distribution. The more the scores are clustered around the average score (as in

TABLE 6-1   *Two sets of hypothetical CRF expertness scores for samples of ten subjects receiving the self-disclosing treatment condition. The mean for each set is 64.0*

A_1	A_2
63	66
65	79
64	49
66	64
63	78
62	32
62	62
64	56
66	82
65	72
$\overline{X}_{A1} = 64$	$\overline{X}_{A2} = 64$

column A_1), the better a particular measure of central tendency represents the performance or score of all participants. Conversely, the more dispersion there is among scores within a group (as in Column A_2), the less the average score depicts a typical score of the participants. But a psychologist cannot rely upon perceptual judgments of frequency distributions to decide whether the variation in scores is minimal or excessive. As with measures of central tendency, the variability must be quantified. Accordingly, there are several statistics to describe the dispersion of the scores.

MEASURES OF VARIABILITY

Range

The simplest measure of variability is called the range. For a set of scores the **range** is computed simply by subtracting the lowest score from the highest score:

$$\text{Range} = X_{\text{highest}} - X_{\text{lowest}}.$$

To illustrate the range, we refer again to the CRF expertness scores in the McCarthy and Betz experiment. The highest and lowest scores for each treatment condition are easily determined from the frequency distributions presented in Table 5–2. For example, the range for the self-disclosing group is 67 ($83 - 16$) and the range for the self-involving participants is 53 ($83 - 30$).

The range clearly describes the overall spread of scores in a distribution. A larger value for the range, as found for the self-disclosing group, indicates greater dispersion between the largest and smallest scores. The range, however, is a relatively unstable measure of variability because it depends upon only two scores in the sample. Any change in either the largest or smallest score will affect the range, even though all other scores may remain unchanged. Moreover, the larger the sample, the more likely it is that one deviant score may be obtained to inflate the value of the range. Where a distribution of scores is skewed with only one extremely low or high score, the range may provide a distorted picture of the dispersion of scores within a group. The range may be used with any measure of central tendency, but because of the limitations we have mentioned, it is not a frequently reported measure of variability.

Interquartile Range

A more informative measure of variability, particularly when the distribution of scores is skewed, is the **interquartile range** (IQR), which describes the range of values for the middle 50 percent of the scores in a distribution. Recall that the median was defined as a score corresponding to the 50th percentile. The interquartile range is obtained by subtracting the score corresponding to the 25th percentile (or first quartile) from the score that falls at the 75th percentile (or third quartile). In notation, the interquartile range is defined as,

$$IQR = Q_3 - Q_1$$

where Q_3 is the score at the 75th percentile and Q_1 is the score at the 25th percentile. Because the interquartile range excludes the top 25 percent and the bottom 25 percent of the scores in a distribution, its value is unaffected by only a few extreme scores.

Obviously the interquartile range will be smaller than the range for a set of scores. For the CRF expertness scores of Table 5–1, the interquartile ranges for the self-disclosing and self-involving groups are 16.6 (where $Q_3 - Q_1 = 74.0 - 57.4$) and 13.0 (where $Q_3 - Q_1 = 76.8 - 63.8$), respectively.[1]

The interquartile range provides useful information about the variability of scores in a distribution, for it reveals the range of scores typical for the middle 50 percent of the individuals grouped around the median. For this reason, the interquartile range is used as a measure of variability when the median is used to describe the central tendency for a set of scores. It is seldom used as a measure of variability with the sample mean.

---

[1] The 75th and 25th percentile scores for both distributions were obtained with a formula that provides a precise value. The formula and discussion of its use may be found in McCall (1980), Chapter 4; Runyon and Haber (1980), Chapter 4; Shavelson (1981), p. 132, and other statistics textbooks.

Semi-Interquartile Range

The **semi-interquartile range** (*SIQR*) is simply one-half of the interquartile range:

$$SIQR = \frac{IQR}{2} = \frac{(Q_3 - Q_1)}{2}.$$

The semi-interquartile range describes the average spread of scores for 25 percent of the scores above and below the median. Only when the distribution is perfectly symmetrical, however, will the semi-interquartile range represent exactly the range of scores for the 25 percent of the scores above the median and the 25 percent of scores below the median.

For the CRF expertness scores in Table 5–1, the semi-interquartile range is 8.3 for the self-disclosing group and 6.5 for the self-involving group. These semi-interquartile ranges indicate that the middle 50 percent of the scores in the self-disclosing condition did not extend more than about 8 rating points above or 8 rating points below the median. Similarly, for the self-involving condition, the middle 50 percent of the scores are in the range of approximately 7 rating points above or below the median. Notice that we have qualified the preceding two statements with the words *about* and *approximately*. Because the frequency distributions for both the self-disclosing and self-involving treatments are somewhat skewed (see Tables 5–2 and 5–3), these semi-interquartile ranges do not include exactly 25 percent of the scores on each side of the median.

Comparing Range Measures

The range, interquartile range, and semi-interquartile range each provide an interval containing a percentage of the scores (e.g., 100 percent for the range) around the central location in a distribution. None of these statistics, however, utilizes all the scores in the distribution for its computation. Further, there are instances when a single number, based upon all of the scores and describing the typical amount of variability in a distribution, is needed. Several such statistics have been developed, utilizing the arithmetic mean as the measure of central tendency. The first such statistic we discuss is the average deviation.

Average Deviation

As we indicated in Chapter 5, the mean is obtained by adding all the scores in a sample and dividing by the number of scores. It is an obvious step, we think, to take a similar approach to deriving a measure of variability. That is, we could subtract the mean from each score, add up all the resulting deviations, and then divide the sum by the number of scores. In notation this measure of variability would be:

$$\frac{\sum (X_i - \bar{X})}{n}.$$

There is a problem, however, with this proposed measure of variability: The sum of $X_i - \bar{X}$ deviations will always equal zero, because the sum of the positive deviations will equal the sum of the negative deviations. Dividing zero by n will provide a useless mean value of zero.[2]

One way to get around this problem is to sum the *absolute values* of the deviations. The absolute value of any number is the number itself, disregarding whether the number is positive or negative. The absolute value of a number is represented by | |, and therefore the absolute deviation of a score from the mean is written as $|X_i - \bar{X}|$ (thus, $|4 - 8| = 4$). Dividing the sum of absolute deviations by n results in a measure of variability called the **average deviation** (abbreviated AD). In notation, the average deviation (also called the *mean deviation,* abbreviated MD) is written:

$$AD = \frac{\sum (|X_i - \bar{X}|)}{n}.$$

The calculation of the average deviation for the ten scores of column A_2 of Table 6–1 is shown in Table 6–2. In this example, the average deviation is 11.4 for the ten scores that had a range of 50 ($82 - 32$). This result indicates that scores, on the average, deviated by 11.4 points in either direction from the mean. For the CRF expertness scores in Table 5–1, the average deviations for the self-disclosing and self-involving groups are 10.7 and 8.3, respectively. As these values demonstrate, scores were more variable for the self-disclosing group.

Example of calculation of the average deviation for the ten scores of column A_2 of Table 6–1.   **TABLE 6–2**

X_i	$\bar{X}_{A2}$		$X_i - \bar{X}_{A2}$	$|X_i - \bar{X}_{A2}|$	Computation
66	64		+2	2	$AD = (|X_i - \bar{X}_{A2}|)/n$
79	64		+15	15	
49	64		−15	15	$AD = 114/10$
64	64		0	0	
78	64		+14	14	$AD = 11.4$
32	64		−32	32	
62	64		−2	2	
56	64		−8	8	
82	64		+18	18	
72	64		+8	8	
		Sums	0	114	

[2]One definition of the arithmetic mean is that the sum of deviations from the mean, i.e., $\sum (X_i - \bar{X})$, always equals zero.

The average deviation is perhaps the most obvious candidate for a measure of variability with the arithmetic mean, for it is a clear analog of the mean. In practice, however, the average deviation is rarely reported. Instead, a closely related measure, the standard deviation, derived from the variance, is more commonly used.

Variance and the Standard Deviation

With the average deviation, the problem of $X_i - \overline{X}$ deviation scores summing to zero was dealt with by taking the absolute value of each deviation, i.e., $|X_i - \overline{X}|$. Another way to eliminate troublesome negative $(-)$ deviation values is to square each deviation score, i.e., $(X_i - \overline{X})^2$, before it is summed. This procedure is used to derive the variance and, subsequently, the standard deviation.

Variance

To obtain the **sample variance** the squared deviations are summed and divided by the number of scores minus one. In notation, the variance is written:[3]

$$s^2 = \frac{\sum (X_i - \overline{X})^2}{n - 1}.$$

The sum of squared deviations, $\Sigma(X_i - \overline{X})^2$, is often simply called the *sum of squares* and represented by the symbol *SS*. Thus, the variance is also defined:

$$s^2 = \frac{SS}{n - 1}.$$

The variance is a very important concept in the statistical analysis of data, and we will return to it in Chapter 8 when we introduce the inferential statistical test known as analysis of variance. It is not particularly useful as a descriptive statistic, though, and it is seldom reported as a measure of variability in summarizing data. One reason is that it is difficult to conceptualize what information an average squared deviation conveys about the variability of scores. The standard deviation, however, which is derived directly from the variance, is a very useful measure of variability.

Standard Deviation

The **standard deviation** is obtained simply by taking the square root of the variance. Thus, the standard deviation reverts values back to the original scale units of the scores that were used to compute the variance, and it provides a

---

[3]You may think that we have made an error in dividing by $n - 1$ rather than by n. But the formula is correct; we explain the reason on page 149.

measure of the deviation of scores from their arithmetic mean. In notation, the sample standard deviation is defined:

$$s = SD = \sqrt{s^2} = \sqrt{\sum (X_i - \bar{X})^2/(n-1)} = \sqrt{SS/(n-1)}.$$

The letter s is typically used to represent the sample standard deviation in statistical notation, although the abbreviation SD is more commonly used when reporting the values in research articles.

The calculation of a standard deviation from the definitional formula is illustrated in Table 6–3. The ten scores used in this example are the same scores used to illustrate the calculation of the average deviation in Table 6–2. For the

Raw-Score Computational Formula for the Standard Deviation

The definitional formula for the standard deviation best conveys conceptually what the standard deviation is. The formula is easy to use when relatively few scores are involved and the scores and mean of the scores are whole numbers. When decimal values are involved with the scores or the mean, however, then the computations become more cumbersome, for the resulting deviation for each score will be a decimal. Therefore, it is often easier to calculate the standard deviation with a raw-score method that uses a mathematically equivalent computational formula. The computational formula is:

$$SD = \sqrt{\frac{\sum X_i^2 - [(\sum X_i)^2/n]}{n-1}}.$$

With this procedure you square each score and add up all the squared values to obtain $\sum X_i^2$. The $\sum X_i$ is then multiplied by itself to obtain the square of the sum of the scores, $(\sum X_i)^2$ [read as "sum of X quantity squared"], and then divided by the number of scores, n. The latter term, $(\sum X_i)^2/n$, is subtracted from the sum of the squared scores, $\sum X_i^2$, to obtain a value equivalent to the sum of squares. The SS is then divided by $n-1$ to obtain the variance, and the square root of the variance yields the standard deviation.

An example of the use of this computational formula to derive the standard deviation for the ten scores of Table 6–3 is shown below.

X_i	X_i^2	Computation
66	4356	$SD = \sqrt{\dfrac{\sum X_i^2 - [(\sum X_i)^2/n]}{n-1}}$
79	6241	
49	2401	
64	4096	$SD = \sqrt{\dfrac{43{,}090 - [(640)^2/10]}{10-1}}$
78	6084	
32	1024	
62	3844	$SD = \sqrt{(43{,}090 - 40{,}960)/9}$
56	3136	
82	6724	$SD = \sqrt{236.667}$
72	5184	$SD = 15.38$
Sums 640	43,090	

TABLE 6-3   *Calculation of the standard deviation using the definitional formula for the ten scores of column A_2 of Table 6-1*

X_i	$\bar{X}_{A_2}$	$X_i - \bar{X}_{A_2}$	$(X_i - \bar{X}_{A_2})^2$	Computation[a]
66	64	2	4	$SD = \sqrt{\sum (X_i - \bar{X}_{A_2})^2/(n-1)}$
79	64	+15	225	
49	64	−15	225	$SD = \sqrt{2130/(10-1)}$
64	64	0	0	
78	64	+14	196	$SD = \sqrt{236.667}$
32	64	−32	1024	
62	64	−2	4	$SD = 15.38$
56	64	−8	64	
82	64	+18	324	
72	64	+8	64	
		Sums 0	2130	

[a]This procedure requires you to first obtain the sum of squared deviations, SS or $\sum (X_i - \bar{X})^2$. This result is found by subtracting the mean from each score, squaring the resulting deviation, and adding all the squared deviations together. The resulting sum is divided by $n - 1$. This procedure yields the variance, s^2; the standard deviation, s or SD, is the square root of the variance.

CRF expertness scores of Table 5–1 the standard deviations for the self-disclosure and self-involving groups are 14.63 and 11.06, respectively. These agree with the values 14.6 and 11.1 reported by McCarthy and Betz in Table 1 of their article.[4]

Because the variance and the standard deviation are such important statistical concepts·in the analysis of data, we think it is useful to review the formulas which we have introduced and which will be referred to again in subsequent chapters. Accordingly, the variance and standard deviation can be expressed in several ways. Each of these formulas provides the same numerical value of the statistic when applied to a set of data.

	Definitional formula	Computational formula	Sum of squares
Variance $(s^2$ or $SD^2)$	$\dfrac{\sum (X_i - \bar{X})^2}{n-1}$	$\dfrac{\sum X_i^2 - \left[\left(\sum X_i \right)^2/n \right]}{n-1}$	$\dfrac{SS}{n-1}$

[4]We recommend that the standard deviation be reported to at least one more decimal place than the value for the mean. Although this suggestion may appear contrary to the rounding rule given in footnote 8 of Chapter 5, the standard deviation is often squared to obtain the variance. Reporting the standard deviation to one additional decimal place reduces rounding error when it is squared to obtain the variance. Accordingly, we report the standard deviations for the McCarthy and Betz data to two decimal places.

	Definitional formula	*Computational formula*	*Sum of squares*
Standard deviation $s = SD = \sqrt{s^2}$	$\sqrt{\dfrac{\sum (X_i - \bar{X})^2}{n-1}}$	$\sqrt{\dfrac{\sum X_i^2 - \left[(\sum X_i)^2/n \right]}{n-1}}$	$\sqrt{\dfrac{SS}{n-1}}$

What Does the Standard Deviation Tell Us?

Standard Deviation and a Normally Distributed Population of Scores

We have stressed the mean and standard deviation because both measures provide a great deal of descriptive information about a distribution of scores. Let us see how. Suppose for a moment that we are dealing with a population of scores that truly is normally distributed. The normal distribution was briefly introduced in Chapter 5. It is a theoretical mathematical distribution that specifies the relative frequency of occurrence of some set of scores.[5] The frequency distribution of a normally distributed set of scores can be completely described if we know two parameters of the population, the mean (μ) and the standard deviation (σ). As you can see, population parameters are distinguished from sample statistics by the notation used. Sample statistics are most commonly represented by roman letters (e.g., $\bar{X}$, SD), and Greek letters are used to represent population parameters. For example, μ (pronounced "mu") is the Greek letter M (for *mean*) and σ (pronounced "sigma") is the Greek S.

Normal Distribution   **BOX 6-1**

The normal distribution as we know it arose from the work of James Bernoulli (1654–1705), Abraham de Moivre (1667–1754), Pierre Rémond de Montmort (1678–1719), Carl Friedrich Gauss (1777–1855), and others. Their major interests were in developing mathematical approximations for probabilities encountered in various games of chance or in the distribution of errors to be expected in various instances of observation, as in astronomy or physics (see Dudycha and Dudycha, 1972, for a detailed history of the development of the normal distribution). The normal distribution soon became an important distribution for statisticians, because many inferential problems in statistics can be solved only if a normal distribution is assumed (Hays, 1973).

The normal distribution gained importance for psychologists because it is reasonable to assume that any behaviors that are determined by a large number of independent variables will be approximately normally distributed in a population. We stress the word *approximately,* for Glass and Stanley (1970) state:

Somehow the misapprehension arises in the minds of many students that there is a necessary link between the normal distribution—an idealized description of *some* frequency distributions—and practically any data they might collect. The normal

(continued)

[5]The mathematical formula may be found in McCall (1980), p. 97; Runyon and Haber (1980), p. 107; or Shavelson (1981), pp. 150–154.

BOX 6-1   *(continued)*

curve is a mathematician's invention that is a reasonably good description of the frequency polygon of measurements on several different variables. A collection of scores that are *exactly* normally distributed has never been gathered and never will be. But much is gained if we can tolerate the slight error in the statement and claim from time to time that scores on a variable are "normally distributed." (p. 104)

The theoretical normal distribution has a number of properties, such as being symmetrical about the mode, median, and mean, which are all equal, being asymptotic (it never touches the baseline) and being unbounded (its limits are plus and minus infinity). These properties are never attained in actual scores collected from a population. Yet, despite these limitations, we have already discovered, and will discover even more in Chapters 7 and 8, that much can be gained by assuming a normal distribution of scores in the population from which a sample is drawn.

In a normally distributed population of scores, 68 percent of the scores fall within a range that extends one standard deviation above and below the mean ($\mu \pm 1\sigma$). Within plus or minus two standard deviations around the mean ($\mu \pm 2\sigma$), 95 percent of the scores occur. Extending the range to three standard deviations around the mean ($\mu \pm 3\sigma$) encompasses more than 99 percent of the scores. These percentages remain the same regardless of the values of μ and σ.[6]

To illustrate the relationships just described, suppose a population of scores is normally distributed with $\mu = 100$ and $\sigma = 15$. In this case, 68 percent of the scores around the mean fall within the range of 85 to 115, because a score of 85 lies one standard deviation below the mean and a score of 115 is one standard deviation above the mean. Similarly, 95 percent of the scores will have values between 70 and 130, and virtually the whole range of scores in the distribution, 99+ percent, will extend from 55 to 145. To summarize, in a normal distribution,

$$\mu \pm 1\sigma = 68\% \text{ of the scores}$$
$$\mu \pm 2\sigma = 95\% \text{ of the scores}$$
$$\mu \pm 3\sigma = 99+\% \text{ of the scores.}$$

These relationships are illustrated in Figure 6–1.

Standard Deviation and a Sample of Scores

The normal distribution is strictly a theoretical mathematical distribution. No behavioral measure in a population of any size is exactly normally distributed.

---

[6]The values that encompass exactly 95 percent and 99 percent of the scores are $\pm 1.96\sigma$ and $\pm 2.58\sigma$, respectively. We have rounded the values to $\pm 2\sigma$ and $\pm 3\sigma$. The exact values can be found in tables of the standard normal curve found in most statistics texts. See McCall (1980), pp. 97–106, or Shavelson (1981), Chapter 5, for a more complete description of the use of the normal distribution in this regard.

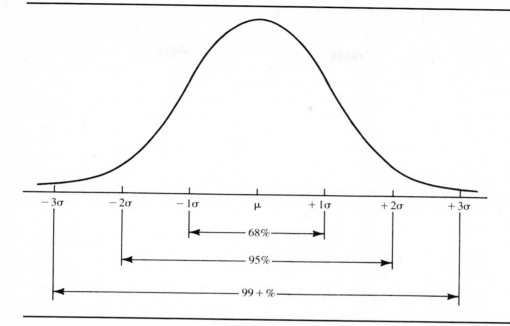

***A normal distribution, illustrating the percentage of scores contained in the ranges
defined by one, two, and three σ around μ.***

FIGURE 6–1

Therefore, the scores obtained from a sample of participants will never be perfectly normally distributed. Inevitably, there will be some skewness, some departure from a perfectly symmetrical distribution. Moreover, the sample standard deviation (*SD*) calculated in experiments is only an estimate of the standard deviation (σ) of the scores in the population to which the subjects belong.

Despite these limitations, in many experiments the well-defined relationship between σ and the percentage of scores located around μ also holds up well with $\overline{X}$ and the *SD*, even when the scores represent only a sample and are not normally distributed. For instance, we have seen that the CRF expertness scores in Table 5–1 are skewed for both treatment conditions. Yet the range $\overline{X} \pm 1SD$ includes just slightly more than 68 percent of the scores; specifically, 72 percent and 74 percent of the scores fall within the range that embraces $\overline{X} \pm 1SD$ for the self-disclosing and self-involving groups, respectively.[7] Also, close to 95 percent of the scores fall within 2*SD* of the sample means (93 percent and 96 percent for the two groups, respectively).

[7]For the self-disclosing group, $\overline{X}_{A1} = 63.1$ and the *SD* = 14.6. Thus, 63.1 − 14.6 = 48.5, and 63.1 + 14.6 = 77.7. By referring to Table 5–2, we determined that 39 of the 54 scores (72 percent) fell within the range of 48.5 to 77.7. For the self-involving group, the $\overline{X}_{A2} \pm 1$ *SD* is 68.5 ± 11.1; thirty-nine of the 53 scores (74 percent) have values between 57.4 and 79.6.

Standard Deviation and Skewness

If you went to the effort of determining the range of expertness scores that fall within $2SD$ of the sample mean for the self-disclosing and self-involving groups, you might notice something peculiar: the range that would embrace about 95 percent of the scores in a normal distribution includes some values that are not on the scale of possible scores! That is, the highest rating a participant could assign to a counselor was 84, but the $\overline{X} \pm 2SD$ range for the self-disclosing data extends to 92.3 and to 90.7 for the self-involving group.[8]

This finding illustrates another informative feature of the standard deviation as a descriptive statistic. The fact that impossible scores are included in the interval of scores within $\overline{X} \pm 2SD$ (or, too, $\overline{X} \pm 3SD$) reveals that scores in a particular group are *not* normally distributed, but skewed. Moreover, for this example, you can readily determine that the scores in both groups are negatively skewed. Let us explain why.

In many experiments, there are limits on the minimum and maximum scores that may be obtained; for example, the CRF scores are limited to a range of 12 to 84. The means obtained by McCarthy and Betz, 63.1 and 68.5, are closer to the upper limit permitted by the rating scale than to the minimum rating score. But it is clear without even seeing the raw data that at least a few individuals gave the counselor relatively low ratings. Several low ratings would deviate from the mean considerably compared to the deviation of other scores and thus be responsible for inflating the value of the SD. Therefore, we infer that a frequency distribution is probably negatively skewed if the mean has a value near the upper limit of possible scores and the range of scores within 2 or $3SD$ of the mean extends beyond the maximum score that can be obtained on the measure of the dependent variable.

A positively skewed distribution can also be detected by knowing only $\overline{X}$ and SD for a set of scores. For example, we recall the results of an experiment conducted by one student in an experimental psychology course. She measured tolerance to thermal pain by recording the duration (in seconds) that a person was able to keep a hand immersed in cold (40° F) water. For one group of subjects she reported that mean tolerance was 58.2 seconds with a standard deviation of 97.0 seconds. Assuming that the distribution of tolerance scores was approximately normal, it was not difficult to infer that some people must have withdrawn their hands from the cold water 40 or more seconds before their hands were even immersed! But, because it is impossible to obtain a tolerance score of negative duration, it is reasonable to assume that a few people who were able to tolerate the cold water for extended periods contributed atypically high scores that skewed the distribution positively and inflated the standard deviation.[9]

[8]The actual ranges are 33.9 to 92.3 for the self-disclosing group and 46.3 to 90.7 for the self-involving group.

[9]Incidentally, this is not an uncommon problem with duration measures of behavior. Such data are likely to be positively skewed, because though 0 seconds is obviously the minimum duration that can be recorded, some individuals may take an extremely long time to respond. When scores with duration measures are so obviously skewed, the median probably is a more appropriate statistic to describe the average score.

You may wonder why one should bother going through an analysis of the shape of a distribution by using the mean and standard deviation when a study of a frequency distribution such as that of Tables 5–2 and 5–3 will provide answers more clearly and precisely. The reason becomes quite evident when you read the published research of psychologists. Frequency distributions of data are rarely presented in published research articles. Most often, authors describe their results with only a mean and standard deviation, as did McCarthy and Betz. Thus, when you are reading published research in psychology you will often have no way of knowing about the shape of the distribution of obtained scores other than by examining the mean and standard deviation.

Comparing Measures of Variability

Table 6–4 presents a summary of the measures of variability for the CRF expertness data of Table 5–1. It is clearly evident that the numerical values for the six measures of variability differ considerably from one another. Because each measure conveys different information about the scores, the numerical values of different measures are not directly comparable to each other. As we indicated earlier in the chapter, however, the six measures can be collapsed into essentially two categories. One type of measure of variability (typified by the range, IQR, and the $SIQR$) describes a distance about an average score containing a certain percentage of participants' scores, for example 100 percent (the range), 50 percent (the interquartile range), or 25 percent (the semi-interquartile range) of the scores. The other measures of variability—the average deviation, the standard deviation, and the variance—provide an index of the average amount by which scores deviate from the mean. For all measures of variability, however, the smaller the value, the less dispersion there is among the scores. If there were no variability at all; that is, if all individuals within a treatment condition had the same scores, then the value for all measures of variability would be zero.

Comparison of measures of variability for the CRF expertness scores in Table 5–1.   **TABLE 6–4**

Measure of variability	Experimental condition	
	Self-disclosing	*Self-involving*
Range	67.0	53.0
Interquartile range (IQR)	16.6	13.0
Semi-interquartile range ($SIQR$)	8.3	6.5
Average deviation (AD)	10.7	8.3
Standard deviation (SD)[a]	14.63	11.06
Variance (s^2)	213.96	122.33

[a]The standard deviation was obtained by taking the square root of the variance and rounding to two decimal places.

Even though each measure of variability provides different information, we notice consistency among them in Table 6–4. For each corresponding pair of variability measures, the value for the self-disclosing scores is larger than the value for the self-involving scores. The greater variability for the self-disclosing group revealed by these descriptive statistics is consistent with the impression formed when we first inspected the frequency distributions in Tables 5–2 and 5–3.

What Is a Large Amount of Variability?

No one rule of thumb is used to determine whether a particular value for any measure of variability reflects a "reasonable" or an excessive amount of dispersion in the scores. For any value of a measure of variability you may ask, "Does that value indicate that there is a lot of variability in the scores?" It may or may not. Whether variability is extensive or not is relative to the magnitude of the units used in measuring the dependent variable and to the possible range of scores that can be obtained on the measure. Senders (1958) illustrates this relation for the standard deviation: "A standard deviation of 3 inches in a set of 100 telegraph poles would not be alarming, but the same standard deviation in a set of 100 noses would be, quite literally, out of this world! Noses are, in general, shorter than telegraph poles" (p. 318).

Practicing researchers often get a sense of the relative amount of variability in an experiment by comparing it to prior research by others on the topic. This, too, is a procedure we recommend to you for gaining a sense of the relative amount of variability to be expected in any research you may conduct.

CHOOSING DESCRIPTIVE STATISTICS

We have discussed a variety of descriptive statistics that are used to describe the average score and the dispersion of scores for a sample of participants. In practice, however, researchers select only one measure of central tendency and of variability to summarize their data from an experiment. Thus, typically, all the scores for a treatment group will be reduced to two numerical values.

Among the different descriptive statistics we have discussed, how does the researcher decide which to use to summarize the data for a group of participants? The selection is not arbitrary. Instead, the choice of a measure of central tendency and measure of variability depends principally upon three considerations: (1) the level of measurement represented by the dependent variable scale, (2) the shape of the frequency distributions of scores, and (3) the intended use of the descriptive statistics for further statistical analysis. Table 6–5 summarizes the recommended measures to use given the level of measurement and shape of the distribution.

Recommended measures of central tendency and variability given levels of measurement of the dependent variable and the shape of the frequency distribution of the obtained scores.   TABLE 6–5

	Shape of the frequency distribution				
	Approximately symmetrical Unimodal			*Heavily skewed Unimodal*	
Level of measurement	*Measure of central tendency*	*Measure of variability*		*Measure of central tendency*	*Measure of variability*
Ordinal	Median	SIQR		Median	SIQR
Interval or ratio	Arithmetic mean	SD		Median	SIQR

Level of Measurement of the Dependent Variable

Nominal Measurement

In Chapter 5 we pointed out that some measurement scales provide greater precision in measuring behavior than others. We said then that nominal measurement is the crudest form of measurement, and we have omitted nominal measurement from Table 6–5 because nominal data do not lend themselves to measures of central tendency and variability. With a nominal measurement scale, participants' responses are classified into categories and all participants within a category are equated behaviorally. Consequently, nominal data can be described only in terms of frequencies (i.e., how many individuals in a group were assigned to one category or another) or percentages.

Ordinal Measurement

With ordinal data the median is the most appropriate measure of central tendency, regardless of the shape of the frequency distribution or what further statistical analyses are intended. Only three measures of variability are appropriate to consider when the median is used as the measure of central tendency—the range, interquartile range, and semi-interquartile range. Of the three, the semi-interquartile range is used most often and is considered the preferred measure of variability with the median. Like the median, the semi-interquartile range is based upon percentiles of scores and thus is determined by counting scores in the frequency distribution. The average deviation, the variance, and the standard deviation do not belong with the median. Each provides a measure with respect to the mean and therefore should be used only with the mean.

Interval and Ratio Measurement

When the frequency distributions are approximately normally distributed, the mean is the preferred measure of central tendency for interval and ratio measures because it offers the potential of being the most representative value, for all the scores in a sample are involved in its computation. The standard deviation is the measure of variability most often reported with the mean. The average deviation and the variance are rarely reported as the only measure of variability for a set of data.

Rating Scales and Levels of Measurement

As we discussed in Chapter 5, data from rating scales lie within a gray area, in that such scores seem to have properties which go somewhat beyond ordinal level of measurement, but which do not attain interval measurement. For purposes of statistical analysis, then, should ordinal or interval level be assumed in treating rating scores? Gardner (1975) suggests that it is appropriate to treat rating-scale scores as interval data. This recommendation is consistent with the practice of most psychologists who use rating scales.

When means and standard deviations are used to describe ratings, it is evidently assumed that the scores are more interval than ordinal in nature. Both Barak and LaCrosse (1975) and McCarthy and Betz (1978) treated the ratings from the Counselor Rating Form as interval level of measurement. The issue is not without controversy, however. Labovitz (1967) agrees with Gardner, but Champion (1968) and Black and Champion (1976) argue that rating scales cannot be defended as representing more than ordinal level of measurement and, therefore, that the mean and standard deviation are not appropriate descriptive statistics for these measures.

Shape of the Frequency Distribution

The shape of the frequency distribution usually is a determinant in choosing the descriptive statistics only when the dependent variable is measured at the interval or ratio level of measurement. If the distribution of scores is approximately symmetrical, then the sample mean and standard deviation are the preferred descriptive statistics. But if the distribution of scores is considerably skewed, then the mean and standard deviation are often not appropriate descriptive measures to use. Instead, the median may be the better choice for a measure of central tendency. Let us use a simple illustration to see why. Suppose you sampled five students to discover the typical family income of students at your college. The family incomes reported by the five students were: $16,500, $18,600, $19,200, $21,300, and $240,700. A frequency distribution of these values is positively skewed, with a median of $19,200 and a mean of $63,260. Clearly, in this example, the median represents a more typical income than the mean. The mean, because it includes the income of each student in its computation, is heavily influenced by the one value that is so obviously deviant in comparison to the others. In this case, it is evident why the median is more representative of the students' family income.

One can usually tell by examining a frequency distribution whether it is skewed. Moreover, if the distribution is skewed, then the values of the mean and median will not agree, and the direction of the difference in the mean and median will reveal whether the distribution is positively or negatively skewed. Because the mean is sensitive to extreme values, deviant scores in the tail of a skewed distribution tend to pull the mean away from the median in the direction of the tail. Therefore, in a negatively skewed distribution the mean will have a lower value than the median; similarly, a few extremely high scores in a positively skewed distribution will inflate the mean with respect to the median.

The degree of skewness in a distribution of scores is reflected by the difference between the mean and median values. The larger the disparity, the more the distribution is skewed. If seriously skewed, then the median is a better choice for a measure of central tendency than the mean. But how do you determine whether a distribution of scores is heavily skewed? In part, skewness is in the (trained) eye of the beholder of the data. One researcher may judge a distribution to be highly skewed and opt to use the median. Another investigator, however, may not regard the data to be so skewed and will choose to use the mean and standard deviation to describe the data.[10]

Using Descriptive Statistics for Further Analysis of Data

The choice of a measure of central tendency (and therefore of variability) is dictated in part by whether the descriptive statistics are to be used for subsequent inferential purposes. Recall that in Chapter 4 we referred to variability among scores within a treatment condition as error variation. We pointed out that error variation is a problem for the investigator because the effect of the independent variable may be obscured by extensive variation among scores within a group. In order for the effect of an independent variable to be detected, the systematic variation (i.e., the differences in the average scores between groups) must be sufficiently greater than the error variation (variability among subjects' scores within groups).

The purpose of inferential statistics is to assess the amount of systematic variation in relation to the amount of error variation of the experiment. For this purpose, the mean, standard deviation, and variance are most often used

---

[10]Numerical measures of skewness have been developed, but psychologists seldom use them. These measures are discussed in Glass and Stanley (1970), pp. 88–90.

because they are related to the known characteristics of the normal distribution. Hence, the statistical tests most frequently used to evaluate whether an independent variable has an effect will analyze sample means. Psychologists often use the sample mean and standard deviation to summarize their data when considerations of level of measurement and shape of the frequency distributions might dictate against it. The issue of making inferences from the data sometimes overrides these other considerations. For this reason you will find that the sample mean and standard deviation are the most frequently utilized descriptive statistics in psychological research.

EXPLORATORY DATA ANALYSIS

We have placed considerable emphasis upon looking at and describing data in the belief that a careful descriptive analysis may be a powerful tool for discovering and understanding psychological phenomena; moreover, it reflects a developing trend in the behavioral sciences (see, for example, Wainer and Thissen, 1981).

Much of the statistical data analysis currently employed in psychological research is *confirmatory;* that is, it is meant to provide statistics that may allow a psychologist to confirm or disconfirm a research hypothesis. This aim is certainly in line with the emphasis placed upon development of theory and formulation of research hypotheses in our discussion in Chapter 2. For this purpose, use of the sample mean and a standard deviation is often most expeditious, for they allow us to use some of the most powerful and flexible inferential statistical tests to draw conclusions about whether there are any "real" differences among sample means due to the effect of the independent variable.

The last several years, however, have seen increasing emphasis on using exploratory as well as confirmatory techniques of analysis on behavioral data. Tukey (1977) has been a leading proponent of exploratory data analysis, which stresses visual techniques and displays for exploring data to find possible relationships among independent and dependent variables. To this end, Tukey has developed a variety of easily constructed visual exploratory techniques, two of which relate readily to our discussion of descriptive statistics.[11]

Stem-and-Leaf Displays

Tukey suggests that rather than plotting simple or grouped frequency distributions of scores such as those in Tables 5–2 and 5–3, one use instead a **stem-and-leaf display** similar to that presented in Table 6–6 for the self-disclosing expertness

---

[11]An excellent review of the work in this area is provided in a chapter by Wainer and Thissen (1981). Tukey (1977) and Mosteller and Tukey (1977) are two basic sources for exploratory data analysis and should be consulted by anyone planning to employ such techniques on their data.

TABLE 6-6

*A stem-and-leaf plot of the self-disclosing condition expertness scores from Table 5–1.
The unit of the stem is 10 rating points and the unit of the leaf is 1 rating point.*

Stem	Leaf
8	0, 1, 1, 2, 3
7	0, 1, 2, 3, 4, 6, 6, 7, 7, 8, 8, 8, 8
6	0, 0, 0, 1, 2, 2, 3, 3, 4, 4, 5, 5, 6, 6, 8, 8, 8, 9, 9
5	2, 6, 7, 7, 7, 7, 8, 8, 9
4	1, 8, 9, 9
3	2
2	6, 6
1	6

scores of Table 5–1. The numbers to the left of the vertical line are the stems and represent the first digit of a participant's score; that is, for a score of 65, the 6 is the stem. The numbers to the right of the vertical line are the leaves and represent the second digit of a response; in the example of 65, a 5. A stem-and-leaf display is easily constructed from the raw data, and no information is lost in doing so, as occurs in a group frequency distribution; all the raw scores can be reconstructed from the display.

By examining Table 6–6 and simply counting the number of scores, one can easily determine that the distribution is bimodal at 57 and 78, it has a median of about 64.5, the range of scores is from 16 to 83, and the 25th and 75th percentiles are about 57 and 74 respectively. Certainly a stem-and-leaf plot can very quickly provide a great deal of descriptive information about a set of scores.

Box-and-Whisker Plots

A second visual display of data is provided by a so-called **box-and-whisker plot**. Box-and-whisker plots for the self-disclosing and self-involving expertness scores of Table 5–1 are presented in Figure 6–2. The median for each set of scores is shown by the dashed line inside the rectangular box. The box itself represents the interquartile range, where the middle 50 percent of the scores in the distribution lie. The range of scores is provided by the solid horizontal lines at the ends of the dashed vertical lines or whiskers.

From the box-and-whisker plot of the data in Table 5–1, one can rather easily see that the distributions of scores are negatively skewed and that the range of scores is quite large, although the middle 50 percent of the scores are close to each other, considering the range of scores. Further, it appears that both the median and the middle 50 percent of the scores for the self-involving group are higher than those of the self-disclosing group.

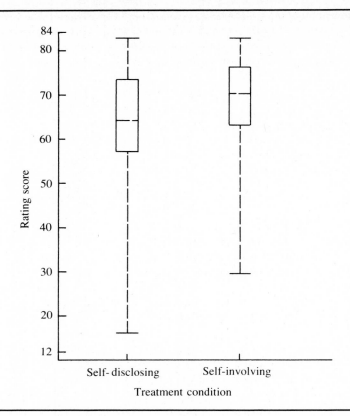

FIGURE 6-2   *Box-and-whisker plot for the self-disclosing and self-involving expertness scores of Table 5-1.*

Although exploratory data analysis and graphic techniques such as the stem-and-leaf display or the box-and-whisker plot are not yet widely used by psychologists, there is little doubt that their use will greatly increase in future years. As Tukey (1969, 1977) has argued, data analysis is often akin to detective work, and a thorough descriptive analysis of the data obtained in an experiment will help the researcher-detective discover important psychological phenomena from the data.

USING STATISTICS FOR INFERENCE AND ESTIMATION

Through most of this chapter and the last, we have emphasized the use of statistics for describing the sample data in an experiment. Summarizing scores with measures of central tendency and variability is, as we have indicated, only the first step in analyzing data, however. Recall that the purpose of conducting an experiment is to test a research hypothesis that states a relationship between independent and dependent variables. But simply summarizing data with descriptive statistics is not sufficient to decide if the data do or do not provide support for a research hypothesis. Because of the ever-present variability in data, visual inspection of descriptive statistics does not permit one to decide if any difference between two or more sample means is a chance difference or a difference due to the independent variable. Thus, it becomes necessary to conduct inferential statistical tests on the data from an experiment.

Psychologists are also often interested in estimating population parameters from the descriptive statistics of a sample. Statistical estimation is widely used in many settings. As we have indicated, in most circumstances it is usually not possible to measure all members of a population that is of interest. For example, market researchers cannot identify or test all potential consumers to determine their acceptance of a product before it is manufactured and distributed. Similarly, it is not possible to measure the amount of alcohol consumed, attitudes toward birth control, frequency of sexual activity, opinions on political matters, and other information among all members of a large population. Instead, it is frequently necessary to estimate population values from descriptive statistics obtained from samples of individuals in a population.

For purposes of both conducting inferential statistical tests and estimating population parameters from descriptive statistics, it is necessary to make inferences from sample data. The word *infer* implies reasoning to something unknown from something known. Translated into the task of the psychological researcher, *statistical inference* is the drawing of conclusions about unknown population values on the basis of statistics provided by the sample data in the experiment. Statistical inference, then, is achieved by estimating unknown population parameters from known sample statistics.

Populations have parameters, such as μ or σ, which describe their characteristics. Any descriptive statistic computed on a sample of measurements provides a possible basis for estimating a corresponding parameter in the population. In this chapter, however, we will be primarily interested in the sample mean ($\bar{X}$) as an estimator of the population mean (μ). In Chapters 7 and 8 we will use the sample variance (s^2) to estimate the population variance (σ^2).

Sample Mean as an Estimator of Population Mean

The sample mean ($\bar{X}$) is often used to estimate a population mean (μ). In the McCarthy and Betz experiment, the sample mean of 63.1 for expertness may be used to estimate the mean of a population who could hypothetically hear self-disclosing statements from a counselor. Using this sample mean would lead to an estimate of 63.1 for the population mean. Likewise, the sample mean of 68.5 may be used to estimate the mean of a population who, in principle, could hear self-involving statements from a counselor. An estimate is just a rough or approximate calculation, however. Whether or not the estimate from the sample is a good estimate of the population parameter depends upon a number of factors, one of which is the representativeness of the sample.

Representativeness and Random Sampling

Any sample from a population will provide some idea about characteristics of that population. Indeed, in the absence of any other information, a single sample mean provides the best guess about the value of a corresponding population mean. To ensure that the sample mean will provide a good estimate of a population mean, however, the characteristics of the individuals in the sample should be similar to those of the individuals in the population that is of interest. The distribution of attributes such as sex, age, intelligence, socioeconomic status, religion, political affiliation, anxiety, height, weight, and so forth should occur in the sample much as they do in a population. In other words, the members of the sample should be *representative* of the population whose parameters are to be estimated. One way to ensure as much as possible that they will be is to select a simple random sample from a population.

Simple random sampling (often merely called **random sampling**) is defined as the selecting of members from a population in such a way that each member of the population has an equal chance of being selected for the sample, and the selection of one member neither influences nor is influenced by the selection of any other member of the population. Therefore, a random sample is one whose members are selected without bias so that the characteristics of the sample should not differ in any systematic way from those of the population from which the sample was selected.

This method of selection does not mean, however, that a particular sample will be exactly representative of a population. Because samples consist of fewer members than the populations, one cannot expect the characteristics of the participants in the sample to be distributed in exactly the same way as those in the population. Moreover, because the characteristics are distributed by chance, some random samples will distribute the characteristics better than others. Some random samples will be quite representative of a population, but a few will be very unrepresentative. Random sampling does ensure, however, that in the long run (i.e., over an infinitely large number of samples) samples will be representative of the population from which they were drawn.

Random sampling should be viewed as an ideal that in practice is rarely achieved in psychological research. A truly random sample is difficult to obtain, for two reasons. First, often it is not possible to identify all the members of a particular population that is of interest, and therefore not every member of such a population will have an equal opportunity of being selected. This limitation

You will recall that in Chapter 3 we discussed randomization in assigning participants to groups. Although the criteria for randomness in assigning and selecting participants are the same, the functions of random sampling and random assignment are different. The purpose of random sampling is to obtain a sample representative of the characteristics of the population, but the purpose of random assignment is to form equivalent groups in an experiment. Although in practice random sampling is rarely achieved in research, there is no reason why—in any true experiment—random assignment cannot be accomplished. No matter how participants are sampled from a population, randomly or otherwise, the individuals who have been selected can be randomly assigned to experimental conditions in true experiments.

obviously precludes drawing a random sample from this population. And the larger the population that is of interest, the more difficult it is to identify the members. Second, if any randomly selected member of a population does not participate in a particular study for any reason, then the randomness, and thus the representativeness, of the sample is impaired. The characteristics of randomly selected individuals who refuse to be interviewed or surveyed, who become no-shows after agreeing to participate, or who simply are unavailable may differ in some systematic way from other randomly selected individuals who do participate. To the extent that this nonparticipation occurs, the representativeness of the sample is compromised.

Random sampling does not guarantee that a sample statistic from a sample will provide a good estimate of the corresponding population parameter. It only ensures that in the sample the distribution of characteristics of members of the population will be left merely to so-called chance factors. Moreover, because a sample mean $\bar{X}$ is derived from fewer individuals than exist in the population that is of interest, it should not be expected that it will be exactly equal to a population mean μ. There should be some error in the estimate and most often there will be. Suppose, for example, that you formed two samples by random selection from a population and obtained measures from the individuals in the two samples. As we know, because of the presence of chance variation in scores, it is likely that the means of both samples will differ. Yet each sample mean provides an estimate of the population mean. One of the two sample means will be a better estimate of the population mean; that is, one of the sample means will more closely approximate the true mean of the population. Because the value of the population mean is unknown, however, you cannot tell which of the sample means is the better estimate. A psychologist can never be sure exactly how good an estimate a sample mean provides. But two major factors influence the accuracy of any such estimate—the sample size and the amount of variation in the scores of a population—and these must be taken into account when assessing the adequacy of an estimate made from a random sample.

Factors Related to Accuracy of Estimation

Sample size   A little reflection will generate some intuitive insight into the way in which sample size influences the accuracy of a particular sample estimate. It should seem obvious that the larger the size of the sample, the better the estimate should be. After all, in larger samples more members of the population will be represented. Therefore, more measures typical of the population members will be obtained. Hence, one would expect more precise and more consistent estimates from large samples than from small samples.

Consider the extreme or most limiting possibilities in sample size. If one were to sample the whole population that is of interest so that the sample consists of an entire population, then obviously the mean of the sample would be the same as that of the population. In this case, there would be no room for error in the sample estimate. Suppose, however, that a sample consisting of only one randomly selected member from a population were obtained. The resulting sample mean (equal to the one score divided by 1) would be as variable from one sample to another as the scores in the population. It is no surprise, then, that better estimates of a population mean should be obtained from larger samples. Clearly, McCarthy and Betz's sample means, based on sample sizes of 54 and 53, are better estimates of their respective population's means than if their sample sizes had been much smaller, with, say, 2 or 3 subjects.

Variability in population measures   Consider the unlikely possibility that the measures or scores for all members of a population are exactly the same. Thus, the score for any individual is equal to the mean of the population. Under these conditions, it is evident that the mean obtained from a sample of any size will be exactly equal to the population mean. There will be no error in the sample estimate. On the other hand, consider a population that has extensive variation among the scores measured. Although it should occur infrequently, by chance alone the scores in one random sample may consist principally of low values; the resulting sample mean, then, would differ considerably from the population mean. Similarly, a relatively poor estimate of the population mean would be obtained if individuals who had primarily high scores were randomly sampled from a population. Thus, the accuracy of a particular sample estimate will be related to the amount of variability in a population. The more extensive the variability in the scores of a population, the less likely it is that a particular sample mean will be an accurate estimate of the population mean.

Sampling Distribution of the Mean

Our discussion has indicated that the accuracy of a sample estimate for a parameter depends upon both sample size and the variation of the scores in a population. Unless the sample encompasses all the scores in a population or there is no variation of scores in the population, the sample statistic is likely to be in error in estimating the value of the population parameter.

A researcher never knows for sure just how accurate a particular sample estimate of a population parameter is. That is, he or she cannot determine precisely how much the sample estimate may deviate from the population parameter. But the investigator can determine the amount of error that can be expected in the estimate. To understand the basis for quantifying the expected error in estimating population parameters from sample statistics, you must understand the concept of sampling distributions. In particular, we will discuss the sampling distribution of the mean, for we emphasize statistical analysis of means in experiments.

As we have pointed out, a psychologist typically measures only one sample of participants in a particular treatment condition in an experiment. From this one sample the experimenter wants to estimate a population mean for that treatment condition. That is, the experimenter wants to use the sample mean ($\bar{X}$) from that treatment condition to estimate a population mean (μ) for the population from which that sample was selected. Therefore, in an experiment, the mean from a single sample of participants in a treatment condition is the only basis the psychologist has for estimating the population mean for that condition.

Suppose, however, that a psychologist obtained not one but many independent random samples from the same population and calculated the mean for each sample on a behavioral measure. In practice, this would not occur, of course, but it is analogous to many investigators obtaining and observing random samples from the same population on a behavioral measure. If a thousand such samples were obtained, then one would have a thousand sample means that estimate a single population mean.

What would one do with a thousand sample means? Recalling Chapter 5, you might consider organizing them into a frequency distribution in which you arrange the values of the sample means from low to high and tally the number of times each value occurs. The resulting frequency distribution of sample means is not simply called a frequency distribution, however. Instead, a frequency distribution of sample means is called a **sampling distribution of the mean.** In general, a frequency distribution for any statistic derived from sample data is called a sampling distribution for that statistic. You will recall from Chapter 5 that a frequency distribution of scores can be summarized in terms of its shape, a measure of central tendency, and a measure of variability. Similarly, because the sampling distribution of the mean is a frequency distribution, it, too, can be described in terms of its shape, mean, and standard deviation.[12]

Shape of a sampling distribution of the mean   A theoretical or idealized sampling distribution of the mean is graphically depicted in Figure 6–3. Observe that the

---

[12]The concept of a sampling distribution applies only to statistics computed on the scores of a sample. There is no sampling distribution of a population parameter, because a parameter is a fixed value that does not vary.

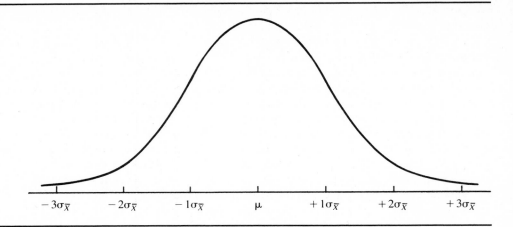

$-3\sigma_{\overline{X}}$ $-2\sigma_{\overline{X}}$ $-1\sigma_{\overline{X}}$ μ $+1\sigma_{\overline{X}}$ $+2\sigma_{\overline{X}}$ $+3\sigma_{\overline{X}}$

FIGURE 6–3   *Theoretical sampling distribution of the mean with mean μ and standard error $\sigma_{\overline{X}}$.*

distribution is perfectly symmetrical and unimodal. Such an idealized sampling distribution is a statistician's invention; that is, it would occur only in the long run with an infinite number of samples. It is important to realize, however, that any sampling distribution of the mean (in the long run) will be approximately normally distributed, whether the shape of the distribution of individual scores in the population is symmetrical or skewed.[13] As we shall see later, as few as 50 or 100 means of random samples will convincingly approximate a normal distribution.

Mean of a sampling distribution of the mean   Because a sampling distribution of the mean is distributed approximately normally, it is reasonable to summarize the distribution of values by describing the mean and the standard deviation of the sample means. As one might expect, the mean of the sample means in a perfectly normal sampling distribution will be equal to the population mean (μ). In an instance with far fewer than an infinite number of sample means, and therefore with less than a perfectly normal distribution, the mean of the sample means will not be exactly equal to the population mean. Yet, as we demonstrate later, it will be remarkably close to the value of the population mean.

Sampling error   In a sampling distribution of the mean, some sample means will provide better or more accurate estimates of a population mean than others. The error in an estimate due to chance factors is called **sampling error.** The amount by which a particular sample mean deviates from the true population mean (i.e., $\overline{X} - \mu$) varies from sample to sample. If the sample mean is exactly the same as the population mean, i.e., if $\overline{X} - \mu = 0$, then there is no sampling error in the

---

[13]In mathematical statistics, this is called the *central limit theorem.* This theorem is discussed in more detail in most introductory-level statistics textbooks.

estimate. The amount of sampling error is measured by the standard error of the mean.

Standard error of the mean In a simple frequency distribution of raw scores (such as that shown in Table 5–2), the amount of variability among the scores can be described by the standard deviation (*SD* or *s*). Similarly, the amount of variability among the sample means in a sampling distribution can be described by the standard deviation computed upon the values of the sample means. This type of standard deviation, however, is not typically called a standard deviation, but rather is called a **standard error of the mean** or simply a **standard error.** Specifically, the true standard error of the mean, $\sigma_{\bar{x}}$, is equal to the standard deviation of the population divided by the square root of the size of the sample. In notation, $\sigma_{\bar{x}} = \sigma/\sqrt{n}$, where σ represents the standard deviation of scores in the population and *n* is the size of the sample. However, σ is a population parameter, and we have said that any population parameter typically is unknown to the researcher (which is why estimates are made from samples to begin with). Therefore, how can one determine the standard error of the mean?

Perhaps you have anticipated that the answer to the question lies in estimating σ from the sample. The sample standard deviation (*s* or *SD*) is an estimate of the population standard deviation (σ). Therefore, although it is rarely possible to determine the standard error of a population, $\sigma_{\bar{x}}$, it is possible to estimate its value. This estimate, referred to as $s_{\bar{x}}$ or *SE*, is based on the sample standard deviation, and is expressed in notation as:

$$s_{\bar{X}} = SE = \frac{s}{\sqrt{n}} = \frac{SD}{\sqrt{n}}.$$

Thus, $s_{\bar{x}}$ is the estimated standard error of the mean. An example of a $s_{\bar{x}}$ can be obtained from McCarthy and Betz's data. For the expertness scores (see Table 6–4), $s_{\bar{x}}$ for the self-disclosing treatment is $14.63/\sqrt{54}$, which equals 1.99, and $s_{\bar{x}}$ for the self-involving treatment is $11.06/\sqrt{53}$, which equals 1.52.

Why Do We Divide by *n* − 1 to Obtain the Variance and Standard Deviation?   BOX 6–3

You may wonder why in the formulas for the variance and the standard deviation presented earlier in the chapter, the sum of squared deviations $\Sigma (X_i - \bar{X})^2$, is divided by $n - 1$ instead of by *n*. We can provide the answer now. Statisticians have determined that the sample variance defined as $\Sigma (X_i - \bar{X})^2/n$ consistently underestimates the actual value of the population variance. That is, it provides a "biased" estimate of the population variance. Subtracting one from *n* is a kind of "correction factor" that has been demonstrated statistically to provide an unbiased estimate of the population variance. Thus, the variance with $n - 1$ in the denominator does not consistently either over- or underestimate the corresponding population parameter. Incidentally, in calculating the sample mean no such correction is needed; the sample mean as defined $\Sigma X_i/n$ provides an unbiased estimate of the population mean.

Distinction between $\sigma_{\bar{X}}$ ***and*** $s_{\bar{X}}$ It is important that you understand the distinction between the two standard errors of the mean, $\sigma_{\bar{X}}$ and $s_{\bar{X}}$ or *SE*. The true standard error, $\sigma_{\bar{X}}$, is a fixed value that can be determined when the population standard deviation σ is known. The $s_{\bar{X}}$ or *SE*, though, because it is an estimate and thus subject to sampling error, will vary from sample to sample. Obviously, different random samples from the same population can be expected to produce different sample variances and standard deviations because of the chance differences in scores that will occur from one sample to another. In any one sample, however, the scores in the sample provide the only basis for estimating the population standard deviation and therefore for estimating the standard error of the mean ($\sigma_{\bar{X}}$).

The formula for the estimated standard error $s/\sqrt{n}$ shows clearly how the variability of sample means in a sampling distribution is related to the variability of scores in the population and to the size of the sample used to estimate the population mean. The larger the standard deviation (s) of scores, the greater the standard error will be. Increasing sample size (n), however, increases the denominator, which contributes to making the standard error smaller.

As we have indicated, the researcher uses the standard error to measure the amount of sampling error and thus to ascertain how well the obtained sample mean estimates a population mean. The smaller the obtained standard error the better the estimate, in the sense that the smaller the standard error, the more confident one can be that the sample mean does not differ substantially from the population mean. The larger the standard error, the greater the error of the estimate is likely to be.[14]

You can understand this concept more easily if you recall that the accuracy of estimation was discussed as being related both to the amount of variation in the scores in a population and to the sample size. In that discussion we indicated that the less the scores vary in the population and the larger the sample size, then the more accurate is the estimate obtained from the sample of scores. Similarly, smaller variation in the scores in a population and a larger sample size lead to smaller values of the standard error. Conversely, the more variation in the population and the smaller the sample size, then the larger the standard error. Thus, the estimated mean is more likely to differ from the true population mean.

Conceptually, both $\sigma_{\bar{X}}$ and $s_{\bar{X}}$ provide the same kind of information about the variability of means in a sampling distribution of means. How well or poorly a particular sample mean $\bar{X}$ will estimate the value of μ depends upon the size of the standard error of the mean. In practice, because σ is usually unknown, investigators estimate $\sigma_{\bar{X}}$ with the $s_{\bar{X}}$ to determine the expected error in the estimate. Typically, when the standard error of the mean is reported in a research article it is the $s_{\bar{X}}$ (or *SE*).

---

[14]It is possible to use the standard error to obtain *confidence intervals* for an estimate of the population mean. These intervals provide a range of scores in which the experimenter can estimate the probability that the interval encompasses the true population mean. The procedure is described in most introductory statistics texts.

Example of a Sampling Distribution of the Mean

To illustrate some of the concepts of sampling distributions we now generate empirical sampling distributions by showing the results of actual sampling from a population in which μ and σ are known. The population in question has 100 scores ($N = 100$). A frequency distribution of the 100 scores is represented graphically in Figure 6–4. As you can see, the distribution of scores in the population is symmetrical and unimodal. The scores range from 8 to 20 with a mean μ of 14.0 and a standard deviation σ of 2.14.

Empirical sampling distributions of the mean were obtained for three different sample sizes by actually drawing random samples from the population with

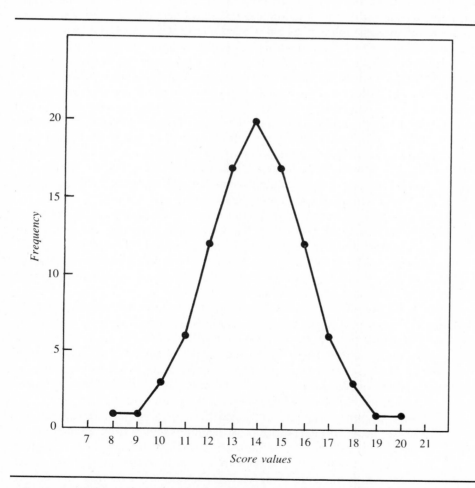

Frequency distribution for a population of 100 scores with $\mu = 14.0$ and $\sigma = 2.14$.   **FIGURE 6–4**

the aid of a computer. First, 100 random samples of two scores ($n = 2$) were obtained and the mean of each sample was calculated. Then, 100 random samples of five scores ($n = 5$) were drawn and the mean of each sample was determined. Finally, 100 random samples of ten scores ($n = 10$) were obtained and the mean of each sample mean was determined. A grouped frequency distribution of the 100 means, i.e., a sampling distribution of the mean, for each of the three sample sizes is presented in Figure 6–5.

Keep in mind that each of the 300 sample means represents an estimate of the same population mean, $\mu = 14$. Yet sampling error among the means is quite evident in each of the three sampling distributions. Observe also that the three sampling distributions in Figure 6–5 are relatively symmetrical and unimodal. Moreover, as expected, in each distribution the values of the sample means are clustered around the true population mean of 14. In fact, the means of the sample means in the three sampling distributions are nearly equal to 14; the mean values are 13.96, 14.14, and 13.99 for distributions (a), (b), and (c), respectively.

It is also evident that the variability in sample means is related to sample size. The values of the 100 sample means in (a) with each mean based on two scores are clearly more dispersed than those in (b) and (c), which were derived from either five or ten scores, respectively. The most deviant sample means occur in the smaller sample sizes. Conversely, the sample mean values are less variable with the larger sample sizes. The largest difference in 100 sample means is found in the sampling distribution in (a), where the highest and lowest sample means, based upon only two scores each, were 17.5 and 10.0—a difference of 7.5. In (c), however, where ten scores were randomly sampled each time, the difference in the largest (15.7) and smallest (12.4) mean values is only 3.3.

Each sampling distribution in Figure 6–5 has its rare or infrequently occurring sample mean value, but a value that may be relatively rare in one distribution [e.g., a sample mean of 15.5 in (c)] is not so unlikely in another [i.e., (a)]. Moreover, the most deviant sample means in the distributions based on larger sample sizes are *all* closer in value to the population mean of 14 than is the one for distributions based upon smaller samples.

We have not illustrated the effects of sampling from populations with different variances on the sampling distributions of means. From our previous discussion, however, you can see that it is evident that the more variation in scores in a population, the more likely it is that the sample means will vary, regardless of sample size. The more spread out or dispersed the scores in the population, the more high or low values can be obtained randomly. Hence, the sample means are more likely to reflect the low or high scores and vary more widely.

We have demonstrated and explained that, in general, a researcher can expect to obtain better estimates with large random samples from populations in which the variability in scores to be sampled is small. Although the investigator can control sample size, little can be done to reduce the variation of scores in the population beyond minimizing error variance associated with measurement of scores. Thus, to increase the accuracy of estimates of population parameters, psychologists typically resort to using larger samples.

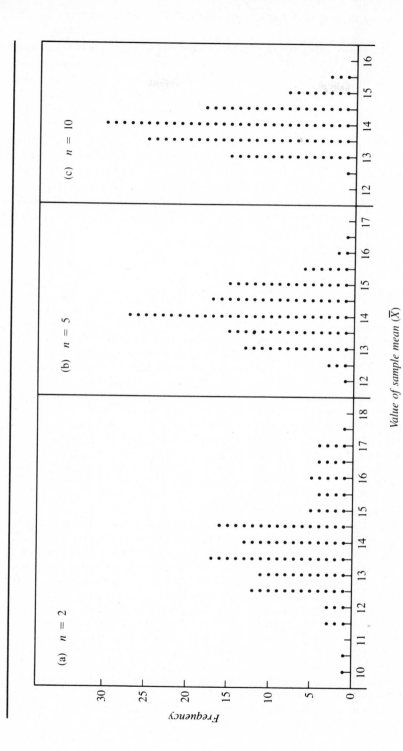

FIGURE 6-5   *Empirical sampling distributions of the means for 100 samples drawn from the population of scores presented in Figure 6–4. The sample sizes are: (a) n = 2, (b) n = 5, (c) n = 10.*

As our discussion in this chapter has indicated, measures of variability, and especially the variance and the standard deviation, have important descriptive and inferential uses in data analysis. As a descriptive statistic, the standard deviation not only indicates the typical deviation of a participant's score from the mean, but it also permits a psychologist to determine a range that encompasses an approximate percentage of scores in the distribution.

In statistical inference, the standard deviation provides a way of determining how accurately a sample mean estimates a population mean. This function becomes increasingly important in the next two chapters on statistical hypothesis testing. In these chapters you will see how psychologists make inferences from samples to populations in order to determine whether the independent variable had an effect. As you will discover, each of the statistical tests we discuss uses measures of variability in a prominent way.

SUMMARY

- Measures of variability are needed to indicate how well a measure of central tendency represents the typical performance of participants in an experiment.
- Measures of variability that are used include the range, the interquartile range, the semi-interquartile range, the average deviation, the variance, and the standard deviation. Of these, the standard deviation is the most useful measure of variability.
- The standard deviation of a set of scores permits one to make inferences about the shape of the distribution of those scores, including whether the shape of the distribution is approximately normally distributed or skewed.
- The choice of which descriptive statistics to use in describing the results of an experiment depends upon three factors: (1) the level of measurement employed in the measure of the dependent variable, (2) the shape of the frequency distribution of the obtained scores, and (3) what further analysis is intended for the data.
- Statistics computed from scores obtained from a sample may be used to estimate the corresponding parameters of a population. As an example, the sample mean ($\overline{X}$) is often used to estimate a population mean (μ).
- In order to be an accurate estimate, a sample statistic must be computed on a sample that is representative of a population. Such representativeness is often obtained by random sampling. The accuracy of the estimate also depends upon the sample size and the variability among scores in the population.
- The sampling distribution of a statistic is the frequency distribution of values that the statistic might take on if an infinite set of samples were drawn from a population. The sampling distribution of the mean $\overline{X}$ is a particularly important sampling distribution for psychologists, for it sets the stage for an understanding of statistical hypothesis testing.
- The variability of a sampling distribution of the mean is given by the standard error of the mean, $SE = SD/\sqrt{n}$.
- The SE provides a measure of the accuracy of a sample mean, $\overline{X}$, as an estimate of a population mean, μ.

7

In this chapter we develop the principles of statistical hypothesis testing and describe two statistical tests you can use to analyze differences between two independent groups. Topics include:

- The "experimenter's dilemma," which demonstrates the need for an inferential model for analyzing data in an experiment
- The logic of statistical testing
- The nature of a test statistic
- Statistical hypotheses
- Decision making with a statistical test
- Errors in statistical decision making
- The *t* test for two independent groups
- The Mann-Whitney *U* test for two independent groups

WHY YOU NEED TO KNOW THIS MATERIAL

Two groups of individuals formed by random assignment will always differ on the value of a measure of central tendency computed on any measurement of behavior. Is this difference a real one due to the independent variable or is it simply a chance difference? To answer this question a psychologist must conduct a statistical test on the data.

Statistical Hypothesis Testing and the *t* Test

From one point of view, significance testing is a device for curbing overenthusiasm about apparent effects in the data.

William H. Kruskal (1968, p. 240)

The goal of any experiment is to determine if the independent variable has an effect. The decision is made by comparing the typical performance of the subjects in the two or more treatment groups. This seemingly easy task, however, poses a dilemma for the experimenter. Let us reexamine the nature of an experiment to see what this dilemma is.

Thus far we have discussed the principal steps in conducting a true experiment:

- A research hypothesis is formulated stating the relationship between the independent variable and the dependent variable.
- Treatment groups are initially formed by randomly assigning participants to one of the two groups. Therefore, both groups should represent the same population of potential participants before the independent variable is manipulated.
- The independent variable is manipulated and scores on the dependent variable are recorded.
- Measures of typical performance, the sample means $\overline{X}_{A_1}$ and $\overline{X}_{A_2}$, are obtained for each treatment group. The sample means provide estimates of the means of the populations (μ) from which the samples were drawn.

These steps set the stage for the appearance of a dilemma for the experimenter. Any inference about the effect or lack of an effect of an independent variable is made from the sample means. In principle, if the sample means are equal to each other, then the treatment had no effect and both sample means are estimates of the same population mean. On the other hand, if the sample means are not equal to each other, then it seems reasonable to assume that the treatment had an effect and that the sample means estimate different population means.

If you stop to think about it for a moment, however, the task is not quite as simple as we have made it appear. Throughout our discussion of research design we have stressed the concept of variation in the data from an experiment. We have argued that subjects given the same treatment condition will not necessarily obtain the same score on the measure of the dependent variable. Scores will differ because of differences in attributes among individuals, any differences in physical extraneous variables present from participant to participant, and from errors of measurement. Indeed, we saw a very clear demonstration of such *error variation* in the raw data of the McCarthy and Betz experiment presented in Table 5–1. Consequently, chance or haphazard differences between the means of different groups are *anticipated* in any experiment, whether or not the independent variable has an effect upon the dependent variable. Thus, our suggested approach of making a decision about the effect of an independent variable simply from any observed differences in sample means is simplistic. Sample means will usually differ, even if the independent variable has no effect whatsoever! The steps in research design leading to this problem are schematized in Figure 7–1. This problem also can be illustrated numerically.

Numerical Illustration of the Experimenter's Dilemma

Consider the outcome of ten hypothetical experiments in which samples of size 5 ($n = 5$) are obtained by random selection from two populations (A_1 and A_2) with equal means. Each of the populations is identical to the population used to generate Figure 6–3, thus $\mu_{A_1} = \mu_{A_2} = \mu_A = 14$. This situation is analogous to an instance in which an independent variable has no effect. The ten outcomes are presented in Table 7–1. Observe that although the true difference between the population means, $\mu_{A_1} - \mu_{A_2}$, is 0, none of the differences between the sample means, $\bar{X}_{A_1} - \bar{X}_{A_2}$, is exactly 0.

An illustration of the ten "experiments" with a treatment effect present is given in Table 7–2. The effect of an independent variable (or treatment effect) is equivalent to changing one of the population means. The sample means from the A_1 population with μ_{A_1} are the same as in Table 7–1. A treatment effect of $+2$ is now reflected, however, in the sample means from the A_2 population with μ_{A_2}; a value of 2 is added to each score to simulate a treatment effect, which increases the population mean by 2. Thus, μ_{A_2} now equals 16, so that $\mu_{A_1} - \mu_{A_2} = -2$ instead of 0. Observe again, however, that none of the differences between sample means,

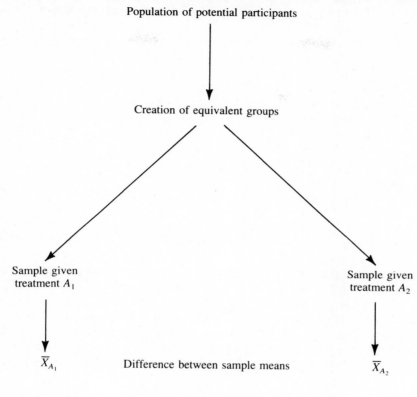

Population of potential participants

Creation of equivalent groups

Sample given
treatment A_1

Sample given
treatment A_2

$\overline{X}_{A_1}$ Difference between sample means $\overline{X}_{A_2}$

?   Experimenter's Dilemma   ?

Is any difference between X_{A_1} and X_{A_2} a "real" difference
due to the independent variable, or a chance difference due to
error variation?

The steps leading to the experimenter's dilemma.   **FIGURE 7-1**

$\overline{X}_{A_1} - \overline{X}_{A_2}$, is exactly equal to the difference between the population means $\mu_{A_1} - \mu_{A_2} = -2$.

Tables 7–1 and 7–2 reflect all that we have already discussed about sampling error, except that now the effect of sampling error is also revealed in the differences between the sample means. Consider the task of the experimenter in the context of this example. He or she obtains two sample means ($\overline{X}_{A_1}$ and $\overline{X}_{A_2}$) and observes the difference between them ($\overline{X}_{A_1} - \overline{X}_{A_2}$). On the basis of this difference the researcher must decide if the two sample means are estimates of identical population means (and, hence, there is no treatment effect present), or if they estimate

TABLE 7-1   *Results of "experiments" in which pairs of means were repeatedly randomly sampled from two populations where $\mu_{A_1} = \mu_{A_2} = 14$. All samples are based upon sample sizes of 5 (n = 5).*

| | Sample means | | Difference |
Experiment	$\bar{X}_{A_1}$	$\bar{X}_{A_2}$	$\bar{X}_{A_1} - \bar{X}_{A_2}$
1	13.6	13.2	+0.4
2	13.0	15.2	−2.2
3	12.2	16.2	−4.0
4	16.4	12.6	+3.8
5	15.2	14.4	+0.8
6	14.0	11.6	+2.4
7	13.4	14.2	−0.8
8	14.8	15.4	−0.6
9	13.8	14.0	−0.2
10	15.0	14.8	+0.2

different population means (thereby indicating a possible treatment effect). Suppose the experimenter obtains a difference between sample means of $\bar{X}_{A_1} - \bar{X}_{A_2} = -4.0$. What should he or she decide about the population means? An observed difference of the magnitude of about −4.0 occurs in both Tables 7–1 and 7–2. Does the observed difference of −4.0 indicate that $\mu_{A_1} = \mu_{A_2}$ or that $\mu_{A_1} \neq \mu_{A_2}$? The experimenter cannot be sure. Suppose, on the other hand, that the experimenter observes a difference of +.4. Differences of +.4 again occur in both

TABLE 7-2   *Results of "experiments" in which pairs of means were repeatedly randomly sampled from two populations where $\mu_{A_1} = 14$ and $\mu_{A_2} = 16$. Thus, μ_{A_2} simulates a treatment effect of +2 added to the scores of Table 7–1 (shown in parentheses) and $\mu_{A_1} - \mu_{A_2} = -2.0$. All samples are based upon sample sizes of 5 (n = 5).*

| | Sample means | | Difference |
Experiment	$\bar{X}_{A_1}$	$\bar{X}_{A_2}$	$\bar{X}_{A_1} - \bar{X}_{A_2}$
1	13.6	15.2 (13.2 + 2)	−1.6
2	13.0	17.2 (15.2 + 2)	−4.2
3	12.2	18.2 (16.2 + 2)	−6.0
4	16.4	14.6 (12.6 + 2)	+1.8
5	15.2	16.4 (14.4 + 2)	−1.2
6	14.0	13.6 (11.6 + 2)	+0.4
7	13.4	16.2 (14.2 + 2)	−2.8
8	14.8	17.4 (15.4 + 2)	−2.6
9	13.8	16.0 (14.0 + 2)	−2.2
10	15.0	16.8 (14.8 + 2)	−1.8

Tables 7–1 and 7–2. What inference about population means and thus the effect of an independent variable should be made from this observed difference between sample means? The experimenter clearly is faced with a dilemma about the inference to be made on the effect of the independent variable from the observed difference of the sample means. The difficulty is resolved by answering the question: "How big a difference between the sample means is big enough to decide that something other than sampling error is at work in the experiment?"

This dilemma is analogous to that faced in an actual experiment when an experimenter has an observed difference between two (or more) treatment means. He or she must decide whether this difference reflects the effect of an independent variable or is due merely to sampling error. As we have seen, the absolute size of the difference between the treatment means is of little help in resolving the problem, for as Tables 7–1 and 7–2 indicate, there may be a great deal of overlap in the size of the differences obtained both with and without a treatment effect. Further, the expected size of the chance differences between the treatment means also depends upon the amount of variation present in the scores, regardless of the possible effect of an independent variable. Greater error variation in scores leads to the possibility of larger chance differences between the sample means. It is important to understand that any systematic effects of an independent variable in an experiment will always be superimposed upon this background of error variation. How, then, does a psychologist tell when those systematic effects are large enough so that they are not reasonably due merely to the presence of error in the data? The experimenter has clearly encountered a dilemma, for he or she has come to a crucial stage in the experiment and now seems to have run into an obstacle.

Statistical Hypothesis Testing: Resolving the Experimenter's Dilemma

Fortunately, the obstacle we have just discussed can be overcome by using statistical tests. In brief, the general approach employed in statistical hypothesis testing is to assume that each sample mean estimates a corresponding population mean. That is, it is assumed that $\overline{X}_{A_1}$ estimates μ_{A_1} and $\overline{X}_{A_2}$ estimates μ_{A_2}. By making this assumption, and then making certain assumptions about the population means, an experimenter can determine the extent of chance differences expected between sample means. Essentially, the experimenter can estimate the differences between sample means that might occur if the independent variable has no effect and those that might occur only because of sampling error. Then, if the obtained difference between the sample means is large enough so that it is an unlikely chance difference, the experimenter decides that the difference is due not to chance, but rather to the effects of the independent variable.

Many inferential statistical tests are suitable for use with diverse types of data and research designs. Regardless of the specific test used, however, basic concepts of hypothesis testing are applicable to all statistical tests. Our purpose in this chapter is to develop these general concepts of statistical hypothesis testing with respect to the sample mean $(\overline{X}_A)$ as the descriptive statistic that is of interest. The mean has a number of desirable mathematical properties that lend it to the development of powerful and useful statistical tests. Then we present a specific test for the difference between two sample means, the t test. We then discuss an alternative to the t test, the Mann-Whitney U test, which does not require the same assumptions as the t. A more versatile statistical test, the F test of the analysis of variance, is introduced in Chapter 8.

STATISTICAL HYPOTHESIS TESTING

Statistical Model for an Experiment

An inferential statistical test is derived from a statistical model that the researcher adopts for the experiment. In a general sense, a model is merely a representation of something. For an experiment, a **statistical model** is a mathematical representation of the experiment. This representation results in a test statistic that permits the researcher to determine the likelihood of a particular difference in sample means occurring if error variation alone is responsible for differences among sample means.[1]

Creating a statistical model for an experiment may sound quite forbidding to you at this stage. The statistical models and their associated inferential statistical tests for various experimental designs are well established, however, and, in most instances, the tests are quickly and easily conducted with the aid of calculators or computers.

Parametric and Nonparametric Statistical Models

All statistical models make certain assumptions about the conditions that are regarded as being true in the experiment. Most of the statistical tests that we discuss in this text are based upon parametric models. **Parametric tests** evaluate relationships among population parameters, such as the population mean μ or variance σ^2. Their appropriate use rests upon these assumptions: (1) the samples of the experiment are randomly drawn from a population of scores and each score is independent of every other score, (2) the scores in the population sampled are normally distributed, and (3) the variances of scores in the populations are equal. Whether these assumptions of random sampling, normal distributions, and

---

[1]In our writing we use the phrases "difference between treatment means" (implying two treatment conditions) and "differences among treatment means" (implying more than two treatment conditions) interchangeably. We have thus far discussed an experiment with only two levels of the independent variable, but the fundamentals of statistical hypothesis testing apply to any number of treatment conditions employed in an experiment.

equality of variances are actually met in the experiment is quite problematic. In most experiments they are not; however, parametric statistical tests such as the *t* test and the analysis of variance are based upon these assumptions.

When the formal assumptions of parametric tests are seriously violated or when the level of measurement of the scores dictates against using the mean and standard deviation to describe the data, then statistical tests based upon nonparametric models are often used. **Nonparametric tests** make no assumptions about the distributions of scores in the populations from which the subjects are sampled. For this reason, nonparametric tests are referred to as *distribution-free tests*. They do not use sample statistics to estimate population parameters and therefore do not test relationships among population parameters.

For many but not all parametric statistical tests, there are alternative nonparametric tests for analyzing the same data. For instance, in this chapter we discuss the *t* test and then its nonparametric counterpart, the Mann-Whitney *U* test. Our approach to developing the concepts of statistical testing is based upon a parametric statistical model. The fundamental concepts of statistical hypothesis testing, though, are very much the same for both parametric and nonparametric tests.

Statistical Tests

Nature of a Test Statistic

Quite simply, a statistical test permits the researcher to determine the probability that a particular difference in sample means $\overline{X}_{A_1} - \overline{X}_{A_2}$ would occur if only sampling error were responsible for the obtained difference. And if the difference in sample means is one that would be very rare if chance alone were responsible, then the possibility is considered that the sample means are not estimates of the same population mean and that the effect of the independent variable was mainly responsible for the obtained difference between the sample means. As we have suggested, however, the simple difference between sample means, $\overline{X}_{A_1} - \overline{X}_{A_2}$, does not provide an adequate basis for making a decision about the equality or inequality of population means because it provides no measure of the amount of sampling error to be expected. Rather, this decision must be made on the basis of a test statistic computed from the sample data.

Fundamentally, most test statistics computed in inferential tests provide some way of comparing the amount of variation in the dependent variable that presumably is due to the independent variable to the amount of variation to be expected from sampling error alone. Often this comparison is a ratio in the general form:

$$\text{test statistic} = \frac{\text{amount of systematic variation}}{\text{amount of error variation}}.$$

The two parametric test statistics that we discuss in this text, the t and the F, utilize variances as the measure of variation; we discuss how to do so later in this chapter and in Chapter 8.

What Does a Statistical Test Actually Test?

The outcome of a statistical test provides the basis for drawing conclusions about the effect of an independent variable and therefore for deciding whether a research hypothesis is or is not supported by the data. A research hypothesis, however, is not tested directly by a statistical test. Rather, a statistical test is a procedure for testing statistical hypotheses. **Statistical hypotheses** are statements about characteristics of populations; for the t and F statistics that we present in this text, the statistical hypotheses always involve statements about population means (μ). Unlike research hypotheses, statistical hypotheses are not declarative sentences stating a relation between independent and dependent variables. Instead, statistical hypotheses are written in notational or symbolic form rather than in sentence form.

Two statistical hypotheses are formulated for any statistical test. These hypotheses are the **null hypothesis** (designated H_0 and pronounced "H naught") and the **alternative hypothesis** (designated H_1 and pronounced "H one"). The null and alternative hypotheses are expressed in such a way that: (1) logically both cannot be true at the same time; that is, they are *mutually exclusive,* and (2) they must include all possible relationships among the parameters involved in the hypotheses. Therefore, one of the statistical hypotheses must represent the true state of affairs with respect to the values of the parameters being tested. For our example in which we wish to determine whether two sample means differ because of the effect of an independent variable, the statistical hypotheses are stated:

H_0: $\mu_{A_1} = \mu_{A_2}$ (null hypothesis)
H_1: not H_0 (alternative hypothesis)

Realize that for any population of scores, one or the other of these hypotheses must be true. It is logically impossible for both to be true at the same time, however.

The null hypothesis does not specify numerical values for population parameters, which, of course, are unknown; it only states symbolically that the population means are equal. Essentially, then, H_0: $\mu_{A_1} = \mu_{A_2}$ corresponds to the situation that would exist if the independent variable had no effect on the dependent variable. If the sample means are not affected by the treatment conditions, then all participants will be representative of a population with the same mean μ_A on a measure of the dependent variable. Under the assumption of the null hypothesis the observed difference between sample means is due merely to chance fluctuations or sampling error.

The alternative hypothesis H_1 is usually stated as simply the *negation* of the null. It states that the population parameters are not equal. They would not be if sample means differed because the participants were not representative of identical populations. One way in which this condition could happen, of course, would be if the independent variable affected the subjects' behavior.

It is evident that support for the research hypotheses of the experiment can be obtained only by refuting the null hypothesis of the statistical test. Indeed, the researcher hopes to reject the null hypothesis in favor of accepting the alternative hypothesis. Rejecting the null hypothesis is equivalent to deciding that the observed difference in sample means is due not merely to sampling error but to a systematic nonchance influence such as would occur if the independent variable did affect the behavior measured.

As an example of this reasoning, McCarthy and Betz's research hypothesis "that the two types of counselor responses would lead to differences in client perceptions of the counselor" (p. 252) is supported only if it is decided that the mean CRF scores for the two treatment conditions estimate different population means. This is the situation implied by the alternative hypothesis. Thus, only if it is decided that H_0 is false, and therefore H_1 is true, can support for the research hypothesis be established. In one respect, then, the null hypothesis is set up as a straw man that the researcher hopes will be knocked down.

The Theoretical Sampling Distribution of a Test Statistic

We have thus far described an inferential statistical test as deriving a test statistic that provides a test of a null hypothesis. The role of the null hypothesis in a statistical test is to establish a situation under which the theoretical sampling distribution of the test statistic may be obtained. Simply defined, a **theoretical sampling distribution** of a test statistic is a distribution specifying the *probability* of obtaining any particular value of that statistic if the null hypothesis is true.

The **probability** (p) of occurrence of a particular value of a test statistic may be defined as:

$$p = \frac{\text{Number of occurrences of a particular value of a test statistic}}{\text{Total number of occurrences of the test statistic}}.$$

For example, if 100 values of a test statistic were obtained, and a particular value of that test statistic occurred 10 times, the probability of that value would be equal to 10/100 or .10. As you can see, the probability of an event has limiting values of 0 and 1.0. A value that is certain never to occur has a probability of 0 and a value that occurs on each trial has a probability of 1.0. Consequently, then, the theoretical sampling distribution of a test statistic specifies the proportion of outcomes of each value of the statistic that would be obtained under the conditions specified in the null hypothesis if an *infinite* set of values of the test statistic were computed.

Most test statistics possess a family of sampling distributions, the exact shape of the distribution depending upon the number of scores entering into that test statistic. For example, in Figure 6–5 (p. 153) we presented empirical sampling distributions for the sample mean $\bar{X}$ for three sample sizes. In this figure the simple frequency of occurrence of each value of the mean is plotted on the ordinate. A theoretical sampling distribution for a test statistic is conceptually very similar to the sampling distribution of the mean except that the probability of a value of the test statistic rather than the frequency of occurrence of the sample mean is plotted on the ordinate. An illustration of a theoretical sampling distribution for a test statistic is illustrated in Figure 7–2. (This sampling distribution is for an *F* statistic, discussed in Chapter 8. Ignore the notation of the critical value and the rejection region for the moment.) For this test statistic, increasing values of the test statistic reflect larger differences among treatment means in relation to error variation.

By knowing the sampling distribution for any test statistic, the researcher can determine how likely or unlikely any particular value or values of the test statistic are when sampling error alone is responsible for the differences between

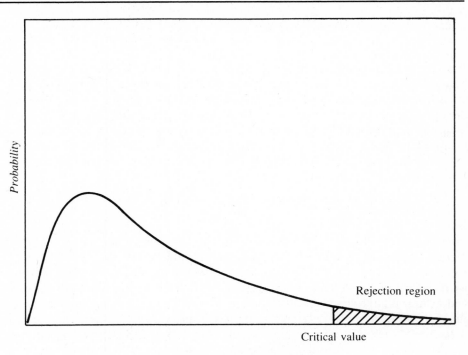

Possible values of the test statistic

FIGURE 7–2   *Example of a theoretical sampling distribution of a test statistic.*

the sample means. Some values of the test statistic will be quite likely to occur by chance alone. Others, particularly those which reflect large differences in treatment means in comparison to a small amount of error variation, will occur quite infrequently under the chance conditions reflected in H_0. The decision about whether the null hypothesis or the alternative hypothesis represents a more plausible situation is made on the basis of these probabilities. We pursue this task in the next section.

Before we discuss making a decision about the statistical hypotheses, two points about sampling distributions of test statistics require further elaboration. First, notice that although H_0: $\mu_{A_1} = \mu_{A_2}$ is the same as stating H_0: $\mu_{A_1} - \mu_{A_2} = 0$, the decision about the statistical hypotheses is not made by deriving a theoretical sampling distributon of $\overline{X}_{A_1} - \overline{X}_{A_2}$ values. We presented $\overline{X}_{A_1} - \overline{X}_{A_2}$ sampling distributions in Tables 7–1 and 7–2 only to illustrate the dilemma faced by an experimenter in attempting to arrive at decisions about the results of an experiment. For making decisions about the statistical hypotheses, the sampling distribution for a *test statistic* is used, because a test statistic takes into account the amount of error variation as well as any systematic variation between treatment means.

Second, you may wonder why the sampling distribution for a test statistic is not obtained under the alternative hypothesis H_1: not H_0. The reason very simply is that the alternative hypothesis is an *inexact* hypothesis that allows many possible relations between population means. But a sampling distribution can be obtained only when the precise relation can be specified among population means.[2] This precision is achieved only in the null hypothesis H_0: $\mu_{A_1} = \mu_{A_2}$. If the experimenter could specify that a treatment has an effect such as +2, so that H_1: $\mu_{A_2} = \mu_{A_1} + 2$, then a sampling distribution for the test statistic under the conditions of H_1 could be obtained. There would be no need to conduct a statistical test under these conditions, however, for the treatment effect, and thus the difference between the population means, would already be known and exactly specified.

Making a Decision about the Statistical Hypotheses

How does a researcher reach a decision about a null hypothesis? First, a criterion must be established for rejecting the null hypothesis. That is, the researcher must decide what would be highly improbable or unlikely values of the test statistic if the null hypothesis is true. Then, the obtained value of the test statistic computed on the sample data is compared to the sampling distribution of the test statistic under the null hypothesis. If the probability of the obtained value of the test statistic is deemed to be too low to have occurred because of sampling error alone if H_0 is true, then the null hypothesis is rejected and treated as false. Because of

---

[2]Notice that in order to obtain the empirical sampling distributions of $\overline{X}_{A_1} - \overline{X}_{A_2}$ in Tables 7–1 and 7–2, we had to specify the exact relation between the population means. For Table 7–1, $\mu_{A_1} = \mu_{A_2}$, and for Table 7–2, $\mu_{A_2} = \mu_{A_1} + 2$. In an experiment, however, the exact treatment effect cannot be specified.

the mutually exclusive property of the statistical hypotheses and the requirement that statistical hypotheses include all possible outcomes, rejection of H_0 implies an acceptance of H_1 as the true state of nature. Rejection of the null hypothesis and acceptance of the alternative hypothesis implies that the difference between the sample means is not just a chance outcome. It is decided that something other than chance is responsible for the outcome.

Significance levels   How improbable under a hypothesis of chance (i.e., under H_0) must the test statistic value be to reject H_0? A rare outcome is defined by the *significance level* or *alpha* (α) *level* adopted by the investigator. Traditionally, psychologists and other scientists have decided that values of the test statistic occurring only five times or fewer in 100 occasions under the null hypothesis are sufficiently rare so that it is more reasonable to decide that the alternative hypothesis, H_1, is true when such a value of the test statistic is obtained. Normally this criterion is stated as a probability value such as $\alpha = .05$. Significance levels other than .05 may be adopted; sometimes a significance level of .01 (or, $\alpha = .01$) is selected.

Rejection regions   The critical values in the sampling distributions of various test statistics for selected significance levels are readily obtained from tables that are presented in most statistical tests. (The relevant tables in this text appear in the Appendix.) The tabled values define the rejection region in the sampling distribution of the test statistic. That is, the rejection region represents the values of the test statistic that have a probability equal to or less than α under the null hypothesis H_0. Thus, the *rejection region* defines the values of the test statistic that meet the criterion for rejecting the null hypothesis H_0 and accepting the alternative hypothesis H_1.

A critical value of a test statistic and the rejection region it defines are shown on the right tail of the sampling distribution in Figure 7–2. Any value of the test statistic calculated on the sample data and falling in the rejection region would be quite improbable or rare if H_0 were true, but would be more likely to occur if H_1 were true. Accordingly, the experimenter bases the decision to reject or not reject H_0 upon whether or not the value of the test statistic lies within the rejection region of the sampling distribution of the test statistic.

Statistically significant difference   If the test statistic obtained falls in the rejection region when the significance level is established as .05, then the experimenter decides that there is only 1 chance in 20 or less that such an obtained difference in sample means would be due to sampling error alone if the null hypothesis were true. The experimenter then decides that it is more likely that the difference in sample means is due to factors other than chance alone. Such differences among sample means are often said to be *statistically significant* (at the .05 level). That is, there is a statistically significant difference at a .05 (or other) level of significance. Statistically significant results often are reported in journal articles as $p < .05$ (the symbol $<$ represents "less than"). The reader thus knows that the null hypothesis was rejected at the .05 level because the probability (p) of obtaining such a difference among sample means when the null hypothesis is true is *equal to* or *less than* .05, i.e., $p < .05$.[3]

Statistically nonsignificant difference   If the obtained value of the test statistic does *not* fall in the rejection region of the theoretical sampling distribution, then the null hypothesis is not rejected and the results are regarded as nonsignificant (at the .05 level). In such an instance, then, a difference between sample means would *not* be statistically significant and $p > .05$. The difference is not regarded as sufficiently unlikely to be explained by anything other than chance variation.

We can summarize the decisions and conclusions reached from statistical tests, where the significance level is set at .05, as follows:

If the test statistic falls into the rejection region for $\alpha = .05$, then:	If the test statistic does *not* fall into the rejection region for $\alpha = .05$, then:
p of the test statistic is less than or equal to .05, or $p < .05$.	p of the test statistic is greater than .05, or $p > .05$.
The null hypothesis (H_0) is rejected.	The null hypothesis (H_0) is not rejected. The sample means estimate the same population mean.
The alternative hypothesis (H_1) is accepted. The sample means estimate different population means.	The alternative hypothesis (H_1) is not accepted.
The differences between the sample means are "statistically significant" (at the .05 level).	The differences between the sample means are "statistically not significant" (at the .05 level), or a "nonsignificant" difference was obtained.
It is decided that something in addition to sampling error is responsible for the differences among the sample means.	It is decided that sampling error is the most plausible explanation of the differences among sample means.

Why is the .05 significance level adopted?   It may appear that researchers are unduly conservative about the criterion that is used to make decisions about the null hypothesis and subsequently to draw conclusions about the effect of an independent variable on a dependent variable. You may ask, for example, "What if the outcome had been statistically significant at the .06 level or even the .10 level? After all, the probability of the results being due to chance alone is still small. Why not regard an outcome as 'probably' significant if the null hypothesis

---

[3]Mathematically, this is indicated by $p \leq .05$, where the symbol $\leq$ is read as "less than or equal to." In published research, however, common practice is simply to indicate probability levels as $p < .05$ or $p < .01$.

could be rejected at the .06 or .07 level? Isn't setting the significance level so that 'it is .05 or nothing at all' an unnecessarily rigid criterion?"

The reservation is understandable, but scientists typically adopt a rather conservative stance in making decisions about data. As our opening quote from Kruskal (1968) indicates, statistical testing is an objective approach to restraining an overenthusiastic investigator from interpreting differences among means that are most reasonably attributed to chance. Thus, although somewhat arbitrary, the .05 significance level is widely recognized as conventional for regarding outcomes as statistically significant or not. Indeed, any difference among sample means that does not reach the usual .05 level of significance is generally viewed skeptically by researchers and interpreted as a chance difference. As you would expect, there is some controversy on this issue (see, for example, Beale, 1972; Schulman, Kupst, and Suran, 1976; or Skipper, Guenther, and Nass, 1967). But, most typically, psychologists adhere to the use of a value of α equal to .05 or less.

Type I and Type II Errors in Statistical Tests

A statistical test leads the experimenter to make one of two decisions about the null hypothesis: to (1) reject, or (2) fail to reject it. Either decision may be correct or wrong depending on whether the null hypothesis is in fact true or not. If a wrong decision about the null hypothesis is made, then an error is committed. A **Type I error** is made if the null hypothesis is rejected when it is actually true. On the other hand, failing to reject H_0 when the alternative hypothesis (H_1) is true results in a **Type II error.**

The true state of the statistical hypotheses and the decisions made from the statistical test with the corresponding correct decisions and errors are presented in Table 7–3. It is important to notice that decisions made about H_0 and H_1 are probabilistic. An experimenter who rejects H_0 at the .05 significance level is in effect concluding that, "The sample means came from different populations, but there is a 1 in 20 chance that I am wrong if the null hypothesis is true." Thus, it is clear that a decision about H_0 and H_1 based upon any one test may be wrong.[4] As Glass and Stanley (1970) observe,

> *In testing any statistical hypothesis the researcher's decision that the hypothesis is true or that it is false is never made with certainty; he [or she] always runs a risk of making an incorrect decision.* The essence of statistical testing is that it is a means of controlling and assessing that risk. (p. 275)

As we see, then, uncertainty is inevitable in any decision about H_0 and H_1.

---

[4]It is important to realize that the risk of committing a Type I or Type II error is inherent in the nature of statistical hypothesis testing. Overt errors in computation or interpretation of the obtained statistic may lead to the same wrong decision as occurs when a Type I or II error is made, but such computational errors have absolutely no relationship to the concepts of Type I and II errors.

The outcomes of statistical decision making.   **TABLE 7–3**

	Decision by the experimenter	
	Fails to Reject H_0	Rejects H_0 Accepts H_1
H_0 True	Correct decision	Type I error
State of nature		
H_1 True	Type II error	Correct decision

From any one experiment, a researcher can never know if a Type I or Type II error was made. This inherent uncertainty associated with statistical decision making is one of the important reasons why an experiment cannot prove that an independent variable did or did not have an effect. A number of factors affect the probability that one of these errors will occur when a statistical decision is made, and we discuss this issue more fully in Chapter 13.

Statistical and Scientific Significance

The use of the word *significant* to characterize a rare outcome in a test of a statistical hypothesis is unfortunate. Perhaps the most typical connotation to something significant is that it is important. Yet, this attribution is totally inappropriate to make to a statistically significant difference in an experiment. In statistical hypothesis testing, significance has one meaning only: a rare outcome, as Carver (1978) indicates quite clearly:

> Statistical significance simply means statistical rareness. Results are "significant" from a statistical point of view because they occur very rarely in random sampling under the conditions of the null hypothesis. (p. 383)

A statistical test has only one function and that is to permit the experimenter to conclude that the differences obtained among sample means are not due to chance by using "formal, objective, communicable, and reproducible procedures rather than by intuition" (Winch and Campbell, 1969, p. 143). If a statistically rare result occurs in an experiment, then the statistical test provides absolutely no indication of the reason for this result. The responsibility for determining the reason rests with the experimenter, who must carefully examine the conditions of the experiment and the manipulation of the independent variable to ascertain the validity of the experiment. This is an involved process, which we treat in detail in Chapter 13.

It is clear that statistical significance bears no relation to scientific significance. The scientific importance of a result is determined long before the data are subjected to statistical analysis. In a well-conceived and well-designed experiment both statistically significant and nonsignificant differences may be scientifically important. Indeed, where a particular predicted relationship is important to a theoretical formulation, failure to find that relationship empirically may have scientific significance. Recall from Chapter 2 that a theory can never be confirmed by empirical results, but can only be disconfirmed when predicted relationships cannot be empirically verified.

We do not want to underplay the role and importance of statistical hypothesis testing in psychological research, but as Lykken (1968) indicates:

> The finding of statistical significance is perhaps the least important attribute of a good experiment; it is *never* a sufficient condition for concluding that a theory has been corroborated, that a useful empirical fact has been established with reasonable confidence—or that an experimental report ought to be published. The value of any research can be determined, not from the statistical results, but only by skilled, subjective evaluation of the coherence and reasonableness of the theory, the degree of experimental control employed, the sophistication of the measuring techniques, the scientific or practical importance of the phenomena studied, and so on. (pp. 158–159)

Relation between Research Hypotheses and Statistical Hypotheses

The word *hypothesis* is repeatedly used in psychological research and statistical methods. Perhaps to your dismay, it is used in many contexts, sometimes incorrectly, often preceded by adjectives indicating that the author has a specified use of the term in mind. We want to ensure that the distinction between research hypotheses and statistical hypotheses is crystal clear in your thinking, for sometimes the appropriate distinction is not even made by researchers. For example, a psychologist may wrongly state null and alternative hypotheses in this form:

> *Null Hypothesis (H₀):* There is no difference in memory for an assault between witnesses exposed to or not exposed to an antirape program.

> *Alternative Hypothesis (H₁):* Witnesses exposed to an antirape program have better memory of an assault than witnesses not exposed to such a program.

Formulating a null and alternative hypothesis in this way leads to potential confusion about the nature and role of hypotheses in an experiment.

A null hypothesis is a statistical hypothesis stated in terms of population parameters (e.g., H_0: $\mu_{A_1} = \mu_{A_2}$), and it forms the basis for the sampling distribution of the inferential statistical test used and nothing more. It is not a statement of a lack of relation between an independent and a dependent variable. Hopkins (1976) calls a hypothesis in the form of the null hypothesis stated above an *unhypothesis* because such a statement of a hypothesis has absolutely nothing to do with the formulation of the research problem, has no relationship to theoretical formulations in the problem area, does not relate to the expected outcome of the experiment, and is not the null hypothesis that provides the sampling distribution for the test statistic.

> The null hypothesis is *not* just a statement that is negative of a positively stated research hypothesis. It is not used in the development of the researcher's hypothesis of expected outcomes of the study (his guess or conjecture). It *is* used as a part of statistically based decision-making procedures. (Hopkins, 1976, p. 47)

The alternative hypothesis stated above is an appropriate example of a *research* hypothesis, but it is *not* an example of an alternative hypothesis (H_1) to a null hypothesis. If this research hypothesis led to testing of memory for a simulated assault between groups exposed to or not exposed to an antirape program, and if statistical tests were then conducted using the memory scores as data, then the null hypothesis of the statistical test would be H_0: $\mu_{A_1} = \mu_{A_2}$ where μ_{A_1} and μ_{A_2} represent the population means of memory scores for individuals given or not given an antirape program, respectively. The alternative hypothesis would be H_1: not H_0. This alternative hypothesis includes one outcome ($\mu_{A_1} > \mu_{A_2}$) that would agree with the research hypothesis, and one outcome ($\mu_{A_1} < \mu_{A_2}$) that would disagree with the research hypothesis. If the obtained outcome agrees with the research hypothesis, (i.e., $\mu_{A_1} > \mu_{A_2}$), then the statistical test provides absolutely no indication of why the population means differ. As Boneau (1961) observes:

> The statistical test cares not whether a Social Desirability scale measures social desirability, or number of trials to extinction is an indicator of habit strength. . . . Given unending piles of numbers from which to draw small samples, the *t* test and the *F* test will methodically decide for us whether the means of the piles are different. (p. 261)

Thus, in summary, although research hypotheses quite obviously relate different independent and dependent variables from experiment to experiment, the statistical hypotheses of a specific test retain the same form in different experiments.

THE *t* TEST FOR INDEPENDENT GROUPS

We have posed the experimenter's dilemma and discussed the basic logic of statistical hypothesis testing that underlies all statistical tests. We now describe a statistical test, the *t* test, which is frequently used to analyze differences between means in a simple between-subjects experiment in which two levels of one independent variable are manipulated.

Earlier in the chapter we pointed out that any test statistic in general represents a ratio of systematic variation to error variation. Following this general approach, the *t* statistic is defined as:

$$t = \frac{(\overline{X}_1 - \overline{X}_2) - (\mu_1 - \mu_2)}{s_{\overline{X}_1 - \overline{X}_2}}.$$

The numerator of the t merely reflects how much an obtained difference between two sample means (i.e., $\bar{X}_1 - \bar{X}_2$)[5] differs from the difference between the two population means (i.e., $\mu_1 - \mu_2$), which the sample means are assumed to estimate. As we shall see, in most instances, the difference between the population means $\mu_1 - \mu_2$ is hypothesized to be zero. The denominator of the t is a measure of error variation called the *standard error of the difference* between two sample means. To understand this term and thus the nature of the test, we must more fully examine the distribution of differences between two sample means.

Sampling Distribution of Differences in Sample Means

In Table 7–1 we presented the outcomes of ten hypothetical experiments, in each of which two samples of size 5 were drawn randomly from two populations with equal means ($\mu_1 = \mu_2 = 14$). For each experiment, then, the null hypothesis H_0: $\mu_1 = \mu_2$ was true. Even though each obtained $\bar{X}_1 - \bar{X}_2$ difference in sample means estimates the same true zero difference in population means, considerable variation in $\bar{X}_1 - \bar{X}_2$ values is still observed. Some $\bar{X}_1 - \bar{X}_2$ values are positive (e.g., +3.8), indicating that $\bar{X}_1$ is larger than $\bar{X}_2$ but others are negative (e.g., −4.0), resulting from $\bar{X}_2$ being larger than $\bar{X}_1$. None of the obtained $\bar{X}_1 - \bar{X}_2$ values is exactly equal to the true $\mu_1 - \mu_2$ difference of zero. Because each mean in a pair of means was sampled randomly from one of two identical populations, only chance factors or sampling error could be responsible for this obtained variation in $\bar{X}_1 - \bar{X}_2$ values.

Suppose we replicated the hypothetical experiment 100 times for each of three sample sizes, $n = 2$, $n = 5$, and $n = 10$, and calculated the resulting $\bar{X}_1 - \bar{X}_2$ values. Plotting a frequency distribution of these differences in sample means, i.e., a distribution of $\bar{X}_1 - \bar{X}_2$ values, results in a sampling distribution of differences in means. We did so, and the resulting sampling distributions of the 100 differences in means of the hypothetical experiment for the three sample sizes are presented in Figure 7–3. Recall from Chapter 6 that a frequency distribution of sample means $\bar{X}$ is called a sampling distribution of the mean. As we discussed in Chapter 6, the theoretical sampling distribution of the mean has several important characteristics about its shape, mean, and standard error. A theoretical sampling distribution of differences in means shares these same characteristics. For example, a sampling distribution of $\bar{X}_1 - \bar{X}_2$ values from an infinite number of random samples will be normally distributed. (This property is often referred to as the *central limit theorem*.) From Figure 7–3 you can see that each of the empirical sampling distributions begins to approximate the shape of a theoretical sampling distribution of differences between means even though only 100 samples were drawn. As expected, then, a sampling distribution of $\bar{X}_1 - \bar{X}_2$ values can be described by its mean and standard error.

----

[5]Previously we have indicated means as $\bar{X}_{A_1}$ or $\bar{X}_{A_2}$. For discussion of the t test we simply use $\bar{X}_1$ and $\bar{X}_2$. This is the notation most frequently used in presentations of the t test. The notations $\bar{X}_{A_1}$, $\bar{X}_{A_2}$, and $\bar{X}_1$, $\bar{X}_2$ are equivalent.

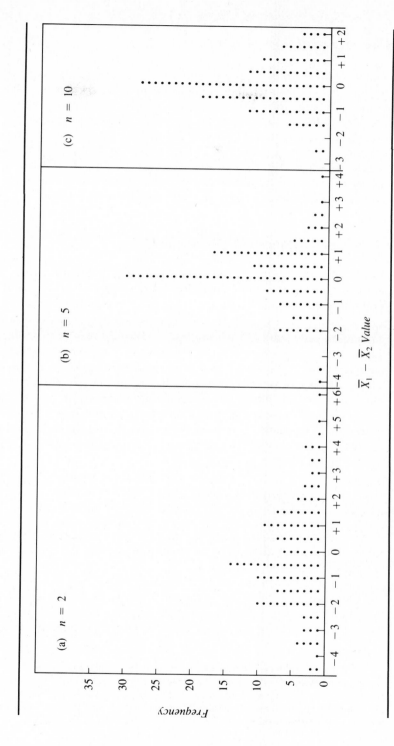

FIGURE 7-3 *Empirical sampling distribution of the difference between two sample means $(\bar{X}_1 - \bar{X}_2)$ for 100 samples drawn from two populations with identical means $(\mu_1 = \mu_2)$. Sampling distributions for samples of size 2, 5, and 10 are shown.*

Mean of a Sampling Distribution of Differences in Means

The mean of the distribution of an unlimited set of $\bar{X}_1 - \bar{X}_2$ values will be equal to the true difference in population means $\mu_1 - \mu_2$. Therefore, when $\mu_1 = \mu_2$, the mean of the obtained $\bar{X}_1 - \bar{X}_2$ values will, in the long run, equal zero and the obtained differences in sample means will be clustered around the true difference of zero in the population means. This characteristic is demonstrated in the distributions shown in Figure 7–3. The means for $n = 2$, $n = 5$, and $n = 10$ are $-.120$, $.070$, and $.019$, respectively. Thus, even with only 100 sets of samples, the means of the $\bar{X}_1 - \bar{X}_2$ differences are quite close to the true difference of zero between the populations from which the samples were selected.

Standard Error of a Sampling Distribution of Differences in Means

The standard deviation of a theoretical sampling distribution of $\bar{X}_1 - \bar{X}_2$ values is called the **standard error of the difference in sample means** and is denoted $\sigma_{\bar{X}_1 - \bar{X}_2}$. You will recall that the standard error for a sampling distribution of the mean (i.e., $\sigma_{\bar{X}} = \sigma/\sqrt{n} = \sqrt{\sigma^2/n}$ is a function of both the variability of scores in the population sampled and the sample size. The smaller the variability of scores in the population (i.e., σ or σ^2) and the larger the sample (n), the less variation or sampling error there will be among means. The effect of sample size, even with a limited number of samples, is evident in Figure 7–3. The distribution of $\bar{X}_1 - \bar{X}_2$ values becomes less spread out as sample size increases from $n = 2$ to $n = 10$.

The standard error of the difference in sample means, often more simply referred to as the **standard error of the difference,** also depends upon the variability of scores in the populations being sampled and the sample sizes. The standard error of the difference is defined as:

$$\sigma_{\bar{X}_1 - \bar{X}_2} = \sqrt{\frac{\sigma_1^2}{n_1} + \frac{\sigma_2^2}{n_2}} \;\; .$$

As you see, the standard error of a theoretical sampling distribution of $\bar{X}_1 - \bar{X}_2$ values is essentially derived by combining or pooling the standard errors of each sampling distribution of means.

In a single experiment, of course, the value of σ or σ^2 is typically not known and therefore the value of $\sigma_{\bar{X} - \bar{X}}$ cannot be determined.[6] But recall from Chapter 6 that the true standard error of the mean $\sigma_{\bar{X}}$ was estimated by $s_{\bar{X}}$. Similarly, the true standard error of the difference between two sample means ($\sigma_{\bar{X} - \bar{X}_2}$) can be

---

[6]If σ is known, then a statistic called the z may be calculated to test the difference between two sample means. Most often, of course, the values of the population variances σ_1^2 and σ_2^2 are not known and therefore $\sigma_{\bar{X} - \bar{X}^2}$ cannot be determined. Accordingly, it is rarely appropriate to use a z test with the z statistic in psychological research. Computational details for the z may be found in most introductory statistics texts.

estimated by using the variances calculated from the sample data. The estimated standard error of the difference for a sampling distribution of $\bar{X}_1 - \bar{X}_2$ values is given by:

$$s_{\bar{X}_1 - \bar{X}_2} = \sqrt{\frac{s_1^2}{n_1} + \frac{s_2^2}{n_2}},$$

where s_1^2 and s_2^2 are the sample variances.

As we have stated, the estimated standard error of the difference is the denominator of the t statistic. Thus, you can see that the t simply reflects how many estimated standard errors away from the mean of the sampling distribution an obtained $\bar{X}_1 - \bar{X}_2$ difference lies. For example, a t value of 1.000 reveals that a $\bar{X}_1 - \bar{X}_2$ difference is one standard error away from the mean of the sampling distribution of $\bar{X}_1 - \bar{X}_2$ values.

Statistical Decision Making with a *t* test for Independent Groups

Throughout this chapter we have emphasized that two sample means are expected to differ whether the independent variable has an effect or not. Indeed, as we have indicated, the purpose of statistical hypothesis testing is to determine whether it is even plausible to consider a nonchance explanation of the difference obtained between sample means. A t test provides an answer to the fundamental statistical question that must be answered before a conclusion is reached about the research hypothesis: What is the probability that the obtained difference in two sample means could occur if chance (i.e., sampling error) alone were responsible?

In conducting a t test to determine whether there is a significant difference between two means, the steps for statistical hypothesis testing are followed:

- A null hypothesis H_0 and alternative hypothesis H_1 are formulated;
- A significance level (usually $\alpha = .05$) is selected. The significance level establishes the rejection region in the theoretical sampling distribution for the t statistic and therefore determines the critical value of t;
- The t statistic is calculated from the data obtained in the experiment; and
- A decision to reject or not reject H_0 is made on the basis of comparing the calculated t to the critical value of t.

We now consider each of these steps in turn and then provide an example of the use of the t test for independent groups.

Null and Alternative Hypotheses

Recall that a statistical hypothesis is a statement about the relationship of population parameters. The parameters relevant to a statistical test of two sample means

$\bar{X}_1$ and $\bar{X}_2$ are the population means μ_1 and μ_2, because each sample mean is an estimate of the population mean. To obtain the theoretical sampling distributions of t, it is assumed that the two treatment groups come from identical populations. For statistical decision making, then, the null hypothesis states that the two population means are equal. In notation, the null hypothesis for the t test for independent groups is usually written:

$$H_0:\ \mu_1 = \mu_2.$$

The situation represented by the null hypothesis is that which is expected to exist when the independent variable has no effect on subjects' behavior. The alternative hypothesis typically is written simply as the negation of the null hypothesis, H_1: Not H_0, or equivalently, $H_1:\ \mu_1 \neq \mu_2$. This is the situation assumed to exist when the independent variable does have an effect. These null and alternative hypotheses are appropriate for any t test on two independent groups.

Calculating the t Statistic

The formula for the t test is, as we have already presented it,

$$t = \frac{(\bar{X}_1 - \bar{X}_2) - (\mu_1 - \mu_2)}{s_{\bar{X}_1 - \bar{X}_2}}.$$

The null hypothesis for the t test, however, $H_0:\ \mu_1 = \mu_2$, is equivalent to $H_0:$ $\mu_1 - \mu_2 = 0$. Thus, the t statistic can be written:

$$t = \frac{(\bar{X}_1 - \bar{X}_2) - (0)}{s_{\bar{X}_1 - \bar{X}_2}}.$$

This formula can then be written even more simply as:

$$t = \frac{\bar{X}_1 - \bar{X}_2}{s_{\bar{X}_1 - \bar{X}_2}}.$$

For ease in computation this definitional formula may be further rewritten:[7]

$$t = \frac{\bar{X}_1 - \bar{X}_2}{\sqrt{\dfrac{s_1^2}{n_1} + \dfrac{s_2^2}{n_2}}}.$$

[7]Other formulas for the t appear in textbooks. These other formulas are computationally equivalent to the one given here, but include the notation for calculating the variance from raw scores. The formula for the $s_{\bar{X}_1 - \bar{X}_2}$ we give assumes that the appropriate descriptive statistics for each group—the sample mean, $\bar{X}$, and standard deviation, SD—are calculated before the inferential statistical test is performed. Therefore, the sample variances, s_1^2 and s_2^2, are readily obtained for computing the t merely by squaring the standard deviation.

With this formula only the sample means, standard deviations, and sample sizes are needed for computing the *t*. Because the descriptive statistics should be obtained before the data are subjected to a statistical test of significance, the *t* statistic is easily calculated by merely substituting the appropriate values into the formula.

We illustrate the computation of the *t* for the CRF expertness scores reported in the McCarthy and Betz (1978) experiment. The only values needed to compute the *t* formula are these:[8]

	Treatment group	
	Self-disclosing	*Self-involving*
n	54	53
M	63.07	68.51
SD	14.63	11.06

The step-by-step computations of *t* for these data are presented in Table 7–4.

The calculated value of $t = 2.172$ agrees with the value of $t = -2.17$ reported by McCarthy and Betz. Notice that in the last computational step we dropped the negative sign $(-)$ in the obtained *t* value. Reporting the *t* as an absolute value rather than as a positive or negative value is conventional. Whether the *t* is positive or negative merely reveals whether $\bar{X}_1$ or $\bar{X}_2$ is the larger value. Which treatment mean is designated $\bar{X}_1$ or $\bar{X}_2$ is often arbitrary. In the McCarthy and Betz experiment, for example, if the self-involving treatment means were designated $\bar{X}_1$, then

---

Steps in computing the t *test for independent groups using the descriptive statistics from the CRF expertness scores.*   **TABLE 7–4**

$$t = (\bar{X}_1 - \bar{X}_2)/\sqrt{(s_1^2/n_1 + s_2^2/n_2)}$$
$$= (63.07 - 68.51)/\sqrt{[(14.63)^2/54 + (11.06)^2/53)]}$$
$$= -5.44/\sqrt{214.0369/54 + 122.3236/53}$$
$$= -5.44/\sqrt{3.9636 + 2.3080}$$
$$= -5.44/\sqrt{6.2716}$$
$$= -5.44/2.5043$$
$$= -2.1723$$
$$= 2.172$$

---

[8]The means and standard deviations are reported to two decimal places to reduce rounding error in calculating the *t*. McCarthy and Betz report corresponding values in their Table 1. They present the values of the means to only one decimal place, however. Using their values leads to a larger rounding error in the calculations.

all reported t values would be positive rather than negative. Normally, then, a t is reported without a $+$ or $-$ sign preceding the value.

You will notice, too, that we reported the calculated t value to three decimal places instead of two. As will be discussed, the tabled critical values of t are given to three decimal places. Accordingly, we think it is more appropriate to report the obtained value of t to three decimal places.

Theoretical Sampling Distributions of t

Both the $\overline{X}_1 - \overline{X}_2$ value in the numerator *and* the $s_{\overline{X}_1 - \overline{X}_2}$ in the denominator of the t statistic are based on sample values and therefore subject to sampling error. Further, the value of $s_{\overline{X}_1 - \overline{X}_2}$ depends upon both the size of the sample variances, s_1^2 and s_2^2, and the samples sizes, n_1 and n_2.

Therefore, the value of t is sensitive to the sizes of the samples. Thus, the sampling distributions of t vary essentially with the sizes of the samples. As a result, the t statistic is not one but a family of theoretical sampling distributions. More specifically, a particular theoretical sampling distribution of t depends upon the degrees of freedom associated with the two samples.

Degrees of freedom   The **degrees of freedom** (abbreviated *df*) refers to the number of scores that are free to vary when we are estimating a population parameter by a sample statistic. To help you understand what is meant by "free to vary" in computing a statistic, an example will be helpful. Suppose you want to calculate the variance on a sample of five scores. To do so you will have to calculate the sums of squares or *SS* for the five scores. To compute the *SS,* you must obtain and square each $X_i - \overline{X}$ value. The first step, then, is to obtain the mean $\overline{X}$. You do this step and find that the mean of the five scores is 13.4. Moreover, you know that four of the five scores have values of 13, 15, 13, and 12. Given that the mean is 13.4, it is possible to determine the value of the fifth score; it must be 14, because no other value of X_i, given that four of the five scores are known, will yield a mean of 13.4. Once $\overline{X}$ is known, then the values of only four of the five scores are free to vary. The value of the fifth score is not free to vary; its value is fixed by the restriction that the value of the mean imposes. Thus, all but one of the scores is free to vary in calculating the sample variance. In this instance, there are four degrees of freedom among the five scores.

In Chapter 6 we pointed out that an unbiased estimate of the population variance is obtained by dividing *SS* by $n - 1$ rather than by n. Because $n - 1$ represents the number of scores free to vary when obtaining a *SS,* the formula for the sample variance can be expressed as the sums of squared deviations (*SS*) divided by the degrees of freedom (*df*), or

$$s^2 = \frac{SS}{df}.$$

Returning to the t statistic, the estimated standard error of the difference $s_{\overline{X}_1 - \overline{X}_2}$ is obtained by calculating the variances from each sample, s_1^2 and s_2^2. Thus, the degrees of freedom for the sampling distribution of the t statistic are based upon the combined df associated with each variance estimate s_1^2 and s_2^2. For a particular sampling distribution of t,

$$df = (n_1 - 1) + (n_2 - 1) = N - 2$$

where N represents the total number of scores in the two samples.

Shape of the* t *distribution Obviously, where the degrees of freedom correspond to all but two subjects (i.e., $N - 2$) in a two-group experiment employing a between-subjects design,[9] the degrees of freedom are directly related to sample size. Because any number of subjects potentially can be selected for an experiment, there is virtually an unlimited number of df and thus theoretical distributions of t. Figure 7–4 illustrates how the shape of the t distribution changes with its degrees of freedom and therefore with sample size. First, notice that the t distribution is similar to the normal distribution in several respects. Each t distribution is symmetrical, unimodal, and has a mean equal to zero. When the null hypothesis H_0: $\mu_1 = \mu_2$ is true, the expected t value will be zero, because the average $\overline{X}_1 - \overline{X}_2$ value in a sampling distribution will be zero. Of course, even when H_0 is true, values of $\overline{X}_1 - \overline{X}_2$ will vary around a mean of zero simply because of sampling error or chance. Further, it is expected that $\overline{X}_1$ will be larger than $\overline{X}_2$ about as often as it is smaller than $\overline{X}_2$. Therefore, in the long run, the $\overline{X}_1 - \overline{X}_2$ values will be positive and negative equally often when, in fact, $\mu_1 - \mu_2$. Consequently, the expected t values will be positive or negative around a mean of zero.

A "Fixed" Score BOX 7–1

Students attempting to understand the concepts associated with degrees of freedom are sometimes confused about the implications of an individual's score being "fixed." How can a score be fixed; that is, have a certain value that is determined by a sample mean and the scores from others in the sample? The answer is, of course, that this can occur only after the data have been collected and the mean for a treatment condition has been determined. During the conduct of the experiment each individual's performance is free to vary and is certainly not fixed by the scores of other participants. Notice that in order to say that a score is fixed, the mean of the sample and all other scores in that sample must be known. The so-called fixed score went into the computation of the mean, and therefore its value becomes determinable only when the mean and all the other scores in the group are known.

---

[9]A t test can also be used to analyze the differences between means in an experiment employing a within-subjects design. In this design the scores in the two treatment conditions are obtained from the same subjects and are not independent; thus, the df for this t are determined differently. For this reason theoretical distributions of t are based upon degrees of freedom rather than upon the number of subjects used. We briefly discuss the use of the t for within-subjects designs in Chapter 11.

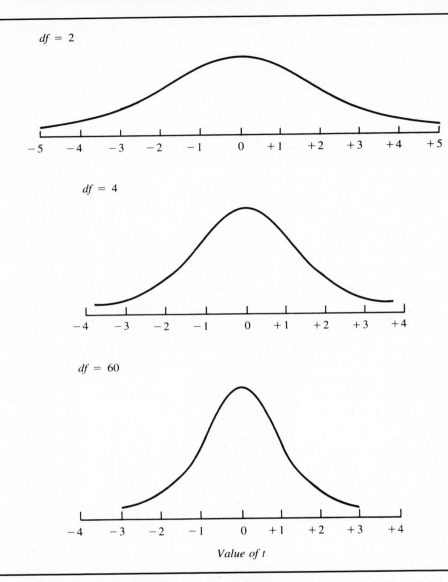

FIGURE 7-4   *Distributions of the* t *statistic for 2, 4, and 60* **df.**

For an infinite number of degrees of freedom (a theoretical but not actual possibility) the distribution of *t* is the same as the normal. All other *t* distributions, however, differ from a normal distribution. In general, the distribution of *t* is flatter (less peaked) and wider (the possible values are more spread out) than a normal distribution is. As you can see in Figure 7–4, the flattest and widest *t* distributions are those based on the smallest sample sizes. In Chapter 6 we discussed ranges within which normally distributed scores were expected to fall. Recall our stating that in a normal distribution a range of $\mu \pm 2\sigma$ encompasses about 95 percent of the scores. More specifically, a range of $\mu \pm 1.96\sigma$ encompasses *exactly* 95 percent of the scores. Because a *t* distribution is spread out more than the normal distribution, however, a larger percentage of *t* values fall in either tail of the distribution than occurs with the normal distribution. Therefore a range of *t* values larger than 0 ± 1.96 will *always* be required to encompass 95 percent of the values of *t*.

Establishing the Rejection Region for t

A rejection region is composed of scores in the theoretical sampling distribution of a statistic that encompass rare values of the statistic when a null hypothesis is true. For the *t* statistic these are values in either tail of the distribution. Let us see why.

As we have seen in Figure 7–4, most values of *t* will be clustered around zero in the middle of the distribution when H_0 is true. By chance alone, however, some value of *t* will fall at either end of the distribution even when H_0 is true. Such values are obtained when the numerator of the statistic (i.e., the difference between the sample means $\overline{X}_1 - \overline{X}_2$) is large compared to the denominator (i.e., the standard error of the difference). But these large values of *t* are rare occurrences under a null hypothesis $H_0: \mu_1 = \mu_2$.

On the other hand, if H_1 is true and $\mu_1 \neq \mu_2$, then large values of $\overline{X}_1 - \overline{X}_2$ and thus of *t* are expected to occur more frequently. Hence, the rejection region for the *t* is composed of large positive and negative values of *t*, which would occur with a probability equal to α if the null hypothesis is true but would occur much more frequently if H_1 is true. Thus, given the alternative hypothesis H_1: Not H_0, the null hypothesis is rejected when an obtained *t* is sufficiently greater than zero in either direction (i.e., when $\overline{X}_1$ is greater than $\overline{X}_2$, or $\overline{X}_1$ is less than $\overline{X}_2$) so that the probability of its occurrence under H_0 is equal to or less than the probability set by the significance level.

Following this logic, then, a rejection region is established in each tail of the theoretical *t* distribution. That is, the total probability of a rare outcome as defined by the significance level is divided between both tails of the *t* distribution. For instance, where $\alpha = .05$, two rejection regions are established—one in each tail of the *t* distribution, each with a probability of .025. Therefore, if the obtained value of *t* falls in the rejection region in either tail of the *t* distribution, then the null hypothesis is rejected and the alternative hypothesis accepted.

The two rejection regions in a theoretical distribution of *t* based upon 8 degrees of freedom are illustrated in Figure 7–5. In this instance, the probability that a *t* value will be at least as large as -2.306 is .025, and the probability that it

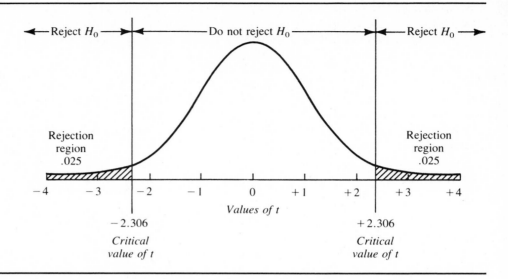

FIGURE 7-5   *Rejection regions for the t distribution for 8 df and $\alpha = .05$.*

will be equal to or larger than +2.306 is also .025 under the null hypothesis. Any obtained *t* value equal to or larger than −2.306 or +2.306 lies within a rejection region; such an outcome will occur only 5 percent of the time when the null hypothesis is true. Thus, the critical value of *t* that establishes the rejection region in both tails of the distribution is 2.306. Any obtained value of *t* equal to or greater than this critical value is regarded as too unlikely to occur by chance or sampling error alone. By establishing two rejection regions, one in each tail of the theoretical *t* distribution, the experimenter covers both possibilities implied by the alternative hypothesis. The total probability of an outcome in either of the two areas by chance is .05.

Using the table of critical **t** *values*   Recall that a particular sampling distribution of *t* depends upon the degrees of freedom involved. Consequently, for a particular significance level (e.g., .05 or .01) the critical *t* values and therefore the rejection regions will differ for experiments employing different sample sizes. Fortunately, precise critical values of *t* for the .05 and .01 significance levels are presented in tables. (See Table A–1 in the Appendix.)

To explain how the table of critical *t* values is used and interpreted, we present in Table 7–5 the critical values of *t* for $\alpha = .05$ and .01. The first column lists degrees of freedom for *t* distributions. The values shown in any row in the .05 or .01 column are the critical values of *t* for the corresponding degrees of freedom for that significance level. For example, we see from the table that where the significance level is .05 the critical *t* value for 8 degrees of freedom is 2.306.

Critical values of the t distribution for α = .05 and α = .01 (two-tailed test).　　**TABLE 7–5**

df	α = .05	α = .01
1	12.706	63.657
2	4.303	9.925
3	3.182	5.841
4	2.776	4.604
5	2.571	4.032
6	2.447	3.707
7	2.365	3.499
8	2.306	3.355
9	2.262	3.250
10	2.228	3.169
11	2.201	3.106
12	2.179	3.055
13	2.160	3.012
14	2.145	2.977
15	2.131	2.947
16	2.120	2.921
17	2.110	2.898
18	2.101	2.878
19	2.093	2.861
20	2.086	2.845
21	2.080	2.831
22	2.074	2.819
23	2.069	2.807
24	2.064	2.797
25	2.060	2.787
26	2.056	2.779
27	2.052	2.771
28	2.048	2.763
29	2.045	2.756
30	2.042	2.750
40	2.021	2.704
60	2.000	2.660
120	1.980	2.617
∞	1.960	2.576

The table shows that the critical values of *t* decrease as the degrees of freedom increase. Recall that the *t* distribution is more spread out when fewer degrees of freedom are involved; the critical *t* values will lie farther from zero. Moreover, a significance level of .01 imposes a more stringent criterion for defining a rare chance outcome. Therefore, for all degrees of freedom the critical *t* value is larger for $\alpha = .01$ than for $\alpha = .05$; any obtained $\overline{X}_1 - \overline{X}_2$ difference will have to be more standard errors away from zero to be regarded as a rare chance occurrence when a .01 significance level is adopted instead of .05.

As a rule of thumb, an obtained t will typically have to be larger than 2.000 to lie in the rejection region. That is, the difference in sample means will have to fall more than about two standard errors away from zero in order to be statistically significant. With 60 or fewer degrees of freedom, and a .05 significance level, all critical t values are 2.000 or larger. Indeed, only for an infinite number of df when the t distribution is exactly the same as the normal distribution does the critical value of t become as small as 1.960.

You will observe that only selected critical values beyond 30 degrees of freedom are included in the table. For many experiments, particularly those employing sample sizes larger than 30, the exact critical values of t are not included. This situation rarely poses a problem for the investigator, however. In such cases we recommend that the critical t value be based upon the number of degrees of freedom in the table that is closest in value to but smaller than the degrees of freedom associated with the calculated t.

As an example, in the McCarthy and Betz experiment each t test on the CRF scores was based on 105 degrees of freedom (as $n_1 + n_2 - 2 = 54 + 53 - 2 = 105$). The table shows critical t values for 60 and 120 df but none between. Thus, following our recommendation, we would use 60 df to determine the critical t (which is 2.000 for $\alpha = .05$) instead of 120 df. This procedure makes the t test slightly more conservative, because the actual significance level used is somewhat smaller than .05. That is, the critical value of t for 60 df is somewhat larger than the critical value for 105 df. If 120 df were used to define the critical value instead, then the significance level would be slightly larger than .05. For the McCarthy and Betz data, the calculated t of 2.172 (see Table 7–4) from the expertness scores exceeds the critical values for both 60 df (2.000) and 120 df (1.980). If the obtained t lies in the rejection region for 60 df, then, of course it will also be in the rejection region for 105 df.[10] Should the calculated t value fall between the tabled values for the next lower (e.g., 60) and the next higher (e.g., 120) df, then a more accurate critical value can be interpolated from the tabulated values.

One-tailed versus two-tailed tests   The t test we have described and illustrated is sometimes referred to as a **nondirectional** or **two-tailed test.** It is so named because the null hypothesis will be rejected and the alternative hypothesis accepted if the calculated t value falls in a rejection region in either tail of the t distribution. Some authors (e.g., Jones, 1952) have argued that when the research hypothesis is directional and a specific relationship is predicted among the means (e.g., $\overline{X}_1 > \overline{X}_2$), then a directional or one-tailed test may be used. In a one-tailed test the rejection region is established in only one tail of the t distribution. Thus, rather

---

[10]The true critical t value for 105 df at $\alpha = .05$ is 1.983, although by linear interpolation of the tabled values for 60 df and 120 df the critical t value becomes 1.985. Either of these values, however, is smaller than the tabled value of t for 60 df (2.000) but larger than the value for 120 df (1.980).

than splitting the value of the significance level between two tails as we have described, a rejection region encompassing the total value of α is established in the tail of the t distribution that corresponds to the direction of the outcome predicted by the research hypothesis.

The advantage of using a directional t test is that a smaller critical value of t is necessary for rejecting H_0, because the entire rejection region lies in only one tail of the distribution. Thus, it is "easier" to reject H_0 in that a smaller difference between sample means will result in a t falling into the rejection region. This advantage poses a problem, however. Remember that the decision to adopt a one-tailed or two-tailed rejection region (and, hence, to conduct a directional or nondirectional t test) must be made before the data are collected and analyzed. If a one-tailed rejection region is adopted, then the experimenter cannot reject the null hypothesis from a difference in means that is in the direction opposite to that hypothesized, because no rejection region for such an outcome has been established. Therefore, it is not appropriate to make any statement about whether the two means differ significantly.

One appealing but wholly unjustifiable strategy is to conduct a one-tailed test if a calculated t narrowly misses statistical significance with a two-tailed test. The problem with such a procedure is that the significance level for the experiment is actually greater than the adopted alpha level. If the calculated t falls into the rejection region in the one-tailed test but not in the two-tailed test, then the probabilities of t in the rejection regions for both tests determine the actual significance level. For example, where the significance level adopted for both the two-tailed and one-tailed test is .05, the actual probability of making a Type I error is closer to .075. Thus, conducting both a two-tailed and a one-tailed test on the same data is hedging on one's predictions and is statistically dishonest.

We recommend that a two-tailed t test be used routinely whether the research hypothesis states a specific outcome or not. We agree with Kimmel (1957), who suggests that a one-tailed test should be used only when one of these three situations exists:

- A difference in the direction opposite to that predicted in the research hypothesis is psychologically meaningless.
- A difference in the opposite direction from that predicted would not affect the future behavior of the experimenter or others working on the problem.
- Results opposite to those predicted by the research hypothesis *cannot* be predicted from any other existing theoretical formulation of the problem.

It seems quite evident that stringent application of these criteria would rule out most potential uses of a one-tailed test in experimental research.

Another problem with a one-tailed t test is that the appropriate sampling distribution of t may be unknown if only positive or only negative t values are considered in establishing a rejection region. Gaito (1977) argues that the sampling distribution of t is developed under a null hypothesis assuming that both positive and negative t values are equally likely occurrences.

Finally, the most widely used statistical test in psychological research for comparing means is a nondirectional test only. The analysis of variance (which we discuss in Chapter 8) is an alternative to the *t* test when comparing two sample means. All values of the test statistic *F* for the analysis of variance are positive, regardless of the direction of the difference between sample means. Thus, there is only one rejection region for all outcomes, whether they are in the hypothesized direction or not.

For the various reasons we have just given, we maintain that rejection regions for the *t* test should routinely be established in both tails of the sampling distribution. Unless there are compelling reasons to do otherwise, we suggest that only a nondirectional or two-tailed *t* test should be used.

Decisions about Statistical Hypotheses

The *t* value of 2.172 calculated from the McCarthy and Betz CRF expertness scores is larger than the tabled critical value of 2.000 and therefore falls into the rejection region for the .05 significance level. Following the decision-making rules discussed earlier in this chapter, the two statistical decisions are then to *reject H_0* and *accept H_1*. From these decisions, it is inferred that the two sample means (63.1 and 68.5) are not estimates of identical population means and that the difference between them is most probably due to something other than mere sampling error. The difference between the sample means is regarded as statistically significant at the .05 level, or, in other words, "The means differ significantly at the .05 level."

If the calculated *t* were smaller than the critical value, then of course just the opposite statistical decisions and inferences would be made. The *t* would not lie within the rejection region, and the decisions would be *fail to reject H_0* and *do not accept H_1*. In such a case it is inferred that the two sample means are estimates of the same population mean and probably differ only because of sampling error. Accordingly, it is appropriate to state that there is no statistically significant difference between the means at the .05 level; or, "The means do not differ significantly at the .05 level."

Reporting Results of Statistical Analysis

In any journal report a brief textual presentation of the data analysis is given in the Results section. Usually concise, the presentation reports both the relevant descriptive and the inferential statistics. We present an example of how the results of the analysis of the CRF expertness ratings might be described in a journal report following the format adopted by journals published by the American Psychological Association:

The mean expertness ratings for the self-disclosing and self-involving conditions were 63.1 ($SD = 14.63$) and 68.5 ($SD = 11.06$), respectively. The means differed significantly, $t(105) = 2.172, p < .05$.

This presentation of the results conveys considerable information about the experiment to the informed reader. Let us see why by examining each of the components of the report of the t test separately:

$t(105)$ identifies the *name of the test statistic* as the t. Therefore, we know that a t test was used to analyze the data, and because a t test may be used to compare only two sample means, two levels of an independent variable were employed in the experiment. The *degrees of freedom* for the test statistic are shown in parentheses. In this example, if we know a between-subjects design was employed for the experiment, then we know that scores were analyzed from 107 different participants (because $df = N - 2$).

$= 2.172$ gives the *calculated value* of the test statistic (not the tabled critical value).

$p < .05$ tells us that (a) the *null hypothesis was rejected;* (b) a .05 *probability level* for alpha was adopted; (c) it is inferred that more than sampling error was responsible for the obtained difference in sample means; and (d) the difference in sample means is "statistically significant" (at the .05 level). The "less than" ($<$) sign indicates that the probability of obtaining the calculated value of t if H_0 were true is less than (or equal to) .05 by chance alone. Therefore H_0 was rejected and the result is statistically significant. If $p > .05$ were reported, then the "greater than" ($>$) sign would indicate that the researcher failed to reject H_0 and the means did not differ significantly at the indicated alpha level.

The same format is used to report the results of analyses using different statistical tests. In all cases, however, the name of the statistic, degrees of freedom, obtained value of the statistic, and the probability (i.e., alpha) level are identified.

The t test is a widely used statistical test for comparing two means, and it appears in the published psychological literature frequently. Therefore, we believe that it is important to understand the concepts of the t test. Another statistical test, however, the analysis of variance, is being used more and more frequently for comparing two means. Moreover, the two tests are closely related. We introduce the analysis of variance in the next chapter.

MANN-WHITNEY *U* TEST

The t test and the analysis of variance (discussed in Chapter 8) are, as we have stated, parametric statistical tests. That is, they use sample statistics (e.g., $\overline{X}$ and

s^2) to estimate the values of population parameters (μ or σ^2). Certain assumptions are made about the populations, for example, that the scores in the population are normally distributed, and the variances of the populations sampled are equal. Relationships among parameters are then hypothesized (e.g., H_0: $\mu_1 = \mu_2$) and used to develop the theoretical sampling distribution of the test statistic.

In some instances of research, however, it is not reasonable to assume that the data come from a normally distributed population or that the variances of the several treatment groups are equal. For example, in measuring the reaction time of an individual to a stimulus, a large majority of the measured reaction times are likely to be very short (e.g., perhaps about 500 milliseconds). No reaction time can be less than 0 seconds, but there is no upper limit on the maximum time that may be measured, and it is likely that a few individuals may have quite long reaction times compared to other people. Thus, distributions of reaction-time measures are very likely to be L-shaped—most reaction times are quite short, a few may be much longer. The frequency distribution of such scores is positively skewed and looks like a capital L.

Should the *t* test be used on such data? It is reasonably tolerant to moderate violations of some of its assumptions; i.e., it is "robust." We discuss robustness of parametric tests more fully in Chapter 8. Many psychologists would argue, however, that the *t* test should not be used in this case. Rather, they would propose using a nonparametric statistical test. Recall that nonparametric or distribution-free tests require no underlying assumptions about the shape of the distribution in the populations from which the samples were drawn, and they do not rely upon sample statistics to estimate any population parameters.

The Mann-Whitney U test is one nonparametric alternative to the *t* test for independent groups. It is an appropriate statistical test for analyzing data from a between-subjects design employing two levels of an independent variable. Before we develop the Mann-Whitney test, however, we will introduce an example experiment that requires a nonparametric statistical test and will also introduce the concept of ranking scores.

Perception of Ambiguous Figures: An Example Experiment

To illustrate the Mann-Whitney U test, we borrow from the research of Reisberg (1983) on the perception of ambiguous figures. Reisberg's work is based upon the theoretical formulation of perception as a cognitive task requiring working memory. Ambiguous figures are simply perceptual stimuli that involve two or more possible perceptual organizations. For example, Figure 7–6 illustrates the Schroeder staircase. This well-known figure has two possible perceptual organizations: In one, a set of stairs appears normal; in the other, the stairs seem upside down. (The stairs will reverse if you view them for a while.) If attention and memory are required to reverse the perception from one organization to the other, then an additional task that occupies attention and memory should prolong the

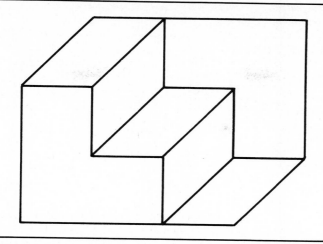

An example of an ambiguous figure, the Schroeder staircase.   **FIGURE 7–6**

amount of time needed to reverse the perception. To test this hypothesis, Reisberg formed two groups of subjects in one of his experiments. Both groups viewed the Schroeder staircase and were to report to the experimenter when they had seen both organizations of the stimulus. The independent variable was a type of interfering task. Subjects in the control group simply viewed the figure and reported the reversal. Subjects in the experimental group were required to count backward by threes from a three-digit number while they viewed the stimulus. It was hypothesized that this task required both attention and memory. Thus, if the perceptual task also required attention and memory, then the counting backward should interfere with its performance and delay the reports of a reversal. The experimenter timed how long it took the subject to make this report. If the subject did not report a reversal at the end of 2 minutes, the test was stopped for that individual and the subject assigned an "infinite" (∞) latency.

Table 7–6 presents hypothetical data for a similar experiment employing nine participants in each of the two treatment conditions. Notice that these scores do not appear to approximate a normal distribution, even if a considerably larger number of scores were to be obtained. Most of the latencies, particularly of the control subjects, are relatively short. For both conditions, however, several of the latencies are quite long, resulting in distributions appearing more L-shaped than normal. In addition, for the experimental group, because one subject did not report a reversal within two minutes, there is an infinite latency that cannot be assigned a numerical value. Either of these two conditions, the L-shaped distribution or the infinitely large score, produces a violation of the assumptions required of the *t* test. Thus, the *t* test is an inappropriate statistical test for these data. For this reason, Reisberg analyzed his data with the Mann-Whitney *U* test.

TABLE 7-6   *Hypothetical reversal latency scores (in seconds) for nine participants in each of two treatment conditions.*

Treatment condition	
No counting	*Counting backward*
(A_1)	(A_2)
2	4
5	10
6	11
8	12
9	14
13	17
15	85
21	98
42	∞[a]

Note. For ease of discussion, the scores are presented in order of increasing latency in each treatment condition. The raw data recorded from subjects as tested would not be so ordered.

[a] This score represents an "infinite" reversal latency; this subject did not see the reversal within the two-minute time limit.

Ranking Scores

Many nonparametric tests, including the Mann-Whitney U test, utilize a ranking of scores in order to develop a test statistic and a sampling distribution of that statistic. This is done even though the recorded scores may represent an interval or ratio level of measurement; the scores are converted to ordinal measurement by ranking them. The first step in ranking scores for the Mann-Whitney U is to combine the scores of both groups (for a total of N scores) and then place the scores in order of increasing magnitude from smallest to largest. In performing the ranking, the group identity of the scores should be maintained. Then the ranks from 1 to N should be assigned to the scores, giving the smallest score the rank of 1 and the largest score the rank of N. These steps are shown in Table 7–7 for the data of Table 7–6.

A simple intuitive statistical test on ranked data may be developed by examining the information in Table 7–7. Consider a statistic formed by summing the ranks of the scores for each group (i.e., ΣR_a). For the example,

$$\sum R_{A_1} = 1 + 3 + \cdots + 14 + 15 = 70, \text{ while}$$

$$\sum R_{A_2} = 2 + 7 + \cdots + 17 + 18 = 101.$$

The total sum of the 18 ranks $\Sigma\Sigma R_A$ equals 171 (i.e., 70 + 101). If a treatment has no effect, then one would expect that when the scores are combined and ordered

Illustration of the rank ordering of scores of Table 7–6.   **TABLE 7–7**

Latency scores ordered from smallest to largest	2	4	5	6	8	9	10	11	12	13	14	15	17	21	42	85	98	∞
Group identity[a]	1	2	1	1	1	1	2	2	2	1	2	1	2	1	1	2	2	2
Rank	1	2	3	4	5	6	7	8	9	10	11	12	13	14	15	16	17	18
Number of times an A_1 score precedes A_2 scores	9		8	8	8	8				5		4		3	3			
Number of times an A_2 score precedes A_1 scores		8					4	4	4		3		2					

[a] 1 indicates the score is from group A_1, 2 indicates the score is from group A_2.

(as they are in Table 7–7), the scores from each group would be approximately equally distributed over the rankings. That is, we would not expect the scores from one condition to be represented exclusively among the lower ranks and the scores of the other condition to be exclusively among the higher ranks. In other words we expect the total sum of the ranks (in our example, 171) to be split about equally between the two treatment conditions (e.g., $\Sigma R_{A_1} = 86$ and $\Sigma R_{A_2} = 85$).

On the other hand, suppose the treatment did have an effect and all the A_1 scores were of less magnitude than the A_2 scores. For our example, the ΣR_{A_1} would then equal 45 ($\Sigma R_{A_1} = 1 + 2 + \cdots + 9$) and the ΣR_{A_2} would equal 126 ($\Sigma R_{A_2} = 10 + 11 + \cdots + 18$). This outcome would certainly be rare by chance if the independent variable had no effect, but much more likely if the independent variable did affect behavior. The probability of such an outcome under chance conditions could be found simply by determining a sampling distribution for either ΣR_{A_1} or ΣR_{A_2}, for if we know $\Sigma\Sigma R_A$, then only one ΣR_A is free to vary.

The Mann-Whitney U test takes the general approach we have just developed but uses a test statistic called U. The U statistic is simply the number of times that the rank of a score in one group precedes the rank of a score in the other group. This approach is illustrated in Table 7–7. For example, the score of 2 from the A_1 group precedes all the A_2 scores in rank. Thus this score precedes 9 of the A_2 scores. Scores of 5, 6, 8, and 9 from the A_1 group each precede eight of the scores in the A_2 group. The total number of times that an A_1 score precedes an A_2 score in rank is 56 (i.e., $9 + 8 + \cdots + 3 + 3 = 56$). Thus, the value of U for the A_1 group is 56. The value of U may also be determined more simply by the formula:

$$U_{A_1} = n_{A_1}n_{A_2} + \frac{n_{A_1}(n_{A_2} + 1)}{2} - \sum R_{A_1},$$

where n_{A_1} is the number of scores in group A_1 and n_{A_2} is the number of scores in the A_2 group. Substituting values into this equation provides:

$$U_{A_1} = (9)(9) + \frac{9(9 + 1)}{2} - 70 = 56.$$

Obviously, there is also a value of U for the A_2 group. This value simply represents the number of times that the rank of an A_2 score precedes the rank of an A_1 score. This operation is also illustrated in Table 7–7 and the value of U_{A_2} is 25. This value may also be obtained from the formula:

$$U_{A_2} = n_{A_1}n_{A_2} + \frac{n_{A_2}(n_{A_1} + 1)}{2} - \sum R_{A_2}.$$

When values are substituted into this formula,

$$U_{A_2} = (9)(9) + \frac{9(9 + 1)}{2} - 101 = 25.$$

The U statistic varies identically with the $\sum R_A$ statistic we discussed earlier. If the treatment has no effect, then we expect the scores from each group to be equally distributed over the rankings and consequently the value of U_{A_1} about equal to U_{A_2} (in this example, about 40). If the treatment has an exceptionally strong effect, however, and all the A_1 scores have lower ranks than the A_2 scores (thus, $\sum R_{A_1} = 45$ and $\sum R_{A_2} = 126$), then the value of U_{A_1} is:

$$(9)(9) + \frac{9(9 + 1)}{2} - 45 = 81,$$

and the value of U_{A_2} equal to

$$(9)(9) + \frac{9(9 + 1)}{2} - 126 = 0.$$

Such values of U would, of course, be quite unlikely by chance alone. Thus, if an experimenter obtains a U equal to 0, he or she would be likely to reject a hypothesis of chance occurrence for this outcome.

Notice that the values of U_{A_1} and U_{A_2} are perfectly inversely related. As U_{A_1} increases, U_{A_2} must decrease by an equal amount. Hence, only one value of U, most typically the smaller value, need be calculated. One can easily determine if the smaller value has been calculated by using the relation:

$$U_{A_2} = n_{A_1}n_{A_2} - U_{A_1}.$$

In our example we could thus find U_{A_2} from U_{A_1} by

$$U_{A_2} = (9)(9) - 56 = 81 - 56 = 25,$$

and this is the smaller of the two values of U for these data.

***Critical values of* U**   The sampling distribution for the smaller value of U for groups ranging in size from 1 to 20 for $\alpha = .01$ and $\alpha = .05$ is presented in Appendix Table A–5. The null hypothesis H_0 under which the sampling distribution of U is developed is:

H_0:   The population distribution of A_1 scores is identical to the population distribution of A_2 scores.

The alternative hypothesis is simply:

H_1:   The population distribution of A_1 scores is not identical to the population distribution of A_2 scores.

Obtained values of U *equal to* or *smaller than* the tabled critical values of U are statistically significant for the value of α selected. For the example data with $U_{A_2} = 25$, $n_{A_1} = 9$, $n_{A_2} = 9$, and $\alpha = .05$ (two-tailed test) the critical value of U is 17. Because the obtained value of U_{A_2} is larger than the tabled value of U, the value of U_{A_2} is nonsignificant. Thus, we fail to reject the null hypothesis at the .05 level for this test. In the actual experiment by Reisberg, however, with 20 subjects in each group, the obtained smaller value of U was 127. Entering Table A–5 for $\alpha = .05$ and $n_{A_1} = 20$, $n_{A_2} = 20$, the critical value of U is 127. The obtained smaller value of U is thus equal to the tabled value of U. Hence, the obtained value of U is statistically significant at the .05 level; the null hypothesis is rejected and the alternative hypothesis is accepted. From this result, Reisberg concluded that the counting-backward treatment increased the latency of reporting a reversal. Table 7–8 presents a summary of the steps we have just discussed in conducting the Mann-Whitney U test.

Characteristics of the Mann-Whitney **U** *Test*

As the null hypothesis for the Mann-Whitney U indicates, the U provides a test of equality of the population distributions from which the samples were selected. It does not test the equality of a parameter such as μ as does the t test. If a significant value of U is obtained, then it is likely, but not necessary, that the medians of the two populations differ. It is possible, however, for the distributions of the two populations to take on considerably different shapes yet have the same median values.

The U requires that the scores of the subjects be rank ordered. Thus, it assumes measurement of at least an ordinal level. In many instances, the raw data will reflect either interval or ratio levels of measurement and these measures will be converted to ranks for application of the Mann-Whitney U. The only other requirement is that the underlying dimension of the dependent variable be continuous in nature even though the actual measurements may be only ordinal in nature.

TABLE 7–8   *Computation and testing of the Mann-Whitney* U

Step 1.	Rank order the combined scores of both groups from the smallest score (rank = 1) to the largest score (rank = N). Maintain the group designation (A_1 or A_2) of each score. This ranking is illustrated in Table 7–7. If scores are tied, assign each of the tied scores the mean of the ranks they would have been assigned if they were not tied.
Step 2.	Find ΣR_{A_1} and ΣR_{A_2}.
Step 3.	Compute U_{A_1} $$U_{A_1} = n_{A_1}n_{A_2} + [n_{A_1}(n_{A_2} + 1)/2] - \Sigma R_{A_1}.$$
Step 4.	Compute U_{A_2} $$U_{A_2} = n_{A_1}n_{A_2} + [n_{A_2}(n_{A_1} + 1)/2] - \Sigma R_{A_2}.$$ or $$U_{A_2} = n_{A_1}n_{A_2} - U_{A_1}.$$
Step 5.	Choose the smaller of the two obtained values of U.
Step 6.	H_0: The distribution of scores in the population from which the A_1 scores were drawn is identical to the distribution of scores in the population from which the A_2 scores were drawn.
	H_1: The distribution of scores in the population from which the A_1 scores were drawn is not identical to the distribution of scores in the population from which the A_2 scores were drawn.
Step 7.	Choose a value of α.
Step 8.	Enter Table A–5 for the value of α chosen and n_{A_1}, n_{A_2} subjects to find the critical value of U.
Step 9.	If the obtained smaller value of U is less than or equal to the tabled U, reject H_0 and accept H_1. If the obtained smaller value of U is greater than the tabled U, fail to reject H_0.
Step 10.	If the group sizes are larger than twenty, refer to Bruning and Kintz (1977), McCall (1980), or Siegel (1956) for alternative computational methods.

Given these relatively few assumptions (which is characteristic of many nonparametric tests), compared to the assumptions required for the use of the *t* test, you may wonder why the *U* test (and other nonparametric tests) is not much more widely used. There are several answers to this question. In general, nonparametric tests are less likely to detect an effect of an independent variable than are parametric tests such as the *t* if the population distributions are indeed normal. That is, they are more likely to lead to Type II errors in this case. Nonparametric tests also typically provide different information than do parametric tests. For example, the *t* test leads to decisions about the equality of the population means, but decisions with the *U* test concern the equality of the population distributions.

Finally, for more complex designs, such as the factorial designs discussed in Chapters 10 and 12, there are often no nonparametric tests that provide as much information as do the appropriate parametric tests for these designs.

When Should a Nonparametric Test Be Used?

There are no hard and fast rules about when nonparametric tests should be employed. The example we used based upon Reisberg's experiment is an unusually clear-cut instance in which a nonparametric statistical test is necessary. One of the scores in this experiment was a nonnumerical infinite value. With such an infinite value, a mean or standard deviation of scores cannot be computed. Obviously then, a parametric test such as the t cannot be used on these data.

Other instances often are not so clear cut, however. For example, how much must the underlying distribution of a population of scores differ from a normal distribution before use of a parametric test is inappropriate? When are the variances of two or more populations considered to be unequal? Psychologists are not in agreement on the answers to these questions; consequently they often do not agree upon whether a parametric or nonparametric test should be used.

Willemsen (1974) argues that psychologists often employ nonparametric statistics when they believe their data do not meet the assumptions necessary for a parametric test. She further contends that many psychologists possess "a general attitude that dictates that research conclusions should be based upon as small a number of untested assumptions as can possibly be arranged" (p. 179). Consequently, when you read the literature of psychology you will find instances when you may disagree with the author of the research on the most appropriate type of statistical test, parametric or nonparametric, to be employed on the data.

We have devoted a considerable amount of discussion to introducing nonparametric statistics and their use, emphasizing the U test. The Mann-Whitney U provides an understanding of the rationale that is employed in developing nonparametric tests. Many of the other nonparametric tests that we introduce in later chapters use the approach of ranking scores and then using ranks to develop a test statistic. The assumptions for these other tests and their appropriate uses are also very similar to the U test. For these reasons, we shall introduce these tests in later chapters in far briefer form than the U.

SUMMARY

- The experimenter's dilemma is to decide whether differences between the sample means in an experiment are "real" differences due to the effect of the independent variable or chance differences due simply to sampling error. The dilemma is resolved by conducting a statistical test derived from a statistical model for the experiment. The statistical model provides a test statistic used to estimate the probability of chance differences between sample means.

- The use of statistical tests follows these steps:
  - ○ The value of a test statistic is computed on the data of the experiment.
  - ○ The sampling distribution of the test statistic under a null hypothesis is determined. The sampling distribution provides the probability of occurrence for values of the test statistic under an assumption of chance differences. A rejection region defined as the set of values of the test statistic that have a probability equal to or less than α is specified in the sampling distribution. The value of α is typically set at .05 (or .01).
  - ○ The null hypothesis (H_0) is rejected and the alternative hypothesis (H_1) is accepted if the obtained value of the test statistic falls into the rejection region.
  - ○ The rejection of a null hypothesis implies that the sample means are not estimates of the same population means. One possible explanation for the difference is, of course, that the independent variable had an effect and is responsible for the differences.
- Two types of potential errors are inherent in testing statistical hypotheses. A Type I error occurs when the null hypothesis is rejected although it is actually true. A Type II error occurs when the null hypothesis is not rejected although it is false. From a single experiment a researcher cannot know if the decision made about the statistical hypothesis represents one of these errors.
- The t test is an example of a parametric statistical test for comparing the difference between two independent means.
- The Mann-Whitney U test is a nonparametric alternative to the t test when the assumptions of the t are not met.

8

In this chapter we develop the principles of a statistical test known as the analysis of variance. Topics include:

- Partitioning a subject's score into components that are responsive either to the effect of the independent variable or to the effects of error variation
- Using these components to obtain two independent variance estimates of the population variance in scores
- Obtaining a test statistic, the F ratio, from the variance estimates
- Using the F ratio to make a decision about the likelihood of chance differences between sample means
- Applying the analysis of variance to the data of McCarthy and Betz

WHY YOU NEED TO KNOW THIS MATERIAL

The analysis of variance is the most widely used statistical test in the behavioral sciences. If you conduct research in psychology or read published reports of research in psychology you will undoubtedly need to use and understand analysis of variance techniques.

One-Factor Between-Subjects Analysis of Variance

The concepts of analysis of variance are fundamental to understanding the basis of much current psychological research methodology. Analysis of variance is by far the most widely used statistical test in psychological research; indeed, Rucci and Tweney (1980) characterize the analysis of variance as "the workhorse statistic of experimental psychology" (p. 166). The **analysis of variance** (abbreviated ANOVA, pronounced "An-Oh-Vah") is a statistical procedure that is used to compare two or more means simultaneously. If used to compare only two sample means, then the results of the analysis of variance are identical to those of a *t* test (see Chapter 7). But if three or more means are compared, then an analysis of variance is needed to determine the probability that the means vary as they do because of sampling error alone.

An understanding of analysis of variance also reinforces the strategies of experimental design discussed in Chapters 3 and 4. The analysis of variance statistical model makes it abundantly clear why researchers attempt to maximize the effect of the independent variable and to minimize the error variation that occurs within treatment conditions. By the end of this chapter you will see that issues of experimental design and statistical analysis are intimately intertwined. In fact, most of the research designs we present in later chapters are sometimes called **analysis of variance designs** because the designs are so closely tied to the analysis of variance model for statistical analysis of the data.

OVERVIEW OF ANALYSIS OF VARIANCE

The approach of the analysis of variance is to sort the variation among all scores in an experiment into components that contribute to the total variation. Essentially, an analysis of variance breaks down the total variation in scores into sources that reflect the systematic effects of an independent variable and the nonsystematic error variation among individual scores. This sorting of the total variation into systematic variance and error variance results in a test statistic called F; the F is named after Sir Ronald A. Fisher (1890–1962), a British statistican who developed the fundamental concepts of analysis of variance.

The test statistic F is a ratio between two variance estimates and may be stated generally as:

$$F = \frac{s^2}{s^2}.$$

Therefore, the F is a ratio of two estimates of the population variance of scores σ^2. The variance estimate in the numerator is derived from the variation in sample means. Recall from Chapter 7 that differences in treatment means result from sampling error and any systematic variation in scores resulting from the effect of an independent variable. Thus, the numerator of the F statistic reflects *systematic variation* as well as variation due to sampling error. The variance estimate in the denominator of the F ratio is based upon variation in scores within treatment conditions, or simply *error variation*. Accordingly, the test statistic F is essentially a ratio of systematic and error variance to error variance, or

$F =$ Systematic and error variance / Error variance.

According to the analysis of variance model, variation in scores due to a treatment effect is independent of variation due to error. If the independent variable has no effect, then the only variation among scores will be due to error; the variance estimates in the numerator and denominator will be about the same, and the F ratio should be about 1.00. When an independent variable has an effect, however, the treatments will increase differences among sample means. In this instance, the variance estimate of the numerator will be greater than that of the denominator and will produce an F ratio with a value larger than 1.00. Thus, the more F exceeds 1.00, the less probable it is that the difference in treatment means is due to sampling error alone.

ANALYSIS OF VARIANCE STATISTICAL MODEL

Constructing a Score

Deriving the analysis of variance and the resulting test statistic F begins by assuming a simple model or representation of an individual's score in an experiment. The model merely states that a score is determined by the effects of the particular treatment administered and the influence of "error" *added to* some baseline level of performance. The baseline level simply represents the typical behavior of an individual in the absence of a treatment effect. This additive model for representing an individual's score can be expressed as

Individual's = Base level + Treatment + Effects
score   effect   of error.   **(Eq. 8–1)**

Scores from ten individuals in a hypothetical experiment with two levels of an independent variable, factor A.   **TABLE 8–1**

Levels of independent variable (factor A)

	A_1	A_2
	13	16
	15	15
	13	13
	12	14
	14	13
$\bar{X}$	13.4	14.2
SD	1.14	1.30

Each of these components of an individual's score can be represented symbolically and expressed numerically. To explain, we introduce in Table 8–1 some sample data from a hypothetical experiment in which there are two levels of an independent variable and five scores in each treatment group.

The scores in Table 8–1 are represented symbolically in Table 8–2. The symbols are similar to those we used earlier. The independent variable is identified as factor A, with two levels, A_1 and A_2. A particular score for an individual is represented by X_i with a numerical subscript to identify the participant (e.g., $X_1, X_2, \ldots, X_{10}$). The sample means for each level of the independent variable are indicated by $\bar{X}_{A_1}$ and $\bar{X}_{A_2}$, or more generally by $\bar{X}_A$. The grand mean, which is the mean of all the scores in the experiment, is labeled $\bar{X}_G$. The number of scores in a level of the independent variable is represented as n_A, and the total number of scores in the experiment is represented by N. For Table 8–1 therefore, $n_{A_1} = 5$, $n_{A_2} = 5$, $N = 10$, $\bar{X}_{A_1} = 13.4$, $\bar{X}_{A_2} = 14.2$, and $\bar{X}_G = 13.8$.

Notational representation of scores from the hypothetical experiment with two levels of an independent variable, factor A.   **TABLE 8–2**

Levels of independent variable (factor A)

A_1	A_2
X_1	X_6
X_2	X_7
X_3	X_8
X_4	X_9
X_5	X_{10}
$\bar{X}_{A_1}$	$\bar{X}_{A_2}$

Using this general notation we can now represent the components of a score previously expressed in words in equation 8–1:

$$X_i \quad = \quad \bar{X}_G \quad + \quad (\bar{X}_A - \bar{X}_G) \quad + \quad (X_i - \bar{X}_A). \qquad \textbf{(Eq. 8–2)}$$

| Individual's score | = Grand mean | + Deviation of individual's treatment-group mean from the grand mean | + Deviation of individual's score from his or her treatment-group mean |

The grand mean is used to represent the "typical" performance of a participant before any treatment effect or error has acted upon his or her score. A treatment effect is expected to affect all individuals who receive a given level of the independent variable *equally* and either adds to or subtracts from the base score of the grand mean. Thus, a treatment effect, if it exists, changes the value of the treatment means. The treatment means will then differ from the grand mean. Hence, the difference $\bar{X}_A - \bar{X}_G$ reflects any effect of an independent variable (the treatment effect in equation 8–1). But, in addition to any treatment effect, the sample means will also differ from each other because of sampling error. Therefore, the deviation of any treatment-group mean from the grand mean reflects both a treatment effect and sampling error.

The deviation of an individual score from a treatment mean $X_i - \bar{X}_A$ reflects only error or chance variation in the experiment. This deviation was introduced in Chapter 6 in the discussion of the standard deviation and variance as measures of variability among scores within a group. Because any treatment effect is assumed to equally increase or decrease the scores of all individuals receiving that treatment, the treatment mean will change accordingly. Thus, the values of $X_i - \bar{X}_A$ reflect only error variation among the scores within a particular treatment condition.

Each score in Table 8–1 may be constructed numerically by substituting the appropriate values into equation 8–2. Let us illustrate this point for one of the scores presented in Table 8–1. For example, subject X_4 has a score of 12.0; this score may be constructed as follows:

$$X_4 = \bar{X}_G + (\bar{X}_{A_1} - \bar{X}_G) + (X_4 - \bar{X}_{A_1})$$
$$12.0 = 13.8 + (13.4 - 13.8) + (12 - 13.4)$$
$$12.0 = 13.8 + (-.4) + (-1.4)$$
$$12.0 = 12.0.$$

This example for an individual's score shows how the analysis of variance model constructs a score by adding together the influence of the several factors that are assumed to contribute to the measured performance of an individual in an experiment.

Deriving Variance Estimates from the Components of Scores

Partitioning a Score

The task ahead is to take this conceptualization of a score and use it to construct a test statistic. For this purpose, it is most useful to treat an individual's score as *deviating* (i.e., differing) from the grand mean of the scores in the experiment. We can do so by transposing $\bar{X}_G$ in equation 8–2 so that it is placed on the other side of the equals sign. Accordingly, we now obtain

$$X_i - \bar{X}_G = (\bar{X}_A - \bar{X}_G) + (X_i - \bar{X}_A). \qquad \textbf{(Eq. 8–3)}$$

Deviation of individual's score from the grand mean	Deviation of individual's treatment-group mean from the grand mean	Deviation of individual's score from his or her treatment-group mean

Using the score of X_4 for an example, equation 8–3 becomes:

$$12.0 - 13.8 = (13.4 - 13.8) + (12.0 - 13.4)$$
or
$$-1.8 = (-0.4) + (-1.4)$$
$$-1.8 = -1.8.$$

Equation 8–3 represents the partitioning of a score, for it separates the total deviation of an individual's score from the grand mean into the components or parts that determine the total deviation. The partitioning shows that an individual's score deviates from the grand mean as much as it does because of the *systematic effects of the treatment received* and because of the *unsystematic influences of error or chance factors*.

The benefit of partitioning a score into several components is that it establishes the basis for deriving the measures of variance necessary for the F statistic. Notice that each term in equation 8–3 is a deviation of a score or of a mean from a mean. Recall from Chapter 6 that a variance is expressed in the general form as

$$s^2 = \frac{SS}{n - 1}.$$

This formula suggests that if each deviation represented in equation 8–3 were squared for each individual and then summed over all individuals in an experiment, then the result would be a sum of squared deviations or SS that is the numerator of a variance estimate. From equation 8–3, three such SS can be obtained. The term $X_i - \bar{X}_G$ leads to SS_{Total}, which is a measure of the total variation of scores from the grand mean. The $\bar{X}_A - \bar{X}_G$ deviation leads to SS_A, which is a measure of *systematic variation* reflecting the influence of the independent variable. Finally, $X_i - \bar{X}_G$ leads to SS_{Error}, which is a measure of *error variation* only in the experiment.

Obtaining Sums of Squares

Let us illustrate how the partitioned scores are used to derive the sums of squares to be used in forming variance estimates of the F statistic. Table 8-3 illustrates the steps in computing the sums of squares for the ten scores shown in Table 8-1.

In Step 1 the scores of all ten subjects in the hypothetical experiment have been partitioned. In Step 2 the numerical values of the deviations are obtained following equation 8-3. Each of the positive and negative deviations is squared in Step 3.[1] Finally, the values of the squared deviations are summed over all individuals in the experiment in Step 4. The result, as expected, is the three sums of squares: SS_{Total}, SS_A, and SS_{Error}.

As shown in Step 4, the SS_{Total} is represented in notation by $\sum_{A=1}^{a} \sum_{n=1}^{n_A} (X_i - \bar{X}_G)^2$.

The double summation sign $\sum_{A=1}^{a} \sum_{n=1}^{n_A}$ merely indicates that the squared deviations $(X_i - \bar{X}_G)^2$ are to be summed over all individuals in each treatment group (from the first, $n = 1$, to the last, n_A, in a particular group) and over all groups (from the first level of the independent variable, $A = 1$, to the last level, a). Similarly, to obtain the SS_A value, the squared deviations of the treatment group mean from the grand mean are summed over all individuals in the experiment; accordingly, SS_A is represented by $\sum_{A=1}^{a} \sum_{n=1}^{n_A} (\bar{X}_A - \bar{X}_G)^2$. Finally the SS_{Error} is obtained by summing each squared deviation of an individual's score from the mean of his or her treatment group, or $\sum_{A=1}^{a} \sum_{n=1}^{n_A} (X_i - \bar{X}_A)^2$.

As shown at the bottom of Table 8-3, an important relationship exists among the sums of squares. The SS_{Total} is equal to the sum of SS_A and SS_{Error}. That is,

$$SS_{Total} = SS_A + SS_{Error}. \qquad \textbf{(Eq. 8-4)}$$

Or in notation,

$$\sum_{A=1}^{a} \sum_{n=1}^{n_A} \left(X_i - \bar{X}_G\right)^2 = \sum_{A=1}^{a} \sum_{n=1}^{n_A} \left(\bar{X}_A - \bar{X}_G\right)^2 + \sum_{A=1}^{a} \sum_{n=1}^{n_A} \left(X_i - \bar{X}_A\right)^2. \qquad \textbf{(Eq. 8-5)}$$

By using SS values to reflect the variation in scores in an experiment, it can be seen that the total variation (SS_{Total}) is the result of systematic variation that occurs between groups receiving different treatments (SS_A, sometimes identified as $SS_{Between\ groups}$) and error variation that occurs within groups of participants receiving the same treatment (SS_{Error}, sometimes expressed as $SS_{Within\ groups}$). Thus, the analysis of variance enables a researcher to break down the total variation in scores into two unique and independent sources of variation.

---

[1]Recall from Chapter 7 that simply adding up the positive and negative deviations over all scores will lead to values of 0 for each component. One of the properties of a mean is that the deviations about it always sum to 0. Squaring the deviations prior to summing avoids this difficulty.

Step 1: Partition scores for the ten subjects (see Table 8–1)

	$X_i - \bar{X}_G$	$=$	$(\bar{X}_A$	$-$	$\bar{X}_G)$	$+$	$(X_i - \bar{X}_A)$
	$13 - 13.8$	$=$	$(13.4$	$-$	13.8	$+$	$(13 - 13.4)$
Subjects	$15 - 13.8$	$=$	$(13.4$	$-$	$13.8)$	$+$	$(15 - 13.4)$
in A_1	$13 - 13.8$	$=$	$(13.4$	$-$	$13.8)$	$+$	$(13 - 13.4)$
	$12 - 13.8$	$=$	$(13.4$	$-$	$13.8)$	$+$	$(12 - 13.4)$
	$14 - 13.8$	$=$	$(13.4$	$-$	$13.8)$	$+$	$(14 - 13.4)$
	$16 - 13.8$	$=$	$(14.2$	$-$	$13.8)$	$+$	$(16 - 14.2)$
Subjects	$15 - 13.8$	$=$	$(14.2$	$-$	$13.8)$	$+$	$(15 - 14.2)$
in A_2	$13 - 13.8$	$=$	$(14.2$	$-$	$13.8)$	$+$	$(13 - 14.2)$
	$14 - 13.8$	$=$	$(14.2$	$-$	$13.8)$	$+$	$(14 - 14.2)$
	$13 - 13.8$	$=$	$(14.2$	$-$	$13.8)$	$+$	$(13 - 14.2)$

Step 2: Perform the subtractions in Step 1 to obtain deviations

$$X_i - \bar{X}_G = (\bar{X}_A - \bar{X}_G) + (X_i - \bar{X}_A)$$

	-0.8	$=$	-0.4	$+$	-0.4
Subjects	$+1.2$	$=$	-0.4	$+$	$+1.6$
in A_1	-0.8	$=$	-0.4	$+$	-0.4
	-1.8	$=$	-0.4	$+$	-1.4
	$+0.2$	$=$	-0.4	$+$	$+0.6$
	$+2.2$	$=$	$+0.4$	$+$	$+1.8$
Subjects	$+1.2$	$=$	$+0.4$	$+$	$+0.8$
in A_2	-0.8	$=$	$+0.4$	$+$	-1.2
	$+0.2$	$=$	$+0.4$	$+$	-0.2
	-0.8	$=$	$+0.4$	$+$	-1.2

Step 3: Square each deviation

	$(X_i - \bar{X}_G)^2$	$(\bar{X}_A - \bar{X}_G)^2$	$(X_i - \bar{X}_A)^2$
	0.64	0.16	0.16
Subjects	1.44	0.16	2.56
in A_1	0.64	0.16	0.16
	3.24	0.16	1.96
	0.04	0.16	0.36
	4.84	0.16	3.24
Subjects	1.44	0.16	0.64
in A_2	0.64	0.16	1.44
	0.04	0.16	0.04
	0.64	0.16	1.44

Step 4: Sum the squared deviations over all subjects

$$\sum_{A=1}^{a} \sum_{n=1}^{n_A} \left(X_i - \bar{X}_G\right)^2 = \sum_{A=1}^{a} \sum_{n=1}^{n_A} \left(\bar{X}_A - \bar{X}_G\right)^2 + \sum_{A=1}^{a} \sum_{n=1}^{n_A} \left(X_i - \bar{X}_A\right)^2$$

13.60	$=$	1.60	$+$	12.00
SS_{Total}	$=$	SS_A	$+$	SS_{Error}

The derivation of *SS* values is the major computational procedure involved in analysis of variance. In practice it is unlikely that one would perform the necessary calculations following the steps presented in Table 8–3. Instead, alternative computational formulas are commonly used to obtain the *SS* values, and we illustrate them later in this chapter.[2] The steps shown in Table 8–3, however, should help you to understand the concept of sums of squares as used in analysis of variance; the computational formulas do not easily lead to this understanding.

Determining Degrees of Freedom

Recall that a sample variance s^2 is defined as $SS/(n - 1)$. In Chapter 6 we stated that the sums of squares are divided by $n - 1$ rather than by n so that the sample variance will provide an unbiased estimate of the population variance σ^2. More generally, as introduced in Chapter 7 (p. 180), $n - 1$ corresponds to the degrees of freedom (*df*) in the variance estimate. As you will recall, the term *degrees of freedom* refers to the number of values that are free to vary in the computation of a statistic.

The formula for a sample variance that provides an unbiased estimate of the population variance can thus be expressed more generally as $s^2 = SS/df$. Using this formula for a variance, we can see that if the appropriate *df* are known, then equation 8–4 permits one to obtain three different variance estimates from the sum of squares of the scores in an experiment. The required *df* are easily determined simply by applying the definition of degrees of freedom to each of the sums of squares components of equation 8–4: SS_{Total}, SS_A, and SS_{Error}. We consider the degrees of freedom for each of these sources in turn.

Total degrees of freedom   To compute the total sum of squares SS_{Total}, the grand mean $\overline{X}_G$ must be known. Because the total sum of squares is based upon the deviation of every score in the experiment from the grand mean, then one less than the total number of scores are free to vary. To illustrate, refer to the data in Table 8–1. The grand mean $\overline{X}_G$ for the ten scores is 13.8. To derive the SS_{Total} the grand mean is subtracted from each of the ten scores. Because the grand mean is based upon the ten scores and the sum of the ten $(X_i - \overline{X}_G)$ deviations must equal 0, then one less than the total number of scores are free to vary. Thus, any nine of the ten scores are free to vary, but the tenth score is fixed. Consequently, there are nine *df* associated with the SS_{Total}. More generally, the total degrees of freedom, or df_{Total}, are equal to one less than the total number of scores analyzed. In notation, $df_{Total} = N - 1$.

Degrees of freedom for SS_A The SS_A is computed from the deviations of the means of the treatment conditions (e.g., $\overline{X}_{A_1}$ and $\overline{X}_{A_2}$) from the grand mean $\overline{X}_G$.

---

[2]Simplified computational procedures to obtain *SS* values for this research design are also found in Bruning and Kintz (1977, pp. 24–27) and in Linton and Gallo (1975, pp. 138–144).

For a research design with two levels of the independent variable and an equal number of scores in each condition, if the grand mean is known, then only one treatment mean is free to vary. For example, where $\bar{X}_G = 13.8$ and $\bar{X}_{A_1} = 13.4$, as in Table 8–1, then $\bar{X}_{A_2}$ is fixed; it must equal 14.2. Any other value of $\bar{X}_{A_2}$ would not be consistent with a grand mean $\bar{X}_G$ of 13.8. Accordingly, there is 1 *df* for SS_A in the example. In general, the *df* for SS_A are equal to one less than the number of levels of the independent variable. In notation, $df_A = a - 1$, where a represents the number of levels of the independent variable A.

***Degrees of freedom for* SS_{Error}** The SS_{Error} is obtained by subtracting the mean of each treatment condition $\bar{X}_A$ from the scores of all individuals within the treatment condition for all the treatment conditions in the experiment. Thus, for each level of the independent variable, once $\bar{X}_A$ is determined only $n - 1$ scores are free to vary within that level. In Table 8–1, only four of the five scores are free to vary within each treatment condition A_1 and A_2. Because there are two levels of the independent variable and four scores are free to vary within each of the levels, there are 8 *df* associated with the SS_{Error} (4 *df* for A_1 plus 4 *df* for A_2). More generally, where a represents the number of levels of the independent variable and n the number of scores within each level of the independent variable, $df_{Error} = a(n - 1)$. Because $(a)(n)$ equals the total number of scores (N), this product may be expressed more simply as the total number of scores minus the number of levels of the independent variable, or $df_{Error} = N - a$.

Additivity of degrees of freedom The degrees of freedom are additive in the same manner as the corresponding sums of squares values. Thus, for this analysis of variance model,

$$df_{Total} = df_A + df_{Error}.$$

In the example, $9 = 1 + 8$.

Calculating variance estimates from SS *and* df: *Mean squares*

We defined a variance estimate s^2 as the sum of squared deviations divided by the degrees of freedom, or $s^2 = SS/df$. Notice that in a sense, a variance estimate is literally a mean squared deviation, for the *sum* of the squared deviations involved in the estimate is divided by the *number* of them (except for those which are not free to vary). Not unreasonably, then, in analysis of variance a variance estimate is usually called a mean square (abbreviated MS). **Mean square** is simply another term for variance estimate, but its use is unique to analysis of variance. Although the terminology may be initially confusing, just keep in mind that a mean square is merely a variance estimate by another name.[3]

[3]The use of the term *variance estimate* in place of *mean square* is gaining limited acceptance in statistical texts. The term *mean square*, however, is still widely used in most texts and journal reports of research.

Following equation 8–4, the two *MS* values used to form the *F* statistic in a one-way between-subjects analysis of variance are derived from the various *SS* and *df* values calculated. One variance estimate, MS_A, is based upon the *systematic variation between groups,* and the other, MS_{Error}, is based upon the *error variation within groups*. More specifically, these mean squares are defined as follows:

$$MS_A = \frac{SS_A}{df_A}$$

$$MS_{Error} = \frac{SS_{Error}}{df_{Error}}.$$

Although it is quite possible to obtain a MS_{Total} by dividing the SS_{Total} by the df_{Total}, the value provides no useful information in the analysis of variance, and therefore it is not typically calculated. For the data in Table 8–1, then, $MS_A = SS_A/df_A$, which equals $1.60/1 = 1.60$; and $MS_{Error} = SS_{Error}/df_{Error}$, which equals $12.00/8 = 1.50$. The *F*-statistic for these data is thus equal to

$$F = \frac{MS_A}{MS_{Error}} = \frac{1.60}{1.50} = 1.07.$$

Summarizing an Analysis of Variance

The results of an analysis are frequently presented in a summary table, which identifies the *sources of variation,* the relevant *SS*, *df*, and *MS* values, and the *obtained value* of the test statistic *F*. Table 8–4 illustrates how such a summary table is organized. For your reference we have also presented in the table the formulas for each of the computations involved using the notation which has been introduced and explained in this chapter. A summary table of the numerical values for the analysis of variance performed on the data of Table 8–1 is presented in Table 8–5.

As we discussed in Chapter 7, the purpose of computing a test statistic such as the *F* ratio is to test a statistical hypothesis. This test allows one to make an

TABLE 8–4   *A notational summary of a one-way analysis of variance.*

Source	SS	df	MS	F
Factor A	$\sum\limits_{A=1}^{a} \sum\limits_{n=1}^{n_A} \left(\bar{X}_A - \bar{X}_G\right)^2$	$a - 1$	SS_A/df_A	MS_A/MS_{Error}
Error	$\sum\limits_{A=1}^{a} \sum\limits_{n=1}^{n_A} \left(X_i - \bar{X}_A\right)^2$	$N - a$	SS_{Error}/df_{Error}	
Total	$\sum\limits_{A=1}^{a} \sum\limits_{n=1}^{n_A} \left(X_i - \bar{X}_G\right)^2$	$N - 1$	Not calculated	

Summary of the analysis of variance on the scores in Table 8-1.   **TABLE 8-5**

Source	df	SS	MS	F
Factor A	1	1.60	1.60	1.07
Error	8	12.00	1.50	
Total	9	13.60		

inference about whether the treatment means differ by more than would be expected from sampling error alone; that is, whether the sample means are estimates of a single common population mean or of different population means. To understand specifically how this decision is made using the F ratio, it is necessary to know what factors in an experiment influence MS_A and MS_{Error}, and the nature of the sampling distribution of the F statistic. We turn first to a discussion of the factors that influence each MS value, and therefore, the value of F.

Mean Squares as Estimates of the Population Variance

As we have shown, mean squares are simply sums of squares divided by degrees of freedom. Consequently, the factors affecting the numerical values of the MS are the same as those which affect the SS. Thus the discussion of the population variances estimated by mean squares must necessarily be somewhat redundant with our earlier discussion of factors affecting the value of sums of squares.

MS_A

The MS_A is a variance estimate responsive to any differences in treatment means that result from the effects of the independent variable, or of any extraneous variable that may be confounded with the independent variable, as well as from sampling error. Let us see why.

The value of MS_A is given by:

$$\frac{\sum_{A=1}^{a} \sum_{n=1}^{n_A} \left(\overline{X}_A - \overline{X}_G \right)^2}{df_A}.$$

From this formula it is clear that the numerical value of MS_A depends upon the means of each level of the independent variable. If each treatment mean is identical to each other treatment mean and thus equal to the grand mean, then the value of MS_A is equal to 0. However, MS_A takes on values different from 0 whenever the means of two or more treatment groups are not equal to each other. As the values of $\overline{X}_A$ become more disparate from each other and, consequently, different from

Raw-Score Computational Formulas for the One-Factor Between-Subjects Analysis of Variance

The definitional formulas for the several sums of squares in an analysis of variance and the computation of *SS* and *MS* by partitioning scores, as in Table 8–3, provide the basis for a conceptual understanding of the analysis of variance. But this approach requires rather tedious computations that are very prone to error. Thus, for computing an analysis of variance in actual research, simplified computational procedures have been developed. These procedures give no conceptual insight into the analysis of variance, but they ease considerably the computations involved.

This section provides the computational format for a one-way between-subjects analysis of variance. We introduce a computational format that will be expanded in later sections to more complex research designs.

The computational formulas are based upon the raw scores, the total of the scores in a treatment (rather than the treatment mean), and the grand total of the scores in the experiment (rather than the grand mean). Accordingly, following the notational representation introduced in Table 8–2, an experiment with two levels of an independent variable *A* and five subjects in each level is represented as:

Levels of the independent variable (factor A*)*

Level A_1	Level A_2	
X_1	X_6	
X_2	X_7	
X_3	X_8	
X_4	X_9	
X_5	X_{10}	
T_{A_1}	T_{A_2}	G (grand total)

where

X_i = raw score of a subject
T_A = total of scores for a treatment condition
G = grand total of the scores
n_A = number of scores in a treatment condition
a = number of levels of independent variable A
N = total number of scores.

Three numerical terms are then computed using these values:

$$[1] = \sum_{A=1}^{a} \sum_{n=1}^{n_A} X_i^2 \qquad \text{the sum of all the raw scores squared}$$

$$[2] = \sum_{A=1}^{a} T_A^2/n_A \qquad \text{the sum of each treatment group total squared, divided by the number of scores in a treatment condition}$$

$$[3] = G^2/N \qquad \text{the grand total squared, divided by the total number of scores.}$$

Using these numerical values, an analysis of variance is computed as follows:

Source of Variance	SS	df	MS	F
Factor A	[2] − [3]	$a - 1$	SS_A/df_A	MS_A/MS_{Error}
Error	[1] − [2]	$N - a$	SS_{Error}/df_{Error}	
Total	[1] − [3]	$N - 1$	Not calculated	

To illustrate the computations, we use the example scores given in Table 8–1 for which an analysis of variance is summarized in Table 8–5.

Factor A	
Level A_1	Level A_2
13	16
15	15
13	13
12	14
14	13
$T_{A_1} = 67$	$T_{A_2} = 71$

$G = 67 + 71 = 138$

and $n_A = 5$, $a = 2$, and $N = 10$.

The values of the necessary numerical computational terms are:

$[1] = 13^2 + \cdots + 14^2 + 16^2 + \cdots + 13^2 = 1918.0$
$[2] = (67^2 + 71^2)/5 = 9530/5 = 1906.0$
$[3] = 138^2/10 = 19044/10 = 1904.4$

Then:

$SS_A = 1906.0 - 1904.4 = 1.6$
$df_A = 2 - 1 = 1$

$SS_{Error} = 1918.0 - 1906.0 = 12.0$
$df_{Error} = 2(5 - 1) = 8$

$SS_{Total} = 1918.0 - 1904.4 = 13.6$
$df_{Total} = 10 - 1 = 9$.

The summary of the analysis of variance is then:

Source	SS	df	MS	F
Factor A	1.6	1	$1.6/1 = 1.6$	$1.6/1.5 = 1.07$
Error	12.0	8	$12.0/8 = 1.5$	
Total	13.6	9	——	

The numerical values obtained by this computational approach are identical to those presented in Table 8–5, obtained from the definitional formulas of an analysis of variance.

the value of $\overline{X}_G$, the numerical value of MS_A becomes larger. The question we now ask is: Why would the treatment means for two or more groups in an experiment differ from each other when the subjects initially were randomly assigned to create equivalent groups? There are three reasons to be considered: (1) sampling error, (2) the effects of the independent variable, and (3) the effects of any extraneous variables that may have been confounded in the experiment. We consider each in turn.

Sampling error and MS_A We have stressed that all measurements of behavior possess some error that leads to variability among the scores obtained. A large portion of the error is due to attribute differences among participants, but as we have indicated, error variation also results from any difference that may occur from time to time in the procedure of the experiment, differences that may occur in the physical setting of the experimental situation, and from errors of measurement. Thus, as we demonstrated in Chapter 7, in any instance where different groups of subjects are formed, it is reasonable to expect differences among the group means on any dependent variable that might be measured, even if no independent variable is manipulated and even if the subjects are randomly assigned. Recall that random assignment of subjects creates equivalent groups, but not equal groups. Equivalent groups are formed when participants are assigned without bias, but this does not mean that the groups will be exactly equal in performance on the dependent variable before the independent variable is introduced. Because of the various sources of error in any experiment, some differences among the sample means of equivalent groups are expected even before the treatments are administered. As we know from Chapter 7, such chance differences in sample means are said to be due to sampling error.

Effects of the independent variable and MS_A If the independent variable does have an effect upon the dependent variable, then that effect will be reflected in differences between the treatment-group means. As an example, suppose that the effect of a particular level of an independent variable is to increase an individual's score by 4. If all scores in that level of the independent variable are increased by 4, then the mean for that treatment condition also increases by 4. This effect of the independent variable causes the difference between each treatment mean ($\overline{X}_A$) and the grand mean ($\overline{X}_G$) to increase. This increase is directly reflected, of course, in the value of MS_A, because MS_A is based upon the values of $\overline{X}_A - \overline{X}_G$. It is for this reason that MS_A is treated as the mean square associated with the systematic variance in an experiment or, in analysis of variance terms, with factor A, the independent variable.

Effects of confounded extraneous variables and MS_A Extraneous variables, as discussed in Chapter 3, are potential independent variables that, if not controlled, may systematically affect the dependent variable being measured. If an extraneous variable is allowed to systematically vary along with the independent variable, its effect will be to increase the size of the differences among the treatment means.

The effect of the independent variable, if any, is confounded with the effect of the extraneous variable, and both will inflate the $\overline{X}_A - \overline{X}_G$ deviations and therefore increase the size of MS_A. If confounding occurs, one cannot determine if a difference between the treatment means is due to the independent variable, the extraneous variable, or both. Of course, the experimenter does not want confounding to occur and will attempt to design an experiment so that it does not occur in order that MS_A will represent only sampling error and the effects of the independent variable.

MS *Error*

The MS_{Error} is an estimate of the population variance due only to error variation in an experiment. This result occurs because the numerical value of MS_{Error} is derived from the deviations of the individual scores from the mean of the treatment group that they are in; i.e., from the $X_i - \overline{X}_A$ deviations. These deviations should not be affected by the independent variable. If an independent variable does have an effect, a treatment should systematically change the scores of all the individuals who receive that treatment. Any systematic changes in scores occurring because of a treatment effect, however, will also be accompanied by a corresponding increase or decrease in the treatment mean. As an example, if the effect of a particular treatment is to increase each individual's score by 3 points on a test, then the corresponding treatment-group mean will also increase by 3 points. Thus, the deviation between an individual's score and the group mean, $(X_i - \overline{X}_A)$, will not change, and the value of MS_{Error} will not be affected by any influence of an independent variable. Hence, MS_{Error} is an estimate of the population variance due only to error variation in the scores. The factors affecting each mean square are summarized in Table 8–6.

Relationship of MS$_A$ *and* MS$_{Error}$

Both MS_A and MS_{Error} are unbiased estimates of the population variance of scores σ^2. This result occurs because in deriving each variance estimate, the sums of squares are divided by degrees of freedom rather than by the actual number of

Factors that affect mean squares in an experiment.   **TABLE 8–6**

Variance estimate	Affected by
MS_A	• Sampling error • Effect of the independent variable • Effect of any confounded extraneous variable
MS_{Error}	• Error variation in scores within treatment conditions

scores involved in computing the variance. As unbiased estimates, neither mean-square value should be systematically smaller or larger than the population variance when error alone is responsible for the variability in scores on which the estimate is based.

The two mean squares are also *independent estimates* of the population variance, which means that either mean square may change in value without affecting the value of the other. We illustrate how a treatment effect influences MS_A but not MS_{Error} and, therefore, why each variance estimate is independent, in Tables 8–7A and 8–7B.

In Table 8–7A we have presented the scores of Table 8–1, which were used to illustrate the steps involved in performing an analysis of variance (shown in Tables 8–3 and 8–5). Although we did not state it earlier, these scores simulate a situation in which the independent variable has no effect, for each sample was randomly selected from a population with a mean μ of 14.0 and a variance σ^2 of 4.56 (the population described in Figure 6–3). Therefore, each of the sample means (13.4 and 14.2) is an unbiased estimate of the same population mean (14.0); the difference between the sample means is due only to sampling error. The MS_A and MS_{Error} values in the summary table (1.60 and 1.50, respectively) are both smaller than the actual population variance they estimate; however, they are unbiased and

TABLE 8-7   **A. Analysis of variance on scores without a treatment effect.**

	A_1	A_2		Source	df	SS	MS	F
	13	16		Factor A	1	1.60	1.60	1.07
	15	15		Error	8	12.00	1.50	
	13	13		Total	9	13.60		
	12	14						
	14	13						
$\overline{X}_A$	13.4	14.2						

B. Analysis of variance on scores with a treatment effect of +2. The treatment added to scores is shown in parentheses.

	A_1	A_2		Source	df	SS	MS	F^a
	13	18	$(16 + 2)$	Factor A	1	19.60	19.60	13.07*
	15	17	$(15 + 2)$	Error	8	12.00	1.50	
	13	15	$(13 + 2)$	Total	9	31.60		
	12	16	$(14 + 2)$	*$p < .05$.				
	14	15	$(13 + 2)$					
$\overline{X}_A$	13.4	16.2						

[a]Significant values of F are indicated by a probability level footnote on a summary table.

independent estimates of σ^2. Because both samples were drawn from the same population, we would not expect them to differ greatly from each other and, as expected, the obtained F ratio of the mean squares, 1.07, is just slightly greater than 1.00.

Table 8–7B shows what happens to MS_A and MS_{Error} when the independent variable does have an effect. Here a treatment effect is simulated by adding +2 to each score in the A_2 column, thus increasing the sample mean $\overline{X}_{A_2}$ from 14.2 to 16.2. This result is equivalent to drawing the A_2 sample from a population with a μ of 16. Notice that as a result of this "treatment effect," SS_A is increased but SS_{Error} remains unchanged. Accordingly, the treatment effect produces an increased value of MS_A; as a result, the obtained F ratio in Table 8–7B is larger than the value in Table 8–7A (13.07 vs. 1.07).

As this demonstration shows, it is evident that if the independent variable has no effect upon the dependent variable and if no extraneous variable covaries with the independent variable, then only error will affect the MS_A and MS_{Error} values. Both mean squares are expected to be approximately equal, and, therefore, the F ratio should be equal to about 1.00. On the other hand, if the independent variable does produce an effect on the behavior measured, then the MS_A reflects the systematic variation contributed by the independent variable in addition to the existing sampling error. Consequently, the MS_A will be larger than the MS_{Error} and the F ratio will be greater than 1.00.

Statistical Decision Making with Analysis of Variance

As we explained in Chapter 7 and have seen with the t test, a conclusion about a research hypothesis is based upon the decisions made about null and alternative hypotheses in a statistical test. Two sample means, $\overline{X}_{A_1}$ and $\overline{X}_{A_2}$, may differ in an experiment. But before the researcher attributes the difference in means to the effect of the independent variable, a fundamental statistical question must be answered: What is the probability that the differences in sample means could be due to sampling error alone? Although the effect of the independent variable may provide a plausible psychological explanation of the possible differences in sample means, the researcher must first determine whether the difference in sample means is even sufficient to require such a nonchance explanation.

The F statistic enables the researcher to determine the probability that the differences obtained among two (or more) sample means would occur if sampling error alone were responsible for the differences. This result is accomplished by following the procedures for statistical testing described in Chapter 7: A null hypothesis H_0 and alternative hypothesis H_1 are formulated; a significance level (usually $\alpha = .05$) is selected that establishes a rejection region in the theoretical sampling distribution of the F statistic and determines the critical value of F; the F statistic is calculated on the data of the experiment; and, finally, a decision to reject or not reject H_0, and therefore to accept or not accept H_1, is made on the basis of comparing the obtained value of F to the critical value of F.

Null and Alternative Hypotheses

For an experiment with two levels of an independent variable the null hypothesis H_0 tested in an analysis of variance is that the populations from which the two samples were obtained are identical and hence have the same means μ. In notation, the null hypothesis may be written:

$$H_0: \mu_{A_1} = \mu_{A_2}.$$

The null hypothesis represents the situation that presumably exists if the independent variable has no effect.

The alternative hypothesis H_1 is stated simply as the negation of the null hypothesis:

$$H_1: \text{Not } H_0,$$

which states that the population means are not equal to each other. This is the situation that presumably exists if the independent variable does have an effect.

Theoretical Sampling Distributions of F

The decision to reject or not reject the null hypothesis depends upon how rare or unlikely an obtained value of the test statistic F would be if H_0 were true. As you recall, the *significance level* defines what the experimenter means by an improbable F value under the conditions of the null hypothesis. The significance level usually adopted in psychological experiments is $\alpha = .05$. Accordingly, the decision to reject or fail to reject the null hypothesis is made by determining whether the chance of obtaining the calculated F value is more than or less than 5 times in 100 when H_0 is true. If the probability of obtaining a particular F value under chance conditions is equal to or less than .05, then the usual decision is to reject the null hypothesis (at the .05 level of significance) and accept the alternative hypothesis.

The probabilities are determined by knowing the *theoretical sampling distribution* of the test statistic F. There is not just one theoretical sampling distribution of F, however. Instead, the sampling distribution of F depends upon the number of means compared and the number of scores in each treatment condition. More specifically, the sampling distributions of F, and therefore the probabilities associated with a particular value of F, differ with the degrees of freedom associated with the numerator and denominator mean squares of the F ratio.

A typical theoretical sampling distribution of F is illustrated in Figure 8–1. Unlike the test statistic t, the distribution of F is positively skewed. The lowest possible value of F is 0; this value would be obtained if all the sample means were equal to each other and the resulting MS_A value were 0. There is no upper limit to the values that F may assume. Indeed, theoretically, F may take on any value between 0 and positive infinity (∞). Because the probability of obtaining a value of F between 0 and positive infinity is 1.00, the area under the curve for any theoretical distribution of F is equal to 1.00.

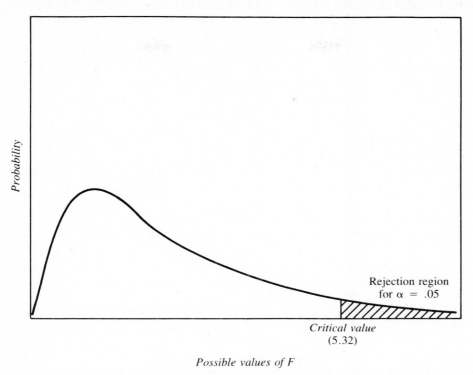

Theoretical sampling distribution of **F** *for 1 and 8 degrees of freedom and rejection region for a significance level of .05.*   **FIGURE 8–1**

Establishing the Rejection Region for F

If the independent variable has no effect and therefore the null hypothesis H_0 is true, then it is expected that the two variance estimates, MS_A and MS_{Error}, will be nearly equal; consequently, the resulting F ratio should be around 1.00.[4] If the independent variable does have an effect on the behavior and therefore H_0 is not true, then the resulting F ratio will be greater than 1.00, because MS_A will be larger than MS_{Error}. In order to reject the null hypothesis, then, the obtained value of F must thus be sufficiently greater than 1.00 so that the probability of such a value occurring if H_0 were true is equal to or less than the alpha level selected. Therefore, it is necessary to determine from the sampling distribution what large values of F would occur so infrequently by chance or error alone. These values lie

[4]The actual expected value of F under the null hypothesis is given by $df_{Error}/(df_{Error} - 2)$, where $df_{Error} > 2$.

in the *rejection region* for the test statistic. The rejection region for F always lies in the tail of the distribution, for only values larger than 1.00 will lead to rejection of H_0. The lower limit of the rejection region for F is defined by the *critical value* of F. Any obtained value of F that equals or exceeds the critical value falls into the rejection region. The probability of obtaining such a value of F if H_0 is true is less than or equal to α. The rejection region for a theoretical sampling distribution of F with 1 and 8 degrees of freedom associated with MS_A and MS_{Error}, respectively, and $\alpha = .05$ is also shown in Figure 8–1.

You should understand that for a particular significance level there is a different critical value of F for every possible theoretical sampling distribution of F. But determining exact critical values from a figure such as Figure 8–1 is very difficult; thus the critical values for the commonly used significance levels (.05 and .01) are presented in tables. (See Table A–2 in the appendix.)

Using the table of critical F values   To see how the tables of F are used, let us refer to the analysis of variance summarized in Table 8–7A. We analyzed hypothetical data on ten individuals who were assigned to one of two groups. Notice that there is 1 *df* for the MS_A and 8 *df* for the MS_{Error} in this analysis. To determine the rejection region it is necessary to find the critical value of F in the theoretical sampling distribution based upon 1 and 8 degrees of freedom.

For illustration, a section of a more complete table of critical F values for the .05 significance level found in Table A–2 in the appendix is presented in Table 8–8. As shown, tables of F values are arranged so that the degrees of freedom associated with the numerator (MS_A) of the F ratio (or df_1) appear in a row across the top of the table. The degrees of freedom for the denominator MS_{Error} (or df_2) appear in the column at the left side of the table.

To find the critical value of F for 1, 8 degrees of freedom, merely find the column with the value 1 designated for df_1 and then locate the value 8 in the row

TABLE 8-8   *Values of F for* $\alpha = .05$.

Degrees of freedom for denominator (df_2)	Degrees of freedom for numerator (df_1)				
	1	2	3	4	5
1	161.4	199.5	215.7	224.6	230.2
2	18.51	19.00	19.16	19.25	19.30
3	10.13	9.55	9.28	9.12	9.01
4	7.71	6.94	6.59	6.39	6.26
5	6.61	5.79	5.41	5.19	5.05
6	5.99	5.14	4.76	4.53	4.39
7	5.59	4.74	4.35	4.12	3.97
8	5.32	4.46	4.07	3.84	3.69
9	5.12	4.26	3.86	3.63	3.48
10	4.96	4.10	3.71	3.48	3.33

representing df_2. For these two degrees of freedom you will find a corresponding value of 5.32 entered in the table. This value is the critical value of the test statistic F, which defines the rejection region in this analysis of variance. It tells us that any calculated value of F with 1, 8 df that is *equal to or larger than* 5.32 lies in the rejection region, for such a value would occur on the average only five or fewer times in every 100 experiments if the null hypothesis were true.

Decisions about the Statistical Hypotheses

In the example from Table 8–7A, the obtained F ratio of 1.07 is smaller than the critical value (5.32) and does not lie in the rejection region. Accordingly, following the rules established in Chapter 7 for statistical decision making, we *fail to reject* H_0 and *do not accept* H_1. Therefore, we decide that the treatment means do not differ significantly at the .05 level and that the two sample means ($\overline{X}_{A_1} = 13.4$ and $\overline{X}_{A_2} = 14.2$) are estimates of the same population mean with the difference between them most probably due to sampling error.

For the analysis presented in Table 8–7B, however, we make just the opposite decisions about H_0 and H_1. In this instance, recall that we simulated a treatment effect by adding $+2$ to every score in the A_2 condition. The resulting obtained F ratio of 13.07 clearly exceeds the tabled critical value of 5.32. Because the obtained F value falls into the rejection region the statistical decisions are to *reject* H_0 and *accept* H_1. It is inferred, then, that the two sample means ($\overline{X}_{A_1} = 13.4$ and $\overline{X}_{A_2} = 16.2$) are not estimates of the same population mean and that the samples are representative of two different populations with means μ_{A_1} and μ_{A_2}, respectively. The null hypothesis is rejected because the obtained F of 13.07 would be a relatively rare occurrence if H_0 were true but a more likely outcome if H_1 were true. Therefore, it is decided that sampling error is an unlikely explanation for the obtained difference in sample means. Accordingly, in this example, there is a statistically significant difference between the treatment means at the .05 level. Table 8–9 summarizes the process of decision making in the analysis of variance.

Remember that when H_0 is rejected and H_1 accepted in an analysis of variance, a research hypothesis is not necessarily supported. The alternative hypothesis H_1 will be accepted if the sample means differ significantly in either

Decisions about the null (H_0) and alternative (H_1) hypotheses with analysis of variance. **TABLE 8–9**

Calculated value of F	*Decisions about* H_0 *and* H_1
Equals or exceeds the critical value (is in the rejection region)	Reject H_0 Accept H_1
Is smaller than the critical value (is outside the rejection region)	Fail to reject H_0 Do not accept H_1

direction, i.e., if $\bar{X}_{A_1} < \bar{X}_{A_2}$ or if $\bar{X}_{A_1} > \bar{X}_{A_2}$. The research hypothesis may specifically state the direction of the difference in means expected, but H_1 merely indicates that the means differ; it does not state the direction of the difference. Moreover, even if the sample means differ in the direction stated by the research hypothesis, the effect of the independent variable may not provide the only possible explanation, for the experiment may have been confounded by an extraneous variable; this issue is pursued in greater depth in Chapter 13.

It is clear that the answers provided by decisions made about statistical hypotheses and research hypotheses are fundamentally different. Before a scientific explanation for a difference between treatment means is introduced, it must first be established that such an explanation is needed. With statistical procedures, such as analysis of variance, statistical hypotheses are tested to determine *whether* sample means differ. Research hypotheses then provide a scientific explanation as to *why* the sample means differ.

Assumptions of Statistical Tests for Between-Subjects Designs

Parametric statistical tests such as the *t* test and the analysis of variance are based upon three formal assumptions about the scores. These assumptions are important because the sampling distributions of the test statistic, *t* or *F*, and therefore the probability values for the statistic (i.e., the critical values given in Tables A–1 and A–2) are generated from populations that meet these assumptions. Specifically, as we mentioned in Chapter 7, these assumptions are:

1.   The samples of the experiment are randomly drawn from a population of scores and each score is independent of each other score.
2.   The scores in the populations are normally distributed.
3.   The variances of scores in the populations are equal.

In practice, however, these assumptions are often not fully met in an experiment; that is, they are *violated*. Yet, researchers typically proceed to use the *t* test or the analysis of variance on the data. This approach raises the question of what assumptions are frequently violated and what the consequences of such violations are.

The subjects in experiments are seldom randomly drawn from any population. The failure to randomly sample does not alter the outcome of the *t* test or the analysis of variance, but, as we discuss more fully in Chapter 13, it limits the ease with which the results can be generalized. Although samples may not be randomly drawn, however, these statistical tests require each score in the experiment to be independent of every other score. That is, they assume that every subject contributes only one score in the experiment. If two or more scores are analyzed for an individual, then a different *t* test or analysis of variance model must be used. The statistical tests for this type of design are discussed in Chapter 11.

Violations of the second (the normal distribution of scores) and the third (the equality of variances, often called the *homogeneity of variances*) assumption can change the probability of obtaining a particular value of a test statistic. Consequently, the actual probability of making a Type I error differs from that established by the value of α.

Until relatively recently the analysis of variance was thought to be very "robust" against violations of these assumptions. **Robustness** means that violating the assumptions has little effect on the probability of obtaining a particular value of the test statistic and thus on the probability of making a Type I error. More recent work by Bradley (1980, 1984) and replications of that work by Wike and Church (1982) has challenged this robustness notion. Bradley argues that there is no one set of conditions under which these assumptions may be violated and the robustness of these tests ensured. Violations of the normality and variance assumptions are more likely to have minimal effects on the probability of making a Type I error, however, when the following conditions are met:

- The number of participants in each treatment condition is the same.
- The shape of the distributions of the scores for each treatment condition is about the same and the distributions are neither very peaked nor very flat.
- The value of α is set at .05.

ANALYSIS OF VARIANCE AND PRINCIPLES OF RESEARCH DESIGN

In Chapters 3 and 4 we stressed that the strategy of experimental design involved maximizing the effect of the independent variable, avoiding confounding by extraneous variables, and minimizing error variation. An understanding of the analysis of variance clearly reveals why these principles were emphasized. In order to reach the conclusion that an independent variable has an effect, the null hypothesis of the analysis of variance must be rejected. This event occurs when the systematic variance in an experiment is sufficiently large that sampling error is ruled out as an explanation for any differences found. As we have discussed, the value of the F ratio is directly responsive to both the effects of the independent variable and the amount of error variation. Increasing the effect of the independent variable increases the value of MS_A and decreasing error variation reduces the value of MS_{Error}. Both processes work to increase the value of the F ratio and thus to increase the likelihood that the null hypothesis will be rejected.

Of course, as we have stated, a confounded extraneous variable will also work to increase systematic variance, and the systematic variance contributed by the confounded variable cannot be separated from the systematic variance contributed by the independent variable. It is therefore clear that a flawed experimental design cannot be rescued by statistical analysis of the data. Experimental design and statistical analysis are closely related. As Fisher (1971) observed, "Statistical procedure and experimental design are only two different aspects of the same whole" (p. 3). Indeed, we believe that neither can be fully understood without an appreciation of the other.

ANALYSIS OF VARIANCE ON THE DATA OF McCARTHY AND BETZ

McCarthy and Betz used the t test as an inferential statistical test for their data. They could, however, have used the analysis of variance instead of the t test on their data. When there are only two levels of the independent variable, the t test and the analysis of variance may be used interchangeably. It is only when the independent variable takes on three or more levels that the analysis of variance necessarily becomes the preferred inferential statistical test.

An analysis of variance summary table for McCarthy and Betz's expertness scores of the CRF is presented in Table 8–10.[5] For $\alpha = .05$, the rejection region for an obtained value of F with 1 and 106 df is defined by values of F equal to or larger than 4.00.[6] The value of F computed on the expertness scores, 4.69, is larger than the critical value of F and hence falls in the rejection region. Thus the decision on the statistical hypotheses associated with this analysis of variance is to reject H_0: $\mu_{A_1} = \mu_{A_2}$ and to accept H_1: not H_0.

After the decision has been made to reject H_0 and accept H_1, the obtained outcome must then be compared to the predicted outcome to find whether the results agree or disagree with the research hypothesis. The decision to accept H_1 merely indicates that the two sample means do not estimate the same population mean. Is μ_{A_1} larger or smaller than μ_{A_2}? To make this decision the psychologist

TABLE 8–10   *Summary of analysis of variance on expertness scores in the McCarthy and Betz experiment*

Source	df	SS	MS	F
Counselor response (A)	1	790.21	790.21	4.69*
Error	105	17,700.95	168.58	
Total	106	18,491.16		

*$p < .05$.

[5]This analysis was conducted on the raw data presented in Table 5–1. As an exercise we suggest you conduct an analysis of variance on these scores using computational procedures.

[6]The exact value of F that defines the rejection region for 1 and 106 degrees of freedom is 3.93, but this value does not appear in tables of critical F values. Therefore, we went to the next smaller number of degrees of freedom in the table, 1 and 60, to obtain the critical value of 4.00. This procedure makes a slightly more conservative test of the analysis of variance, because essentially a significance level smaller than .05 is adopted. If the obtained value should be extremely close to the critical value, then the critical value can be interpolated from the table. But such marginal cases should not occur often, and therefore it is useful to find the critical value that corresponds to the next lowest number of df for the denominator of the F ratio.

must visually inspect the two treatment means.[7] We observe that $\bar{X}_{A_2}$ (the sample mean for the self-involving condition) is greater than $\bar{X}_{A_1}$ (the sample mean for the self-disclosing condition). Because $\bar{X}_{A_1}$ estimates μ_{A_1} and $\bar{X}_{A_2}$ estimates μ_{A_2}, it is concluded that μ_{A_2} is greater than μ_{A_1}. This is the only logically consistent conclusion that may be reached based upon the analysis of variance and visual inspection of the two means.

We have presented a much more extensive discussion of this analysis of variance and the interpretation of it than would typically be presented in a journal report of this research. Following the guidelines of the *American Psychological Association Publication Manual* (1983), the obtained values of the test statistic F, df, MS_e (i.e., the MS for the error term in the denominator of the F ratio), and significance level are reported in only a few sentences such as these:

> The mean expertness ratings for the self-disclosing and self-involving conditions were 63.1 ($SD = 14.63$) and 68.5 ($SD = 11.06$), respectively. The means differed significantly, $F(1, 105) = 4.69$, $MS_e = 168.58$, $p < .05$.

To summarize, then: From the analysis of variance on McCarthy and Betz's data we have concluded that the two treatment means for expertness scores do not estimate the same population mean and that the sample mean for self-involving responses estimates a higher population mean than the sample mean for self-disclosing responses. In comparison to the t test on these data, there are no advantages or disadvantages to conducting an analysis of variance; the decisions arrived about the statistical hypotheses are identical.

Relationship between t and F

We have pointed out that the t test and the analysis of variance are so closely related that they lead to the same statistical decisions when analyzing data from two treatment groups. If one were to reject the null hypothesis at the .05 level with the t test (two-tailed), then one would also reject H_0 with an analysis of variance on the same data. Moreover, if one were to conduct a t test, then the value of F from an analysis of variance on the same data can readily be determined without even computing the mean squares. The reason is that the test statistics t and F are related in such a way that $t^2 = F$ or $t = \sqrt{F}$. To illustrate this relationship, we see that the t value reported by McCarthy and Betz in the analysis of expertness scores is -2.17; when the t is squared the resulting value becomes 4.69, which is equal to the F calculated and reported in Table 8–10.

This relation also holds for the tabled critical values of t and F for the analysis of two sample means when the same significance level is adopted. As an example, for $\alpha = .05$ the critical value of F for 1, 8 df is 5.32. The critical value of t for 8 df and $\alpha = .05$ in a two-tailed test is 2.306, which is the square root of 5.32. Thus, $2.306^2 = 5.32$, and $t^2 = F$.

---

[7]If H_0 and H_1 had involved more than two population means, then a test of multiple comparisons would be used to determine which pairs of means differ significantly (see Chapter 9).

SUMMARY

- The analysis of variance is a statistical test used to determine whether the differences between two or more sample means may reasonably be attributed to sampling error alone.
- The analysis of variance partitions each subject's score into a component that reflects the effect of the independent variable and a component that is due to error. The components for each subject's score are squared, summed, and divided by degrees of freedom to obtain two variance estimates: MS_A and MS_{Error}.
- MS_A is responsive to sampling error, the effect of the independent variable, and any confounded extraneous variables.
- MS_{Error} is responsive to sampling error alone.
- The test statistic F is a ratio of two variance estimates; i.e., $F = MS_A/MS_{Error}$.
- If the obtained value of F falls into the rejection region of the theoretical sampling distribution of F, then the null hypothesis, $H_0: \mu_{A_1} = \mu_{A_2}$, is rejected and the alternative hypothesis, $H_1:$ not H_0, is accepted.
- Rejection of the null hypothesis implies that the differences among the sample means are rare occurrences under a null hypothesis that only chance is responsible for the difference. One possible inference from this decision is that the sample means differ because of the different treatments administered.

9

PREVIEW

This chapter extends the analysis of variance to experiments involving three or more levels of an independent variable. We also introduce multiple comparison tests and strength of association measures. Topics include:

- Computing F and its interpretation when there are three or more groups in an experiment
- The need for multiple comparison tests following analysis of variance
- Three multiple comparison procedures: the multiple F test, Tukey's test, and the Scheffé test
- The misuse of multiple comparison tests for data fishing
- Two measures of strength of association: η^2 (eta squared) and ω^2 (omega squared)
- The nonparametric Kruskal-Wallis one-way analysis of variance by ranks

WHY YOU NEED TO KNOW THIS MATERIAL

Many experiments employ three or more levels of an independent variable. A significant F ratio in an analysis of variance merely indicates that at least one pair of means differs. Follow-up tests are needed to determine exactly which means differ from the others. Strength of association measures are used to estimate the magnitude of the independent variable's effect. You will encounter these different tests and measures when you read published research articles in psychology journals.

One-Factor Multilevel Designs: Analysis of Variance, Follow-up Tests, and Strength of Association Measures

Our discussion of research design and analysis of data has focused on the simplest instance of an experimental design—a one-factor between-subjects design with two levels of the independent variable. In principle, however, there is no limit to the number of levels the independent variable may take on. The number of levels is determined by the research hypothesis being tested, the nature of the independent variable being manipulated, and the investigator's resources.

An extension of a one-factor between-subjects design to more than two levels (sometimes called a **multilevel design**) merely requires a straightforward application of the principles discussed in Chapters 3 and 4. The researcher attempts to *maximize* the effect of the independent variable, *minimize* the error variation, and *control* extraneous variables so that they do not confound the experiment. The descriptive analysis of data is identical to that conducted on an experiment with two treatments. The only new concepts associated with introducing three or more levels of the independent variable arise in the interpretation of the inferential data analysis.

Computing the analysis of variance is a simple extension of the analysis presented in Chapter 8. The new aspect of the analysis arises when a statistically significant F ratio occurs. A significant F ratio merely indicates that there is at least one significant difference among the several means being compared. But it does not indicate specifically which of the means differ. Therefore in multilevel experiments specific differences among various means must be determined by follow-up tests to the analysis of variance.

To illustrate the issues involved in multilevel experiments, we will introduce a new research area, dealing with tonic immobility in certain animals. We limit the design of the example experiment to only three levels of the independent variable, but everything presented in this chapter applies to any number of levels of the independent variable. To set the stage for the experimental example we briefly provide background information on tonic immobility.

TONIC IMMOBILITY AS A RESEARCH PROBLEM

A sometimes-reported observation of human behavior is that in periods of intense fear, people may "freeze" or become immobile in a particular position, even though it may be advantageous to do something else. People often use expressions such as being "scared stiff" or "frozen with fear." Similar behavior appears to occur in many animals—birds, fish, insects, reptiles, and possibly even primates—when they are suddenly restrained (Gallup, 1974). The phenomenon is sometimes called *animal hypnosis,* but is more specifically called *tonic immobility.*

The idea of animal hypnosis is very old; it is mentioned in the Old Testament of the Bible (Gallup, 1974), and an example of a tonically immobile "furiously

---

BOX 9-1   **Basic Research—A Comment**

Experimental psychologists often do not feel that they must be able to demonstrate practical applications for the results of their research. Their posture is that so-called *basic research* (as we might call the tonic immobility research) will provide greater knowledge of natural processes than will research on truly applied problems. No one can know all the potential applications of his or her research or even if the research will have any practical application. Certainly B. F. Skinner did not envision the myriad applications of his work in operant conditioning when he began his research on pigeons.[a]

Recently it has become fashionable to disparage basic research. Many newspapers carry brief columns decrying the senseless expenditure of tax dollars and often list several grants for research in the social sciences while asking readers to judge their merits merely by the title of the research. One member of the U.S. Senate even gave out so-called "golden fleece" awards to federally funded social science projects that he thought had no merit.

We think that the research we have described on tonic immobility is the kind of research that might invite a variety of criticisms on its value. At first glance, tonic immobility in chickens may not appear to have any relevance to human behavior. Suarez and Gallup (1979), however, have noticed very striking similarities in the behavior of animals in a tonically immobile state and the form of paralysis that appears to occur in victims during rape. Further, many similarities have been noticed among the characteristics of tonic immobility in animals and the catatonic stupor exhibited in certain forms of schizophrenia (Ratner, Karon, VandenBos, and Denny, 1981; Suarez and Gallup, 1979).

We do not know if knowing about tonic immobility in chickens will help psychologists to understand the behavior of rape victims or schizophrenic individuals. That is for the future to reveal. We do know, however, that criticizing research for its apparent lack of immediate relevance is a dangerous practice. No one can predict from what research the next major discovery in understanding behavior will spring![b]

---

[a]See Skinner (1960) for a delightful essay on an attempt to use pigeons as a guidance mechanism for a rocket-powered missile in World War II.

[b]A book by Pick, Leibowitz, Singer, Steinschneider, and Stevenson (1978) specifically addresses this problem and provides a variety of examples of applications from basic research in psychology.

exasperated hen" was reported by Daniel Schwenter in 1636 (Völgyesi, 1966). In recent years, a considerable amount of research has been done on the topic, and Suarez and Gallup (1979) summarize some characteristics of tonic immobility: profound motor inhibition, Parkinson's-like tremors, suppressed vocal behaviors, no loss of consciousness, apparent analgesia, reduced body-core temperature, abrupt onset and termination, and aggressive reactions at termination.[1]

A number of theoretical explanations have been proposed for tonic immobility; one current explanation is that the phenomenon may be the result of intense fear (Gallup, 1974; Thompson and Joseph, 1978). This view is based on the assumption that certain aversive or noxious environmental events will evoke an innate fear response and that immobility is one such innate response (Gallup, 1974).

One important environmental stimulus for enhancing tonic immobility seems to be the eyes of a potential predator. Research by several investigators (e.g., Gallup, Nash, and Ellison, 1971; O'Brien and Dunlap, 1975) indicates that viewing a potential predator's eyes may considerably increase a period of tonic immobility. Subsequently Gagliardi, Gallup, and Boren (1976) attempted to discover more specifically what feature of the eye was responsible for the increase in tonic immobility. They focused upon one variable feature, the size of the pupil in relation to total eye size. Because their work was exploratory, Gagliardi et al. did not state an explicit directional research hypothesis on the effect of pupil size in their paper.

To investigate the effect of pupil-to-eye-size ratio, Gagliardi et al., employed a between-subjects design with seven levels of the independent variable of simulated pupil-to-eye-size ratio. Their subjects, chickens, were randomly assigned to one level of the independent variable, and tonic immobility was induced by restraining the chicken for 15 seconds.[2] The appropriate eye spot was then presented to the immobile chicken and the duration of tonic immobility was measured. A clear effect for pupil-to-eye-size ratio was found; a simulated ratio of 11 to 20 led to a larger increase in tonic immobility than any of the other eye-size ratios.

EXAMPLE OF A MULTILEVEL ONE-FACTOR DESIGN

The example we introduce to illustrate a between-subjects design with three or more levels of the independent variable is modeled on the research of Gagliardi et

---

[1]If you are interested in pursuing the literature on tonic immobility, a special issue of *The Psychological Record,* 1977, Volume 27, Number 1, pages 1–218 was devoted to the topic.

[2]Almost all procedures for induction of tonic immobility utilize some form of manual restraint. Gagliardi et al. used the procedure of placing the chicken on its right side and gently holding it down for 15 seconds. The period of tonic immobility began after the chicken was released and continued until the chicken righted itself. Based upon the data from their article, periods of tonic immobility in excess of 190 seconds occurred in some treatment conditions.

al. (1976). To simplify the presentation, however, we use only three levels of the independent variable of pupil-to-eye-size ratio. For the experiment, pupil-to-eye-size ratios of 6/20, 11/20, and 15/20 were used, with ten chickens randomly assigned to each treatment condition. Figure 9–1 illustrates the eye spots. Assume that the basic tonic immobility procedure of Gagliardi et al. was followed and that the hypothetical data presented in Table 9–1 were obtained.

Analyzing Data of a Multilevel Experiment

The data analysis for multilevel one-factor between-subject designs proceeds just as it did for the two-level design discussed in Chapters 5, 6, and 8; it begins with a descriptive analysis and is followed by an analysis of variance.

Descriptive Statistics

The means and standard deviations of the duration of tonic immobility for each level of the independent variable are presented in Table 9–2. Differences among these means reflects the treatment effect, if any, in the experiment. Again, how-

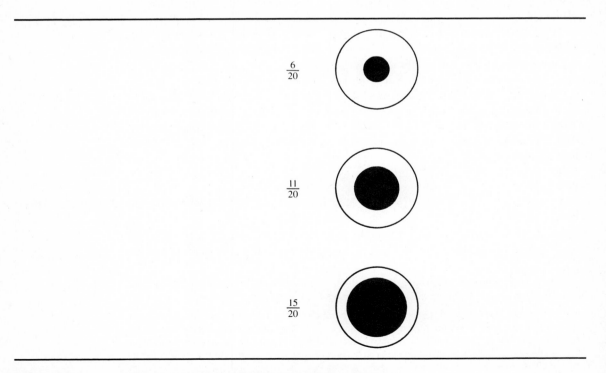

FIGURE 9–1   *The eyespots used in the tonic immobility experiment.*

Hypothetical duration of tonic immobility scores (in seconds) for each chicken as a function of pupil-to-eye-size ratios.   **TABLE 9–1**

Pupil-to-eye-size ratio		
6/20	11/20	15/20
72	117	103
89	98	96
117	139	113
78	121	94
108	148	122
96	104	130
103	132	92
84	133	108
92	112	98
81	126	104

ever, any systematic differences appear against a background of sampling error. From the raw data of Table 9–1 and the standard deviations of Table 9–2, it is apparent that there is considerable variation among the scores within a level of the independent variable as well as substantial overlap among the scores across treatment conditions. Clearly, a simple visual inspection of the means is insufficient to decide whether or not the obtained differences among the means reflect systematic variation or only chance differences due to sampling error.

Inferential Statistics: Analysis of Variance

The inferential statistical test appropriate for the multilevel one-factor design is again the analysis of variance. The partitioning of sources of variance and computations involved is identical to those for comparing two groups, except that, in this instance, the sums of squares are computed on the scores of participants in three treatment groups. For computation, the steps outlined in Chapter 8 (pp. 212 to 213) may be followed. An analysis of variance summary table for the data of Table 9–1 is presented in Table 9–3.

Means (M) and standard deviations (SD) of tonic immobility scores (in seconds) as a function of pupil-to-eye-size ratio.   **TABLE 9–2**

	Pupil-to-eye-size ratio		
	6/20	11/20	15/20
M	92.0	123.0	106.0
SD	14.2	15.7	12.5

TABLE 9–3   *Analysis of variance summary table for tonic immobility scores as a function of pupil-to-eye-size ratio.*

Source	df	SS	MS	F
Eye-size ratio (A)	2	4820.00	2410.00	11.99*
Error	27	5428.00	201.04	
Total	29	10,248.00		

*$p < .05$.

Notice several points about the analysis summarized in Table 9–3. The degrees of freedom are determined by applying the procedure detailed in Chapter 8 and summarized in Table 8–4. Mean squares are obtained simply by dividing each sum of squares by its appropriate *df*. The sources of variation affecting each *MS* are identical to those of the analysis of variance with two levels of the independent variable (see Table 8–6 for a summary of the factors affecting the value of each *MS*). Thus, an *F* ratio is formed by dividing the MS_A by the MS_{Error}. The null hypothesis, H_0, is a simple extension of the null hypothesis for the design with only two levels of the independent variable. Because three sample means are being tested by this analysis, the null hypothesis in notation is H_0: $\mu_{A_1} = \mu_{A_2} = \mu_{A_3}$. That is, the null hypothesis states that the means of the populations from which the three samples were obtained are identical. This null hypothesis determines the sampling distribution for the *F* ratio. The alternative hypothesis is most easily written as H_1: not H_0. An alternative hypothesis expressed in this form is often called an omnibus alternative hypothesis because many possible relationships among the population means could occur if "not H_0" were true. Figure 9–2 presents, symbolically and graphically, some of the relationships that may occur under H_1 for an experiment with three treatment conditions.

The tabulated critical value of *F* that defines the rejection region for 2 and 27 *df* with a significance level of .05 is 3.35 (see Table A–2). The obtained value of *F* in Table 9–3, $F(2,27) = 11.99$, lies within the rejection region and leads to the decision to reject H_0 and accept H_1 at the .05 level of significance. The inference from this decision is that not all the sample means in Table 9–2 are estimates of the same population mean. But, as Figure 9–2 illustrates, many relationships are possible among the three means when the alternative hypothesis is true. Which of the sample means differ from the others? An answer to this question cannot be obtained with three or more sample means by a simple visual inspection alone. Follow-up tests to the analysis of variance are required to determine which means differ significantly from which other treatment means. Such follow-up tests are most generally referred to as multiple comparison procedures.[3]

---

[3]Multiple comparison tests are also called *tests for specific comparisons* or *analytic comparisons*.

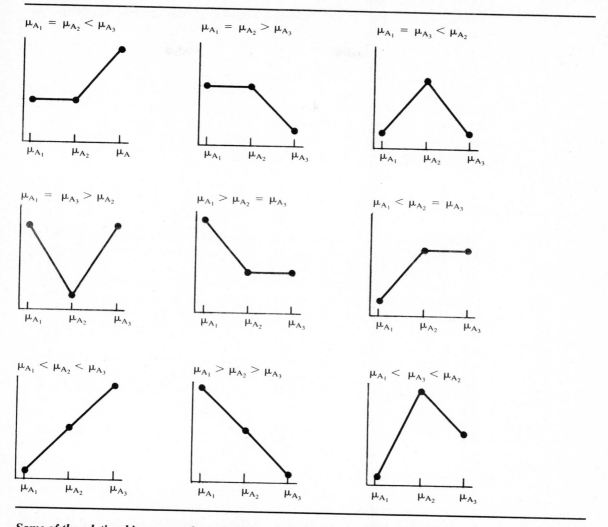

Some of the relationships among three population means that are possible under H_1: not H_0.

FIGURE 9–2

MULTIPLE COMPARISON PROCEDURES

Multiple comparison procedures are statistical tests used to find which means differ from one another in a multilevel one-factor design. They are most typically employed as a follow-up to a significant multilevel analysis of variance. We venture to guess that the topic of multiple comparisons is one of the most confusing in psychological research for the beginning student. It is difficult, not because of the logic behind making comparisons, but because so many comparison techniques have been developed, each slightly different from another. The varied techniques have been developed in an attempt to address one or more problems when making multiple comparisons. In our approach, we will briefly introduce the simple comparison and the problems associated with making such comparisons. Then we will develop a general approach to the comparison problem, followed by several modifications for this approach. Notice that although the example and discussion deal with only three sample means, the techniques developed are appropriate for comparing any number of means from a one-factor experiment.

A Simple Comparison

Given the three sample means from the tonic immobility experiment, an investigator could make three simple two-mean (i.e., pairwise) comparisons among them: $\bar{X}_{A_1}$ compared to $\bar{X}_{A_2}$ (i.e., $\bar{X}_{A_1} - \bar{X}_{A_2}$), $\bar{X}_{A_1}$ compared to $\bar{X}_{A_3}$ (i.e., $\bar{X}_{A_1} - \bar{X}_{A_3}$) and $\bar{X}_{A_2}$ compared to $\bar{X}_{A_3}$ (i.e., $\bar{X}_{A_2} - \bar{X}_{A_3}$). From these three pairwise comparisons one could infer which, if any, of the relationships among the population means shown in Figure 9–2 is the most probable for the experiment. One way of making these comparisons would be to use the t test for differences between groups. This method would involve simply conducting three t tests, one for each comparison. From these three comparisons, a researcher could determine which means differ significantly from each other. Unfortunately, however, the issue is not quite so easily resolved: Several problems arise whenever multiple-comparison tests are needed.

Problem of Type I Errors

One problem that arises has to do with the probability of a Type I error occurring in the comparisons to be made. Recall that for the overall analysis of variance on the experiment (reported in Table 9–3), the probability of a Type I error is equal to the value of α. But when conducting multiple comparisons, an investigator runs many more statistical tests, the exact number depending upon the number of comparisons to be made. For the pairwise comparisons in the experiment we initially suggested using three t tests. If, for each comparison, the probability of a Type I error is equal to α, as it is with separate t tests for each comparison, then the probability of making at least one Type I error among the comparisons becomes progressively greater with an increasing number of comparisons. Very quickly this probability attains a value quite unacceptable to the researcher. As an example, for three sample means, there are three possible comparisons. But only two of them are independent comparisons because each mean is involved in two of the three possible comparisons.[4] If, for each of these two independent comparisons, the probability of a Type I error is equal to $\alpha = .05$, then the probability of making a Type I error over the two comparisons is nearly .10.

To see why this problem occurs, suppose that one of the three means deviates extensively from the others merely because of sampling error. If a t test reveals that it differs significantly from one of the other two means, then a Type I error will be made in rejecting the null hypothesis. This deviant mean is also likely to differ significantly from the third mean, thus resulting in another Type I error. If one conducts the three possible comparisons, then the probability of a Type I error will be even larger; but the exact probability cannot be exactly specified because the three comparisons are not all independent of one another.

Error Rates

The **error rate** in an experiment is the probability of making at least one Type I error in the various statistical comparisons conducted. The error rate increases very rapidly with a growing number of comparisons. For example, consider employing the t test for five independent comparisons among six means with $\alpha = .05$ for each comparison. The probability of at least one Type I error in the five comparisons is .23. This error rate is obviously too high for most researchers. It is for this reason that the simple t test as presented in Chapter 7 is not often used to make multiple comparisons.

Planned vs. Post Hoc Comparisons

The willingness of a researcher to risk a Type I error depends upon whether the comparisons to be conducted are *planned* on the basis of the research hypothesis prior to conducting the experiment (called **planned** or **a priori comparisons**) or are comparisons *suggested* by the pattern of means obtained in the experiment (called **post hoc, a posteriori,** or **incidental comparisons**). Fundamentally, the issue relates to the discussion in Chapter 2 that predictions of behavior are more valuable scientifically than after-the-fact, post hoc attempts to interpret and explain the data. Scientists believe that planned comparisons, made on the basis of predicted relationships among the means, are less likely to capitalize on chance differences among the means than are unplanned, post hoc comparisons

---

[4]Independent comparisons are those which do not depend upon the outcome of any other comparison. Here is a simple analogy: If you know three means, e.g., 8, 10, and 12, you can obtain three possible differences between pairs of two means: 8-10, 8-12, and 10-12. Notice, however, that only two of them are independent; if you know the numerical value of any two of them, then you know the third. For independent comparisons, the probability of a Type I error is equal to $1 - (1 - \alpha)^k$, where k is the number of independent comparisons.

suggested by the pattern of means of the obtained data. For this reason, researchers are more willing to risk a Type I error when they are conducting planned comparisons than when they are "data snooping" with post hoc comparisons.

A number of multiple comparison procedures have been developed as solutions to the Type I error-rate problem for both planned and post hoc comparisons. All the different tests are fundamentally similar in that they reduce the value of α for each comparison made so that the probability of a Type I error over all the comparisons made is held to some acceptable level. We next introduce a general approach suitable for planned comparisons. Modifications of this approach will then make it suitable for post hoc comparisons.

Comparison Procedure for Multiple *F* Tests

The approach we present is called the *analysis of variance multiple* F *tests comparison procedure*. A survey of one widely read psychology journal revealed that this technique is one of the multiple-comparison procedures most frequently used for planned comparisons (Gaito and Nobrega, 1981). The multiple *F* test procedure has the added benefit of building directly upon the analysis of variance and being easily modified for making post hoc multiple comparisons.

The multiple *F* test procedure obtains a critical value (CV), which specifies the minimal difference between two treatment means that is statistically significant at the α level chosen. The actual difference between the means in each comparison of interest is then compared against this CV. If the obtained difference between the compared means is equal to or larger than the CV, then the obtained means are significantly different from each other and are treated as estimates of different population means. The CV is given by

$$(\sqrt{2F_\alpha}) \left(\sqrt{\frac{MS_{\text{Error}}}{n}} \right)$$

The MS_{Error} is the error term from the analysis of variance, F is the critical value of F with 1, df_{Error} degrees of freedom for the significance level chosen,[5] and n is the number of scores in each treatment condition. Alternatively, a tabled critical value of t may be used to calculate the CV by

$$(\sqrt{2})(t_\alpha) \left(\sqrt{\frac{MS_{\text{Error}}}{n}} \right).$$

This approach, often called the *least significant difference* (LSD), gives a CV identical to the multiple *F* test CV.

To illustrate the use of this critical-value approach, we compute the CV for the three possible two-mean comparisons of the means in Table 9–2, using the multiple *F* test formula. For 1 and 27 *df* and $\alpha = .05$, the critical value of F is

---

[5]The value of F is multiplied by 2 because the comparison involves two means.

4.21. Substituting this value and the values of MS_{Error} and n into the formula for the CV, leads to:

$$CV = (\sqrt{2(4.21)}) \left(\sqrt{\frac{201.04}{10}} \right) = 13.0.$$

Thus, the CV is 13.0. Any difference between two treatment means *equal to or larger* in absolute value (the value without considering the $+$ or $-$ sign) than 13.0 is a statistically significant difference at the .05 level. The absolute differences among the three treatment means of the experiment are shown in Table 9–4. (Ignore the footnotes to the table for the moment.) As you can see, each of the obtained differences exceeds the CV. Thus, each mean is significantly different from each other mean and the null hypothesis (e.g., H_0: $\mu_{A_1} = \mu_{A_2}$) of each comparison is rejected.

    If specific predictions about the relationship among the population means had been made before conducting the experiment, and the three comparisons had been made in response to these predictions (i.e., they were planned comparisons), then a researcher could conclude that each treatment mean differs significantly from each other treatment mean. Thus, each of the sample means estimates a different population mean (μ_A). In order, from producing most to least tonic immobility, the treatments are eye-size ratios of 11/20, 15/20, and 6/20 respectively. We emphasize, however, that this inference would be appropriate only if the comparisons had been dictated by well-formulated predictions expressed in the research hypothesis. A mere statement prior to conducting the experiment that all comparisons will be conducted is *not* an example of a planned comparison. A planned comparison implies there is a well-developed theoretical or empirical

Means and differences between the means for the three pupil-to-eye-size ratios. The mean for each eye-size ratio is shown in parentheses. The absolute values of the differences between the corresponding means are presented. **TABLE 9–4**

		Eye-size ratio		
		6/20 (92)	11/20 (123)	15/20 (106)
Eye-	6/20 (92)	—	31[a,b,c]	14[a]
size-	11/20 (123)		—	17[a,b,c]
ratio	15/20 (106)			—

[a] $p < .05$, Multiple F test; $CV = 13.0$.
[b] $p < .05$, Tukey test; $CV = 15.8$.
[c] $p < .05$, Scheffé test; $CV = 16.4$.

reason for expecting that the means to be compared will differ. Thus, each planned comparison should provide meaningful information about the experiment.[6]

Post Hoc Comparisons and Control of Type I Errors

The Type I error rate for the multiple F test approach is equal to α for each comparison made. Consequently, as we have explained, if an experimenter conducts a number of multiple comparisons, the probability of making a Type I error becomes rather substantial. The problem is usually not a major one if the comparisons made are planned. As we have stressed, such comparisons should be limited in number and should reflect a prediction made from a theoretical understanding of the topic.

With post hoc comparisons, however, the problem of Type I errors becomes more severe, especially if there are many levels of the independent variable and all possible comparisons among the treatment means are to be made. In an attempt, then, to control the Type I rate of error, a large number of techniques have been developed. All the techniques take a common approach in that they essentially begin with the multiple F test approach and then reduce the probability of a Type I error for each individual comparison so that the Type I error rate over all the comparisons made is held to some low, specifiable level (e.g., .05). Let us see how this is done.

Consider the equation for the CV by the multiple F test approach:

$$CV = (\sqrt{2F_\alpha}) \left(\sqrt{\frac{MS_{\text{Error}}}{n}} \right).$$

Almost all the multiple comparison procedures that have been developed for post hoc tests use the term $\sqrt{MS_{\text{Error}}/n}$ in their formula. Rather than multiplying by $\sqrt{2F_\alpha}$, however, the other techniques use a larger multiplier, thereby creating a larger CV. And, with a larger CV, fewer comparisons among the treatment means will differ significantly. Therefore the probability of a Type I error will be reduced. The specific value of the multiplier depends upon what types and how many comparisons the test permits, and how the Type I error rate is to be controlled.

Post Hoc Comparison Procedures

Two post hoc comparison procedures, the Tukey test and the Scheffé test, are widely used.

---

[6]There is some controversy in the psychological literature about whether planned comparisons should also be orthogonal; that is, independent. We have taken the approach that the comparisons need not be independent, but that they should be planned to provide meaningful information about the results of an experiment. See Keppel (1982) for a summary of the issues.

Tukey Test   In the Tukey test, often referred to as the *honestly significant differ-ence (HSD)* test or as the Tukey *a* test, a critical value is calculated as

$$CV = q_k \left(\sqrt{\frac{MS_{\text{Error}}}{n}} \right).$$

The value of q_k depends upon the value of α chosen, the number of means to be compared, and the *df* for MS_{Error}. Values of q_k are given in Table A–3.

Scheffé Test   The critical value for the Scheffé test is obtained by

$$CV = (\sqrt{a - 1})\,(\sqrt{2F_\alpha}) \left(\sqrt{\frac{MS_{\text{Error}}}{n}} \right)$$

where *a* represents the number of levels of factor *A* and F_α is the critical value of *F* for $a - 1$ and MS_{Error} degrees of freedom.

Characteristics of the multiple *F* test, least significant differences test, Tukey test, and Scheffé test are summarized in Table 9–5.

Summary of multiple comparison tests.   **TABLE 9–5**

	Multiple F	Least significant Differences	Tukey test	Scheffé test
Formula for CV	$(\sqrt{2F_\alpha})\,(\sqrt{MSe/n})$	$(\sqrt{2})\,(t_\alpha)\,(\sqrt{MSE/n})$	$q_k(\sqrt{MSe/n})$	$(\sqrt{a-1})\,(\sqrt{2F_\alpha})\,(\sqrt{MSe/n})$
Recommended use	All planned comparisons	All planned comparisons	All post hoc comparisons between two means	All possible post hoc comparisons
	Multiple *F* and least significant differences are identical tests			
Approximate probability of a Type I error	Equal to α for each comparison	Equal to α for each comparison	Equal to α for the total of all two-mean comparisons	Equal to α for the total of all possible comparisons
Relative rating of probability of a Type I error	High	High	Low	Very low
Relative rating of probability of a Type II error	Low	Low	High	Very high

Note: MSE is the mean square error from the analysis of variance.

Choosing a Test of Multiple Comparisons

Tests for Planned Comparisons

The multiple F test approach, or equivalently, the least significant differences test, is recommended for planned comparisons. The number of planned comparisons should be no greater than the number of groups being compared, however. For example, if there are four group means then no more than four planned comparisons should be conducted. And, we reiterate, they should be planned to provide meaningful information about the results of the experiment.

Tests for Post Hoc Comparisons

Post hoc comparisons should be conducted only if a significant value is obtained for the independent variable in the overall analysis of variance. The recommended follow-up test then depends upon whether only pairwise or all possible comparisons are to be made.

Pairwise comparisons   When the only comparisons to be made are those involving treatment means taken two at a time (i.e., pairwise comparisons), the Tukey test is the one recommended. Another test, the Newman-Keuls, is also widely used for pairwise comparisons. This test requires that the means be ordered according to magnitude. A different CV is then found for each comparison. The size of the CV depends upon the number of steps (i.e., the number of other ordered means) between the two means being compared.[7]

All possible comparisons   When all possible comparisons are to be made, including pairwise and more complex comparisons, such as

$$\bar{X}_{A_1} - \left(\frac{\bar{X}_{A_2} + \bar{X}_{A_3}}{2}\right),$$

the Scheffé test is recommended.

The next section illustrates the different decisions that are reached by applying the multiple F, Tukey, and Scheffé approaches to the tonic immobility data.

Multiple Comparisons on the Tonic Immobility Experiment

When introducing the tonic immobility experiment, we indicated that the experiment was exploratory. Although Gagliardi et al. expected the duration of tonic

---

[7]Procedures for conducting the Newman-Keuls test are detailed in Bruning and Kintz (1978), pp. 119–122; and in Linton and Gallo (1975), pp. 324–327.

immobility to vary with the pupil-to-eye-size ratio, they did not make a specific prediction on the relationship expected among the population means. Thus, planned comparisons are not appropriate for this experiment. Rather, any follow-up tests should employ a post hoc multiple comparison procedure. For the sake of illustration, however, we will compare the results of using the multiple F test, Tukey, and Scheffé procedures on the treatment means of Table 9–2.

As we have already found, the CV for the multiple F test approach on the hypothetical data is 13.0. For the Tukey test, the CV is:[8]

$$(3.53)\left(\sqrt{\frac{201.04}{10}}\right) = (3.53)(4.48) = 15.8.$$

The CV using the Scheffé test is:

$$(\sqrt{2})(\sqrt{(2)(3.35)})\left(\sqrt{\frac{201.04}{10}}\right) = (3.66)(4.48) = 16.4.$$

As you notice, the critical values for both the Tukey test and the Scheffé test are larger than the CV of the multiple F test approach. Consequently, using these two procedures leads to fewer statistically significant differences and thus a lower probability of Type I error than does the multiple F test approach. This result is clearly shown in Table 9–4. Significant differences between the treatment means employing the three critical values are indicated by the several footnotes in the table. The multiple F test approach leads to significant differences among all three means. Both the Tukey and Scheffé tests result in significant differences in only two comparisons, those between the means of eye-size ratios 11/20 and 6/20, and 15/20 and 11/20.

Obviously, then, different decisions may be reached from the same data depending upon which follow-up test is used. Which, if any, is the "correct" test to use? The answer to this question hinges on our previous discussion of planned and post hoc comparisons. If the comparisons were planned prior to conducting the experiment and were clearly based upon predictions of the research hypothesis, then the multiple F test approach is appropriate. If the comparisons were prompted by the results obtained; that is, prompted by a question of the kind, "Hmmm, I wonder if these two means differ," and if the comparisons to be made are those involving only two means at a time, then the Tukey test is most appropriate. This is the case represented by the tonic immobility example. Should the experimenter want to conduct more complex comparisons such as the mean of the 11/20 against the combined mean of the 6/20 and 15/20 conditions, as well as the simple pairwise comparisons, then the Scheffé test is the most appropriate.

---

[8]The value of q_k used is for 24 *df* for error. The value of 27 *df* is typically not tabled.

In general, the multiple F test is the most sensitive for detecting differences between treatment means, but it provides the least protection against making Type I errors. On the other hand, the Scheffé test provides most protection against Type I errors but is the least sensitive for detecting treatment effects. Thus, the same numerical differences between treatment means might lead to considerably different decisions depending upon the specific test used and whether the comparisons are planned or post hoc.

PITFALLS OF DATA FISHING

Perhaps it has crossed your mind that one way of doing research is to collect data on a large number of different groups and then look for statistically significant differences among the groups by using post hoc tests, an approach often called *data fishing* or *data snooping*. But most psychologists would disagree; let us illustrate why by using two examples taken from newspaper reports of research.

Several years ago it was reported that extremely obese children, who were in the 95th to 100th percentiles for weight-height ratio, had significantly higher measured intelligence than extremely lean children in the 0 to 5th percentiles in weight-height ratio. Dividing the children into quintiles (five-percentile groupings) based upon their weight-height ratio gave the experimenters twenty different mean intelligence-test scores to be compared. Suppose, for illustration, the experimenters conducted nineteen independent comparisons using an approach that held the probability of a Type I error equal to .05 for each comparison (e.g., the multiple F test approach). The probability of a Type I error is then:

$$p(\text{Type I error}) = 1 - (1 - .05)^{19} = .62.$$

With nineteen independent comparisons and $\alpha = .05$ for each comparison, the probability of concluding that there is at least one statistically significant difference when H_0 is really true is .62. Does the difference in intelligence between the extremely obese and extremely lean children represent this Type I error? We cannot know from this study alone. But we can argue that most researchers would not place much credence in this difference unless there were some conceptually sound reasons to expect it.

A second instance of the possibility of many comparisons arises in epidemiological studies of physical or mental health problems. For example, states typically maintain records on cancer deaths by communities. One possible way, then, of detecting communities where there may be environmental problems leading to increased cancer rates (e.g., chemical dumps, contaminated water, and so on), is to compare each town or city's cancer rate to some statewide or national mean. Using Massachusetts with 351 towns or cities as an example, we could conduct 350 independent comparisons between two means. If the probability of a Type I error is equal to .05 for each comparison, then the probability of at least one Type I error occurring over the 350 comparisons is $1 - (1 - .05)^{350} = .9999999840316$, or effectively 1.00! Thus, we are virtually assured of at least one Type 1 error, a decision that would lead to the conclusion that a town has a cancer rate significantly higher than the statewide average when it really does not.

Such a study apparently was conducted in Massachusetts, and at least several towns were found to have a significantly higher rate of a type of cancer than other towns of equivalent size. Do such statistically signficant differences reflect a real problem that must be addressed, or could they merely be Type I errors? From the statistical test alone one cannot tell, and the health workers doing this study were quite aware of this doubt; they were quoted as saying, "It's very difficult to be certain that this is not a chance occurrence"; "Statistically rare events, like an inside straight in poker, do occur"; "You always see these crazy ups and downs with chance fluctuations." Indeed, if the null hypothesis is true, then we would expect about 17 (i.e., $.05 \times 350$) statistically significant comparisons on the basis of chance alone. Thus, by exhaustive statistical testing, researchers may be led on a fruitless search seeking a variable that causes a presumed effect when in reality there is no effect larger than that which can be accounted for by sampling error alone.

As we have illustrated, merely collecting data followed by large numbers of multiple comparison tests may lead researchers on nonproductive excursions. For this reason, psychological researchers should do only those comparisons which make sense from either a theoretical perspective or from previous empirical work on the problem.

STRENGTH OF A TREATMENT EFFECT

Measuring Strength of Association with a Significance Test

A statistically significant difference merely indicates that an independent variable has an effect in an experiment. It does not, however, measure the strength of the relationship between the independent and dependent variables. Yet psychologists often are also interested in knowing the magnitude of a treatment effect, as you can see when reading journals. Frequently, differences among treatment means are reported as "highly significant ($p < .001$)" or as just "significant ($p < .05$)." The implication from reporting results in this manner is that the "highly significant" difference reflects a greater treatment effect than does the "significant" difference. This inference is quite inappropriate to make from a significance test, however; let us explain why.

Recall that the value of a t or an F depends not only upon the difference between the means of the treatment groups but also upon the error variability in the experiment. Thus, two experiments, each with the same difference between the means of the treatment groups, may well result in differing values of t or F because of different amounts of error variability in the experiments. One of the differences may be reported as "highly significant" and the other merely as "significant," yet both may reflect the same treatment effect, as evidenced by the actual difference between treatment means. A test of statistical signficance could be used to compare magnitudes of treatment effects in two experiments only if the error terms were identical for both experiments. But this identity would rarely happen. Therefore, a significance test is not an appropriate measure of the effect of a treatment, even if researchers sometimes misuse it for this purpose.

Measures of Strength of Association

A number of statistical measures have been developed for quantifying the magnitude of effect of an independent variable. These statistics are referred to as **strength of association measures, magnitude of effect measures,** or **utility indices.** The measures represent the proportion of the total variation in an experiment that is systematic variation. Thus, a strength of association measure indicates how much of the total variation in an experiment (represented by SS_{Total}) is "accounted for" by the independent variable. Two of the most commonly used strength of association measures are eta squared, and omega squared.[9] We describe them here.

Eta Squared: A Descriptive Measure of Strength of Association

Eta squared (η^2), also called the *correlation ratio,* provides a descriptive measure of the strength of association for the *particular samples tested.* For the *t* test, η^2 is obtained from the squared *t* value and degrees of freedom by

$$\eta^2 = \frac{t^2}{t^2 + df}.$$

For the analysis of variance, η^2 is simply the ratio of the sums of squares associated with the treatment effect to the total sums of squares:

$$\eta^2 = \frac{SS_A}{SS_{Total}}.$$

Where only the *F* and the *df* are known for a one-way between-subjects analysis of variance, η^2 can be obtained by

$$\eta^2 = \frac{df_A(F)}{df_A(F) + df_{Error}}.$$

The value of η^2 reveals proportion of the total variation of the dependent variable in the *samples* measured is due to the effect of the independent variable in the experiment.

[9]Maxwell, Camp, and Arvey (1981) and Sechrest and Yeaton (1981) discuss and compare a number of the strength of association measures. Dodd and Schultz (1973) present computational procedures for determining the strength of association in a wide variety of research designs.

Omega Squared: An Inferential Measure of the Strength of Association

An inferential measure of the strength of association is given by the value of **omega squared** (ω^2). The value of ω^2, too, is a proportion reflecting the ratio of systematic variance to the total variance in the scores of the dependent variable. In contrast to η^2, however, ω^2 is used to estimate the proportion of total variance that is accounted for by the independent variable in the *population* from which the samples were selected. But this population estimate is limited to the specific levels of the independent variable employed in the experiment.

Computationally, ω^2 is derived from a result of a t test by

$$\omega^2 = \frac{t^2 - 1}{t^2 + n_1 + n_2 - 1}.$$

From an analysis of variance summary table, ω^2 is found from the SS and df by

$$\omega^2 = \frac{SS_A - (a - 1)(MS_{\text{Error}})}{SS_{\text{Total}} + MS_{\text{Error}}}.$$

When only the value of F and degrees of freedom are known, ω^2 may be obtained by

$$\omega^2 = \frac{df_A(F - 1)}{df_A(F) + df_{\text{Error}} + 1}.$$

Examples of Using Strength of Association Measures

Let us illustrate how η^2 and ω^2 measures are computed by substituting appropriate values into the formulas for the effect of type of counselor response on expertness scores in the McCarthy and Betz experiment. The self-disclosing and self-involving means differed significantly, as revealed by both a t test (Chapter 7), $t(105) = 2.172$, $p < .05$, and an analysis of variance (Chapter 8), $F(1,105) = 4.69$, $p < .05$. By also using the value in the summary table for the analysis of variance (Table 8–10), we can see how the same η^2 value of .04 is obtained in several ways:

$$\eta^2 = \frac{t^2}{t^2 + df} \qquad = \frac{(2.172)^2}{(2.172)^2 + 105} = .04, \text{ or}$$

$$\eta^2 = \frac{SS_A}{SS_{\text{Total}}} \qquad = \frac{790.21}{18,491.16} = .04, \text{ or}$$

$$\eta^2 = \frac{df_A(F)}{df_A(F) + df_{\text{Error}}} = \frac{1(4.69)}{1(4.69) + 105} = .04.$$

For the same data, the ω^2 value of .03 is found as follows:

$$\omega^2 = \frac{t^2 - 1}{t^2 + n_1 + n_2 - 1}$$

$$= \frac{(2.172)^2 - 1}{(2.172)^2 + 54 + 53 - 1} = .03, \text{ or}$$

$$\omega^2 = \frac{SS_A - (a - 1)(MS_{\text{Error}})}{SS_{\text{Total}} + MS_{\text{Error}}}$$

$$= \frac{790.21 - 1(168.50)}{17,700.95 + 168.50} = .03, \text{ or}$$

$$\omega^2 = \frac{df_A(F - 1)}{df_A(F) + df_{\text{Error}} + 1}$$

$$= \frac{1(4.69 - 1)}{1(4.69) + 105 + 1} = .03.$$

Similarly, for the data of the tonic immobility example experiment in this chapter, where a significant difference was found among the three means, $F(2,27) = 11.99$, $p < .05$, $\eta^2 = .47$, and $\omega^2 = .42$. As you can see, ω^2 is slightly smaller than η^2 in each of these examples. It will always be so because ω^2 is a population estimate and η^2 is not.

Interpreting Measures of the Strength of Association

What specifically do these strength of association values mean? Where $\eta^2 = .04$ for type of counselor response, is 4 percent a small, medium, or large amount of the total variance to account for? In comparison to a maximum 100 percent to be accounted for, 4 percent is obviously quite small. But what percentage of the variance can one realistically expect to account for by an independent variable?

Accounting for 100 percent of the variance in an experiment is an impossible goal. In all instances, some of the variance in a dependent measure is due to errors of measurement and to uncontrolled extraneous variables. As we have discussed, errors of measurement typically do not occur in any systematic fashion in an experiment; hence, it is very unlikely that they can be entirely eliminated. Further, as we have indicated in previous chapters, not all extraneous variables can be controlled in any one experiment. Consequently, there will always be error variance in an experiment, and an investigator will thus have to settle for accounting for less than 100 percent of the total variance.

Cohen (1977) provides a rule of thumb for evaluating the strength of the effect of an independent variable; he suggests that an effect accounting for about 1 percent of the variance represents a *small* effect, 6 percent a *medium* effect, and 15 percent a *large* effect. But application of this rule of thumb must be tempered by the number of extraneous variables that may be influencing a particular dependent variable and the extent to which the independent variable was maximized in its manipulation. For example, in Chapters 3 and 4, we pointed out several potential independent variables that may affect the perceived expertness of a counselor. McCarthy and Betz attempted to control these variables in their experiment so that they would not contribute variance to the experiment. It is very likely that there are as many more unknown extraneous variables affecting perceived expertness as there are known variables. No doubt, these unknown variables were at work in McCarthy and Betz's experiment and they contributed to the considerable error variance.

It is therefore quite reasonable to expect that no one independent variable will account for a large proportion of the variance in an experiment. Indeed, Keppel (1982, pp. 94–95) argues that in "healthy" areas of psychological research one may expect to find a preponderance of experiments that account for only small amounts of the variance in the dependent variable. He explains that as psychologists research particular problems and attempt to develop explanations for the phenomenon that is of interest, their manipulations of independent variables will come to be directed by the theoretical explanations offered and will be aimed at falsifying research hypotheses deduced from a theory. Often the manipulations needed to test a research hypothesis will be small and therefore unlikely to account for a large proportion of the variance in the experiment. Yet a subtle manipulation and subsequent small effect may be of considerable theoretical importance. In this context, the manipulation of type-of-counselor reponse by McCarthy and Betz was quite subtle. Someone not familiar with the literature and theoretical formulations in this topic may indeed expect such a manipulation to have little or no effect on perceived expertness.

It is thus very difficult to specify what value of η^2 or ω^2 reflects an important amount of variance accounted for. In exploratory research, where one has attempted to achieve the maximum possible effect of the independent variable, values such as .25 or even the $\eta^2 = .47$ of the tonic immobility experiment might be quite reasonable to expect. But in research based upon well-defined conceptualizations of a problem and with rather subtle manipulations of the independent variable, 4 percent or 5 percent of the variance accounted for may be a most reasonable expectation.

This argument finds support in the published literature of psychology. For example, Haase, Waechter, and Solomon (1982) calculated η^2 on 11,044 tests of statistical significance reported in issues of the *Journal of Counseling Psychology* published between 1970 to 1979. They found a median η^2 of .083 with an interquartile range of .043 to .268. More than half the values of η^2 were .09 or less. Linton and Gallo (1975) report a similar study they conducted "on most of the published studies in American Psychological Association journals for the year 1964" (p. 330). They found strength of association values of less than .05 for more than 50 percent of the published studies. This result should give you some idea of the typical strength of association found in current psychological research and provide you with a basis for evaluating the magnitude of an effect from a strength-of-association measure.

KRUSKAL-WALLIS ANALYSIS OF VARIANCE BY RANKS

The Kruskal-Wallis one-way analysis of variance by ranks is a nonparametric alternative to the one-way between-subjects analysis of variance for multilevel designs. The approach of this test is very similar to that of the Mann-Whitney U test (see Chapter 7). All the scores obtained from three or more independent groups are ranked in order from the smallest to the largest score. An H test statistic is then obtained by:

$$H = \left[\left(12 \right) \big/ N \left(N + 1 \right) \right] \left[\sum_{A=1}^{a} \left(\left(\sum_{n=1}^{n_A} R_a \right)^2 \big/ n_a \right) \right] - 3 \left(N + 1 \right).$$

In this equation, N is the total number of scores over all levels of the independent variable, $\sum_{n=1}^{n_A} R_a$ is the sum of the ranks for scores in level A of the experiment, n_a is the number of scores in level A, and a is the number of levels of the independent variable.

The statistical hypotheses for the H statistics are:

H_0: The distributions of scores in the population from which the groups were sampled are identical.
H_1: The distributions of scores in the population from which the groups were sampled are not identical.

For three independent groups with ns ranging from 1 to 5, selected critical values of H for $\alpha = .05$ are presented in Appendix Table A–6. Obtained values of H equal to or larger than the tabled critical value are statistically significant at the .05 significance level. When the sample size is larger than five for each group, the sampling distribution of the test statistic H corresponds to the distribution of a χ^2 (pronounced "chi square") statistic. Therefore, when n is greater than five for each group, Table A–9 in the Appendix may be used to test for the statistical significance of H. The critical value of H in Table A–9 is defined for a $- 1$ df; an obtained value of H equal to or larger than the tabled value of χ^2 is significant at the α level chosen.

To illustrate the computation of the H statistic we use the hypothetical duration of tonic immobility scores presented in Table 9–1. These scores provide an interesting example in the choice of type of statistical test. As we indicated in Chapter 7, response latency or duration scores often tend to be skewed. For example, with the phenomenon of tonic immobility it is possible that some chickens may remain immobile for an unusually long period in comparison to the majority of the subjects in the experiment. This condition will result in a positively skewed distribution of scores. Such skewed distributions violate the normality assumptions for the analysis of variance and sometimes render it an inappropriate statistical test for the data.

The tonic immobility scores obtained by Gagliardi et al. (1976) were positively skewed; we know that they were because the authors stated that they had "several unusually high scores" (p. 59). To eliminate this skewing Gagliardi et al. winsorized their data. With a *winsorization procedure* the highest and lowest extreme values are replaced by the next-to-the-highest and the next-to-the-lowest scores. Then, an arithmetic mean is calculated on the resulting data, producing a *winsorized mean*. Because the extreme scores that are excluded are replaced with other scores, the size of the original sample is retained. Winsorized means are essentially treated as arithmetic means for further statistical analysis. In their experiment, Gagliardi et al. conducted an analysis of variance on the winsorized means. This method for dealing with atypical scores, however, should be used only if there is reason to believe that the few extreme observations were due to unusual circumstances that can be explained "after the fact" (Winer, 1971). A malfunction with a recording apparatus or a participant's apparent failure to follow instructions may obviously be responsible for producing "outliers" or "wild shots," as such questionable scores are sometimes called. Winsorization is not appropriate if it is used to routinely deal with the problem of skewed data. If the distribution of scores were inherently skewed by the nature of the behavior measured, then statisticians would contend that the data should be analyzed by a nonparametric statistical test that does not require assuming a normally distributed population of scores.

The computations involved in obtaining the *H* statistic are shown in Table 9–6. As you can see, the value of *H* computed on the hypothetical tonic immobility data is significant at the .05 level. Thus, for the data in Table 9–1, both the analysis of variance and the Kruskal-Wallis analysis of variance by ranks lead to rejection of the null hypothesis. The example data, however, were not skewed as were those of Gagliardi et al. In instances with severely skewed distributions there is no assurance that the two tests will lead to the same decisions. We suspect that many psychologists would prefer to use the Kruskal-Wallis test over the winsorization procedure and analysis of variance in this instance.

When there are three or more treatment groups in an experiment and the null hypothesis is rejected using the Kruskal-Wallis test, then follow-up tests must be conducted to determine specifically which of the distributions differ significantly from one another. The problems faced in conducting nonparametric follow-up tests are identical to those faced when employing parametric tests such as the analysis of variance. One approach is simply to use multiple Mann-Whitney *U* tests to make comparisons of two groups at a time. Running multiple Mann-Whitney *U* tests, however, poses the same problem as using multiple *t* tests following an analysis of variance. Both tests lead to an inflated Type I error rate for the experiment. Thus, the Mann-Whitney *U* is appropriate only if the follow-up tests are *planned* comparisons and few in relation to the total number of comparisons that may be made.

Several nonparametric follow-up tests for post hoc comparisons have been developed. They are, however, beyond the scope of this text. Ryan's procedure,

TABLE 9–6   *Computing the Kruskal-Wallis* **H** *for the data of Table 9–1*

Step 1. Rank each score from the smallest (rank $= 1$) to the largest (rank $= N$). The scores from all groups are combined for the ranking, but the group identity of the scores is maintained. With tied scores assign the mean of the ranks they would have received had they not been tied. This process is shown in the table below.

		Pupil-to-eye-size ratio			
6/20 (A_1)		11/20 (A_2)		15/20 (A_3)	
Score	*Rank*	*Score*	*Rank*	*Score*	*Rank*
72	1	117	21.5	103	13.5
89	5	98	11.5	96	9.5
117	21.5	139	29	113	20
78	2	121	23	94	8
108	17.5	148	30	122	24
96	9.5	104	15.5	130	26
103	13.5	132	27	92	6.5
84	4	133	28	108	17.5
92	6.5	112	19	98	11.5
81	3	126	25	104	15.5
② $\left(\sum\limits_{n=1}^{n_A} R_a \right) =$ 83.5		229.5		152.0	
③ $\left(\sum\limits_{n=1}^{n_A} R_a \right)^2 = $ 6972.25		52,670.25		23,104.00	
④ $\left(\sum\limits_{n=1}^{n_A} R_a \right)^2 / n_a = $ 6972.25/10		52,670.25/10		23,104.00/10	
697.255		5267.025		2310.400	

Step 2. Find the sum of the ranks $\left(\sum\limits_{n=1}^{n_A} R_a \right)$ for each group; this sum is shown in row ② in the table.

Step 3. Square the sum of the ranks $\left(\sum\limits_{n=1}^{n_A} R_a \right)$ for each group to obtain $\left(\sum\limits_{n=1}^{n_A} R_a \right)^2$. This procedure is shown in row ③ in the table. Divide each $\left(\sum\limits_{n=1}^{n_A} R_a \right)^2$ by n_a to obtain $\left(\sum\limits_{n=1}^{n_A} R_a \right)^2 / n_a$ for each treatment condition. This procedure is shown in row ④ in the table.

Step 5. Sum the values of $\left(\sum\limits_{n=1}^{n_A} R_a \right)^2 / n_a$ to obtain $\sum\limits_{A=1}^{a} \left(\left(\sum\limits_{n=1}^{n_A} R_a \right)^2 / n_a \right)$. For the example, this sum is $697.225 + 5267.025 + 2310.400 = 8274.65$.

Step 6. Compute the value of H:

$$H = \left[\left(12 \right) \middle/ N \left(N + 1 \right) \right] \left[\sum_{A=1}^{a} \left(\left(\sum_{n=1}^{n_A} R_a \right)^2 \middle/ n_a \right) \right] - 3 \left(N + 1 \right).$$

For the example,

$$H = [(12)/30(30 + 1)][8274.65] - [3(30 + 1)]$$
$$H = 13.769$$

Step 7. The statistical hypotheses that provide the sampling distribution of H are:

H_0:   The population distributions from which the scores are sampled are identical.

H_1:   The population distributions from which the scores are sampled are not identical.

For values of n_a equal to or less than 5 with a equal to 3, selected critical values of H for $\alpha = .05$ are presented in Table A–6. For values of n_a greater than 5 and a equal to or greater than 3, critical values of H are the same as the χ^2 values presented in Table A–9. The df for use of this table are equal to $a - 1$.

Step 8. Select a value of α and find the critical value of H. For our example, the value of n_a is greater than 5 for each group; thus Table A–9 provides the critical value. For $\alpha = .05$ and $df = 3 - 1 = 2$, the critical value of H is 5.99. The obtained value of H is larger than the critical value; thus the null hypothesis is rejected and the alternative hypothesis is accepted.

Correction for Ties. If many scores have tied ranks, the value of H may be corrected for ties using this formula:

$$H^* = H \middle/ 1 - \left[\sum \left(t^3 - t \right) \middle/ \left(N^3 - N \right) \right]$$

where H^* is the value of H corrected for ties and t is the number of tied scores in a set of tied scores. For our example there are two tied scores in each set of tied scores (e.g., scores of 117 in A_1 and 117 in A_2) and seven sets of tied scores. Thus, the value of $\sum (t^3 - t)$ for each tie equals $(2^3 - 2)$ or 6. Over the seven sets of ties, the $\sum (t^3 - t)$ equals 42. The value of H^* then becomes:

$$H^* = 13.769/[1 - (42/(30^3 - 30))]$$
$$H^* = 13.785$$

As this illustration demonstrates, the correction for ties has the effect of slightly increasing the value of H. If the value of H is statistically significant before being corrected for ties, then the correction is unnecessary. Because the effect of correcting for ties is so small, it typically need be computed only if the value of H uncorrected for ties is of marginal significance (e.g., $.05 < p < .10$) or if the number of ties constitutes a substantial proportion of the scores (e.g., 25 percent or more).

For further information on the use of the Kruskal-Wallis analysis of variance on ranks, we refer you to Linton and Gallo (1975), Marascuilo and McSweeney (1977), and Siegel (1956).

which holds the probability of a Type I error equal to α for all possible comparisons, is discussed in Linton and Gallo (1975). Marascuilo and McSweeney (1977, pp. 306–312) present several follow-up tests, including a nonparametric analog of the Tukey test.

SUMMARY

- The analysis of variance may be employed with more than two levels of an independent variable. The computation of the F ratio in this case is identical to that for two levels of an independent variable.

- If the F ratio is statistically significant, multiple comparison procedures are necessary to determine which of the three or more sample means differ. The significant value of F simply indicates that at least one significant difference exists among the means being compared.

- Several problems arise when additional statistical tests must be conducted on the same data: (1) The probability that a difference between means simply represents a Type I error increases with each additional statistical test conducted, and (2) additional statistical tests may be prompted by the outcome of the experiment (post hoc comparisons) rather than planned before the experiment is conducted (planned comparisons). Post hoc comparisons may capitalize upon chance differences among the means.

- Multiple comparison procedures include the multiple F test, Tukey's test, and the Scheffé test.

- The choice of the appropriate multiple comparison procedure depends upon whether the comparisons to be made are planned or post hoc and upon the number of comparisons to be made.

- The strength of a treatment effect may be estimated either by eta squared (η^2), which provides a measure of strength of association for the sample, or by omega squared (ω^2), which provides a measure of strength of association for the population.

- The Kruskal-Wallis one-way analysis of variance by ranks is a nonparametric alternative to the one-way between-subjects analysis of variance for multilevel designs. It may be used when the data violate the assumptions of the analysis of variance.

10

In this chapter we introduce the two-factor between-subjects design. Topics include:

- The benefits of factorial designs
- The information obtained from factorial designs—main effects and interactions of the independent variables
- The data analysis of a factorial design, including the analysis of variance of a 2×2 between-subjects design
- Various types of between-subjects factorial designs

WHY YOU NEED TO KNOW THIS MATERIAL

Factorial designs are the workhorse designs of psychology. Anyone who reads or conducts research in psychology needs to clearly understand them.

Factorial Designs and
Two-way Analysis of Variance

The one-factor experimental design that we have discussed introduces most of the fundamental principles of research design and analysis of data in psychological research. But the one-factor design is often limited in its application because it permits us to manipulate only one independent variable at a time. As you are aware, most behaviors probably are multiply determined, i.e., affected by two or more independent variables. Mills and Aronson (1966), for example, found that the amount of opinion change in a member of an audience listening to a speaker depends upon both the physical attractiveness of the speaker and the speaker's announced desire to influence or not influence listeners. O'Brien and Wolford (1982) found that memory for a list of noun pairs depends upon the ability of the person learning the list to image, the type of image provided to the learner, and the length of the retention interval. One-factor designs do not permit us to manipulate more than one independent variable at a time; thus, to study the influence of two or more independent variables in combination, both Mills and Aronson, and O'Brien and Wolford used factorial designs in their experiments.

The word *factor* is simply another term for *independent variable*. Hence, **factorial designs** are research designs in which two or more independent variables are simultaneously varied. In the simplest factorial design, two independent variables are manipulated and each variable assumes two levels. Such a design is often called a 2×2 ("two-by-two") design. The first 2 indicates the two levels of the first independent variable and the second indicates the number of levels of the second independent variable. This was the research design used by Mills and Aronson. One of their independent variables was attractiveness of the speaker, which was varied over two levels—attractive and unattractive. Their other independent variable was the speaker's expressed desire for persuasion, which again had two levels—either to persuade the audience or not persuade them. O'Brien and Wolford employed a $2 \times 2 \times 2$ design. They had three independent variables—imagery ability, type of image, and length-of-retention interval—and each

257

independent variable varied over two levels. Among the many possible factorial designs are 2 × 4 (two levels of the first factor, four levels of the second), 3 × 3 × 2 (three levels of two factors, two levels of the third factor), 2 × 2 × 2 × 2 (four factors with two levels of each), and so on. Factorial designs may also be totally between-subjects, totally within-subjects, or a combination of the two, resulting in a mixed design. In this chapter we discuss only between-subjects factorial designs. Within-subjects and mixed factorial designs are developed in Chapter 12.

THE 2 × 2 BETWEEN-SUBJECTS DESIGN

The 2 × 2 between-subjects design is most convenient for discussing and illustrating the important concepts associated with factorial designs. This design is represented in Table 10–1. The table illustrates two independent variables or factors simply identified as *A* and *B,* each taking on two levels—independent variable *A* with levels A_1 and A_2, and independent variable *B* with levels B_1 and B_2. More generally, there are *a* levels of factor *A* and *b* levels of factor *B*. For the Mills and Aronson experiment, factor *A* is attractiveness of the speaker, with two levels, attractive (A_1) and unattractive (A_2), and factor *B* is the expressed desire to persuade, with two levels, persuade (B_1) and nonpersuade (B_2). The combination of the two independent variable creates four treatment conditions, often called *cells,* in the table: A_1B_1, A_1B_2, A_2B_1, and A_2B_2. Each cell or treatment condition actually represents a combination of treatments corresponding to one level of each independent variable. In the Mills and Aronson example, the treatment combinations are attractive-persuade (A_1B_1), attractive-nonpersuade (A_1B_2), nonattractive-persuade (A_2B_1), and nonattractive-nonpersuade (A_2B_2).

TABLE 10–1   *Plan of a two-factor between-subjects design with two levels of each independent variable.*

		Levels of independent variable A (Factor A)	
		A_1	A_2
Levels of independent variable B (Factor B)	B_1	A_1B_1 treatment condition (A_1B_1 cell)	A_2B_1 treatment condition (A_2B_1 cell)
	B_2	A_1B_2 treatment condition (A_1B_2 cell)	A_2B_2 treatment condition (A_2B_2 cell)

An equal number of participants typically are randomly assigned to each of four treatment combinations in a between-subjects factorial design. Thus, if a total of forty participants is to be utilized in a 2 × 2 design, ten individuals are randomly assigned to each treatment condition or cell. Although the experiment has four treatment conditions, an individual experiences only one of those conditions.

Information Obtained from a Factorial Design

As we have indicated, factorial designs are employed to simultaneously investigate the effects of two or more independent variables. From such a design, information is obtained about the main effects of each independent variable and about the interaction of the two independent variables. That is, a factorial design allows the investigator to determine the effect of each independent variable separately and also their joint effect.

Main Effects of Independent Variables

Table 10–2A illustrates the various sample means that may be calculated in a 2 × 2 factorial design. The **main effect means** for factor *A,* which reflect the *overall effect* of independent variable *A,* are given by $\bar{X}_{A_1}$ and $\bar{X}_{A_2}$. These means, sometimes called *column means,*[1] are obtained essentially by treating the design as a one-factor design manipulating only factor *A* and ignoring factor *B*. We do so by collapsing the data over levels of factor *B*. That is, the mean is found for all

Main effects in a 2 × 2 between-subjects factorial design.   **TABLE 10–2**

a. Cell means that may be calculated	b. Main effect means for factor *A*	c. Main effect means for factor *B*
	Ignore classification of scores for factor *B* to obtain main effect means for factor *A*.	Ignore classification of scores for factor *A* to obtain main effect means for factor *B*.

[1]Main effect means are also sometimes referred to simply as *marginal* means.

subjects given either treatment A_1 or A_2 while disregarding which level of factor B they received, as shown in Table 10–2B. The main effect for independent variable A is then the difference $\overline{X}_{A_1} - \overline{X}_{A_2}$. If factor A has an effect upon the dependent variable, then this effect will be reflected in the value of $\overline{X}_{A_1} - \overline{X}_{A_2}$.

A similar logic applies to obtaining the main effect for independent variable B. The design is now treated as a one-factor design manipulating only factor B. The treatment means for factor B (sometimes called *row means*) are obtained by collapsing over factor A as shown in Table 10–2C. The main effect for independent variable B is the difference $\overline{X}_{B_1} - \overline{X}_{B_2}$.

Interaction of the Independent Variables

Two things are said to *interact* when they act upon each other. In an experiment an **interaction** occurs when the *effect* of one independent variable (e.g., factor A) *depends* upon the level of the other independent variable (e.g., B_1 or B_2) with which it is manipulated. Thus, an interaction of independent variables is their *joint* effect upon the dependent variable, which cannot be predicted simply by knowing the main effect of each independent variable separately. Consequently, the occurrence of an interaction must be analyzed by comparing differences among the cell means rather than among the main effect means. We introduce a technique for identifying an interaction among cell means later in the chapter.

Importance of Factorial Designs and Interactions

The study of interactions among independent variables represents complex thinking about the determinants of behavior. Indeed, interactions of variables are the substance of many of the important relationships psychologists have discovered. Much of the substantive material in psychology textbooks deals with interactions of independent variables, although frequently these findings are not explicitly identified as interactions. For example, social psychology texts are rife with reported interactions.

- The influence of a message on opinion change depends upon the complexity of the message and the mode of its presentation. Difficult-to-comprehend messages lead to more opinion change when they are presented in a written format; easy-to-comprehend messages lead to more change when they are presented in a videotaped format.
- Whether a person will offer aid to a victim in distress may depend upon the race of the victim and the number of potential helpers present. Whites are equally likely to help a white victim whether other potential helpers are

present or not, but they are more likely to help a black victim when no other potential helpers are present.

- The style of leadership interacts with the setting to determine the effectiveness of a leader. For instance, directive leaders are most effective when tasks are unstructured, but nondirective leaders are most effective when tasks are highly structured.
- Men value the creative work of other men more highly and women value the creative work of other women more highly.

Newspapers and other popular media also often report interactions in articles on behavior and health. Recent examples that we have found include:

- The effect of alcoholic beverages on driving behavior depends upon the amount of time passed since drinking and personality traits such as aggressiveness or submissiveness.
- How comfortable a stranger will feel with you is a result of interaction of the sex of the stranger and the direction from which you approach; males approached from the side, but females approached from the front, will feel more comfortable.
- Females respond more openly to a nun wearing a habit, while males respond more openly when the nun is wearing street clothes.
- How well you withstand pain depends upon the type of pain and certain personality characteristics.
- Drugs frequently interact with one another; when combined one drug may greatly strengthen the effect of another, or conversely, it may inhibit the effect of the other. For example, avoid taking sleeping pills if you are taking other medications; sleeping pills can interact fatally with other drugs.

Interactions, not main effects, seem to be the rule rather than the exception in the study of behavior. In many instances, the effect of an independent variable is related to the personality traits of individuals. Walter Mischel, a leading personality theorist, writes in his book:

> The effects of conditions depend on the individuals in them, and . . . the *interaction* of individual differences and specific conditions is usually crucial. For example, the impact of different types of classroom arrangements depends on the particular students in them; small group discussion that might be helpful for some students might be a bore or even a handicap for others. (1976, p. 498)

This view suggests that it is probably futile to search for main effects of personality traits that predict behavior in many situations. It is most likely that treatment effects depend upon the attributes of people. Cronbach (1975) implores, "We need to reflect on what it means to establish empirical generalizations in a world in which most effects are interactive" (p. 121).

EXAMPLE OF A 2 × 2 BETWEEN-SUBJECTS DESIGN

To illustrate a 2 × 2 between-subjects design, we use an experiment conducted by Edward J. O'Brien as an undergraduate student. The experiment, conducted on a problem of his choice in a course in experimental psychology, was O'Brien's first research work in psychology and led to the more extensive research in graduate school that was published by O'Brien and Wolford (1982).

O'Brien's experiment dealt with the effects of a word-pegging mnemonic (memory) aid on the immediate recall of a list of words. The word-pegging technique employed was one often recited by children, "one is a bun, two is a shoe, three is a tree, four is a door," and so on, in which a word is rhymed with a number. After the rhyme is learned, a bizarre mental image is associated with each number-word pair. With "three" one might imagine a huge Christmas tree bent over and held down by an object represented by the third word in the list to be learned. The goal of the scheme, then, is to remember the object holding down the Christmas tree. The technique may be employed when attempting to learn a list of objects or words. Suppose you are asked to learn the list *luggage, pancake, garage,* and *paddle*. Employing the word-pegging technique, the third item in the list, *garage,* might be remembered by forming a mental image of a garage holding down a Christmas tree. When the time came to recall the list, you would run through the mnemonic "one, two, three," and so on. The word *three* would prompt the image of the Christmas tree and the object, the garage, holding it down.

Although the word-pegging aid appears complex, it is actually quite easy to use. O'Brien hypothesized, however, that the word-pegging technique should be effective only if the list of words to be learned is composed of concrete nouns, words one can easily image, because they refer to objects in the environment. He reasoned that a list of abstract nouns, such as *debt, heat,* or *bliss,* which refer to concepts and not objects, would not benefit from application of word pegging; the word-pegging technique requires forming an image of the word to be remembered, but abstract nouns do not lend themselves easily to the formation of mental images. Hence, O'Brien formulated a research hypothesis predicting an interaction of the *type of learning strategy* applied to learning a list with the *type of words* to be learned. More specifically, he hypothesized that a word-pegging mnemonic technique is beneficial in comparison to no mnemonic technique if a list of concrete nouns is to be learned, but word pegging is of no benefit compared to no mnemonic aid if a list of abstract nouns is to be learned.

To test this research hypothesis empirically, O'Brien used a 2 × 2 between-subjects design. Two independent variables were manipulated, the type of learning strategy employed (factor A) and the type of word list (factor B). Each independent variable had two levels. For the type of learning strategy, subjects were either instructed in the use of word pegging (pegging, level A_1) or were not instructed (no pegging, level A_2). For the type of word list, the lists were either twenty unrelated concrete nouns (level B_1: nouns such as *bamboo, razor, saucer, fiddle, chisel*) or twenty unrelated abstract nouns (level B_2: nouns such as *love, thought, apathy, calamity, vanity*). Five subjects were randomly assigned to each of the four possible treatment combinations of the experiment: pegging-concrete nouns (A_1B_1); no pegging-concrete nouns (A_2B_1); pegging-abstract nouns (A_1B_2); and no pegging-abstract nouns (A_2B_2). All subjects were given one trial to learn the entire list of twenty nouns. After the learning trial, the subjects were asked to recall the words in the order presented. An individual's score was the number of words out of twenty that could be recalled.

Descriptive Data Analysis of a Factorial Experiment

Table 10–3 presents the raw data for the twenty subjects of the experiment. As with the data of a one-factor design, the first step in data analysis begins with computing measures of central tendency, specifically sample means.

From the data in Table 10–3, nine sample means may be calculated: four cell means, four main-effect means, and one grand mean. These means are presented in Table 10–4.

Cell Means

A cell mean $(\overline{X}_{AB})$ is simply the mean of the n scores for a particular treatment combination (e.g., $n = 5$ in A_1B_1 for this experiment). The cell means describe the typical performance of subjects receiving each treatment combination.

Scores for twenty subjects in the example two-factor experiment.   **TABLE 10–3**

	Type of strategy (Factor A)	
	Pegging (A_1)	*No pegging (A_2)*
Concrete (B_1)	17	11
	20	9
	14	12
	16	8
	17	13
Type of word (Factor B)		
Abstract (B_2)	12	12
	10	9
	14	15
	8	11
	11	13

TABLE 10-4   *Means (M) for the data of Table 10–3. Standard deviations (SD) are given in parentheses.*

	Type of strategy (Factor A)		Main effect for type of word
	Pegging (A_1)	*No pegging (A_1)*	
Concrete (B_1)	16.8	10.6	13.7
Type of word (Factor B)	(2.2)	(2.1)	
Abstract (B_2)	11.0	12.0	11.5
	(2.2)	(2.2)	
Main effect for type of strategy	13.9	11.3	Grand mean 12.6

Main Effect Means

Main effect means are obtained by finding the mean of the scores for one level of an independent variable collapsed over the levels of the other factor. Following the approach illustrated in Table 10–2, the main effect means ($\overline{X}_A$) for factor A, the type of strategy, in Table 10–3, are based upon the ten scores of individuals given either the pegging or no-pegging strategy. Type of word (factor B) is ignored while determining these main effect means. The main effect means ($\overline{X}_B$) for factor B, type of word, are similarly obtained. In this case, type of strategy (factor A) is ignored when the means are computed. The main effects represent the typical performance in a level of one of the independent variables while ignoring the other independent variable.

Grand Mean

The grand mean ($\overline{X}_G$) is found simply by obtaining the mean of all the scores in the table. For the data in Table 10–3, the grand mean is the mean of all twenty scores. Because the grand mean represents average performance over all treatment conditions, it is not typically presented as a descriptive statistic. But it is a valuable statistic for deriving an analysis of variance for such a design. This use will become apparent in later sections of this chapter.

It may be useful for you to take a few minutes to compute these means from the data of Table 10–3 to ensure your understanding of their computation.

Measures of Variability

As we discussed in Chapter 6, the measure of variability most typically used in conjunction with the mean is the standard deviation (*SD*). The standard deviations for the data in each cell of Table 10–3 are also presented in Table 10–4. In a factorial design the *SD* is typically calculated only for the cell means as we have illustrated, because the cell mean represents only the participants receiving the same treatment condition.

INFERENTIAL DATA ANALYSIS OF A FACTORIAL DESIGN

An Overview

The statistical model used to represent the factorial design is again the analysis of variance. As you will recall from Chapter 8, the analysis of variance model partitions the total variation in scores into unique sources of variation that are independent of each other. The one-way between-subjects analysis of variance discussed in Chapter 8 has two independent sources of variation: the effect of the independent variable (i.e., factor *A*) and the effects of uncontrolled extraneous variables and errors of measurement (i.e., error). In a two-way factorial design, however, two independent variables are manipulated or employed. Thus, the total variation of all scores is attributed to four sources:

1. the effect of the particular treatment level of factor *A*
2. the effect of the particular treatment level of factor *B*
3. the interaction of factors *A* and *B*; i.e., the unique effect of a particular combination of independent variables *A* and *B*
4. the effects of error from uncontrolled extraneous variables and errors of measurement; i.e., error variation.

The approach taken by the two-factor analysis of variance model is to partition a score into a set of four components, each component reflecting one of the sources of variation in the score. Then, like the one-way analysis of variance, a mean square is obtained from each component of the partitioned scores of all individuals. Following this step, three separate *F* ratios are generated, one for each main effect, *A* and *B*, and one for the *A* × *B* interaction. Each of the three obtained values of *F* is then compared to tabled values of *F* from the sampling distribution under a null hypothesis to determine the statistical rarity of the obtained value of *F* if sampling error alone is responsible for any obtained differences in sample means. Three null hypotheses and alternative hypotheses are tested by these *F* ratios. The specific statistical hypotheses tested for the main effects and interaction are presented in a later section of this chapter.

Components of a Score

In a two-factor between-subjects design it is assumed that a subject's score is influenced by the four sources of variance described. Specifically, a score is "constructed" by beginning at some base level and adding to it the effects of factor *A*, factor B, the $A \times B$ interaction, and, of course, error. Conceptually, a score is constructed as follows:

Score $X_i =$ Base level $+$ Effect of factor A $+$ Effect of factor B
$+$ Effect of interaction of factors A and B $+$ Error.

In notation, the construction of a score is represented by:

$$X_i = \bar{X}_G + (\bar{X}_A - \bar{X}_G) + (\bar{X}_B - \bar{X}_G) +$$
$$[(\bar{X}_{AB} - \bar{X}_G) - (\bar{X}_A - \bar{X}_G) - (\bar{X}_B - \bar{X}_G)] + (X_i - \bar{X}_{AB}). \quad \textbf{(Eq. 10–1)}$$

This equation shows that the grand mean of the scores ($\bar{X}_G$) is considered to be the base level for a score. If there is no systematic variation at all in the experiment, then the grand mean should adequately represent a "typical" score. A treatment effect is reflected by the deviation of the mean for the level of the independent variable received by the subject from the grand mean. For factor A this figure is given by $\bar{X}_A - \bar{X}_G$ and for factor B by $\bar{X}_B - \bar{X}_G$. The interaction of the two independent variables is expressed in more complex form. Fundamentally, however, it is the remaining deviation of the cell mean from the grand mean after the main effects of each independent variable have been removed. This calculation is shown here:

$$A \times B \quad = \quad (\bar{X}_{AB} - \bar{X}_G) \quad - \quad (\bar{X}_A - \bar{X}_G) \quad - \quad (\bar{X}_B - \bar{X}_G).$$

Interaction of A and B	Deviation of cell mean from grand mean	Main effect of factor A	Main effect of factor B

Carrying out the algebraic manipulations results in the expression of the interaction as:

$$\bar{X}_{AB} - \bar{X}_A - \bar{X}_B + \bar{X}_G.$$

Finally, the error in the score reflects how much the individual's score deviates from the mean of the treatment condition ($X_i - \bar{X}_{AB}$). Essentially it is what is left over in the score after the main effects of both factors and their interaction have been taken into account. As in a one-way analysis of variance, it reflects the uniqueness of a subject's score in a group of individuals all of whom received the same treatment. By substituting the less complex form of the interaction, equation 10–1 can be simplified as follows:

$$X_i = \bar{X}_G + (\bar{X}_A - \bar{X}_G) + (\bar{X}_B - \bar{X}_G)$$
$$+ (\bar{X}_{AB} - \bar{X}_A - \bar{X}_B + \bar{X}_G) + (X_i - \bar{X}_{AB}). \quad \textbf{(Eq. 10–2)}$$

To illustrate the use of this equation, we "construct" one of the scores presented in Table 10–3. Let us see, for example, how the score for the third individual in the pegging-abstract word-treatment group (A_1B_2) is constructed by substituting appropriate values into equation 10–2. The specific main effect and cell means are identified in notation as,

$$X_i = \bar{X}_G + (\bar{X}_{A_1} - \bar{X}_G) + (\bar{X}_{B_2} - \bar{X}_G)$$
$$+ (\bar{X}_{A_1 B_2} - \bar{X}_{A_1} - \bar{X}_{B_2} + \bar{X}_G) + (X_i - \bar{X}_{A_1 B_2}).$$

Substituting numerical values, we obtain

$$14.0 = 12.6 + (13.9 - 12.6) + (11.5 - 12.6)$$
$$+ (11.0 - 13.9 - 11.5 + 12.6) + (14.0 - 11.0).$$

We can demonstrate that this is an equation simply by carrying out the arithmetic functions indicated. And,

$$14.0 = 12.6 + (1.3) + (-1.1) + (-1.8) + (3.0).$$

Therefore,

$$14.0 = 12.6 + 1.3 - 1.1 - 1.8 + 3.0$$

and

$$14.0 = 14.0.$$

Deriving Variance Estimates from the Components of Scores

Partitioning a Score

In order to obtain mean squares from the model of a score expressed in equation 10–2, the scores must be *partitioned*. Following the approach of a one-factor analysis of variance, we partition by transposing $\bar{X}_G$ in equation 10–2 so that it is placed on the other side of the equals sign. Accordingly, we obtain:

$$(X_i - \bar{X}_G) \quad = \quad (\bar{X}_A - \bar{X}_G) \quad + \quad (\bar{X}_B - \bar{X}_G)$$

Deviation of a score from the grand mean	Deviation of factor A main effect mean from the grand mean	Deviation of factor B main effect mean from the grand mean

$$+ \quad (\bar{X}_{AB} - \bar{X}_A - \bar{X}_B + \bar{X}_G) \quad + \quad (X_i - \bar{X}_{AB}).$$

Deviation of a cell mean from the grand mean after main effects of factors A and B have been removed; i.e., interaction

Deviation of a score from the treatment-group mean; i.e., error

(Eq. 10–3)

This equation states that a score deviates from the grand mean because of the systematic influences of the two treatments received and their interaction, and because of the unsystematic influence of error variation. By partitioning a score into these several components, we have established the basis for deriving four mean squares. To do so, we must first obtain values for the sums of squares for each partitioned component.

Deriving Sums of Squares from Partitioned Scores

Using the approach presented in Chapter 8, sums of squares (*SS*) are obtained by partitioning each individual's score in the form of equation 10–3. This procedure is illustrated in Step 1 of Table 10–5 for each of the scores of Table 10–3. Next,

TABLE 10–5   *Deriving sums of squares for a two-way analysis of variance.*

Step 1: Partition scores for the twenty subjects (see Table 10–4)

$$X_i - \bar{X}_G = (\bar{X}_A - \bar{X}_G) + (\bar{X}_B - \bar{X}_G) + (\bar{X}_{AB} - \bar{X}_A - \bar{X}_B + \bar{X}_G) + (X_i - \bar{X}_{AB})$$

Subjects in A_1B_1

$17 - 12.6 = (13.9 - 12.6) + (13.7 - 12.6) + (16.8 - 13.9 - 13.7 + 12.6) + (17 - 16.8)$
$20 - 12.6 = (13.9 - 12.6) + (13.7 - 12.6) + (16.8 - 13.9 - 13.7 + 12.6) + (20 - 16.8)$
$14 - 12.6 = (13.9 - 12.6) + (13.7 - 12.6) + (16.8 - 13.9 - 13.7 + 12.6) + (14 - 16.8)$
$16 - 12.6 = (13.9 - 12.6) + (13.7 - 12.6) + (16.8 - 13.9 - 13.7 + 12.6) + (16 - 16.8)$
$17 - 12.6 = (13.9 - 12.6) + (13.7 - 12.6) + (16.8 - 13.9 - 13.7 + 12.6) + (17 - 16.8)$

Subjects in A_2B_1

$11 - 12.6 = (11.3 - 12.6) + (13.7 - 12.6) + (10.6 - 11.3 - 13.7 + 12.6) + (11 - 10.6)$
$9 - 12.6 = (11.3 - 12.6) + (13.7 - 12.6) + (10.6 - 11.3 - 13.7 + 12.6) + (\ 9 - 10.6)$
$12 - 12.6 = (11.3 - 12.6) + (13.7 - 12.6) + (10.6 - 11.3 - 13.7 + 12.6) + (12 - 10.6)$
$8 - 12.6 = (11.3 - 12.6) + (13.7 - 12.6) + (10.6 - 11.3 - 13.7 + 12.6) + (\ 8 - 10.6)$
$13 - 12.6 = (11.3 - 12.6) + (13.7 - 12.6) + (10.6 - 11.3 - 13.7 + 12.6) + (13 - 10.6)$

Subjects in A_1B_2

$12 - 12.6 = (13.9 - 12.6) + (11.5 - 12.6) + (11.0 - 13.9 - 11.5 + 12.6) + (12 - 11.0)$
$10 - 12.6 = (13.9 - 12.6) + (11.5 - 12.6) + (11.0 - 13.9 - 11.5 + 12.6) + (10 - 11.0)$
$14 - 12.6 = (13.9 - 12.6) + (11.5 - 12.6) + (11.0 - 13.9 - 11.5 + 12.6) + (14 - 11.0)$
$8 - 12.6 = (13.9 - 12.6) + (11.5 - 12.6) + (11.0 - 13.9 - 11.5 + 12.6) + (\ 8 - 11.0)$
$11 - 12.6 = (13.9 - 12.6) + (11.5 - 12.6) + (11.0 - 13.9 - 11.5 + 12.6) + (11 - 11.0)$

Subjects in A_2B_2

$12 - 12.6 = (11.3 - 12.6) + (11.5 - 12.6) + (12.0 - 11.3 - 11.5 + 12.6) + (12 - 12.0)$
$9 - 12.6 = (11.3 - 12.6) + (11.5 - 12.6) + (12.0 - 11.3 - 11.5 + 12.6) + (\ 9 - 12.0)$
$15 - 12.6 = (11.3 - 12.6) + (11.5 - 12.6) + (12.0 - 11.3 - 11.5 + 12.6) + (15 - 12.0)$
$11 - 12.6 = (11.3 - 12.6) + (11.5 - 12.6) + (12.0 - 11.3 - 11.5 + 12.6) + (11 - 12.0)$
$13 - 12.6 = (11.3 - 12.6) + (11.5 - 12.6) + (12.0 - 11.3 - 11.5 + 12.6) + (13 - 12.0)$

Step 2: Perform the subtractions in Step 1 to obtain deviations

Subjects in A_1B_1

$+4.4 = +1.3 + +1.1 + +1.8 + +0.2$
$+7.4 = +1.3 + +1.1 + +1.8 + +3.2$
$+1.4 = +1.3 + +1.1 + +1.8 + -2.8$
$+3.4 = +1.3 + +1.1 + +1.8 + -0.8$
$+4.4 = +1.3 + +1.1 + +1.8 + +0.2$

Subjects in A_2B_1

$-1.6 = -1.3 + +1.1 + -1.8 + +0.4$
$-3.6 = -1.3 + +1.1 + -1.8 + -1.6$
$-0.6 = -1.3 + +1.1 + -1.8 + +1.4$
$-4.6 = -1.3 + +1.1 + -1.8 + -2.6$
$+0.4 = -1.3 + +1.1 + -1.8 + +2.4$

Subjects in A_1B_2									
-0.6	$=$	$+1.3$	$+$	-1.1	$+$	-1.8	$+$	$+1.0$	
-2.6	$=$	$+1.3$	$+$	-1.1	$+$	-1.8	$+$	-1.0	
$+1.4$	$=$	$+1.3$	$+$	-1.1	$+$	-1.8	$+$	$+3.0$	
-4.6	$=$	$+1.3$	$+$	-1.1	$+$	-1.8	$+$	-3.0	
-1.6	$=$	$+1.3$	$+$	-1.1	$+$	-1.8	$+$	$+0.0$	

Subjects in A_2B_2									
-0.6	$=$	-1.3	$+$	-1.1	$+$	$+1.8$	$+$	$+0.0$	
-3.6	$=$	-1.3	$+$	-1.1	$+$	$+1.8$	$+$	-3.0	
$+2.4$	$=$	-1.3	$+$	-1.1	$+$	$+1.8$	$+$	$+3.0$	
-1.6	$=$	-1.3	$+$	-1.1	$+$	$+1.8$	$+$	-1.0	
$+0.4$	$=$	-1.3	$+$	-1.1	$+$	$+1.8$	$+$	$+1.0$	

Step 3: Square each deviation

	$(X_i - \bar{X}_G)^2$	$(\bar{X}_A - \bar{X}_G)^2$	$(\bar{X}_B - \bar{X}_G)^2$	$(\bar{X}_{AB} - \bar{X}_A - \bar{X}_B + \bar{X}_G)^2$	$(X_i - \bar{X}_{AB})^2$
Subjects in A_1B_1	19.36	1.69	1.21	3.24	.04
	54.76	1.69	1.21	3.24	10.24
	1.96	1.69	1.21	3.24	7.84
	11.56	1.69	1.21	3.24	.64
	19.36	1.69	1.21	3.24	.04
Subjects in A_2B_1	2.56	1.69	1.21	3.24	.16
	12.96	1.69	1.21	3.24	2.56
	.36	1.69	1.21	3.24	1.96
	21.16	1.69	1.21	3.24	6.76
	.16	1.69	1.21	3.24	5.76
Subjects in A_1B_2	.36	1.69	1.21	3.24	1.00
	6.76	1.69	1.21	3.24	1.00
	1.96	1.69	1.21	3.24	9.00
	21.16	1.69	1.21	3.24	9.00
	2.56	1.69	1.21	3.24	0.00
Subjects in A_2B_2	.36	1.69	1.21	3.24	0.00
	12.96	1.69	1.21	3.24	9.00
	5.76	1.69	1.21	3.24	9.00
	2.56	1.69	1.21	3.24	1.00
	.16	1.69	1.21	3.24	1.00

Step 4: Sum the squared deviations for each component over all subjects

$$\sum_{A=1}^{a}\sum_{B=1}^{b}\sum_{n=1}^{n_{AB}}(X_i - \bar{X}_G)^2 = \sum_{A=1}^{a}\sum_{B=1}^{b}\sum_{n=1}^{n_{AB}}(\bar{X}_A - \bar{X}_G)^2 + \sum_{A=1}^{a}\sum_{B=1}^{b}\sum_{n=1}^{n_{AB}}(\bar{X}_B - \bar{X}_G)^2$$

$$+ \sum_{A=1}^{a}\sum_{B=1}^{b}\sum_{n=1}^{n_{AB}}(\bar{X}_{AB} - \bar{X}_A - \bar{X}_B + \bar{X}_G)^2 + \sum_{A=1}^{a}\sum_{B=1}^{b}\sum_{n=1}^{n_{AB}}(X_i - \bar{X}_{AB})^2$$

$198.8 =$	33.8	$+$	24.2	$+$	64.8	$+$	76.0
$SS_{Total} =$	SS_A	$+$	SS_B	$+$	$SS_{A\times B}$	$+$	SS_{Error}

we obtain the numerical value of each of the deviations (Step 2), we square the values of each of the positive and negative deviations (Step 3), and then we sum the squared deviations over all participants in the experiment (Step 4). The result is five sums of squares: SS_{Total}, SS_A, SS_B, $SS_{A \times B}$, and SS_{Error}.

Notationally the steps and resulting sums of squares are indicated by:

$$\sum_{A=1}^{a} \sum_{B=1}^{b} \sum_{n=1}^{n_{AB}} (X_i - \bar{X}_G)^2 = \sum_{A=1}^{a} \sum_{B=1}^{b} \sum_{n=1}^{n_{AB}} (\bar{X}_A - \bar{X}_G)^2 + \sum_{A=1}^{a} \sum_{B=1}^{b} \sum_{n=1}^{n_{AB}} (\bar{X}_B - \bar{X}_G)^2$$

$$+ \sum_{A=1}^{a} \sum_{B=1}^{b} \sum_{n=1}^{n_{AB}} (\bar{X}_{AB} - \bar{X}_A - \bar{X}_B + \bar{X}_G)^2 + \sum_{A=1}^{a} \sum_{B=1}^{b} \sum_{n=1}^{n_{AB}} (X_i - \bar{X}_{AB})^2. \quad \textbf{(Eq. 10-4)}$$

The summing notation $\sum_{A=1}^{a} \sum_{B=1}^{b} \sum_{n=1}^{n_{AB}}$ indicates that each term is first summed over all the n_{AB} subjects within a treatment condition, then summed over all b levels of factor B, and finally summed over all a levels of factor A. In sums-of-squares notation, equation 10-4 may be written:

$$SS_{\text{Total}} = SS_A + SS_B + SS_{A \times B} + SS_{\text{Error}}. \quad \textbf{(Eq. 10-5)}$$

The sources of variance, SS, and the definitional formula for each SS are shown in columns 1, 2, and 3, respectively, of Table 10-6.

TABLE 10-6   *Formulas for analysis of variance for a two-factor between-subjects design.*

① Source of variance	② SS	③ Definitional formula of SS	④ Fixed term for df	⑤ Term free to vary for df	⑥ General formula for df[a]	⑦ df for example[b]	⑧ MS
Factor A	SS_A	$\sum_{A=1}^{a} \sum_{B=1}^{b} \sum_{n=1}^{n_{AB}} (\bar{X}_A - \bar{X}_G)^2$	$\bar{X}_G$	$\bar{X}_A$	$a - 1$	1	$SS_A/(a-1)$
Factor B	SS_B	$\sum_{A=1}^{a} \sum_{B=1}^{b} \sum_{n=1}^{n_{AB}} (\bar{X}_B - \bar{X}_G)^2$	$\bar{X}_G$	$\bar{X}_B$	$b - 1$	1	$SS_B/(b-1)$
Interaction of A *and* B	$SS_{A \times B}$	$\sum_{A=1}^{a} \sum_{B=1}^{b} \sum_{n=1}^{n_{AB}} (\bar{X}_{AB} - \bar{X}_A - \bar{X}_B + \bar{X}_G)^2$	$\bar{X}_A, \bar{X}_B, \bar{X}_G$	$\bar{X}_{AB}$	$(a-1) \times (b-1)$	1	$SS_{A \times B}/(a-1)(b-1)$
Error	SS_{Error}	$\sum_{A=1}^{a} \sum_{B=1}^{b} \sum_{n=1}^{n_{AB}} (X_i - \bar{X}_{AB})^2$	$\bar{X}_{AB}$	X_i	$ab(n-1)$	16	$SS_{\text{Error}}/ab(n-1)$
Total	SS_{Total}	$\sum_{A=1}^{a} \sum_{B=1}^{b} \sum_{n=1}^{n_{AB}} (X_i - \bar{X}_G)^2$	$\bar{X}_G$	X_i	$N - 1$	19	Not calculated

[a] a = number of levels of factor A.
 b = number of levels of factor B.
 n = number of scores in each treatment condition.
[b] 2×2 design with five subjects per cell.

Determining Degrees of Freedom for Each Sum of Squares

Variance estimates, or mean squares (*MS*), are obtained by dividing the sums of squares by the appropriate degrees of freedom (*df*). Recall that degrees of freedom are defined as the number of scores that are free to vary in the computation of a statistic. Using this definition it is quite simple to calculate the *df* for each term of equation 10–4. Following the procedure outlined in Chapter 8, the "fixed" term of each *SS* is ascertained. The fixed term (S) for each *SS* is shown in column 4 of Table 10–6. Then, assuming this fixed term, we count how many other terms or scores are free to vary in the determination of the particular *SS* (see column 5). This count is then expressed in more general notation applicable to any two-factor between-subjects analysis (column 6). The outcome of applying the procedure to the example data in Table 10–4 is also presented (column 7).

Calculating Variance Estimates from SS *and* df: *Mean Squares*

There are four sources of variation in scores from a two-factor experiment; thus, four variance estimates may be obtained from the partitioning of scores. Dividing each *SS* by its corresponding *df* produces the four mean squares: MS_A, MS_B, $MS_{A \times B}$, and MS_{Error} (see column 8 of Table 10–6). Each *MS* is responsive to different sources of variation in the experiment.

Mean Squares as Estimates of the Population Variance

In the instance where neither of the independent variables has an effect on the dependent variable and there is no interaction of the independent variables, then each *MS* is an estimate of only error variation. Under these circumstances, all the four mean squares should be approximately equal in value and reflect only the effects of error. But if either or both of the independent variables have a main effect, or if they interact, the effect is reflected in the value of the corresponding *MS*. Thus, for example, if factor *A* produces a main effect, MS_A will increase in value relative to MS_{Error}, but MS_B, $MS_{A \times B}$, and MS_{Error} will not be affected by the main effect of factor *A*. A similar situation holds if factor *B* has an effect, and for $MS_{A \times B}$ if the independent variables interact. The MS_{Error}, however, is not affected by either main effects or interaction of the independent variables. It always reflects only error variance in the experiment. The sources of variance, the four mean squares, and the factors affecting each *MS* are summarized in columns 1, 2, and 3 of Table 10–7.

TABLE 10-7   *Overview of a two-factor between-subjects analysis of variance.*

① Source of variance	② MS	③ Responsive to	④ F ratio	⑤ Statistical hypotheses
Factor A	MS_A	Systematic variance due to A Sampling error	MS_A/MS_{Error}	H_0: $\mu_{A_1} = \mu_{A_2}$ H_1: not H_0
Factor B	MS_B	Systematic variance due to B Sampling error	MS_B/MS_{Error}	H_0: $\mu_{B_1} = \mu_{B_2}$ H_1: not H_0
Interaction of factors A and B	$MS_{A \times B}$	Systematic variance due to interaction of A and B Sampling error	$MS_{A \times B}/MS_{Error}$	H_0: all $(\mu_{AB} - \mu_A - \mu_B + \mu_G) = 0$ H_1: not H_0
Error	MS_{Error}	Error variance		
Total	MS_{Total}	All systematic and error variance		

Statistical Decision Making with Factorial Analysis of Variance

The F Statistic

As you know, the statistic employed in the analysis of variance is the F. An F statistic is formed by the ratio of two mean squares, one MS a variance estimate responsive to the effects of an independent variable as well as to sampling error, and the other MS responsive only to error variance in the experiment. In a one-factor design only one F statistic is derived in the analysis. In the two-factor experiment, however, there are three possible sources of systematic variation. Thus, three F ratios are formed; they are shown in column 4 of Table 10–7. Each of these ratios employs MS_{Error} as the denominator and the appropriate MS for the independent variable or the interaction as the numerator. If the independent variable affecting the MS in the numerator of a particular F ratio does *not* have an effect, then that F ratio should be about equal to 1.00, for both the numerator and denominator MS reflect only error variation in the experiment. But if the independent variable does have an effect, the value of the MS for that variable will become larger and the particular value of F for that factor will become greater than 1.0. This reasoning is, of course, identical to that expressed in Chapter 8 for the one-factor analysis of variance.

Statistical Hypotheses for Factorial Analyses

To determine how large a value of F is necessary to decide that the value is not reasonably attributed simply to error variance requires us to test a null hypothesis and generate the sampling distribution for F under that null hypothesis. Because there are three different F ratios for a two-factor between-subjects design, three different null hypotheses are tested, one for each F ratio that is calculated. The null and alternative hypotheses for each F ratio are presented in column 5 of Table 10–7. As you will notice, the null and alternative hypotheses for the main effects of factors A and B are identical in form to the expression of statistical hypotheses for the one-way analysis of variance. For the main effect of an independent variable, therefore, the analysis of variance treats the data as if they were obtained from a one-factor design, a point emphasized in Table 10–2.

The null hypothesis for the interaction takes a form slightly different from the statistical hypotheses for main effects. Simply, this null hypothesis states that in the population, if no interaction occurs, the deviation of the cell mean μ_{AB} from the grand mean μ_G will be equal to 0 after the main effects of each independent variable; that is, $\mu_A - \mu_G$ and $\mu_B - \mu_G$, have been taken into account and subtracted from it. In other words, this null hypothesis states that with no interaction the value of each cell mean may be exactly predicted from the main effects of the independent variables. The alternative hypothesis merely states that this prediction is not true.

Decision Making from the F Ratio

Statistical decision making from an obtained value of F in a factorial design is identical to the process followed in a one-factor analysis of variance. A value of α defining the size of the critical region is chosen prior to conducting the analysis. The sampling distribution of F under H_0 is then determined for each of the three F ratios. This step requires looking up three critical values of F with the appropriate numerator and denominator df in Table A–2. Then, for each of the obtained F ratios, if the obtained value of F is *equal to or larger than* its corresponding critical value, the null hypothesis H_0 for that F is *rejected* and the alternative hypothesis H_1 is *accepted*. On the other hand, if the obtained value of an F is *less than* its critical value, then the decision is to *fail to reject* the null hypothesis and to *not accept* the alternative hypothesis for that source of variance. To illustrate this process, we turn to an analysis of variance on the example data in Table 10–3.

Analysis of Variance on the Example Data

A summary of the analysis of variance on the data of Table 10–3 is presented in Table 10–8. The values for the sums of squares were obtained from the computations in Table 10–5 and the degrees of freedom from Table 10–6. Following column 4 of Table 10–7, each MS responding to systematic variance was divided by MS_{Error} to find the value of F for each of the factors and their interaction. In this example, each F statistic has 1 df for its numerator and 16 df for its denominator. Hence, each of the three values of F has the same critical value and rejection

TABLE 10–8   *Analysis of variance summary table for example experiment.*

Source	SS	df	MS	F
Type of strategy (*A*)	33.80	1	33.80	7.12*
Type of word (*B*)	24.20	1	24.20	5.09*
A × *B*	64.80	1	64.80	13.64*
Error	76.00	16	4.75	
Total	198.80	19		

*p < .05.

region. This result is not necessarily the same in all factorial designs. Depending upon the number of levels of each factor, it is quite possible for each value of *F* to have a different numerator *df*; thus each value will have a different rejection region.

Setting $\alpha = .05$, the critical value of *F* with 1, 16 *df* is 4.49 (obtained from Table A–2). Hence, for each of the three values of *F* in Table 10–8 the rejection region consists of obtained values of *F* equal to or larger than 4.49. Because each of the obtained values of *F* is larger than 4.49, each falls in the rejection region. Thus the appropriate null hypothesis is rejected and the corresponding alternative hypothesis is accepted for each of the three *F* ratios in this example.

Raw-Score Computational Formulas for the Two-Factor Between-Subjects Analysis of Variance

The notational representation for computing an analysis of variance of a two-factor between-subjects design with two levels of each factor and five subjects per cell is:

		Factor A		
		A_1	A_2	
	B_1	X_1 X_2 X_3 X_4 X_5 $T_{A_1B_1}$	X_{11} X_{12} X_{13} X_{14} X_{15} $T_{A_2B_1}$	T_{B_1}
Factor B	B_2	X_6 X_7 X_8 X_9 X_{10} $T_{A_1B_2}$	X_{16} X_{17} X_{18} X_{19} X_{20} $T_{A_2B_2}$	T_{B_2}
		T_{A_1}	T_{A_2}	G

where X_i = raw score of a subject

T_A = total of scores for a main effect of factor A

T_B = total of scores for a main effect of factor B

T_{AB} = total of scores in a cell

G = grand total of scores

n_{AB} = number of scores in a cell

a = number of levels of independent variable A

b = number of levels of independent variable B

N = total number of scores.

The numerical values needed to obtain *SS* are:

$[1] = \Sigma_{A=1}^{a} \Sigma_{B=1}^{b} \Sigma_{n=1}^{n_{AB}} X_i^2$ the sum of all the raw scores squared

$[2] = \Sigma_{A=1}^{a} \Sigma_{B=1}^{b} T_{AB}^2/n_{AB}$ the sum of each cell total squared, divided by the number of scores in a cell.

$[3] = \Sigma_{A=1}^{a} T_A^2/bn_{AB}$ the sum of each main effect total for factor A squared, divided by the number of scores entering into that total

$[4] = \Sigma_{B=1}^{b} T_B^2/an_{AB}$ the sum of each main effect total for factor B squared, divided by the number of scores entering into that total

$[5] = G^2/N$ the grand total squared, divided by the total number of scores.

Using these numerical values, an analysis of variance is computed as follows:

Source	SS	df	MS	F
Factor A	$[3] - [5]$	$a - 1$	SS_A/df_A	MS_A/MS_{Error}
Factor B	$[4] - [5]$	$b - 1$	SS_B/df_B	MS_B/MS_{Error}
$A \times B$	$[2] - [3]$ $- [4] + [5]$	$(a - 1)x$ $(b - 1)$	$SS_{A \times B}/df_{A \times B}$	$MS_{A \times B}/MS_{Error}$
Error	$[1] - [2]$	$ab(n - 1)$	SS_{Error}/df_{Error}	
Total	$[1] - [5]$	$N - 1$	Not calculated	

To illustrate the computations, we use the example scores given in Table 10–3 for which an analysis of variance is summarized in Table 10–8.

	Factor A			
	A_1		A_2	
B_1	17 20 14 $T_{A_1B_1} = 84$ 16 17		11 9 12 $T_{A_2B_1} = 53$ 8 13	$T_{B_1} = 137$
Factor B				
B_2	12 10 14 $T_{A_1B_2} = 55$ 8 11		12 9 15 $T_{A_2B_2} = 60$ 11 13	$T_{B_2} = 115$
	$T_{A_1} = 139$		$T_{A_2} = 113$	$G = 252$

(continued)

Raw-Score Computational Formulas for the Two-Factor Between-Subjects Analysis of Variance (continued)

$[1] = 17^2 + \ldots + 17^2 + 11^2 + \ldots + 13^2 + 12^2 + \ldots + 11^2 + 12^2 + \ldots + 13^2 = 3374.0$
$[2] = (84^2 + 53^2 + 55^2 + 60^2)/5 = 16,490/5 = 3298.0$
$[3] = (139^2 + 113^2)/(2)(5) = 32,090/10 = 3209.0$
$[4] = (137^2 + 115^2)/(2)(5) = 31,994/10 = 3199.4$
$[5] = 252^2/20 = 63,504/20 = 3175.2$

Then:

$$SS_A = 3209.0 - 3175.2 = 33.8$$
$$df_A = 2 - 1 = 1$$

$$SS_B = 3199.4 - 3175.2 = 24.2$$
$$df_B = 2 - 1 = 1$$

$$SS_{A \times B} = 3298.0 - 3209.0 - 3199.4 + 3175.2 = 64.8$$
$$df_{A \times B} = (2 - 1)(2 - 1) = 1$$

$$SS_{\text{Error}} = 3374.0 - 3298.0 = 76.0$$
$$df_{\text{Error}} = (2)(2)(5 - 1) = 16$$

$$SS_{\text{Total}} = 3374.0 - 3175.2 = 198.8$$
$$df_{\text{Total}} = 20 - 1 = 19$$

The summary of the analysis of variance is then:

Source	SS	df	MS	F
Factor A	33.8	1	$33.8/1 = 33.80$	$33.80/4.75 = 7.12$
Factor B	24.2	1	$24.2/1 = 24.20$	$24.20/4.75 = 5.09$
$A \times B$	64.8	1	$64.8/1 = 64.80$	$64.80/4.75 = 13.64$
Error	76.0	16	$76.0/16 = 4.75$	
Total	198.0	19		

The numerical values obtained by this computational approach are identical to those presented in Table 10–8, obtained from the definitional formulas of an analysis of variance.

Interpreting an Analysis of Variance

Computing a two-factor analysis of variance and making decisions with respect to the statistical hypotheses becomes quite routine with sufficient practice. The interpretation of the outcome of such an analysis of variance with respect to the data obtained, however, is not routine. It requires very careful examination of the various treatment means obtained in the experiment. To do this examination, it is often useful to present the sample means in graphic as well as tabular form, such as that shown in Table 10–4. In addition, the occurrence of a significant interaction requires that we prepare a table of the simple effects for each independent variable. We turn first to these two tasks.

Graphic Presentation of Treatment Means

In published articles, the cell means are frequently presented graphically in a figure rather than in a table such as Table 10–4. Compared to a table, a graphic presentation often provides a much clearer portrayal of any interaction that may have occurred. But it may require some effort by the reader to determine any main effects from a graphic presentation. For this reason, we present a brief discussion of plotting and interpreting a figure of cell means from a factorial experiment.

The cell means from Table 10–4 are plotted in Figure 10–1. Each cell mean is identified in this figure, but this is *not* done with figures in published articles. When plotting such a figure, one of the independent variables is always plotted on the abscissa (horizontal axis) and the measure of the dependent variable is always plotted on the ordinate (vertical axis). Which of the two independent variables should be plotted on the abscissa? The rule most generally followed is that the independent variable that is more *quantitative* or with a more continuous underlying dimension is plotted on the abscissa. In the example experiment this variable would seem to be factor *A,* the type of word, as the concreteness-abstractness dimension of words is a continuum. The second independent variable, type of strategy instruction, is represented by the two functions within the figure. Each of the lines on the figure represents one level of this factor.

The cell means are the only values presented in a figure; main effect means are not plotted. Thus, to identify main effect means from a figure, it is often necessary to perform some perceptual gymnastics with the plotted cell means. You have to use a process that may be called *perceptual averaging.* That is, you isolate the cell means involved for one level of a factor and average them by visually combining them; then you do the same thing with the plotted means involved in the other level(s) of the same factor.

One mnemonic device that appears to work well for remembering how to obtain main effect means from the cell means of a figure is what we call *squishing and sliding.*[2] Using this memory aid to find the main effects for type of word (factor *B*) from the data in Figure 10–1, you "squish" together the two concrete noun cell means (pegging-concrete—A_1B_1, and no pegging-concrete—A_2B_1) to find the main effect mean for the concrete-word condition ($\bar{X}_{B_1}$). The main effect mean is the midpoint of the "squished" means. Similarly, you squish together the two

---

[2]This mnemonic aid was suggested to us by one of our students, Lauren J. MacArthur. "Squashing and sliding" may be more semantically correct, but squishing and sliding seems more euphonious to us. The procedure provides correct main effect means as long as each cell of the experiment contains an equal number of scores.

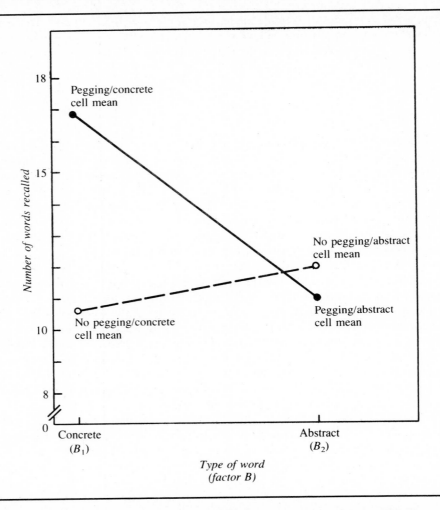

FIGURE 10–1   *Mean number of words recalled in the experiment of our example as a function of the type of word (concrete versus abstract) and the type of mnemonic strategy employed (word pegging versus no pegging).*

abstract-word-condition cell means (pegging-abstract—A_1B_2, and no pegging-abstract—A_2B_2) to obtain the main effect mean for the abstract-word condition ($\bar{X}_{B_2}$). The main effect for type of word is then the difference between the midpoints obtained by squishing ($\bar{X}_{B_1} - \bar{X}_{B_2}$). The process of squishing is illustrated in Figure 10–2.

The main effect means for type of strategy (factor A) are obtained by "slid-

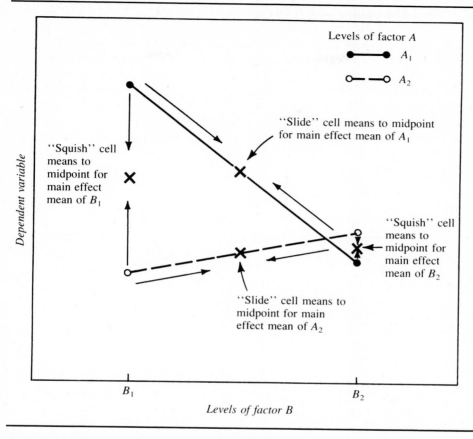

An illustration of squishing and sliding to obtain main effect means from a figure of the cell means in a 2 × 2 design.

FIGURE 10-2

ing" each of the cell means toward the midpoint of the line connecting those cell means. The sliding process is also illustrated in Figure 10–2. Thus, the main effect mean ($\overline{X}_{A_1}$) for the pegging condition is obtained by sliding the pegging-concrete (A_1B_1) and the pegging-abstract (A_1B_2) cell means toward the midpoint of the line connecting them. The main effect mean for the no-pegging condition ($\overline{X}_{A_2}$) is similarly obtained by sliding the no-pegging-concrete (A_2B_1) cell mean and the no-pegging-abstract (A_2B_2) cell mean toward the midpoint of the line connecting them. The main effect for the type of strategy is the difference between the two midpoint values obtained in this manner ($\overline{X}_{A_1} - \overline{X}_{A_2}$). The main effect means obtained by the technique of squishing and sliding are numerically equivalent to those obtained by finding the mean of the appropriate cell means in Table 10–4.

Tabular Presentation of Sample Means and Simple Effects

Earlier in the chapter we defined an interaction of two independent variables as occurring when the effect of one independent variable *depends* upon the level of the other independent variable with which it is combined. The occurrence of an interaction in experimental data must thus be analyzed by comparing differences among the cell means. These differences reveal the simple effects of the independent variables. The **simple effect** of an independent variable in a factorial design is the effect of that independent variable at only one level of the other independent variable. Table 10–9 illustrates the four simple effects comparisons as well as the two main effect comparisons in a 2 × 2 design.

TABLE 10–9   *Simple and main effects in a 2 × 2 between-subjects design.*

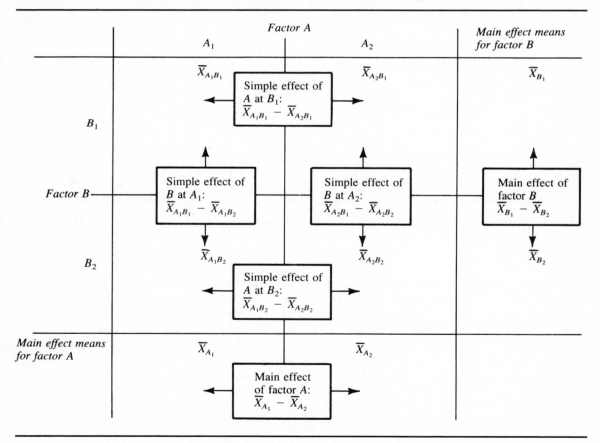

Take a moment to study Table 10–9. Although it may appear complex, the information in it is easily grasped. The various simple effects for each independent variable are presented in the rectangular boxes between cells. In a 2×2 design, there are only two simple effect comparisons for each independent variable. The simple effect of factor A at level B_1 of factor B is given by $\bar{X}_{A_1B_1} - \bar{X}_{A_2B_1}$. This simple effect reveals the influence, if any, of factor A at level B_1 of factor B. Similarly, the simple effect of factor A at level B_2 of factor B, $\bar{X}_{A_1B_2} - \bar{X}_{A_2B_2}$, reveals the effect of factor A at level B_2. There are also two possible simple effects for factor B; the simple effect of factor B at level A_1 of factor A, $\bar{X}_{A_1B_1} - \bar{X}_{A_1B_2}$, and the simple effect of factor B at level A_2 of factor A, $\bar{X}_{A_2B_1} - \bar{X}_{A_2B_2}$. Each of these simple effects reveals the effect of factor B at only one level of factor A.

If an interaction of the independent variables occurs, then the two simple effects for a factor will not be equal to each other or to the main effect for that factor. Thus, if there is an interaction, the simple effect of factor A at level B_1, $\bar{X}_{A_1B_1} - \bar{X}_{A_2B_1}$, will not equal the simple effect of factor A at level B_2, $\bar{X}_{A_1B_2} - \bar{X}_{A_2B_2}$, and neither of these simple effects of factor A will be equal to the main effect of factor A, $\bar{X}_{A_1} - \bar{X}_{A_2}$. This description will also apply to the simple effects of factor B. If an interaction occurs, then the simple effect of factor B at level A_1, $\bar{X}_{A_1B_1} - \bar{X}_{A_1B_2}$, will not equal the simple effect of B at level A_2, $\bar{X}_{A_2B_1} - \bar{X}_{A_2B_2}$, and neither of these simple effects will equal the main effect of factor B, $\bar{X}_{B_1} - \bar{X}_{B_2}$.

If no interaction among the independent variables occurs, then the simple effects and the main effect for a factor will be equal to each other. This equivalency will apply to each of the independent variables; the simple effects of factor A will be equal to each other and to the main effect of factor A, and the simple effects of factor B will be equal to each other and to the main effect of factor B. But notice that the lack of an interaction does not mean that the simple effects of factor A will equal the simple effects of factor B. This equality will occur only if there is also no main effect for either independent variable.

The numerical values of the simple- and main effect differences from the means of Table 10–4 are presented in Table 10–10. The main effect and simple effect differences between means are shown in the rectangular boxes. The direction of the comparison is indicated by the arrow attached to the box. For example, the simple effect of type of strategy for abstract words (the simple effect of factor A at B_2) is $\bar{X}_{A_1B_2} - \bar{X}_{A_2B_2} = 11.0 - 12.0 = -1.0$ word. Likewise, the simple effect of type of word under a pegging strategy (the simple effect of B at A_1) is $\bar{X}_{A_1B_1} - \bar{X}_{A_1B_2} = 16.8 - 11.0 = 5.8$ words. It is important to maintain a consistency of direction in the comparisons and to retain the sign ($+$ or $-$) of the effect.

A table such as this is *never* presented in published research, but it is helpful when attempting to understand the outcome of an experiment. Notice that Tables 10–4 and 10–10 and Figure 10–1 present the same information, but each in a different form. Both the tabular and graphic approaches will be useful as we discuss interpretation of the analysis of variance with respect to the main effects and interaction of the example experiment.

TABLE 10–10   *Main effect and simple effect differences among the means of the example experiment.*

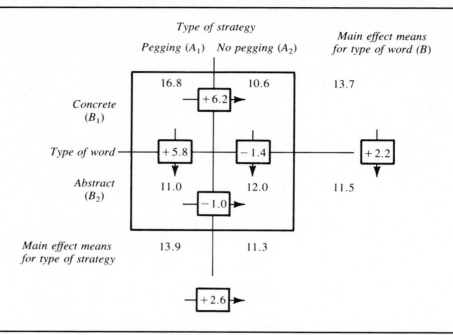

Interpreting the Analysis of Variance on the Example Experiment

Identifying the main effect for independent variable* A: *Type of strategy   Based upon the obtained value of $F(1,16) = 7.12$ in Table 10–8, the null hypothesis $H_0: \mu_{A_1} = \mu_{A_2}$ for factor A, type of strategy, is rejected and the alternative hypothesis, H_1: not H_0, is accepted. This decision implies that the main effect means for type of strategy (13.9 and 11.3) are *not* estimates of a common population mean μ_A. Rather, each estimates a different population mean, μ_{A_1} and μ_{A_2}, respectively. The main effect difference between the column means, 2.6 words (shown in Table 10–10), is thus considered to be a "real" difference and not merely a value that deviates from a true difference of 0 because of sampling error alone. Because only two means are involved in the comparison, a visual inspection is sufficient to indicate that the direction of the difference is for greater recall in the pegging condition.

Identifying the main effect for independent variable* B: *Type of word   The obtained value of F for factor B, the type of word in the example experiment, is 5.09. This value is statistically significant with $\alpha = .05$, hence the null hypothesis for factor B, $H_0: \mu_{B_1} = \mu_{B_2}$ is rejected and the alternative hypothesis is accepted. The implication is that the main effect means for type of word (13.7 and 11.5) are not estimates of a common population mean μ_B. Once again, each of the two sample means is treated as estimating a different population mean, μ_{B_1} and μ_{B_2} respectively. The main effect difference of 2.2 words between the row means (illustrated in Table 10–10) is considered to be "real" and not merely a chance difference due only to sampling error. Visual inspection indicates that the mean for the concrete-word condition is the greater of the two means involved in the comparison.

Identifying the interaction of independent variables A and B　　Based upon the obtained value of $F(1, 16) = 13.64$ in Table 10–8, the null hypothesis for the interaction of factors A and B, H_0: all $(\mu_{AB} - \mu_A - \mu_B + \mu_G) = 0$, is rejected and the alternative, H_1: not H_0, is accepted. In equation 10–2 (p. 266) we showed how a score is constructed from several components. To illustrate the meaning of an interaction, let us use this equation to predict the values of cell means from the *main effect means alone* of Table 10–4. We do so by starting with the grand mean and adding to it the main effects for the appropriate level of each independent variable. Thus, to predict the value of the pegging-concrete (A_1B_1) cell mean from main effects, we begin with the grand mean (12.6) and add to it the main effects of a pegging strategy ($13.9 - 12.6 = 1.3$) and a concrete word ($13.7 - 12.6 = 1.1$). The resulting value is 15.0 ($12.6 + 1.3 + 1.1 = 15.0$). This is the *expected* value of the pegging-concrete cell mean if no interaction occurs in the experiment and the value of the cell mean can be exactly predicted from main effects alone. Following this approach for each of the four cell means of the experiment results in the predicted cell means presented in Table 10–11.

　　Table 10–11 presents the outcome expected if *no* interaction of the independent variables occurs in the experiment. Observe here that the simple effects of an independent variable and the main effects of that independent variable are equal to one another. If there is no interaction, then the effect of one independent variable does *not* depend upon the level of the other independent variable. Thus, in Table 10–11, a change from a pegging to a no-pegging strategy results in an expected decrease of 2.6 words recalled for both concrete and abstract words. Similarly, a change from concrete to abstract words results in an expected decrease in recall of 2.2 words for both pegging and no-pegging conditions.

　　The cell means actually obtained (shown in Table 10–10), however, reflect the occurrence of an interaction. Thus, they present a much different pattern of relationships than do the hypothetical cell means presented in Table 10–11. In Table 10–10 you can clearly see that the simple effects for type of strategy differ for concrete and abstract words. That is, the simple effect of factor A at B_1 (i.e., $+6.2$ words) does *not* equal the simple effect of factor A at B_2 (i.e., -1.0 word). In addition, neither of these simple effects equals the main effect for type of strategy (i.e., $+2.6$ words). Similarly, the simple effects for type of word (factor B) depend upon the type of strategy used (i.e., $+5.8$ words for pegging, -1.4 words for no pegging), and neither of the simple effects is equal to the main effect for type of word (i.e., $+2.2$ words).

TABLE 10–11   *Simple effect differences expected among cell means if no interaction of the independent variables occurs.*

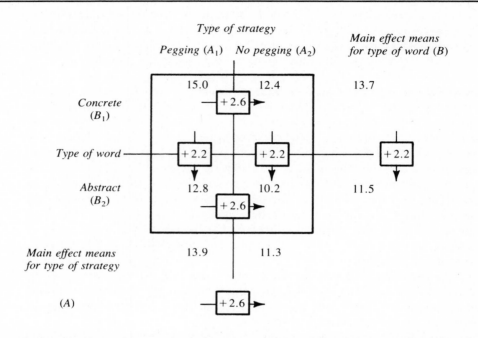

Figure 10–1 also illustrates these differences in the simple effects for each of the two independent variables. For example, from the figure you can see that the simple effect for type of strategy (factor A) is different for concrete and abstract words. The "it depends" nature of an interaction becomes quite clear from this illustration. If you were asked "What is the effect of type of strategy on amount recalled?" the answer would have to be, "It depends upon the type of word learned." Likewise, if you were asked, "What is the effect of type of word on recall?" the answer would take the form, "It depends upon the type of strategy used."

Notice that the lines connecting data points in Figure 10–1 are *nonparallel,* a distinguishing characteristic of a plot of an interaction. Because an interaction implies that the simple effects of an independent variable are not equal to its main effect, the plot of an interaction necessarily yields nonparallel lines. But the lines need not cross as they do in Figure 10–1; they will do so only when the simple effects for an independent variable have opposite signs as they do in this example.

In practice, it is rare to find any two lines in a figure exactly parallel geometrically. Because of sampling error, the lines will not be precisely parallel, even when there is no statistically significant interaction. Thus, visual inspection alone is insufficient to determine whether or not the lines are to be treated as *statistically parallel*. This decision is made only after a statistically significant value of F is obtained for the interaction term in an analysis of variance.

The pattern among the cell means in the experiment is only one of many that may result in a statistically significant interaction. Obtaining a significant interaction in the analysis of variance ensures only that the simple effect and main effect differences for an independent variable will not be equal. It does not provide further information about the numerous possible ways in which this result may occur. The exact nature of the interaction can be determined only by carefully analyzing the relationships among the cell means as we have done here. As part of this analysis it may be necessary to conduct follow-up statistical tests on the values of the simple effects. These tests are discussed in a later section of this chapter.

Interpreting main effects when an interaction occurs   When a statistically significant interaction occurs, the main effects for the independent variables may not lend themselves to meaningful interpretation. This condition happens because the main effect of an independent variable is merely the mean of the simple effects for that variable. For example, the main effect for type of strategy $(+2.6)$ in Table 10–10 is simply the mean of the simple effects for concrete and abstract words (i.e., $[(+6.2) + (-1.0)]/2 = 2.6$). A similar relationship holds for the simple and main effects for type of word (i.e., $[(+5.8) + (-1.4)]/2 = 2.2$). For both independent variables it appears that the main effect differences do not represent the appropriate simple effects very well, as we can easily see in Figure 10–1. The main effect for type of strategy suggests that recall is higher when a pegging strategy is used. But a pegging strategy leads to better recall only when it is used with concrete words. With abstract words, performance under pegging conditions is little different (or perhaps even poorer) from performance under no-pegging conditions. Thus it is misleading to conclude there is an interpretable main effect for type of strategy when pegging recall scores were higher for concrete nouns but not for abstract nouns.

Similarly, there is no meaningful or interpretable main effect difference in recall for type of words. Although the main effect difference suggests that concrete words are better recalled than abstract words, examining the simple effects and Figure 10–1 indicates that they are so only when a pegging strategy is employed.

This example illustrates that the main effect of each independent variable is an *artificial result* of the pattern of simple effects for that variable. More simply, the main effects in the example experiment are artifacts of the interaction. The occurrence of a significant interaction in analysis of variance is always a warning signal to carefully examine any significant main effects to find whether or not they lend themselves to a meaningful interpretation.

A Journal Summary of the Results of the Example Experiment

A journal summary of these results would probably provide descriptive statistics in the form of either a table (such as Table 10–4) or a figure (similar to Figure 10–1). The textual presentation of the results might be similar to the following:

> As predicted, there was a significant interaction of type of word with type of strategy, $F(1, 16) = 13.64$, $MS_e = 4.75$, $p < .05$. There was also a significant main effect for type of strategy, $F(1, 16) = 7.12$, $MS_e = 4.75$, $p < .05$, with higher recall for pegging ($M = 13.9$) than for no pegging ($M = 11.3$). In addition, the main effect for type of word was significant, $F(1, 16) = 5.09$, $MS_e = 4.75$, $p < .05$, with greater recall for concrete words ($M = 13.7$) than for abstract words ($M = 11.5$).

EXTENSIONS OF THE 2 × 2 DESIGN

Number of Subjects Required

For simplicity's sake, our discussion has been limited to the 2 × 2 between-subjects design. Factorial designs need not be limited, however, to two levels of each independent variable or to two independent variables. It is quite possible to have two-factor designs such as a 2 × 3, 2 × 4, 3 × 4, 4 × 4, 4 × 7, 6 × 6, and so on. The only limitation arises in the number of participants necessary to complete the design. If you were to use a 2 × 2 between-subjects design and wished to have ten participants in each treatment combination, then a total of forty subjects would be necessary. On the other hand, if you wished to investigate the same two independent variables but planned to have six levels of each (i.e., a 6 × 6 between-subjects design), then a total of 360 participants would be necessary if ten individuals are to be assigned to each of the 36 treatment combinations.

More than two independent variables may also be varied in a between-subjects design. Thus, psychologists may use three-factor designs such as 2 × 2 × 2, 3 × 2 × 2, and 2 × 2 × 6; four-factor designs such as 2 × 2 × 2 × 2, or 3 × 3 × 2 × 4; and even five- or six-factor designs. The number of participants needed to complete such designs increases rapidly as either more independent variables or more levels of the independent variables are added. Thus, to have ten subjects per cell in a 3 × 4 × 5 design requires a total of 600 individuals for assignment to the sixty treatment combinations. Therefore, with factorial designs having three or more independent variables, experimenters often manipulate one or more of those variables as a within-subjects variable rather than as a between-subjects variable. Recall that in a within-subjects design, a participant is exposed to all levels of the treatment; thus, the number of individuals needed is reduced dramatically from the number needed for a between-subjects manipulation of that variable. Factorial designs employing within-subjects variables are discussed in Chapter 12.

Analysis of Variance

The analysis of variance for between-subjects designs employing three or more independent variables is very similar to the approach taken for the analysis with two independent variables. The basic approach of the analysis of variance does not differ for two or twenty levels of the independent variable. The number of interactions to be analyzed increases dramatically, however, as factorial designs become more complex. This increase is illustrated in Table 10–12. In complex analyses of variance there will be one main effect for each independent variable. But each independent variable may interact with one or more other factors, depending on how many independent variables are manipulated in an experiment. For instance, for a three-factor design, there will be four interactions, three two-way ($A \times B$, $A \times C$, and $B \times C$) and one three-way interaction ($A \times B \times C$).[3] Observe, however, that for a four-factor design there are ten interactions to analyze. A five-factor design produces 26 possible interactions, and in a six-factor design 57 interaction terms emerge!

As more factors are added to an experiment the interpretation of results becomes more and more complex. Describing and interpreting a two-way interaction is usually manageable. Interpreting a three-way interaction is more difficult. But making sense out of multiple three-way or four-way interactions in one experiment is an extremely arduous task. Although in principle there may be no limit to the number of independent variables that may be manipulated in an experiment, obviously very practical limitations are dictated by the need to be able to understand the outcome of the experiment. Accordingly, most of the experiments reported in psychological journals employ two or three independent variables. Five- and six-factor designs are less often used.

Main effects and interactions in factorial designs.   **TABLE 10–12**
Independent variables are identified as factors A, B, C, and D.

Number of independent variables	Main effects	Interactions
2 (A, B)	A, B	$A \times B$
3 (A, B, C)	A, B, C	$A \times B, A \times C, B \times C$ $A \times B \times C$
4 (A, B, C, D)	A, B, C, D	$A \times B, A \times C, A \times D$ $B \times C, B \times D, C \times D$ $A \times B \times C, A \times B \times D$ $A \times C \times D, B \times C \times D$ $A \times B \times C \times D$

[3]Computations for a three-factor between-subjects analysis of variance are given by Bruning and Kintz (1977), pp. 31–38, and Linton and Gallo (1975), pp. 156–164.

FOLLOW-UP TESTS FOR THE ANALYSIS OF VARIANCE

After obtaining the statistically significant value of F for the interaction in Table 10–8, we interpreted the interaction effect among the cell means (Figure 10–1 and Table 10–10) by simple visual inspection. But this is not a rigorously correct approach to the problem. As we discussed in Chapter 9 with a one-factor design, if a null hypothesis involving more than two population means (i.e., there are three or more levels of one independent variable) is rejected, then follow-up or multiple-comparisons tests are needed to find exactly which means differ. Mere visual inspection of the means is not a satisfactory basis for making such a decision. The same problem arises in factorial designs, for interpreting both statistically significant main effects and interactions.

Follow-up Tests for Statistically Significant Main Effects

The procedure for determining a main effect in a factorial design is equivalent to treating the scores for the factor as a one-factor design. If only two means are involved in a main effect (i.e., the independent variable has only two levels), then a statistically significant main effect may be interpreted by visually inspecting the means. If, however, the main effect involves three or more means (i.e., the independent variable has three or more levels), then a statistically significant main effect requires a follow-up test to find which pairs of means differ from each other. Depending upon whether the follow-up comparison is a *planned* or a *post hoc* comparison, any of the tests identified in Table 9–5 may be used if the appropriate MS_{Error} is employed. The value of n is the number of scores that entered into the means to be compared. Interpretation of these multiple comparisons is identical to the interpretation for the one-factor experiment discussed in Chapter 9.

Follow-up Tests for a Statistically Significant Interaction

The approach we have taken to interpreting an interaction is to analyze the simple effects of each independent varable. In a 2×2 experiment this analysis involves four comparisons—two simple effects for each independent variable. A simple-effect comparison is an **unconfounded comparison** of cell means. These comparisons are unconfounded because the two treatment conditions being compared involve different levels of one independent variable but only one level of the other (see Tables 10–9 and 10–10). For example, if the simple effect of 6.2 words difference between pegging-concrete and no pegging-concrete conditions is statistically significant, then the difference can be attributed to the type of strategy used, for these treatment conditions differed only on the level of this independent variable.

Confounded comparisons may also be made among the treatment combinations in a factorial experiment. Confounded comparisons involve cell means that differ on levels of both independent variables. For example, in Table 10–10 comparisons of pegging-concrete versus no pegging-abstract treatment conditions, or pegging-abstract versus no pegging-concrete treatment conditions are confounded comparisons. If the means for either of these comparisons differ significantly, then we cannot know whether the pegging instructions or the type of noun is responsible for the difference; one group used pegging and the other did not, but also, one group had concrete nouns and the other had abstract nouns. Follow-up comparisons to determine the nature of a statistically significant interaction typically involve tests on the unconfounded simple effect differences. Although not recommended, psychologists may sometimes also do tests on confounded comparisons.

The procedure used to test if the simple effect differences are statistically significant is a familiar one; a *critical value* (*CV*) for a comparison is determined. If the obtained value for that comparison is equal to or exceeds the *CV*, the comparison is statistically significant at the significance level adopted. The two approaches most frequently used are Scheffé's test and Tukey's test. For all possible comparisons, confounded as well as unconfounded, Scheffé's test is often recommended. The *CV* for Scheffé's test is given by:

$$CV = (\sqrt{ab - 1})(\sqrt{2F_\alpha})\left(\sqrt{\frac{MS_{\text{Error}}}{n}}\right),$$

where n is the number of scores entering into the cell means and F_α is the critical value of F for $ab - 1$, MS_{Error} degrees of freedom.

Applying this formula to the analysis of the example experiment with $\alpha = .05$, the *CV* equals:

$$(\sqrt{(2)(2) - 1})(\sqrt{2(3.24)})\left(\sqrt{\frac{4.75}{5}}\right) = 4.30.$$

Thus the *CV* is 4.30. Any simple effect differences greater in absolute value than 4.30 are significant at the .05 level. From Table 10–10, you can see that the simple effect for type of strategy for concrete words (+6.2) and the simple effect for type of word with a pegging strategy (+5.8) are significant at the .05 level with Scheffé's procedure.

If only unconfounded comparisons are to be made, a modification of Tukey's test is often used. This test modifies the value of q_k (see Table A–3), depending upon the number of unconfounded comparisons to be made. For the frequently used 2×2 design that we have illustrated, the *CV* is given by:

$$CV = q_k\left(\sqrt{\frac{MS_{\text{Error}}}{n}}\right),$$

where q_k is the value of q_k obtained from Table A–3 for three means being compared and *df* for MS_{Error}. For our example, with 16 *df* for MS_{Error}, and $\alpha = .05$, the value of q_k is 3.65. Hence, the numerical value of the Tukey *CV* is:

$$3.65 \left(\sqrt{\frac{4.75}{5}} \right) = 3.56.$$

Any simple-effect differences greater than 3.56 in absolute value are significant at the .05 level. In our example, the Tukey test leads to the same significant differences in Table 10–10 as does the Scheffé test. The Tukey *CV*, however, is always smaller than the Scheffé *CV* because the Tukey test is appropriate only for unconfounded comparisons, but the Scheffé procedure is appropriate for both confounded and unconfounded comparisons. For the unconfounded simple effect comparisons of Table 10–10, the Tukey test is the procedure to choose.

When other than 2×2 designs are used, the value of q_k must be adjusted to reflect the number of possible unconfounded comparisons that can be made. Computational details may be found in Cicchetti (1972) or Linton and Gallo (1975).

TYPES OF INDEPENDENT VARIABLES IN FACTORIAL DESIGNS

The independent variables employed in factorial designs may be either active or attribute variables. When both independent variables are active variables the design is often called a **treatments-by-treatments design.** Usually the research interest in a treatments-by-treatments design is in the interaction of the independent variables rather than in the main effect of those variables. The experiment in our example employed a treatments-by-treatments design, and clearly interest was concentrated on the potential interaction of the variables.

When one of the independent variables is an active-independent variable and the other an attribute variable, the design is frequently called a **treatments-by-levels design,** where the term *levels* refers to levels of the attribute variable. Treatments-by-levels designs have two major uses. In one use, the attribute variable is introduced as a second independent variable simply to reduce error variance. In this instance, the attribute variable is a form of control and is used to statistically minimize the variation due to extraneous variables in the experiment (as we discussed in Chapter 4). The attribute variable is expected to affect the dependent variable; therefore, it is statistically analyzed in the experiment so that the variance it contributes may be separated from the error variance of the experiment.

A second use of treatments-by-levels designs is to study attribute-by-treatment (also referred to as aptitude-by-treatment) interactions. In this use, the levels of the attribute variable are levels of an aptitude or of a personality trait that the experimenter expects will interact with the treatment variable. As we indicated earlier in the chapter, Cronbach (1957, 1975) states that the effect of many experimental treatments may well depend upon various characteristics or attributes of the subjects receiving the treatment. For example, it may be that the effectiveness of a form of teaching may depend upon the presence of certain characteristics in the learner. If those characteristics are present, then the teaching method may be very effective; if those characteristics are not present, then another teaching method may be more effective. The interest in such studies is clearly in the interaction of the attribute variable with the treatment.

Finally, on occasion, factorial designs employ two attribute variables. Such designs have no specific name assigned to them, but consistency in terminology would indicate they should be called **attribute-by-attribute designs.** The interest here is again primarily in the possible interaction of the two independent variables.

Notice that the use of attribute variables in factorial designs is open to all the difficulties of the ex post facto design that were discussed in Chapter 3. Although participants may be randomly assigned to a treatment condition, they essentially self-select into levels of the attribute variable. Thus, the psychologist cannot be sure that the dimension characterized by the attribute variable is the only one on which the subjects differ.

Examples of Various Types of Between-Subjects Factorial Designs

Treatment-by-treatment, treatment-by-levels, and attribute-by-attribute designs are all forms of between-subjects designs. The statistical analysis for each of these designs is identical to the analysis of variance presented in this chapter. Examples of each use of these factorial designs and representative outcomes are presented in Figure 10–3. Each panel (*a* to *h*) shows an outcome adapted from a published study. The summarized analysis of variance reported by each author is included so that you may practice interpreting the results of factorial designs. We suggest that you take the time to squish and slide to estimate the main effects and simple effects in each figure; this exercise will help you to see how the data agree with statistical results for each example. Also carefully notice the variety of patterns of main effects and interactions that may occur in a factorial design. In some instances, apparent interactions observed in the pattern of means are not statistically significant.

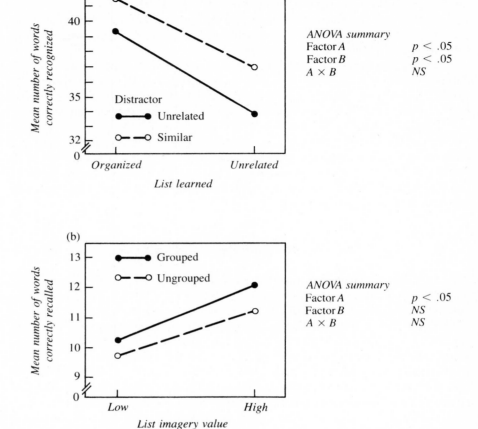

FIGURE 10-3   *Outcomes of research illustrating use of treatment-by-treatment (Figures 10a and 10b), treatment-by-attribute (Figures 10c–e), and attribute-by-attribute (Figures 10f–h) designs. The outcome of an analysis of variance on each study is summarized next to each figure (p < .05 = statistically significant at the .05 level, NS = statistically nonsignificant).*

FIGURE 10-3a   *Mean number of words correctly recognized as a function of the organization of the list to be learned (factor A, words organized by conceptual categories versus unrelated words) and the type of distractors used in the recognition task (factor B, conceptually similar to the words to be recognized versus unrelated to the words to be recognized.). (Adapted from Table 1 of Hall, 1982, p. 36.)*

FIGURE 10-3b   *Mean number of nouns correctly recalled as a function of imagery value of the nouns (factor A) and the grouping of the nouns on a page (factor B). (Adapted from Table 1 of Decker and Wheatley, 1982, p. 46.)*

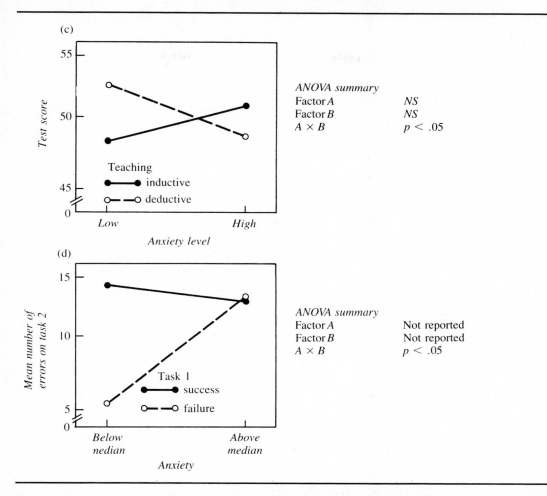

(c)

Test score

ANOVA summary
Factor A   NS
Factor B   NS
A × B   p < .05

Teaching
●——● inductive
○——○ deductive

55

50

45

0

Low   High

Anxiety level

(d)

Mean number of errors on task 2

ANOVA summary
Factor A   Not reported
Factor B   Not reported
A × B   p < .05

Task 1
●——● success
○——○ failure

15

10

5

0

Below
median

Above
median

Anxiety

Score on a test of course content as a function of student's anxiety level (factor A) and the   **FIGURE 10–3c**
type of teaching strategy employed (factor B: inductive or deductive exposition).
(Adapted from Table 2 of Tallmadge and Shearer, 1971, p. 34.)

Mean number of errors on a second concept-identification task as a function of level of   **FIGURE 10–3d**
manifest anxiety (factor A: above or below the group median on the Test of Manifest
Anxiety) and success or failure on a first concept-identification task (factor B). (Adapted
from Table 1 of Meites, Pishkin, and Bourne, 1981, p. 294.)

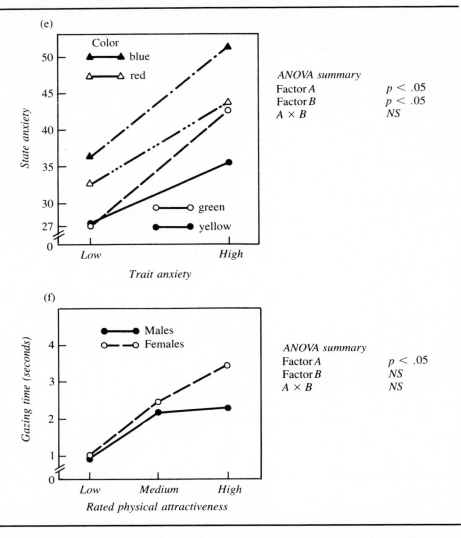

FIGURE 10–3e   *Level of state anxiety (a measure of transitory anxiety) as a function of trait anxiety (factor A: a measure of anxiety as a stable personality trait) and exposure to one of four colors for an eight-minute period (factor B). (Adapted from Table 1 of Reeves, Edmonds, and Transou, 1978, p. 857.)*

FIGURE 10–3f   *Self-awareness measured by amount of time gazing in a reflecting window as a function of rated physical attractiveness (factor A) and sex of the participant (factor B). (Adapted from Table 1 of McDonald and Eilenfield, 1980, p. 394.)*

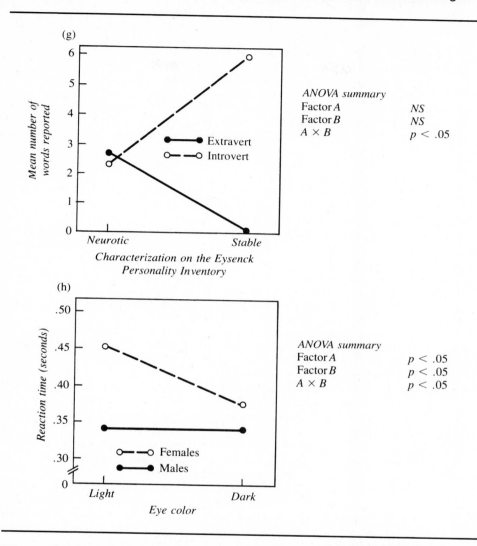

(g)

ANOVA summary
Factor *A*   NS
Factor *B*   NS
A × *B*   *p* < .05

(h)

ANOVA summary
Factor *A*   *p* < .05
Factor *B*   *p* < .05
A × *B*   *p* < .05

Mean number of perceived words reported in the autokinetic technique as a function of characterization of the participant on the Neuroticism-Stability dimension (factor A) and the Extraversion-Introversion dimension (factor B) of the Eysenck Personality Inventory. (Adapted from Table 1 of Frigon, 1977, p. 913.)

FIGURE 10-3g

Reaction time (in seconds) on a simple task as a function of eye color (factor A) and sex of the participant (factor B). (Adapted from Table 1 of Tedford, Hill, and Hensley, 1978, p. 504.)

FIGURE 10-3h

SUMMARY

- Factorial designs involve the concurrent manipulation of two or more independent variables. The major benefit of such designs is that the interaction effect of the independent variables may be investigated as well as the main effect of each independent variable.
- The analysis of variance for a two-factor between-subjects design partitions the total variance in the experiment into four components:
  - MS_A, which is responsive to systematic variance due to factor A and to sampling error;
  - MS_B, which is responsive to systematic variance due to factor B and to sampling error;
  - $MS_{A \times B}$, which is responsive to systematic variance due to the interaction of factors A and B and to sampling error, and
  - MS_{Error}, which is responsive only to error.
- Three F ratios are formed using these variance estimates, one for each source of systematic variance. These F ratios are tested for statistical significance following the procedures discussed in Chapter 8.
- To interpret the outcome of the analysis of variance, simple effects and main effects must be analyzed for each independent variable.
  - The main effect of an independent variable is the overall effect of that variable, disregarding the other independent variable.
  - The simple effect of an independent variable is the effect of that variable at only one level of the other independent variable. A significant interaction indicates that the two (or more) simple effects for a particular factor are not equal to each other.
- Factorial designs may be expanded to any number of independent variables and levels of each variables. Analysis of data and interpretation become increasingly difficult, however, when more than three independent variables are manipulated.
- Follow-up tests are needed for significant effects of an independent variable with more than two levels or when a significant interaction occurs. Two frequently used tests are Scheffé's test and Tukey's test.
- Either active or attribute independent variables may be employed in a factorial design. Classification of factorial designs by type of independent variable employed leads to three categories of between-subjects factorial designs.
  - Treatments-by-treatments designs: both independent variables are active variables.
  - Treatments-by-levels designs: one independent variable is an active variable, the other is an attribute variable.
  - Attribute-by-attribute: both independent variables are attribute variables.

11

In this chapter we develop the concepts of the one-factor within-subjects design; topics discussed include:

- The characteristics of a within-subjects design
- Statistical tests for analyzing data from a within-subjects design, including the analysis of variance, the t test for related measures, the Wilcoxon signed-ranks test, and the Friedman analysis of variance by ranks
- Considerations in choosing whether to use a between-subjects or a within-subjects design

WHY YOU NEED TO KNOW THIS MATERIAL

Within-subjects designs are widely used alternatives to the between-subjects design. They have both advantages and disadvantages compared to between-subjects designs.

One-Factor Within-Subjects Designs and Analysis of Variance

We have discussed only between-subjects designs in which each treatment condition is administered to a different group of participants. A second major type of research design is the **within-subjects design**. With this design one group of subjects is exposed to all levels of each independent variable. In the simplest type of a within-subjects design only one independent variable is employed and each individual is exposed to and measured under two or more levels of the independent variable. Because participants are measured repeatedly in a within-subjects design, these designs are also often referred to as *repeated-measures designs*.[1]

EXAMPLE OF A WITHIN-SUBJECTS EXPERIMENT

Psychologists have long been interested in the relationship between level of bodily arousal and task performance. Arousal level is a theoretical construct used to characterize the total neural activity of the body. Much of the interest in the relationship between arousal and performance stems from research by Yerkes and Dodson (1908). They discovered that, for mice learning to discriminate among stimuli of varying brightness by being punished with electrical shock for incorrect responses, there was an optimal intensity of shock for proficient learning.

Over the intervening years, a great deal of research has supported the hypothesis that the arousal-performance relationship often takes the form of an inverted U (see Figure 4–1, page 77). That is, at low levels of arousal, performance too will be at a low level. As arousal increases, performance increases up to some optimal level of arousal. After the optimal level of arousal, further increases in arousal lead to decreases in task performance.[2]

[1] These designs are also designated treatments-by-subjects or correlated-groups design.

[2] See Kling and Riggs (1971), pp. 831–845, for a review of arousal research and a critique of the conceptual status of arousal. Revelle, Humphreys, Simon, and Gilliland (1980) apply the arousal model to research involving personality characteristics, time of day, and caffeine ingestion. Eysenck (1976) reviews the relationship between arousal and learning and memory.

Although the arousal-performance relationship seems to be reasonably well established for many types of task performance, very little research has been done on the possible relationship between arousal and perceptual sensitivity. One instance of such a study, however, is an experiment by Halpin (1978) on the effects of arousal level on olfactory sensitivity. Halpin hypothesized, basing his prediction upon the inverted-U relationship between arousal and performance, that olfactory sensitivity would be greatest for a moderate level of arousal and would decrease for both lower and higher levels of arousal. To test this hypothesis Halpin employed a within-subjects design with three levels of arousal. A low level of arousal was induced experimentally by having participants listen to relaxation instructions suggesting that they imagine relaxing scenes. A moderate level of arousal was created by having the individual listen to white noise (a sound like the rushing noise on a television set tuned to a channel that is not broadcasting). For the high level of arousal, participants were led to believe they would receive at least one slightly painful electric shock while olfactory sensitivity was being measured; no shocks were actually given, however. The participant also heard occasional loud burst of noise and static during this time.

Olfactory senstitivity was measured by having participants smell solutions of 1-propanol in distilled water. The odor of this substance is similar to that of rubbing alcohol. Seventeen solution strengths ranging from .001 percent propanol by volume (a very weak solution) to 65 percent propanol by volume (a strong solution) were employed. For each measurement of olfactory sensitivity a determination was made of the weakest concentration the subject could detect; that is, a *detection threshold* was measured: Under each level of arousal, two measures of sensitivity were obtained and the mean of the two measures was recorded as the individual's threshold.

Altogether, thirty-six subjects were employed. Each was tested under each of the three levels of arousal. Induction of arousal and measurement of olfactory sensitivity took approximately four to six minutes, depending upon the treatment conditions. The interval between the arousal conditions was two to three minutes.

CHARACTERISTICS OF WITHIN-SUBJECTS DESIGNS

Table 11–1 presents the design for a one-factor within-subjects experiment with three levels of an independent variable and six subjects. It is clear that the independent variable must be an *active independent variable*. If a participant is to be tested under each level of the independent variable, then the variable must be one that the experimenter can actively manipulate, such as level of arousal in Halpin's experiment. When the experimenter's interest is in an attribute variable, such as a personality variable or gender of the subjects, use of a within-subjects design is precluded and only a between-subjects design can be used.

Within-subject designs have several characteristics that distinguish them from between-subjects designs. In general, they (1) require fewer participants, (2) may

Design of a one-factor within-subjects experiment with three levels of the independent variable and six subjects.   TABLE 11-1

	Independent variable A			
Subjects	A_1	A_2	A_3	Means for subjects
S_1	X_1	X_2	X_3	$\bar{X}_{S_1}$
S_2	X_1	X_2	X_3	$\bar{X}_{S_2}$
S_3	X_1	X_2	X_3	$\bar{X}_{S_3}$
S_4	X_1	X_2	X_3	$\bar{X}_{S_4}$
S_5	X_1	X_2	X_3	$\bar{X}_{S_5}$
S_6	X_1	X_2	X_3	$\bar{X}_{S_6}$
Means for factor A	$\bar{X}_{A_1}$	$\bar{X}_{A_2}$	$\bar{X}_{A_3}$	$\bar{X}_G$

offer more sensitivity for detecting the effects of the independent variable, and (3) are susceptible to multiple-treatment effects.

Number of Participants Required

A subject in a within-subjects design is measured under each treatment condition; thus, fewer participants are needed than would be required for a corresponding between-subjects design. In the example shown in Table 11-1, six scores are obtained under each of the three levels of the independent variable, but only six participants are required to obtain these eighteen scores. For a corresponding between-subjects design, eighteen individuals would have to be used to obtain eighteen scores.

The reduced number of subjects needed in a within-subjects design can be of real benefit to a researcher, particularly when two or more independent variables are manipulated. In Chapter 10 we illustrated one of the difficulties of the between-subjects factorial designs: the very rapid increase in number of participants needed as independent variables are added or the number of levels of an independent variable are increased. Thus, an advantage of within-subjects designs, particularly in factorial designs, is that fewer participants are needed.

Sensitivity of Within-Subjects Designs

A within-subjects design is often more sensitive for detecting the effects of an independent variable than a between-subjects design because each subject is tested and measured on each level of the independent variable. For example, the scores X_1, X_2, and X_3 in the row labeled S_3 of Table 11–1 are all obtained from the same subject. Whether or not an independent variable has an effect, it is quite reasonable to expect that three scores from one individual will be more alike than will three scores obtained from three people, as would occur in a between-subjects design. Consequently, as we shall see, error variation in a within-subjects design is potentially less than that in a corresponding between-subjects design. This difference, in turn, increases the sensitivity of the design for detecting possible treatment effects.

Multiple-Treatment Effects

In a within-subjects design a participant is given a sequence of treatments over a period of time. The number of treatments given is equal to the number of levels of the independent variable. This sequence of treatments opens the within-subjects design to **multiple-treatment effects** (sometimes also called *sequencing* or *context effects*); the effect of a treatment administered later in the sequence may depend upon the treatments preceding it. Three general types of multiple-treatment effects may occur in within-subjects designs: practice effects, treatment-carryover effects, and demand characteristics.

Practice Effects

In any experiment, participants typically are given a treatment and then are measured on some task. If an individual is repeatedly measured on the same task, such as detecting an odor in Halpin's experiment, his or her performance may change from trial to trial, even if the various treatments administered have no effect on the performance. Such changes in task performance, which occur merely because of the subject's repeatedly performing the task, and not because of any specific effects of the independent variable, are called **practice effects**. (They are also sometimes referred to as *order, time-related,* and *progressive-error effects.*) Practice effects may be either positive or negative.

    Positive-practice effects occur when task performance improves simply because the subject is repeatedly tested on a task. Figure 11–1 illustrates positive-practice effects in an experiment with three measurements of a dependent variable. In the example experiment people may become better at detecting odors simply because of experience on the task. Remember that these effects occur regardless of any effect of the particular treatment administered.

    Negative-practice effects arise when task performance decreases over repeated task measurements. Such effects may be due to fatigue (indeed, some authors refer to negative-practice effects as *fatigue effects*) or boredom increasing over time. The results of these effects are shown in Figure 11–1. As an example, our illustrative experiment is quite vulnerable to negative-practice effects. As you have no doubt experienced, the olfactory system rapidly adapts to the continued

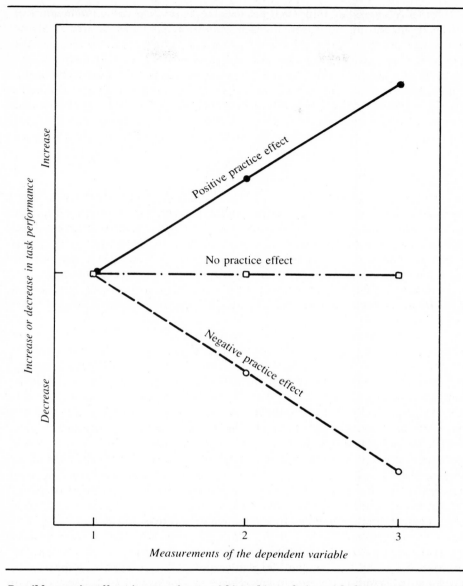

***Possible practice effects in a one-factor within-subjects design with three measurements of
a dependent variable.***   **FIGURE 11-1**

presence of odorants. Thus it is likely that subjects in the experimental example
could become less sensitive over repeated trials. It is also possible, of course, that
no practice effects may occur and that performance will not change from trial to
trial. This condition is also shown in Figure 11–1.

Practice effects are important because they *confound* the experiment. Suppose a treatment has no effect, but a positive-practice effect occurs. If all the treatment conditions are administered to all individuals in the same sequence, then performance for the last treatment will be superior to that for the first. Here one might wrongly conclude that the different treatments were responsible for the improvement in performance when in fact performance was facilitated simply by repeatedly "practicing" the task. Fortunately, however, practice effects often can be controlled in a within-subjects design so that they do not confound the experiment. We discuss several methods of control in a later section of this chapter.

Treatment-Carryover Effects

Treatment-carryover effects (sometimes called *treatment-transfer effects*) are the specific effects that may carry over or transfer from one treatment to affect the performance measured during a subsequent treatment. These effects may be of specific interest to the experimenter or they may be a nuisance to be controlled. An instance of the useful variety is the within-subjects variable of trials on a learning task. Here the experimenter is looking for improvement from trial to trial and assumes that the improvement is due to learning that occurred on and carried over from the previous trial.

In many other instances, however, a psychologist is interested in the effect of the treatment itself and does not want the results to be contaminated by previous treatments. Using a within-subjects design, Holen and Kinsey (1975) asked participants to evaluate how effective three therapeutic approaches (behavioral, client-centered, and psychoanalytic) were on a common problem of patients. In this task, it is quite likely that the approach the participant first experienced affected the rated effectiveness of the two approaches experienced on the subsequent trials. That is, the individual probably rated the effectiveness of the second therapeutic approach compared with that of his or her judgment about the effectiveness of the first approach heard. Likewise, the third approach probably was judged in comparison to the first two approaches experienced. Holen and Kinsey were, of course, aware of this possibility and took appropriate steps to ensure that their experiment was not confounded by these possible carryover effects.

The various carryover effects from one treatment condition to another may be equal or unequal. In the Holen and Kinsey experiment, it is likely that the carryover from the first psychotherapeutic approach experienced to the second was equal to the carryover from approaches 2 to 1 or from 1 to 3, 3 to 1, 2 to 3, or from 3 to 2. But the carryover does not always happen so. With some treatment conditions carryover effects may be unequal or differential; the carryover from treatment 1 to 2 may not be the same as that from treatment 2 to treatment 1. A facetious but illustrative example would be comparing performance in a "drunk" and a "sober" condition in a within-subjects design. Suppose the two conditions were tested within ten minutes of each other. You will easily recognize that the carryover effects from a sober-to-drunk sequence are not equivalent to the carryover effects from a drunk-to-sober sequence.

In many other instances, differential treatment-carryover effects may occur in within-subjects designs, and a researcher must always be aware of this possibility. In the experiment by Halpin it is possible that the carryover effects from each level of arousal may be unequal. The effects of a high level of arousal may be more intense and lasting than effects of either a low- or moderate-arousal level. As we discuss in a later section, differential carryover effects are not easily controlled for in a within-subjects design.

Demand Characteristics

Demand characteristics are subtle cues in an experiment that a subject may use to guide his or her behavior in the experiment (Orne, 1962). When such cues are present, participants may attempt to respond as they think the experimenter would like them to respond. Presumably they do so by using these cues to make a guess about the hypothesis of the experiment and then to behave in accord with this perceived hypothesis. Within-subjects designs are particularly open to the effects of demand characteristics. Because a participant in a within-subjects design experiences all the treatment conditions, he or she is given more opportunity to arrive at some reasonably accurate guess about the hypothesis or expected outcome than is an individual in a corresponding between-subjects experiment. For example, a subject in the Holen and Kinsey experiment on evaluating psychotherapeutic techniques experienced all three therapeutic approaches. Thus, each subject was given more than one opportunity to formulate a hypothesis about the purpose of the experiment. Subjects would be less likely to experience this effect if they evaluated only one psychotherapeutic approach. Hence, a psychologist must pay particular attention to the possible confounding effect of demand characteristics when employing a within-subjects design.

Control of Multiple-Treatment Effects

Two broad strategies for controlling extraneous variables were introduced in Chapter 4: (1) holding the extraneous variable constant, and (2) holding the effects of the variable constant by balancing the effects equally across treatment conditions. These two strategies form the nucleus of control procedures for multiple-treatment effects in a within-subjects design.

Holding the extraneous variable constant   The strategy of holding the extraneous variable constant may be used to control practice effects and some instances of carryover effects and demand characteristics. Positive-practice effects may be held constant by using subjects who are highly practiced in the task measured in the experiment. If individuals have had extensive experience, then there should be no improvement on the task across the levels of the experiment due to positive practice effects alone. Positive-practice effects are then constant across all levels of the independent variable and are thus eliminated as an extraneous variable in the experiment.

Negative-practice effects may be held constant by introducing sufficient time between the repeated tests for any effects of fatigue or boredom to dissipate (such as recovery from adaptation to olfactory stimulation, as in Halpin's experiment). Keppel and Saufley (1980) suggest also that monetary incentives for performance or instructions may hold negative-practice effects constant over the levels of the independent variable.

Differential-carryover effects that dissipate relatively soon (for instance, recovering from the "drunk" condition in our drunk-sober illustration) may be held constant by introducing sufficient time between tests. Many differential-treatment effects, however, do not dissipate rapidly. The effects of a treatment, such as learning a task, may be lasting. In this instance, introducing time between treatments will not control for unequal carryover effects.

Demand characteristics may on occasion be held constant and may even be eliminated from the experiment by introducing deceptive cues and disguising the apparent purpose of the experiment. This technique cannot be accomplished in all cases, however, and may, in certain experiments, lead to conflict with ethical practices in research.

Counterbalancing   Balancing is a procedure for holding the effects of an extraneous variable constant. The principle of balancing is that different levels of an extraneous variable are equally distributed across levels of the independent variable so that the effects of the extraneous variable are balanced across treatments. This is a widely used procedure for holding the effects of an extraneous variable constant when the variable itself cannot be eliminated from the experiment. Balancing techniques do not eliminate either practice effects or carryover effects; they merely ensure that these effects are spread evenly across treatments so that the effects of the extraneous variable do not covary with levels of the independent variable and confound the experiment.

Various balancing procedures are commonly used in within-subjects designs. The general procedure followed in all balancing procedures is to present the levels of the independent variable in different orders so that one treatment does not always occur in the same position (such as first or last), and so that one treatment is not always followed or preceded by another specific treatment. This sequencing is done by counterbalancing the order of treatments among participants. Treatments may be completely counterbalanced, partially counterbalanced, or randomly ordered.

Complete counterbalancing among participants requires determining all possible orders in which the levels of the independent variable may be presented and then using each order an equal number of times in the experiment. Each subject is to be randomly assigned to one of the orders of treatment. If an experiment has only two levels of an independent variable, A_1 and A_2, then there are only two possible orders for administering the treatments—A_1, A_2 and A_2, A_1. For three levels of an independent variable, A_1, A_2, and A_3, the treatments may be administered in six possible orders. A complete counterbalancing of three treatments is shown in Table 11–2A. In complete counterbalancing, each level of the independent variable occurs an equal number of times in each position of administration (i.e., first, second, or third for the three treatment conditions), and immediately precedes and follows each other treatment an equal number of times. The number of participants required in a completely counterbalanced order is some multiple of the number of possible orders (e.g., 6, 12, 18, or 24 individuals if three treatments are completely counterbalanced). Halpin employed complete counterbalancing by forming six subgroups of six subjects each. Within each subgroup each individual received one of the six possible sequences of arousal level. This procedure controls for carryover effects of arousal, however, only if the carryover effects are equal from one level of arousal to another.

Complete counterbalancing of treatment orders is the approach that most assuredly distributes multiple-treatment effects equally over all levels of the independent variable. But there is a potential limitation to complete counterbalancing: the number of possible orders of treatments increases very rapidly with an increase

Illustration of counterbalancing procedures for a one-factor within-subjects design with three levels of an independent variable.　　　　**TABLE 11–2**

	Order in which levels of the independent variable are presented to participants			
	First	*Second*	*Third*	*Participant*[a]
(A) Complete counterbalancing among participants (multiples of six participants required)	A_1	A_2	A_3	3
	A_1	A_3	A_2	6
	A_2	A_1	A_3	1
	A_2	A_3	A_1	5
	A_3	A_1	A_2	4
	A_3	A_2	A_1	2
(B) Partial counterbalancing (multiples of three participants required)	A_1	A_2	A_3	2
	A_2	A_3	A_1	3
	A_3	A_1	A_2	1
(C) Random ordering (any number of participants may be employed)	A_2	A_1	A_3	4
	A_1	A_3	A_2	1
	A_2	A_3	A_1	2
	A_3	A_2	A_1	3

[a]Participants have been randomly assigned to treatment orders.

in the number of levels of the independent variable.[3] With three treatments there are six possible orders. With four levels of the independent variable, however, the number of possible orders increases to 24. Thus, to completely counterbalance the order of presentation of four treatments, at least 24 participants are required. For five levels of an independent variable there are 120 possible treatement orders and thus at least 120 subjects are needed. Six treatments requires 720 participants. With seven treatments the number of possible orders jumps to 5040. With this rapid growth in the need for subjects, you can understand why psychologists often utilize approaches other than complete counterbalancing to balance the effects of extraneous variables over treatment conditions.

Partial counterbalancing (often also called *incomplete counterbalancing* or a *Latin squares design*) requires using only as many orders of administration of the treatments as there are levels of the independent variable. Over all orders, each treatment condition appears once in each position of administration. A partial counterbalancing of three treatment conditions is shown in Table 11–2B. From this table you can see that over the three orders of presentation each treatment appears only once in each position. Thus fewer participants are required to partially counterbalance the order of treatments than are needed to completely counterbalance. At least three participants are required for three treatment conditions, four participants for four treatment conditions, and so on.

Partial counterbalancing, because it requires fewer participants, is frequently employed in within-subjects designs. It has the disadvantage, however, that each treatment does not necessarily precede or follow each other treatment an equal number of times.[4] For example, as shown in Table 11–2B, treatment A_1 immediately precedes treatment A_2 twice (in orders assigned to subjects 1 and 2), but it does not immediately precede treatment A_3. Likewise, treatment A_2 immediately precedes treatment A_3 twice, but precedes treatment A_1 not at all. If the carryover effects are equal for all treatments, then this procedure poses no difficulties in balancing carryover effects among all the treatments. But if the treatments have unequal carryover effects (for example, treatment A_2 has a greater carryover effect than treatment A_1), then carryover effects will not be balanced equally over all treatment conditions.

Random ordering of treatments is another method used to balance practice and carryover effects in a within-subjects design. One possible random order of three treatment conditions is shown in Table 11–2C. The orders were selected from a table of random numbers. The assumption in random ordering is that practice and carryover effects will eventually balance out over all treatments. Any number of participants may be employed, but the larger the number of partici-

---

[3]The number of possible orders is determined by $a!$ (read "a factorial"), where a is the number of levels of factor A. We compute $a!$ by $a! = (a)(a-1)(a-2) \ldots (1)$. For example, $3! = (3)(2)(1) = 6$, and $4! = (4)(3)(2)(1) = 24$.

[4]If the design has an even number of levels of the independent variable (e.g., 2, 4, 6, etc.), then it is possible to have each treatment precede or follow each other treatment equally often.

Control of multiple-treatment effects in a within-subjects design.

TABLE 11–3

Effect	Control procedure	Comments
Practice		
Positive practice	Use highly practiced participants	Holds the level of practice constant
	Counterbalance order of treatments	Holds the effect of practice constant
Negative practice	Introduce rest period between tests	Holds the level of practice constant
	Counterbalance order of treatments	Holds the effect of practice constant
Treatment carryover		
Equal carryover	Counterbalance order of treatments	Holds the effect of carryover constant
Unequal carryover	Introduce time between treatments	Holds the level of carryover constant if carryover effect dissipates with time
Demand characteristics		
	Disguise the apparent purpose of the experiment	Holds demand characteristics constant and eliminates them as a variable

pants the more likely it is that practice and carryover effects will be equally distributed among treatments.

Complete counterbalancing, partial counterbalancing, and random ordering are appropriate balancing techniques only when practice and carryover effects are approximately equal from treatment to treatment. But when carryover effects are not equal from one treatment to another, using these balancing techniques will not prevent confounding. The procedures for controlling multiple-treatment effects in a within-subjects design are summarized in Table 11–3.

Controlling Differential-Carryover Effects and Demand Characteristics

One approach to resolving the problem of differential-carryover effects is to introduce sufficient time between treatments that the carryover effects may dissipate. As we indicated earlier, however, not all treatment effects dissipate rapidly. If treatments involve different instructional conditions or the learning of different tasks, then it is unlikely that any carryover effects will dissipate over a reasonably short time. Then the only alternative is to abandon the within-subjects design.

A between-subjects design is always preferable whenever there are relatively permanent unequal carryover effects among treatments or whenever practice effects are not equal from trial to trial. Within-subjects designs simply offer no adequate method of balancing to avoid confounding under these circumstances. A between-subjects design is also often the design to choose whenever demand characteristics threaten to confound the experiment. Because participants in a between-subjects design experience only one treatment condition, they are less likely to perceive and respond to subtle cues that may introduce demand characteristics in the experiment.

ANALYZING DATA OF A ONE-FACTOR WITHIN-SUBJECTS DESIGN

To illustrate the analysis of data for a one-factor within-subjects design we present hypothetical data similar to those which Halpin may have obtained. For ease of illustration and discussion, however, we present data for only six subjects who received the treatments in a completely counterbalanced order. The order in which they received the arousal treatment and their propanol-detection thresholds for each condition are given in Table 11–4. Remember that greater sensitivity is revealed by detection of weaker concentrations of propanol.

Although Table 11–4 illustrates the order in which the treatments were administered, it does not permit easy computation of descriptive statistics or visual inspection of the possible effects of the treatments. Thus in Table 11–5 the data are rearranged so that each subject's score for a level of the independent variable appears in the same column. In this form the data are useful for further statistical analysis, and this is how the raw data normally are presented.

TABLE 11–4   *Hypothetical threshold data for six subjects given three levels of arousal. The treatment orders are completely counterbalanced. The order in which the treatments were given and the threshold are shown for each subject.*

Subject	Treatment order					
	1		2		3	
1	A_2	.256	A_3	.512	A_1	.512
2	A_1	1.024	A_3	.768	A_2	.288
3	A_3	.256	A_1	.256	A_2	.064
4	A_1	.768	A_2	.128	A_3	.768
5	A_3	.512	A_2	.256	A_1	.768
6	A_2	.096	A_1	.512	A_3	.256

Note. Thresholds are expressed in percent concentrations. A_1 = low arousal, A_2 = moderate arousal, A_3 = high arousal.

Hypothetical propanol thresholds in Table 11–4 rearranged by treatments. Thresholds are given in percent concentration.   **TABLE 11–5**

| Subject | Arousal level (A) | | | Subject means |
	A_1 Low	A_2 Moderate	A_3 High	
1	.512	.256	.512	.426
2	1.024	.288	.768	.693
3	.256	.064	.256	.192
4	.768	.128	.768	.555
5	.768	.256	.512	.512
6	.512	.096	.256	.288
M	.640	.181	.512	
SD	.268	.096	.229	

Grand mean = .444

Descriptive Analysis of Data

As with the one- and two-factor between-subjects designs, the analysis for the data in Table 11–5 begins with computing descriptive statistics. The treatment means and standard deviations are shown at the bottom of each column in the table. Visual examination of these means suggests that level of arousal may have affected olfactory sensitivity. As you know, however, the differences between the means must be viewed against a background of error variation. Visual inspection alone does not permit one to assess whether the systematic variation is relatively greater than the error variation. As before, we resolve this decision-making problem by adopting a statistical model and testing a null hypothesis with an inferential statistical test. Again we will use an analysis of variance.

One-Factor Within-Subjects Analysis of Variance

An Overview

The analysis of variance for a one-factor within-subjects design is sometimes called a *treatments-by-subjects* analysis of variance, a reminder that each subject is tested under all levels of the independent variable. The analysis of variance partitions the total variation of a one-factor within-subjects experiment into three sources: (1) that due to the effect of the independent variable (A), (2) that due to the effect of the individual differences among subjects (S), and (3) that due to the interaction of the treatments with the subjects ($A \times S$).

To understand how sources of variance from a within-subjects design are partitioned, it is useful to think of the within-subjects design as a two-factor design with the independent variable as one factor (A) and the subjects themselves as the second factor (S). Because each subject is tested under each level of the independent variable, a one-factor within-subjects design can be regarded as an $A \times S$ factorial design with a levels of factor A and as many levels of factor S as there are subjects. Thus there is a total of AS conditions, or cells, and each condition represents one level of the independent variable combined with a particular subject. In our present example, there are three arousal conditions and six subjects; therefore the experiment can be viewed as employing a 3 (level of arousal) $\times$ 6 (number of subjects) factorial design producing a total of 18 treatments-by-subjects (AS) conditions. But only one score is obtained for each of the AS cells.

Similarly, we can think of the analysis of variance as two-factor analysis of variance with "main effect" means derived for factors A and S. Notice that in Table 11–5 the means for each row of scores as well as for each column have been computed. The three column means are the treatment means that are of interest for evaluating the effect of the independent variable. Each of the six row means is derived by averaging the scores obtained from one individual in all treatment conditions. Thus, the mean for each row represents the typical performance of a subject over all levels of the independent variable. These row means reflect individual differences in performance among the various participants in a within-subjects experiment. Although these subject means are relevant to the analysis of variance, these values typically are not reported as descriptive statistics for experiments using a within-subjects design.

Thinking of a one-factor within-subjects design as a kind of two-factor design and the analysis of variance as a two-factor analysis does not change the experiment; only one independent variable is manipulated and its effect analyzed. Conceptualizing the design in this way, however, should help you to understand the introduction of the $A \times S$ interaction term in the one-factor within-subjects analysis of variance.

The total sums of squares (calculated as usual) in a one-factor within-subjects design is partitioned into three independent sources that reflect the effect of treatments (factor A), individual differences among subjects (factor S), and the interaction of treatments with subjects ($A \times S$). This partitioning accounts for all the variance in the experiment. Because there is only one score per subject per treatment condition, the value in each cell may be regarded as a mean of one score! Accordingly, there is no way to obtain an estimate of within-cells variance as is done for the two-factor between-subjects analysis of variance.

If the independent variable does have an effect, then all participants should have a tendency to increase or decrease their scores under particular treatment conditions. For example, if a treatment has the effect of increasing performance, then such an effect should be reflected in a higher mean for that level of the independent variable. Even if the independent variable has no effect, however, some variation in repeated measures on the same participant—an increase or decrease from one treatment to the next—is still expected. This chance variation from treatment to treatment is reflected in the treatments-by-subjects ($A \times S$) interaction. Thus, the $A \times S$ interaction represents the variation in scores that cannot be attributed to the effects of the treatments alone (A) or to individual differences among subjects (S). Consequently, the treatments-by-subjects mean square is used as the *error term* in the one-factor within-subjects analysis of variance.

Partitioning a Score

A participant's score in a one-factor within-subjects design may be thought as beginning at some base level and then having added to it or subtracted from it the effects of the independent variable (factor A), individual differences (factor S), and the treatments-by-subjects interaction ($A \times S$). This result may be expressed conceptually as shown below:

X_i = Base level + Effect of A + Individual differences +
　　　　　　　Effect of treatments-by-subjects interaction.

In notation, an individual's score is constructed thus:

$$X_i = \bar{X}_G + (\bar{X}_A - \bar{X}_G) + (\bar{X}_S - \bar{X}_G)$$
$$+ [(X_i - \bar{X}_G) - (\bar{X}_A - \bar{X}_G) - (\bar{X}_S - \bar{X}_G)].$$ **(Eq. 11-1)**

The equation shows that, as with the previous analyses of variance that we have discussed, the grand mean of the scores is considered to be the base for a subject's score. Indeed, if there are no treatment effects, individual differences, or treatments-by-subject interactions, then the grand mean should adequately reflect the "typical" score. The main effect for the independent variable is reflected by the deviation of a treatment mean from the grand mean ($\bar{X}_A - \bar{X}_G$). Individual differences are similarly reflected by the deviation of the subject's mean from the grand mean ($\bar{X}_S - \bar{X}_G$). The interaction is the remaining deviation in the subject's score when the effects of the treatment (A) and the influence of individual differences (S) are removed from this score. This is the interaction:

$A \times S$	=	$[(X_i - \bar{X}_G)$	−	$(\bar{X}_A - \bar{X}_G)$	−	$(\bar{X}_S - \bar{X}_G)].$
Treatments-by-subjects interaction		Deviation of subject's score from grand mean		Deviation of treatment mean from grand mean		Deviation of subject's mean from grand mean

Carrying out the algebraic manipulations permits us to write the interaction component more simply as:

$$A \times S = (X_i - \bar{X}_A - \bar{X}_S + \bar{X}_G).$$

Transposing the grand mean to the other side of the equals sign in equation 11-1 and substituting the shortened interaction component results in the partitioning equation:

$$X_i - \bar{X}_G = (\bar{X}_A - \bar{X}_G) + (\bar{X}_S - \bar{X}_G) + (X_i - \bar{X}_A - \bar{X}_S + \bar{X}_G).$$

| Deviation of score from grand mean | Because of treatment *A* | Because of individual differences | Because of treatments-by-subjects interaction |

(Eq. 11–2)

Obtaining Mean Squares

To complete the analysis of variance, each score in the experiment is partitioned, the terms on both sides of the equation are then squared, and the numerical values of the squared components are summed over all subjects. In notation, these steps for obtaining the sums of squares are expressed by:

$$\sum_{A=}^{a} \sum_{n=1}^{n_s} (X_i - \bar{X}_G)^2 = \sum_{A=}^{a} \sum_{n=1}^{n_s} (\bar{X}_A - \bar{X}_G)^2 + \sum_{A=}^{a} \sum_{n=1}^{n_s} (\bar{X}_S - \bar{X}_G)^2$$

$$+ \sum_{A=}^{a} \sum_{n=1}^{n_s} (X_i - \bar{X}_A - \bar{X}_S + \bar{X}_G)^2. \qquad \textbf{(Eq. 11–3)}$$

Therefore,

$$SS_{Total} = SS_A + SS_S + SS_{A \times S}. \qquad \textbf{(Eq. 11–4)}$$

The similarity between the one-factor within-subjects analysis of variance and two-factor between-subjects analysis of variance is revealed in the derivation of sums of squares values. The computations for the sums of squares are systematically performed in exactly the same way for both analyses. Recall from Chapter 10 that the total sums of squares for a two-factor between-subjects design is partitioned into four independent sources. The sums of squares reflect variations among the means in (1) columns (factor *A*), (2) rows (factor *B*), and (3) cells (*A* × *B* interaction); the fourth sums of squares comes from the variation of scores within cells. Similarly, for a one-factor within-subjects analysis of variance the partitioning of the total sums of squares proceeds by looking at the variation among means in (1) columns (factor *A*), (2) rows (factor *S*), and (3) cells (*A* × *S* interaction), where each cell "mean" is based upon a single score. But the partitioning can go no further, because with one value per cell no within-cell variation can occur. Thus, there are three possible sources of total variation in a one-factor within-subjects experiment with one score from each subject in each treatment condition.

To obtain the mean squares for each source in the analysis of variance, the *SS* is divided by its corresponding degrees of freedom. The general approach to finding degrees of freedom is again to find the "fixed" term in each SS and then determine how many other terms or scores are free to vary in that particular SS. Table 11-6 presents the definitional formula for each SS, fixed terms, terms free to vary, df, and MS for each source of variance.

Deriving the F Ratio

The F ratio for the one-factor within-subjects design is given by $MS_A/MS_{A\times S}$. As with a between-subjects design, the mean square for the independent variable (MS_A) is responsive to any systematic variance created by the independent variable. However, MS_A is also responsive to error, that is, to the interaction of the treatment with the subjects. Not all subjects necessarily respond similarly to a particular treatment. As a mundane example, consider the possibility that a particular perfume scent may arouse some men but make other men sneeze! Moreover, the amount of chance variation from one treatment to the next is likely to differ among individuals. These points are illustrated in Figure 11-2, which graphically depicts the hypothetical data in Table 11-5. The three levels of arousal are represented on the abscissa. The functions within the figure depict the three scores obtained from the six subjects. Observe that although some subjects are more sensitive than others to propanol under all arousal conditions, thresholds for all individuals are lowest for the moderate-arousal condition. Thus, there is an apparent effect of arousal level on threshold. By "sliding" the means for each subject, you

Formulas for analysis of variance for a one-factor within-subjects design.   **TABLE 11-6**

Source of variance	SS	Definitional formula	Fixed terms	Terms free to vary	df[a]	MS
Factor A	SS_A	$\sum\limits_{A=1}^{a}\sum\limits_{n=1}^{n_s}(\bar{X}_A - \bar{X}_G)^2$	$\bar{X}_G$	$\bar{X}_A$	$a-1$	$SS_A/(a-1)$
Factor S	SS_S	$\sum\limits_{A=1}^{a}\sum\limits_{n=1}^{n_s}(\bar{X}_S - \bar{X}_G)^2$	$\bar{X}_G$	$\bar{X}_S$	n_s-1	$SS_s/(n_s-1)$
$A \times S$	$SS_{A\times S}$	$\sum\limits_{A=1}^{a}\sum\limits_{n=1}^{n_s}(X_i - \bar{X}_A - \bar{X}_S + \bar{X}_G)^2$	$\bar{X}_A, \bar{X}_S, \bar{X}_G$	X_i	$(a-1)\times (n_s - 1)$	$SS_{A\times S}/(a-1)(n_s-1)$
Total	SS_{Total}	$\sum\limits_{A=1}^{a}\sum\limits_{n=1}^{n_s}(X_i - \bar{X}_G)^2$	$\bar{X}_G$	X_i	$N-1$	Not calculated

[a] a = number of levels of factor A, n_s = number of subjects.

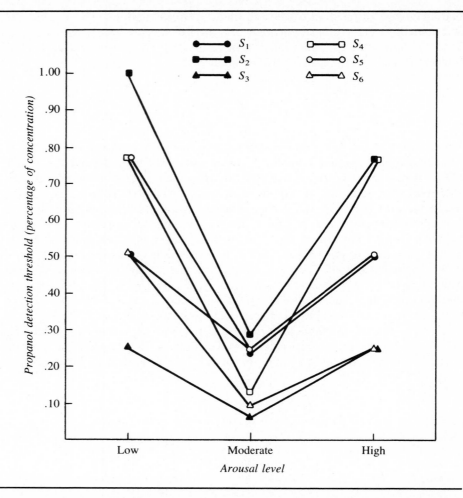

FIGURE 11–2   *Propanol detection thresholds for each subject at low-, moderate-, and high-arousal levels.*

can see that individual differences in odor sensitivity exist among subjects regardless of arousal level. Because the six functions are not parallel, however, a treatments-by-subjects interaction is present, too. As Table 11–5 and Figure 11–2 show, for some subjects the low- and high-arousal thresholds are the same (e.g., subjects 1 and 3), but for others the low-arousal threshold is higher than the high-arousal threshold (e.g., subjects 2 and 5). Thus the effect of the arousal treatment or the amount of chance variation from one measure to another is not the same for all subjects.

If a treatment interacts with subjects, then the implication is that a participant's performance cannot be predicted from treatment effects and individual

Overview of a one-factor within-subjects analysis of variance. **TABLE 11-7**

Source of variance	MS	Responsive to:	F ratio	Statistical hypotheses
A	MS_A	Systematic variance $A \times S$ variance	$MS_A / MS_{A \times S}$	H_0: $\mu_{A_1} = \mu_{A_2} = \mu_{A_3}$ H_1: not H_0
S	MS_S	Individual differences	None[a]	
$A \times S$	$MS_{A \times S}$	$A \times S$ variance		

[a]There is no F ratio for the subjects factor employing MS_S because there is no appropriate error term to use for such an F ratio. Even under the condition in which there are no individual differences, MS_S and $MS_{A \times S}$ are not responsive to the same factors and thus are not estimates of the same variance.

differences alone. Such a treatments-by-subject interaction not only affects the value of $MS_{A \times S}$, it also affects the value of the treatment means and consequently MS_A. This information is summarized in Table 11-7. The table reveals that if there is no systematic variance in the experiment, then both MS_A and $MS_{A \times S}$ are independent estimates of only treatments-by-subject variance. Under these conditions, the F ratio formed by $MS_A / MS_{A \times S}$ should approximately equal 1.00. On the other hand, if the independent variable does have an effect, then MS_A increases in size compared to $MS_{A \times S}$ and the F ratio formed by the two variance estimates becomes larger than 1.00.

Statistical Decision Making

The statistical decision-making process in a one-factor within-subjects design is identical to that followed in the one-factor between-subjects analysis of variance. A value of α defining the size of the critical region for F is chosen prior to conducting the analysis. The sampling distribution of F under H_0 is then determined by finding the critical value of F with the appropriate numerator and denominator df in Table A-2. If the obtained value of F is less than the critical value of F, then the decision is to fail to reject the null hypotheses. The treatment means are thus considered to be estimates of the same population mean and the differences between treatment means due only to error variance. If the obtained value of F is equal to or larger than the critical value of F, however, then the obtained value of F falls in the rejection region. Accordingly, the null hypothesis is rejected and the alternative hypothesis is accepted. In this instance, we conclude that the treatment means do not estimate the same population mean; rather, at least one of them is an estimate of a different population mean. All other things being equal (that is, if the experiment is not confounded), the differences among the sample means are attributed to the effects of the independent variable.

Assumptions of Statistical Tests for Within-Subjects Designs

Four assumptions are presumed to be met by the data when a one-factor within-subjects analysis of variance is employed:

1. Each participant is tested under each level of the independent variable.
2. The scores in the populations are normally distributed.
3. The variances of scores in the populations are equal.
4. The contribution of the individual differences of a subject remains the same for his or her scores over all treatment conditions.

The first assumption is necessary for the within-subjects analysis of variance to be the appropriate statistical model for the data; thus, it cannot be violated. The second and third assumptions are identical to assumptions for a between-subjects analysis of variance. They are often violated in experiments, but the analysis of variance maintains some robustness toward such violations. The fourth assumption states that the subject's behavior, independent of the treatment effect, remains stable over all levels of the independent variable. It is quite likely that this assumption is violated in many cases of psychological research. The effect of such a violation is to increase the probability of making a Type II error.

Most of the work on the robustness of the analysis of variance against violations of assumptions has been done with between-subjects designs. Generalizing from this work to the within-subjects design, it is likely that violations of the assumptions have the least effect on the probability of making a Type I error when:

•   The shape of the distributions of the scores for each treatment condition is about the same and the distributions are neither very peaked nor very flat.
•   The significance level is set at .05.

If any of these assumptions is seriously violated, then the nonparametric Wilcoxon signed-ranks test or the Friedman analysis of variance may be used in place of the parametric analysis of variance. These tests are presented later in this chapter.

Analysis of Variance on the Data from the Example

An analysis of variance of the hypothetical scores from Halpin's experiment in Table 11–5 is summarized in Table 11–8. For $\alpha = .05$, the critical value of F with 2 and 10 *df* is 4.10. The obtained value of F, 20.01, falls in the rejection region. Hence, the null hypothesis H_0: $\mu_{A_1} = \mu_{A_2} = \mu_{A_3}$ is rejected and the alternative hypothesis H_1: not H_0 is accepted at the .05 level. With respect to the treatment means of Table 11–5, the implication is that the sample means are not all estimates of the same population mean, μ_A. This decision merely indicates, however, that there is at least one difference among the three means. It does not indicate exactly

Raw-Score Computational Formulas for the One-Factor Within-Subjects Analysis of Variance

The notational representation for computing an analysis of variance of a one-factor within-subjects design with three levels of an independent variable and six subjects is:

Subjects	Independent variable A			
	A_1	A_2	A_3	
S_1	X_1	X_2	X_3	T_{S_1}
S_2	X_1	X_2	X_3	T_{S_2}
S_3	X_1	X_2	X_3	T_{S_3}
S_4	X_1	X_2	X_3	T_{S_4}
S_5	X_1	X_2	X_3	T_{S_5}
S_6	X_1	X_2	X_3	T_{S_6}
	T_{A_1}	T_{A_2}	T_{A_3}	G

where

X_i = raw score of a subject
T_A = total of scores for a treatment condition
T_S = total of scores for a subject
G = grand total of scores
n_s = number of subjects
a = number of levels of independent variable A
N = total number of scores.

The numerical values needed to obtain SS are:

$[1] = \sum_{A=1}^{a} \sum_{n=1}^{n_s} X_i^2$ the sum of all the raw scores squared

$[2] = \sum_{A=1}^{a} T_A^2 / n$ the sum of each treatment condition total squared, divided by the number of scores in a treatment condition

$[3] = \sum_{n=1}^{n_s} T_{Si}^2 / a$ the sum of each subject's scores squared, divided by the number of scores entering into that total

$[4] = G^2 / N$ the grand total squared, divided by the total number of scores

Using these numerical values, an analysis of variance is computed as follows:

Source	SS	df	MS	F
Factor A	$[2] - [4]$	$a - 1$	SS_A / df_A	$MS_A / MS_{A \times S}$
Subjects	$[3] - [4]$	$n_s - 1$	SS_S / df_S	
$A \times S$	$[1] - [2] - [3] + [4]$	$(a - 1) \times (n_s - 1)$	$SS_{A \times S} / df_{A \times S}$	
Total	$[1] - [4]$	$N - 1$	Not calculated	

To illustrate the computations, we use the scores given in Table 11–5 for which an analysis of variance is summarized in Table 11–8.

(continued)

Raw-Score Computational Formulas for the One-Factor Within-Subjects Analysis of Variance *(continued)*

	Factor A			
Subject	A_1	A_2	A_3	
1	.512	.256	.512	$T_{S_1} = 1.280$
2	1.024	.288	.768	$T_{S_2} = 2.080$
3	.256	.064	.256	$T_{S_3} = 0.576$
4	.768	.128	.768	$T_{S_4} = 1.664$
5	.768	.256	.512	$T_{S_5} = 1.536$
6	.512	.096	.256	$T_{S_6} = 0.864$
$T_A =$	3.840	1.088	3.072	$G = 8.000$

$$[1] = .512^2 + \cdots + .512^2 + .256^2 + \cdots + .096^2 + .512^2 + \cdots + .256^2 = 4.8968$$

$$[2] = (3.840^2 + 1.088^2 + 3.072^2)/6 = 25.3665/6 = 4.2278$$

$$[3] = (1.280^2 + 2.080^2 + 0.576^2 + 1.664^2 + 1.536^2 + 0.864^2)/3 = 12.1713/3 = 4.0571$$

$$[4] = 8^2/18 = 64/18 = 3.5556$$

Then:

$$SS_a = 4.2278 - 3.5556 = 0.6722$$
$$df_A = 3 - 1 = 2$$

$$SS_S = 4.0571 - 3.5556 = 0.5015$$
$$df_S = 6 - 1 = 5$$

$$SS_{A \times S} = 4.8968 - 4.2278 - 4.0571 + 3.5556 = 0.1675$$
$$df_{A \times S} = (3 - 1)(6 - 1) = 10$$

$$SS_{\text{Total}} = 4.8968 - 3.5556 = 1.3412$$
$$df_{\text{Total}} = 18 - 1 = 17$$

The summary of the analysis of variance is:

Source	*SS*	*df*	*MS*	*F*
Factor *A*	0.6722	2	$0.6722/2 = .3361$	$.3361/.0168 = 20.01^*$
Subjects	0.5015	5	$0.5015/5 = .1003$	
$A \times S$	0.1675	10	$0.1675/10 = .0168$	
Total	1.3412	17	————	

$^*p < .05$.

The numerical values obtained by this computational approach are identical to those presented in Table 11–8.

Analysis-of-variance summary table for hypothetical data of Halpin's experiment. **TABLE 11–8**

Source	df	SS	MS	F
Arousal level (A)	2	0.6722	.3361	20.01*
Subjects (S)	5	0.5015	.1003	
A × S	10	0.1675	.0168	
Total	17	1.3412		

p < .05.

Note. This analysis of variance was performed on the scores presented in Table 11–5 and shown in Figure 11–2.

which means differ from each other. To locate the difference or differences among the means, a follow-up test must be conducted.

Follow-up Tests for Within-Subjects Analysis of Variance

The problems and issues of follow-up tests for the within-subjects design are the same as those discussed in Chapter 9 for the between-subjects design. Depending upon the types of comparisons to be made, any of the procedures presented in Table 9–5 may be used. The value of MS_{Error} is simply the error term from the one-factor within-subjects analysis of variance; that is, $MS_{A \times S}$. For the experimental example we illustrate the use of the multiple F test approach. This is the approach to choose for this experiment, for the research hypothesis (see page 300) indicated only two planned comparisons to be made: the mean threshold for the moderate level of arousal compared to the means of the low- and high-arousal conditions.

The critical value for the multiple F test approach is given by:

$$CV = (\sqrt{2F_\alpha})\left(\sqrt{\frac{MS_{A \times S}}{n}}\right)$$

where n is the number of scores in the means being compared. Substituting numerical values, we obtain:

$$CV = [\sqrt{(2)(4.96)}]\left[\sqrt{\frac{.0168}{6}}\right] = .167.$$

Thus, for each of the two planned comparisons, a difference between the sample means larger in absolute value than .167 is a statistically significant difference at the 0.5 level. The comparisons are shown in Table 11–9. Each comparison is statistically significant. Hence it is concluded that the population mean estimated by the sample mean for the moderate-arousal condition (μ_{A_2}) is less than the population mean estimated by the sample means for either the low- (μ_{A_1}) or high- (μ_{A_3}) arousal conditions.

TABLE 11-9   *Means and differences between means for the three levels of arousal of the experimental example. The mean for each level of arousal is shown in parentheses. The absolute values of the differences are presented.*

	Level of arousal		
	Low (.640)	*Moderate* (.181)	*High* (.512)
Low (.640)	——	.459*	Not planned
Moderate (.181)		——	.331*
High (.512)			——

*$p < .05$., multiple F test $CV = .167$.

Journal Summary of the Results from the Experimental Example

A brief description of the results of the analysis on the hypothetical data (Table 11–5) might be written for the Results section of an article as follows:

> The mean propanol thresholds for the low-, moderate-, and high-arousal conditions are .640, .181, and .512 (percent concentrations) respectively. An analysis of variance indicates that the means differ significantly, $F(2, 10) = 20.01$, $MS_e = .0168$, $p < .05$. Multiple F tests on the two planned comparisons reveal that both the low- and high-arousal thresholds are significantly higher than the moderate-arousal threshold, $p < .05$ ($CV = .167$).

THE *t* TEST FOR RELATED MEASURES

When only two levels of an independent variable are manipulated in a within-subjects design, the t test for related measures may be used to test for significant differences between the two sample means. This t statistic is defined as:

$$t = \frac{(\bar{X}_1 - \bar{X}_2) - (\mu_1 - \mu_2)}{s_D}$$

where s_D is the standard error of the mean difference between each X_1 and X_2 score. Because the same subjects are measured under each treatment condition, the two sets of scores are not independent of each other; they are correlated to some extent. Therefore, this t test employs a computational formula different from that of the t test for independent groups presented in Chapter 7. Other than differences in deriving the t value, however, the t test for related measures is interpreted identically to the t test for independent groups.

When the null hypothesis H_0: $\mu_1 = \mu_2$ is tested, the computational formula for the t test for related measures is given by:

$$t = \frac{\bar{X}_1 - \bar{X}_2}{\sqrt{\dfrac{\sum\limits_{n=1}^{n_s} D^2 - \left(\sum\limits_{n=1}^{n_s} D\right)^2 \Big/ N}{N(N-1)}}}$$

The value of D is the difference between the two scores of a subject, and N represents the number of pairs of scores, or, equivalently, the number of subjects. The denominator of this t test is simply the standard error of the mean difference between the X_1 and X_2 scores; i.e., s_D. The df are equal to $N - 1$, which represents the number the number of pairs of scores that are free to vary.

To illustrate the use of this t test, suppose our experimental example on olfactory thresholds employed only two levels of arousal, low (A_1) and moderate (A_2), and the scores obtained were those in the first two columns of Table 11–5. The step-by-step computations for the t on these scores are presented in Table 11–10.

The remaining steps in the use of the t test for related measures are identical to those for the t test for the independent groups. A value of α is selected and the critical value of t is obtained from Table A–1. If the obtained value of t is equal to or greater than the critical value, then the null hypothesis H_0: $\mu_1 = \mu_2$ is rejected and the alternative hypothesis H_1: Not H_0 is accepted.

For the t calculated in Table 11–10, the df are $N - 1 = 5$. Thus, for a 0.5 significance level, the critical value of t for a two-tailed rejection region is 2.571. The obtained t of 5.281 is greater than the critical value; hence, H_0 is rejected and H_1 is accepted. The difference between the sample means is significant at the .05 level.

CHOICE OF RESEARCH DESIGN: BETWEEN-SUBJECTS OR WITHIN-SUBJECTS

How does a psychologist decide whether to use a between-subjects or within-subjects research design to evaluate a research hypothesis? Halpin, for example, might have used a between-subjects design instead of a within-subjects design. Why did he choose the within-subjects design over a between-subjects design? Although we cannot know his exact reasons, several issues are to be considered when making such a decision. Each type of design has its advantages and limitations.

Multiple-Treatment Effects

The effect of an independent variable investigated in a between-subjects design may be different from its effect with the same levels in a within-subjects design. Grice and Hunter (1964) demonstrated this effect rather convincingly in a study

TABLE 11-10   *Computing the* t *test for related measures*

Subject	Arousal level (A)		D	D^2
	A_1 Low	A_2 Moderate		
1	.512	.256	+.256	.065536
2	1.024	.288	+.736	.541696
3	.256	.064	+.192	.036864
4	.768	.128	+.640	.409600
5	.768	.256	+.512	.262144
6	.512	.096	+.416	.173056
$\bar{X}$	.640	.181	Sum +2.752	1.488896

$$t = (\bar{X}_1 - \bar{X}_2) / \sqrt{\left[\sum_{n=1}^{n_s} D^2 - \left(\sum_{n=1}^{n_s} D \right)^2 / N \right] / [N(N-1)]}.$$

$$= (.640 - .181) / \sqrt{[1.488896 - (2.752)^2 / 6] / [(6)(5)]}$$

$$= (.640 - .181) / \sqrt{[1.488896 - (7.573504/6)] / 30}$$

$$= .459 / \sqrt{(1.488896 - 1.262251)/30}$$

$$= .459 / \sqrt{(.226645/30)}$$

$$= .459 / \sqrt{.007555}$$

$$= .459 / .086920$$

$$= 5.281$$

Note. In this example, all $\bar{X}_1 - \bar{X}_2$ difference scores are positive. Usually, however, some *D* values will be negative. The sum of the difference scores, $\sum_{n=1}^{n_s} D$, must take into account the + or − values of the difference scores. All computations have been carried to six decimal places in order to avoid rounding error in the value of *t*.

on classical conditioning of an eyeblink to a tone. For one set of participants a within-subjects design was used and all subjects received both a loud and a soft tone as a conditioned stimulus.[5] For another set of participants, a between-subjects

[5]People normally do not blink reflexively when a tone is sounded. Grice and Hunter (1964) used a classical conditioning procedure to get individual to blink to a tone. To do so, they sounded a tone and .5 second after the tone sounded they directed a puff of air at the eye. The normal response by the eye to a puff of air is a reflexive blink. Grice and Hunter wanted the participants to blink to the tone. After many pairings of the tone and the air puff, they measured how many eyeblinks responded to the tone prior to the onset of the air puff. They reported their results as the percentage of trials on which an eyeblink occurred to the tone (i.e., the percentage of conditioned or learned responses). Classical conditioning is a basic type of learning and is often thought to be the way in which we learn emotional responses to objects and people.

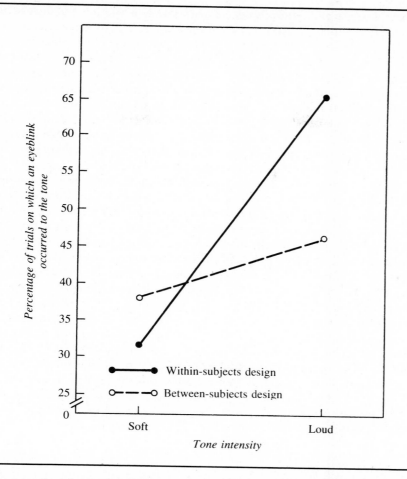

Percentage of trials in Grice and Hunter's experiment, on which a conditioned eyeblink occurred to the soft and loud tones for participants in a between-subjects design and for participants in a within-subjects design. (Adapted from data presented by Erlebacher, 1977.)

FIGURE 11–3

design was employed, in which each subject received only one of the tone intensities, either loud or soft, but not both. Figure 11–3 presents the results of their study. Notice that the figure depicts an interaction of the tone intensity (one independent variable) with the type of research design (the other independent variable). That is, the effect of the tone intensity on the dependent variable (conditioned eyeblinks) depends upon the type of research design used. The difference in the percentage of eyeblinks between loud and soft tones is much larger for the within-subjects design than it is for the between-subjects design.

Clearly, Grice and Hunter's results demonstrate a multiple-treatment effect or a *range effect* (Poulton, 1973, 1975) for the tone-intensity variable in a within-subjects design. In the within-subjects design the percentage of eyeblinks to a particular tone intensity depends upon the range of intensities of the other tones that are being employed. Poulton cites numerous studies in learning, perception, memory, stress, and psychophysical scaling in which range effects have occurred when within-subjects designs were employed. He concludes that such effects may mislead psychologists about the effectiveness of a variety of independent variables. He remarks, "The day should soon be approaching when no reputable psychologist will use a within-subjects design, except for a special purpose, without combining it with a separate-groups [i.e., between-subjects] design" (1975, p. 29).

Not all psychologists are as pessimistic about the influence of multiple-treatment effects as Poulton is. Greenwald (1976) contends that there are many instances where these effects are of interest; for example, in determining how well a participant can discriminate slight differences in levels of the independent variable. Also, within-subject designs may sometimes more closely approximate the so-called real world, in which people normally experience a wide variety of stimulus intensities or "treatments." Greenwald provides an example of such "natural" treatments in the study of the effects of source credibility on persuasion. In everyday life people are exposed to many kinds of messages, designed to persuade, which come from sources of varying credibility. That is, there is a naturally occurring variation of source credibility. Thus, if one is interested in generalizing laboratory research on source credibility to the real world, then it may be useful to manipulate the variable in a within-subjects design. Within-subjects designs thus may be quite useful where the generalizability of the research is of considerable importance. Moreover, because within-subjects designs are widely used in psychological research, it is apparent that many psychologists are not overly bothered by the threat of multiple-treatment effects in these designs.

Statistical Considerations

In a within-subjects design each subject receives each level of the independent variable and therefore is exposed to all treatment conditions. Normally, less variation in performance from one treatment to another is expected from the same person than if two peopled experienced the two treatments. In an analysis of variance, such decreased variation is reflected in a smaller error term. Further, a within-subjects analysis of variance partitions out the variability due to individual differences among subjects (MS_S) so that it does not contribute to the error variance. In a between-subjects design, this variation is included in the MS_{Error}. In general, then, if an independent variable has an effect on performance that could be detected with either a between-subjects or a within-subjects design, the within-subjects analysis of variance in principle is more likely to detect that effect. We

Simulated scores for two levels of an independent variable with six scores for each level. In Part A the results of a between-subjects analysis of variance on the twelve different scores are presented. In Part B, a within-subjects analysis was conducted on the same twelve scores from six subjects who received both Levels A_1 and A_2.

TABLE 11-11

	Factor A	
	A_1	A_2
	7.0	9.0
	9.0	10.0
	8.0	9.0
	8.0	8.0
	6.0	8.0
	10.0	11.0
M	8.0	9.2

A. Between-subjects analysis of variance

Source	df	SS	MS	F
Factor A	1	4.08	4.08	2.43
Error	10	16.83	1.68	
Total	11	20.92		

B. Within-subjects analysis of variance

Source	df	SS	MS	F
Factor A	1	4.08	4.08	14.57*
Subjects	5	15.42	3.08	
$A \times S$	5	1.42	0.28	
Total	11	20.92		

$*p < .05.$

demonstrate this point with an example. Table 11–11 presents a research design with two levels of an independent variable and six scores under each level. The scores in level A_1 were sampled from a population with $\mu_{A_1} = 8$ and scores in level A_2 were sampled from a population with $\mu_{A_2} = 9$. Part A of the table presents an analysis of variance where a between-subjects design is assumed. Part B presents an analysis of variance in which the data are treated as arising from a within-subjects design. Notice that the SS_{Total} and SS_A are the same for both analyses. The error variance in the between-subjects analysis, however, is separated into two components in the within-subjects analysis: variation due to individual differences among subjects (MS_S) and variation due to the interaction of the independent variable with subjects ($MS_{A \times S}$). The $MS_{A \times S}$ is the appropriate error term for the F ratio in the within-subjects analysis; consequently it is much smaller than the error term in the between-subjects analysis of variance (MS_{Error}). Hence, the F ratio in the within-subjects analysis is statistically significant at the .05 level, while the F value for the between-subjects analysis is nonsignificant.

To further demonstrate the greater sensitivity of within-subjects designs, we analyzed data sampled from two populations in five "experiments" in which different treatment effects were simulated. The mean of population A_1 remained the same ($\mu_{A_1} = 8.0$), but the mean of population A_2 varied in each instance ($\mu_{A_2} = 8.5, 9.0, 9.5, 10.0$, or 10.5). Thus, ignoring the direction of the difference, treatment effects represented by $\mu_{A_1} - \mu_{A_2}$ were .5, 1.0, 1.5, 2.0, and 2.5. For each "experiment," two sets of six scores ($n = 6$) were randomly sampled, one from population A_1 and the other from A_2. Both a one-factor between-subjects and a one-factor within-subjects analysis of variance were conducted on each set of twelve scores. The resulting F values are presented in Table 11–12. Notice that a larger value of F is required for significance in the within-subjects design because of fewer df for the error term. Significant differences at the .05 level were obtained, however, with the within-subjects analysis for all but the smallest treatment effect, but only the largest treatment effect was significant with the between-subjects analysis.[6] In other words, within-subjects analyses are more likely to find small differences between means to be statistically significant than between-subjects analyses. The general point is that if the independent variable has the same effect in a between-subjects design or a within-subjects design, then it is more likely that smaller effects of the independent variable will be detected with a within-subjects design. Thus within-subjects designs are regarded as more sensitive than between-subjects designs.

TABLE 11–12   *Obtained values of* F *for five simulated treatment effects. The data have been analyzed with both a between-subjects and within-subjects analysis of variance.*

	Treatment effect ($\mu_{A_1} - \mu_{A_2}$)				
	.5	1.0	1.5	2.0	2.5
Difference in sample means	.7	1.2	1.5	1.7	2.5
Between-subjects analysis	.69	2.43	3.14	4.31	11.03*
Within-subjects analysis	2.50	14.57*	19.29*	15.53*	40.00*

*$p < .05$. Where $\alpha = .05$, the critical value of F is 4.96 for each between-subjects analysis of variance; for each within-subjects analysis the critical value is 6.61.

[6]You may be puzzled about why the value of F for the within-subjects design with a difference between population means of 2.0 ($F = 15.63$) is smaller than the F for a difference in means of 1.5 ($F = 19.29$). The reason is that we did not add a constant to each score to create the differences between the means. Rather, for each mean difference, a new population of A_2 was created and a sample of six scores was drawn from it. For a difference of 2.0, the scores sampled increased the $MS_{A \times S}$ and thus resulted in a lower value of F for that difference.

For detecting treatment effects statistically, the within-subjects design would appear to be preferable to the between-subjects design. A large "catch" must be considered, though. Practice effects and carryover effects will always undermine the statistical sensitivity of a within-subjects design.[7] Counterbalancing, as a control procedure, does not eliminate these effects; rather, it only prevents the effects from adding to systematic variation that would confound the experiment. To achieve this result, counterbalancing distributes these effects evenly over all treatment conditions; as a result, an individual's score for a treatment condition administered early in the sequence may be different than if the treatment were given later. Because subjects receive the treatments in different orders, the practice and carryover effects can differentially influence the patterns of subjects' scores across treatments. Such effects will add to the treatments-by-subjects ($A \times S$) interaction that is the error term in the within-subjects analysis of variance.

Increasing the error term in an F ratio, of course, produces a smaller value of F. Therefore, a within-subjects design may lead to an F ratio for the independent variable that is smaller than expected from the size of the treatment effect. Gaito (1958, 1961) observes, then, that counterbalancing can lead to *negatively biased F* ratios, and the probability of obtaining a significant F for any given treatment effect may be reduced.

The point of this discussion is that practice and carryover effects pose a problem in any within-subjects design. If such effects are anticipated in an experiment (and one must assume they will always be present to some extent), then the researcher can deal with the problem in one of two ways: either (1) take steps to minimize the effects (see Table 11–3), or (2) use a between-subjects design.

The Research Hypothesis

The research hypothesis being tested should always remain paramount in the choice of either a between- or within-subjects design. Therefore, the research design we choose should be the one most appropriate for providing an empirical test of the research hypothesis (Greenwald, 1976). Will the design permit clear decisions to be made about the effectiveness of the independent variable? Does one design permit greater generalizability than another? These are relevant questions a researcher must consider when contemplating the choice of either a between-subjects or within-subjects research design.

NONPARAMETRIC STATISTICAL ANALYSES FOR ONE-FACTOR WITHIN-SUBJECTS DESIGNS

Several nonparametric statistical tests are appropriate for one-factor within-subject designs. We consider two here, the Wilcoxon signed-ranks test for within-subjects

[7] Further statistical difficulties that may arise in a within-subjects design are discussed by Gaito (1973) and Knapp (1982).

designs with two levels of an independent variable and the Friedman analysis of variance by ranks test that is appropriate when three or more levels of one independent variable are manipulated. Each of these tests assumes only that the underlying dimension of behavior measured is continuous and that subjects' scores may be placed in rank order. In a fashion similar to the Mann-Whitney U test (Chapter 7) and the Kruskal-Wallis analysis of variance of ranks (Chapter 9), ranked scores are used to obtain a test statistic for which a sampling distribution is known.

An Experimental Example

To provide an example of the computation and interpretation of these statistical tests, we introduce a fictitious experiment adapted after an actual experiment reported by Cosmides (1983). Cosmides was interested in the general problem of how emotion is expressed in voice patterns. More specifically, she wanted to know whether vocal expression of emotion is similar from person to person as is the facial expression of emotion. To investigate this problem, she measured certain sound characteristics of a subject's speech as he or she read a part from a script. Her experimental design and data analyses were rather complex; the important point for our purposes, however, is that one of her dependent variables, the frequency span of sounds in a subject's utterance, required using nonparametric statistical analyses.

After this brief introduction to the problem, suppose that we employ a one-factor within-subjects design with two levels of an independent variable to find the range of auditory frequencies emitted in vocal expressions in different situations. The independent variable is the type of script a subject is to read—a script reflecting a happy scene and a script reflecting a sad scene. In each condition the subject's task is simply to read the script to themselves and, on signal from the experimenter, say aloud the words "I'll do it."[8] The frequency span of the vocal expression of "I'll do it" is the dependent variable for each subject and is measured in cycles per second (cps, or Hertz). That is, a score is the range of the highest vocal frequency minus the lowest vocal frequency in a subject's expression of the three words.

Suppose the frequency spans for ten subjects tested under both script conditions are those presented in Table 11–13. The means and standard deviations for these scores are also shown here. Notice that not only do the mean frequency ranges appear to differ, but there is also a large difference in the variability of the

---

[8] Assume that appropriate control techniques have been employed to prevent confounding of the experiment by carryover effects or other threats to the validity of this research design. Our purpose here is only to briefly illustrate the nonparametric statistical analysis of such a design. Cosmides introduced a variety of controls in her experiment to ensure that the research would be valid.

Hypothetical data for vocal-frequency span (in Hertz) as a function of types of script read.

TABLE 11–13

Subject	Type of script	
	Happy	Sad
1	305	214
2	275	385
3	360	519
4	299	307
5	317	483
6	326	454
7	284	501
8	347	463
9	331	382
10	314	297
M	315.8	400.5
SD	26.54	101.40
SD^2	704.37	10,281.96

two conditions. Recall that the t test requires the sample variances to be estimates of the same population variance. Clearly, it appears that the two variances (SD^2) of the experimental example are unequal. Thus the t test is not an appropriate statistical test for these data. The same problem was faced by Cosmides, and she resolved it by conducting a nonparametric test on her data.

Wilcoxon Signed-Ranks Test

The appropriate nonparametric test for the one-factor within-subjects design with two levels of an independent variable is the **Wilcoxon signed-ranks test.** This test is the nonparametric analog of the t test for two related groups. The test statistic for the Wilcoxon test is called the T, and it is simply the smaller sum of the ranks from the two treatment conditions. The statistical hypotheses tested with T are similar to those tested by the Mann-Whitney U test or the Kruskal-Wallis analysis of variance on ranks; however, the results reflect differences in the distributions of scores in related rather than independent groups. These hypotheses are:

H_0: The population distributions of the related A_1 and A_2 scores are identical.

H_1: The population distributions of the related A_1 and A_2 scores are not identical.

The computation and interpretation of the Wilcoxon test for the data in Table 11–13 appears in Table 11–14.

TABLE 11-14   *Computation and interpretation of the Wilcoxon Test on the data of Table 11-13. The numbers above each column correspond to the numbered steps below.*

Subject	Type of script Happy (A_1)	Sad (A_2)	(1) d_i	(2) $\|d_i\|$	(3)	(4)
1	305	214	+ 91	91	4	+ 4
2	275	385	−110	110	5	− 5
3	360	519	−159	159	8	− 8
4	299	307	− 8	8	1	− 1
5	317	483	−166	166	9	− 9
6	326	454	−128	128	7	− 7
7	284	501	−217	217	10	−10
8	347	463	−116	116	6	− 6
9	331	382	− 51	51	3	− 3
10	314	297	+ 17	17	2	+ 2

Step 1.   Find the difference ($d_i = A_1 - A_2$) between the subject's two scores as shown in column (1). Maintain the sign (+ or −) of the difference.

Step 2.   Find the absolute values of the differences (the value without regard to sign) as shown in column (2).

Step 3.   Rank the absolute differences from smallest (rank = 1) to largest (rank = N) as shown in column (3). Differences of 0 are not ranked. Tied values of d_i should be assigned the mean of the ranks that would have been assigned had no tie occurred.

Step 4.   Give each rank the sign of the difference found in Step 1. This procedure is illustrated in column (4).

Step 5.   Sum the ranks of like sign (i.e., the sum of the positive ranks and the sum of the negative ranks). For example, the sum of the positive ranks in column (4) equals 6 (i.e., 4 + 2) and the sum of the negative ranks equals 49.

Step 6.   Choose the smaller of the two sums of the ranks. In this case it is 6, the sum of the positive ranks. This sum is the value of the test statistic T.

Step 7.   The sampling distribution of T is obtained under the statistical hypotheses:

   H_0:   The population distributions of the related A_1 and A_2 scores are identical.
   H_1:   The population distributions of the related A_1 and A_2 scores are not identical.

Step 8. Critical values in the sampling distribution of T for $\alpha = .05$ and $\alpha = .01$ are presented in the Appendix, Table A–7. Obtained values of T *equal to or less than* those presented in the table fall into the rejection region for the value of α selected. For values of N larger than 50, consult Siegel (1956).

Step 9. For our example with $N = 10$ and $\alpha = .05$, the rejection region is defined by values of T equal to or less than 8. The obtained value of T is 6; hence this value is significant at the .05 level. Thus, the null hypothesis is rejected and the alternative hypothesis is accepted. The conclusion is that the scores in A_1 and A_2 do not come from identical populations.

Friedman Analysis of Variance by Ranks

The **Friedman analysis of variance by ranks** is the nonparametric alternative to the one-factor within-subjects analysis of variance. It is an appropriate nonparametric test to employ when three or more levels of an independent variable are manipulated. To illustrate how the Friedman test is used, we expand the study of acoustic expression of emotion to include a third level of type of script—a neutral script. Hypothetical frequency-range scores for this experiment are presented in Table 11–15.

Computing the Friedman analysis of variance on hypothetical vocal-frequency span scores of ten subjects for three levels of type of script.　　　　**TABLE 11–15**

Hypothetical scores for vocal-frequency span in Hertz as a function of type of script read.

Subject	Type of script		
	Happy (A_1)	*Sad* (A_2)	*Neutral* (A_3)
1	305	214	231
2	275	385	195
3	360	519	200
4	299	307	174
5	317	483	214
6	326	454	237
7	284	501	172
8	347	463	209
9	331	382	187
10	314	297	219
M	315.8	400.5	203.8
SD	26.54	101.40	22.30
SD^2	704.37	10281.96	497.29

(continued)

TABLE 11–15   *(continued)*

Step 1.   Rank the scores for each subject across the *a* levels of the independent variable. This ranking for the hypothetical scores is shown below. Rank from the lowest (rank = 1) to the highest scores (rank = *a*). Each subject thus has *a* ranked scores. Tied scores of an individual are given the mean of the ranks that would be assigned if no ties had occurred.

Subject	Type of script		
	Happy (A_1)	Sad (A_2)	Neutral (A_3)
1	3	1	2
2	2	3	1
3	2	3	1
4	2	3	1
5	2	3	1
6	2	3	1
7	2	3	1
8	2	3	1
9	2	3	1
10	3	2	1
Sum of ranks $\sum_{n=1}^{n_s} R_a$	22	27	11

Step 2.   Sum the ranks in each column, as shown in the table above.

Step 3.   Compute the value of the statistic χ_r^2 (chi square).

$$\chi_r^2 = [12/na(a + 1)]\left[\sum_{A=1}^{a} \left(\sum_{n=1}^{n_s} R_a \right)^2 \right] - 3(n)(a + 1)$$

For our example these computations equal:

$$\chi_r^2 = [12/(10)(3)(3 + 1)][(22)^2 + (27)^2 + (11)^2] - 3(10)(3 + 1)$$

$$\chi_r^2 = 13.4$$

Step 4.   The sampling distribution for χ_r^2 is determined under the null hypothesis:

H_0:   The population distributions of the related A_1, A_2, and A_3 scores are identical.

The alternative hypothesis is:

H_1:   The population distributions of the related A_1, A_2, and A_3 scores are not identical.

Step 5.   The critical value of χ_r^2 depends upon the number of subjects in the group and the number of levels of the independent variable. For three levels of the independent variable ($a = 3$) with between 2 and 9 subjects and for four levels of the independent variable ($a = 4$) with between 2 and 4 subjects, critical values of χ_r^2 for $\alpha = .05$ are given in the Appendix, Table A–8. For $a = 3$, n greater than 9; $a = 4$, n greater than 4; and $a = 5$ or more, critical values of χ_r^2 are given in the Appendix, Table A–9. The *df* for use of Table A–9 are $a - 1$. Obtained values of χ_r^2 *equal to or greater than* those tabled are significant at the level of α chosen.

Step 6. The obtained χ_r^2 for the example data is 13.40. For $a = 3$ and $n = 10$, the critical value of χ_r^2 is given in Table A–9. With $\alpha = .05$ and $2 - 1$ *df*, the critical value of χ_r^2 is 5.99. The obtained value of 13.40 is greater than the critical value, hence the obtained χ_r^2 is significant at the .05 level. The null hypothesis is rejected and the alternative hypothesis that the scores are not from identical populations is accepted.

Examining the variances of these scores $(SD)^2$ reveals that they are not equal for the three treatment conditions. The inequality of variance is quite marked and thus an assumption required by the analysis of variance is evidently not met by these data. In this instance, many investigators would prefer to analyze the data by the nonparametric Friedman analysis of variance by ranks as did Cosmides for parts of her experiment. The Friedman test simply assumes that the scores to be analyzed have an underlying continuous dimension and can be ranked.

Table 11–15 illustrates the computational steps for the Friedman test on the data of the example. The statistic computed and tested in the Friedman analysis of variance by ranks is χ_r^2 (pronounced "chi square sub *r*"). Notice that a statistically significant value of χ_r^2 simply permits one to conclude that the scores in the several treatment conditions do not come from related populations with identical distributions. To determine exactly which distributions do differ significantly, follow-up tests are needed. For a limited number of planned comparisons, the Wilcoxon signed-ranks test may be used to compare scores from two treatment conditions at a time. The Wilcoxon test does not, however, control the Type I error rate. Thus if a number of comparisons are made, using the Wilcoxon test may lead to an unacceptably high Type I error rate. Marascuilo and McSweeney (1977) describe alternative follow-up tests which control the Type I error rate and which may be used for planned or post hoc comparisons.

SMALL-*N* DESIGNS: A SPECIAL CASE OF THE WITHIN-SUBJECTS DESIGN

The research designs we have discussed have all involved administering different treatments to different groups of subjects (the between-subjects design) or repeatedly administering different treatments to the same group of subjects (the within-subjects design). Each of these designs requires a reasonably large number of participants in a group (e.g., usually ten or more individuals in each group of a between-subjects design; see Chapter 4). In some instances this need for a number of subjects may pose hindrances to reseach. For example, in evaluating a particular therapy for a behavior disorder, there may not be enough individuals with the same disorder to form the two groups needed for a between-subjects design. In such instances, researchers often employ research designs known as small-N designs. **Small-N designs,** also called *single case* or *$N = 1$ designs,* typically use one or only a few subjects to test the effect of an independent variable.

Reversal Design

The most common small-N design is the reversal design illustrated in Figure 11–4. The **reversal design** (also called the *withdrawal design*) is often characterized as an *ABAB* design. The *A* represents a period of measurement of baseline behavior when no treatment is present. **Baseline behavior** (sometimes also referred to as *basal level* or *operant level*) is the existing amount or rate of the behavior that exists when a treatment is not present. The *B* represents the application of the treatment condition. The approach of the reversal design, then, is to measure

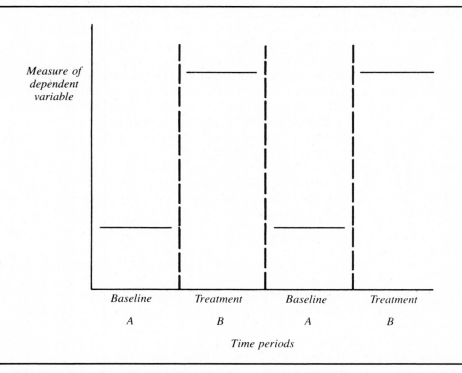

FIGURE 11–4   *Illustration of an ABAB reversal design with an idealized outcome of results.*

behavior prior to administering a treatment (*A*), administer the treatment and observe any changes in the behavior (*B*), withdraw the treatment to see if the behavior returns to baseline (*A*), and then readminister the treatment and again observe any changes in the behavior (*B*). An idealized outcome of an *ABAB* design is represented in Figure 11–4. Here you will notice that the behavior or performance measure increases when the treatment is administered and returns to the baseline level when the treatment is withdrawn. If all extraneous variables are carefully controlled, then the most parsimonious explanation for the behavior change is that the manipulation of the independent variable is responsible. It is this systematic manipulation of an independent variable and the careful control of extraneous variables that distinguishes small-*N* designs from a case study (discussed in Chapter 14). Although case studies often involve only one individual, they are typically more descriptive, less manipulative, and less controlled than a small-*N* design.

As an example of a reversal design, Fantuzzo and Smith (1983) employed an *ABAB* reversal design as part of a larger study to teach a severely autistic child to dress himself. The baseline (*A*) was a measure of the amount that the child dressed himself (percentage dressed) in a nine-minute period. The treatment condition (*B*) was the introduction of a reinforcement of chocolate milk for appropriate dressing behavior. The results of the *ABAB* portion of their study are shown in Figure 11–5. Visual inspection of this figure clearly shows the effect of the treatment condition. The behavior, though variable from day to day, occurs considerably more often under the treatment conditions (*B*) than under baseline measurement conditions (*A*).

Subjects in a Reversal Design

The "subject" in a small-*N* design need not always be an individual. The design may be employed using the patients on a psychiatric ward of a hospital as the "subject." In this case the dependent variable is some collective behavior of all the individuals on the ward (e.g., work on some simple task) and the goal is to determine if a treatment affects this behavior. Similar examples may involve using all the students in a class or all members of a family as one subject. For example, Palmer, Lloyd, and Lloyd (1977) investigated the effect of providing cost information on usage of electricity by a family. In one of the conditions they employed an *ABAB* reversal design, as illustrated in Figure 11–6. Here the subject was all members of the family and the dependent variable was the daily usage of electricity by this "subject."

Characteristics of Reversal Designs

As our examples illustrate, reversal designs have important characteristics. The independent variable must be an active variable for which a treatment may be

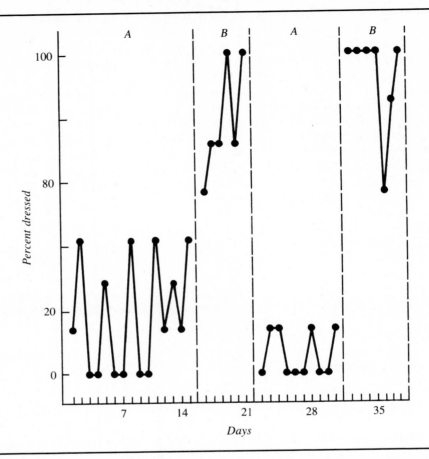

FIGURE 11–5   *The results of Fantuzzo and Smith's (1983) ABAB reversal design for dressing behavior in an autistic child. A = baseline, B = reinforcement condition. Reprinted with permission of authors and publisher from: J. W. Fantuzzo and C. S. Smith. Programmed generalization of dress efficiency across settings for a severely disturbed, autistic child.* **PSYCHOLOGICAL REPORTS**, *1983,* **53,** *871–879, Figure 1.*

applied and withdrawn by the experimenter. The effects of the independent variable should also be reversible if a reversal design is employed. Reversibility means that the independent variable should have virtually no carryover effects. The small-*N* example of Fantuzzo and Smith employed a reversible independent variable. The chocolate-milk reinforcer for dressing behavior could be withdrawn at any time, and the chocolate milk itself would have no carryover effects.

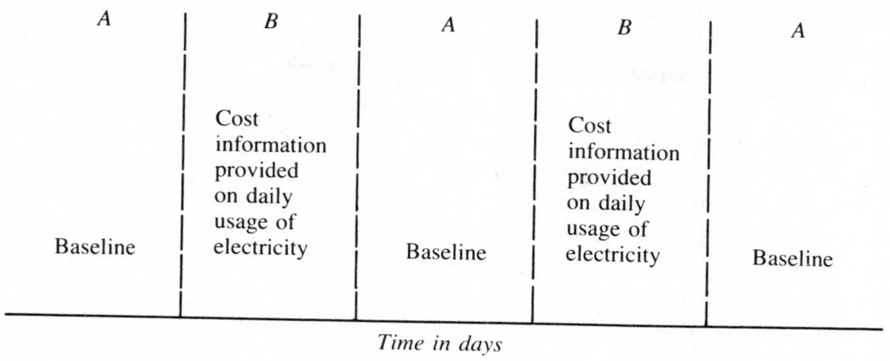

A	B	A	B	A
Baseline	Cost information provided on daily usage of electricity	Baseline	Cost information provided on daily usage of electricity	Baseline

Time in days

Illustration of the *ABABA* reversal design employed by Palmer et al. (1977). The dependent variable measured was the daily consumption of electricity by the family.

FIGURE 11–6

On the other hand, if the treatment were a surgical operation to create a brain lesion, then the effects of the treatment would be irreversible and a carryover effect would be present. In most instances, if a carryover effect is present, then a reversal design is inappropriate for investigating the effect of a treatment. Where carryover effects exist, more complex small-*N* designs such as the multiple-baseline design are often used.

In the **multiple-baseline design,** two or more baseline behaviors are identified and measured. After the baseline behaviors have become stable, a treatment expected to affect only one of the baseline behaviors is introduced. The effect of the treatment is then assessed by observing the changes in the baseline behavior affected by the treatment and comparing this behavior to the baseline behaviors unaffected by the treatment. A number of variations of multiple-baseline designs are discussed more fully in Hersen and Barlow (1976) and Robinson and Foster (1979).

Reversal designs depend very heavily upon the control technique of constancy to isolate the effects of the independent variable. Extraneous variables must be held constant. If an extraneous variable is allowed to covary along with the independent variable manipulated, then the design is confounded and the reason for any changes in the dependent variable cannot be determined. Accordingly, only one independent variable should be manipulated at a time in a reversal design. Indeed, Hersen and Barlow (1976) point out that this is a cardinal rule for this design. If more than one independent variable is manipulated at a time, then any changes in behavior must be considered as due to the joint effect of the two variables. Reversal designs do not permit an investigator to separate out the individual effects of the two or more independent variables manipulated.

Analyzing Data for Reversal Designs

The statistical analysis of reveral designs typically involves plotting raw data, computing descriptive statistics such as the median or mean on the dependent variable for each *A* and *B* period, and carefully inspecting the results visually. Because most conclusions about the effectiveness of an independent variable are drawn from visual inspections of the data, the behavior measured should be quite stable and should exhibit minimal variability during baseline periods. Baseline behaviors which are quite variable from measurement to measurement or which show increasing or decreasing trends over time make it more difficult to confidently conclude that the independent variable is responsible for changes in behavior.

Traditional analysis of variance or *t* tests are not applicable when only one subject is employed in a design. These familiar statistical models have been modified, however, for use in small-*N* designs, but not without some controversy as to their appropriate use. The issues involved are discussed more fully by Gentile, Roden, and Klein (1972), Michael (1974a, b), and Shine and Bower (1971).

The reversal design as we have presented it is only one of a number of variations. Further, there are approaches to the small-*N* design beyond the reversal design and the multiple-baseline design. These designs are discussed and illustrated in Hersen and Barlow (1976) and Robinson and Foster (1979).

SUMMARY

- In a within-subjects design one group of participants is exposed to all levels of the independent variable.
- The characteristics of a within-subjects design include these:
  - The independent variable must be an active independent variable,
  - Fewer participants are required than for a corresponding between-subjects design.
  - Within-subjects designs may be more statistically sensitive in detecting the effect of an independent variable, and
  - It is more open to confounding by multiple treatment effects than is a corresponding between-subjects design. Multiple-treatment effects may be controlled by several procedures including practice, introducing rest periods between treatments, and counterbalancing the order of treatments.
- The analysis of variance for a one-factor within-subjects design provides a statistical test for the effect of the independent variable manipulated.
- When only two levels of an independent variable are manipulated, the *t* test for related measures may be used in place of the analysis of variance.
- The Wilcoxon signed-ranks test is a nonparametric alternative to the *t* test for related measures.
- The nonparametric Freidman analysis of variance by ranks is used when three or more levels of the independent variable are manipulated.

- Several considerations are involved in deciding whether to use a between-subjects or a within-subjects design in an experiment. They include:
  - ○ The likelihood of the occurrence of multiple-treatment effects,
  - ○ The differences between within-subjects and between-subjects analyses in statistical sensitivity to a treatment effect, and
  - ○ The research hypothesis being tested.
- Small-*N* designs are a special case of the within-subjects design. They typically employ one or only a few subjects. The reversal design is a very common small-*N* design.

12

PREVIEW

In this chapter we introduce two additional factorial designs: the two-factor within-subjects design and the two-factor mixed design. Topics include:

- The design and the analysis of data for a two-factor within-subjects design
- The design and analysis of data for a two-factor mixed design
- Considerations in choosing among the three major types of factorial designs discussed in this text

WHY YOU NEED TO KNOW THIS MATERIAL

In this chapter we describe two other types of commonly used factorial designs. Knowledge of these designs will familiarize you with many of the factorial designs used in psychological research.

Two-Factor Within-Subjects and Mixed Designs and Analyses of Variance

We introduced the fundamental concepts of a factorial design in Chapter 10. In that chapter we described the design and statistical analysis for an experiment in which two independent variables are manipulated as between-subjects factors. As we pointed out, a two-factor between-subjects design is simply a logical extension of a one-factor between-subjects design. Similarly, as an extension of the one-factor within-subjects design, two (or more) independent variables may be manipulated in a factorial design as within-subjects factors in which each individual is exposed to all treatment conditions. A third possibility for a factorial design is to manipulate at least one independent variable as a between-subjects factor and at least one variable as a within-subjects factor. In this design each subject receives only one level of a between-subjects independent variable but is tested under all levels of a within-subjects factor. This approach leads to a so-called mixed factorial design. In this chapter we describe within-subjects and mixed factorial designs, limiting our discussion to two-factor designs.

TWO-FACTOR WITHIN-SUBJECTS DESIGN

In a one-factor within-subjects design each participant is exposed to each level of the independent variable and thus is measured repeatedly. It follows, then, that in a **two-factor within-subjects design** each participant also receives each treatment condition. The simplest instance of a two-factor within-subjects design is again a 2×2 design. The plan of such a design with ten participants is presented in Table 12–1. With two levels of factor A (A_1 and A_2) and two levels of factor B (B_1 and B_2), each participant is measured under each of the four conditions that result from the AB treatment combinations A_1B_1, A_1B_2, A_2B_1, and A_2B_2. For this example, then, a total of forty scores is obtained from the ten subjects. Consequently, all comparisons that can be made among the various means derived from the scores—the main effects for factors A and B, and the simple effects that reveal any $A \times B$ interaction—are within-subjects comparisons.

TABLE 12–1   *Plan of a two-factor within-subjects design with two levels of each independent variable. The scores of ten participants are represented.*

		Factor A				Main effect means of factor B
		A_1		A_2		
		X_1		X_1		
		X_2		X_2		
		X_3		X_3		
		X_4		X_4		
	B_1	X_5	$\overline{X}_{A_1 B_1}$	X_5	$\overline{X}_{A_2 B_1}$	$\overline{X}_{B_1}$
		X_6		X_6		
		X_7		X_7		
		X_8		X_8		
		X_9		X_9		
		X_{10}		X_{10}		
Factor B						
		X_1		X_1		
		X_2		X_2		
		X_3		X_3		
		X_4		X_4		
	B_2	X_5	$\overline{X}_{A_1 B_2}$	X_5	$\overline{X}_{A_2 B_2}$	$\overline{X}_{B_2}$
		X_6		X_6		
		X_7		X_7		
		X_8		X_8		
		X_9		X_9		
		X_{10}		X_{10}		
Main effect means of factor A		$\overline{X}_{A_1}$		$\overline{X}_{A_2}$		

Characteristics of Within-Subjects Factorial Designs

The characteristics of a within-subjects factorial design are the same as those of the one-factor within-subjects design. In comparison to a corresponding between-subjects design, a within-subjects factorial design requires fewer participants, is more sensitive in statistically detecting treatment effects, and is very susceptible to multiple-treatment effects. The latter characteristic is a major problem. Even with the simplest within-subjects factorial design, the 2×2 design, an individual is measured under four treatment conditions. Thus, an experimenter must carefully guard against practice effects, treatment-carryover effects, and demand characteristics that may jeopardize the conclusions from any within-subjects design.

The procedures for controlling these multiple-treatment effects are identical to those summarized in Table 11–3 (page 309). Counterbalancing procedures are routinely employed in factorial within-subjects designs to control for any confounding that can be caused by the order of the treatments and practice from repeated experience on the task. In a 2×2 factorial design a minimum of twenty-four participants will be needed to completely counterbalance the sequences of the treatments. In practice, however, fewer than twenty-four subjects are often used in experiments, and therefore partial counterbalancing procedures are employed.

Descriptive Analysis of Data

Data obtained from an experiment employing a within-subjects factorial design are analyzed using the same general approach employed for the between-subjects factorial design. To illustrate the data analysis, forty hypothetical heart-rate scores from an experiment employing a 2 (task difficulty) $\times$ 2 (noise level) within-subjects design are presented in Table 12–2. Heart rate in beats per minute (BPM) was

Heart-rate scores as a function of task difficulty (factor A) and noise level (factor B). The means for each subject over all four treatment conditions are presented in the column at the right of the scores.   **TABLE 12–2**

	Task difficulty (factor A)			
	Easy (A_1)	Difficult (A_2)		
	78	79		
	81	79		
	86	84		
	76	76	Subject	Mean
Soft (B_1)	82	84		
	77	78	1	80.00
	81	80	2	80.75
	83	83	3	86.00
	74	72	4	76.75
	79	80	5	84.00
Noise level (factor B)	81	82	6	77.75
	82	81	7	81.00
	89	85	8	83.75
	77	78	9	73.25
Loud (B_2)	85	85	10	79.25
	76	80		
	81	82		
	84	85		
	73	74		
	79	79		

measured when ten subjects performed tasks that were either easy (A_1) or difficult (A_2), performing them in the presence of either soft (B_1) or loud (B_2) noise. Therefore, heart rate was measured in all subjects under four conditions combining task difficulty and noise level: easy-soft, easy-loud, difficult-soft, and difficult-loud.

The mean heart rates for each of the four treatment conditions are presented in Table 12–3. As in the between-subjects factorial design, these and the main effect means are the means compared in a two-factor analysis of variance to determine whether the main effects for factors A and B and the $A \times B$ interaction are statistically significant. An analysis of variance, of course, is necessary to find out whether differences in means are more likely to be caused by chance factors or by systematic factors operating in the experiment.

Two-Factor Within-Subjects Analysis of Variance

You will recall that the two-factor between-subjects analysis of variance partitioned the total variation in scores into four sources, that due to factor A, factor B, the $A \times B$ interaction, and error, and produced three F ratios (for factor A, factor B, and $A \times B$). The two-factor within-subjects analysis also yields three F ratios for the same factors, but the total variation is partitioned into seven sources. At first this analysis of variance model may appear to be somewhat imposing. As you will see, however, the two-factor within-subjects analysis of variance is merely a logical extension of a one-factor within-subjects analysis.

Sources of Variation

Main effects   The approach to partitioning the total variation into its sources for a two-factor within-subjects design proceeds as we have previously described for other analyses of variance. First, as with the two-factor between-subjects analysis of variance (Chapter 10), we know that some of the total variation in scores will

TABLE 12–3   *Mean heart rate as a function of task difficulty and noise level. Standard deviations are given in parentheses.*

		Task difficulty	
		Easy	*Hard*
Noise level	*Soft*	79.7 (3.59)	79.5 (3.72)
	Loud	80.7 (4.69)	81.1 (3.54)

be due to any main effect influences of the independent variables. The difference in main effect column means for factor A (80.2 for A_1, the easy task, and 80.3 for A_2, the difficult task) reflects the amount of total variation in heart rate that can be attributed to the effect of task difficulty alone. Hence, one source of total variation in the two-factor within-subjects design is factor A (i.e., task difficulty in our example).

Similarly, the influence of factor B alone can be obtained from the difference in the B_1 and B_2 main effect row means. For the noise-level factor of the example the main effect is represented by the difference in the soft and loud noise-level heart rate means, 79.6 (B_1) and 80.9 (B_2), respectively. A second source of total variation, then, is factor B. Thus, in our example, some of the variation in heart-rate measures is due to the influence of noise level presented while performing the tasks.

Even though only two independent variables are manipulated in a two-factor within-subjects design, a third "main effect" source of variation is derived in the analysis of variance. To understand this third main effect, it is again helpful to think of the subjects themselves as a factor in the analysis. (Recall that subjects were treated as a second factor in a one-factor within-subjects analysis of variance.) Therefore, the two-factor within-subjects design, for purposes of statistical analysis, can be viewed as a three-factor design, with subjects as the third factor. Let us see why.

In a two-factor within-subjects design each subject is tested under all levels of both factors A and B. In a sense, then, the participants are factorially combined with the two independent variables, for each subject is measured in each AB treatment condition. Thus, in the example shown in Table 12–2, there are $2 \times 2 \times 10$ or 40 ABS conditions, with one score in each condition. Therefore, each individual can be considered a level of a subjects factor, factor S. Each "main effect" mean for the subjects factor is actually the mean of the scores recorded in all the AB experimental treatment conditions for a particular individual only.

Means for the ten subjects in the example are also shown in Table 12–2. (Notice, though, that subject means typically are not presented in tables or figures in research reports.) As the table shows, the mean of subject 1 is 80.00. This mean is the average of heart-rate scores in the four-treatment condition; that is, the mean of four ABS scores—78 ($A_1B_1S_1$), 79 ($A_2B_1S_1$), 81 ($A_1B_2S_1$), and 82 ($A_2B_2S_1$). Subject 3 had the highest mean, with a heart rate of 86.00, and subject 9 exhibited the lowest overall heart rate, with a mean of 73.25. Thus, you can see that the ten "main effect" subject means vary more extensively than the two main effect means associated with the task-difficulty and noise-level factors. Because the mean score for a subject is collapsed across the levels of factor A and factor B, differences in subject means cannot be due to any systematic influences of the independent variables. Accordingly, variation in subjects' means reflects individual differences; that is, some subjects will tend to give higher scores than other subjects regardless of the effects of the independent variables. It is apparent, then, that some of the total variation in heart-rate scores is due to a third source, *factor S*, the individual differences among subjects. For this reason a two-factor within-subjects design is also referred to as a treatments-by-treatments-by-subjects design, as a two-factor repeated-measures design, or as an $A \times B \times S$ design with a levels of factor A, b levels of factor B, and s levels of factor S, where s corresponds to the number of subjects.

Interactions   In addition to their main effect influences on the total variation, each of the three factors (i.e., factor A, factor B, and factor S) may interact with the other factors. That is, the effect of one factor may depend upon the level of one or both of the other factors. One obvious interaction involves the independent variables of the experiment, factor A and factor B. In our example, suppose that heart rate differs when performing easy and difficult tasks only in the presence of loud-noise conditions but not when the tasks are performed in soft-noise conditions. That is, task difficulty (factor A) may interact with noise level (factor B). The $A \times B$ interaction, then, is a fourth source of variation in a two-factor experiment.

The remaining interactions involve the subjects factor. As we explained when describing a one-factor within-subjects design, the effect of an independent variable may not be the same for all individuals. Some subjects can be affected more than others by a treatment, or they may show greater chance fluctuations from one measurement to another. That is, there may be an interaction of either independent variable (factor A or factor B) with the subjects (factor S). For instance, an $A \times S$ interaction is seen in the hypothetical heart-rate scores in Table 12–2. Subject 1 had a heart rate of 78 in the easy task-soft noise (A_1B_1) condition and 81 in the easy task-loud noise (A_1B_2) condition. The mean of the two scores, 79.5, represents the individual's behavior overall in the easy task (A_1) condition; similarly, the subject's behavior for the difficult task (A_2) treatment is represented by a score of 80.5 (the mean of 79 and 82). The difference between these two scores (i.e., $79.5 - 80.5 = -1.0$) is a measure of the effect of task difficulty (factor A) on that subject. The A_1 score for subject 1 is lower than the A_2 score. Now consider the A_1 and A_2 heart rates for subject 2; in this case the A_1 score (81.5) is higher than the A_2 score (80.0) and the apparent effect of factor A is different (i.e., $81.5 - 80.0 = +1.5$). Subjects 1 and 2 do not exhibit the same changes in heart rate under the two task-difficulty levels. This example illustrates that the effect of an independent variable may depend upon the individual receiving the treatments. Task difficulty (factor A), in this example, interacts with subjects (factor S). Individuals may respond differently to various levels of an independent variable either because the treatments do in fact affect participants differently or because of chance fluctuations from one measurement to the next. Thus, whatever the reason for the differences in pattern of subjects' scores across treatment conditions, the $A \times S$ interaction is a fifth source of the total variation.

Similarly, factor B may also interact with subjects. That is, the effect of factor B may also depend upon the subject receiving the treatment. Accordingly, a sixth source of the total variation is the $B \times S$ interaction.

A final source of variation is the interaction of all three factors, factor A, factor B, and factor S. Thus far we have described how differing responses by subjects to the independent variables are reflected in $A \times S$ and $B \times S$ interactions. Similarly, an interaction effect of the two independent variables ($A \times B$) may not necessarily be the same for all subjects. That is, the overall $A \times B$ interaction effect itself may interact with subjects. This condition suggests, therefore, that all three "factors" (A, B, and S) can interact, thereby producing a complex $A \times B \times S$ interaction.

The basis for an $A \times B \times S$ interaction can be seen with the scores in Table 12–2. The interaction is evident where the scores of two individuals exhibit an $A \times B$ interaction but the pattern of the interaction is not the same for the two subjects. For example, look at the scores of subjects 4 and 5. For subject 4 the heart-rate scores for easy and difficult tasks (treatments A_1 and A_2, respectively) in the presence of soft noise (B_1) are the same (both are 76), showing no apparent effect of task difficulty (factor A); but notice that in the loud-noise condition (level B_2), the A_1 heart rate (77) is lower than the A_2 measure (78). Thus, for this subject, heart rate does not differ while performing easy or difficult tasks in the presence of soft noise, but it does differ when the tasks are performed under loud-noise conditions. Subject 5 shows an exactly opposite pattern; heart rate differs for easy and difficult tasks with soft noise present but does not change when the tasks are performed with loud noise. You see, then, that an $A \times B$ interaction effect can vary among individuals who receive the same treatments. Therefore, a seventh source of total variation results from the interaction of all three factors, the $A \times B \times S$ interaction.

All possible ways of partitioning the total variation into independent sources are now exhausted. All main effects and interactions among the scores have been identified. No within-cell variation can be isolated as an additional source because each ABS cell in the data table contains only one score.

To summarize, then, in a two-factor within-subjects analysis of variance the total variation is partitioned into seven sources: factor A, factor B, factor S, and the $A \times B$, $A \times S$, $B \times S$, and $A \times B \times S$ interactions. These sources are identified in column ① of Table 12–4. Although we have described the subjects factor as a third source of variation, you see that it appears as the first source in the table. We have placed it there merely so that the three effects that are of interest (i.e., factor A, factor B, and $A \times B$) appear together in the table.

Obtaining Sums of Squares

The sources of variation that we have described for a two-factor within-subjects analysis of variance lead to conceptualization of a subject's score as deviating from the grand mean of the experiment (i.e., $X_i - \bar{X}_G$) because

TABLE 12-4   *Structure of an analysis of variance for a two-factor within-subjects design.*

① Source	② SS	③ df	④ MS	⑤ Responsive to	⑥ F ratio	⑦ Statistical hypotheses[a]
Subjects (S)	SS_S	$s-1$	MS_S	Individual differences		
Factor A	SS_A	$a-1$	MS_A	Effects of factor A Interaction of $A \times S$ Chance fluctuations	$MS_A/MS_{A \times S}$	H_0: $\mu_{A_1} = \mu_{A_2}$ H_1: Not H_0
Factor B	SS_B	$b-1$	MS_B	Effects of factor B Interaction of $B \times S$ Chance fluctuations	$MS_B/MS_{B \times S}$	H_0: $\mu_{B_1} = \mu_{B_2}$ H_1: Not H_0
Interaction of A and B ($A \times B$)	$SS_{A \times B}$	$(a-1) \times (b-1)$	$MS_{A \times B}$	Interaction of $A \times B$ Interaction of $A \times B \times S$ Chance fluctuations	$MS_{A \times B}/MS_{A \times B \times S}$	H_0: all $(\mu_{AB} - \mu_A - \mu_B + \mu_G) = 0$ H_1: Not H_0
$A \times S$	$SS_{A \times S}$	$(a-1) \times (s-1)$	$MS_{A \times S}$	Interaction of $A \times S$ Chance fluctuations		
$B \times S$	$SS_{B \times S}$	$(b-1) \times (s-1)$	$MS_{B \times S}$	Interaction of $B \times S$ Chance fluctuations		
$A \times B \times S$	SS_{ABS}	$(a-1) \times (b-1) \times (s-1)$	MS_{ABS}	Interaction of $A \times B \times S$ Chance fluctuations		
Total	SS_{Total}	$abs-1$	Not calculated	All systematic and error variance		

[a] The statistical hypotheses stated are appropriate for a 2 × 2 design.

1. the factor A treatment had an effect (A),
2. the factor B treatment had an effect (B),
3. the individual is different from other subjects (S),
4. the factor A and factor B effects interact ($A \times B$),
5. the effect of factor A is different from its effect on other individuals ($A \times S$),
6. the effect of factor B is different from its effect on other individuals ($B \times S$),
7. the interaction effect of factor A and factor B is different from its effects on other individuals ($A \times B \times S$).

Each of these seven influences that are assumed to contribute to an individual's score and therefore to the deviation of an individual's score from the grand mean can be quantified as sums of squares deviations. We present the procedure for deriving sums of squares using the raw-score computational formulas only, however, because the deviational formulas are quite cumbersome. But conceptually, understand that for each subject deviations for each source are obtained and squared. The resulting squared deviations are then summed over all subjects to obtain the sum of squared deviations, where

$$SS_{\text{Total}} = SS_A + SS_B + SS_S + SS_{A \times B} + SS_{A \times S} + SS_{B \times S} + SS_{A \times B \times S}.$$

Column ② of Table 12–4 presents the sums of squares for each source of variation in the experiment.

Obtaining Degrees of Freedom

The degrees of freedom for any main effect or interaction of a factorial within-subjects analysis of variance are obtained in the same way as in the two-factor between-subjects analysis of variance. For MS_A and MS_B the degrees of freedom correspond to the number of levels of the independent variable minus one. That is, $df_A = a - 1$ and $df_B = b - 1$. For any interaction term the degrees of freedom are obtained by multiplying the degrees of freedom for each factor involved in the interaction. Thus, $df_{A \times B} = (a - 1)(b - 1)$. The degrees of freedom for each of the sources involving an interaction with subjects are obtained in the same way. Therefore, $df_{A \times S} = (a - 1)(s - 1)$, $df_{B \times S} = (b - 1)(s - 1)$, and $df_{A \times B \times S} = (a - 1)(b - 1)(s - 1)$. These formulas for obtaining the df for each sum of squares are summarized in column ③ of Table 12–4.

Mean Squares

Mean squares are, of course, again calculated by dividing the sum of squares for a source of variation by the appropriate number of degrees of freedom for that source, i.e., $MS = SS/df$. The mean squares for each source of variation in the experiment are identified in column ④ of the table.

Deriving F *Ratios and Statistical Decision Making*

The purpose of performing an analysis of variance on data from a two-factor within-subjects design is the same as for the two-factor between-subjects design. The investigator wants to determine whether there is a statistically significant main effect or interaction for factors A and B. Therefore, three F ratios have to be calculated and decisions made about the statistical hypotheses associated with each F ratio.

Recall that in constructing an F ratio the idea is to find two mean squares that will have about the same values when it is assumed that the null hypothesis is true. That is, it is necessary to find mean squares from two independent sources of variation that respond to the same error influences when H_0 is true. When H_0 is false, however, because there is a main effect or interaction effect, then one of the variance estimates should respond to the systematic influence of that effect as well as to the various error influences operating in the experiment. This mean square is then divided by a second mean square, which responds only to the same error influences but not to any systematic influences of that factor. The resulting value is the F ratio. If there is an effect of the independent variables and H_0 is false, then the F ratio will be larger than 1.00. On the other hand, if the independent variable or interaction has no effect, then both mean squares presumably respond to the same error influences and both should therefore have about the same value. The resulting F ratio should then be equal to about 1.00.

In deriving F ratios for a two-factor within-subjects analysis of variance, the numerator MS values again are those associated with the main effects and interaction of the independent variables, MS_A, MS_B, and $MS_{A \times B}$, respectively. You will recall that in a two-factor between-subjects analysis of variance the same denominator MS value—the MS_{Error}—was used for each of the three F ratios. In contrast, in a two-factor within-subjects analysis, each of the F ratios has a different error term or denominator MS. The denominator for each F ratio is always the MS of the interaction of that factor with subjects.

As an example, for factor A the F ratio is formed by dividing the MS_A by the $MS_{A \times S}$. The basis for the use of $MS_{A \times S}$ in this F ratio can be seen by examining column ⑤ of Table 12–4. As we have indicated, $MS_{A \times S}$ is responsive to both an $A \times S$ interaction and chance fluctuations in scores from measurement to measurement. On the other hand, the MS_A is responsive to both the systematic effects of the independent variable and to the various error influences that the $MS_{A \times S}$ alone reflects. If factor A has no effect on the scores, then both the MS_A and $MS_{A \times S}$ are determined by the same error influences. Each mean square will provide an equally good but independent estimate of the population variance in scores, and the F ratio will be about 1.00.[1] But when the independent variable has

---

[1]You may notice that the value of F for task difficulty in Table 12–5 is .04. This value simply reflects chance variation in two independent estimates (MS_A and $MS_{A \times S}$) of the same population variance.

an effect, the MS_A will increase in value and the $MS_{A \times S}$ will not. The resulting F value then becomes larger than 1.00.

A similar logic applies to the F ratios for factor B and for the $A \times B$ interaction. Accordingly, the F ratios for the main effects and interactions of factors A and B are formed as follows:

- Main effect for factor A $F = MS_A / MS_{A \times S}$
- Main effect for factor B $F = MS_B / MS_{B \times S}$
- $A \times B$ interaction effect $F = MS_{A \times B} / MS_{A \times B \times S}$.

These F ratios are presented in column ⑥ of Table 12–4. Notice that although we earlier identified factor S as a third "main effect" in the two-factor within-subjects analysis, no F ratio is obtained for this factor. This source is responsive only to individual differences and there is no appropriate error term in the analysis for this factor.

The statistical hypotheses and decision-making procedures for each main effect (i.e., factor A and factor B) and interaction (i.e., $A \times B$) are identical to those for the two-factor between-subjects analysis of variance. The statistical hypotheses for each of the three F ratios for a 2×2 within-subjects design are shown in column ⑦ of Table 12–4. Depending upon the number of levels of the independent variables, each F ratio potentially has a different number of degrees of freedom in the numerator and denominator. Hence, for the analysis of variance, three different critical values and rejection regions may have to be established for the one significance level adopted, one for each F ratio. Then, as with all the previous analyses of variance that we have discussed, if the obtained value of F falls into its rejection region, the null hypothesis for that source of variation is rejected and the alternative hypothesis is accepted.

Raw-Score Computational Formulas for the Two-Factor Within-Subjects Analysis of Variance

The notational representation for computation of an analysis of variance for a two-factor within-subjects design with two levels of each factor and ten subjects is:

	Factor A			
	A_1		A_2	
	X_1		X_1	
	X_2		X_2	
	X_3		X_3	
	X_4		X_4	
B_1	X_5	$T_{A_1 B_1}$	X_5	$T_{A_2 B_1}$ T_{B_1}
	X_6		X_6	
	X_7		X_7	
	X_8		X_8	
	X_9		X_9	
	X_{10}		X_{10}	

(continued)

Raw-Score Computational Formulas for the Two-Factor Within-Subjects Analysis of Variance *(continued)*

Factor B

		X_1		X_1		
		X_2		X_2		
		X_3		X_3		
		X_4		X_4		
B_2		X_5	$T_{A_1 B_2}$	X_5	$T_{A_2 B_2}$	T_{B_2}
		X_6		X_6		
		X_7		X_7		
		X_8		X_8		
		X_9		X_9		
		X_{10}		X_{10}		
		T_{A_1}		T_{A_2}		G

where

X_i = raw score of a subject
T_A = total of scores for a main effect of factor A
T_B = total of scores for a main effect of factor B
T_{AB} = total of scores in a cell
G = grand total of scores
n = number of scores in a cell
a = number of levels of independent variable A
b = number of levels of independent variable B
N = total number of scores
s = number of subjects.

In addition, three other totals involving subjects are required, but are not shown in the notational representation. The totals are:

$T_{Si \text{ for } A}$ = the total of a subject's scores for a level of factor A (over all levels of B).
$T_{Si \text{ for } B}$ = the total of a subject's scores for a level of factor B (over all levels of A).
T_{Si} = the total of a subject's scores over all levels of both independent variables.

The numerical values needed to obtain SS are:

$$[1] = \sum_{A=1}^{a} \sum_{B=1}^{b} \sum_{n=1}^{ns} X_i^2 \qquad \text{the sum of all the raw scores squared.}$$

$$[2] = \sum_{A=1}^{a} \sum_{B=1}^{b} T_{AB}^2/n \qquad \text{the sum of each cell total squared, divided by the number of scores in a cell.}$$

$$[3] = \sum_{A=1}^{a} T_A^2/bn \qquad \text{the sum of each main effect total for factor } A \text{ squared, divided by the number of scores entering into that total.}$$

$$[4] = \sum_{B=1}^{b} T_B^2/an \qquad \text{the sum of each main effect total for factor } B \text{ squared, divided by the number of scores entering into that total.}$$

$$[5] = \sum_{n=1}^{ns} T_{Si \text{ for } A}^2/a \qquad \text{the sum of each subject's scores for each level of factor } A \text{ squared, divided by the number of scores entering into that total.}$$

$[6] = \sum_{n=1}^{n_s} T_{Si \text{ for } B}^2/b$ the sum of each subject's scores for each level of factor B squared, divided by the number of scores entering into that total.

$[7] = \sum_{n=1}^{n_s} T_{Si}^2/ab$ the sum of each subject's scores over all levels of factors A and B squared, divided by the number of scores entering into that total.

$[8] = G^2/N$ the grand total squared, divided by the total number of scores.

Using these numerical values, an analysis of variance is computed as follows:

Source	SS	df	MS	F
Subjects	$[7] - [8]$	$s - 1$	SS_S/df_S	
Factor A	$[3] - [8]$	$a - 1$	SS_A/df_A	$MS_A/MS_{A \times S}$
Factor B	$[4] - [8]$	$b - 1$	SS_B/df_B	$MS_B/MS_{B \times S}$
$A \times B$	$[2] - [3] - [4] + [8]$	$(a-1) \times (b-1)$	$SS_{A \times B}/df_{A \times B}$	$MS_{A \times B}/MS_{A \times B \times S}$
$A \times S$	$[5] - [3] - [7] + [8]$	$(a-1) \times (s-1)$	$SS_{A \times S}/df_{A \times S}$	
$B \times S$	$[6] - [4] - [7] + [8]$	$(b-1) \times (s-1)$	$SS_{B \times S}/df_{B \times S}$	
$A \times B \times S$	$[1] - [2] - [5] - [6] - [8] + [3] + [4] + [7]$	$(a-1) \times (b-1) \times (s-1)$	$SS_{A \times B \times S}/df_{A \times B \times S}$	
Total	$[1] - [8]$	$N - 1$	Not calculated	

To illustrate the computations, we use the following forty hypothetical scores. Assume that these scores were obtained from ten subjects (identified S_1 through S_{10}), who were exposed to all four treatment conditions in the experiment.

		Factor A A_1		Factor A A_2		
	S_1	78		79		
	S_2	81		79		
	S_3	86		84		
	S_4	76		76		
B_1	S_5	82	$T_{A_1B_1} = 797$	84	$T_{A_2B_1} = 795$	$T_{B_1} = 1592$
	S_6	77		78		
	S_7	81		80		
	S_8	83		83		
	S_9	74		72		
	S_{10}	79		80		
Factor B						
	S_1	81		82		
	S_2	82		81		
	S_3	89		85		
	S_4	77		78		
B_2	S_5	85	$T_{A_1B_2} = 807$	85	$T_{A_2B_2} = 811$	$T_{B_2} = 1618$
	S_6	76		80		
	S_7	81		82		
	S_8	84		85		
	S_9	73		74		
	S_{10}	79		79		
		$T_{A_1} = 1604$		$T_{A_2} = 1606$		$G = 3210$

(continued)

Raw-Score Computational Formulas for the Two-Factor Within-Subjects Analysis of Variance *(continued)*

$[1] = 78^2 + \cdots + 79^2 + 79^2 + \cdots + 80^2 + 81^2 + \cdots + 79^2 + 82^2 + \cdots + 79^2$
$\quad = 258,172$
$[2] = (797^2 + 795^2 + 807^2 + 811^2)/10 = 2,576,204/10$
$\quad = 257,620.4$
$[3] = (1604^2 + 1606^2)/(2)(10) = 5,152,052/20$
$\quad = 257,602.6$
$[4] = (1592^2 + 1618^2)/(2)(10) = 5,152,388/20$
$\quad = 257,619.4$

To obtain values [5], [6], and [7], the following format is useful:

S	$T_{S \text{ for } A_1}$	$T_{S \text{ for } A_2}$	$T_{S \text{ for } B_1}$	$T_{S \text{ for } B_2}$	T_{S_i}
1	159	161	157	163	320
2	163	160	160	163	323
3	175	169	170	174	344
4	153	154	152	155	307
5	167	169	166	170	336
6	153	158	155	156	311
7	162	162	161	163	324
8	167	168	166	169	335
9	147	146	146	147	293
10	158	159	159	158	317

$[5] = (159^2 + 161^2 + \cdots + 158^2 + 159^2)/2 = 516,276/2$
$\quad = 258,138$
$[6] = (157^2 + 163^2 + \cdots + 159^2 + 158^2)/2 = 516,286/2$
$\quad = 258,143$
$[7] = (320^2 + \cdots + 317^2)/4 = 1,032,470/4$
$\quad = 258,117.5$
$[8] = 3210^2/40 = 10,304,100/40$
$\quad = 257,602.5$

Then:

$SS_S = 258,117.5 - 257,602.5 = 515$
$df_S = 10 - 1 = 9$

$SS_A = 257,602.6 - 257,602.5 = .1$
$df_A = 2 - 1 = 1$

$SS_B = 257,619.4 - 257,602.5 = 16.9$
$df_B = 2 - 1 = 1$

$SS_{A \times B} = 257,620.4 - 257,602.6 - 257,619.4 + 257,602.5 = .9$
$df_{A \times B} = (2 - 1)(2 - 1) = 1$

$SS_{A \times S} = 258,138 - 257,602.6 - 258,117.5 + 257,602.5 = 20.4$
$df_{A \times S} = (2 - 1)(10 - 1) = 9$

$$SS_{B \times S} = 258{,}143 - 257{,}619.4 - 258{,}117.5 + 257{,}602.5 = 8.6$$
$$df_{B \times S} = (2 - 1)(10 - 1) = 9$$

$$SS_{A \times B \times S} = 258{,}172 - 257{,}620.4 - 258{,}138 - 258{,}143 - 257{,}602.5 + 257{,}602.6$$
$$+ 257{,}619.4 + 258{,}117.5 = 7.6$$
$$df_{A \times B \times S} = (2 - 1)(2 - 1)(10 - 1) = 9$$

$$SS_{\text{Total}} = 258{,}172 - 257{,}602.5 = 569.5$$
$$df_{\text{Total}} = 40 - 1 = 39$$

The summary of the analysis of variance is then derived by:

Source	SS	df	MS	F
Subjects	515.0	9	515.0/9 = 57.22	
Factor A	.1	1	.1/1 = .10	.10/2.27 = .04
Factor B	16.9	1	16.9/1 = 16.90	16.90/.96 = 17.60*
$A \times B$	.9	1	.9/1 = .90	.90/.84 = 1.07
$A \times S$	20.4	9	20.4/9 = 2.27	
$B \times S$	8.6	9	8.6/9 = .96	
$A \times B \times S$	7.6	9	7.6/9 = .84	
Total	569.5	39		

*$p < .05$.

Summarizing the Analysis of Variance

A complete summary of the analysis of variance on the heart-rate data in our example (Table 12–2) is shown in Table 12–5. The analysis of variance reveals that the main effect for noise level (factor B) is significant at the .05 level. The obtained F value of 17.60 clearly exceeds the tabled critical value of 5.12 for 1 and 9 df where $\alpha = .05$; hence, the calculated F falls into the rejection region. Thus, the null hypothesis H_0: $\mu_{B1} = \mu_{B2}$ is rejected because the probability is so low (less than .05) that the main effect means of 79.6 and 80.9 differ as much as they do because of chance variation only. Consequently, each main effect mean for noise level ($\bar{X}_B$) is considered to be an estimate of a different population mean. Neither the main effect of task difficulty (factor A) nor the task difficulty $\times$ noise level ($A \times B$) interaction is statistically significant with F values of .04 and 1.07, respectively.

Here is an example of how the results of our hypothetical experiment might be presented in the text of a journal article:

> The mean heart-rate measures in BPM are presented in Table 1. An analysis of variance reveals a significant main effect for noise level, $F(1, 9) = 17.60$, $MS_e = 2.27$, $p < .05$, with heart-rate higher overall in the loud-noise ($M = 80.9$) than in the soft-noise ($M = 79.6$) condition. Neither the main effect for task difficulty, $F(1, 9) = .04$, $MS_e = .10$, $p > .05$, nor the task difficulty $\times$ noise-level interaction, $F(1, 9) = 1.07$, $MS_e = .84$, $p > .05$, were significant.

TABLE 12–5   *Summary of analysis of variance on the hypothetical heart-rate scores as a function of task difficulty and noise level.*

Source	SS	df	MS	F
Subjects (*S*)	515.00	9	57.22	
Task difficulty (*A*)	.10	1	.10	.04
Noise level (*B*)	16.90	1	16.90	17.60*
A $\times$ *B*	.90	1	.90	1.07
A $\times$ *S*	20.40	9	2.27	
B $\times$ *S*	8.60	9	.96	
A $\times$ *B* $\times$ *S*	7.60	9	.84	
Total	569.50	39		

*$p < .05$.

Example of a Two-Factor Within-Subjects Experiment

Do people sometimes have difficulty recognizing their own voices? This was the question investigated by Douglas and Gibbins (1983), employing a two-factor within-subjects design. In a 1979 experiment, Gur and Sackeim had people listen to a series of recorded voices, one of which was the participant's own voice. The person was asked to identify his or her own voice from among the recordings. While performing this task, the individual's galvanic skin response (GSR) was also recorded. The GSR is a measure of the electrical conductivity of the skin and is thought to be a measure of emotional response or physiological arousal; it is one of the physiological measures used in a lie-detector test.

Gur and Sackeim found that even though individuals often denied recognizing their own voice, they showed a heightened GSR when it was presented. They interpreted these results to indicate that individuals often unknowingly deceive themselves, perhaps in order to avoid confronting some disliked part of themselves (e.g., their voice). Douglas and Gibbins (1983) offered an alternative explanation of these results. They argued that Gur and Sackeim's subjects had to pick out their own voice from a series of unknown voices. If the GSR is an index of general arousal, then perhaps the GSR would respond to identifying any voice known to the participant, not only to his or her own voice. If this response occurs, they reasoned, then Gur and Sackeim's results may have been due only to the arousal associated with attempting to identify any known stimulus, and not due to self-deception.

To test this hypothesis, Douglas and Gibbins asked thirty female undergraduate students to identify a known voice from among other less familiar voices.[2] Subjects listened to voice segments presented for 2, 4, 6, 12, or 24 seconds.

---

[2]Douglas and Gibbins actually had individuals participate in two experiments; in the other they attempted to distinguish their own voice from among other voices. We report only part of their study here.

In one condition, the voices presented for each of the durations were those of persons well known to the participant (the *target voice* condition); in a second condition the voices were those of individuals less well known to the participant (the *other voice* condition). Thus, the authors employed a 2 × 5 within-subjects design with two levels of type of voice and five levels of duration of voice presentation. Each subject, then, was presented with both target voices and other voices, with each type of voice presented at five different durations. The dependent variable was the GSR response after each voice was presented.

The mean GSR reactivity scores[3] for the target voice and other voice conditions at each of the five durations are shown in Table 12–6. An incomplete summary of the analysis of variance on the GSR measures, showing the sources, degrees of freedom, and obtained *F* values, is presented in Table 12–7. The analysis of variance shows that only the main effect for type of voice was statistically significant, because the obtained *F* value of 19.67 exceeds the critical value of 4.18 for 1 and 29 *df*, where $\alpha = .05$. Because the *F* values for duration of presentation and the interaction are both less than 1.00 we know that they cannot be statistically significant.

If you were to plot the ten means and "squish and slide" to compute the main effects and simple effects, you should readily see that the outcome of the analysis of variance is congruent with the impression formed from examining the pattern of means. We can see by inspecting the data, for instance, that the mean GSR measure in the target voice condition for the five durations is about 1.00, because they vary from .80 to 1.15. It is also evident that the GSR values for the other voice condition are consistently close to .50, varying only from .45 to .55 at the five durations. Thus, it appears that the two main effect means for

Mean GSR reactivity (in microhms) as a function of type of voice and duration of voice presentation.   **TABLE 12–6**

		Duration of presentation (seconds)				
		2	4	6	12	24
Type of voice	Target	1.00	1.15	.95	1.00	.80
	Others	.55	.50	.45	.45	.45

Note. The means are interpolated from Figure 2 in the Douglas and Gibbons (1983) article. Each mean is based upon thirty scores. It is conventional to represent the independent variable with the largest number of levels as the column variable and the other as the row variable. For analysis of variance, however (see Table 12–7), the type of voice variable is identified as factor *A*.

[3]The GSR is measured in microhms. An ohm is a measure of resistance to the flow of electrical current. A microhm is one-millionth of an ohm. For more information on the measurement of the GSR, see Edelberg (1972).

TABLE 12–7   *Incomplete summary of analysis of variance for GSR reactivity as a function of type of voice and duration of voice presentation in the Douglas and Gibbons (1983) experiment.*

Source	df	F
Subjects (S)	29	
Type of voice (A)	1	19.67*
Duration of presentation (B)	4	0.67
A × B	4	0.62
A × S	29	
B × S	116	
A × B × S	116	
Total	299	

*p < .05.

type of voice should be about 1.00 and .50 for the target-voice and other-voice conditions, respectively. (The actual main effect means calculated from the values given in Table 12–6 are .98 and .48.) The analysis of variance indicates that this difference between the two main effect means is improbable if chance factors alone were responsible for the difference and therefore is a significant difference at the .05 level.

It is also apparent that all five main effect means for duration of presentation should be close to .75; indeed, they are .78, .83, .70, .73, and .63. And the analysis of variance reveals that the variation among these five main effect means is most probably due to chance fluctuations and therefore not statistically significant at the .05 level. The simple effect differences for type of voice are about the same at each of the five durations (about .50). Therefore, there is no apparent interaction among the independent variables. The analysis of variance substantiates the lack of interaction between the two independent variables.

To illustrate again how results from experiments employing factorial designs are reported, we present an excerpt from the Results section of Douglas and Gibbins's article. Here, they describe the results of a two-factor analysis of variance on the GSR scores. Notice that they identify the duration-of-presentation factor as a trials factor. They also report the probabilities of the F ratios to levels that *would* meet significance (i.e., *a posteriori* significance levels), although these probabilities do not reflect the actual (or *a priori*) significance level that was adopted in the experiment, which probably was .05.

> A two factor (Target vs. Other Condition × Trials) repeated-measures ANOVA on GSR scores showed a main effect of target versus other condition, $F(1, 29) = 19.67$, $p < .001$. There was no significant main effect of trials, $F(4, 116) = .67, p < .25$, and again there was no significant interaction effect, $F(4, 116) = .62, p < .25$. (p. 590)

Based upon this outcome, and the results of the second experiment, in which subjects were to identify their own voice from among other voices, Douglas and

Gibbins concluded that a higher GSR to one's own voice does not necessarily show self-deception, because the same effect can be shown with identification of another's voice. As Douglas and Gibbins state, "We were able to replicate Gur and Sackeim's findings of high GSR when a person's own voice was present, irrespective of whether recognition was reported. But the same results were also obtained when the voice to be recognized was not the subject's own. Clearly, the effect has not been proven to be due to self-deception" (p. 592).

TWO-FACTOR MIXED DESIGN

As we have pointed out, the **two-factor mixed design** is a design in which one independent variable is manipulated as a between-subjects variable and one independent variable is manipulated as a within-subjects variable.[4] Again, the simplest instance of a mixed design is a 2×2 design. The plan of such a design with twenty participants is presented in Table 12–8. Factor A is the between-subjects variable.[5] In the example, the twenty subjects are randomly assigned to either level A_1 or A_2. After random assignment ten individuals will be assigned to level A_1 and ten different subjects will be assigned to level A_2. Factor B is the within-subjects variable. Each participant assigned to A_1 receives both levels B_1 and B_2 of factor B. Likewise, each of the participants assigned to A_2 also receives both levels of factor B. Hence, in Table 12–8 the score X_1 of the A_1B_1 cell arises from the same individual as the score X_1 from the A_1B_2 cell. Similarly, subject 6 of the A_2B_1 cell is the same individual as subject 6 of the A_2B_2 cell.

The two-factor mixed design permits an experimenter to evaluate main effects for each independent variable and the possible interaction of the independent variables. As can be seen from Table 12–8, the comparison of main effect means for factor A is a between-subjects comparison; one set of subjects contributes the scores entering into $\bar{X}_{A1}$ and another set of participants contributes the scores entering into $\bar{X}_{A2}$. The comparison of the main effect means for factor B is a within-subjects comparison because all the participants in the experiment have been tested under both levels of factor B. Correspondingly, for the simple effects comparisons needed to determine the nature of an interaction, the simple effect comparisons of factor A are between-subjects comparisons and the simple effect comparisons of factor B are within-subjects comparisons.

[4]Not all psychologists use the word *mixed* to refer to a design in which one factor is a between-subjects variable and the other a within-subjects variable. Some authors use the designation of mixed designs for instances in which one independent variable is a fixed factor; that is, the experimenter has arbitrarily selected the levels of the factor, and the other independent variable is a random factor, where the experimenter randomly selected the levels to be employed from the population of levels that the independent variable may take on. All the analyses of variance presented in this text, however, assume fixed-effects independent variables.

[5]We have here reversed our usual designation of A for the columns factor and B for the rows factor. This choice follows the common practice of most authors and journals.

TABLE 12–8   *Plan of two-factor mixed design with two levels of each independent variable. Factor A is the between-subjects independent variable and factor B is the within-subjects independent variable. The scores for ten participants in each level of factor A are represented.*

		Factor B			Main effect means of A
		B_1		B_2	
A_1		X_1		X_1	
		X_2		X_2	
		X_3		X_3	
		X_4		X_4	
		X_5 $\bar{X}_{A_1B_1}$		X_5 $\bar{X}_{A_1B_2}$	$\bar{X}_{A_1}$
		X_6		X_6	
		X_7		X_7	
		X_8		X_8	
		X_9		X_9	
		X_{10}		X_{10}	

Factor A

Between-subjects comparison

		B_1		B_2	
A_2		X_{11}		X_{11}	
		X_{12}		X_{12}	
		X_{13}		X_{13}	
		X_{14}		X_{14}	
		X_{15} $\bar{X}_{A_2B_1}$		X_{15} $\bar{X}_{A_2B_2}$	$\bar{X}_{A_2}$
		X_{16}		X_{16}	
		X_{17}		X_{17}	
		X_{18}		X_{18}	
		X_{19}		X_{19}	
		X_{20}		X_{20}	

Main effect means of B $\bar{X}_{B_1}$ $\bar{X}_{B_2}$

Within-subjects comparison

Characteristics of a Mixed Factorial Design

The mixed design rather obviously possesses characteristics of both the between- and within-subjects factorial designs. Because subjects are measured at least twice on the within-subjects variable, the design is open to practice effects, treatment-carryover effects, and demand characteristics as potential confounding variables for the manipulation of the within-subjects independent variable. Again, procedures for controlling these multiple-treatment effects are identical to those employed with one-factor within-subjects designs and are summarized in Table

11–3 (page 309). In this respect, notice that mixed designs are often employed in experiments in which there is specific interest in a practice or treatment-carryover effect. For example, many experiments in learning use mixed designs where the between-subjects factor may be type of material to be learned and the within-subjects variable is learning trials. Here, the experimenter is interested in the amount of improvement from trial to trial (i.e., a practice effect). In such instances, counterbalancing procedures are not used with the within-subjects independent variable.

Other characteristics of the mixed design in comparison to the between-subjects and within-subjects factorial designs are discussed later in this chapter.

Descriptive Analysis of Data

Data obtained from an experiment employing a mixed factorial design are analyzed using the same general approach employed for the between-subjects factorial design and the within-subjects factorial design. To illustrate the data analysis, the forty hypothetical heart-rate scores of Table 12–2 are again presented in Table 12–9. Now, however, assume that they were obtained from twenty individuals in a mixed-design experiment, in which ten of the individuals were assigned to level A_1 (soft noise) of the between-subjects factor (factor A—noise level). These subjects were measured on both levels of task difficulty, factor B (B_1—easy task, B_2—difficult task). Likewise, the remaining ten subjects were assigned to level A_2 (loud noise) and measured on both levels B_1 and B_2 of factor B. The main effect and cell means of these data are, of course, identical to those presented in Table 12–3. Again, an analysis of variance is necessary to determine whether the main effects for factors A and B and the $A \times B$ interaction are statistically significant.

Two-Factor Mixed-Design Analysis of Variance

Sources of Variation

The analysis of variance for a two-factor mixed design is procedurally similar to that of the two-factor between-subjects and the two-factor within-subjects analysis of variance. Again, F ratios are obtained for factor A, factor B, and the $A \times B$ interaction. In this model, however, the total variation of the scores is partitioned into five sources rather than four or seven sources, which is done for the two-factor between-subjects and within-subjects analysis of variance, respectively. Two of the five sources are due to *between-subjects variation:* the effects of the between-subjects independent variable (factor A) and the error variation of subjects within each group. The remaining three sources are due to *within-subjects variation:* the effects of the within-subjects independent variable (factor B), the joint effect of factors A and B ($A \times B$ interaction), and the error within subjects, which is reflected in the interaction of factor B with subjects ($B \times S$).

TABLE 12–9   *Heart-rate scores as a function of noise level (factor A) and task difficulty (factor B). The means for each subject over the two levels of task difficulty are presented in the column at the right of the scores.*

| | Task difficulty (factor B) | | | |
	Easy (B_1)	Difficult (B_2)	Subject	Mean
	78	79	1	78.5
	81	79	2	80.0
	86	84	3	85.0
	76	76	4	76.0
Soft (A_1)	82	84	5	83.0
	77	78	6	77.5
	81	80	7	80.5
	83	83	8	83.0
	74	72	9	73.0
	79	80	10	79.5
Noise level (factor A)				
	81	82	11	81.5
	82	81	12	81.5
	89	85	13	87.0
	77	78	14	77.5
Loud (A_2)	85	85	15	85.0
	76	80	16	78.0
	81	82	17	81.5
	84	85	18	84.5
	73	74	19	73.5
	79	79	20	79.0

Although there are both between-subjects and within-subjects sources of variation in a mixed design, the main effect sources (factor A and factor B) and the interaction of the two independent variables ($A \times B$) are obtained and interpreted in exactly the same way as they are for any other two-factor analysis of variance. In effect, the analysis of variance ignores whether the differences between main effect means and the differences among cell means that contribute to the interaction arise from between-subjects or within-subjects comparisons. But it is evident that "error" terms for evaluating the significance of the main effects and interaction must take into account whether the scores are independent (as in a between-subjects design) or whether they are repeated measures (as in a within-subjects design). In order to understand the two remaining sources of error variation in the analysis, it is helpful to draw parallels from both a one-factor between-subjects analysis of variance (Chapter 8) and a one-factor within-subjects analysis of variance (Chapter 11).

Between-subjects error variation Recall that in a one-factor between-subjects analysis of variance, the error variation is composed of a term that reflects the difference between a subject's score and the mean of the treatment condition he or she is in (i.e., $X_i - \overline{X}_A$). This error reflects individual differences and chance differences among subjects. A similar source of error variation occurs in a two-factor mixed analysis of variance. In this design, subjects again differ from each other not only because of the level of the between-subjects independent variable that they receive (factor A) but also because of individual differences. In this case, however, the individual differences among subjects are reflected by the differences between a subject's *mean* and the mean of the treatment group he or she is in, i.e., $\overline{X}_S - \overline{X}_A$. For example, in Table 12–9, subject 7 in the soft-noise condition has a mean heart rate of 80.5, which is the average of the easy (B_1) and difficult (B_2) task scores. The uniqueness of this individual's mean is represented by the difference between this mean and the mean of the soft-noise group (i.e., $80.5 - 79.6 = .9$). This difference cannot be due to any systematic effect of the between-subjects independent variable, noise level, because this subject was exposed to only the soft-noise level. An analogous situation holds for the other subjects in the soft-noise condition as well as for subjects in the loud-noise condition. Thus, another source of variation in scores is due to individual and chance differences in subjects' scores from the mean of the treatment group to which they belong. Because these differences add to between-subjects variation, they form the basis for a fourth source of the variation in heart-rate scores, subjects within groups. This term reflects chance and individual differences between subjects and is often called *between-subjects error*.

Within-subjects error variation The final source of variation in a two-factor mixed analysis of variance is due to any interaction effect between the subjects and the within-subjects independent variable (factor B) and chance differences that may occur from measurement to measurement. This source is conceptually identical to the treatments-by-subjects interaction of the one-factor within-subjects analysis of variance. For an illustration, observe the scores of subjects 12 and 19 in Table 12–9. For subject 12 a change in the within-subjects variable, factor B, from an easy task to a difficult task, decreases the heart rate from 82 to 81. On the other hand, for subject 19, a change from easy to difficult task results in an increase of heart rate from 73 to 74. Thus, we see that the effect of the within-subjects variable depends upon the subject. That is, there is a treatments-by-subjects ($B \times S$) interaction. This $B \times S$ *interaction* is the fifth source of total variation in heart-rate scores. Because this term also includes any chance error that may occur from repeated measurements of the subject and that cannot be separated from the $B \times S$ interaction, it is often referred to as *within-subjects error*.

All possible ways of partitioning the total variation into independent sources are now exhausted. All main effects, interactions, and sources of error have been identified. Summarizing, then, in a two-factor mixed analysis of variance, the total variation is partitioned into five sources:

Between-subjects
  1.   Factor *A*
  2.   Error (between-subjects)
Within-subjects
  3.   Factor *B*
  4.   *A* × *B* interaction
  5.   Error (within-subjects)

These sources are identified in column ① of Table 12–10.

Obtaining Sums of Squares

The sources of variation that we have described for a two-factor mixed design lead to conceptualization of a subject's score as deviating from the grand mean of the experiment (i.e., $X_i - \bar{X}_G$) because:

  1.   the factor *A* treatment had an effect (*A*),
  2.   the factor *B* treatment had an effect (*B*),
  3.   the factor *A* and factor *B* effects interact (*A* × *B*),
  4.   the individual is different from other subjects (error between subjects),
  5.   the effect of factor *B* is different from its effect on other individuals (error within subjects).

In a two-factor mixed-design analysis of variance we assume that each of these five influences contributes to an individual's score. Therefore, the deviation of an individual's score from the grand mean can be quantified as sums of squares deviations. Again the deviational formulas are quite cumbersome, however; thus we present the procedure for deriving sums of squares using the raw-score computational formulas only. But understand that, in principle, deviations for each source are obtained and squared for each subject. The resulting squared deviations are then summed over all subjects to obtain the sum of squared deviations, where

$$SS_{\text{Total}} = SS_A + SS_B + SS_{A \times B} + SS_{\text{Error (between subjects)}} + SS_{\text{Error (within subjects)}}.$$

The sums of squares corresponding to each source of variation are presented in column ② of Table 12–10.

Obtaining Degrees of Freedom

The degrees of freedom for the main effects and interaction of the treatments for a two-factor mixed design are obtained exactly as for the two-factor between-subjects or two-factor within-subjects designs. Thus, for SS_A and SS_B, the *df* are $a - 1$ and $b - 1$, respectively. Similarly, for $SS_{A \times B}$, $df_{A \times B}$ are equal to $(a - 1)(b - 1)$.

TABLE 12-10   *Structure of an analysis of variance for a two-factor mixed design.*

① Source	② SS	③ df	④ MS	⑤ Responsive to	⑥ F ratio	⑦ Statistical hypotheses[a]
(Between subjects)						
Factor A	SS_A	$a-1$	MS_A	Effects of factor A Error between subjects	$MS_A / MS_{\text{Error (b. subj.)}}$	$H_0: \mu_{A_1} = \mu_{A_2}$ $H_1:$ Not H_0
Error (b. subj.)	$SS_{\text{Error (b. subj.)}}$	$a(s-1)$	$MS_{\text{Error (b. subj.)}}$	Error between subjects		
(Within subjects)						
Factor B	SS_B	$b-1$	MS_B	Effects of factor B Error within subjects	$MS_B / MS_{\text{Error (w. subj.)}}$	$H_0: \mu_{B_1} = \mu_{B_2}$ $H_1:$ Not H_0
Interaction of $A \times B$	$SS_{A \times B}$	$(a-1) \times (b-1)$	$MS_{A \times B}$	Interaction of $A \times B$ Error within subjects	$MS_{A \times B} / MS_{\text{Error (w. subj.)}}$	$H_0:$ all $(\mu_{AB} - \mu_A - \mu_B + \mu_G) = 0$ $H_1:$ Not H_0
Error (w. subj.)	$SS_{\text{Error (w. subj.)}}$	$a(b-1) \times (s-1)$	$MS_{\text{Error (w. subj.)}}$	Error within subjects		
Total	SS_{Total}	$abs-1$	Not calculated	All systematic and error variance		

[a]The statistical hypotheses stated are appropriate for a 2×2 design.

Degrees of freedom for the two sources of error variation are easily determined by returning to our conceptualization of fixed scores and scores free to vary. The between-subjects error variation is composed of the deviations of the individual subject means from the mean of the treatment group they are in. Using the scores in Table 12–9 as an example, if the treatment mean ($\overline{X}_A$) is known, then only nine of the ten subject means in a treatment group are free to vary. The tenth subject mean is fixed. Thus, in each level of the between-subjects variable of this example, nine subject means are free to vary. Because there are two treatment levels, a total of eighteen subject means are then free to vary for the between-subjects error. More generally, the *df* for between-subjects error, *df*Error (b. subj.), may be expressed for any number of levels of the between-subjects variable and any number of subjects in each treatment level as $a(s-1)$, provided that the number of subjects is equal for each treatment group.

The error within subjects reflects the variation in a subject's score that cannot be accounted for by the main effects of each factor, the $A \times B$ interaction, or the between-subjects error. Conceptually, the question of *df* for this term resolves to the number of a subject's scores that are free to vary when cell means ($\overline{X}_{AB}$) and subject means ($\overline{X}_S$) are known. By looking at Table 12–9, we can see that for the example data, if each $\overline{X}_S$ is known, then only one of the two scores of a subject is free to vary. The other score is fixed. If $\overline{X}_{AB}$ is also known, however, then the scores of only nine of the ten subjects in a treatment group are free to vary. For example, in the soft-noise condition of Table 12–9, after the scores of subjects 1 to 9 are known, both scores of subject 10 are fixed because this subject's scores must lead to a subject mean of 79.5 and cell means of 79.7 and 79.5 for $\overline{X}_{A_1B_1}$ and $\overline{X}_{A_1B_2}$, respectively. Thus, in the experimental example, nine scores are free to vary for each level of factor A. Hence, there are eighteen *df* for error within subjects. More generally, for any two-factor mixed analysis of variance, the *df*Error (w. subj.) is equal to $a(b-1)(s-1)$. The *df* for each source of variation and *SS* are presented in column ③ of Table 12–10.

Mean squares for each source of variation in the two-factor mixed design are, as with all analyses of variance, obtained simply by dividing each *SS* by its corresponding *df*. The resulting mean squares are identified in column ④ of Table 12–10.

Mean Squares

Mean squares for each source of variation in the two-factor mixed design are, as with all analyses of variance, obtained simply by dividing each *SS* by its corresponding *df*. The resulting mean squares are identified in column ④ of Table 12–10.

Deriving F Ratios and Statistical Decision Making

The two-factor mixed analysis of variance permits a statistical test of significance of the main effects of factors A and B and their interaction ($A \times B$). The F ratio for factor A is formed by dividing MS_A by the $MS_{\text{Error (b. subj.)}}$. As summarized in column ⑤ of Table 12–10, both MS_A and $MS_{\text{Error (b. subj.)}}$ are responsive to the variation due to between-subjects error. However, MS_A also responds to the effects of the between-subjects independent variable, factor A. Thus, if factor A does have an effect, then MS_A will be larger than $MS_{\text{Error (b. subj.)}}$ and the value of the F ratio formed by these variance estimates will be greater than 1.00.

The F ratios for the within-subjects independent variable, factor B, and the $A \times B$ interaction are formed using $MS_{\text{Error (w. subj.)}}$ as the denominator. The logic for this step can be seen by examining Column ⑤ of the table. If there is no main effect of factor B or no $A \times B$ interaction, then MS_B, $MS_{A \times B}$, and $MS_{\text{Error (w. subj.)}}$ are independent estimates of the within-subjects error in the experiment. If there is a main effect of Factor B or an A $\times$ B interaction, however, then MS_B or $MS_{A \times B}$, respectively, will increase in value while $MS_{\text{Error (w. subj.)}}$ will remain unchanged. The three F ratios of the two-factor mixed analysis of variance are summarized in column ⑥ of the table.

The decision-making procedures for the three F ratios are identical to those of the two-factor between-subjects and the two-factor within-subjects analyses of variance. Critical values and rejection regions are established for each F ratio. If an obtained value of F falls into its rejection region, then the null hypothesis associated with that F ratio is rejected and the corresponding alternative hypothesis is accepted. The statistical hypotheses for each F ratio of a 2×2 mixed analysis of variance are presented in column ⑦ of the table.

Raw-Score Computational Formulas for the Two-Factor Mixed-Design Analysis of Variance

Notation used for computing a two-factor mixed-design analysis of variance with two levels of each factor. Factor A is the between-subjects variable and factor B is the within-subjects variable.

	Factor B				
	B_1		B_2		
	X_1		X_1		T_{S_1}
	X_2		X_2		T_{S_2}
	X_3		X_3		T_{S_3}
	X_4		X_4		T_{S_4}
A_1	X_5	$T_{A_1 B_1}$	X_5	$T_{A_1 B_2}$	T_{S_5}	T_{A_1}
	X_6		X_6		T_{S_6}
	X_7		X_7		T_{S_7}
	X_8		X_8		T_{S_8}
	X_9		X_9		T_{S_9}
	X_{10}		X_{10}		$T_{S_{10}}$

(continued)

Raw-Score Computational Formulas for the Two-Factor Mixed-Design Analysis of Variance *(continued)*

			Factor A			
A_2	X_{11} X_{12} X_{13} X_{14} X_{15} X_{16} X_{17} X_{18} X_{19} X_{20}	$T_{A_2 B_1}$	X_{11} X_{12} X_{13} X_{14} X_{15} X_{16} X_{17} X_{18} X_{19} X_{20}	$T_{A_2 B_2}$	$T_{S_{11}}$ $T_{S_{12}}$ $T_{S_{13}}$ $T_{S_{14}}$ $T_{S_{15}}$ $T_{S_{16}}$ $T_{S_{16}}$ $T_{S_{17}}$ $T_{S_{18}}$ $T_{S_{20}}$	T_{A_2}
	T_{B_1}		T_{B_2}		G	

where

X_i = raw score of a subject
T_A = total of scores for a main effect of factor A
T_B = total of scores for a main effect of factor B
T_{AB} = total of scores in a cell
T_{S_i} = total of scores for a subject (over all levels of factor B)
G = grand total of scores
n = number of scores in a cell
a = number of levels of independent variable A
b = number of levels of independent variable B
N = total number of scores
s = number of subjects.

The numerical values needed to obtain SS are:

$$[1] = \sum_{A=1}^{a} \sum_{B=1}^{b} \sum_{n=1}^{n_s} X_i^2 \qquad \text{the sum of all the raw scores squared.}$$

$$[2] = \sum_{A=1}^{a} \sum_{B=1}^{b} T_{AB}^2/n \qquad \text{the sum of each cell total squared, divided by the number of scores in a cell.}$$

$$[3] = \sum_{A=1}^{a} T_A^2/bn \qquad \text{the sum of each main effect total for factor } A \text{ squared, divided by the number of scores entering into that total.}$$

$$[4] = \sum_{B=1}^{b} T_B^2/an \qquad \text{the sum of each main effect total for factor } B \text{ squared, divided by the number of scores entering into that total.}$$

$$[5] = \sum_{n=1}^{n_s} T_{Si}^2/b \qquad \text{the sum of each subject's scores squared, divided by the number of scores entering into that total.}$$

$$[6] = G^2/N \qquad \text{the grand total squared, divided by the total number of scores.}$$

Using these numerical values, an analysis of variance is computed as follows:

Source	SS	df	MS	F
(Between)				
Factor A	$[3] - [6]$	$a - 1$	SS_A/df_A	$MS_A MS_{\text{Error (b. subj.)}}$
Error (between subjects)	$[5] - [3]$	$a(s - 1)$	$SS_{\text{Error (b. subj.)}}/df_{\text{Error (b. subj.)}}$	
(Within)				
Factor B	$[4] - [6]$	$b - 1$	SS_B/df_B	$MS_B/MS_{\text{Error (w. subj.)}}$
$A \times B$	$[2] - [3] - [4] + [6]$	$(a - 1) \times (b - 1)$	$SS_{A \times B}/df_{A \times B}$	$MS_{A \times B}/MS_{\text{Error (w. subj.)}}$
Error (within subjects)	$[1] - [2] - [5] + [3]$	$a(b - 1) \times (s - 1)$	$SS_{\text{Error (w. subj.)}}/df_{\text{Error (w. subj.)}}$	
Total	$[1] - [6]$	$N - 1$	Not calculated	

To illustrate the computations, we used the following forty hypothetical scores. Assume that these scores were obtained from ten subjects assigned to each level of the between-subjects variable (factor A). Each subject is exposed to each level of the within-subjects variable (factor B).

		Factor B			
		B_1	B_2	T_S	
	S_1	78	79	157	
	S_2	81	79	160	
	S_3	86	84	170	
	S_4	76	76	152	
A_1	S_5	82 $T_{A_1 B_1} = 797$	84 $T_{A_1 B_2} = 795$	166 $T_{A_1} = 1592$	
	S_6	77	78	155	
	S_7	81	80	161	
	S_8	83	83	166	
	S_9	74	72	146	
	S_{10}	79	80	159	
Factor A					
	S_{11}	81	82	163	
	S_{12}	82	81	163	
	S_{13}	89	85	174	
	S_{14}	77	78	155	
A_2	S_{15}	85 $T_{A_2 B_1} = 807$	85 $T_{A_2 B_2} = 811$	170 $T_{A_2} = 1618$	
	S_{16}	76	80	156	
	S_{17}	81	82	163	
	S_{18}	84	85	169	
	S_{19}	73	74	147	
	S_{20}	79	79	158	
	$T_{B_1} = 1604$		$T_{B_2} = 1606$	$G = 3210$	

$[1] = 78^2 + \cdots + 79^2 + 79^2 + \cdots + 80^2 + 81^2 + \cdots + 79^2 + 82^2 + \cdots + 79^2$
$= 258,172$

$[2] = (797^2 + 795^2 + 807^2 + 811^2)/10 = 2,576,204/10$
$= 257,620.4$

$[3] = (1592^2 + 1618^2)/(2)(10) = 5,152,388/20$
$= 257,619.4$

(continued)

Raw-Score Computational Formulas for the Two-Factor Mixed-Design Analysis of Variance *(continued)*

$[4] = (1604^2 + 1606^2)/(2)(10) = 5,152,052/20$
$\qquad = 257,602.6$
$[5] = (157^2 + \cdots + 159^2 + 163^2 + \cdots + 158^2)/2 = 516,286/2$
$\qquad = 258,143$
$[6] = 3210^2/40 = 10,304,100/40$
$\qquad = 257,602.5$

Then:

$SS_A = 257,619.4 - 257,602.5 = 16.9$
$df_A = 2 - 1 = 1$

$SS_{\text{Error (b. subj.)}} = 258,143 - 257,619.4 = 523.6$
$df_{\text{Error (b. subj.)}} = 2(10 - 1) = 18$

$SS_B = 257,602.6 - 257,602.5 = .1$
$df_B = 2 - 1 = 1$

$SS_{A \times B} = 257,620.4 - 257,602.6 - 257,619.4 + 257,602.5 = .9$
$df_{A \times B} = (2 - 1)(2 - 1) = 1$

$SS_{\text{Error (w. subj.)}} = 258,172 - 257,620.4 - 258,143 + 257,619.4 = 28.0$
$df_{\text{Error (w. subj.)}} = 2(2 - 1)(10 - 1)$

$SS_{\text{Total}} = 258,172 - 257,602.5 = 569.5$
$df_{\text{Total}} = 40 - 1 = 39$

The summary of the analysis of variance is then derived as follows:

Source	SS	df	MS	F
(Between)				
Factor A	16.9	1	$16.9/1 = 16.90$	$16.90/29.09 = .58$
Error (b. subj.)	523.6	18	$523.6/18 = 29.09$	
(Within)				
Factor B	.1	1	$.1/1 = \quad .10$	$.10/1.56 = .06$
$A \times B$	.9	1	$.9/1 = \quad .90$	$.90/1.56 = .58$
Error (w. subj.)	28.0	18	$28.0/18 = \quad 1.56$	
Total	569.5	39		

Summarizing the Analysis of Variance

Table 12–11 presents a complete summary of a two-factor within-subjects analysis of variance on the example data of Table 12–9. This analysis of variance reveals that neither of the main effects nor the interaction of factors A and B are statistically significant at the .05 level. Accordingly, the decision is to "fail to reject" for each of the three statistical hypotheses of this analysis.

Summary of a two-factor mixed analysis of variance on the hypothetical heart-rate scores as a function of task difficulty and noise level.   **TABLE 12–11**

Source	SS	df	MS	F
(Between subjects)				
Noise level (*A*)	16.90	1	16.90	0.58
Error (b. subj.)	523.60	18	29.09	
(Within subjects)				
Task difficulty (*B*)	0.10	1	.10	0.06
A × *B*	0.90	1	.90	0.58
Error (w. subj.)	28.00	18	1.56	
Total	569.50	39		

Example of a Two-Factor Mixed Experiment

A two-factor mixed design was employed by Forte, Mandato, and Kayson (1981) to investigate the effects of sex-role stereotyped advertising on recall of those advertisements by male and female subjects. They were interested in a possible interaction effect of the type of advertisement with the sex of the subject, hypothesizing that subjects would best recall sex-role stereotyped ads showing people of the same sex as the subject. To study the problem, they used two groups, one composed of twenty males, the other of twenty females. Each participant viewed two types of advertisement—those showing men in traditional sex-stereotyped occupations (e.g., a construction worker) and those showing women in sex-stereotyped occupations (e.g., a nurse). To avoid confounding multiple-treatment effects with the type of advertisement variable, Forte et al. presented the two types of advertisements to each subject in a different random order. In this experiment, then, a 2 (sex of subject) × 2 (type of advertisement) mixed design was employed. Sex of the subject was the between-subjects independent variable, and type of advertisement was the within-subjects independent variable.

After viewing the advertisements, participants recalled as many details of the ads as they could. The recall scores for each individual could vary from 0 to 14 details for each type of advertisement. The mean number of details recalled for each condition and an incomplete summary table of the analysis of variance are presented in Tables 12–12 and 12–13, respectively. Forte et al. described these results as follows:[6]

---

[6]The style of presentation of the *F* ratios, *df*, and *MS*Error has been modified from the original article to be in agreement with the new requirements of the *Publication Manual of the American Psychological Association* (1983). Forte et al. published this work in a journal requiring a slightly different editorial style.

The 2×2 mixed analysis of variance performed on the recall scores gave a significant effect of sex of the subject, $F(1, 38) = 50.4$, $MS_e = 3.11$, $p < .001$, as well as a significant interaction between type of advertisement and sex of the subject, $F(1, 38) = 11.25$, $MS_e = 1.08$, $p < .005$. Females recalled more details ($M = 11.6$) than males ($M = 8.9$). As expected, male subjects recalled more details from male-related ads ($M = 9.4$) than from female-related ads ($M = 8.4$), but female subjects recalled an almost equal number of details from both types of ads ($Ms = 11.4$ and 11.9) for male- and female-oriented advertisements, respectively. (pp. 620–621)

Again, we suggest that you compute main effects and simple effect differences on the means presented in Table 12–12. Then plot the means in a figure and "squish and slide" the means to relate the results in the table and your figure to the outcome of the analysis of variance presented in Table 12–13.

TABLE 12–12   *Mean number of details correctly recalled in the Forte, Mandato, and Kayson (1981) experiment as a function of type of advertisement and sex of the subject.*

		Type of advertisement	
		Male stereotyped	Female stereotyped
	Male	9.4	8.4
Sex of subject			
	Female	11.4	11.9

TABLE 12–13   *Incomplete summary of analysis of variance for number of details recalled as a function of sex of subject and type of advertisement in the Forte et al. (1981) experiment. Values in the table are those presented in the published report of the experiment.*

Source	df	MS	F
(Between subjects)			
Sex of subject (A)	1	156.74	50.40*
Error (b. subj.)	39	3.11	
(Within subjects)			
Type of advertisement (B)	1	.80[a]	.74[a]
A × B	1	12.15	11.25*
Error (w. subj.)	38	1.08	
Total	79		

[a] Estimated from main effect means.

*$p < .05$.

COMPARISON OF FACTORIAL DESIGNS

The between-subjects, within-subjects, and mixed-factorial designs are three fundamental types of factorial designs that a psychologist may employ. The designs may be expanded beyond those described here to include three or more independent variables. Each design, however, possesses characteristics that make it especially suited or unsuited for investigation of certain types of problems. Our purpose here is to compare and contrast the designs on several characteristics.

Type of Independent Variables That May Be Used

The designs may be compared on the type of independent variables that may be employed. Because a between-subjects manipulation of an independent variable involves different groups of subjects in each treatment condition, either active or attribute-independent variables may be used. A within-subjects manipulation of an independent variable, of course, requires an active-independent variable. Row 1 of Table 12–14 summarizes the types of independent variables that may be employed in each type of factorial design.

Number of Participants Required

Consider an experiment with two independent variables, A and B, with two levels of each factor (A_1, A_2 and B_1, B_2), which could be conducted as either a between-subjects, within-subjects, or mixed design. Suppose further that ten scores were to be obtained under each AB treatment condition. With a between-subjects design, ten participants would be required for each AB cell. Because there are four treatment combinations, a total of forty participants would be required in the between-subjects design. For a within-subjects design, each subject is tested under each treatment combination and therefore only ten individuals would be required. Finally, in a mixed design, assuming that factor A is the between-subjects variable, ten participants would be required for each level of factor A. But each individual would be given both levels of factor B; thus a total of twenty participants would be needed to obtain the forty scores. The relationship among the designs with respect to the number of participants needed to obtain a constant total of scores is shown in row 2 of Table 12–14.

Sensitivity to Multiple-Treatment Effects

Clearly, the between-subjects design is the least efficient and the within-subjects design the most efficient with respect to the total number of participants needed to obtain a fixed number of scores. But this advantage is gained at the cost of

TABLE 12–14   *Comparison of factorial designs*

	Between-subjects	*Within-subjects*	*Mixed*
Type of independent variable permissible	Active Attribute	Active	Active or attribute for between-subjects variable Active for within-subjects variable
Number of participants	*s* for each *A B* cell	*s*	*s* for each level of between-subjects variable
Sensitivity to multiple-treatment effects	Low	High	Low for between-subjects variable High for within-subjects variable
Statistical sensitivity to treatment effects	Low	High	Low for between-subjects variable High for within-subjects variable

much greater sensitivity to multiple-treatment effects in the within-subjects design. Because a participant in a within-subjects design serves in all treatment combinations, it may often be easy for an individual to formulate hypotheses about the study and have his or her responses influenced by demand characteristics. There are many types of experimental treatments that, because of their carry-over effects and the ease with which they lend themselves to guessing the nature of the hypotheses of the experiment, simply are not appropriately investigated with a within-subjects manipulation of that variable. Row 3 of Table 12–14 summarizes the sensitivity of the three designs to multiple-treatment effects.

Statistical Sensitivity to Treatment Effects

The three designs are also not equally sensitive statistically to treatment effects. To illustrate this characteristic, suppose the heart-rate scores in Table 12–2 were obtained from either a between-subjects design with forty participants, a within-subjects design with ten participants, or a mixed design (where *A* is the between-subjects and *B* is the within-subjects variable) with twenty participants.[7] Summary tables for the appropriate analysis of variance conducted on the data for each design are presented in Table 12–15.

As you can see, the total sums of squares for each analysis of variance are equal. That is, the total variation in the scores is the same regardless of the type of

---

[7] In an actual experiment, of course, only one of the designs would have been employed.

TABLE 12-15 *Analysis of variance summary tables for data treated as obtained from (a) a between-subjects design, (b) a within-subjects design, and (c) a mixed design*

(a) Between-subjects

Source	df	SS	MS	F
A	1	0.10	0.10	0.01
B	1	16.90	16.90	1.10
A × B	1	0.90	0.90	0.06
Error	36	551.60	15.32	
Total	39	569.50		

(b) Within-subjects

Source	df	SS	MS	F
Subjects	9	515.00	57.22	
A	1	.10	.10	0.04
B	1	16.90	16.90	17.60*
A × B	1	.90	.90	1.07
A × S	9	20.40	2.27	
B × S	9	8.60	0.96	
A × B × S	9	7.60	0.84	
Total	39	569.50		

*$p < .05$.

(c) Mixed

Source	df	SS	MS	F
A (between)	1	16.90	16.90	0.58
Error (b. subj.)	1	523.60	29.09	
B (within)	1	0.10	0.10	0.06
A × B	1	0.90	0.90	0.58
Error (w. subj.)	18	28.00	1.56	
Total	39	569.50		

Note. Recall that for a mixed design, the designation of *A* and *B* factors is reversed, as the usual procedure is to designate the row variable as the between-subjects factor and the column variable as the within-subjects factor. Hence, factor *A* for the mixed analysis corresponds to factor *B* for the between-subjects and within-subjects analyses.

analysis of variance applied to them. Similarly, the sums of squares for factors A and B and the $A \times B$ interaction are comparable across the designs. This result occurs because the main effect differences and the interaction remain the same regardless of the analysis of variance model used. The situation changes, however, with the remaining sources of variation in each analysis. In the between-subjects design, any variance in scores that cannot be accounted for by the main effects of the independent variable or the interaction becomes "error" variation. In the within-subjects design this error variation is further partitioned into variation due to subjects (S) and $A \times S$, $B \times S$, and $A \times B \times S$ interactions. In the mixed design the error variation is partitioned into error between subjects and error within subjects. The net result is that the within-subjects design is statistically more sensitive to treatment effects. As you can see in our example, the within-subjects analysis is able to detect a treatment effect for factor A, whereas this effect is not detected in either of the other analyses. Row 4 of Table 12–14 summarizes the statistical sensitivity of each of the three analyses.

In general, then, a within-subjects manipulation of a variable allows an experimenter to detect smaller effects of an independent variable than does a between-subjects manipulation of the same variable, because in a within-subjects manipulation each subject acts as his or her "own control." Thus, for research problems that lend themselves equally well to either a between-subjects or within-subjects manipulation of an independent variable, the within-subjects manipulation would seemingly be the design to choose. But, as we have discussed, multiple-treatment effects present serious limitations to the use of within-subjects designs. Thus, in most instances, research problems do not lend themselves equally well to all three types of designs, and the choice of design will depend upon a variety of factors in addition to the relative sensitivity of the statistical test.

SUMMARY

- In a two-factor within-subjects design, both independent variables are manipulated as within-subjects variables; therefore, each subject is tested under all treatment conditions.
  - A two-factor within-subjects analysis of variance is used to analyze the data.
  - The analysis of variance provides information about the main effect of each independent variable and the interaction of the independent variables.
- In a two-factor mixed design, one independent variable is manipulated as a between-subjects variable and the other independent variable is manipulated as a within-subjects factor.
  - A two-factor mixed analysis of variance is used to analyze the data. As with other factorial designs, this design provides information about the main effect of each independent variable and the interaction of the independent variables.

The choice of a between-subjects, within-subjects, or mixed factorial design for an experiment depends upon several considerations, including:

○   The type of independent variable employed. Attribute variables may typically be investigated only by use of between-subjects manipulations.

○   The number of participants to be used. Within-subjects manipulations require fewer subjects than do corresponding between-subjects manipulations.

○   The potential of multiple-treatment effects is higher in within-subjects manipulations.

○   The need for statistical sensitivity to detect treatment effects. Error variance is often smaller with within-subjects designs than with between-subjects designs.

13

In this chapter we identify the types of validity of an experiment and discuss several threats to each type of validity. Topics include:

- The role of replication in establishing the validity of an experiment
- Statistical-conclusion validity
- Internal validity
- Construct validity
- External validity

WHY YOU NEED TO KNOW THIS MATERIAL

The effect of an independent variable may explain the outcome of an experiment, but the investigator cannot be certain. The process of establishing the validity of an experiment involves ruling out plausible alternative hypotheses as explanations for the results. In this chapter we explain why psychological "facts" based upon research are "probabilistic" and therefore cannot be "proven."

Validity of Experiments

To perceive a fact of nature which had never been seen before by any human eye or mind, to discover a new truth in any field, to uncover an event of past history or discern a hidden relation, these experiences the fortunate bearer will cherish throughout his life. But let the pains of research not be overlooked. Hardly has the new discovery been made when its author begins to question its validity. How the heart can seem to cease beating when a loophole is perceived! In such a moment the heaven-high jubilance of the discoverer turns into deathly sadness. And it is not sickly indecision which brings this sudden despair; rather it is the investigator's task to doubt and to doubt again.

Curt Stern (1965, p. 772)

The **validity** of an experiment describes the correctness of the conclusions reached from that experiment. In any instance of research, four issues of validity matter: (1) **statistical-conclusion validity**—examining the correctness of the decisions made about the statistical hypotheses, (2) **internal validity**—establishing whether there is any effect due to the independent variable as it was manipulated, (3) **construct validity**—determining that the manipulated and measured variables adequately represent the conceptual independent and dependent variables, and (4) **external validity**—considering how far the results may be generalized to other people, other settings or environments, or other times. To assess the validity of an experiment one seeks answers to these questions and weighs the pitfalls that may ensnare any research.

ROLE OF REPLICATION IN ESTABLISHING VALIDITY

In Chapter 2 we indicated that replicability of research results by other researchers in other settings was one criterion of the scientific method. The question of replication is one of, "If this experiment were to be conducted again, would the results be the same?" Replication, then, is the basis for establishing each of the types of validity for a research finding (D. E. Campbell, 1982).

Types of Replication

A psychologist may repeat an experiment in many ways. Lykken (1968) identifies three forms of replication that may occur in psychological research: literal, operational, and constructive. We add a fourth form to this list, partial replication.

A **literal replication** exactly duplicates the entire method of the experiment being replicated. Sampling of participants, manipulation of the independent variable, and measurement of the dependent variable are conducted exactly as they were in the original experiment. Lykken (1968) states that, "Asking the original investigator to simply run more subjects would perhaps be about as close as we could come to attaining literal replication" (p. 155). To conduct a literal replication of an experiment one would need more information than is typically found in the method section of a report. A literal replication of McCarthy and Betz's experiment, for example, would require knowing exactly how they sampled their participants and precisely how they were assigned to treatment groups. One would also need the script used in the experiment (presented in Table 3–1), the instructions (see Table 4–1) and the procedures used for analyzing the content of the participants' responses (see Table 4–2). Given these requirements for a literal replication of an experiment, it is not difficult to understand why very few literal replications occur in psychological research.

An **operational replication** is an attempt to duplicate an experimental result merely from the information provided in the Method section of a report on that experiment. To conduct an operational replication of McCarthy and Betz's research, one would use the description of their method to construct instructions and simulated counseling sessions, select subjects, and score responses. As you might expect, in most instances an operational replication will involve some differences between the original and the replicated experiment in the methods of sampling and assigning individuals and in the procedures used to manipulate and measure the variables. An operational replication thus provides information about whether following the described operations will lead to the same results.

A **constructive replication** is conducted by merely knowing the conclusion drawn from the first experiment. A psychologist conducting a constructive replication of McCarthy and Betz's research would need only their conclusion that, "Counselor use of self-involving responses enhances his or her expertness and trustworthiness to a greater extent than does counselor use of self-disclosing responses" (McCarthy and Betz, 1978, p. 255). Using only this conclusion as a basis for research, the psychologist would then design a study to test this so-called fact. Such a replication would then use different operational definitions and empirical referents to manipulate and measure the constructs of the original research.

Lykken's three types of replication are conceptually clear and each is especially useful in answering one of the validity questions raised at the beginning of the chapter. But pure instances of any of the three types of replications are quite rare in published research. Rather, published replications of research are usually attempts to expand the research being replicated. We call such forms of replication partial replications. Typically, in a **partial replication** the methodology of the original author is employed but without the adherence to the reported method demanded of operational replications. In most instances, this research will provide an operational replication of the original research and will also incorporate manipulation of additional independent variables (Ostrom, 1971).

As we indicated earlier in this discussion, the validity of an instance of research is fundamentally established by replicating that research. We now turn to a discussion of validity issues in psychological research and the role of various types of replication in establishing validity. Following the lead of Cook and Campbell (1979) we will address four validity topics: statistical-conclusion validity, internal validity, construct validity, and external validity.

STATISTICAL-CONCLUSION VALIDITY

Statistical-conclusion validity refers to whether the decisions made about the null and alternative hypotheses from the statistical test are correct or not. This is a critical issue in any investigation, because the conclusion arrived at about the effect of an independent variable on a dependent variable (and therefore about the research hypothesis tested) is based upon the statistical conclusions that are drawn. Recall that the purpose in conducting a statistical test is to determine whether the differences in the dependent variable among treatment conditions are likely to be due to chance or to nonchance factors. Only if the null hypothesis is rejected does the experimenter have a basis for concluding that the independent variable has an effect on the behavior.

In Chapter 7 we indicated that whenever a decision is made about a statistical hypothesis, there is always a possibility that the decision represents either a Type I or a Type II error. If the null hypothesis is either wrongly rejected (Type I error) or not rejected (Type II error), then the experiment will lack statistical-conclusion validity. Obviously, an experimenter does not want to make either of these errors. If a treatment effect is present, then the experimenter wants to detect it; after all, this is the reason for conducting an experiment in the first place. But an experimenter also does not want to conclude that a treatment has an effect when it really does not. Accordingly, we will examine the factors that affect the probability of making a Type I or Type II error in an experiment.

BOX 13-1   Do Scientists Fudge Data?

Our entire discussion of the validity of an experiment rests on the assumption that scientists actually collect the data they report in their experiments. Unfortunately, in some cases this assumption is unwarranted, for scientists sometimes appear to fabricate or "fudge" the data of their experiments. It is relatively difficult to substantiate this charge, however. Scientists who fudge their data typically do not admit it; consequently, most evidence for fudging is circumstantial.

One possible instance in psychology involves the work of Sir Cyril Burt (1883–1971), an English psychologist who spent a lifetime investigating the genetic and environmental bases of intelligence. Several psychologists (see, for example, Dorfman, 1978; McAskie, 1978; or Wade, 1976) have argued that at least some of the data that Burt reported in published studies were fabricated, and the evidence for their contention seems quite solid.

Is the Burt case merely the tip of an iceberg or an isolated instance? Obviously it is difficult to support an answer to this question with any evidence. It is probably safe to state, though, that total fabrication of data in psychological research is rare (Barber, 1976). Although there are motivations in science for fudging data—prestige, recognition, financial grants, and so on—there are also strong motivations for honesty in scientific research. Recall that our arguments for the validity of research are all concentrated on replicability. It is quite unlikely that fudged results could be consistently replicated by others. Though it is quite possible that any honestly conducted study may not be replicable by others, a series of unreplicable fabricated studies by an individual would soon lead to a cloud of doubt from the scientific community.

The scientific community can be ruthless in its treatment of dishonesty. McCain and Segal (1973) contend, "A scientist can be an alcoholic, a braggart, a lecher, a thief, a murderer, a traitor (outside his discipline), or even a member of a civic club and still be forgiven, but one instance of his deliberately falsifying data brings eternal condemnation by his peers" (p. 130). The scientific community demands honesty of its members and is quite intolerant of any breaches of this demand; falsifying data virtually ends a scientist's career (Fisher, 1982).

We suggest that there may be instances of fabricated data in the literature, yet we feel that such occurrences are rare. For that reason, unless there is specific evidence to the contrary, examination of the validity of experiments can proceed on the assumption that data were actually collected under the conditions indicated in the research report.

Factors Affecting Statistical-Conclusion Validity

Three major factors affect statistical-conclusion validity in an experiment: (1) the significance level adopted (i.e., the value of α); (2) the magnitude of the effect induced by the independent variable; and (3) the amount of variability in the measure of the dependent variable.

The Significance Level (Alpha Level)

The probability of making a Type I or Type II error depends upon the significance level adopted. Recall from Chapter 7 that α, which defines the significance level for an experiment, is the probability of obtaining a value of the test statistic that leads to rejection of the null hypothesis when the null hypothesis is indeed true. The value of α therefore defines the probability of making a Type I error. Thus, when the alpha level is selected for a statistical test, the risk of making a Type I error is established. With a .05 significance level, for example, the experimenter knows that if H_0 is true, then the probability of wrongly rejecting the null hypothesis is .05. Similarly, if the alpha level is established at .01, then there is only a 1 in 100 chance of making a Type I error by incorrectly rejecting the null hypothesis when it is true.

The probability of making a Type II error also depends upon the significance level adopted. The effect of changing the value of α is reflected in the rejection region established for the test statistic. As the value of α is decreased (say from .05 to .01), the critical value of the test statistic establishing the rejection region is increased (for t and F and most other parametric tests). Thus, it becomes less likely that small but real differences between population means will lead to values of an obtained test statistic that fall into the rejection region. Consequently, the experimenter is less likely to accept a true alternative hypothesis and more likely to commit a Type II error.

This relationship is illustrated in Figure 13–1, using the theoretical sampling distribution of F for 1 and 8 degrees of freedom (given by the distribution plotted in solid lines). The distribution represented by the dashed lines is one possible sampling distribution of F that may occur when H_1 is true. Notice that by decreasing α from .05 to .01, the critical value of F for rejecting H_0 increases and therefore fewer values of F will fall into the rejection region when H_1 is true.

As you can see from Figure 13–1, there is a kind of inverse relationship between Type I and Type II errors. It is not possible to maximize protection against both types of errors in an experiment. If the researcher takes steps to minimize the likelihood of making a Type I error, then it is more likely that a Type II error will occur. Similarly, the probability of making a Type II error can be decreased by increasing the risk of making a Type I error. For this reason, .05 is the usual significance level adopted for experiments, for it represents an "acceptable" risk for making a Type I error while allowing reasonable protection against a Type II error.

Size of Effect of the Independent Variable

The probability of making a correct decision also varies with the size of the effect induced by the independent variable. In the context of statistical-hypothesis testing, the effect of the independent variable is to increase the differences among the population means. For each possible difference in population means (i.e., treatment effect), there is a different (but always unknown) sampling distribution of the test statistic. This relation is illustrated in Figure 13–2 for the theoretical sampling distribution of the F statistic under H_0, and under two hypothetical instances of H_1, a smaller and a larger treatment effect. As you can see, the larger

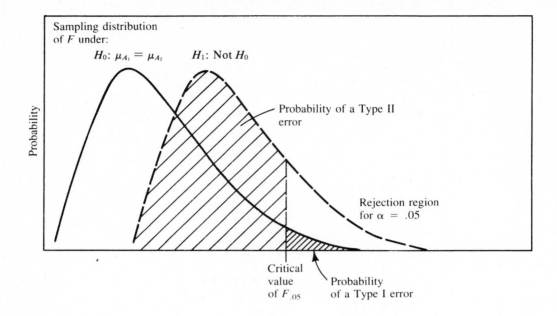

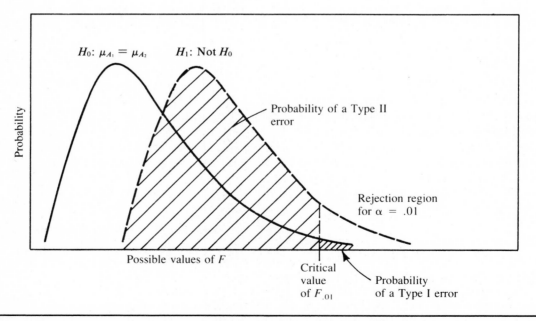

FIGURE 13–1   *Probability of Type I and II errors as a function of the significance level. Significance levels of $\alpha = .05$ and $\alpha = .01$ are illustrated.*

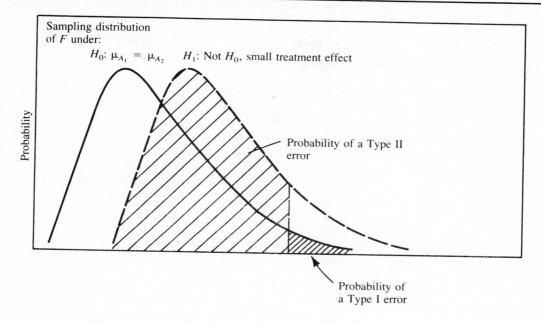

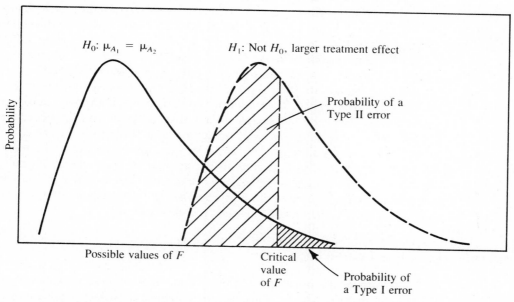

Probability of Type I and II errors as a function of size of effect of the independent variable. A smaller and a larger treatment effect are illustrated.

FIGURE 13–2

the treatment effect, the less likely it becomes that a Type II error will be made. It is more likely, therefore, that the null hypothesis will be correctly rejected.

Amount of Variation in the Dependent Variable

The decisions about H_0 and H_1 also depend upon the amount of variability in the scores within treatment conditions. Both the t test and the analysis of variance essentially compare the differences between the sample means of groups given different levels of the independent variable (i.e., systematic variation) to differences among scores within the same treatment conditions (i.e., error variation). If the test statistic indicates that the systematic variation is sufficiently greater than the error variation (i.e., the test statistic falls into the rejection region), then H_0 is rejected and H_1 accepted. Clearly, then, the decision about whether a given difference between sample means is a chance occurrence or not depends upon the amount of error variation in the experiment.

An example of this relationship is shown in Table 13–1. The table illustrates two sets of samples of size 5, each selected from two populations whose means differed by a value of 2.0.[1] The difference between the sample means for both sets 1 and 2 is 3.4. Consequently, in the analysis of variance of each sample presented in Table 13–1, MS_A is the same for each set ($MS_A = 28.90$). The scores were selected, however, so that in set 1 the error variation is greater than in set 2. This difference can be seen by comparing the standard deviations associated with set 1 (3.51 and 1.87) to those associated with set 2 (1.41 and 1.14). This difference is also reflected in the analysis of variance, where the MS_{Error} for set 1 (7.90) is nearly five times greater than the MS_{Error} for set 2 (1.65). For $\alpha = .05$, the obtained value of F for set 1 is statistically nonsignificant, and the obtained F for set 2 is statistically significant. Hence, for set 1, H_0 is not rejected, but in set 2, H_0 is rejected and H_1 accepted. The important point here is that given the same numerical difference between the sample means, two different conclusions about the statistical hypotheses are reached; the decision with respect to set 1 reflects a Type II error, but the decision with respect to set 2 is correct. Of course, the reason for these two differing decisions rests in the amount of error variance among the scores in each of the two samples. The relevance of this example is clear. In the design and conduct of research, a psychologist should make all efforts to reduce sources of error variation affecting the dependent variable.

When Is Statistical-Conclusion Validity Achieved?

In one experiment a researcher can never know if he or she has made a Type I or II error in that experiment. This decision can arise only from replications of the study. The most efficacious approach is a literal replication of the experiment

[1] The procedure used to generate the populations was identical to that used in creating Table 6–2.

Two sets of two randomly drawn samples of size 5 each. Sample A_1 was drawn from a population with a mean $= \mu_1$. Sample A_2 was drawn from a population with a mean $= \mu_1 + 2$.

TABLE 13–1

	Set 1		Set 2	
	A_1	A_2	A_1	A_2
	10	17	14	18
	14	14	14	17
	14	18	12	19
	11	17	14	17
	19	19	16	16
M	13.6	17.0	14.0	17.4
SD	3.51	1.87	1.41	1.14

Analysis of variance summary tables

		Set 1					Set 2		
Source	df	SS	MS	F	Source	df	SS	MS	F
Factor A	1	28.90	28.90	3.66	Factor A	1	28.90	28.90	17.52*
Error	8	63.20	7.90		Error	8	13.20	1.65	
Total	9	92.10			Total	9	42.10		
					*$p < .05$				

with different subjects. If the original difference between treatment means is due only to sampling error (i.e., a Type I error), then it is very unlikely that a literal replication would lead to the same difference.

Literal replications of research are not frequently done; however, when they are, interesting outcomes may occur. Layton and Turnbull (1975) attempted to manipulate male and female subjects' belief in, and evaluation of, extrasensory phenomena (ESP) by having an experimenter describe studies that either supported an ESP interpretation or did not. The task of the participants was to attempt to match an unseen target list of 100 randomly ordered digits from 1 to 5. In the first experiment, Layton and Turnbull found that males told there was no evidence for ESP and females told there was evidence for ESP scored greater than chance on the ESP task. Based upon the differences of this experiment, Layton and Turnbull felt "fairly confident in claiming that subjects' belief and evaluation of ESP influenced their performance on the ESP task" (p. 174).

Layton and Turnbull then conducted a literal replication of the study, using different participants drawn from the same population. In this replication they failed to find any statistically significant differences for their manipulated variables. A compelling argument for these differing results is that the differences found in the first experiment represent a Type I error, and that is what Layton and Turnbull concluded: "The apparent occurrence of psi effects in the first experiment is thus interpreted as a Type I error" (p. 177). This conclusion, however, was reached only after presenting arguments that the outcome of the literal replication did not represent a Type II error.

Most often, however, judgments about statistical-conclusion validity must be drawn from partial replications. Because such replications typically make changes in the manipulations and procedures of the experiment, however, decisions about the statistical-conclusion validity of the replicated experiment are often not as directly or as quickly reached as in Layton and Turnbull's work. But if one study indicates an effect for an independent variable, and this effect cannot be reliably obtained in subsequent partial replications, then it is quite possible that a Type I error occurred in the original study (see Greenwald, 1975, for examples).

Although a psychologist cannot establish the statistical-conclusion validity of any one study from that study alone, he or she should make all efforts to maximize such validity in a study, including (1) choosing a value of α that reflects the relative importance of Type I and II errors; (2) attempting to maximize the effect of the independent variable; and (3) attempting to minimize the error variance. In other words, a psychologist should attempt to employ a sensitive research design, as we emphasized in Chapter 4.

INTERNAL VALIDITY

After statistical-conclusion validity has been examined and it is decided that differences exist in sample means, a question arises: is the obtained difference due to the effect of the *independent-variable-as-manipulated* on the *dependent-variable-as-measured*? This is the issue of **internal validity** of the research, "the validity with which statements can be made about whether there is a causal relationship from one variable to another in the form in which the variables were manipulated or measured" (Cook and Campbell, 1979, p. 38). A threat to internal validity, then, is any event in the experiment that weakens the possibility of reaching a conclusion that the independent-variable-as-manipulated caused the observed effect on the dependent-variable-as-measured. Such threats may offer a plausible alternative or rival explanation for the effect found.

Two of the threats we discuss are of more importance to between-subjects designs, two are of more consequence to within-subjects designs, and one is relevant to either design. It is also quite possible for more than one threat to operate in an experiment and for the threat to diminish as well as to enhance the effect of the independent-variable-as-manipulated.

Threats to Internal Validity of Experiments

Threats to Between-Subjects Designs

Subject mortality   If participants are dropped from an experimental condition because of the particular treatment, then subject mortality has occurred. Subject mortality does not imply that the participants died, but merely that they did not complete the testing in a treatment condition because of the rigor of the treatment (e.g., difficulty of learning, excessive fatigue, length of time needed to complete the task, and so on). New subjects may be selected to replace those who are lost through attrition. But in doing so the equivalence of groups created by random assignment prior to introduction of the independent variable is jeopardized. A difficult treatment condition may have been completed by only those participants capable of withstanding the rigors of the treatment. In an experiment by Runquist, Pullyblank, and Whyte (1982) on learning word lists, the data from 29 of 109 participants were discarded, mostly because the individuals were unable to learn the lists. The largest number was lost from the most difficult learning condition. Consequently, Runquist et al. had no assurance that their treatment groups were equivalent.[2]

Selection biases   This threat describes the instance when the two or more treatment groups are not equivalent prior to introduction of the independent variable. Although this result can happen in many ways, it often occurs when, in place of random assignment, participants in an experiment are *selected* for treatment conditions on the basis of some irrelevant attribute. One unusual but real example in the experience of one of the authors occurred when a male student was running an experiment with two levels of an active-independent variable that required different amounts of time in contact with the participants. This student admitted that he assigned females to the longer-duration treatment condition so that he would have more time in contact with them. Males were all assigned to the shorter-duration treatment condition. Obviously, this experimenter had no assurance that his groups were equivalent prior to introduction of the independent variable.

   We stress that in an experiment, selection biases can typically be avoided by randomly assigning subjects to levels of the independent variable. Selection biases, however, are an especially serious threat in ex post facto studies, where participants are not randomly assigned to a level of the independent variable, but are selected because they possess the attribute that is of interest. As we pointed out in Chapter 3, psychologists can never be sure that the groups formed in an ex post facto study differ only on the attribute of interest and not on any other attributes.

Threats to Within-Subjects Designs

As we have discussed, in a within-subjects design, a participant is measured on each level of the independent variable. Consequently, each individual is measured at least twice, and possibly many more times. These repeated measurements allow several possible threats to internal validity to arise.

---

[2]Runquist et al., of course, were aware of this problem and were appropriately cautious in interpreting their results.

History   If events outside the experimental situation occur between the several treatments administered to a participant and affect the measured behavior, then the history of the individual has affected the outcome of the experiment. The events considered under history are, of course, events that may affect the behavior of all subjects, not just the events unique to one individual. Differences in history are likely to be nonexistent in a typical laboratory experiment when the several measures occur successively in time. Such differences are much more likely to occur, however, if a considerable time, such as weeks or months, intervenes between the measurements. For example, this effect may be a problem in long-term studies of attitude change: Events in the environment outside the experimental situation may substantially alter an individual's attitude during the period of the experimental study.

Maturation   Administering several treatments and measurements to a subject usually takes time. Between the treatments, various processes within the individual may change and affect behavior. Depending upon the interval between the treatments, the participant may become fatigued, sleepy, hungry, and will most assuredly grow older, if only by a small amount. If any of these maturational processes affect the behavior being measured, then they affect the outcome of the experiment. Notice that history refers to specific events occurring in the environment, and maturation refers to processes within the individual.

Threat to Either Between-Subject or Within-Subject Designs

Instrumentation   Instrumentation is the possibility that the characteristics of the measuring instrument for the dependent variable may systematically change over the time needed either to test one participant or to conduct the entire experiment. Changes in accuracy of measurement are very possible if another person (e.g., the experimenter) is the measuring instrument. Experimenters, as well as subjects, may be affected by maturational processes. And these maturational processes (e.g., fatigue, hunger, motivation) may also affect the accuracy of data collection as well as the participant's performance. As an example, notice that in Table 4–2, the scoring procedure used by McCarthy and Betz, they urged the individuals scoring the responses to be consistent from participant to participant (statement VI.3).

When Is Internal Validity Achieved?

Decisions about the internal validity of the research come most directly from careful examination of the design and procedure of the experiment and from operational replications of it. Cook and Campbell (1979) urge each psychologist, in assessing internal validity, to be his or her own best critic of possible threats to internal validity. Additional support for internal validity is gained from operational replications of the research. Recall that an operational replication essentially provides a test of the described method of the replicated experiment. If the results of a study can be replicated by following the published method of that study, then psychologists are more confident of the internal validity of the original research.

Unfortunately, few operational replications of experiments are published in psychology and decisions about internal validity must most often be reached from partial replications. In a partial replication, however, the method of the experiment to be replicated is often elaborated and changed; hence decisions reached from the replication about internal validity of the original study must remain tenuous. Failures to replicate may then be due to changes in the method rather than lack of internal validity in the original experiment.

CONSTRUCT VALIDITY

For an experiment to possess **construct validity** the conceptual variables involved in the research hypothesis must be appropriately manipulated and measured by the empirical referents used. Conceptual variables are operationally defined routinely in experiments. But how do psychologists know that a procedure with an empirical referent "truly" manipulates or measures the psychological construct that is of interest? For example, how does one know that the Counselor Rating Form really measures the concept of expertness or that the words "Well, I like the good things I've seen about you" (see Table 3–1) demonstrate counselor self-involvement? The issue of construct validity, then, has to do with how well the empirical referents relate to the conceptual variables of the experiment.

As a major aspect in assessing the validity of an experiment, construct validity is a recent development.[3] The concept of construct validity of psychological measurement has, however, a relatively long history in psychology (Cronbach and Meehl, 1955). We will first discuss the construct validity of independent and dependent variables with respect to the adequacy of the empirical referents used to define them. Next, we consider various sources of confounding by the participant and the experimenter that threaten the construct validity of an experiment.

Theoretical Constructs

In Chapter 3 we stated that theoretical constructs are invented concepts which are neither tangible nor readily observable and which enter into relationships with

---

[3]Construct validity was apparently introduced as a major aspect in assessing the validity of experiments by Cook and Campbell (1976). Construct validity, however, has been discussed in several contexts and identified by different names by various authors. For example, Campbell and Stanley (1963) initially treated it as one component of external validity and Berkowitz and Donnerstein (1982) continue this usage. Bracht and Glass (1968) spoke of ecological validity within the broader categorization of external validity, and Mahoney (1978) discussed theoretical validity.

other constructs in a theory in an attempt to explain certain behaviors. You will recall that for such constructs to be scientifically useful it must be possible to relate them to observable variables (i.e., empirical referents) via operational definitions.[4] Theoretical constructs are, however, what Meehl (1970b) has identified as "open concepts." That is, because the definition of a construct is given by the theory in which it is embedded, and because that theory is always open to change and reconceptualization on the basis of empirical research, the theoretical construct is never fully defined; it is "open" to additional meanings and relationships. For example, Cronbach and Meehl (1955) state, "We will be able to say 'what anxiety is' when we know all of the laws involving it; meanwhile, since we are in the process of discovering these laws, we do not yet know precisely what anxiety is" (p. 294). Thus, any theoretical construct offers the possibility of many potentially different operational definitions and, therefore, empirical referents. Some empirical referents may more validly represent the construct than others.

Development of Empirical Referents

Almost anyone can construct a rating scale or write a sentence for a counselor to speak, and specify the operations used to do so. But merely specifying the empirical referents and how they were manipulated or measured does not ensure that they validly represent the conceptual variables of the experiment. An empirical referent must have some clear relationship to the features of the construct it is to represent. But this relation cannot be established unless the theoretical construct is itself clearly formulated. A vaguely limned theoretical construct with ill-defined relationships to other constructs will hardly permit us to develop empirical referents having construct validity. Hence, the basis for construct validity begins with clearly and precisely defined conceptual variables.

In determining the essential features of a construct, we begin by seeking its definition in a good dictionary or in one of the specialized dictionaries of psychological terms. A dictionary definition does *not* provide an operational definition; rather, it provides what Kerlinger (1973) calls a *constitutive definition* in terms of other words or constructs. But a constitutive definition will help us to identify the inherent, essential features of a construct. A definition of *expert* in a dictionary is "having, involving, or displaying special skill or knowledge derived from training or experience" (*Webster's Ninth New Collegiate Dictionary,* 1983, p. 437). From this constitutive definition, it is clear that the concept of "expert" implies possessing acquired knowledge or skills in a particular area. Thus any empirical referent for the concept of expertness should reflect these features.

After the essential aspects of the construct have been identified, a psychologist consults the psychological literature to see how others have manipulated or

---

[4]As Underwood (1975) argues, "Nothing is more conducive to the infection of a theory by ploglies and homunculi than a free-floating intervening process" (p. 131). A homunculus is a supposed little man, often thought to "live in the head," who directs behavior. Do you know what Underwood means by "ploglies"?

measured the construct that is of interest. Doing so does not mean that new operational definitions for empirical referents should not be developed and used; they certainly should be whenever a need arises. But they should be developed with an understanding of how others have manipulated or measured the conceptual variable. McCarthy and Betz provide an excellent example of this practice. In the introduction to their article they present a critical examination of the features of the construct of self-disclosure, others' definitions of the construct and the deficiencies of those definitions, and the argument for their own empirical referents of the construct.

It is apparent, however, that no one empirical referent can fully manipulate or measure a construct. McCarthy and Betz's two sentences (see Table 3–1) are certainly not the only possible empirical manipulations of the type of counselor statement. And the CRF does not fully measure what is commonly conceived of as expertness. The validity of any empirical referent as a manipulation of a construct is, at best, only tentative. Validity is gained for the particular manipulation when one can show that it affects behavior in the direction predicted by the construct. Thus, the empirical manipulation of counselor self-involvement and self-disclosure by McCarthy and Betz gains validity as further studies show that it influences behavior in accord with the expected effects of type of counselor statement. Validity is also gained when other empirical manipulations of counselor self-involvement and self-disclosure lead to the same results as do McCarthy and Betz's manipulations. This is a procedure known as *converging operations,* the convergence of several empirical manipulations or operations on the same construct (Garner, Hake, and Eriksen, 1956).

Likewise, the CRF gains validity as a measure of the concept of expertness as one can demonstrate that it (1) agrees with other previously used empirical measures of expertness, (2) can differentiate expert from nonexpert counselors, and (3) shows low relationships to empirical measures of other constructs such as empathy, friendliness, or attractiveness. Ultimately, then, the construct validity of an experiment is an accretionary process dependent upon replicating findings by other experimenters using a variety of manipulations and measurements of the conceptual variables.

Threats to Construct Validity of Experiments

We now discuss a variety of threats to the construct validity of experiments. These threats are potential sources of confounding variables. Hence, our primary interest here is in the construct validity of the independent variable rather than that of the dependent variable.[5] Realize, however, that the issue of construct validity of the dependent variable is equally important in determining the construct validity of an experiment.

[5]Our approach follows that of Cook and Campbell (1979), who emphasize the construct validity of manipulations in an experiment. A more complete listing and discussion of threats is found in Bracht and Glass (1968) under the heading, ecological validity.

Reactive Nature of Experiments

One potential pitfall to establishing construct validity is that many, if not most, experiments are reactive; the subject is aware of being in an experiment. Consequently, the experimenter must be wary lest such obtrusive measures alter individuals' "natural" behavior. Several threats to construct validity resulting from the reactive nature of experiments have been identified and investigated by psychologists.

Subject roles   A number of psychologists have suggested that participants may attempt to adopt a "role" either as a good or a negativistic subject in an experiment (Weber and Cook, 1972). The good subject is thought to want to provide responses that will support the experimenter's research hypothesis. The negativistic subject, on the other hand, is thought to attempt to provide responses that will sabotage the experiment. The importance of subject roles in an experiment is often closely tied to a second presumed threat to construct validity, that of demand characteristics of the experiment. Whether or not a participant assumes a role may depend upon the demand characteristics of the experiment.

Demand characteristics   Orne (1962) argues that the experience of a participant in an experiment is one of problem solving, in which an individual attempts to identify the hypothesis of the study so that he or she may try to respond in accordance with the experimenter's hypothesis. Orne feels that most individuals will want to be good subjects and will be sensitive to cues in the experiment, such as the experimenter's tone of voice or some cues in the instructions that may indicate how they should behave. These cues, often quite subtle, are called the *demand characteristics* of the experimental situation. Orne proposes that an individual's behavior in an experiment will be determined by both the manipulated independent variable and the demand characteristics perceived in the experiment. If demand characteristics are important determinants of behavior in an experimental situation, then the construct validity of the experiment may be low. Participants may be deliberately responding as they perceive they should, which may negate the effect of the independent variable.

There is growing doubt, however, about the pervasiveness of both subject roles and demand characteristics in psychological research. Weber and Cook (1972) argue that these factors may be important only when a participant is both motivated to adopt a specific role and cues in the experiment allow the individual to ascertain the responses appropriate to the role he or she has elected to play. Most experimenters, however, take precautions to employ a **single-blind procedure;** that is, to prevent the subject from knowing whether he or she is receiving a control treatment or an experimental treatment. This procedure reduces the risk of a participant's responding in accordance with the perceived hypothesis of the experimenter. The single-blind procedure, of course, does not rule out the possible presence of cues that subjects may use to guide their behavior. But it is quite unlikely that individuals will know exactly what role or behaviors would provide support for the research hypothesis or evidence against it. Consequently, Berkowitz and Donnerstein (1982) comment, "Future historians of social science surely will marvel at how this reasoning [i.e., that subjects adopt a role and try to provide "good" data by responding to demand characteristics] has been accepted in the absence of clear evidence supporting it" (p. 250). They state there is little empirical evidence in support of subject roles and demand characteristics being an important factor in most research.

Evaluation apprehension   Individuals in psychology experiments may also often show apprehension about the possibility of their performance being evaluated by a psychologist (Rosenberg, 1969). A psychologist may be perceived as possessing unique abilities to assess a person's intelligence, motivation, or emotional state. Because of evaluation apprehension, individuals may thus behave differently toward a treatment than they would if the apprehension were not present. Or the behavior may be due only to the evaluation apprehension and not at all to the independent variable. In such instances a psychologist may arrive at wrong conclusions about the effect of the independent variable.

A good amount of evidence indicates that evaluation apprehension may play an important role in determining the outcome of many experiments (Barber, 1976; Berkowitz and Donnerstein, 1982; Weber and Cook, 1972). Individuals want to appear "normal" in most experiments and may avoid giving any responses that they think may be abnormal.

Multiple-Treatment Effects

As we discussed in Chapter 11, if a participant is exposed to two or more treatments sequentially, the apparent effects of later treatments may depend upon the exposure to earlier treatments. Practice effects, either positive or negative, may linger from one measurement to another. Or the effects of one treatment may carry over and affect another treatment. Also, demand characteristics are more likely to have an effect when a participant receives several treatment conditions. In most instances, however, multiple-treatment effects may be controlled by using the procedures presented in Chapter 11.

Experimenter Effects

A number of so-called experimenter effects may threaten the construct validity of an experiment (see Barber, 1976). We discuss two here: experimenter attribute effect and experimenter expectancy effect.

Experimenter attribute effect   The personal attributes of an experimenter, such as sex, age, physical appearance, or friendliness may affect the behavior of subjects in an experiment (Rosenthal, 1966). Young-adult male subjects may behave differently with a young female experimenter than they would with an older male experimenter. After reviewing the research in this area, however, Barber (1976) concludes, "All that can be said with confidence at the present time is that an experimenter's sex, age, race, prestige, anxiety, friendliness, dominance, etc. may *at times* affect how subjects perform in the experiment, but we can rarely predict beforehand what experimenter attributes will exert what kind of effects on subjects' performance on what kinds of experimental tasks" (p. 52). For this reason, Barber suggests that an experiment incorporate a number of experimenters who differ on potentially relevant attributes. This recommendation, however, has not been widely acted upon by psychologists.

Experimenter expectancy effect   Experimenters also have expectancies about the behavior of participants in an experiment and the outcome of the experiment. By subtle transmission of cues (e.g., facial expressions, verbal expressions, voice inflections) it appears possible that experimenters might be a source of demand characteristics that unwittingly influence subjects to behave as the experimenter hypothesized or expected (Rosenthal, 1966). But Barber (1976) believes the evidence for this effect is also quite weak, especially where the procedures of the experiment are carefully controlled and the criteria for categorizing participants' responses are clearly defined. The possibility of such an effect can be further minimized by using a double-blind procedure in experiments. Earlier we stated that most experiments employ a single-blind procedure; that is, the participants are not aware of the research hypothesis. In a **double-blind procedure,** neither the experimenter nor the subjects are aware of the research hypothesis. This security is achieved by having people other than the investigator who formulated the research hypothesis conduct the experiment.[6] But, though the double-blind procedure is often very desirable, it may be difficult to achieve for the investigator who has no source of funds to pay someone for conducting the experiment.

Pre- and Posttest Sensitization

A participant sometimes is given a pretest; that is, a test or measure of the dependent variable prior to administration of the independent variable to measure

---

[6]One of our colleagues, Dr. Barrie Westerman, observes with tongue in his cheek, that novice experimenters may often employ a "polyblind" procedure that provides several dubious advances beyond the conventional double-blind control. In a polyblind procedure the experimenter does not know the rationale for the research, the research hypothesis, or the appropriate statistical analysis for the data. The participants, on the other hand, do not know when or where the experiment is taking place. In short, no one involved with the experiment knows anything about anything—a total blind or polyblind procedure.

a baseline performance of behavior. When, subsequently, a treatment intended to alter that behavior is administered, it is possible that the independent variable had an effect only because the individual had been sensitized to the effects of that treatment by the pretest. Had the pretest not been given, the treatment would not have had an effect. For example, pretest sensitization may be a particular problem in studies of attitude change. Often, in such studies, people are pretested on various attitudes that they hold. They are then presented with a message designed to alter those attitudes and are again measured on the attitude to see if a change in attitude has occurred. If a change is found, it may not be due to the message (the manipulated independent variable) alone. It is possible that the message had an effect only because the people were sensitized by the pretest to the attitude for which the message was intended. If the person had not been sensitized by the pretest, the message might have had no effect.

A similar situation may hold for posttest sensitization. Suppose participants are presented with a message designed to produce attitude change but no pretest is given. After the message has been delivered, the participants are then given a questionnaire about the attitude the message was designed to change. A change in attitude may then not be due to the message alone. The message may have an effect only when the person is sensitized to the potentially changed attitude by a questionnaire following the message. That is, the independent variable may have an effect only because the subject is sensitized to its effects by the subsequent measurement of the dependent variable.

It is, of course, possible for both pre- and posttest sensitization to occur in the same experiment. Although the problems of pretest sensitization may often be avoided by using alternative experimental designs, there are no easy solutions to the posttest sensitization problem. Typically, a dependent variable must be measured after an independent variable is administered in order to assess whether the independent variable is effective. One solution is to use nonreactive measures of the dependent variable; the researcher could measure the behavior without the individual's being aware of the observation. This is often a very difficult task, however, and may pose problems of its own, both procedurally and ethically (see Webb, Campbell, Schwartz and Sechrest, 1966, for more information).

When Is Construct Validity Achieved?

Each of the threats to construct validity that we have discussed may be seen as a potential second independent variable (i.e., an extraneous variable) that may be confounded with the conceptual independent variable. It may indeed be this second, confounding variable that is responsible for systematic differences in the participants' behavior. If it is, then wrong conclusions may be drawn about the reasons for differences found among the treatment groups. Therefore, the threats to construct validity offer rival hypotheses to the research hypotheses of the experiment. To gain construct validity, the rival hypotheses involving the threats must then be shown to be implausible.

The most immediate source of support for the construct validity of an experiment is a constructive replication of that experiment based only on the conclusions of the first study and using different operational definitions and empirical referents for the conceptual variables. If the results of the constructive replication are the same as in the original experiment, then we gain confidence that the constructs are related in the manner found in the original research.

Constructive replications are rather rare, however, in the literature of psychology. Thus, as with statistical-conclusion validity and internal validity, inferences about construct validity must typically be reached from partial replications. To the extent that a partial replication provides different empirical manipulations and measures for the conceptual independent and dependent variables, the construct validity of the first experiment is strengthened.

EXTERNAL VALIDITY

The issue of external validity is one of deciding to what universe the results of an experiment may be generalized. Cook and Campbell (1979) characterize the problem as one of generalizing to different populations and settings. Bracht and Glass (1968) discuss these as issues of population validity and ecological validity, respectively, and we employ that distinction here.

Population Validity

Population validity refers to the population to which the effect of the independent variable can be generalized. As we discussed in Chapter 6, psychologists always work with samples, but they are interested in making inferences beyond the samples. The broader interest extends to what population a result may be generalized. To define the problem more clearly, we first discuss the typical subjects in psychological research.

Who Are the Participants in Psychological Research?

The study of psychology is sometimes facetiously characterized as the study of the college sophomore and the white rat. The characterization is not completely accurate, but it has a germ of truth.

Human participants   Prior to about 1970, many universities and colleges with psychology departments active in research maintained what is known as a "subject pool." The members of this pool were students who were enrolled in the introductory psychology course at that college. Often, as part of the course requirement, these students were required to serve in psychology experiments conducted by faculty members of the department. Smart (1966) surveyed studies published in two prominent psychology journals in the early 1960s. He found that 80 percent of the studies used college students and 37 percent used students from introductory psychology courses. Parenthetically, a preponderance of these studies used males only (28 percent) compared to studies with females only (9 percent).

In the 1970s the subject-pool practices of colleges and universities began to change because of a new code of ethics published by the American Psychological Association in 1973. Currently, although many colleges still maintain a subject pool, few make participation in research a requirement for introductory psychology courses. Instead, many institutions give students extra credit for participating in experiments or let them substitute other options, such as writing a paper or book report (Miller, 1981). Many times, where there are neither financial resources nor need to maintain a subject pool, experimenters obtain their participants by recruiting volunteers from classes, dormitories, cafeterias, or lounges. Samples obtained by any of these methods are often called *accidental samples* (Cook and Campbell, 1979) or *convenience samples*.

Regardless of changes in the subject-pool practices, college students still appear to be the participants in a majority of psychological studies. For example, in the area of social psychology, Higbee, Millard, and Folkman (1982) report that approximately 70 percent of the published studies still employ college students as participants.

Surveys by Miller (1981) and Jung (1982) indicate that psychologists are moving toward use of volunteer subjects. Rosenthal and Rosnow (1969, 1975) propose, however, that using volunteers in research may severely limit the population validity of the research. Volunteers tend to be better educated, of higher social class, more intelligent, more sociable, and in greater need of social approval than nonvolunteers. Not all psychologists believe, however, that using volunteers

The Typical Human Participant　　　　　　　　　　　　　　　　　　　　　　　**BOX 13-2**

And so we have the human subject who actually enters the laboratory and provides the data for our study of human behavior. He is primarily a male college student and is often enrolled in a psychology class. At least some of the time he will be a subject because he happened to be in class on the day volunteers were recruited or because his own personal characteristics and/or some aspect of the recruiting situation led him to volunteer. If a course requirement dictates that he serve as a subject, and if he has a choice among experiments, his own personal characteristics may lead him to choose one kind of experiment as opposed to another.

　　Are our subjects chosen at random? Are they representative of the general population, of the population of college students, of the population of college sophomores, or even of the sophomores of their own college? The answer to all of these questions, for much of our reported research, would seem to be a taunting and haunting No.

　　Duane P. Schultz (1969). The human subject in psychological research. *Psychological Bulletin, 72,* p. 219.

places stringent limitations upon the population validity of psychological research. Kruglanski (1973), for example, argues that there is no evidence for generalized "volunteer effects" in psychological research.

Animal subjects   The other popular subject in psychological research is the white laboratory rat, *Rattus norvegicus var. albinus,* a domesticated variant of the wild Norway rat. There is some question, though, whether the laboratory rat is representative even of other rats. Lockard (1968) argues that the breeding of a domestic laboratory rat has led to an animal well suited for survival in an environment in which even an "idiot" rat could survive. The laboratory rat often shows little social or aggressive behavior and no fear of or flight from man. Moreover, many of the behaviors that allow the rat to survive so well in the wild seem to have disappeared. The learning capability of the laboratory rat also appears to differ from that of the wild rat.

How widely is the white rat used in psychological research employing animals? Beach (1950) tabulated animal studies published between 1911 and 1948 in the *Journal of Comparative and Physiological Psychology.* He found that laboratory rats were the subjects in about 50 percent of the studies published. Porter, Johnson, and Granger (1981) updated this tabulation for the years 1961 to 1976 and found that laboratory rats were subjects in 58 percent of the nearly 2,000 articles they examined. Whether the proportion of animal studies employing the white rat is actually this high is open to some controversy. By surveying other journals, departments of psychology, and their colleagues, Snowden (1982) and Erwin (1982) suggest that the proportion of animal studies employing the white rat is much less than 50 percent, perhaps between 10 and 40 percent. In any event, the white rat appears to be the chosen subject in a rather sizable proportion of psychological studies of animal behavior.

Generalization from the Sample

Psychological research is based upon the fundamental, although often implicit, assumption that the sample of participants is representative of some larger population. It is to this larger population that a psychologist wishes to generalize. **Generalization** is the making of inferences from a sample to an experimentally accessible population and then from the experimentally accessible population to a target population (Bracht and Glass, 1968). The **experimentally accessible population** is the population that, in practice, is available to the experimenter. Even though a psychologist may be interested in making statements about all college students in the United States, the experimentally accessible population from which a sample is drawn is usually much more limited. In many instances it may be the students at the college where a psychologist teaches. For clinical psychologists, the accessible population may be composed of patients at nearby mental hospitals or outpatients at a community clinic.

The **target population,** on the other hand, is a total population that a psychologist is attempting to generalize to and make statements about. It might be all college students, all persons exhibiting neurotic syndromes, all children in kindergarten, or any other group of people or animals. The target population is often elusive and difficult or impossible to enumerate. Think of all the people in the state of Kentucky on any particular day as a target population. Do you think anyone could easily (or even with difficulty) enumerate all members of this target population, including people briefly passing through the state on their way to somewhere else? Obviously, random selection of an accessible population from a target population is usually beyond reach for most psychological researchers.

The issue of generalizing from a sample to a population thus resolves to two inferential jumps—from sample to accessible population and from accessible population to target population. The sample may or may not be randomly sampled from the accessible population. If the accessible population is clearly and rigorously defined and the sample is randomly selected from the accessible population, then the first inference—from sample to accessible population—can be made quite easily and confidently. If, however, a convenience sample from the accessible population is obtained, then the inference from sample to accessible population may be and often is difficult.

The difficulty of the inference will, of course, depend upon the independent and dependent variables being employed. For example, in research dealing with sensory capabilities such as visual or auditory acuity where little difference among people with normal sensory abilities is expected, it may not matter whether participants are conveniently or randomly sampled. It is unlikely that the effect of the independent variable would depend upon whether the subject was a volunteer or not. But what of the experiment dealing with variables affecting altruism? Would you expect the results obtained with volunteers to be the same as those obtained with nonvolunteers? Unfortunately, the answer to the question is not readily obtainable. How does a psychologist get the nonvolunteers to participate in research? And if a psychologist does get them to participate, are they still nonvolunteers?

The second inference, from the accessible population to the target population, is fraught with danger under almost all circumstances because it is almost impossible to randomly sample from an accessible population. Also, accessible populations, which at first inspection seem to be samples of the same target population, may, in reality, not be so. For example, it may appear that students enrolled in introductory psychology at two universities are representative of the same target population, college students in the United States. They are, however, very likely not to be. Differences between the accessible populations are likely to be major; e.g., socioeconomic status or year in college, which would indicate that these students are not representing the same target populations. If the effect of the independent variable depends upon the characteristics of the accessible population, then a subject attribute interacts with the independent variable. That is, the effect of the independent variable occurs only when a particular attribute is present in the subjects. Should this limitation occur, then any generalization on the effectiveness of the independent variable must be limited to populations that also possess the characteristic. Unfortunately, however, psychologists seldom know if such a characteristic is present in their accessible populations and, if so, whether the effect of the independent variable depends upon the presence of the characteristic. If such an interaction occurs, then any inference from accessible population to target population becomes extremely difficult. Thus, a major threat to population validity is the possibility of an interaction of the independent variable with an attribute of the participants.

How Important Is Random Sampling for Population Validity?

In an experiment   As we have discussed, random selection from both accessible and target populations is, in principle, important to generalization. But random selection from any population is not easily achieved, and most psychological research does *not* involve random sampling of subjects (Kazdin, 1981). Does this mean that the generalizability of the results cannot go beyond the sample of individuals employed in the experiment? Not necessarily.

Several authors have argued that the ultimate test of generalization is the test of replication (Cook and Campbell, 1979; Kazdin, 1981). Can the results be replicated in an operational, partial, or constructive replication with another sample of participants drawn from a different population? The more frequently one can answer yes to this question, the more confidence one may have in generalizations to the other populations, even though none of the samples may have been randomly selected from a population.

Others contend that random sampling in experiments is not even a critical requirement for generalization. Kruglanski (1976), for example, proposes that when an experiment is conducted to test a research hypothesis derived from a theory, then any subjects encompassed within the domain of people or animals described by the theory are representative participants. In this case he maintains that random sampling of subjects is irrelevant.

This position seems to be gaining support among researchers. For example, Calder, Phillips, and Tybout (1981) emphasize that a test of a theory is an attempt to refute the theory. A refutation is achieved by obtaining statistically significant differences among treatment groups that disagree with the predictions of the research hypothesis derived from the theory. As we have discussed, significant differences among treatment conditions are most easily detected when error variation in the experiment is relatively small. One way of reducing error variation is by selecting participants with homogeneous (i.e., similar) characteristics. This selection is more likely to occur using some nonrandom sampling method, such as convenience sampling from a readily accessible population, rather than by employing random sampling. Following this line of thinking in theories of consumer behavior, Lynch (1982) reasons that "The representativeness of the sample is not seen to be an issue, because if a theory is supposed to apply to 'consumers in general,' it can be rejected if its predictions are falsified for any subgroup of consumers" (p. 226).

For estimating a population parameter   Although many psychologists, either by words or actions, indicate that random sampling of subjects is not of major interest in an experiment, the method of obtaining a sample is crucial when the sample is

---

Description of Participants   **BOX 13-3**

In recent years psychologists have been placing greater emphasis on considering the population validity of their research. For the reader of research to arrive at some tentative decisions on the generalizability of results, he or she must have adequate knowledge about the participants in the research. But how frequently is the reader provided with this information?

In a survey of an important psychology journal, Schultz (1969) found that in about 4 percent of the articles he could not discover who the subjects were, how they were obtained, or whether they were male or female. White and Duker (1973) surveyed journals publishing research on child development and found, "Journals' reporting of the characteristics of children in samples is a hit-and-miss affair. The reader is always told the number of children in the sample, and his chances of finding out their sex, age, and grade are 2 out of 3, but beyond that point, it is reader beware" (pp. 700–701). More recently, Janssen (1979) reported that about 23 percent of the approximately 5,000 participants in the studies he reviewed in German psychology journals could not be identified, even whether they were adults, children, adolescents, or students.

Perhaps in response to criticisms such as these, the *Publication Manual of the American Psychological Association* (1983) indicates that the subjects section of a research article should provide information on who the subjects were, how they were selected, and how many were used. The manual states too that demographic information such as sex and age, information about payment for participation, any promises made to the participants, and the geographic location and type of institution or organization from which the participants came should also be reported.

White and Duker (1973) suggest the following format for a description of participants:

> This sample was drawn from the university laboratory school because of its availability to research [a good case might be made that this is an important service for the laboratory school to offer]; only second graders were considered for the project because of their age range. Of 37 second graders available, 4 were too young for the age criterion and were dropped. This left an eligible pool of 33, of whom 31 participated on the pretest (1 was ill; 1 was on a trip) and 28 completed the posttest (2 were absent; the third did not fill anything in on his paper despite the entreaties of his teacher, the junior investigator, and his father, the senior investigator). (p. 703)

This description is phrased for a sample of children, but its style could easily be adapted to any sample.

being used to estimate the precise value of a population parameter. Exact estimates of a population parameter from a representative sample are often critical for the user of the estimate.

We are all aware that television networks rely upon ratings to make programming decisions and to determine the amount that advertisers can be charged for commercials. The ratings are provided to the networks by television rating services that estimate the number of people who watch specific television programs; that is, they estimate a population parameter. Quite obviously, it would be impossible to measure the entire United States population in any one-hour period to determine which, if any, television program was being watched at the time. Therefore, the estimates that provide the ratings are computed from a relatively small sample of carefully selected families (often fewer than 1,000) whose viewing habits are recorded in logs or monitored electronically. It is evident that given the use to which television ratings are put, obtaining an accurate estimate of the population's viewing habits is of primary importance. Thus, samples of viewers are very carefully selected to be representative of the population of viewers.

If researchers are too casual about the manner in which they obtain samples, then the resulting estimates and inferences may be very misleading. Some types of convenience samples may make it difficult to arrive at any reasonable population estimates. An example of the inferential problems that can be posed by sampling merely those individuals who are most accessible is found in the Hite (1981) survey on male sexuality. To obtain her sample, Hite distributed about 119,000 questionnaires by sending them to a variety of organizations to which men belong, having the questionnaire printed in several magazines, and inviting men to send for it. About 6 percent of the distributed questionnaires were returned. From this sample, it is difficult to ascertain how adequately the respondents represent the beliefs, attitudes, and behaviors of the population of married men, or even of the population to whom the questionnaire was distributed. It is possible, for example, that those who responded were men who were most willing to disclose their own sexual activities. Thus, although Hite's survey may represent the characteristics of those men who responded to the survey, it does not easily lend itself to generalization to any other population of American adult males.

Ecological Validity

Ecological validity deals with the issue of generalizing to settings other than the experimental laboratory. Here the issue is one of possible interaction between the independent variable and the experimental setting. The effect of the treatment may depend upon a particular experimental setting. Because of this possibility, many authors have called for abandoning laboratory experimentation in favor of field experimentation. (For some reviews of the issues, see Aronson and Carlsmith, 1968; Berkowitz and Donnerstein, 1982; Henshel, 1980; Petrinovich, 1979; and

Tunnell, 1977.) Their argument is that the introduction of mundane (i.e., real-world) realism into the experimental setting will help increase the ecological validity of psychological research.

Kazdin (1981) proposes, however, that it is not so much the specific setting in which the research is conducted that determines its generalizability to other settings, but how well the conditions for administering the independent variable can be adhered to in other settings. Findings established in the well-controlled environment of the laboratory may not be replicable in settings where a variety of factors are allowed to fluctuate. On this question, Dipboye and Flanagan (1979) compared numerous laboratory studies to field studies in industrial and organizational psychology. In many instances they found an equally restricted variety of settings and limited sampling of subjects in both laboratory and field studies. They thus concluded that there was no necessary difference in the ecological validity of the two types of research and that one cannot more readily generalize to other settings from field studies than from laboratory studies.

When Is External Validity Achieved?

External validity is threatened when the effect of an independent variable depends upon a characteristic of the participants or the setting in which the experiment was conducted. If this threat occurs, then replication of the experiment with participants who do not possess the characteristic or who are tested in a different setting may result in a different effect of the independent variable.

The external validity of any experiment cannot be determined from that experiment alone. The question can be resolved only by replicating the findings with different participants in different settings. Evidence for external validity can be garnered from operational, partial, and constructive replications, for each of these replications typically employs subjects selected from different accessible populations and different experimental settings. Like other forms of validity, external validity for a research hypothesis gradually accumulates with increasing research on the topic.

SOME CONCLUDING COMMENTS ON VALIDITY

Table 13–2 summarizes the types of validity, the various threats to each type, and means of establishing each type of validity that we have discussed. It is clear that no one single experiment can be perfectly valid. Attempts to increase one type of validity (e.g., statistical-conclusion validity) may decrease another validity (e.g., population validity). And, although we have categorized specific threats to types of validity, in actual research threats may not be so neatly defined.

TABLE 13–2   *Summary of validity types in an experiment.*

	Types of validity		
Statistical Conclusion	*Internal*	*Construct*	*External*
Correctness of decision made from the statistical test.	The effect of the independent-variable-as-manipulated on the dependent-variable-as-measured.	What psychological constructs were manipulated and measured by the empirical referents?	Population validity: To what populations may the results be generalized? Ecological validity: To what settings may the results be generalized?
	Threats to validity		
Type I errors Type II errors	Subject mortality Selection biases History Maturation Instrumentation	Reactive nature Participant roles Demand characteristics Evaluation apprehension Multiple-treatment effect Experimenter effects Pre- and posttest sensitization	Interaction of independent variable with participant attributes Interaction of independent variable with experimental setting
	Validity established by		
Literal replication	Careful control of design and procedure of the experiment Operational replication	Careful control of design and procedure of the experiment Constructive replication	Replication using different samples Replication using different settings

    The importance of replicating results in scientific research is also evident from the discussion presented in this chapter. As Bauernfeind (1968) observes, replicability of results is a cornerstone of modern science. The strength and generality of current psychological knowledge, along with limitations in its application, will necessarily grow slowly. Judgments about a specific phenomenon must await outcomes of investigations in widely varied settings with different manipulations and measures and with clearly described samples from defined populations.

Even though we have stressed carefully examining the validity of any experiment, we want to make it clear that one should *not* become a nitpicker on questions of validity. Such an approach is likely to lead to overlooking important empirical and theoretical contributions of an experiment (Nisbett, 1978). Certainly, each threat to the validity of an experiment may offer a possible rival hypothesis or explanation for the results of an experiment. Realize, however, that possible existence of a threat to validity does not ensure that it is also a plausible explanation for the results. Freese and Rokeach (1979) maintain that any form of empirical research will contain some "impurities" and potential extraneous variables that may offer the possibility of plausible rival hypotheses. Obviously, all the potential extraneous variables in any experiment cannot be controlled. But to offer a rival explanation by one of these extraneous variables, one must show not only that the variable was uncontrolled, but that it has an established effect in settings similar to those in the research being considered. As D. T. Campbell (1969) remarks, "It is not failure-to-control in general that bothers us, but only those failures of control which permit *truly plausible* rival hypotheses, laws with a degree of scientific establishment comparable to or exceeding that of the law our experiment is designed to test" (p. 356). Thus, the validity of the experiment should not be automatically discounted merely because an alternative explanation is possible.

SCIENTIFIC UNDERSTANDING

In Chapter 2 we presented a conception of scientific knowledge as a process of theory falsification. We reasoned that scientific knowledge was at best uncertain and, as Bronowski (1973) eloquently states, "tolerant." A scientist can never show a theory to be true; the best he or she can do is to show, at least under some circumstances, that it is not false. This decision is to be based upon how congruent the observations of an empirical phenomenon are with the predictions from the theory. We have seen, however, that comparing observations and predictions is a task containing many possible pitfalls and uncertainties. Indeed, as Stern states in the quotation opening this chapter, it is the researcher's responsibility to challenge and question his or her own findings.

You should now understand why the word "proof" is not an active part of the psychologist's vocabulary. No empirical research, regardless of the design or statistical analysis used, can ever prove a theory or an explanation. Research studies only probe a theory and provide evidence that may be used to falsify a theory (Winch and Campbell, 1969). Confidence in a theory and the research hypotheses deduced from it grows as other investigations are able to confirm the relationships found, particularly as the experimental settings, the operational manipulations and measures of the conceptual variables, and the types of participants are varied (Bolles, 1962; Winch and Campbell, 1969).

McCarthy and Betz's research provides us with an opportunity to briefly illustrate some of these validity issues. It is clear from the tenor of their discussion that they believe the statistically significant differences found do not reflect a Type I error, that threats to internal validity cannot account for the differences between the groups, and that their manipulations and measures in the experiment adequately represent the conceptual independent and dependent variables. As a reader and consumer of their research, however, you must make your own judgments about these considerations from the information they have presented in the introduction and Method sections.

In any area of research, finding apparent answers to some questions raises many more, as in McCarthy and Betz's work. For instance, what is the range over which self-disclosing and self-involving statements are effective? Are self-disclosing and self-involving statements two levels of a broader conceptual variable—willingness to put oneself at risk? Is the type of counselor statement effective in a real counseling situation with people actually seeking counseling? Does the type of statement have the same effect with same-sex and opposite-sex client-counselor pairs? Is the type of statement effective in other than a counseling situation, such as a student-teacher learning situation?

These are all relevant questions, but they cannot be answered just on the basis of the one experiment by McCarthy and Betz. Such questions can be answered only by additional research. Subsequent work by McCarthy (1979, 1982), McCarthy and Schmeck (1982), DeForest and Stone (1980), Dowd and Boroto (1982), LaCrosse (1980), and others has sought to provide answers for these and other questions related to the effects of counselor self-disclosure.

IS THERE A SEX BIAS IN PSYCHOLOGICAL RESEARCH?

We have mostly painted a picture of psychological research as an objective pursuit of knowledge, free of the experimenter's values and preconceptions. But this is perhaps characterizing a nonexistent ideal. Scientists, too, are human, and in their research may not be able to shed cultural stereotypes and biases. In particular, cultural stereotypes of sex differences and appropriate sex roles appear to be prevalent in the research literature of psychology. Grady (1981) has identified five aspects of psychological research that appear to reflect a sex bias.

Choice of Research Topics

A 1975 survey of seven leading psychology journals published by the American Psychological Association indicated that only about 8 percent of the articles dealt with topics of particular importance to women. The author of the survey, Florence Denmark, president of the American Psychological Association in 1980, suggests that this small percentage is due to rejection of articles dealing with women's issues by predominantly white male journal editors (Grady, 1981).

Scientific Understanding

BOX 13-4

The scientist gains his understanding through the rejection or confirmation of scientific hypotheses, but this depends upon much more than merely rejecting or failing to reject the null hypothesis. It depends partly upon the confirmation from other investigators . . . particularly as the experimental conditions are varied. . . . Confirmation of scientific hypotheses also depends in part upon whether they can be incorporated into a larger theoretical framework. . . . Final confirmation of scientific hypotheses and the larger theories they support depends upon whether they can stand the test of time.

These processes have to move slowly. As Bakan (1953) has observed, the development of a scientific idea is gradual, like learning itself; its probability of being correct increases gradually from one experimental verification to the next, as response probability increases from one trial to the next. The effect of any single experimental verification is not to confirm a scientific hypothesis but only to make its *a posteriori* probability a little higher than its *a priori* probability.

Reprinted with permission of author and publisher from: Bolles, Robert C. "The difference between statistical hypotheses and scientific hypotheses." *Psychological Reports,* 1962, *11,* 639–645.

Participants Employed

Although national census figures usually indicate there are slightly more females than males in the United States, a number of surveys indicate that the ratio of male to female subjects in published research may be as high as 2 to 1 (Carlson, 1971; McKenna and Kessler, 1977; Schultz, 1969; Signorella, Vegega, and Mitchell, 1981; Smart, 1966). McKenna and Kessler (1977) suggest various possible motives for such a bias in selection of subjects, including such arguments as that male psychologists may feel they better understand males than females, that males are more likely to exhibit some behaviors (such as aggression) in the environment, that females are more variable in their behaviors and thus it may be more difficult to get results in agreement with the research hypothesis, and a reluctance to induce certain behaviors or feelings (e.g., aggression or anxiety) in females.

Empirical Referents Used

When dealing with the same conceptual variable, psychologists may employ systematically different empirical referents for males and females. In reviewing studies of aggression, McKenna and Kessler (1977) found that with males the independent variables employed were those which aroused strong feelings or exposed the subject to an action or threat by another. For females, on the other hand, the independent variables were typically more "passive," such as presentation of stories. A similar distinction was found for the dependent variables; males were most frequently asked to shock another, and females were most frequently asked to rate aggressive feelings and behaviors. From their research, McKenna and Kessler conclude that some topics in psychology may be sex-role stereotyped by investigators (e.g., aggression is a "masculine area") and the empirical referent employed for a conceptual variable may depend upon the sex of the participants used in the experiment.

Statistically Testing for Sex Differences

If both male and female subjects are used in an experiment, then often it is possible, by employing sex as a second independent variable, to test for any sex differences in the behavior measured. A survey by Signorella et al. (1981) indicates that in studies employing males and females, sex differences are tested for about 50 percent of the time in journals representing developmental psychology and about 40 percent of the time in journals publishing social psychology literature. Many of the studies that tested for such differences did not, however, hypothesize such differences. Apparently, then, much of the testing for sex differences is not based upon a clear theoretical explanation for predicting and understanding any differences found. The difficulty with such an approach is summarized by Grady (1981):

> One of the most important by-products of atheoretical testing for sex differences is that negative findings tend to stay out of the literature and positive ones are reported. The nature of the null hypothesis is such that a finding of no difference cannot be "accepted"; rather, it can only be interpreted as "no decision can yet be made". . . . Thus, we can never develop a literature of sex similarities but only a literature of sex differences. (p. 632).

Grady clearly believes that such routine testing for sex differences is why "Psychology is replete with inconsequential, accidental, and incidental findings of 'sex differences'" (p. 632).

Conclusions Reached from the Results

Research employing males often leads to broader generalizations than does research with females. Schwabacher (1972, cited in Grady, 1981) found that generalizations from research with males are likely to be about "individuals," and generalizations from research employing females are likely to be about "women, girls, or females." Dan and Beekman (1972) argue, "The habit of mind which allows that males are more representative of the human race than females should be recognized as a potentially serious bias in our psychological research and theory" (p. 1078).

What Can Be Done?

Perhaps the most important corrective action is to expose the research biases we have discussed to the light of day. Making psychological researchers aware of the covert biases in their research is likely to lead to careful examination of research procedures. Many of the criticisms that Grady (1981) and others have made can be rectified by careful and thoughtful planning of research and explicit attention to each of the five biases we have discussed.[7]

SUMMARY

- The validity of an experiment is determined by the correctness of the conclusions reached from the results of that experiment. The ultimate test of the validity of an experiment lies in replicating the experiment. Four types of replication—literal, operational, constructive, and partial—are recognized.
- Statistical-conclusion validity refers to the correctness of the decisions reached from the statistical test. Threats to statistical-conclusion validity include Type I and Type II errors.
- Internal validity refers to the validity of drawing conclusions about the effect of the independent-variable-as-manipulated on the dependent-variable-as-measured. Threats to internal validity include subject mortality, selection biases, subject histories, maturation, and instrumentation.
- Construct validity concerns the validity of drawing inferences to psychological constructs from the empirical referents of the experiment. Threats to construct validity include the reactive nature of experiments, multiple-treatment effects, and pretest and posttest sensitization.
- External validity is considered in two categories, population validity and ecological validity.
  - Population validity deals with the problem of to what populations of subjects the results can be generalized. Population validity is threatened by interaction of the independent variable with attributes of the participants in the experiment.
  - Ecological validity considers the settings to which the results can be generalized. Ecological validity is threatened by interactions of the independent variable with experimental-setting variables.

---

[7]A task force of the American Psychological Association Division 35, Psychology of Women, has prepared *Guidelines for Nonsexist Research* (1982). In addition, a monograph, *Understanding the Manuscript Review Process: Increasing the Participation of Women* (1982) has been prepared by the American Psychological Association. Information on these materials may be obtained from:
Women's Program Office
American Psychological Association
1200 Seventeenth Street N.W.
Washington, D.C. 20036

14

In this chapter we introduce three types of nonexperimental research methods and relevant statistical techniques. Topics discussed include:

- The correlational approach and correlation coefficients (r and r_s)
- Naturalistic observation
- Case-study method
- The chi square (χ^2) test

WHY YOU NEED TO KNOW THIS MATERIAL

Many problems that interest psychologists cannot be studied using the experimental method. To investigate these problems, psychologists use various nonexperimental methods. In this chapter we introduce you to the fundamental types of nonexperimental research methods.

Nonexperimental Research Methods

A true experiment is characterized by manipulation of active independent variables, random assignment of participants to treatment conditions, and control of extraneous variables to prevent confounding with the independent variable. But many variables that psychologists want to investigate are not open to active manipulation and control. Attribute variables such as gender, age, intelligence, and handedness, for example, cannot be actively manipulated. Other attributes such as smoking behavior, amount of schooling, or drug use can, in principle, be manipulated; obviously, though, ethical considerations prohibit true experimentation with these variables. If a psychologist wishes to compare illegal drug users and nonusers on a particular measure of behavior, then in most instances he or she must select individuals who are already drug users to compare with individuals who are not drug users. Because of the potential harmful effects, it would be unethical to administer an illegal substance to a randomly assigned group of participants.

A variety of nonexperimental methods have been developed to investigate problems that do not lend themselves to study by a true experiment. The methods share two characteristics: The independent variable that is of interest cannot be actively manipulated, and participants cannot be randomly assigned to treatment conditions. We discuss three types of nonexperimental methods in this chapter: the correlational approach, naturalistic observation, and the case study.

CORRELATIONAL APPROACHES TO RESEARCH

Variables that are related or that vary together are said to be *correlated*. Thus, studies utilizing a **correlational approach** are attempts to establish the extent to which two or more nonmanipulated variables are related. No variables are manipulated; the investigator simply measures naturally occurring events, behaviors, or personality characteristics. Psychologists have explored the relationship between birth order and intelligence, attendance at classes in college and course grades,

415

avocational interests and career success, scholastic aptitude and academic performance, and eye color and reaction time. None of these or other potentially important attributes or environmental variables are easily or ethically open to active manipulation.

The correlational method typically involves obtaining pairs of observations or measures on the variables that are of interest from a relatively large number of individuals. Each pair of observations consists of a measure obtained for each variable from one individual. The paired measures are then plotted and statistically analyzed (often by using a correlation coefficient) to determine if any relationship exists between them.

An example of this method is the work of Windholz and Diamant (1974), who explored relationships between certain personality characteristics and belief in extraordinary phenomena such as reincarnation, witchcraft, astrology, and extrasensory perception. They had 297 college students complete a *Scale of Belief in Extraordinary Phenomena* (SOBEP) questionnaire and one of three personality inventories, such as the Thorndike Dimensions of Temperament personality inventory (Thorndike, 1966). Thus, for each subject a score on belief in extraordinary phenomena as well as scores on various personality traits were obtained. Windholz and Diamant then examined the various sets of scores to see if belief in extraordinary phenomena was correlated with any of the personality traits measured. In one analysis they examined the relation of SOBEP scores for the reflective personality trait. Reflective individuals are characterized by interest in ideas and knowledge for its own sake rather than for immediate application. Suppose the reflective scores (designated variable X) and the SOBEP scores (designated variable Y) for ten subjects are those presented in Table 14–1. In this example, individuals with higher scores are more reflective or possess more belief in extraordinary phenomena.

TABLE 14–1   *Hypothetical scores for ten subjects on the reflective scale of the* Thorndike Dimensions of Temperament *(Thorndike, 1966) and on the* Scale of Belief in Extraordinary Phenomena *(SOBEP, Windholz and Diamant, 1974).*

Subject	Reflective Score (X)	SOBEP (Y)
1	9	3
2	10	2
3	16	4
4	5	1
5	9	4
6	7	1
7	5	3
8	11	5
9	1	2
10	17	5

Are these scores related? Are higher SOBEP scores associated with higher reflective scores and are lower scores on the SOBEP related to lower scores on reflectivity? One way to gain a visual impression of the relationship is to construct a scatterplot or scattergram of the scores as we have done in Figure 14–1. In a **scatterplot** one of the two measures (typically the variable labeled *X*) is represented on the horizontal axis (abscissa) and the other measure (the *Y* variable) is plotted on the vertical axis (ordinate). The score of a subject on each of the two measures is then depicted by one point on the scatterplot. In Figure 14–1, the scores for subject 1 are plotted at the point within the figure that intersects a value of 9 on the reflective scale and 3 on the SOBEP scale. To more clearly illustrate how the scatterplot was constructed, we have identified each individual by placing a number next to the point that represents his or her scores on both measures. Typically only the scores are plotted, however; participants are not identified by name or number on a scatterplot.

The scatterplot seems to indicate that there is a relationship between belief in extraordinary phenomena and the reflective personality trait. Generally, higher

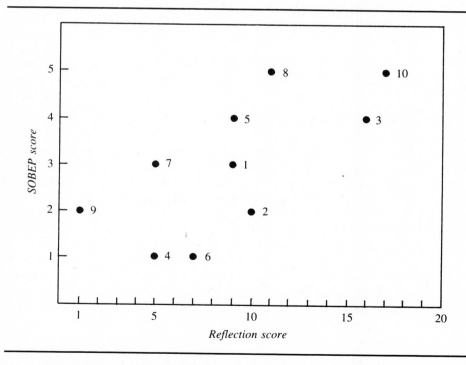

Scatterplot of **Reflective** *scores and* **Scale of Belief in Extraordinary Phenomena**   **FIGURE 14–1**
(SOBEP) *scores for ten participants. The numbers next to the plotted scores identify the individuals.*

SOBEP scores appear to be associated with higher scores on the reflective trait measure. Visual inspection of a scatterplot alone, however, is not sufficient to determine whether there is an association between two variables. The relationship depicted in the figure needs to be described quantitatively. Descriptive statistics expressing the degree of relation between the two variables are called *correlation coefficients.*

Pearson Product-Moment Correlation Coefficient

A variety of types of correlation coefficients have been developed to numerically describe the relationship between two variables. The most commonly employed correlation coefficient for interval or ratio measures is the **Pearson product-moment correlation coefficient,** symbolized as *r*. Numerically, the value of *r* for two variables designated *X* and *Y* is found by

$$r = \frac{\sum_{n=1}^{n_S} (X_i - \bar{X})(Y_i - Y)}{\sqrt{\left[\sum_{n=1}^{n_S} (X_i - \bar{X})^2\right]\left[\sum_{n=1}^{n_S} (Y_i - \bar{Y})^2\right]}}.$$

In this formula, X_i is the score of a participant on the *X* variable, $\bar{X}$ is the mean of all scores on the *X* variable, Y_i is the score of a participant on the *Y* variable, and $\bar{Y}$ is the mean of all scores on the *Y* variable.

An examination of terms in the numerator and denominator of this formula helps clarify the meaning of the *Pearson r,* as this correlation coefficient is often called. The numerator in the formula simply represents the *covariation* of the *X* and *Y* variables. If *X* and *Y* vary together so that values of *X* larger than the mean of the *X* scores are associated with values of *Y* larger than the mean of the *Y* scores (and values of *X* smaller than the $\bar{X}$ are associated with values of *Y* smaller than $\bar{Y}$), then the value of the numerator will be positive (+). Conversely, if values of *X* above the mean of the *X* scores are associated with values of *Y* below the mean of the *Y* scores (and *X* values below $\bar{X}$ are associated with *Y* values larger than $\bar{Y}$), then the value of the numerator will be negative (−).

The denominator in the formula reflects the amount of variability of the *X* and *Y* variables. Because the terms in the denominator involve squared deviations, the denominator will always take on positive values. Thus, the sign of the value of the correlation coefficient will be determined by the sign of the numerator; accordingly, the correlation coefficient may be either positive or negative in value.

The computation of the correlation coefficient using this formula on the ten scores in Table 14–1 is illustrated in Table 14–2. This definitional formula for *r* is seldom used to compute the correlation coefficient, however. Rather, an alternative computational formula that simplifies the calculations is often used to calculate *r*.

You see that either formula produces identical values for the data in Table 14–1, where $r = +.70$. We turn next to a more complete explanation of the meaning of the Pearson r.

Meaning of the Pearson r

The Pearson r is a statistic that reveals both the direction and the degree of *linear* relationship between two variables. The direction of the relationship is indicated by the positive or negative sign of the correlation coefficient. The numerical values of r may range from -1.00 through $.00$ to $+1.00$. The absolute value of r ($.00$ to 1.00) indicates the degree to which the points on the scatterplot lie in a straight line.

A **positive correlation coefficient** means that there is a direct relationship between the two variables. High scores on one variable are associated with high scores on the other variable (and therefore low scores on one variable are related to low scores on the other). A direct relationship is illustrated by the scores in Figure 14–1. As another example of a direct relationship, we might expect the

Calculation of Pearson r on scores of Table 14–1.   **TABLE 14–2**

Subject	Reflective			SOBEP			
	X_i	$X_i - \bar{X}$	$(X_i - \bar{X})^2$	Y_i	$Y_i - \bar{Y}$	$(Y_i - \bar{Y})^2$	$(X_i - \bar{X})(Y_i - \bar{X})$
1	9	0	0	3	0	0	0
2	10	+1	1	2	−1	1	−1
3	16	+7	49	4	+1	1	+7
4	5	−4	16	1	−2	4	+8
5	9	0	0	4	+1	1	0
6	7	−2	4	1	−2	4	+4
7	5	−4	16	3	0	0	0
8	11	+2	4	5	+2	4	+4
9	1	−8	64	2	−1	1	+8
10	17	+8	64	5	+2	4	+16
	Mean 9		Sum 218	Mean 3		Sum 20	Sum +46

$$r = \sum_{n=1}^{n_s} (X_i - \bar{X})(Y_i - \bar{Y}) / \sqrt{\left[\sum_{n=1}^{n_s} (X_i - \bar{X})^2\right]\left[\sum_{n=1}^{n_s} (Y_i - \bar{Y})^2\right]}.$$

$r = 46/\sqrt{(218)(20)}$

$r = 46/\sqrt{4360}$

$r = 46/66.03$

$r = +.70$

Raw-Score Computational Formula for the Pearson *r*.

The notational representation for computation of *r* for ten subjects is:

Subject	X_i	Y_i	X_i^2	Y_i^2	$X_i Y_i$
1	X_1	Y_1	X_1^2	Y_1^2	$X_1 Y_1$
2	X_2	Y_2	X_2^2	Y_2^2	$X_2 Y_2$
3	X_3	Y_3	X_3^2	Y_3^2	$X_3 Y_3$
4	X_4	Y_4	X_4^2	Y_4^2	$X_4 Y_4$
5	X_5	Y_5	X_5^2	Y_5^2	$X_5 Y_5$
6	X_6	Y_6	X_6^2	Y_6^2	$X_6 Y_6$
7	X_7	Y_7	X_7^2	Y_7^2	$X_7 Y_7$
8	X_8	Y_8	X_8^2	Y_8^2	$X_8 Y_8$
9	X_9	Y_9	X_9^2	Y_9^2	$X_9 Y_9$
10	X_{10}	Y_{10}	X_{10}^2	Y_{10}^2	$X_{10} Y_{10}$
	ΣX_i	ΣY_i	ΣX_i^2	ΣY_i^2	$\Sigma X_i\ Y_i$

Where

X_i equals the raw score of a subject on the X variable.
Y_i equals the raw score of a subject on the Y variable.
X_i^2 equals the raw score of a subject on the X variable squared.
Y_i^2 equals the raw score of a subject on the Y variable squared.
$X_i Y_i$ equals the raw score on the X variable multiplied by the raw score on the Y variable.
N equals the number of subjects.

Using these numerical values, *r* is computed as follows:

$$r = \frac{N\Sigma X_i Y_i - (\Sigma X_i)(\Sigma Y_i)}{\sqrt{[N\Sigma X_i^2 - (\Sigma X_i)^2][N\Sigma Y_i^2 - (\Sigma Y_i)^2]}}$$

To illustrate the computations we use the sample scores given in Table 14–1.

Subject	X_i	Y_i	X_i^2	Y_i^2	$X_i Y_i$
1	9	3	81	9	27
2	10	2	100	4	20
3	16	4	256	16	64
4	5	1	25	1	5
5	9	4	81	16	36
6	7	1	49	1	7
7	5	3	25	9	15
8	11	5	121	25	55
9	1	2	1	4	2
10	17	5	289	25	85
Sums	90	30	1028	110	316

Then

$$r = \frac{(10)(316) - (90)(30)}{\sqrt{[(10)(1028) - (90)^2][(10)(110) - (30)^2]}}$$

$$r = (3160 - 2700)/\sqrt{(10{,}280 - 8100)(1100 - 900)}$$

$$r = 460/\sqrt{(2180)(200)}$$

$$r = 460/\sqrt{436{,}000}$$

$$r = 460/660.30$$

$$r = +.70$$

The numerical value obtained by this computational approach is identical to that obtained in Table 14–2.

---

number of classes attended by students to be positively correlated with course grades, where the students who receive higher grades attend classes more frequently than those who get lower grades. On the other hand, an inverse relationship is indicated by a **negative correlation coefficient,** where high scores on one variable are associated with low scores on the other variable and low scores on one variable are related to high scores on the other. We might expect number of absences from class and course grades to be inversely related, with students who are frequently absent earning lower grades than students who miss fewer classes. Be careful not to attribute more meaning to the sign of the relationship than it represents. A positive relationship between variables is not inherently better in any way than a negative relationship. The sign merely indicates the direction, not the degree, of a relationship.

The numerical value of the correlation coefficient indicates how well the relationship between the two variables is described by a straight line. A Pearson *r* value of 1.00 means that the relationship is perfectly linear; all points in the scatterplot lie in a straight line. Scatterplots showing correlations of +1.00 and −1.00 are shown in Figures 14–2a and 14–2b, respectively. In these instances, for every value of one measure there is one and only one corresponding value of the other measure.

At the other extreme, if the value of the correlation coefficient equals .00, then no linear relationship exists between the two variables. A particular value of one measure is not systematically associated with a value of the other. Such an instance is shown in Figure 14–2c. Values of the correlation coefficient between .00 and 1.00 indicate that there is some, but not a perfect, relationship among the variables. Two such relationships are shown in Figure 14–2d and 14–2e.

We emphasize that the Pearson *r* is a measure of the linear or straight-line relationship between two variables. If the relationship between two variables is curvilinear, as illustrated in Figure 14–2f, then *r* does not adequately represent the association between the variables; other correlational measures should be used.

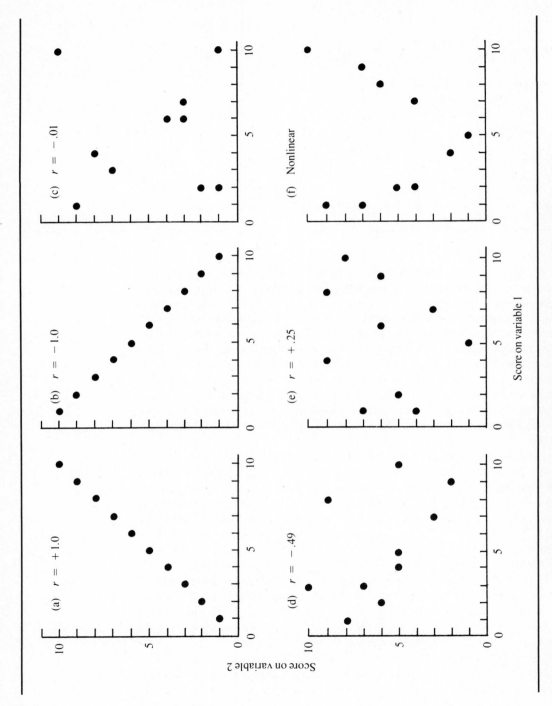

FIGURE 14-2   *Scatterplot illustrating various correlations between scores on variable 1 and variable 2 for ten scores. The value of the Pearson Product Moment Correlation coefficient between the sets of scores is given by* r.

Correlation coefficients may be tested for statistical significance to determine if it is likely that the relationship between the variables observed in the sample reflects more than a chance difference from a true zero relationship in the population. The null hypothesis tested is that the population correlation (indicated by the Greek letter *rho, ρ*) is 0, or $H_0: \rho = 0$, and the alternative hypothesis is $H_1: \rho \neq 0$. Rejecting the null hypothesis leads to the inference that the observed correlation in the sample represents more than sampling error and that a real relationship exists between the variables in the population from which the sample was obtained.

Testing the null hypothesis is quite straightforward. The rejection region for a theoretical sampling distribution of *r* must first be established. Critical values of *r* that define the statistical significance of *r* for $\alpha = .05$ and $\alpha = .01$ are presented in the Appendix, Table A–4. As with most other statistical tests, the critical value of *r* depends upon degrees of freedom. The *df* for *r* are equal to $N - 2$, where *N* is the number of pairs of scores from which the correlation coefficient is calculated. The null hypothesis is rejected at the selected significance level if the obtained value of *r* is *equal to or larger than the critical value*. You will see in Table A–4 that the larger the *df,* and hence sample size, the smaller the value of *r* needed to reject the null hypothesis. This relationship makes sense, because one expects that there will be less sampling error with large samples and that *r* will provide a better estimate of *ρ*.

We illustrate a test of statistical significance for *r* with the ten pairs of scores presented in Table 14–1. The critical value of *r* for $\alpha = .05$ and 8 *df* is .632 (see Table A–4). The calculated value, $r = +.70$, exceeds the critical value; thus, the null hypothesis is rejected and the alternative hypothesis is accepted at the .05 level. The correlation between reflective scores and SOBEP scores in our example is statistically significant, $r(8) = .70$, $p < .05$. The results indicate, therefore, that reflective individuals have a greater tendency to believe in extraordinary phenomena.[1]

A clear distinction should be made between the correlational approach to research for discovering relationships between variables, and correlational statistics which quantify such relationships. Correlational statistics are usually employed with correlational studies, but they may also be utilized to analyze data obtained from

---

[1]The value of $r = +.70$ is higher than the actual correlation found by Windholz and Diamant. For 103 participants they found a correlation of $+.27$. This value, too, is statistically significant at the .05 level. They concluded that this relationship implies "a greater tendency of the believers in extraordinary phenomena to be interested in ideas, and to speculate and reflect, especially on the more abstract level" (p. 126).

experiments. The Pearson r is a useful statistic whenever one wants a measure of a linear relationship between two variables. For example, in the McCarthy and Betz experiment one might want to know how the various dimensions of the CRF are related to one another. As one instance, we find that the correlation between the expertness and the attractiveness ratings of the self-involving counselor is $+.75$. (The Pearson r was calculated on the data presented in Table 5–1.) By consulting Table A–4 and using the degrees of freedom closest in value to but lower than 52 (as $N - 2 = 54 - 2$), we find that the critical value of r at the .05 level with 50 *df* is .231. Consequently, the obtained value of $r = +.75$ is statistically significant at the .05 level, and H_0: $\rho = 0$ is rejected. Thus, for counselors employing self-involving statements, ratings of expertness and attractiveness are positively related, $r(52) = .75$, $p < .05$. Moreover, the correlation coefficient reveals that there is a relatively strong relationship between the two measures. This issue is discussed next.

r^2 *as a Measure of Strength of Association*

A statistically significant Pearson r merely indicates that the two variables are related, i.e., that the correlation is not zero. The value of r may be statistically significant, however, even when the relationship is weak, i.e., when it is only somewhat different from zero.

In Chapter 9 we introduced the concept of the strength of association between an independent variable and a dependent variable. Eta squared (η^2) and omega squared (ω^2) were discussed as two measures of the strength of the effect of the independent variable on behavior. In correlational studies, the **coefficient of determination,** r^2 (the squared value of the correlation coefficient), provides a measure of the strength of association between two variables that have been correlated.

The interpretation of r^2 is similar to that of η^2 and ω^2. That is, r^2 indicates the proportion of variance in one measure that is related to the variance in the other measure. To illustrate, for the ten hypothetical SOBEP and reflective-trait scores (Table 14–1), r^2 is equal to $(+.70)^2$ or .49. This value means that these pairs of scores have 49 percent of their variance in common. In other words, 49 percent of the variance in scores for one variable is associated with the variance in the other measure.

Relationship between r ***and*** r^2 It is evident that the strength of association between two variables is related to the size of the correlation coefficient. Obviously, the closer the value of r is to 1.00, the greater is the linear relationship between the two variables. However, r^2 is not directly related to r. Larger correlation coefficients account for a proportionally larger amount of the common variance than do smaller correlations. As shown below, a correlation coefficient of $r = .50$, a value midway between .00 and 1.00, accounts for only 25 percent of the common variance. Indeed, less than 50 percent of the variance is shared by the two measures for values of *r* between .00 and .70. Yet the remaining 50 percent of the possible common variance is accounted for by correlation coefficients whose values range from .70 to 1.00.

r	r^2
.00	.00
.10	.01
.20	.04
.30	.09
.40	.16
.50	.25
.60	.36
.70	.49
.80	.64
.90	.81
1.00	1.00

Virtually any value of *r* that differs from zero will be statistically significant if the sample size (and therefore *df*) is sufficiently large. After all, with larger samples it should be easier to detect any nonzero relationship that exists between two variables in a population. But a statistically significant relationship obtained with large samples is not necessarily an important one. A value of *r* as small as .062 is statistically significant at the .05 level with 1000 *df*. With a correlation this small, however, less than 1 percent of the variance in one measure is related to the other ($r^2 = .062^2 = .0038$). Incidentally, such small but statistically significant correlations are not uncommon. In many settings, such as the military or in college aptitude testing, test batteries are administered to thousands of individuals. Many correlations between the variables measured are subsequently analyzed, some of which represent very weak but statistically significant relationships.

To illustrate the use of the coefficient of determination, in the Windholz and Diamant (1974) study, SOBEP and personality-trait scores were correlated on samples of 72 to 122 individuals, depending upon how many of the 297 participants received one of the three personality instruments. Six of the 21 correlation coefficients reported were statistically significant at the .05 level, with significant Pearson *r* values ranging from +.21 (for SOBEP and neuroticism scores) to +.36 (for SOBEP and hypomania scores). Accordingly, coefficients of determination for the statistically significant correlation coefficients range from .04 to .13. The smallest significant correlation (*r* = +.21), therefore, accounts for only 4 percent of the variance, meaning that 96 percent of the variance in neuroticism scores is *not* related to belief in extraordinary phenomena scores. In this instance, we find a statistically significant but weak relationship between the two variables.

You can see how misleading the statistical significance of a correlation coefficient is per se. Thus, we caution you to carefully evaluate whether the statements made about the data from correlational studies are warranted by the size of correlation coefficients that may be statistically significant. For reasons we have discussed, many researchers regard the coefficient of determination as more informative and meaningful than the correlation coefficient.

Spearman Rank-Order Correlation Coefficient

The Pearson r is appropriate when the measures on the two variables to be correlated represent interval or ratio measurement. Sometimes, however, the subjects may be rank ordered on both variables. Either the subjects' scores will be recorded as ranks initially, or the original measures may be converted to ranks for one reason or another. As an example of the latter instance, you will recall that rating scores so frequently used in psychological studies have no clear identity with respect to level of measurement (see Chapter 5). As we pointed out, rating scale measures lie within a gray area; they do not possess true interval measurement properties, yet they seem to provide more information than purely ordinal measurement. Because the Pearson r requires interval measurement of both variables, one might consider transforming rating scores to ranks. Ranked scores, of course, are purely ordinal measures. The statistic commonly used to describe the relationship between two sets of ranked scores from a sample of subjects is the **Spearman rank-order correlation coefficient,** which is symbolized by r_s.

The formula for computing r_s is

$$r_s = 1 - \frac{6 \sum_{n=1}^{n_s} D^2}{N(N^2 - 1)}$$

where D is the difference in a pair of ranked scores for an individual and N equals the number of pairs of ranks (and, therefore, the number of subjects in the study).

Example of Use of r_s

It is well established that chickens and other social animals establish dominance relationships (Collias, 1950; Guhl, 1953). Suppose an investigator wants to find out whether the dominance order within a flock of hens remains stable from one day to the next. To do so, he or she might observe the interactions of the hens in a feeding situation on two consecutive days and each day rank order the birds from most to least dominant on a variety of behavioral criteria. For example, the observer might take into account how much time the birds spend feeding, instances of fighting or threat postures, and so forth.

Ranks of ten hens on day 1 and day 2 from a hypothetical study are presented in Table 14–3. In these measures of food-getting dominance the most dominant hen receives a rank of 1 and the most submissive, a rank of 10. If two birds are judged to be equal in dominance, then both a.e assigned the same rank, which is the average of the two ranks in question. In the example, tied ranks are assigned to subjects 1 and 10 on day 2; each is given a rank of 6.5.

The procedures involved in calculating r_s are relatively simple. The first step, as illustrated in Table 14–3, is to find the difference in each pair of ranks by subtracting one rank from the other, e.g., the rank for day 1 minus the rank for day 2. Then square each of the differences and find the sum of the resulting D^2 values. Next, substitute the D^2 and N values into the formula. In our example, $r_s = +.645$.

Statistical Significance of Spearman Rank-Order Correlation

As with the Pearson r, values of r_s may be positive or negative and may range from -1.00 through .00 to $+1.00$. To test for the statistical significance of r_s, the null hypothesis assumes that the actual rank-order correlation in the population is zero, i.e., $H_0: \rho_s = 0$. The usual alternative hypothesis, then, states that the population correlation is not zero, or $H_1: \rho_s \neq 0$. Minimum values of r_s needed for

Calculating the Spearman rank-order correlation coefficient on dominance rankings of ten hens on day 1 and day 2. **TABLE 14–3**

Subject	Day 1	Day 2	D	D^2
1	4	6.5	−2.5	6.25
2	6	8	−2	4
3	8	4	4	16
4	2	1	1	1
5	7	5	2	4
6	5	9	−4	16
7	10	10	0	0
8	3	2	1	1
9	1	3	−2	4
10	9	6.5	2.5	6.25

Sum 58.5

$$r_s = 1 - \left[6 \sum_{n=1}^{n_s} D^2 / N(N^2 - 1) \right]$$
$$= 1 - [6(58.5)/10(10^2 - 1)]$$
$$= 1 - [351/10(99)]$$
$$= 1 - 351/990$$
$$= 1 - .355$$
$$r_s = +.645$$

statistical significance at the .05 and .01 levels are presented in the Appendix, Table A–10. Notice that the critical values are based upon N—the number of pairs of ranks—rather than degrees of freedom. As before, if the obtained r_s value from the sample is equal to or larger than the critical value, then the decision is to reject H_0 and accept H_1.

The critical value of r_s for $N = 10$ and $\alpha = .05$ is .648. Because the obtained r_s value of .645 in our example is smaller than the critical value, the null hypothesis is not rejected at the .05 level. Therefore, the relationship between the ranks on day 1 and day 2 is not statistically significant, $p > .05$. Accordingly, the results of this study indicate that the dominance order in the flock of hens was not stable over two days.

One should not routinely convert scores to ranks merely because the Spearman r_s may be easier to compute than the Pearson r. We remind you that ordinal measures provide less information than interval or ratio measures. Moreover, the Spearman correlation is not a measure of the degree of linear relationship between two variables. Instead, as Hays (1973) suggests, the Spearman correlation coefficient shows "the tendency of two rank orders to be similar" (p. 787). Consequently, although r_s^2 provides a measure of the strength of association of the two variables, the meaning of the squared correlation is not so clear. Because differences in ranks do not correspond to equal differences in the behavior measured, r_s cannot be interpreted strictly as the proportion of variance accounted for by the two variables. Finally, perhaps the most important point is that the Spearman r_s is less sensitive in detecting a statistically significant relationship than is the Pearson r if the latter is suitable for analyzing two sets of scores.

Ex Post Facto Studies as Correlational Research

In Chapter 3 we introduced the ex post facto study in which participants were selected on the basis of possessing a particular attribute, placed in groups differing on that attribute, and then measured on a dependent variable. To illustrate such a study, we employed an example comparing smokers with nonsmokers on health. Recognize, however, that ex post facto studies are essentially correlational studies; individuals are measured on two variables, and neither one is actively manipulated. The investigator, therefore, obtains pairs of measures from individuals to analyze.

Ex post facto studies do, however, differ in several respects from the correlational approach described in this chapter. In an ex post facto study the variable regarded as the independent variable is usually measured first; in correlational studies the variables are measured in no typical order. Second, in ex post facto research the levels of the independent variable often represent nominal measurement; subjects are frequently classified in categories on the basis of possessing or not possessing the characteristic (e.g., smokers or nonsmokers) or possessing qualitatively different characteristics (e.g., male or female, left-handed or right-handed,

Sprague-Dawley or Wistar strain of rat). In contrast, in a correlational study the range of values that both variables assume is usually more extensive. A third difference is that ex post facto studies usually afford more control over other extraneous variables that may influence the values obtained from the second variable designated as the dependent variable; this control occurs because ex post facto studies are often conducted in laboratory environments similar to those arranged for true experiments, and correlational studies usually are not. An additional major difference between ex post facto and correlational studies has to do with the way the data are analyzed. In ex post facto studies, you will recall, measures of central tendency and variability are calculated on the scores. Thus, instead of calculating and evaluating the statistical significance of correlation coefficients, a *t* test or analysis of variance is often employed to analyze the data in an ex post facto study. As we shall explain in the next section, however, the conclusions derived from analyses of means in ex post facto studies are no different from those permitted from correlational analyses. It is mainly because of this limitation that ex post facto studies are regarded as basically correlational.

In an ex post facto study, Saklofske, Kelly, and McKerracher (1982) investigated the relationship between astrological birth sign and the personality characteristics of extraversion-introversion and neuroticism. Participants were divided into two groups based upon whether the individual's birthdate was under an even or odd astrological sign (e.g., 1—Aries and 3—Gemini are odd astrological signs, and 2—Taurus and 4—Cancer are even astrological signs) and then measured on extraversion-introversion and neuroticism with psychological tests. Subjects in this study could not be randomly assigned to astrological sign groups; rather astrological sign is an attribute possessed by reason of birth. Thus, participants were simply measured on birth sign and two personality traits in an attempt to see if birth sign is related to personality characteristics. Because the measurement of birth sign divided the individuals into two groups (even vs. odd birth sign) the groups were tested for differences on the personality measures by an analysis of variance rather than by correlating birth sign with personality characteristics. Yet this method is correlational even though analysis of variance was used to compare the two groups. The type of statistics used to analyze the data does not change the nature of the research. Parenthetically, Saklofske et al. found no significant differences in personality dimensions in the two birth-sign groups.

As we pointed out in Chapter 3, ex post facto research is very prevalent in the social and behavioral sciences. By including ex post facto studies within the broader context of correlational research, it is probably accurate to state that the majority of investigations in psychology are correlational studies rather than true experiments.

In Chapter 3 we also pointed out the difficulties of establishing cause-and-effect relationships between the independent and dependent variables employed in an ex post facto design. These difficulties extend more generally to all correlational studies. We turn to this problem next.

Correlation and Causality

Many psychological variables are highly correlated, but the mere existence of a correlational relationship between two variables does not imply a causal relationship between them. The variables may be causally related, but because of the so-called third variable problem this connection cannot be determined from the measured correlation alone.

We now explain the *third variable problem:* Suppose two variables such as the reflective personality trait (variable X) and belief in extraordinary phenomena (variable Y) are positively correlated; people who are more reflective have stronger belief in extraordinary phenomena. Which variable, if either, affects the other? Does X cause Y? Or does Y cause X? Perhaps neither of these applies and both are caused by a third variable, Z. This last possibility is illustrated in Figure 14–3. Perhaps those individuals who are both highly reflective and believe in extraordinary phenomena received an education (i.e., variable Z) in which they were taught to contemplate abstract ideas but were not taught physical laws or encouraged to seek empirical evidence for their beliefs. On the other hand, perhaps people who score low on both the reflective trait and belief in extraordinary phenomena had an education wherein they were taught to demand data to support their beliefs and learned the physical laws of nature that are violated by purported extraordinary phenomena.

If a third variable explains the observed relationship between two variables, then the correlation between X and Y is *spurious* or false. Although on the surface a relationship exists between X and Y, the causal relationship is between Z and X, and between Z and Y. From the correlation of X and Y alone, however, a psychologist cannot determine which of these possibilities exists among the variables studied.

The third variable problem often leads to misreporting of correlational studies in the popular media. Recent newspaper articles have discussed studies showing an inverse relationship between alcohol consumption and the probability of having a heart attack: "If you drink approximately three beers a day, it could stop you from having a heart attack." This statement implies that beer consumption produces a healthier heart. But can you conclude this kind of causal relationship from a correlational study that simply measured beer drinkers and nondrinkers on heart attack rates? Perhaps the real relationship is between amount of stress and heart-attack rate, and people who experience less stress in their lives both drink beer and have lower heart-attack rates.

Another study reported an inverse relationship between reported amount of sleep per night and energy levels during the day. Should you conclude from this finding that if you lack energy during the day then you should sleep less during the night? Again, this is a correlational relationship and does not allow you to jump to causal conclusions. Probably a third variable is present that accounts for the observed relationship, perhaps some organic condition that affects both your daytime energy level and the amount of sleep you need.

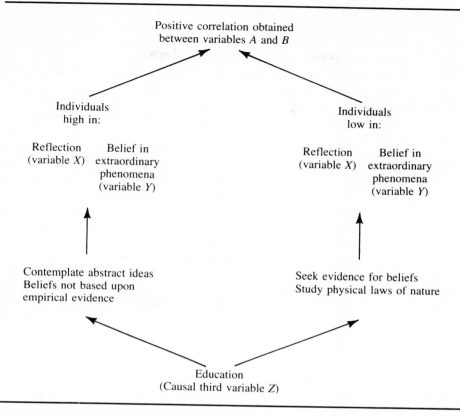

The third variable problem in correlation.

FIGURE 14–3

A curious direct relationship between use of cellophane tape and margarine has also been reported in a study conducted by an advertising-research firm. Here you are unlikely to fall in the causality trap; it is doubtful you would believe that eating margarine leads one to use more cellophane tape or vice versa. Obviously, a third variable underlies this reported relationship. We will let you speculate about what it may be.

NATURALISTIC OBSERVATION

The term **naturalistic observation** usually refers to research composed purely of observation of behaviors in natural settings. No independent variables are manipulated or varied and typically no interaction occurs between the psychologist and the participants. In naturalistic observation, all potential independent variables essentially vary simultaneously; for this reason, much of naturalistic observation research has been purely descriptive of behaviors occurring in a natural environment. It is quite possible, however, to test research hypotheses using naturalistic observation research, and we present an example shortly. In addition, much emphasis in naturalistic observation has been on studies of animal behavior, but its use appears to be becoming more prevalent in other areas of psychology as well, particularly in infant and child development (e.g., see Resch, 1981).

Psychologists engage in naturalistic observation research for many reasons. The starting point for all research is an observation of some behavioral phenomenon in either human beings or animals. Often, a psychologist will want to study a naturally occurring behavior to find potentially important variables controlling that behavior before the problem is studied in the laboratory under more controlled conditions. Moreover, the generality of laboratory findings may also be investigated by naturalistic observation. This function relates back to the issue of the ecological and population validity of a laboratory experiment that we discussed in Chapter 13. Finally, some problems cannot easily be brought into the laboratory for study, such as the interaction of marriage partners in a natural setting or the agonistic behavior of different species of animals in their normal environment. The argument for studying behavior in more natural settings and using a natural range of settings as independent variables is gathering strength in psychology (e.g., Petrinovich, 1979; Tunnell, 1977), and it is likely that there will be many developments in this area in coming years.

Observation in Naturalistic Observation

The role of observation obviously assumes considerable importance in the success or failure of a naturalistic observation study. In Chapter 2 we discussed some characteristics of scientific observation: Observations are directed by theoretical conceptualizations, they are descriptions of behaviors and not of inferred entities, and they must be reliable. In the context of research, making observations in a laboratory experiment is usually quite clear-cut because only one, or at most several features of a subject's behavior are observed at any one time. Further, the collection of observations is often automated or even recorded by the participant in the form of a response to a scale or questionnaire.

Observing in naturalistic situations is considerably more difficult. Many behaviors from many subjects may be occurring simultaneously. So that a scientist will not see only what he or she wants to see in the situation being observed, a schedule to be used in making the observations usually is carefully planned before making the observations. In a laboratory experiment the schedule of observations is usually implicit in the design; a psychologist observes and records the participant's behavior on every "trial" of the experiment. An experimenter does not eliminate or omit observations on certain trials merely because those observations are not in accord with the research hypothesis. Likewise, when making observations in natural settings, the investigator must ensure that behaviors not in accord with a research hypothesis are not overlooked or omitted from observation.

Schedules of Observation

A schedule of observation may require an observer to write a complete, continuous narrative description of the behavior observed. Recently, videotapes and films have sometimes been used in place of such a written narrative (see, e.g., Resch, 1981). Because behavior is so complex, however, and because often more than one behaving organism is observed in the setting, a researcher is likely to use a sampling procedure such as event or time sampling.

Event sampling In event sampling certain behaviors (events) are targeted for observation and these behaviors are observed and recorded whenever they occur. Only the targeted behaviors are recorded, however.

Time sampling In time sampling, a schedule of time is developed when a specific person (or animal) is to be observed. During that time all behaviors of that person are observed. A psychologist may observe and record all the behaviors of a person for a predetermined 20-second period out of every 2 minutes. Other types of observational schedules and techniques have been developed for various problems (see Bouchard, 1976; Brandt, 1972).

Categorizing Responses

In naturalistic observation the criteria for categorizing the observed behavior must also be defined. The issue here is what constitutes a behavioral act. As a simplistic example, if you observed a person walking toward a refrigerator you could categorize this act on a *molar* level (referring to the behavior "as a whole") as one behavioral act—the behavior of walking to the refrigerator. On the other hand, you could categorize the act on a *molecular* level (referring to a simpler, smaller, or more basic level) as a series of behaviors, each step, for example, being treated as one act of behavior. Of course, the molar-molecular categorization is quite relative; no absolute distinction of molar or molecular levels of observation can be made. Moreover, there is no one "correct" way of classifying behavior; the decision must be based on the question for which an answer is being sought. Both molar and molecular categorizations are used in naturalistic observation studies.

Example of Naturalistic Observation

To illustrate the characteristics of naturalistic observation, we utilize the work of Fagot and Patterson (1969), who were interested in patterns of reinforcement of behavior among preschool children and teachers in a nursery school setting. Their study was based upon theorizing about development of appropriate sex-role behaviors in children. A synopsis of their theorizing follows; in their article it was more fully developed and supported by citations to relevant research.

The essence of Fagot and Patterson's theorizing is that a child may initially perform a response because he or she sees a parent or someone else emit the response, but for the child to continue emitting the response, the response must be reinforced. In many instances reinforcement might be praise or attention from a parent or other person. Some evidence indicates that reinforcement for a response is most likely to come from an individual who already possesses that response. That is, you are more likely to reinforce in others behaviors similar to those you possess. It follows that males would be more likely to reinforce male behavior in others and females would be more likely to reinforce female behavior in others. Extrapolating this theory to children leads to the expectation that boys will reinforce "boys'" behavior of others, whether the others are male or female, and girls will reinforce "girls'" behavior of others whether the others are male or female. Fagot and Patterson applied this theorizing to preschool children in a nursery school situation and predicted that: (1) "Since the teachers were female, they would reinforce female-preferred behaviors more than male-preferred behaviors," and (2) "that peers would reinforce same-sex behaviors; therefore, most peer reinforcement would come from those of the same sex" (p. 564).

Because we are most interested here in the methodology of naturalistic observation, we present the Method section of Fagot and Patterson's article in its entirety. Remember that although they are employing naturalistic observation as a method, their goal is to test a research hypothesis and empirically evaluate a theory. To this end, they had to obtain observations that could be compared to the predictions of their research hypothesis. Study Fagot and Patterson's Method section carefully; they deal with many problems of control and observation that we have raised both here and in earlier chapters.

The Method section provides a rather detailed description of the participants and the setting in which observations were made. This information is necessary in order to be able to evaluate the validity of the results. The reader can judge if there are any unique characteristics of either the subjects or the setting that might limit generalizations or inferences to similar people and settings.

Fagot and Patterson also provided empirical referents for the conceptual dependent variables expressed in the research hypotheses. They did not establish an arbitrary list of categories of behavior before conducting their observations; rather, they conducted pilot (or trial) observations to discover what behaviors occurred naturally. From these pilot observations they developed the list of behaviors and consequences that are presented in their Method section.

They categorized behaviors at a molar rather than at a molecular level. That is, they categorized complete patterns of behavior such as "painting at easel" rather than "picks up paintbrush," "puts paintbrush in paint," and so on. The categorization of behaviors as male- or female-preferred is presented not in the Method

Method Section of Fagot and Patterson

Method

Subjects

The data reported in this paper were collected at two nursery schools in Eugene, Oregon (during the period from September 1964 to May 1965).[4] At the beginning of the study, both boys and girls ranged in age from 37 months to 46 months, with a mean of 41.8 months for the boys and 41.1 months for the girls, and were from white upper-middle-class homes. The group met twice a week for 3 hours throughout the year. There were 18 children in each school, with the sexes divided equally in both schools.

Setting Variables

The two nursery schools were similar in physical facilities and in the area of the city in which they were located. Both schools were nonsectarian, although classes were held in church buildings, and both were administered by lay boards consisting of mothers of nursery school children. While the educational level of the teachers was similar, they did have different teaching experiences. In School 1, both teachers had at least 10 years' experience teaching nursery school, while in School 2 the teachers had taught primarily in the first and second grades.

Behavior Checklist

In a pilot study, an attempt was made to list exhaustively all the possible play behaviors and the social consequences of these behaviors. From this preliminary list were selected the 28 responses and the 10 possible consequences that seemed to summarize adequately most of the subjects' behavior. These lists are as follows:

Behaviors

1. Painting at easel.
2. Cutting, pasting, drawing with crayons or chalk.
3. Playing with clay.
4. Play at cornmeal table or sandbox outside.
5. Play with water, blowing bubbles.

6. Design board, puzzles, tinker toys, snakes, flannel boards, marble games.
7. String beads.
8. Build blocks, set up farms and villages.
9. Hammering.
10. Playing toy trucks, planes, boats, trains, tractors.
11. Play with steering wheel, dashboards.
12. Play in kitchen, large playhouse, or extended kitchen activities.
13. Play with dollhouse.
14. Play with dolls.
15. Dress in like-sex costume.
16. Dress in opposite-sex costume.
17. Use like-sex tools.
18. Use opposite-sex tools.
19. Sing, listen to records, play musical instruments.
20. Look at books or listen to story.
21. Science table, science observation, dinosaurs.
22. Play with live animals or toy animals.
23. Sit and do nothing, wander, follow teacher around.
24. Help teacher.
25. Climb, or hide in pipes.
26. Ride trikes, cars, horses, skates, wagons, boats.
27. Swing, slides, teeter totter, or bounce on tires.
28. Throw rocks, hit with an object, push.

Consequences

1. Teacher initiates new behavior.
2. Teacher comments favorably.
3. Teacher joins in activity.
4. Teacher criticizes.
5. Child imitates another child.
6. Child joins another child in parallel play.
7. Child joins another child in interactive play.
8. Child stands and watches another child.
9. Child continues alone.
10. Child criticizes another child.

Observation

The observers were instructed to remain as much in the background as possible, preferably in one position. However, as both schools had two different play areas, it was necessary for the observer to change positions quite often. The observers avoided interacting with the children unless

[4] The authors gratefully acknowledge the cooperation of the staff of the Congregational and Presbyterian Nursery Schools.

Method Section of Fagot and Patterson *continued*

the child demanded a response. If such a demand was made, the observer responded as quickly as possible and then moved away from the child. After the first session, the observer was ignored except on rare occasions.

The observation study began September 9. 1964, and continued intermittently throughout the school year. The first 6 sessions at the beginning of the study were used to develop the checklist and the next 12 sessions to obtain the observer reliability data. The collection of the observation data reported on in this study began during the nineteenth session. The first series of observations lasted for 12 sessions (November to January 1964). A second series of observations of 12 sessions was completed during April and May 1965.

During an observation session, the children were observed during a 70-minute free play period. Each child was observed for a 10- to 15-second interval about once every 5 minutes. Usually it was necessary to code only one behavior per time interval. The observer simply indicated the

code numbers and the consequence for each subject.

Three observers were used for this study. Five children from each school were randomly selected to participate in the observer reliability study. Two observers rated at a time, with the third observer serving as a timekeeper. The timekeeper gave the child's name to be rated at the start of a 60-second period and continued the procedure for each of the five children and then started the list again. Each child was rated 12 times on the behavior checklist. The procedure was repeated three times at each school so that each observer was compared with the other two at both schools. The observer reliability study took a total of 12 nursery school days to complete.

The observers had to give exactly the same code number on each observation to be considered in agreement. There was a total of 120 observations on each of the two scales for each pair of observers. The pairs of observers were able to agree 99% of the time on behaviors and 85–92% of the time on the consequences.

---

section but in the Results section. They determined preference by counting the number of times that males and females engaged in the various categorized behaviors described in the Method section. Thus, whether a behavior was male-preferred or female-preferred was determined empirically from the behaviors of the children.

The various aspects of observation—observer influence, schedule of observations, and reliability of observations—are also addressed in the Method section. They describe the position of the observer at both schools; however, they leave it to the reader to decide whether the presence of an observer influenced the behavior exhibited and, if so, whether it represents a plausible rival hypothesis to the research hypothesis for explaining the results.

The specific scheduling technique used for the observation sessions was time sampling; each child was observed for 10 to 15 seconds out of every 5 minutes. Although Fagot and Patterson do not say so, the observation time for each child was scheduled prior to making the observation; the observation did not depend upon the child's emitting a certain behavior (e.g., they did not see a child painting and then decide to observe). Had they made the observations dependent upon the behavior being emitted (i.e., event sampling), they would have been unable to test their research hypotheses and the results would be misleading.

Finally, Fagot and Patterson concentrated on the reliability of their observations. They wanted to ensure that the same behaviors would be placed in the same categories by different observers. To do so, they compared how the three observers categorized the same observed behavior. Their agreement was not perfect; reliability of measurements among different observers rarely is, but for scientific observation it was quite high and acceptable.[2]

Our major purpose in presenting the Fagot and Patterson study is to demonstrate the methodology of naturalistic observation. The remainder of their paper deals with the results and conclusions from the results. The data analysis techniques associated with naturalistic observation typically are those which we have already discussed. If measures such as the number of responses emitted by boys or girls are analyzed, then a t test or an analysis of variance may be used to determine if systematic differences occur between the groupings. Sets of observations on the same participants often are analyzed by correlational statistics to determine if they are related.

Recent appeals have been made to psychologists to pay greater attention to the ecological validity of their research and to try to use more natural environments in research (e.g., McCall, 1977; McGuire, 1973; Miller, 1977; Zimmer, 1978). With this increasing emphasis on research in natural environments, it is quite reasonable to expect that naturalistic observation will become a more frequently used method of research in future years.

CASE-STUDY METHOD

A **case study** is an intensive, descriptive study of one individual, organization, or event. The case study originated in medicine and its use in psychology came via psychiatry (Bolgar, 1965). Consequently, case studies in psychology often deal with individual cases in psychopathology and psychotherapy. Frequently, case studies are used to evaluate psychotherapeutic treatment with one individual exhibiting pathological behavior and undergoing treatment for the disturbance. But the use of case studies has not been limited to this area. An early use of the case study was that of Preyer (cited in Bolgar, 1965) who made careful observations and notes on his own child. The approach has been widely used since then in studying child behavior and is particularly evident in the highly regarded work of Piaget (1952, 1970). From careful observation of his own children, Piaget proposed many important concepts of cognitive development in children. There are numerous other examples of case studies; biographies and autobiographies are forms of nonscientific case studies with which we are all familiar.

---

[2]It is not unusual for two people observing the same person to not always agree on categorizing what that individual is doing. This is a characteristic of human observation that has many implications in areas such as law and eyewitness testimony. See, for example, the work of Loftus and her associates (Loftus, 1979).

Characteristics of the Case Study

A case study is usually a **longitudinal investigation,** one in which an individual or individuals are studied over a long period such as months or years. Most of the designs we have discussed study individuals for very limited periods (perhaps an hour or less). Although one is not inherently prevented from using experimental designs to study individuals over a long time, pragmatic considerations often limit the number and length of longitudinal experimental studies in psychology.

The case study is also typically descriptive rather than inferential. A case study usually describes one individual thoroughly, but there is seldom major interest in attempting to extend inferences to other individuals or situations. In contrast, though research utilizing experimental designs seldom studies individuals in great depth, the interest in such research is to make inferences to other individuals and other settings.

A case study involves numerous potential independent and dependent variables. Because the case study usually deals with an individual in nonlaboratory situations for quite a long time, there can be many potential independent variables affecting behavior and many behaviors being affected. In contrast, experimental studies most frequently deal with only a few independent and dependent variables at a time.

Sometimes a case study is conceived of as a simplistic experimental design in which a treatment is administered to one individual or a small group of people and then a single measure of behavior is taken. This use of the case study has been soundly criticized (see Campbell and Stanley, 1963; Kerlinger, 1973). The critics point out that because there is no individual or group of people who do not receive the treatment, a psychologist cannot tell what effect, if any, the treatment has on the behavior measured. Essentially, because a control condition is lacking, there is no way to establish either the internal or construct validity of the study.

In many case studies, however, extensive descriptions of various behaviors are obtained both before and after a treatment is administered (Campbell, 1975; Runyan, 1982). In these instances, despite the lack of a control group, a psychologist may feel confident that any changes in behavior that occurred after a treatment was administered were due to the treatment and not to other variables. This is not to say that this use of the case-study approach is not open to threats to internal validity and construct validity. But because of the extensive data collected on the individual, a psychologist may feel confident that such threats do not offer plausible explanations for the behavioral changes he or she observed in the case studied.

A case study is also open to the *post hoc, ergo propter hoc* fallacy. The Latin phrase means "after this, therefore because of this." The fallacy here is in believing that any behavioral changes observed after a treatment is administered are necessarily due to the treatment because they came after it. The skilled researcher, however, is aware of this fallacy in thinking and will be cautious in developing causal relationships from case study data.

Example of a Case Study

To more clearly illustrate the characteristics of a case study we present one conducted by Robert J. Gatchel (1977). This study involves one individual undergoing treatment for phobic behavior. As you read the study, take note of its longitudinal and descriptive characteristics. Also notice the very important interplay between the particular case Gatchel describes and the application of findings from experimental studies to the treatment of this case.

Value of Case Studies

The study by Gatchel is an excellent illustration of the characteristics and usefulness of the case study method. Gatchel did not merely administer a treatment and then take a single measure of behavior; rather, he took many measures of behavior at various times. Before administering the treatment he attempted to discover under what conditions and how often the client experienced anxiety attacks. During treatment, between treatment sessions, and for two weeks after training, the client was asked to record the number and severity of anxiety attacks.

From this rather extensive observation of the client, Gatchel was quite sure that the change in frequency and severity of the anxiety attacks after treatment was due to the total complex of treatment administered. Certainly there is no indication that the client's anxiety attacks were decreasing in severity and frequency in the two-year period prior to entering the experimental treatment. Thus, it is quite unlikely that anxiety would have reduced spontaneously over the two months required for therapy if no therapy had been given.

Although one can be reasonably confident that the behavior change was due to the treatment, one cannot be sure what specific component of the treatment complex was responsible for the change in behavior. For example, Gatchel induced a strong expectancy effect in the client: "High expectancy for improvement was introduced" (p. 690), along with biofeedback on heart rate. From this case alone one cannot tell what specific aspect of the treatment was crucial for behavior change—expectancy, biofeedback, their interaction, or even some other factor operating in the treatment. To determine this aspect, experimental research employing appropriate control conditions is needed. And this is exactly what Gatchel and his associates have done. On the basis of the experimental work cited in his study, Gatchel has found that biofeedback of heart rate is a necessary component of the treatment, although inducing expectancy of improvement facilitates the effect of the biofeedback.

Many psychologists argue that the case study is very valuable as a source of research hypotheses to be tested using some form of research design (Bolgar, 1965; Neale and Liebert, 1980). The case study may also be very useful in providing

Case Study

Therapeutic Effectiveness of Voluntary Heart Rate Control in Reducing Anxiety

Robert J. Gatchel
University of Texas at Arlington

This study demonstrates the therapeutic effectiveness of heart rate control training in the treatment of a phobia. A time-series analysis of pretreatment and posttreatment assessment indicated significant fear reduction due to the biofeedback intervention. The results of this study serve to further illustrate that learned control of heart rate deceleration is an effective self-control skill for coping with anxiety.

A recent study by Gatchel and Proctor (1976) investigated whether learned control of heart rate is an effective treatment strategy for bringing about fear reduction. Heart rate was focused upon because it is strongly associated with fear (Lang, Rice, & Sternbach, 1972), and it was thought that self-control over this visceral response might be the most direct method of producing a low state of sympathetic arousal to compete against the stress response. Results from Gatchel and Proctor clearly demonstrated that learned control of heart rate deceleration significantly reduced verbal, overt–motor, and physiological components of public-speaking anxiety. It should also be noted that therapeutic expectancy was experimentally manipulated in this study, and it was found to contribute to the effectiveness of the biofeedback procedure. However, control of heart rate was found to be the major active ingredient that accounted for therapeutic improvement, with expectancy factors playing a subordinate role.

On the basis of these results, learned control of heart rate was viewed as a self-control skill for effectively coping with anxiety. In an attempt to further assess the utility and generality of this "stress-inoculation" training procedure, the present study reports the use of learned control

of heart rate in treating a claustrophobic problem behavior. The results of this clinical case study serve to compliment the findings of the controlled analogue research study by Gatchel and Proctor (1976) in demonstrating the therapeutic effectiveness of the heart rate biofeedback treatment approach.

The client was a 23-year-old married male university student. As a young child, the client had developed an extreme fear of receiving injections. Approximately 2 years ago, he developed an infection that required the attention of a physician. After making an appointment with the physician, he experienced an extreme amount of anxiety in anticipation of possibly receiving an injection for the infection. At the physician's office, it was determined that an injection of medication was indeed needed, and a nurse proceeded to administer one. Immediately upon administration, the client reported that his ears began "ringing," his heart started to rapidly palpitate, and he then momentarily "blacked out" for a few seconds. The nurse apparently became panic stricken because he remembered hearing her hysterically shouting for the doctor, who was with another patient. The client reported that the experience was highly traumatic, with the feeling of being immobilized and trapped in the small examination room, with his ears ringing, heart palpitating, and a frantic nurse shouting for the doctor. He also reported being extremely embarrassed by the entire incident afterwards.

His physician assessed that the short black out was not due to any allergic reaction caused by the medication because the client had no history of such an allergy, having received the medication many times in the past. There were also no physiological aftereffects. The physician suggested that the high degree of anxiety associated with receiving the injection most probably prompted the fainting spell.

Later that day, the client felt well enough to return to his part-time job. While working alone in a small enclosed area at his place of employment, the client started to reexperience the ringing sensation in his ears and heart palpitations that had preceeded the brief fainting spell earlier that day. He immediately exited from his working area for fear that he might black out once again. As soon as he left, the symptoms subsided. Ever since that day, whenever in an enclosed area, he became hypersensitive to the emergence of these symptoms. Whenever he perceived the onset of the symptoms, he immediately attempted to escape from the situation. The success in alleviating the symptoms apparently reinforced his escape behavior. He also attempted to avoid situations that he thought might precipitate an attack. He subsequently quit his part-time job because he was experiencing an increasing number of anxiety attacks that seriously disrupted his work routine and created a great deal of discomfort. These attacks also disrupted his course work at the university. In all of his classes, he had to sit close to an exit in the event that he might experience the onset of an attack. He had frequent episodes during the course of a day, prompting him to leave the classroom with the resultant disruption of his class work. Even everyday activities such as going shopping with his wife were seriously curtailed due to his fear of having an anxiety attack in the middle of the store with no ready access to an exit.

The client initiated contact with me after hearing about a heart rate biofeedback experiment that I was conducting. From reading articles in the popular press, he became aware of the ways in which biofeedback techniques were being applied to clinical disorders. He requested to participate in the experiment and learn to control his heart rate as a possible means of coping with his anxiety, since the perception of an increase in heart rate was a major component of his anxiety attacks. He had previously been treated, ineffectively, by a psychiatrist with short-term psychotherapy and chemotherapy in an attempt to reduce the anxiety episodes.

After a complete medical examination revealed no physiological causes for the attacks, and after conducting an extensive diagnostic interview, it was decided to offer biofeedback training to the client to provide him with a self-control technique to combat the anxiety. High expectancy for improvement was introduced to mobilize the patient for active participation in the treatment and also because high therapeutic expectancy was found to contribute to the effectiveness of the biofeedback procedure in the Gatchel and Proctor (1976) study. He was informed that the training procedure would provide him with an effective coping skill that he could actively use in reducing tension in a variety of anxiety-provoking situations.

The treatment program consisted of training the subject to control his heart rate. It should also be noted that, since the biofeedback training required the client to remain in a small enclosed subject cubicle for the length of each training session, a "built-in" feature of the therapy procedure was extensive exposure to aversive claustrophobic cues.

Method

The client received 14 sessions of biofeedback training over the course of 2 months. Heart rate, as well as blood pressure, integrated frontalis electromyogram, respiration rate, and skin conductance level, was continuously recorded throughout each session on a Narco Bio-Systems Physiograph. Each training session lasted approximately 1 hour and followed a standard automated format. The timing of each session and

Case Study *continued*

presentation of instructions and feedback were all accomplished automatically using a digital logic circuitry. A detailed description of this automated feedback training procedure can be found in Gatchel and Proctor (1976).

The client was requested to practice heart rate control between sessions whenever possible. He was encouraged to actively use the learned control skill in vivo whenever he felt himself becoming anxious. Also, 2 weeks prior to the initiation of biofeedback training, during the training period, and for 2 weeks after the end of training, the client was requested to keep a daily record of the number and severity of anxiety attacks that he experienced during the course of the day. A 5-point scale was used on which the client was asked to rate the severity of each anxiety attack (5 = extreme amount of anxiety; one = slight amount of anxiety).

Results and Discussion

By the end of the biofeedback training sessions, the client had learned to decelerate his heart rate an average of 7.6 beats/min below resting base level. This performance is comparable to the learned heart rate deceleration found in previously reported controlled experimental studies that used the same automated feedback procedure as the present case study (Gatchel, 1974; Gatchel & Proctor, 1976).

An interrupted time-series analysis (Gottman, 1973) was performed on the sum of the anxiety severity ratings for each pretreatment and posttreatment assessment day (14 pretreatment and 14 posttreatment assessment days) to statisically evaluate the therapeutic effectiveness of the biofeedback intervention. This analysis indicated a significant reduction in the number and severity of anxiety attacks experienced by the client for level, $t(25) = -3.123$, $p < .01$. Before treatment, the mean of the sum of the anxiety severity ratings was 13.1; during the posttreatment phase, the mean decreased to .3.

A follow-up interview session, conducted 6 months later, indicated a maintenance of therapeutic improvement. Since the termination of treatment, the client has not experienced any anxiety attacks that have disrupted his ongoing behavior. He reported complete satisfaction with the biofeedback treatment program in eliminating the formerly frequent anxiety episodes.

The results of this case study demonstrate the therapeutic effectiveness of learned heart rate control in the treatment of a claustrophobic problem behavior. The data indicate that anxiety can be effectively inhibited through control of the heart rate component of sympathetic arousal. Together with the analogue treatment study by Gatchel and Proctor (1976), which demonstrated the effectiveness of heart rate control in reducing speech anxiety, these results serve to further illustrate that learned control of heart rate deceleration is an effective self-control skill for coping with anxiety. Future controlled analogue studies of this effect, similar to that of Gatchel and Proctor, and case studies such as the present study, with other phobic stimuli will further test the utility of the biofeedback technique in the prevention and reduction of anxiety responses.

References

Gatchel, R. J. Frequency of feedback and learned heart rate control. *Journal of Experimental Psychology*, 1974, *103*, 274–283.

Gatchel, R. J., & Proctor, J. D. Effectiveness of voluntary heart rate control in reducing speech anxiety. *Journal of Consulting and Clinical Psychology*, 1976, *44*, 381–389.

Gottman, J. M. N-of-one and N-of-two research in psychotherapy. *Psychological Bulletin*, 1973, *80*, 93–105.

Lang, P. J., Rice, D. C., & Sternbach, R. A. Psychophysiology of emotion. In N. Greenfield & R. Sternbach (Eds.), *Handbook of psychophysiology*. New York: Holt, Rinehart & Winston, 1972.

Received October 3, 1975 ∎

Reprinted from the *Journal of Counseling and Clinical Psychology,* Volume 45 (1977), pages 689–691. Copyright 1977, American Psychological Association. Reprinted by permission of the publisher and author.

descriptive accounts of infrequent or rare behavior, such as the so-called multiple-personality phenomenon (see Thigpen and Cleckley, 1954). It may be quite impossible to study such rare behaviors by any other technique because of their very infrequent occurrence.

ANALYSIS OF FREQUENCY DATA: THE CHI SQUARE TEST

Nonexperimental research methods often lead to collection of data that merely indicate whether a behavior occurred or not. For example, in a naturalistic observation study a psychologist may record only whether a subject does or does not emit a behavior. Such scores represent nominal measurement; the scores simply fall into mutually exclusive categories. A tally of the frequency of occurrence of responses in the various categories may be obtained, but the individual scores themselves convey no numerical information about the subject's response. Statistical tests such as the analysis of variance or *t* test, which assume that a score conveys some numerical information about a subject's behavior, are inappropriate for analyzing frequency data. The nonparametric tests that we have discussed so far, such as the Mann-Whitney *U* test, assume that scores can be ranked. Hence these tests are also inappropriate for simple frequency data. Another nonparametric test, however, the chi square test (χ^2 test), provides an appropriate test for these data. The **chi square test** (pronounced "ky square") is a widely used statistical test for scores that simply represent the frequency of a response observed in subjects.

Example Employing a Chi Square Analysis

The work of McCloskey and his associates on intuitive physics is an example of a study utilizing a chi square analysis of frequency measures. McCloskey, Washburn, and Felch (1983) were interested in studying people's knowledge of falling objects. In some of their studies they presented subjects with a so-called *walker problem.* In this problem, subjects are shown a side view of a man walking at a constant speed. The walker is holding his arm straight out from the shoulder and is holding a small metal ball in his hand. As he is walking, the man drops the ball. The task of the subject is to indicate on the picture where he or she believes the ball will fall. The correct answer is that the ball, because it is moving at the same forward speed as the walker, will fall in a forward arc and land even with the walker. The majority of people, however, indicate that the ball will fall straight down or in a backward arc.

In one study McCloskey et al. used this task to compare subjects who had training in physics (physics-trained) against subjects who did not have training in physics (physics-untrained) to see if there was any difference in their response to the problem. Suppose the results of a similar ex post facto study employing forty physics-trained and forty physics-untrained students were those shown in Table 14–4. A table such as this is often called a *contingency table*. An individual's response was classified as either correct or incorrect. This measure represents nominal level of measurement; a response was simply assigned to one of two mutually exclusive categories (i.e., it is either correct or incorrect, but it cannot be both). Thus, the values in Table 14–4 designated by *O* (for observed) represent the frequency of correct and incorrect answers given by the subjects. Each subject contributed only one response to the table. These frequencies are referred to as the *observed* or *obtained frequencies*. The row and column totals shown in the table are often called *marginal frequencies*. Because the data are categorized by type of subject and type of response, the data in our example are presented in a 2 × 2 contingency table.

Let us consider the scores in Table 14–4 for a moment. Correct responses were given by thirty-four participants and incorrect responses by forty-six participants. If the type of response is not related to the type of subject, then it would be reasonable to expect that of the thirty-four correct responses, about half (i.e., seventeen) would be given by physics-trained subjects and about half by physics-untrained subjects. These are called *expected frequencies*. A similar expectation holds for the incorrect responses if there is no relation between type of subject and type of response. About twenty-three incorrect responses should be given by each type of subject group. The expected frequencies under chance conditions where type of subject and type of response are completely unrelated are also shown in Table 14–4 by the value of *E* (for expected) in each cell.

The chi square test uses these expected frequencies obtained under a chance hypothesis to develop a test statistic. If there is no relation among variables in the population sampled, then the observed frequencies should typically be about the same as the expected frequencies. Large deviations of the observed frequencies

TABLE 14–4   *Hypothetical data for responses of physics-trained and physics-untrained students on the walker problem. The values given by* O *are the obtained frequencies. The values given by* E *are the expected frequencies obtained from the marginal frequencies.*

		Type of student (*A*)		
		Physics-trained	*Physics-untrained*	*(Marginal)*
	Correct	$O = 26$ $E = 17$	$O = 8$ $E = 17$	34
Type of response (*B*)				
	Incorrect	$O = 14$ $E = 23$	$O = 32$ $E = 23$	46
	(Marginal)	40	40	(Total) 80

from the expected frequencies should occur rarely by chance if the variables are not associated. If the variables are related in the population sampled, however, then the observed frequencies should differ from the expected frequencies by larger amounts. For example, if the frequency of correct and incorrect responses is related to the type of student, as McCloskey et al. hypothesized, then it is likely that the physics-trained students will produce more correct responses than the seventeen expected by chance and that the physics-untrained students will produce more incorrect answers than the twenty-three expected.

Computing the χ^2 Statistic

The chi square test measures this deviation of the obtained frequencies from the expected frequencies obtained under a hypothesis of chance with the test statistic:

$$\chi^2 = \sum_{A=1}^{a} \sum_{B=1}^{b} \frac{(O_{ab} - E_{ab})^2}{E_{ab}}.$$

In this formula O_{ab} is the observed frequency in the ab cell, E_{ab} is the expected frequency of the ab cell, a is the number of levels of the A variable (type of subjects in this example), and b is the number of levels of the B variable (type of response in this example).

The null hypothesis under which the sampling distribution of χ^2 is developed and under which expected frequencies for each cell are found is:

H_0:   There is no relationship between the two categorical variables in the population.

The alternative hypothesis is:

H_1:   The two categorical variables are related in the population.

The expected frequencies for each cell of the table may be obtained from the marginal frequencies as follows:

$$\text{Expected frequency of a cell} = \frac{(\text{Row marginal for cell})(\text{column marginal for cell})}{\text{Total number of responses}}$$

For example, the expected frequency for the physics-trained, correct response cell is found by

$$\text{Expected frequency} = \frac{(34)(40)}{80} = 17.$$

Notice that this is the same numerical value of the expected frequency as that shown in Table 14–4.

The numerical value of χ^2 for the sample data with the expected frequencies shown in Table 14–4 is found as follows:

$$\chi^2 = \frac{(26 - 17)^2}{17} + \frac{(14 - 23)^2}{23} + \frac{(8 - 17)^2}{17} + \frac{(32 - 23)^2}{23}$$

$$\chi^2 = \frac{81}{17} + \frac{81}{23} + \frac{81}{17} + \frac{81}{23}$$

$$\chi^2 = 16.57.$$

The df for this χ^2 statistic are found by $(a - 1)(b - 1)$. For the example, $a = 2$, $b = 2$, thus the $df = (2 - 1)(2 - 1) = 1$. Critical values for $\alpha = .05$ and $\alpha = .01$ from the sampling distribution of χ^2 at various df are given in Appendix Table A–9. Obtained values of χ^2 *equal to or greater than* the tabled critical value are significant at the value of α selected.

The critical value of χ^2 for $\alpha = .05$ from Table A–9 is 3.84. The obtained χ^2 value of 16.57 is larger than the critical value; hence, the null hypothesis is rejected and the alternative hypothesis is accepted at the .05 level. The results indicate that the relative frequencies of correct and incorrect responses are not the same for physics-trained and physics-untrained students, $\chi^2(1) = 16.57$, $p < .05$.

Correction for Continuity in a 2 × 2 Contingency Table

When the χ^2 is applied to a 2 × 2 contingency table such as Table 14–4, many authors suggest that a corrected form of the χ^2 formula be used. This formula, with a correction for continuity, is given by:

$$\chi^2 = \sum_{A=1}^{a} \sum_{B=1}^{b} \frac{(O_{ab} - E_{ab} - .5)^2}{E_{ab}}.$$

The corrected formula provides a smaller value of χ^2 than does the uncorrected formula, e.g., 14.78 versus 16.57, respectively, for our example. There is controversy over whether this formula should be used with a 2 × 2 contingency table; however, it is often used and reported in published research.

Limitations on Use of a Chi Square Test

A chi square test may be used on a contingency table of any size (e.g., 3 × 4). Several restrictions apply to its use, however:

- Each subject may contribute only one response to the contingency table.
- The number of responses recorded should be large enough so that no expected frequency is less than 10 in a 2 × 2 contingency table or less than 5 in a contingency table larger than 2 × 2. If this condition is not met, either

more responses should be collected or an alternative test such as the Fisher exact test should be used.

Further details on use of a chi square test and alternative tests for frequency data may be found in Marascuilo and McSweeney (1977) or Siegel (1956).

SUMMARY

- Nonexperimental research methods are characterized by lack of manipulation of the independent variable and inability to randomly assign participants to treatment conditions.
- In the correlational approach the psychologist typically obtains pairs of measures from a group of participants. The measures are then statistically analyzed to determine if a relationship exists between them. Statistical measures of the relationship between two variables are provided by correlation coefficients (e.g., the Pearson r and Spearman r_s). Ex post facto studies (discussed in Chapter 3) are essentially correlational studies. Causality cannot be inferred simply from a significant correlation between two variables or from a significant difference between groups in an ex post facto study. The observed relationship may be due to a third causal variable.
- Naturalistic observation consists of observing the occurrence of behaviors in a natural setting. These observations typically are made according to schedules such as event sampling or time sampling.
- The case-study method involves an intensive, descriptive study of one individual, organization, or event. A case study typically is a longitudinal investigation, descriptive rather than inferential, and often involves numerous potential independent and dependent variables.
- The chi square test is a nonparametric test used for analyzing simple frequency data.

15

PREVIEW

In this chapter we explain the written research report. Topics discussed include:

- APA style requirements
- Content of a research report
- Suggestions for writing a research report
- A sample laboratory report

WHY YOU NEED TO KNOW THIS MATERIAL

The major vehicle for communicating scientific knowledge is the research report. Students are typically expected to both read research reports and write reports describing their own research.

Writing the Research Report

Knowledge needs to be shared with others if it is to be of value to the scientific community. The major vehicle for sharing knowledge in psychology is the journal article. Hundreds of journals around the world publish psychological research. Indeed, publication is so vital that the American Psychological Association publishes a handbook, the *Publication Manual of the American Psychological Association* (1983), which provides comprehensive instructions for preparing articles for publication in a journal. The *Manual* is so useful that many non-APA journals adopt the APA style requirements, colloquially known as "APA style."[1]

Many departments require their students to follow APA style in preparing research reports—that is, laboratory reports—for courses in experimental psychology. In fact, it is not unusual for instructors of experimental psychology courses to adopt the *Publication Manual* as a required "text." We recommend that all psychology students obtain a personal copy of the *Publication Manual* whether it is specifically required for a course or not. It is a valuable guide for writing. Moreover, few style conventions and writing guidelines described in the *Manual* are not relevant to writing student laboratory reports or term papers.[2]

In this chapter we introduce the general requirements of APA style. But we do not discuss or even attempt to summarize most of the style requirements outlined in the 200-page *Manual.* Our approach is to discuss issues in report writing which often prove troublesome to students and which are not discussed in the *Publication Manual.* At the end of the chapter we have included a sample laboratory report prepared in APA style. This report (somewhat revised) was submitted by one of our students, Barbara A. Nesman, to meet a requirement in her experimental psychology course. It describes research that she planned and

---

[1]Thus it is often said that "psychologists do it APA style."

[2]The *Publication Manual* may be ordered from:
Order Department
American Psychological Association
1200 Seventeenth Street, N.W.
Washington, DC 20036

conducted on a problem in music perception, and we refer to it to illustrate points in our discussion on preparing research reports.

The sample laboratory report is probably more extensive (thirty typewritten pages) than a manuscript of the research submitted for journal publication. If Nesman were to describe the same research for publication, then it is likely that the typewritten manuscript would be considerably shorter, for most journals limit the length of articles. In the following discussion, however, we assume you are writing a laboratory report and not an article for publication. The distinction is important, because in a laboratory report one is often not subject to the stringent limitations on length that are imposed on published articles. For a published article the *Publication Manual* states that you should assume that you are writing for a reader with knowledge in the problem area. In a laboratory report, though, you are writing so that an instructor may assess *your* knowledge of the subject.

OVERVIEW OF A RESEARCH REPORT

All research reports that conform to the APA editorial requirements are composed of these major sections:

- Title
- Abstract
- Introduction
- Method
- Results
- Discussion
- References

Each of these parts in a manuscript is illustrated in the sample report that begins on page 466 as well as in the McCarthy and Betz article in Chapter 1.

Title

The title should be a short (12- to 15-word) statement clearly identifying the main topic of the report. Because the title of a published report is used to index that report in *Psychological Abstracts* and other indexing services, it is important that the title accurately reflects the content of the study. It is the reader's first contact with the report and it provides the basis for deciding whether the report is of interest or not. For this reason, a good title often includes the conceptual independent and dependent variables.

Notice that the title with author's name and affiliation is typed on a separate page. The "running head" at the bottom of the page is a shortened version of the title (50 characters maximum) that appears at the top of each page of the published report.

Abstract

The abstract is a short, nonevaluative summary of the research reported that should be no longer than 150 words. The abstract for a published article is entered into a comprehensive indexing system of the published literature of psychology called Psychological Abstracts Information Services that is maintained by the American Psychological Association. Psychological Abstracts Information Services publishes a monthly periodical, *Psychological Abstracts,* which contains abstracts of current psychological research appearing in more than 1000 international journals. *Psychological Abstracts* is used by scientists to "search the literature" for research relevant to their interests.

The abstract should briefly but accurately state the problem investigated, the subjects of the research, the apparatus and materials used, the procedure followed, the results, and the conclusions reached from the results. Any information that appears in the abstract should be presented more fully in the body of the report. For this reason, it is recommended that you write the abstract after preparing the remainder of the report. The abstract is also presented on a separate page.

Introduction

The introduction to your laboratory report is the section in which you introduce the research problem investigated in your study, the theoretical formulations (if any) and relevant empirical work in the problem area, alternative hypotheses and explanations of the empirical findings, unresolved issues, and the rationale for your research hypotheses. By no means is this an easy task! In fact, the introduction is often the most difficult section of a report to write.

The introduction begins on a separate page and is *not* preceded by a heading entitled "Introduction." It is simply assumed that the main body of the report will begin with an introduction.

Problem

For the reader to understand your research, he or she must know the problem you investigated. Therefore, we suggest that you begin your introduction with a statement indentifying the research problem. Nesman's paper begins with the statement, "Appreciation of the musical work of many composers depends upon being able to extract a major theme from a series of variations of that theme." This statement clearly lets the reader know the direction of the research to follow. In the remainder of the first paragraph of the sample paper she then amplifies the nature of this problem. Notice from the example, however, that a problem statement is usually presented in general terms; it does not state a specific research hypothesis. The research hypothesis comes at the end of the introduction.

After the problem statement has been presented the introduction typically proceeds in one of two directions—presentation of the theoretical explanations of the problem area or a review of the empirical research in the area.

Review of Theoretical Explanations

Many problem areas in psychology have some tentative explanations for phenomena associated with the problem. These explanations may be well formulated as a theory or much less well formulated and incomplete. When an explanation is available in the literature for the problem you are interested in, it is often effective to introduce and detail this explanation immediately after you have introduced the problem. By doing so, you will organize the problem area for your reader (and probably for yourself) and identify the important conceptual independent and dependent variables in that area. Additionally, many research hypotheses that have been tested in the empirical research on the problem area are likely to follow from these theoretical explanations. Thus, by presenting the theory or explanation early in your introduction you aid the reader in his or her attempts to understand the problem area and the research that has been done on the problem.

Review of Relevant Empirical Research

All reports require a critical review of the relevant, recent research on the problem. As we have suggested, this task is often more easily accomplished if theoretical formulations are available and have already been presented in your report. The theoretical conceptualizations provide an organization about which you may discuss the empirical findings. In many instances, though, no theoretical formulations may be available to organize the empirical research. If not, the review of the previous empirical research usually follows immediately after statement of the problem. In either case, we present several suggested guidelines for presenting a review of the empirical literature.

- A literature review usually is based upon primary sources of information. A **primary source** of information on a topic is typically an article published in a journal summarizing the research of an experimenter and written by that experimenter. In contrast, a **secondary source** is a report of original research as reported by someone else. In this sense, then, the typical textbook is a secondary source of information for most topics.
- Present your review of others' research in your own words; do not paraphrase from the study itself. To do so, you will have to be very knowledgeable about the research and you should attempt to write your own review without having a copy of the article in front of you for reference. After you have written the review, however, check the details of what you have written against the study itself.

- Present sufficient information about a study so that your reader will know why the study was done, what was done, and what was found. You do not need to describe in detail all the studies that you review, only those which are clearly relevant to the development of your rationale in the problem you investigate. Research that is germinal to the problem area, either because of the method employed or the results obtained, is clearly information that your reader should understand in order to be able to follow your research, and it should be reviewed fully.

- If several studies employed essentially the same design and procedure, you need not present each in detail. Present only one in detail, state that the others were similar, and then briefly summarize the results of the others.

- Be *critical* in your review of the literature. Carefully examine the research that you are reviewing and look for errors in conceptualization, design, and analysis of data, and whether the reported results provide support for the conclusions drawn by the author(s). Also attempt to consider rival or alternative explanations of the results that have not been discussed by the author(s).

- Attempt to give your reader a summary of the empirical support for any theoretical formulations you present in your introduction. Point out, also, where the empirical work has been inconclusive and any unresolved issues connected with the problem.

- Organize your review around variables important in the explanation of the problem or around research with inconclusive and conflicting findings. This structure will help your reader integrate the knowledge of the important variables in the problem area. A chronological review of the literature (i.e., a review in the order in which the research was published) is seldom successful. Reviewing articles in a chronological order usually does not lend itself to integrating the issues and findings.

Rationale for the Research Hypothesis

The review of the relevant literature should lead to a rationale for your specific study and, therefore, for your research hypothesis. Developing an explicit rationale for a particular research hypothesis is a most vexing task for many students. The word *rationale* means *reason* or *basis*. Thus, when you write the rationale for your research hypothesis, you are stating the reasons for your specific hypothesis. The reasons obviously must be related to, and follow from, the literature that you have reviewed. It is your task to ensure that the reader: (1) understands why your experiment needs to be done (i.e., it should be explicitly clear what contribution to the published literature on the problem your experiment *potentially* makes), and (2) clearly sees how your research hypothesis develops from the literature reviewed. A rationale for a research hypothesis is illustrated in the sample paper on page 476. Notice that the author indicates how her research hypotheses follow from the literature that she has reviewed.

Some Suggestions for Writing the Introduction

Use published research reports as models   When you read the literature in the problem area that interests you, read not only for the substantive content of the article, but pay attention also to the form and style of the report. Notice the organization used by the author and the development of his or her rationale for the research hypotheses. Careful attention to these aspects of an article will be beneficial not only for writing your introduction, but for all sections of your laboratory report. We have two cautions, however: (1) Not all published research reports are good models or examples of the suggestions we have presented, and (2) be very careful that you do not plagiarize the published reports that you do use as models.

Organization of paragraphs   Paragraphs should begin with a **topic sentence,** a general statement providing the major idea of the paragraph. For example, the third paragraph of Nesman's paper begins with the sentence, "The work of Franks and Bransford (1971) provides a representative example of the abstraction of prototypes from repeated experience with a set of visual stimuli." This sentence clearly states the major idea of the paragraph. Even without knowing the literature in this area you can anticipate that the paragraph will describe the work of Franks and Bransford. The McCarthy and Betz article in Chapter 1 also provides examples of the excellent use of topic sentences in writing an introduction.

A sentence such as "In a study by Welker (1982), it was found . . ." is usually *not* a suitable topic sentence for a paragraph. With such a sentence the reader is often left uncertain about the relevance of the point the writer presumably is trying to make and is asking, "So? What is the relevance of this sentence? What is the point the writer is trying to make?"

Giving credit when credit is due   One of the most difficult tasks in preparing a scientific research report is giving appropriate credit to your predecessor in a line of research. Using the ideas of others without giving credit to the individual who formulated those ideas constitutes plagiarism. *Plagiarism* is defined as "to steal and pass off (the ideas or words of another) as one's own" (*Webster's Ninth New Collegiate Dictionary,* 1983, p. 898). Thus, a plagiarist is one who steals or uses the words or ideas of others and does not give appropriate credit for development of those words or ideas.

One way to discover how to appropriately credit the work of other authors is to see how they have given credit to those who preceded them. To avoid plagiarism, it is essential that you know thoroughly the studies that you are citing and that you are able to describe these studies *in your own words*. Merely changing a word or two in sentences from any source is literary thievery.

Quotations?   You may think that the way to avoid plagiarism is to directly quote from the references that you cite. This is not so. Direct quotations, even if properly documented, are rarely appropriate for laboratory reports. Use quotations only when you need to present the exact definition of a term or concept used by another author or if you wish to take issue with a specific statement or conclusion made by an author. In reviewing the literature of your problem area, you will notice the minimal use of quotations in published articles. Sometimes students are tempted to introduce quotations when they do not understand what an author has written. This is *not* good scholarship. If you do not understand some of the material in your references, then seek assistance so that you can come to understand what the author has written and so that you will be able to discuss it in your own words. Do not present information that you do not comprehend.

Your first draft should not be your last draft   The introduction to your laboratory report should be substantially completed before you begin conducting research with subjects. Consider this your first draft of the introduction. A good policy for writing is to put this first draft away while you are conducting the research. When you return to it later, some of the details of the studies you cited and the logic in the derivation of your research hypotheses will not be quite so fresh to you. At this time you can be a better critic of your own writing. Can you understand the theoretical conceptualizations and empirical findings from what you have written? Is the rationale for your research hypotheses clearly derived? Do your research hypotheses make the predictions that you intend? When you have answered these questions you are ready to revise the first draft.

Students sometimes ask how many drafts and revisions of the introduction are necessary. We can give no definite answer to this question; we recommend that you allow sufficient time in preparing your report that your submitted report will not be a hurried first draft. Professional scientists write many drafts of their work before it is published and frequently submit some of these drafts to their colleagues for review and criticism before publication.

Method

The Method section of a report presents the details of how the study was conducted. A Method section will typically identify the subjects used in the experiment, the experimental design used, the apparatus, materials, or stimuli employed, and the procedure followed in running the experiment. This section should provide sufficient information that the reader can replicate your experiment. Therefore, this section should be quite detailed in describing how the experiment was conducted. Because of space constraints in journals you will frequently find that some important details are omitted from the Method sections in published articles. For laboratory reports, however, instructors do not usually impose such restrictions. Therefore, the Method section of a laboratory report may be expected to be more detailed than that of a published article.

The Method section is always divided into subsections. The purpose of these subsections is to logically organize the important information necessary for replicating the experiment. The subsections also aid in organizing the information that needs to be presented. Laboratory reports will typically contain at least these subsections in the Method section:

- Subjects
- Design
- Apparatus or Materials
- Procedure

If you need to, use additional subsections.

Subjects

The Subjects subsection should state who participated as subjects in the research, how they were selected, and how many participated. Be specific, but concise, in stating how subjects were selected. Seldom, if ever, will you randomly select subjects; rather they will be obtained from classes, student lounges, dormitories, or other places. State this information in your report as Nesman did in the sample report (see p. 477). If subjects had to meet any requirements for selection, then mention the criterion (or criteria), e.g., visual acuity, handedness, college major. Report how many subjects were disqualified from participation because they could not meet the criterion. Provide any other demographic information about your subjects that may be relevant for your reader to know, such as average age, number of males and females, and so forth.

Design

A Design subsection is particularly useful when a factorial design is used in an experiment. Identify the type of experimental design (e.g., two-factor between-subjects design, two-factor within-subjects design, two-factor mixed design), and the independent variables manipulated and their levels. It is clear in the sample report that a two-factor mixed design was employed and that subjects who received either low- or high-structured musical themes were tested on six transformations of a theme.

Apparatus

In this subsection you describe the apparatus, materials, and stimuli used in the experiment—and their function. A mere listing of the equipment used to present stimuli or record responses is not adequate. For instance, students sometimes are inclined to write, "A Kodak projector was used." For conciseness and clarity it is better to write, "The stimuli were projected with a Kodak Carousel slide projector." Similarly, rather than state that "A stopwatch was used," it is better to explain what it was used for. For example, "A stopwatch was used to record the time it took each subject to perform the task."

Identify commercially available laboratory equipment (e.g., a conditioning chamber, pursuit rotor, reaction-time apparatus, tachistoscope) by the manufacturer's name and the model number. Describe equipment that is constructed for the experiment and therefore not available from a commercial supplier·in enough detail that it can be reconstructed by the reader.

The stimuli or materials used in the experiment must also be described. If the stimuli or materials are rather simple, then it is often appropriate to describe such stimulus materials within the Apparatus subsection or in a subsection identified as Apparatus and Stimuli. If your stimuli or materials are similar to or based on those used by another researcher, then also cite the source of the original stimuli or materials.

In some experiments, however, you may construct your own materials or complex stimuli (e.g., a survey questionnaire, drawings, word lists). In these instances, it makes sense to include a separate Materials or Stimuli subsection in which these stimuli or materials are completely described. Nesman's paper illustrates use of a Stimuli subsection in place of an Apparatus subsection. Her apparatus was simply a piano and a tape recorder. Her stimuli, though, were complex and require considerable explanation in order to make us understand how they were constructed. Hence, in this instance, a Stimuli subsection results in a more complete report and also clarifies the method of the research for the reader.

Procedure

In the Procedure subsection you state explicitly how you executed the research. The major emphasis in this subsection is on stating clearly and concisely what you did with each subject. To that end, state how the subjects were assigned to experimental conditions, how the independent variable(s) was (were) manipulated, and how extraneous variables were controlled. Sometimes the task or procedure is modeled on one reported in a related, published study; if so, cite the reference but describe the procedure that you used.

All relevant control techniques should be described in the Procedure subsection. The reader should be able to evaluate whether you took appropriate steps to avoid confounding the experiment. Therefore, describe any randomization and counterbalancing that you used. For example, state that "subjects were randomly assigned to treatment groups" or that "the order of presentation of the three treatments was completely counterbalanced." Another example: If you randomized the order in which stimuli were presented to each subject, then state that here. Point out, too, environmental features such as ambient noise level, lighting conditions, temperature, and so forth, which were held constant in the experimental situation.

One aspect of the procedure that sometimes causes difficulty for students is describing the instructions given to the subjects. We suggest the following:

- If the instructions are experimentally manipulated as an independent variable; that is, if groups of subjects are given different instructions and you are interested in the effect of those instructions, then present the instructions verbatim in the Procedure subsection.
- If the instructions are not an independent variable and all subjects in essence receive the same instructions, then present a brief summary or paraphrasing of the instructions in the Procedure subsection. In laboratory reports the complete instructions may be included in an appendix.

Other Subsections

The trend among psychological journals appears to be toward greater use of subsections in order to more clearly describe the method of the research. Scanning the Method sections of some journals that adhere to APA style reveals subsections such as these: Memory Lists, Instructions, Criteria for Learning, Visual Task, Auditory Task, Rating Procedure, Judgment Tasks, Trial Sequence, Testing Procedure, Nature of the Noise, Sample, Measures, and Questionnaires. The authors of these articles obviously felt that some aspect of their method was particularly complex and required a separate subsection for clearest presentation. You too may find it appropriate to use additional subsections in your report. Perhaps you have developed a unique task that requires extensive presentation, or perhaps you have constructed a questionnaire that must be presented in detail if your reader is to understand the results. If so, then you should have a subsection of the Method called Task or Questionnaire. Using subsections properly will greatly enhance the clarity of your Method section.

Results

The purpose of the Results section is to present and summarize the statistically analyzed data; raw data are not included in this section. Accordingly, descriptive statistics (e.g., means and standard deviations) and the outcomes of statistical tests on the data (e.g., *t* test, analysis of variance) are reported. The analyzed data to be presented are those which are relevant for drawing conclusions about the research hypothesis that you tested.

The Results section is usually the briefest in the report. Keep in mind that in this section you report simply what you found, not what the findings mean. Therefore, present the organized, statistically analyzed data in an objective, matter-of-fact manner, with no editorializing—explanations of unexpected findings, conclusions, implications—these are not appropriate here.

The Results section consists of a textual presentation and usually tables or figures or both of the analyzed data. As a rule, we believe that the written description of the results in a laboratory report should be complete so that the reader does not have to consult the tables and figures in order to understand the major findings of the research. Therefore, from the textual presentation alone the reader should know (1) the scores that were analyzed, (2) the measures of central tendency and variability that were used, (3) the directions of the differences in the descriptive statistics among the treatment conditions, and (4) the differences, if any, that are statistically significant. On the other hand, from the tables and figures alone the reader should be able to obtain essentially the same information.

The *Publication Manual* is rather vague about the appropriate organization for a Results section. Thus, we provide below some suggestions on organizing and preparing this section that we think provide for logical and complete presentation of the results for any experiment.

Subjects' Scores

With few exceptions, *only one score per subject per treatment condition is statistically analyzed.* Make sure that the reader knows how each subject's score that you analyzed was derived and what the score means. Sometimes, from the information you present in the Method section, it is obvious what individual scores were used for the analysis. In other cases, it is not so evident. For example, often many responses may be recorded in each treatment condition for each subject in the experiment. Recall that McCarthy and Betz analyzed the sum of the twelve different 7-point ratings by each subject for each dimension of counselor effectiveness. Another example: In reaction-time experiments a subject's reaction time is usually measured many times in one treatment condition. Therefore, it is likely that an average of the recorded reaction times (e.g., a single mean or median) will be obtained to represent an individual's reaction-time score. Notice in the sample report (p. 480) that the Results section begins with a description of how a music-recognition score was obtained for each subject by using both the "yes-no" responses and a confidence rating for each musical transformation.

Descriptive Statistics

Next, present the descriptive statistics (e.g., means, standard deviations) for the treatment conditions. If you employed more than two conditions in the experiment, i.e., a multilevel one-factor design or a factorial design, then the descriptive results normally should be presented in a table (such as Table 1 in Nesman's report) or a figure. Any table or figure that you use should be mentioned in the text of the Results section and typed on a separate page. For example, in the sample report, Nesman introduces Table 1 in the text on page 481. The table itself, however, appears separately on page 488 in the report. Notice that the approximate location at which the table should appear in a published report is indicated in the text with the instructions, "Insert Table 1 about here" (see p. 481). Typically, the numerical values that are presented in a table or figure should not also be recited in the text.

Advantages of tables and figures   Tables and figures each have their advantages for presenting descriptive data. Where the values depicted in figures are necessarily less precise, exact values can be provided in tables. Moreover, even for the most complex designs, measures of variability (e.g., standard deviations) can be included in tables. For factorial designs, depicting both measures of central tendency and variability in a figure may result in a cluttered "picture" of the results. Therefore, it is often better to present only measures of central tendency in a figure without measures of variability.

Well-prepared figures, however, illustrate patterns of results more clearly than tables, especially interactions in factorial designs. Thus, the *Publication Manual,* on the choice of a table or a figure for presenting the data, advises the author to "choose the medium that presents them clearly and economically" (p. 27). Figures are more expensive than tables to reproduce for publication, but obviously expense of reproduction is not relevant to you in preparing laboratory reports in which figures are prepared on graph paper.

Statistical Tests

We think it makes sense to present the results of any statistical tests (e.g., χ^2, t test, analysis of variance) after—not before—descriptive statistics are presented. For example, if a t test is used, then it is reasonable to know first what two means are analyzed for statistical significance. Realize, however, that this practice is not always observed in published articles.

Summarize the results of any statistical test of significance in the text. For example, as we illustrated in Chapter 7 when describing the outcome of a t test on the expertness scores of McCarthy and Betz, "The mean expertness ratings for the self-disclosing and self-involving conditions were 63.1 ($SD = 14.63$) and 68.5 ($SD = 11.06$), respectively. The means differed significantly, $t(105) = 2.172$, $p < .05$." In the sample paper the results of the analysis of variance are summarized similarly for each main effect and interaction (p. 481).

Reporting analysis of variance results   If an analysis of variance is used, then we suggest that for each analysis you also present a summary table showing the sources of variation, *df, SS, MS,* and *F* values. Such a table is illustrated by

Table 2 in the sample report. You will find that such summary tables do not often appear in published articles. It is costly to print tables, and the results (F, df, MS_e, p) are usually summarized in the textual presentation anyway. Again, however, there are no such cost considerations for laboratory reports, and we think the information provided by a complete summary table is informative to the reader.

When reporting significant effects in the textual presentation, be sure to describe the direction of the difference. When only two means are compared by a t test or analysis of variance, then visual inspection is all that is necessary to reveal which mean is significantly larger. When three or more means are compared in an analysis of variance, though, then multiple comparison tests are needed to describe which means differ significantly.

Tests of multiple comparisons   Identify the name of the multiple comparison test used after the analysis of variance (e.g., multiple F test, Scheffé test, or Tukey's test). Because some follow-up tests are identified by various names, it is sometimes useful to cite the source of the test you use (e.g., Linton and Gallo, 1975). We also recommend that you state the critical values used to determine the minimal difference in means needed to meet statistical significance and the significance level adopted (e.g., .05). If possible, especially for data from factorial designs, present a table of the comparisons made and the outcomes of these comparisons. The sample report provides an example of such a table using Tukey's test (see Table 3, p. 490).

Strength of association measures   Estimates of the proportion of variance accounted for by an independent variable (e.g., eta squared or omega squared) are presented for statistically significant effects only. The sample report includes presentation of an η^2 value for the significant main effect of musical transformation (see p. 482).

In the Results section you should present a complete, concise, and objective summary of the findings of your experiment. Present all the relevant analyzed data for the report in this section. Do not hold back some results to spring upon the reader in the Discussion section.

Discussion

The results are interpreted in the Discussion section. Here you tell the reader what the results mean. Therefore, in this section you draw conclusions, relate results to previous work, discuss the implications of the results and provide explanations for the findings, consider possible shortcomings of the study, and provide suggestions for further research.

The key to writing a complete and informed discussion is to prepare a good introduction. It is very difficult to write an adequate discussion of the results if you have not reviewed the previous literature and clearly formulated the rationale and research hypotheses. If you do not clearly understand the relationship between your study and previous research, then your discussion of the results will necessarily lack substance.

Drawing Conclusions

The first issue to address is whether the results agree with the research hypothesis. Indeed, the *Publication Manual* states that the discussion should open with "a clear statement of support or nonsupport for your original hypothesis" (p. 27). Nesman's first two sentences in her Discussion state that her results fail to support one of her research hypotheses, but do support the other.

Relating Results to Previous Research

Discuss your results and conclusions in the context of the research cited in the introduction. Thus, it is often appropriate to briefly mention which studies your results are consistent with and, too, those studies in the problem area which are not in agreement.

Implications and Explanations of Results

The research reviewed in the introduction establishes the basis for your research. Your results, then, should have implications for the previous research. Perhaps your results extend the findings of others to different settings. Maybe your results suggest how the generality of previous findings is limited. Whatever the outcome, your results should suggest some implications regarding theoretical issues or previous findings.

Be cautious in speculating on any practical applications suggested by the results of your study. Students sometimes are inclined to try to explain how their results have practical relevance and may go far beyond what is warranted by the data from a single experiment. Address any potential applications briefly. If no practical application is apparent, then we suggest that you do not broach the issue.

Negative Results

So-called negative results; that is, failure to obtain a statistically significant outcome, are usually disappointing. Negative results are difficult to discuss. The *Publication Manual* advises that "negative results should be accepted without an undue attempt to explain them away" (p. 28). Knowing that most published articles report "positive" results, it is understandable that one would react to the negative findings by asking, "What did I do wrong?" It is appropriate to offer some explanation for the lack of an expected effect of the independent variable, but resist the temptation to merely explain away the data by proposing a list of excuses. You should, however, thoughtfully consider issues on statistical-conclusion validity, internal validity, and construct validity. It is quite possible, for example, that the results represent a Type II error. Be aware that if there is no clearly formulated rationale for conducting the research and hence for the research hypothesis, then there will be little of substance to say. Offering superficial excuses and providing unsubstantiated speculation will not prove fruitful.

Nesman obtained negative results for her research hypothesis on the effect of type of musical structure. Because her hypothesis was clearly developed from the literature, though, she was able to discuss the implications of this result and to suggest situations in which musical structure may have an effect.

Evaluating Your Research

Particularly when dealing with negative results, students tend to be critical of their research and point to numerous flaws in the study. But we have observed that experiments with positive results usually do not undergo such intensive scrutiny by the author. Regardless of the outcome of the experiment, any methodological problems encountered in executing an experiment should be cited with a brief but specific explanation about how the results could have been affected. It is better to discuss fewer problems specifically than to prepare a shopping list of perceived flaws. Avoid taking a shotgun approach in identifying possible problems with the methodology. If you are too critical of your research, then you may create the impression that it was not well planned or was carelessly conducted. Any flaws that if corrected would not be likely to change the outcome should be mentioned briefly, if at all.

Suggestions for Further Research

It is not uncommon to find Discussion sections in lab reports ending with the statement, "Further research needs to be done in this area." We would no doubt agree that more research is warranted in any area. But such a statement is trite and conveys no meaningful information. Instead, be specific in proposing any further research that should be undertaken. Explain why the problem deserves study and suggest how it could be investigated.

References

All research reports include a list of references. These are the bibliographic citations to the work that is cited in the report. All references cited in the report should be included in the References section, and all references included in the References section should be cited in the body of the report itself.

Students sometimes have occasion to cite secondary sources in lab reports. The *Publication Manual* does not illustrate citation of secondary sources in the textual presentation, for psychologists preparing manuscripts for journal publication are expected to rely principally on primary sources. Suppose, though, that you report the results of several experiments that were described in a review article, another published research report, or a book. How can you make it clear to the reader that your review of previous work is based upon a secondary source? Several ways of handling the citations, using sources included in the sample report for hypothetical examples, are suggested below:

> Cuddy, Cohen, and Mewhort (1981), according to Welker (1982), found that musically trained individuals are. . . .

> As reported by Welker (1982), Cuddy, Cohen, and Mewhort (1981) found that. . . .

> Cuddy, Cohen, and Mewhort (1981; cited by Welker, 1982) found that. . . .

> According to Welker (1982), several researchers have found that musical training may affect ability to abstract a theme (Cuddy, Cohen, & Mewhort, 1981; DeWar, Cuddy, & Mewhort, 1977).

Include all primary and secondary sources cited in the report in the References section.

Appendix

An Appendix section is seldom included in published research, but it may be required in a laboratory report. The purpose of such a requirement is to ensure that all information that the instructor requires to evaluate your work is included in the laboratory report you submit. The additional material required for this evaluation is normally not appropriate for inclusion in the body of the report itself. The Appendix should not contain any material that the reader needs to understand the research presented in the laboratory report. For this reason, do not refer to the Appendix in any portion of the report. If the reader needs to see the material presented in the Appendix in order to understand the research being reported, then that material should be incorporated in the appropriate section of your report rather than in the Appendix.

The following materials may be included in an Appendix.

- A copy of the *informed consent form* used to inform prospective subjects of the nature of the research. A sample form is illustrated in Appendix A of the example report (see p. 494).
- A copy of the *instructions* given to subjects if those instructions were not presented verbatim in the Method section of the report. If word-for-word

instructions are included in the Method section, then they do not need to be included in the Appendix. If only a summary of the instructions is presented in the Method section, however, then the complete instructions may be given in the Appendix.

- Any *figures or tables* that present information relevant to your method (e.g., a complete set of stimuli used in the experiment). These materials should not be necessary for understanding the method or needed to perform an operational replication of the research. If they are essential to presentation of the method, then they should be included in the Method section.

- A *table of the subjects' scores*. These should be the scores from individual subjects that were used for the data analysis (e.g., computing treatment means, standard deviations, analysis of variance). The subjects are not to be identified by name, but the table should clearly identify the treatment for which the score was obtained. With the data presented in this table, the reader should be able to perform the same analyses that are reported and summarized in the Results section.

- The *computations* of your data analysis, or, if the analysis was done on a computer, a copy of the computer printout of the results. A table of the computational steps followed for any follow-up tests (e.g., Tukey's test) that you may have conducted also would be appropriate here.

SUMMARY

- The major vehicle for communicating scientific knowledge in psychology is the written research report.
- Psychological research reports typically follow the editorial style requirements described in the *Publication Manual of the American Psychological Association*.
- APA-style research reports are organized in four major sections that tell the reader why the research was done (Introduction), how it was conducted (Method), what was found (Results), and what the results mean (Discussion).
- A sample laboratory report of original research conduced by an undergraduate student is presented here.

Sample Laboratory Report

*A short title
with page
numbers appears
on each page.*

*The title should
be informative
and identify
the independent
variables.*

High and Low Musical

1

The Effect of High and Low Musical Structure

upon Abstraction of Themes and Variations

Barbara A. Nesman

Framingham State College

Running head: HIGH AND LOW MUSICAL STRUCTURE

High and Low Musical

2

Abstract

The abstraction of a musical prototype from transformations of high and low structure was investigated. In a procedure analogous to that of Welker (1982), a musical prototype and 5 ordered transformations were generated for music of either high or low structure as defined by rules of formal musical analysis. The prototype theme was the central tendency of the set and the transformations were variations of the theme. Forty subjects were tested for abstraction in a 2 x 6 mixed design, 20 in a high structure condition and 20 in a low structure condition. Evidence of abstraction was provided by false recognition of the prototype and ordering of transformations in relation to the prototype. Contrary to predictions, subjects abstracted equally well in both structure conditions. The main effect for recognition ratings among the ordered transformations was significant, $p < .05$. The results provide evidence for the robustness of the abstraction phenomenon in music perception.

The abstract is a concise summary of the research limited to 150 words.

The Effect of High and Low Musical Structure

upon Abstraction of Themes and Variations

Appreciation of the musical work of many composers depends
upon being able to extract a major theme from a series of
variations of that theme. A musical theme is a short, simple
melody, generally presented early in a composition, which
subsequently appears in varied forms as the musical work
progresses (Copland, 1957). A listener, therefore, is required
to extract and recognize this theme when it is varied in order
to comprehend and appreciate the music. For example, Branms'
<u>Variations on a Theme by Paganini</u> requires the listener to
abstract a theme from a number of variations. Although
composers have long assumed that individuals are capable of
such tasks, until recently there has been very little empirical
evidence to support this assumption.

The task faced in recognition and abstraction of a theme
in music appears quite analogous to the abstraction of
prototypes from a related set of patterns in visual
perception. A prototype is simply a basic pattern of a
stimulus which represents the elements of a larger set of
stimuli (Klatzky, 1975). For example, the prototype of a <u>table</u>
may be thought of as a horizontal flat surface with four legs.
All tables that actually exist, then, are some variation of

No heading is used for the introduction section.

The first paragraph indentifies the research problem.

Subsequent paragraphs develop the review of relevant literature.

this prototype. A considerable amount of evidence indicates
that individuals are able to abstract or draw out the essential
features of a prototype pattern simply by viewing a series of
variants of that pattern without ever having seen the prototype
itself. In a sense, then, an individual may form a cognitive
representation of the prototype.

The work of Franks and Bransford (1971) provides a
representative example of the abstraction of prototypes from
repeated experience with a set of visual stimuli. They
performed a series of experiments on visual recognition using
geometric forms that were related to one another by a set of
systematic variations, called transformations, from a prototype
stimulus. For example, one prototype stimulus employed was a
large blue square on the left and a large green circle on the
right of an index card. A small red triangle was in the center
of the square and a small yellow diamond was in the center of
the circle. Alterations of this stimulus configuration
involved systematically changing the size or location of the
shapes on the card, deleting one of the shapes, or substituting
a different shape for one of the shapes. As an example, one
alteration was simply putting the circle and diamond on the
left of the card and the square and triangle on the right.
Another alteration involved deleting the large blue square on
the left while retaining the small triangle and the circle and
diamond on the right of the card. Transformations of the

The author and date are used for reference citation in the text. (All reference citations must be included in the References section.)

Notice that the report is typed double spaced throughout.

prototype were then constructed by systematically varying the number of alterations on a card. In a first-order transformation, for instance, only one alteration occurred, whereas a second-order transformation contained two combined alterations, a third-order transformation three alterations, and so on.

Franks and Bransford gave subjects an acquisition phase which consisted of viewing and then reproducing 16 transformations of a prototype. This was followed by a recognition task composed of a set of new transformations and the prototype. The subjects demonstrated that they had cognitively abstracted the prototype form in the acquisition phase by recognizing it with high confidence when it was presented in the recognition test. Furthermore, the subjects expressed the highest confidence in actually having seen the prototype during the acquisition phase (although they had not), and the confidence ratings of the transformations were ordered such that the highest recognition ratings were given for transformations closest to the prototype.

The validity of Franks and Bransford's findings for visual perception has been supported by a variety of experiments (e.g., Posner, Goldsmith, & Welton, 1967; Posner & Keele, 1968; Reed, 1972). Recently, Welker (1982) has shown that individuals possess a similar capability with respect to musical stimuli. Welker had subjects mentally rehearse 17 ordered transformations of a prototype musical theme in a 10-second silent period following the presentation of each transformation. These melodies were called the acquisition list. Following two presentations of the acquisition list, the subjects drew a contour or an outline which depicted the successive upward and downward movement in pitch for the 10 tones which they felt best described the average of the set of melodies they heard. The subjects then listened to a new set of melodies (called the recognition list) which contained the prototype theme of the acquisition list and 15 transformations of the prototype different from those of the acquisition list. Following the presentation of each melody, subjects were asked to report whether or not they recognized the melody and to provide a confidence rating of their decision on a scale of 1 (low confidence) to 5 (high confidence). The subjects expressed the greatest amount of confidence in having heard the musical prototype which, in actuality, they had not. They also expressed progressively less confidence in recognition of the melodies as the transformations differed more extensively from the prototype.

The results of the Welker (1982) and Franks and Bransford (1971) experiments demonstrate the generality of the ability of individuals to abstract a prototype pattern after listening to or viewing a series of transformations of that pattern. What factors affect this capability? Welker's prototype melody was highly structured and there is some evidence to suggest the ability to recognize and recall a melody may vary with the structure of the prototype stimulus. Musical structure refers to the relationships among the tones contained within a major scale pattern (Cuddy, Cohen, & Mewhort, 1981). A scale is simply a succession of tones in order of their alphabetical letter names that begins and ends on the same tone (e.g., the C major scale is C-D-E-F-G-A-B-C). In melodies, these tonal relationships (called harmonic progressions) are described by formal musical rules which classify the tones in the order of their importance to this scale pattern. Closely associated with this scale pattern is the concept of "key," which implies that one tone of the pattern is the most salient and that the other tones of the melody are perceived in relation to this fundamental tone. Melodies often begin on this tone, and they are also expected to end on it through a prescribed sequence of notes, called cadence, which provides the listener with a sense of closure or finality (Jones, 1974). For example, in the C major scale, C is the most important note in the scale and the scale begins and ends on C.

Music which is composed in strict accordance with these formal rules of musical analysis may be conceived as highly structured, and music which violates these principles may be considered as low structured (Cuddy et al., 1981). Welker's prototype was composed in strict accordance with these rules and may therefore be regarded as highly structured. His

prototype was based upon both the scale pattern and the key of

C, began on the note C, and followed the most common harmonic

progression to the most common cadence used in music, ending

once again upon C.

Although no studies have been done relating abstraction of

musical prototypes to type of musical structure, recent

evidence suggests that high musical structure favorably

influences recall and recognition of music. For example,

Deutsch (1980) investigated the role that musical structure

plays in the recall of tones. She presented musically trained

subjects with either a set of highly structured short melodies

or a low structured set which contained the same tones in

random order. Recall, as assessed by writing the notation

(i.e., the notes) for the melodies was significantly higher for

the highly structured set than for the low structured set.

Deutsch proposes, therefore, that highly structured melodies

may be more efficiently processed in memory than low structure

melodies. She further speculates that highly structured

musical sequences may improve recall simply because subjects

can relate what they hear to a familiar scale pattern.

Although Deutsch's subjects were all musically trained,

Cuddy et al. (1981) discovered that untrained subjects can also

perceive structure and its degradation in short melodies. In

an experiment that factorially combined harmonic progression,

contour of the notes, key, and scale, structure was
systematically manipulated from high to low over five levels.
Cuddy et al. found that when musically trained and untrained
subjects were asked to compare correct transposed sequences
(i.e., the same scale but in a different key) with incorrect
transposed sequences (one wrong tone inserted), recognition of
the correct sequence declined as the levels of structure
deteriorated for both types of subjects. Further, the pattern
of recognition ratings was the same for both types of subjects.

   A second experiment by Cuddy et al. provided evidence
confirming that ease of recognition is related to musical
structure and is not dependent upon musical training. The
experiment showed that subjects who were trained with informal
lessons on one musical instrument, but untrained in regard to
musical analysis evaluated structured melodies in a fashion
similar to subjects highly trained at the music conservatory
level. Using 32 melodies previously analyzed by faculty
musicians for varying degrees of musical structure, Cuddy et
al. asked these trained and untrained subjects to rate the
melodies in terms of structure, sense of completeness, and
confirmation of expectations. Again they found a high
similarity in the pattern of the ratings of the two types of
subjects. More important, an inverse relationship was found
between subjects' perceptual ratings and the number of
analytical or structural possibilities in the music as

determined by faculty musicians. In other words, sequences
with only one analytical solution (i.e., only one way a
harmonic progression could be expected to go) were rated as
highly structured, whereas sequences with several possible
solutions were rated as low in structure. Based upon these
results, Cuddy et al. suggest that high structure leads to high
certainty in musical perception because musical expectations
are confirmed, and low structure predicts low certainty in that
low structure does not facilitate musical expectations. Cuddy
et al. hypothesize, therefore, that even untrained listeners
may perceive musical sequences by the detection of their
underlying structure in a manner similar to that used in formal
musical analysis.

A question that follows from this work is whether
recognition of a melody is related to the amount of information
imparted by the context in which the tone appears. Dewar,
Cuddy, and Mewhort (1977) manipulated single tones which were
embedded in a series of random notes or in a series of highly
structured notes; they found that the highly structured
condition led to significantly better recognition of that tone
in a subsequent listening task which compared a correct
transposed sequence (i.e., the key was changed) with a
transposed sequence with one altered tone. Dewar et al.
suggest, therefore, that highly structured tonal sequences may
possess relational cues which result in improved recognition

performance. It should be noted, however, that they found an
interaction of structure with number of repetitions of the
task. The low structure performance improved greatly with
repetition and approached the performance of the high structure
condition after about 100 test trials.

It is reasonable to expect, then, that to the extent that
memory and recognition are involved in pattern perception,
abstraction of a musical prototype would be facilitated by
music of high structure. Furthermore, music adhering to formal
rules of musical analysis should provide the listener with
tonal cues relating to an underlying scale pattern which could
make abstraction of a prototype easier simply because the tonal
relationships are familiar. It is the purpose of this study,
therefore, to examine the role of musical structure in the
formation of prototypes. Based upon the reported effects of
musical structure on melody and tonal recognition, a main
effect was hypothesized for musical structure, with the
expectation of higher confidence in the selection of a
prototype, and higher confidence ratings of the transformations
of that prototype for music of high structure than for music of
low structure. A main effect was also predicted for
transformational distance with the expectation that false
recognition confidence ratings would be highest for the musical
prototype and progressively lower as the distance increases for
music of both high and low structure. No interaction of the

The rationale for the research is explicitly presented here.

The research hypotheses are stated here.

High and Low Musical

12

independent variables was expected.

Method

Subjects

The subjects were 42 undergraduate students from
Framingham State College who reported normal hearing. Previous
musical training was not a consideration in their selection.
The subjects were obtained by approaching individuals on the
campus and asking them if they would volunteer for a short
experiment on music recogniton. Two subjects failed to
complete the recognition questionnaire correctly and their data
were discarded. The task was completed by 40 subjects.

Design

A 2 x 6 mixed design was employed. Type of musical
structure (high or low) was the between-subjects variable, and
level of transformation (prototype and 1st- to 5th-order) was
the within-subjects variable.

Stimuli

The patterns consisted of 10 melodic sequences played upon
a recently tuned Yamaha piano and recorded on cassette tape.
The highly structured prototype was similar to Welker's in that
it was a 10-tone pattern which followed common rules of musical
analysis. Tne pattern was generated on a C major scale and
followed a common progression to a common cadence ending once
again on C. Tne low structured prototype did not adhere to any
particular scale, and the harmonic progression was random. The

*Notice the use
of subheadings
to organize the
description of
the method.*

high structured prototype is illustrated in Figure 1 and the
low structured prototype is shown in Figure 2. The contour of
both prototypes was identical. The alterations on the low
structure prototype were composed in such a way that the
distance between the successive tones deviated from the
corresponding highly structured transformation by no more than
a musical whole step (e.g., from C to D on a piano). The sum
of the differences in intervals between the high and low
structured prototypes were approximately the same.

Insert Figures 1 and 2 about here

Following Welker's procedure, the transformations were
generated by altering either the A or B phrase of the
prototype. Application of one alteration rule to either the A
or B portion of the melody resulted in a first-order
transformation. Second through fifth-order transformations
were accomplished by combining from two to five alterations
respectively, using both the A and B phrases of the prototype.
A brief summary of the alteration rules derived from those used
by Welker follows: (a) inversion, melodic reversal which
maintains the distance between tones; (b) syncopation, changing
the rhythm of the melody by inserting rests or changing the
duration of tones; (c) decrease intervals, reduction of the
distance between tones; (d) elaboration, addition of extra

Underlining (to be used sparingly) is used here to introduce key terms.

tones between the prototypical tones; and (e) <u>deletion</u>, removal
of any one measure in the A or B phrase. Examples of these
alterations for high and low structured transformations are
shown in Figures 1 and 2, respectively.

The acquisition list contained two sets of 17
transformations of the prototype--8 first-order
transformations, 6 second-order transformations, and 3
third-order transformations. The recognition list contained
the prototype and three new transformations for each
transformational order from first through fifth, for a total of
16 melodic sequences.

A practice tape which contained three different 10-tone
sequences presented in the key of A was also composed. For all
prepared tapes each tonal sequence was preceded by a hand clap
and followed by 10 seconds of silence. The word "ready"
introduced the practice tape, the acquisition list, and the
recognition list. Each melodic sequence was played at 1.67
beats per second. A 10-second silent period followed each
tonal sequence on the tapes. The stimulus tapes were played on
a Sharp Educator cassette tape recorder (model R.D. 660 AVI) at
a volume that was judged comfortable by each of the subjects.

Procedure

The subjects were randomly assigned to the high or low
structure conditions and one to four subjects were tested at a
time. The practice tape was played for each subject prior to

the listening task. The subjects were told to listen closely
to the 34 transformations of the prototype on the acquisition
list and to mentally rehearse each stimulus in the 10-second
silent period following its presentation. Rehearsal was
described by telling subjects to think about the tonal sequence
they had just heard.

After listening to the acquisition list, the subjects were
given written instructions for the recognition procedure. The
instructions explained that 16 melodies would be presented,
some of which had been heard before, and some of which had
not. The subjects were asked to check "yes" on an answer sheet
if they thought that they had heard the melody before and "no"
if they had not. In addition, the subjects were asked to rate
each decision with a confidence level ranging from 1 (very low
confidence in having heard the melody before) to 5 (very high
confidence). Following the instructions the subjects listened
to the tape containing the prototype and the 15 new
transformations.

Results

Following the approach used by Welker, a subject's score
was a measure combining the recognition response ("yes" or
"no") with the confidence rating associated with the
recognition of the stimulus. These scores created a 10-point
scale where "yes" (i.e., a false recognition of the prototype
or transformation) accompanied by a high confidence rating

*The Results section
begins with an
explanation of
what scores
were analyzed.*

High and Low Musical

16

(i.e., 5) equaled a +5, and "no" (i.e., a correct judgment that the stimulus had not been heard before) accompanied by a high confidence rating (i.e., 5) equaled a -5. On this scale, then, the lowest confidence level for a stimulus is reflected in +1 and -1 scores. Each subject gave one such rating for the prototype and three for each of the five transformations. A mean was then computed of the three ratings for each subject at each of the five levels of transformational distance. Thus, the analyzed data consisted of six scores for each subject--one score for the prototype and one score for each of the transformational distances. The means and standard deviations of these scores for each treatment condition are presented in Table 1.

Insert Table 1 about here

Table 2 presents a summary of the analysis of variance on the scores. No significant main effect was found for type of musical structure, $F(1, 38) = 0.31$, $p > .05$. There was, however, a significant main effect for transformational distance, $F(5, 190) = 41.54$, $p < .05$; but there was no interaction of the variables, $F(5, 190) = 1.12$, $p > .05$.

Insert Table 2 about here

Present descriptive statistics before the results of statistical tests on the data.

The results of the analysis of variance are summarized concisely in textual presentation.

A description of follow-up tests to the analysis of variance is illustrated here.

A Tukey's test was performed on the main effect means for transformational distance. The results of the test are presented in Table 3. Significant differences were found among all levels of transformational distance with tne exception of most immediately adjacent transformations, $\underline{p} <$ .05, with a critical difference value of 1.11 for the mean differences.

Insert Table 3 about here

A strength of association measure, eta squared, indicated 46% of the variance in scores is accounted for by the transformational distance variable.

Discussion

The discussion section begins with a statement of whether the results are, or are not, in agreement with the research hypothesis.

The results fail to support the hypothesis that type of musical structure influences the abstraction of a musical theme and the confidence judgments of its variations. However, the results do support and extend Welker's (1982) findings on subjects' abilities to abstract a melodic theme and to order the variations of that theme in terms of transformational distance. The evidence as a whole certainly suggests that pattern perception in music is a robust phenomenon that occurs whether or not a prototype possesses high musical structure.

In light of these results, it is interesting to consider the nature of the task faced by subjects when attempting to recognize a stimulus. Visual stimuli such as Franks and

High and Low Musical

18

Bransford's (1971) geometric shapes can probably be
comprehended simultaneously in their entirety (i.e., in a
parallel fashion) when viewed by subjects. This is not the
case for musical stimuli, however. Melodies by their very
nature must be comprehended sequentially over time.
Comprehension of melodies, it would seem, must therefore entail
memory for each consecutive tone in its context, subjective
judgments about distances between the tones, and subjective
judgments of the contour which the consecutive tones form.
This would seem to be a formidable task indeed for subjects who
were selected with no regard for musical training from a
college which does not offer a major in music. Yet subjects
demonstrated order in their responses.

Additionally, it is noted that Welker's subjects were
asked to draw a contour representing the average of what they
thought they heard before they were given the recognition
task. This certainly could be construed by subjects as a cue
that they were expected to detect some sort of typical or
average melody in the recognition task. No such cuing occurred
in the present experiment. This provides further evidence that
subjects were abstracting and ordering the stimuli in a
meaningful way without instructions or cues to suggest that
they should do so.

One might conclude from the present results, then, that
subjects ignore the aesthetics and clues offered by musical

Notice that the results are related to previous research.

An explanation is provided for unexpected results.

structure in the abstraction process, and, instead, simply rely upon the patterns provided by the distance between tones. This would be analogous perhaps to the process by which Franks and Bransford's subjects perceived geometric shapes. However, this conclusion may be premature. It should be pointed out that experiments showing greater recognition in highly structured musical situations (e.g., Dewar et al., 1977) were designed so that subjects were presented with a structured sequence followed by a difficult recognition or recall task. The difficulty of the task may have induced a reliance upon structural musical cues. Had subjects been given the opportunity to learn the low structured sequences through repetition, then they might no longer have relied upon these structural cues.

In the present experiment, as well as in the work of Welker, subjects were provided with a great deal of repetition of correct portions of the melodies in the acquisition phase. In light of the Dewar et al. results, where the low structure performance condition benefited most from repetition, it is possible that a condition which provides subjects with fewer repetitions of the pattern would show an effect for type of structure.

High and Low Musical

20

References

Copland, A. (1957). <u>What</u> <u>to</u> <u>listen</u> <u>for</u> <u>in</u> <u>music</u>. New York: McGraw-Hill.

Cuddy, L. L., Cohen, A. J., & Mewhort, D. J. K. (1981). Perception of structure in short melodic sequences. <u>Journal</u> <u>of</u> <u>Experimental</u> <u>Psychology</u>: <u>Human</u> <u>Perception</u> <u>and</u> <u>Performance</u>, <u>7</u>, 869-883.

Deutsch, D. (1980). The processing of structured and unstructured tonal sequences. <u>Perception</u> <u>&</u> <u>Psychophysics</u>, <u>28</u>, 381-389.

Dewar, K. M., Cuddy, L. L., & Mewhort, D. J. K. (1977). Recognition memory for single tones with and without context. <u>Journal</u> <u>of</u> <u>Experimental</u> <u>Psychology</u>: <u>Human</u> <u>Learning</u> <u>and</u> <u>Memory</u>, <u>3</u>, 60-67.

Franks, J. J., & Bransford, J. D. (1971). Abstraction of visual patterns. <u>Journal</u> <u>of</u> <u>Experimental</u> <u>Psychology</u>, <u>90</u>, 65-74.

Jones, T. J. (1974). <u>Music</u> <u>theory</u>. New York: Barnes & Noble.

Klatzky, R. L. (1975). <u>Human</u> <u>memory</u>. San Francisco: Freeman.

Posner, M. I., & Keele, S. W. (1968). On the genesis of abstract ideas. <u>Journal</u> <u>of</u> <u>Experimental</u> <u>Psychology</u>, <u>77</u>, 353-363.

Posner, M. I., Goldsmith, R., & Welton, K. E., Jr. (1967). Perceived distance and the classification of distorted patterns. <u>Journal</u> <u>of</u> <u>Experimental</u> <u>Psychology</u>, <u>73</u>, 28-38.

References begin on a new page.

Reed, S. K. (1972). Pattern recognition and categorization. Cognitive Psychology, 3, 382-407.

Welker, R. L. (1982). Abstraction of themes from melodic variations. Journal of Experimental Psychology: Human Perception and Performance, 8, 435-447.

Author Notes

This paper was submitted in partial fulfillment of the requirements of an experimental psychology course at Framingham State College. Portions of the paper were presented at the Greater Boston Undergraduate Research Paper Conference, Bridgewater State College, April 1984.

Table 1

Mean Recognition Scores for Different Melodic Patterns

Type of Structure P[a]		Transformational Distance				
		1	2	3	4	5
High						
M	3.20	3.00	1.83	1.54	-.57	-1.07
SD	2.04	1.66	1.09	1.58	1.70	2.29
Low						
M	3.10	2.88	2.18	0.28	-.50	-.85
SD	1.74	1.82	1.40	1.95	1.87	1.52

Note. The minimum score was -5 (very confident the sequence was not heard before) and the maximum score was +5 (very confident the sequence was heard before).

[a]prototype.

Table 2

<u>Analysis of Variance of Music Recognition Scores</u>

Source	<u>df</u>	<u>SS</u>	<u>MS</u>	<u>F</u>
Between Subjects				
Structure (A)	1	1.16	1.16	0.31
Error	38	140.02	3.69	
Witnin Subjects				
Distance (B)	5	608.56	121.71	41.54*
A x B	5	16.44	3.29	1.12
Error	190	555.75	2.93	
Total	239	1321.93		

*$\underline{p} < .05$.

Table 3

<u>Results of Tukey's Test on Main Effect Means for Transformational</u>

<u>Distance</u>

Transformational Distance

	P[a]	1	2	3	4	5
	(3.15)	(2.94)	(2.01)	(0.91)	(−0.54)	(−0.96)
P[a] (3.15)	---	.21	1.14*	2.24*	3.69*	4.11*
1 (2.94)		---	.93	2.03*	3.48*	3.90*
2 (2.01)			---	1.10	2.55*	2.97*
3 (0.91)				---	1.45*	1.87*
4 (−.54)					---	.42
5 (−.96)						---

<u>Note</u>. The main effect means are presented in parentheses. The minimum difference between means required to meet significance at the .05 level is 1.11.

[a]Prototype.

*$p < .05$.

Figure Captions

<u>Figure 1</u>. Prototype for high musical structure and examples of first-, second-, and third-order transformations.

<u>Figure 2</u>. Prototype for low musical structure and examples of first-, second-, and third-order transformations.

The figure captions are typed on a separate page.

Write the figure number, short title, and the word TOP lightly in pencil on the top back of the figure.

High and Low Musical

29

Appendix A

Informed Consent Form

Research conducted by Barbara A. Nesman, Framingham State College, in partial fulfillment of the requirements of course 42.450 Experimental Psychology.

In agreeing to participate in this research I understand the following:

. The experiment will involve listening to a series of short melodies followed by a second series of melodies. On the second series I will indicate whether I have heard the melody before and how confident I am of my judgment.

. The entire experiment will take about 40 minutes.

High and Low Musical

30

- All data from the experiment will remain anonymous. The data from all subjects shall be compiled, analyzed, and submitted in a laboratory report to the course instructor. No participant's data shall be identified by name at any stage of the data analysis or in the laboratory report.

- At the conclusion of the experiment I will be given information concerning my performance and any questions that I may have will be clearly and fully answered.

- I may withdraw from this experiment at any time.

- There are no special benefits to me for participating in this experiment, and it will not affect my status at Framingham State College.

Name (Please print) _____

Signed _____

Date _____

High and Low Musical

31

Appendix B

Instructions for the Recognition List

You will now hear sixteen melodies, some of which you have
heard before, and some of which you have not. Check "Yes" next
to the correct number if you think you have heard it before, and
"No" if you think you did not. Also, please rate your
confidence in your decision on a scale of 1 to 5, 5 meaning very
high confidence, and 1 meaning very low confidence.

High and Low Musical

32

Appendix C

Subject Recognition Score Means as a Function of

Transformational Distance

High Structure

Transformational Distance

Subject	P[a]	1	2	3	4	5
1	4.00	3.33	2.67	-0.33	-0.33	-3.33
2	2.00	0.33	0.67	1.67	1.67	-1.00
3	3.00	3.67	3.67	2.00	1.67	1.67
4	-1.00	3.33	2.00	-0.33	-1.00	1.33
5	5.00	4.00	4.00	2.67	-2.00	-1.67
6	3.00	0.33	1.67	0.67	-2.67	-2.67
7	4.00	5.00	2.00	1.67	-1.67	-1.33
8	5.00	4.67	2.00	0.33	-1.33	-4.33
9	-1.00	2.67	2.00	4.00	1.67	-1.00
10	4.00	1.33	1.67	-0.67	-3.67	-2.00
11	3.00	0.67	1.33	0.33	-1.33	-3.33
12	5.00	5.00	2.33	4.33	-2.00	-5.00
13	5.00	5.00	2.00	4.33	2.33	3.67
14	4.00	4.33	2.00	1.00	-1.00	-3.33
15	5.00	4.00	2.33	3.67	-3.00	1.67
16	4.00	1.00	-0.33	-0.33	1.00	-0.33
17	-1.00	4.00	1.67	1.67	1.33	-0.33

(table continues)

High Structure

Transformational Distance

Subject	P[a]	1	2	3	4	5
18	4.00	1.00	-0.67	1.33	0.67	2.00
19	5.00	4.00	2.33	1.67	-0.33	-0.33
20	2.00	2.33	1.33	1.00	-0.33	1.67

Low Structure

Transformational Distance

Subject	P[a]	1	2	3	4	5
21	3.00	0.33	1.00	0.67	0.00	0.00
22	3.00	2.00	1.00	0.33	1.67	-2.33
23	2.00	4.00	4.00	0.33	-3.00	1.67
24	4.00	5.00	1.33	-0.33	-0.67	-2.00
25	4.00	1.33	1.00	3.00	2.33	-3.00
26	5.00	4.67	4.00	3.00	-1.00	-3.67
27	3.00	4.33	4.33	-0.33	-3.33	-0.33
28	-2.00	4.00	3.33	1.33	-2.67	0.67
29	5.00	2.00	2.33	1.33	1.67	1.33
30	5.00	5.00	4.33	1.33	-2.00	-1.33
31	5.00	4.00	3.67	-3.33	-1.67	-3.00
32	4.00	3.67	1.00	-1.00	-2.67	0.67
33	3.00	-0.33	1.00	0.67	-1.33	0.33
34	5.00	2.33	3.67	1.00	2.33	0.33

(table continues)

Low Structure

Transformational Distance

Subject	P[a]	1	2	3	4	5
35	3.00	4.67	1.33	1.00	1.33	0.33
36	1.00	2.00	1.00	2.67	-2.00	-1.00
37	2.00	2.67	2.33	-3.33	1.00	-1.00
38	1.00	-1.33	1.33	0.67	0.00	-1.33
39	3.00	3.33	1.67	0.67	-1.33	-2.00
40	3.00	4.00	0.00	-4.00	1.33	-1.33

References

Adams, J. S. (1963). Toward an understanding of inequity. *Journal of Abnormal and Social Psychology, 67,* 422–436.

American Psychological Association. (1973). *Ethical principles in the conduct of research with human participants.* Washington, DC: Author.

American Psychological Association. (1982). *Ethical principles in the conduct of research with human participants.* Washington, DC: Author.

American Psychological Association. (1983). *Publication manual of the American Psychological Association* (3rd ed.). Washington, DC: Author.

Aronson, E., & Carlsmith. J. M. (1968). Experimentation in social psychology. In G. Lindzey & E. Aronson (Eds.), *The handbook of social psychology* (2nd ed.) (Vol. 2) (pp. 1–79). Reading, MA: Addison-Wesley.

Austin, W., & Walster, E. (1974). Reactions to confirmations and disconfirmations of expectancies of equity and inequity. *Journal of Personality and Social Psychology, 30,* 208–216.

Bachrach, A. J. (1981). *Psychological research: An introduction* (4th ed.). New York: Random House.

Bakan, D. (1953). Learning and the principle of inverse probability. *Psychological Review, 60,* 360–370.

Barak, A., & LaCrosse, M. B. (1975). Multidimensional perception of counselor behavior. *Journal of Counseling Psychology, 22,* 471–476.

Barber, T. X. (1976). *Pitfalls in human research: Ten pivotal points.* New York: Pergamon Press.

Bauernfeind, R. H. (1968). The need for replication in educational research. *Phi Delta Kappan, 50,* 126–128.

Beach, F. A. (1950). The snark was a boojum. *American Psychologist, 5,* 115–124.

Beale, D. K. (1972). What's so significant about .05? *American Psychologist, 27,* 1079–1080.

Berkowitz, L., & Donnerstein, E. (1982). External validity is more than skin deep. *American Psychologist, 37,* 245–257.

Black, J. A., & Champion, D. J. (1976). *Methods and issues in social research.* New York: Wiley.

Bolgar, H. (1965). The case study method. In B. B. Wolman (Ed.), *Handbook of clinical psychology* (pp. 28–39). New York: McGraw-Hill.

Bolles, R. C. (1962). The difference between statistical hypotheses and scientific hypotheses. *Psychological Reports, 11,* 639–645.

Boneau, C. A. (1961). A note on measurement scales and statistical tests. *American Psychologist, 16,* 260–261.

Boring, E. G. (1957). *A history of experimental psychology* (2nd ed.). New York: Appleton-Century-Crofts.

Bouchard, T. J., Jr. (1976). Field research methods: Interviewing, questionnaires, participant observation, systematic observation, unobtrusive measures. In M. D. Dunnette (Ed.), *Handbook of industrial and organizational psychology* (pp. 363–413). Chicago: Rand McNally.

Bowman, J. T., Roberts, G. T., & Giesen, J. M. (1978). Counselor trainee anxiety during the initial counseling interview. *Journal of Counseling Psychology, 25,* 137–143.

Bracht, G. H., & Glass, G. V. (1968). The external validity of experiments. *American Educational Research Journal, 5,* 437–474.

Bradley, J. V. (1980). Nonrobustness in classical tests on means and variances: A large-scale sampling study. *Bulletin of the Psychonomic Society, 15,* 275–278.

Bradley, J. V. (1984). The complexity of nonrobustness effects. *Bulletin of the Psychonomic Society, 22,* 250–253.

Brandt, R. M. (1972). *Studying behavior in natural settings.* New York: Holt, Rinehart and Winston.

Bronowski, J. (1973). *The ascent of man.* Boston: Little, Brown.

Brown, B. W., Jr. (1972). Statistics, scientific method, and smoking. In J. M. Tanur (Ed.), *Statistics: A guide to the unknown* (pp. 40–51). San Francisco: Holden Day.

Bruning, J. L., & Kintz, B. L. (1977). *Computational handbook of statistics* (2nd ed.). Glenview, IL: Scott Foresman.

Calder, B. J., Phillips, L. W., & Tybout, A. M. (1981). Designing research for application. *The Journal of Consumer Research, 8,* 197–207.

Campbell, D. E. (1982). Lunar-lunacy research: When enough is enough. *Environment and Behavior, 14,* 418–424.

Campbell, D. T. (1969). Prospective: Artifact and control. In R. Rosenthal & R. L. Rosnow (Eds.), *Artifact in behavioral research* (pp. 351–382). New York: Academic Press.

Campbell, D. T. (1975). "Degrees of freedom" and the case study. *Comparative Political Studies, 8,* 178–193.

Campbell, D. T., & Stanley, J. C. (1963). *Experimental and quasi-experimental designs for research.* Chicago: Rand McNally.

Carlson, R. (1971). Where is the person in personality research? *Psychological Bulletin, 75,* 203–219.

Carver, R. P. (1978). The case against statistical significance testing. *Harvard Educational Review, 48,* 378–399.

Champion, D. J. (1968). "Some observations on measurement and statistics": Comment. *Social Forces, 46,* 541.

Cicchetti, D. V. (1972). Extension of multiple-range tests to interaction tables in the analysis of variance: A rapid approximate solution. *Psychological Bulletin, 77,* 405–408.

Cohen, J. (1977). *Statistical power analysis for the behavioral sciences* (Rev. ed.). New York: Academic Press.

Collias, N. E. (1950). Some variations in grouping and dominance patterns among birds and mammals. *Zoologica, 35,* 97–119.

Cook, S. (1981). Ethical implications. In L. H. Kidder, *Selltiz, Wrightsman, and Cook's Research Methods in Social Relations* (4th ed.) (pp. 364–417). New York: Holt, Rinehart and Winston.

Cook, T. D., & Campbell, D. T. (1976). The design and conduct of quasi-experiments and true experiments. In M. Dunnette (Ed.). *Handbook of industrial and organizational psychology.* Skokie, IL: Rand McNally.

Cook, T. D., & Campbell, D. T. (1979). *Quasi-experimentation.* Chicago: Rand McNally.

Cosmides, L. (1983). Invariance in the acoustic expression of emotion during speech. *Journal of Experimental Psychology: Human Performance and Perception, 9,* 864–881.

Cowles, M. P. (1974). N = 35: A rule of thumb for psychological researchers. *Perceptual and Motor Skills, 38,* 1135–1138.

Cronbach, L. J. (1957). The two disciplines of scientific psychology. *American Psychologist, 12,* 671–684.

Cronbach, L. J. (1975). Beyond the two disciplines of scientific psychology. *American Psychologist, 30,* 116–127.

Cronbach, L. J., & Meehl, P. E. (1955). Construct validity in psychological tests. *Psychological Bulletin, 52,* 281–302.

Dan, A. J., & Beekman, S. (1972). Male versus female representation in psychological research. *American Psychologist, 27,* 1078.

Decker, W. H., & Wheatley, P. C. (1982). Spatial grouping, imagery, and free recall. *Perceptual and Motor Skills, 55,* 45–46.

Deese, J. (1972). *Psychology as science and art.* New York: Harcourt Brace Jovanovich.

DeForest, C., & Stone, G. L. (1980). Effects of sex and intimacy level on self-disclosure. *Journal of Counseling Psychology, 27,* 93–96.

Dethier, V. G. (1962). *To know a fly.* San Francisco: Holden Day.

Dipboye, R. L., & Flanagan, M. F. (1979). Research settings in industrial and organizational psychology. *American Psychologist, 34,* 141–150.

Dixon, R. A. (1980). A note on the analysis of causation in psychological research: The influence of theory. *The Psychological Record, 30,* 271–276.

Dodd, D. H., & Schultz, R. F., Jr. (1973). Computational procedures for estimating magnitude of effect for some analysis of variance designs. *Psychological Bulletin, 79,* 391–395.

Dorfman, D. D. (1978). The Cyril Burt question: New findings. *Science, 201,* 1177–1186.

Douglas, W., & Gibbins, K. (1983). Inadequacy of voice recognition as a demonstration of self-deception. *Journal of Personality and Social Psychology, 44,* 589–592.

Dowd, E. T., & Boroto, D. R. (1982). Differential effects of counselor self-disclosure, self-involving statements, and interpretation. *Journal of Counseling Psychology, 29,* 8–13.

Dudycha, A. L., & Dudycha, L. W. (1972). Behavioral statistics: An historical perspective. In R. E. Kirk (Ed.), *Statistical issues* (pp. 2–25). Monterey, CA: Brooks/Cole.

Edelberg, R. E. (1972). Electrical activity of the skin: Its measurement and uses in psychophysiology. In N. S. Greenfield & R. A. Sternback (Eds.), *Handbook of psychophysiology* (pp. 367–418). New York: Holt, Rinehart and Winston.

Ellsworth, P. C. (1977). From abstract ideas to concrete instances. *American Psychologist, 32,* 604–615.

Engen, T. (1971). Psychophysics: II. Scaling methods. In J. W. Kling & L. A. Riggs (Eds.), *Woodworth & Schlosberg's Experimental Psychology* (3rd ed.) (pp. 47–86). New York: Holt, Rinehart and Winston.

Erlebacher, A. (1977). Design and analysis of experiments contrasting the within- and between-subjects manipulation of the independent variable. *Psychological Bulletin, 84,* 212–219.

Erwin, J. (1982). Who do comparative psychologists think they are? *Comparative Psychology Newsletter, 2*(1), 8–12.

Etaugh, C. (1980). Effects of nonmaternal care on children. *American Psychologist, 35,* 309–319.

Eysenck, M. W. (1976). Arousal, learning, and memory. *Psychological Bulletin, 83,* 389–404.

Fagot, B. I., & Patterson, G. R. (1969). An in vivo analysis of reinforcing contingencies for sex-role behaviors in the preschool child. *Developmental Psychology, 1,* 563–568.

Fantuzzo, J. W., & Smith, C. S. (1983). Programmed generalization of dress efficiency across settings for a severely disturbed, autistic child. *Psychological Reports, 53,* 871–879.

Farrant, R. H. (1977). Can after-the-fact designs test functional hypotheses, and are they needed in psychology? *Canadian Psychological Review, 18,* 359–364.

Fisher, K. (1982). The spreading stain of fraud. *APA Monitor, 13* (November), pp. 1, 7, 8.

Fisher, R. A. (1971). *The design of experiments* (8th ed.). New York: Hafner.

Forte, F. L., Mandato, D., & Kayson, W. A. (1981). Effect of sex of subject on recall of gender-stereotyped magazine advertisements. *Psychological Reports, 49,* 619–622.

Freese, L., & Rokeach, M. (1979). On the use of alternative interpretations in contemporary social psychology. *Social Psychology Quarterly, 42,* 195–201.

Frigon, J. Y. (1977). Autokinetic word technique and personality. *Perceptual and Motor Skills, 45,* 911–915.

Gagliardi, G. J., Gallup, G. G., Jr., & Boren, J. L. (1976). Effect of different pupil to eye size ratios on tonic immobility in chickens. *Bulletin of the Psychonomic Society, 8,* 58–60.

Gaito, J. (1958). Statistical dangers involved in counterbalancing. *Psychological Reports, 4,* 463–468.

Gaito, J. (1961). Repeated measurements designs and counterbalancing. *Psychological Bulletin 58,* 46–54.

Gaito, J. (1973). Repeated measurements designs and tests of null hypotheses. *Educational and Psychological Measurement, 33,* 69–75.

Gaito, J. (1977). Directional and nondirectional alternative hypotheses. *Bulletin of the Psychonomic Society, 9,* 371–372.

Gaito, J., & Nobrega, J. N. (1981). A note on multiple comparisons as an ANOVA problem. *Bulletin of the Psychonomic Society, 17,* 169–170.

Gallup, G. G., Jr. (1974). Animal hypnosis: Factual status of a fictional concept. *Psychological Bulletin, 81,* 836–853.

Gallup, G. G., Jr., Nash, R. F., & Ellison, A. L., Jr. (1971). Tonic immobility as a reaction to predation: Artifical eyes as a fear stimulus for chickens. *Psychonomic Science, 23,* 79–80.

Gardner, P. L. (1975). Scales and statistics. *Review of Educaitonal Research, 45,* 43–57.

Garner, W. R., Hake, H. W., & Eriksen, C. W. (1956). Operationism and the concept of perception. *Psychological Review, 63,* 149–159.

Gatchel, R. J. (1977). Therapeutic effectiveness of voluntary heart rate control in reducing anxiety. *Journal of Consulting and Clinical Psychology, 45,* 689–691.

Gentile, J. R., Roden, A. H., & Klein, R. D. (1972). An analysis-of-variance model for the intrasubject replication design. *Journal of Applied Behavior Analysis, 5,* 193–198.

Gillis, J. S. (1976). Participants instead of subjects. *American Psychologist, 31,* 95–97.

Glass, G. V., & Stanley, J. C. (1970). *Statistical methods in education and psychology.* Englewood Cliffs, NJ: Prentice-Hall.

Grady, K. E. (1981). Sex bias in research design. *Psychology of Women Quarterly, 5,* 628–636.

Greenwald, A. G. (1975). Consequences of prejudice against the null hypothesis. *Psychological Bulletin, 82,* 1–20.

Greenwald, A. G. (1976). Within-subjects designs: To use or not to use? *Psychological Bulletin, 83,* 314–320.

Greenwald, A. G. & Ronis, D. L. (1981). On the conceptual disconfirmation of theories. *Personality and Social Psychology Bulletin, 7,* 131–137.

Grice, G. R., & Hunter, J. J. (1964). Stimulus intensity effects depend upon the type of experimental design. *Psychological Review, 71,* 247–256.

Guhl, A. M. (1953). Social behavior of the domestic fowl. *Technical Bulletin of the Kansas Agricultural Experimental Station, 73.*

Guilford, J. P. (1954). *Psychometric methods.* New York: McGraw-Hill.

Gur, R. C., & Sackeim, H. A. (1979). Self-deception: A concept in search of a phenomenon. *Journal of Personality and Social Psychology, 37,* 147–169.

Haase, R. F., Waechter, D. M., & Solomon, G. S. (1982). How significant is a significant difference? Average effect size of research in counseling psychology. *Journal of Counseling Psychology, 29,* 58–65.

Hall, J. F. (1982). List organization and recognition memory. *Bulletin of the Psychonomic Society, 20,* 35–36.

Halpin, B. (1978). Effects of arousal level on olfactory sensitivity. *Perceptual and Motor Skills, 46,* 1095–1102.

Hanson, N. R. (1958). *Patterns of Discovery.* Cambridge: Cambridge University Press.

Hart, G. (1973). A programmed approach to increased counselor open-mindedness. *Journal of Counseling Psychology, 20,* 569–570.

Hartnett, J., Rosen, F., & Shumate, M. (1981). Attribution of age-discrepant couples. *Perceptual and Motor Skills, 52,* 355–358.

Hays, W. L. (1973). *Statistics for the social sciences* (2nd ed.). New York: Holt, Rinehart and Winston.

Henry, D. L., & Jacobs, K. W. (1978). Color eroticism and color preference. *Perceptual and Motor Skills, 47,* 106.

Henshel, R. L. (1980). The purposes of laboratory experimentation and the virtues of deliberate artificiality. *Journal of Experimental Social Psychology, 16,* 466–478.

Hersen, M., & Barlow, D. H. (1976). *Single case experimental designs.* New York: Pergamon Press.

Higbee, K. L., Millard, R. J., & Folkman, J. R. (1982). Social psychology research during the 1970s: Predominance of experimentation and college students. *Personality and Social Psychology Bulletin, 8,* 180–183.

Hite, S. (1981). *The Hite report on male sexuality.* New York: Knopf.

Holen, M. C., & Kinsey, W. M. (1975). Preferences for three theoretically derived counseling approaches. *Journal of Counseling Psychology, 22,* 21–23.

Holmes, C. B. (1979). Sample size in psychological research. *Perceptual and Motor Skills, 49,* 283–288.

Hopkins, C. D. (1976). *Educational research: A structure for inquiry.* Columbus, OH: Merrill.

Huck, S. W., & Sandler, H. M. (1979). *Rival hypotheses.* New York: Harper & Row.

Isaac, S., & Michael, W. B. (1971). *Handbook in research and evaluation.* San Diego, CA: Edits.

Jahn, R. G. (1982). The persistent paradox of psychic phenomena: An engineering perspective. *Proceedings of the IEEE, 70,* 136–170.

Janssen, J. P. (1979). Students: The typical subjects of psychological experiments—thoughts on a research practice. *Psychologische Rundschau, 30,* 99–109. (From *Psychological Abstracts,* 1981, *65,* Abstract No. 9130.)

Jensen, A. R. (1974). Cumulative deficit: A testable hypothesis? *Developmental Psychology, 10,* 996–1019.

Jones, L. V. (1952). Test of hypotheses: One-sided vs two-sided alternatives. *Psychological Bulletin, 49,* 43–46.

Jung, J. (1982). *The experimenter's challenge.* New York: Macmillan.

Kagan, J. (1976). Emergent themes in human development. *American Scientist, 64,* 186–196.

Kaplan, A. (1964). *The conduct of inquiry.* San Francisco: Chandler.

Kazdin, A. E. (1981). External validity and single-case experimentation: Issues and limitations (A response to J. S. Birnbrauer). *Analysis and Intervention in Developmental Disabilities, 1,* 133–143.

Keppel, G. (1982). *Design and analysis: A researcher's handbook* (2nd ed.). Englewood Cliffs, NJ: Prentice-Hall.

Keppel, G., & Saufley, W. H., Jr. (1980). *Introduction to design and analysis.* San Francisco: Freeman.

Kerlinger, F. N. (1969). Research in education. In R. Ebel, V. Noll, & R. Bauer (Eds.). *Encyclopedia of educational research* (4th ed.) (pp. 1127–1144). New York: Macmillan.

Kerlinger, F. N. (1973). *Foundations of behavioral research* (2nd ed.). New York: Holt, Rinehart and Winston.

Kerlinger, F. N. (1979). *Behavioral research: A conceptual approach.* New York: Holt, Rinehart and Winston.

Kerlinger, F. N., & Pedhazur, E. J. (1973). *Multiple regression in behavioral research.* New York: Holt, Rinehart and Winston.

Kimmel, H. D. (1957). Three criteria for the use of one-tailed tests. *Psychological Bulletin, 54,* 351–353.

Kling, J. W., & Riggs, L. A. (1971). *Woodworth & Schlosberg's experimental psychology* (3rd ed.). New York: Holt, Rinehart and Winston.

Knapp, T. R. (1982). A case against the single-sample repeated measures experiment. *Educational Psychologist, 17,* 61–65.

Kruglanski, A. W. (1973). Much ado about the "volunteer artifacts." *Journal of Personality and Social Psychology, 28,* 348–354.

Kruglanski, A. W. (1976). Outcome validity in experimental research: A re-conceptualization. *Representative Research in Social Psychology, 7,* 166–178.

Krumboltz, J. D., Becker-Haven, J. F., & Burnett, K. F. (1979). Counseling psychology. *Annual Review of Psychology, 30,* 555–602.

Kruskal, W. H. (1968). Tests of significance. In D. L. Sills (Ed.), *International encyclopedia of the social sciences* (Vol. 14) (pp. 238–250). New York: Macmillan and Free Press.

Kuhn, T. S. (1970). *The structure of scientific revolutions* (2nd ed.). Chicago: University of Chicago Press.

Kulick, J. A. (1973). *Undergraduate education in psychology.* Washington, DC: American Psychological Association.

Kurtz, P. (1978, Winter). Is parapsychology a science? *The Skeptical Inquirer, 3*(2), 14–32.

Labovitz, S. (1967). Some observations on measurement and statistics. *Social Forces, 46,* 151–160.

LaCrosse, M. B. (1980). Perceived counselor social influence and counseling outcomes: Validity of the Counselor Rating Form. *Journal of Counseling Psychology, 27,* 320–327.

Layton, B. D., & Turnbull, B. (1975). Belief, evaluation, and performance on an ESP task. *Journal of Experimental Social Psychology, 11,* 166–179.

LeTourneau, J. E. (1976). Effects of training in design on magnitude of the Müller-Lyer illusion. *Perceptual and Motor Skills, 42,* 119–124.

Levitt, E. E. (1967). *The psychology of anxiety.* London: Staples.

Lindman, H. R. (1981). An improved text in behavioral research. *Contemporary Psychology, 26,* 853–854.

Linton, M., & Gallo, P. S., Jr. (1975). *The practical statistician: Simplified handbook of statistics.* Monterey, CA: Brooks/Cole.

Lockard, R. B. (1968). The albino rat: A defensible choice or a bad habit? *American Psychologist, 23,* 734–742.

Loftus, E. F. (1979). *Eyewitness testimony.* Cambridge, MA: Harvard University Press.

Lykken, D. T. (1968). Statistical significance in psychological research, *Psychological Bulletin, 70,* 151–159.

Lynch, J. G., Jr. (1982). On the external validity of experiments in consumer research. *Journal of Consumer Research, 9,* 225–239.

McAskie, M. (1978). Carelessness or fraud in Sir Cyril Burt's kinship data? *American Psychologist, 33,* 496–498.

McCain, G., & Segal, E. M. (1973). *The game of science* (2nd ed.). Monterey, CA: Brooks/Cole.

McCall, R. B. (1977). Challenges to a science of developmental psychology. *Child Development, 48,* 333–344.

McCall, R. B. (1980). *Fundamental statistics for psychology* (3rd ed.). New York: Harcourt Brace Jovanovich.

McCarthy, P. R. (1979). Differential effects of self-disclosing versus self-involving counselor statements across counselor-client gender pairings. *Journal of Counseling Psychology, 26,* 538–541.

McCarthy, P. R. (1982). Differential effects of counselor self-referent responses and counselor status. *Journal of Counseling Psychology, 29,* 125–131.

McCarthy, P. R., & Betz, N. E. (1978). Differential effects of self-disclosing versus self-involving counselor statements. *Journal of Counseling Psychology, 25,* 251–256.

McCarthy, P. R., & Schmeck, R. R. (1982). Effects of teacher self-disclosure on student learning and perceptions of teacher. *College Student Journal, 16,* 45–49.

McCloskey, M., Washburn, A., & Felch, L. (1983). Intuitive physics: The straight-down belief and its origin. *Journal of Experimental Psychology: Learning, Memory and Cognition, 9,* 636–649.

McDonald, P. J., & Eilenfield, V. C. (1980). Physical attractiveness and the approach/avoidance of self-awareness. *Personality and Social Psychology Bulletin, 6,* 391–395.

McGuigan, F. J. (1978). *Experimental psychology* (3rd ed.). Englewood Cliffs, NJ: Prentice-Hall.

McGuire, W. J. (1973). The yin and yang of progress in social psychology: Seven koan. *Journal of Personality and Social Psychology, 26,* 446–456.

McKenna, W. & Kessler, S. J. (1977). Experimental design as a source of sex bias in social psychology. *Sex Roles, 3,* 117–128.

Mahoney, M. J. (1978). Experimental methods and outcome evaluation. *Journal of Consulting and Clinical Psychology, 46,* 660–672.

Marascuilo, L. A., & McSweeney, M. (1977). *Nonparametric and distribution-free methods for the social sciences.* Monterey, CA: Brooks/Cole.

Marks, L. E. (1982). Bright sneezes and dark coughs, loud sunlight and soft moonlight. *Journal of Experimental Psychology: Human Perception and Performance, 8,* 177–193.

Marx, M. H. (1976a). Formal theory. In M. H. Marx & F. E. Goodson (Eds.). *Theories in contemporary psychology* (2nd ed.) (pp. 234–260). New York: Macmillan.

Marx, M. H. (1976b). Theorizing. In M. H. Marx & F. E. Goodson (Eds.). *Theories in contemporary psychology* (2nd ed.) (pp. 261–286). New York: Macmillan.

Marx, M. H., & Hillix, W. A. (1973). *Systems and theories in psychology* (2nd ed.). New York: McGraw-Hill.

Maxwell, S. E., Camp, C. J., & Arvey, R. D. (1981). Measures of strength of assocation: A comparative examination. *Journal of Applied Psychology, 66,* 525–534.

Meehl, P. E. (1970a). Nuisance variables and the ex post facto design. In H. Feigl & G. Maxwell (Eds.), *Minnesota studies in the philosophy of science. Vol. IV: Analysis of theories and methods of physics and psychology* (pp. 373–402). Minneapolis: University of Minnesota.

Meehl, P. E. (1970b). Some methodological reflections on the difficulties of psychoanalytic research. In H. Feigl & G. Maxwell (Eds.), *Minnesota studies in the philosophy of science. Vol. IV: Analysis of theories and methods of physics and psychology* (pp. 403–416). Minneapolis: University of Minnesota.

Meites, K., Pishkin, V., & Bourne, L. E., Jr. (1981). Anxiety and failure in concept identification. *Bulletin of the Psychonomic Society, 18,* 293–295.

Michael, J. (1974a). Statistical inference for individual organism research: Some reactions to a suggestion by Gentile, Roden, and Klein. *Journal of Applied Behavior Analysis, 7,* 627–628.

Michael, J. (1974b). Statistical inference for individual organism research: Mixed blessing or curse? *Journal of Applied Behavior Analysis, 7,* 647–653.

Miller, A. (1981). A survey of introductory psychology subject pool practices among leading universities. *Teaching of Psychology, 8,* 211–213.

Miller, D. (1977). Roles of naturalistic observation in comparative psychology. *American Psychologist, 32,* 211–219.

Mills, J., & Aronson, E. (1965). Opinion change as a function of the communicator's attractiveness and desire to influence. *Journal of Personality and Social Psychology, 1,* 173–177.

Mischel, W. (1976). *Introduction to personality* (2nd ed.). New York: Holt, Rinehart and Winston.

Moskowitz, H. R. (1971). Intensity scales for pure tastes and for taste mixtures. *Perception and Psychophysics, 9,* 51–56.

Mosteller, F., & Tukey, J. W. (1977). *Data analysis and regression.* Reading, MA: Addison-Wesley.

Murphy, G. (1963). Robert Sessions Woodworth. 1869–1962. *American Psychologist, 18,* 131–133.

Nagel, E. (1961). *The structure of science. Problems in the logic of scientific explanation.* New York: Harcourt, Brace and World.

Neale, J. M., & Liebert, R. M. (1980). *Science and behavior* (2nd ed.). Englewood Cliffs, NJ: Prentice-Hall.

Nisbett, R. E. (1978). A guide for reviewers: Editorial hardball in the '70s. *American Psychologist, 33,* 519–520.

O'Brien, E. J., & Wolford, C. R. (1982). Effect of delay in testing on retention of plausible versus bizarre mental images. *Journal of Experimental Psychology: Learning, Memory, and Cognition, 8,* 148–152.

O'Brien, T. J., & Dunlap. W. P. (1975). Tonic immobility in the blue crab (*Callinectes sapidus,* Rathbun): Its relation to threat of predation. *Journal of Comparative and Physiological Psychology, 89,* 86–94.

Orne, M. T. (1962). On the social psychology of the psychological experiment: With particular reference to demand characteristics and their implications. *American Psychologist, 17,* 776–783.

Osis, K., Turner, M. E., Jr., & Carlson, M. L. (1971). ESP over distance: Research on the ESP channel. *The Journal of the American Society for Psychical Research, 65,* 245–288.

Ostrom, T. M. (1971). To replicate or explicate. *American Psychologist, 26,* 312.

Palmer, M. H., Lloyd, M. E., & Lloyd, K. E. (1977). An experimental analysis of electricity conservation procedures. *Journal of Applied Behavior Analysis, 10,* 665–671.

Petrinovich, L. (1979). Probabilistic functionalism: A conception of research method. *American Psychologist, 34,* 373–390.

Piaget, J. (1952). *The child's conception of number* (C. Gattegno & F. M. Hodgson, Trans.). London: Routledge & Kegan Paul.

Piaget, J. (1970). *The child's conception of time* (A. J. Pomerans, Trans.). New York: Basic Books.

Pick, H. L., Jr., Leibowitz, H. W., Singer, J. E., Steinschneider, A., & Stevenson, H. W. (1978). *Psychology: From resarch to practice.* New York: Plenum Press.

Popper, K. R. (1959). *The logic of scientific discovery.* New York: Basic Books.

Popper, K. R. (1963). Science: Problems, aims, responsibilities. *Federation Proceedings, 22,* 961–972.

Popper, K. R. (1970). Normal science and its dangers. In I. Lakatos & A. Musgrave (Eds.). *Criticism and the growth of knowledge* (pp. 51–58). Cambridge: Cambridge University Press.

Porter, J. H., Johnson, S. B., & Granger, R. G. (1981). The snark is still a boojum. *Comparative Psychology Newsletter, 1*(5), 1–3.

Poulton, E. C. (1973). Unwanted range effects from using within-subjects experimental designs. *Psychological Bulletin, 80,* 113–121.

Poulton, E. C. (1975). Range effects in experiments on people. *American Journal of Psychology, 88,* 3–32.

Pratt, J. G., & Keil, H. H. J. (1973). Firsthand observations of Nina S. Kulagina suggestive of PK upon static objects. *The Journal of the American Society for Psychical Research, 67,* 381–390.

Pratt, J. G. & Stevenson, I. (1976). An instance of possible metal-bending indirectly related to Uri Geller. *The Journal of the American Society for Psychical Research, 70,* 79–93.

Rakover, S. S. (1981). Social psychological theory and falsification. *Personality and Social Psychology Bulletin, 7,* 123–130.

Ransom, C. (1971). Recent criticisms of parapsychology: A review. *The Journal of the American Society for Psychical Research, 65,* 289–307.

Ratner, S. C., Karon, B. P., VandenBos, G. R., & Denny, M. R. (1981). The adaptive significance of the catatonic stupor in humans and animals from an evolutionary perspective. *Academic Psychology Bulletin, 3,* 273–279.

Reeves, R. A., Edmonds, E. M., & Transou, D. L. (1978). Effects of color and trait anxiety on state anxiety. *Perceptual and Motor Skills, 46,* 855–858.

Reisberg, D. (1983). General mental resources and perceptual judgments. *Journal of Experimental Psychology: Human Performance and Perception, 9,* 966–979.

Resch, R. C. (1981). Natural observational studies: Methodology and video-recording in spontaneous behavior settings. *Infant Mental Health Journal, 2,* 176–187.

Revelle, W., Humphreys, M. S., Simon, L., & Gilliland, K. (1980). The interactive effect of personality, time of day, and caffeine: A test of the arousal model. *Journal of Experimental Psychology: General, 109,* 1–31.

Roberts, C. C., Hoffman, M. A., & Johnson, W. L. (1978). Effects of jury deliberation on the verdicts and social perceptions of simulated jurors: Vidmar revisited. *Perceptual and Motor Skills, 47,* 119–124.

Robinson, P. W. & Foster, D. F. (1979). *Experimental psychology: A small-N approach.* New York: Harper & Row.

Roll, W. G., & Klein, J. (1972). Further forced-choice ESP experiments with Lalsingh Harribance. *The Journal of the American Society for Psychical Research, 66,* 103–112.

Rosenberg, M. J. (1969). The conditions and consequences of evaluation apprehension. In R. Rosenthal & R. L. Rosnow (Eds.), *Artifact in behavioral research* (pp. 280–349). New York: Academic Press.

Rosenthal, R. (1966). *Experimenter effects in behavioral research.* New York: Appleton-Century-Crofts.

Rosenthal, R., & Rosnow, R. L. (1969). The volunteer subject. In R. Rosenthal & R. L. Rosnow (Eds.), *Artifact in behavioral research* (pp. 59–118). New York: Academic Press.

Rosenthal, R., & Rosnow, R. L. (1975). *The volunteer subject.* New York: Wiley.

Rucci, A. J., & Tweney, R. D. (1980). Analysis of variance and the "second discipline" of scientific psychology: A historical account. *Psychological Bulletin, 87,* 166–184.

Rundquist, W. N., Pullyblank, J. C., & Whyte, D. (1982). Differential encoding of nominally similar cues and interference in recall. *Journal of Experimental Psychology: Learning, Memory, and Cognition, 8,* 225–236.

Runyan, W. M. (1982). In defense of the case study method. *American Journal of Orthopsychiatry, 52,* 440–446.

Runyon, P. R., & Haber, A. (1980). *Fundamentals of behavioral statistics* (4th ed.). Reading, MA: Addison-Wesley.

Rutman, L. (1977). Formative research and program evaluability. In L. Rutman (Ed.), *Evaluation research methods: A basic guide* (pp. 59–71). Beverly Hills, CA: Sage.

Saklofske, D. H., Kelly, I. W., & McKerracher, D. W. (1982). An empirical study of personality and astrological factors. *The Journal of Psychology, 110,* 275–280.

Sarason, I. G. (1972). Experimental approaches to test anxiety: Attention and the uses of information. In C. D. Spielberger (Ed.), *Anxiety: Current trends in theory and research* (Vol. 2) (pp. 381–403). New York: Academic Press.

Schmeidler, G. R. (1973). PK effects upon continuously recorded temperature. *The Journal of the American Society for Psychical Research, 67,* 325–340.

Schulman, J. L., Kupst, M. J., & Suran, B. G. (1976). The worship of "*p*": Significant yet meaningless research results. *Bulletin of the Menninger Clinic, 40,* 134–143.

Schultz, D. P. (1969). The human subject in psychological research. *Psychological Bulletin, 72,* 214–228.

Schwabacher, S. (1972). Male vs. female representation in psychological research: An examination of the *Journal of Personality and Social Psychology,* 1970, 1971. *Catalogue of Selected Documents in Psychology, 2,* 20–21.

Sechrest, L., & Yeaton, W. (1981). Estimating magnitudes of experimental effects. *Catalog of Selected Documents in Psychology, 11,* (Ms 2355). Washington, DC: American Psychological Association.

Selltiz, C., Wrightsman, L. S., & Cook, S. W. (1976). *Research methods in social relations* (3rd ed.). New York: Holt, Rinehart and Winston.

Senders, V. L. (1958). *Measurement and statistics.* New York: Oxford University Press.

Shavelson, R. J. (1981). *Statistical reasoning for the behavioral sciences.* Boston: Allyn and Bacon.

Shine, L. C. II, & Bower, S. M. (1971). A one-way analysis of variance for single-subject designs. *Educational and Psychological Measurement, 31,* 105–113.

Siegel, S. (1956). *Nonparametric statistics for the behavioral sciences.* New York: McGraw-Hill.

Signorella, M. L., Vegega, M. E., & Mitchell, M. E. (1981). Subject selection and analyses for sex-related differences: 1968–1970 and 1975–1977. *American Psychologist, 36,* 988–990.

Skinner, B. F. (1960). Pigeons in a pelican. *American Psychologist, 15,* 28–37.

Skinner, B. F. (1975). The steep and thorny way to a science of behavior. *American Psychologist, 30,* 42–49.

Skipper, J. K., Jr., Guenther, A. L., & Nass, G. (1967). The sacredness of .05: A note concerning the uses of statistical levels of significance in social science. *The American Sociologist, 2,* 16–18.

Smart, R. (1966). Subject selection bias in psychological research. *Canadian Psychologist, 7a,* 115–121.

Smith, T. W., Snyder, C. R., & Handelsman, M. M. (1982). On the self-serving function of an academic wooden leg: Test anxiety as a self-handicapping strategy. *Journal of Personality and Social Psychology, 42,* 314–321.

Snowdon, C. T. (1982). Not all of our snarks are boojums. *Comparative Psychology Newsletter, 2*(1), 5–6.

Spielberger, C. D., Gorsuch, R. L., & Lushene, R. E. (1970). *State-trait anxiety inventory.* Palo Alto, CA: Consulting Psychologists Press.

Spielberger, C. D., & Smith, L. H. (1966). Anxiety (drive), stress, and serial-position effects in serial-verbal learning. *Journal of Experimental Psychology, 72,* 589–595.

Steiner, I. D. (1972). The evils of research: Or what my mother didn't tell me about the sins of academia. *American Psychologist, 27,* 766–768.

Stern, C. (1965). Thoughts on research. *Science, 148,* 772–773.

Stevens, S. S. (1951). Mathematics, measurement, and psychophysics. In S. S. Stevens (Ed.), *Handbook of experimental psychology* (pp. 1–49). New York: Wiley.

Stevens, S. S. (1957). On the psychophysical law. *Psychological Review, 64,* 153–181.

Stevens, S. S. (1962). The surprising simplicity of sensory metrics. *American Psychologist, 17,* 29–39.

Suarez, S. D., & Gallup, G. G., Jr. (1979). Tonic immobility as a response to rape in humans: A theoretical note. *The Psychological Record, 29,* 315–320.

Tallmadge, G. K., & Shearer, J. W. (1971). Interactive relationships among learner characteristics, types of learning, instructional methods, and subject matter variables. *Journal of Educational Psychology, 62,* 31–38.

Tedford, W. H., Jr., Hill, W. R., & Hensley, L. (1978). Human eye color and reaction time. *Perceptual and Motor Skills, 47,* 503–506.

Thigpen, C. H., & Cleckley, H. (1954). A case of multiple personality. *Journal of Abnormal and Social Psychology, 49,* 135–151.

Thomas, H. (1982). IQ, interval scales, and normal distributions. *Psychological Bulletin, 91,* 198–202.

Thompson, R. W., & Joseph, S. (1978). The effect of norepinephrine on tonic immobility in chickens. *Bulletin of the Psychonomic Society, 12,* 123–124.

Thorndike, R. L. (1966). *Thorndike dimensions of temperament.* New York: The Psychological Corporation.

Tukey, J. W. (1969). Analyzing data: Sanctification or detective work? *American Psychologist, 24,* 83–91.

Tukey, J. W. (1977). *Exploratory data analysis.* Reading, MA: Addison-Wesley.

Tunnell, G. B. (1977). Three dimensions of naturalness: An expanded definition of field research. *Psychological Bulletin, 84,* 426–437.

Underwood, B. J. (1975). Individual differences as a crucible in theory construction. *American Psychologist, 30,* 128–134.

Vandervert, L. R. (1980). Operational definitions made simple, lasting, and useful. *Teaching of Psychology, 7,* 57–59.

Völgyesi, F. A. (1966). *Animal hypnosis* (2nd ed.) (M. W. Hamilton, Trans.). Hollywood, CA: Wilshire.

Wade, N. (1976). IQ and heredity: Suspicion of fraud beclouds classic experiment. *Science, 194,* 916–919.

Wainer, H., & Thissen, D. (1981). Graphical data analysis. *Annual Review of Psychology, 32,* 191–241.

Walster, E., Walster, G. W., & Berscheid, E. (1978). *Equity: Theory and research.* Boston: Allyn and Bacon.

Webb, E. J., Campbell, D. T., Schwartz, R. D., & Sechrest, L. (1966). *Unobtrusive measures: Nonreactive research in the social sciences.* Chicago: Rand McNally.

Webb, W. B. (1961). The choice of the problem. *American Psychologist, 16,* 223–227.

Weber, S. J., & Cook, T. D. (1972). Subject effects in laboratory research: An examination of subject roles, demand characteristics, and valid inference. *Psychological Bulletin, 77,* 273–295.

Webster's ninth new collegiate dictionary. (1983). Springfield, MA: G. & C. Merriam.

White, M. A., & Duker, J. (1973). Suggested standards for children's samples. *American Psychologist, 28,* 700–703.

Wike, E. L., & Church, J. D. (1982). Nonrobustness in *F* tests: 1. A replication and extension of Bradley's study. *Bulletin of the Psychonomic Society, 20,* 165–167.

Willemsen, E. W. (1974). *Understanding statistical reasoning.* San Francisco: W. H. Freeman.

Winch, R. F., & Campbell, D. T. (1969). Proof? No. Evidence? Yes. The significance of tests of significance. *American Sociologist, 4,* 140–143.

Windholz, G., & Diamant, L. (1974). Some personality traits of believers in extraordinary phenomena. *Bulletin of the Psychonomic Society, 3,* 125–126.

Winer, B. J. (1971). *Statistical principles in experimental design* (2nd ed.). New York: McGraw-Hill.

Wolman, B. B. (1965). Toward a science of psychological science. In B. B. Wolman (Ed.), *Scientific psychology.* New York: Basic Books.

Yaremko, R. M., Harari, H., Harrison, R. C., & Lynn, E. (1982). *Reference handbook of research and statistical methods in psychology.* New York: Harper and Row.

Yerkes, R. M., & Dodson, J. D. (1908). The relation of strength of stimulus to rapidity of habit-formation. *Journal of Comparative Neurology and Psychology, 18,* 459–482.

Zimmer, J. (1978). Concerning ecology in counseling. *Journal of Counseling Psychology, 25,* 225–230.

Zusne, L., & Jones, W. H. (1982). *Anomalistic psychology.* Hillsdale, NJ: Erlbaum.

Appendix

Critical values of the t distribution for $\alpha = .05$ *and* $\alpha = .01$ *(two-tailed test).* **TABLE A–1**

df	$\alpha = .05$	$\alpha = .01$	df	$\alpha = .05$	$\alpha = .01$
1	12.706	63.657	18	2.101	2.878
2	4.303	9.925	19	2.093	2.861
3	3.182	5.841	20	2.086	2.845
4	2.776	4.604	21	2.080	2.831
5	2.571	4.032	22	2.074	2.819
6	2.447	3.707	23	2.069	2.807
7	2.365	3.499	24	2.064	2.797
8	2.306	3.355	25	2.060	2.787
9	2.262	3.250	26	2.056	2.779
10	2.228	3.169	27	2.052	2.771
11	2.201	3.106	28	2.048	2.763
12	2.179	3.055	29	2.045	2.756
13	2.160	3.012	30	2.042	2.750
14	2.145	2.977	40	2.021	2.704
15	2.131	2.947	60	2.000	2.660
16	2.120	2.921	120	1.980	2.617
17	2.110	2.898	∞	1.960	2.576

Reprinted with permission from Table IV.1, Percentage Points, Student's *t*-Distribution, *CRC Handbook of Tables for Probability and Statistics* (2nd ed.). Copyright 1968, CRC Press, Inc., Boca Raton, Florida.

TABLE A-2   *Critical values of the F distribution for α = .05.*

Degrees of freedom for the numerator

denom	1	2	3	4	5	6	7	8	9	10	12	15	20	24	30	40	60	120	∞
1	161.4	199.5	215.7	224.6	230.2	234.0	236.8	238.9	240.5	241.9	243.9	245.9	248.0	249.1	250.1	251.1	252.2	253.3	254.3
2	18.51	19.00	19.16	19.25	19.30	19.33	19.35	19.37	19.38	19.40	19.41	19.43	19.45	19.45	19.46	19.47	19.48	19.49	19.50
3	10.13	9.55	9.28	9.12	9.01	8.94	8.89	8.85	8.81	8.79	8.74	8.70	8.66	8.64	8.62	8.59	8.57	8.55	8.53
4	7.71	6.94	6.59	6.39	6.26	6.16	6.09	6.04	6.00	5.96	5.91	5.86	5.80	5.77	5.75	5.72	5.69	5.66	5.63
5	6.61	5.79	5.41	5.19	5.05	4.95	4.88	4.82	4.77	4.74	4.68	4.62	4.56	4.53	4.50	4.46	4.43	4.40	4.36
6	5.99	5.14	4.76	4.53	4.39	4.28	4.21	4.15	4.10	4.06	4.00	3.94	3.87	3.84	3.81	3.77	3.74	3.70	3.67
7	5.59	4.74	4.35	4.12	3.97	3.87	3.79	3.73	3.68	3.64	3.57	3.51	3.44	3.41	3.38	3.34	3.30	3.27	3.23
8	5.32	4.46	4.07	3.84	3.69	3.58	3.50	3.44	3.39	3.35	3.28	3.22	3.15	3.12	3.08	3.04	3.01	2.97	2.93
9	5.12	4.26	3.86	3.63	3.48	3.37	3.29	3.23	3.18	3.14	3.07	3.01	2.94	2.90	2.86	2.83	2.79	2.75	2.71
10	4.96	4.10	3.71	3.48	3.33	3.22	3.14	3.07	3.02	2.98	2.91	2.85	2.77	2.74	2.70	2.66	2.62	2.58	2.54
11	4.84	3.98	3.59	3.36	3.20	3.09	3.01	2.95	2.90	2.85	2.79	2.72	2.65	2.61	2.57	2.53	2.49	2.45	2.40
12	4.75	3.89	3.49	3.26	3.11	3.00	2.91	2.85	2.80	2.75	2.69	2.62	2.54	2.51	2.47	2.43	2.38	2.34	2.30
13	4.67	3.81	3.41	3.18	3.03	2.92	2.83	2.77	2.71	2.67	2.60	2.53	2.46	2.42	2.38	2.34	2.30	2.25	2.21
14	4.60	3.74	3.34	3.11	2.96	2.85	2.76	2.70	2.65	2.60	2.53	2.46	2.39	2.35	2.31	2.27	2.22	2.18	2.13
15	4.54	3.68	3.29	3.06	2.90	2.79	2.71	2.64	2.59	2.54	2.48	2.40	2.33	2.29	2.25	2.20	2.16	2.11	2.07
16	4.49	3.63	3.24	3.01	2.85	2.74	2.66	2.59	2.54	2.49	2.42	2.35	2.28	2.24	2.19	2.15	2.11	2.06	2.01
17	4.45	3.59	3.20	2.96	2.81	2.70	2.61	2.55	2.49	2.45	2.38	2.31	2.23	2.19	2.15	2.10	2.06	2.01	1.96
18	4.41	3.55	3.16	2.93	2.77	2.66	2.58	2.51	2.46	2.41	2.34	2.27	2.19	2.15	2.11	2.06	2.02	1.97	1.92
19	4.38	3.52	3.13	2.90	2.74	2.63	2.54	2.48	2.42	2.38	2.31	2.23	2.16	2.11	2.07	2.03	1.98	1.93	1.88
20	4.35	3.49	3.10	2.87	2.71	2.60	2.51	2.45	2.39	2.35	2.28	2.20	2.12	2.08	2.04	1.99	1.95	1.90	1.84
21	4.32	3.47	3.07	2.84	2.68	2.57	2.49	2.42	2.37	2.32	2.25	2.18	2.10	2.05	2.01	1.96	1.92	1.87	1.81
22	4.30	3.44	3.05	2.82	2.66	2.55	2.46	2.40	2.34	2.30	2.23	2.15	2.07	2.03	1.98	1.94	1.89	1.84	1.78
23	4.28	3.42	3.03	2.80	2.64	2.53	2.44	2.37	2.32	2.27	2.20	2.13	2.05	2.01	1.96	1.91	1.86	1.81	1.76
24	4.26	3.40	3.01	2.78	2.62	2.51	2.42	2.36	2.30	2.25	2.18	2.11	2.03	1.98	1.94	1.89	1.84	1.79	1.73
25	4.24	3.39	2.99	2.76	2.60	2.49	2.40	2.34	2.28	2.24	2.16	2.09	2.01	1.96	1.92	1.87	1.82	1.77	1.71
26	4.23	3.37	2.98	2.74	2.59	2.47	2.39	2.32	2.27	2.22	2.15	2.07	1.99	1.95	1.90	1.85	1.80	1.75	1.69
27	4.21	3.35	2.96	2.73	2.57	2.46	2.37	2.31	2.25	2.20	2.13	2.06	1.97	1.93	1.88	1.84	1.79	1.73	1.67
28	4.20	3.34	2.95	2.71	2.56	2.45	2.36	2.29	2.24	2.19	2.12	2.04	1.96	1.91	1.87	1.82	1.77	1.71	1.65
29	4.18	3.33	2.93	2.70	2.55	2.43	2.35	2.28	2.22	2.18	2.10	2.03	1.94	1.90	1.85	1.81	1.75	1.70	1.64
30	4.17	3.32	2.92	2.69	2.53	2.42	2.33	2.27	2.21	2.16	2.09	2.01	1.93	1.89	1.84	1.79	1.74	1.68	1.62
40	4.08	3.23	2.84	2.61	2.45	2.34	2.25	2.18	2.12	2.08	2.00	1.92	1.84	1.79	1.74	1.69	1.64	1.58	1.51
60	4.00	3.15	2.76	2.53	2.37	2.25	2.17	2.10	2.04	1.99	1.92	1.84	1.75	1.70	1.65	1.59	1.53	1.47	1.39
120	3.92	3.07	2.68	2.45	2.29	2.17	2.09	2.02	1.96	1.91	1.83	1.75	1.66	1.61	1.55	1.50	1.43	1.35	1.25
∞	3.84	3.00	2.60	2.37	2.21	2.10	2.01	1.94	1.88	1.83	1.75	1.67	1.57	1.52	1.46	1.39	1.32	1.22	1.00

Degrees of freedom for the denominator

Reprinted with permission from Table VI.1, Percentage Points, *F*-Distribution, *CRC Handbook of Tables for Probability and Statistics* (2nd ed.). Copyright 1968, CRC Press, Inc., Boca Raton, Florida.

514

TABLE A-2   *Critical values of the F distribution for* $\alpha = .01$.

Degrees of freedom for the numerator

Degrees of freedom for the denominator	1	2	3	4	5	6	7	8	9	10	12	15	20	24	30	40	60	120	∞
1	4052	4999.5	5403	5625	5764	5859	5928	5982	6022	6056	6106	6157	6209	6235	6261	6287	6313	6339	6366
2	98.50	99.00	99.17	99.25	99.30	99.33	99.36	99.37	99.39	99.40	99.42	99.43	99.45	99.46	99.47	99.47	99.48	99.49	99.50
3	34.12	30.82	29.46	28.71	28.24	27.91	27.67	27.49	27.35	27.23	27.05	26.87	26.69	26.60	26.50	26.41	26.32	26.22	26.13
4	21.20	18.00	16.69	15.98	15.52	15.21	14.98	14.80	14.66	14.55	14.37	14.20	14.02	13.93	13.84	13.75	13.65	13.56	13.46
5	16.26	13.27	12.06	11.39	10.97	10.67	10.46	10.29	10.16	10.05	9.89	9.72	9.55	9.47	9.38	9.29	9.20	9.11	9.02
6	13.75	10.92	9.78	9.15	8.75	8.47	8.26	8.10	7.98	7.87	7.72	7.56	7.40	7.31	7.23	7.14	7.06	6.97	6.88
7	12.25	9.55	8.45	7.85	7.46	7.19	6.99	6.84	6.72	6.62	6.47	6.31	6.16	6.07	5.99	5.91	5.82	5.74	5.65
8	11.26	8.65	7.59	7.01	6.63	6.37	6.18	6.03	5.91	5.81	5.67	5.52	5.36	5.28	5.20	5.12	5.03	4.95	4.86
9	10.56	8.02	6.99	6.42	6.06	5.80	5.61	5.47	5.35	5.26	5.11	4.96	4.81	4.73	4.65	4.57	4.48	4.40	4.31
10	10.04	7.56	6.55	5.99	5.64	5.39	5.20	5.06	4.94	4.85	4.71	4.56	4.41	4.33	4.25	4.17	4.08	4.00	3.91
11	9.65	7.21	6.22	5.67	5.32	5.07	4.89	4.74	4.63	4.54	4.40	4.25	4.10	4.02	3.94	3.86	3.78	3.69	3.60
12	9.33	6.93	5.95	5.41	5.06	4.82	4.64	4.50	4.39	4.30	4.16	4.01	3.86	3.78	3.70	3.62	3.54	3.45	3.36
13	9.07	6.70	5.74	5.21	4.86	4.62	4.44	4.30	4.19	4.10	3.96	3.82	3.66	3.59	3.51	3.43	3.34	3.25	3.17
14	8.86	6.51	5.56	5.04	4.69	4.46	4.28	4.14	4.03	3.94	3.80	3.66	3.51	3.43	3.35	3.27	3.18	3.09	3.00
15	8.68	6.36	5.42	4.89	4.56	4.32	4.14	4.00	3.89	3.80	3.67	3.52	3.37	3.29	3.21	3.13	3.05	2.96	2.87
16	8.53	6.23	5.29	4.77	4.44	4.20	4.03	3.89	3.78	3.69	3.55	3.41	3.26	3.18	3.10	3.02	2.93	2.84	2.75
17	8.40	6.11	5.18	4.67	4.34	4.10	3.93	3.79	3.68	3.59	3.46	3.31	3.16	3.08	3.00	2.92	2.83	2.75	2.65
18	8.29	6.01	5.09	4.58	4.25	4.01	3.84	3.71	3.60	3.51	3.37	3.23	3.08	3.00	2.92	2.84	2.75	2.66	2.57
19	8.18	5.93	5.01	4.50	4.17	3.94	3.77	3.63	3.52	3.43	3.30	3.15	3.00	2.92	2.84	2.76	2.67	2.58	2.49
20	8.10	5.85	4.94	4.43	4.10	3.87	3.70	3.56	3.46	3.37	3.23	3.09	2.94	2.86	2.78	2.69	2.61	2.52	2.42
21	8.02	5.78	4.87	4.37	4.04	3.81	3.64	3.51	3.40	3.31	3.17	3.03	2.88	2.80	2.72	2.64	2.55	2.46	2.36
22	7.95	5.72	4.82	4.31	3.99	3.76	3.59	3.45	3.35	3.26	3.12	2.98	2.83	2.75	2.67	2.58	2.50	2.40	2.31
23	7.88	5.66	4.76	4.26	3.94	3.71	3.54	3.41	3.30	3.21	3.07	2.93	2.78	2.70	2.62	2.54	2.45	2.35	2.26
24	7.82	5.61	4.72	4.22	3.90	3.67	3.50	3.36	3.26	3.17	3.03	2.89	2.74	2.66	2.58	2.49	2.40	2.31	2.21
25	7.77	5.57	4.68	4.18	3.85	3.63	3.46	3.32	3.22	3.13	2.99	2.85	2.70	2.62	2.54	2.45	2.36	2.27	2.17
26	7.72	5.53	4.64	4.14	3.82	3.59	3.42	3.29	3.18	3.09	2.96	2.81	2.66	2.58	2.50	2.42	2.33	2.23	2.13
27	7.68	5.49	4.60	4.11	3.78	3.56	3.39	3.26	3.15	3.06	2.93	2.78	2.63	2.55	2.47	2.38	2.29	2.20	2.10
28	7.64	5.45	4.57	4.07	3.75	3.53	3.36	3.23	3.12	3.03	2.90	2.75	2.60	2.52	2.44	2.35	2.26	2.17	2.06
29	7.60	5.42	4.54	4.04	3.73	3.50	3.33	3.20	3.09	3.00	2.87	2.73	2.57	2.49	2.41	2.33	2.23	2.14	2.03
30	7.56	5.39	4.51	4.02	3.70	3.47	3.30	3.17	3.07	2.98	2.84	2.70	2.55	2.47	2.39	2.30	2.21	2.11	2.01
40	7.31	5.18	4.31	3.83	3.51	3.29	3.12	2.99	2.89	2.80	2.66	2.52	2.37	2.29	2.20	2.11	2.02	1.92	1.80
60	7.08	4.98	4.13	3.65	3.34	3.12	2.95	2.82	2.72	2.63	2.50	2.35	2.20	2.12	2.03	1.94	1.84	1.73	1.60
120	6.85	4.79	3.95	3.48	3.17	2.96	2.79	2.66	2.56	2.47	2.34	2.19	2.03	1.95	1.86	1.76	1.66	1.53	1.38
∞	6.63	4.61	3.78	3.32	3.02	2.80	2.64	2.51	2.41	2.32	2.18	2.04	1.88	1.79	1.70	1.59	1.47	1.32	1.00

Reprinted with permission from Table VI.1, Percentage Points, *F*-Distribution, *CRC Handbook of Tables for Probability and Statistics* (2nd ed.). Copyright 1968, CRC Press, Inc., Boca Raton, Florida.

TABLE A-3   *Values of the studentized range statistic q_k, for $\alpha = .05$.*

		2	3	4	5	6	7	8	9	10
		\multicolumn{9}{c}{*Number of means being compared*}								
	1	17.97	26.98	32.82	37.08	40.41	43.12	45.40	47.36	49.07
	2	6.08	8.33	9.80	10.88	11.74	12.44	13.03	13.54	13.99
	3	4.50	5.91	6.82	7.50	8.04	8.48	8.85	9.18	9.46
	4	3.93	5.04	5.76	6.29	6.71	7.05	7.35	7.60	7.83
	5	3.64	4.60	5.22	5.67	6.03	6.33	6.58	6.80	6.99
	6	3.46	4.34	4.90	5.30	5.63	5.90	6.12	6.32	6.49
	7	3.34	4.16	4.68	5.06	5.36	5.61	5.82	6.00	6.16
Degrees	8	3.26	4.04	4.53	4.89	5.17	5.40	5.60	5.77	5.92
of	9	3.20	3.95	4.41	4.76	5.02	5.24	5.43	5.59	5.74
freedom	10	3.15	3.88	4.33	4.65	4.91	5.12	5.30	5.46	5.60
for	11	3.11	3.82	4.26	4.57	4.82	5.03	5.20	5.35	5.49
MS_{Error}	12	3.08	3.77	4.20	4.51	4.75	4.95	5.12	5.27	5.39
	13	3.06	3.73	4.15	4.45	4.69	4.88	5.05	5.19	5.32
	14	3.03	3.70	4.11	4.41	4.64	4.83	4.99	5.13	5.25
	15	3.01	3.67	4.08	4.37	4.59	4.78	4.94	5.08	5.20
	16	3.00	3.65	4.05	4.33	4.56	4.74	4.90	5.03	5.15
	17	2.98	3.63	4.02	4.30	4.52	4.70	4.86	4.99	5.11
	18	2.97	3.61	4.00	4.28	4.49	4.67	4.82	4.96	5.07
	19	2.96	3.59	3.98	4.25	4.47	4.65	4.79	4.92	5.04
	20	2.95	3.58	3.96	4.23	4.45	4.62	4.77	4.90	5.01
	24	2.92	3.53	3.90	4.17	4.37	4.54	4.68	4.81	4.92
	30	2.89	3.49	3.85	4.10	4.30	4.46	4.60	4.72	4.82
	40	2.86	3.44	3.79	4.04	4.23	4.39	4.52	4.63	4.73
	60	2.83	3.40	3.74	3.98	4.16	4.31	4.44	4.55	4.65
	120	2.80	3.36	3.68	3.92	4.10	4.24	4.36	4.47	4.56
	∞	2.77	3.31	3.63	3.86	4.03	4.17	4.29	4.39	4.47

Values of the studentized range statistic q_k, for $\alpha = .01$.   **TABLE A-3**

		Number of means being compared								
		2	3	4	5	6	7	8	9	10
	1	90.03	135.0	164.3	185.6	202.2	215.8	227.2	237.0	245.6
	2	14.04	19.02	22.29	24.72	26.63	28.20	29.53	30.68	31.69
	3	8.26	10.62	12.17	13.33	14.24	15.00	15.64	16.20	16.69
	4	6.51	8.12	9.17	9.96	10.58	11.10	11.55	11.93	12.27
	5	5.70	6.98	7.80	8.42	8.91	9.32	9.67	9.97	10.24
	6	5.24	6.33	7.03	7.56	7.97	8.32	8.61	8.87	9.10
	7	4.95	5.92	6.54	7.01	7.37	7.68	7.94	8.17	8.37
Degrees	8	4.75	5.64	6.20	6.62	6.96	7.24	7.47	7.68	7.86
of	9	4.60	5.43	5.96	6.35	6.66	6.91	7.13	7.33	7.49
freedom	10	4.48	5.27	5.77	6.14	6.43	6.67	6.87	7.05	7.21
for	11	4.39	5.15	5.62	5.97	6.25	6.48	6.67	6.84	6.99
MS_{Error}	12	4.32	5.05	5.50	5.84	6.10	6.32	6.51	6.67	6.81
	13	4.26	4.96	5.40	5.73	5.98	6.19	6.37	6.53	6.67
	14	4.21	4.89	5.32	5.63	5.88	6.08	6.26	6.41	6.54
	15	4.17	4.84	5.25	5.56	5.80	5.99	6.16	6.31	6.44
	16	4.13	4.79	5.19	5.49	5.72	5.92	6.08	6.22	6.35
	17	4.10	4.74	5.14	5.43	5.66	5.85	6.01	6.15	6.27
	18	4.07	4.70	5.09	5.38	5.60	5.79	5.94	6.08	6.20
	19	4.05	4.67	5.05	5.33	5.55	5.73	5.89	6.02	6.14
	20	4.02	4.64	5.02	5.29	5.51	5.69	5.84	5.97	6.09
	24	3.96	4.55	4.91	5.17	5.37	5.54	5.69	5.81	5.92
	30	3.89	4.45	4.80	5.05	5.24	5.40	5.54	5.65	5.76
	40	3.82	4.37	4.70	4.93	5.11	5.26	5.39	5.50	5.60
	60	3.76	4.28	4.59	4.82	4.99	5.13	5.25	5.36	5.45
	120	3.70	4.20	4.50	4.71	4.87	5.01	5.12	5.21	5.30
	∞	3.64	4.12	4.40	4.60	4.76	4.88	4.99	5.08	5.16

TABLE A-4   *Critical values of r for* $\alpha = .05$ *and* $\alpha = .01$ *(two-tailed test).*

df^a	$\alpha = .05$	$\alpha = .01$
1	.99692	.999877
2	.9500	.99000
3	.878	.9587
4	.811	.9172
5	.754	.875
6	.707	.834
7	.666	.798
8	.632	.765
9	.602	.735
10	.576	.708
11	.553	.684
12	.532	.661
13	.514	.641
14	.497	.623
15	.482	.606
16	.468	.590
17	.456	.575
18	.444	.561
19	.433	.549
20	.423	.537
25	.381	.487
30	.349	.449
35	.325	.418
40	.304	.393
45	.288	.372
50	.273	.354
60	.250	.325
70	.232	.302
80	.217	.283
90	.205	.267
100	.195	.254

[a] df are equal to $N - 2$ where N is the number of paired observations.

Reprinted with permission from Table IX.1, Percentage Points, Distribution of the Correlation Coefficient, When $\rho = 0$, *CRC Handbook of Tables for Probability and Statistics* (2nd ed.). Copyright 1968, CRC Press, Inc., Boca Raton, Florida.

Critical values of U in the Mann-Whitney test for $\alpha = .05$ *(two-tailed test). If the group sizes are unequal, n_1 is the smaller group.*   **TABLE A-5**

		n_2																		
		1	2	3	4	5	6	7	8	9	10	11	12	13	14	15	16	17	18	19	20
	1																				
	2								0	0	0	0	1	1	1	1	1	2	2	2	2
	3				0	1	1	2	2	3	3	4	4	5	5	6	6	7	7	8
	4			0	1	2	3	4	4	5	6	7	8	9	10	11	11	12	13	13
	5		0	1	2	3	5	6	7	8	9	11	12	13	14	15	17	18	19	20
	6		1	2	3	5	6	8	10	11	13	14	16	17	19	21	22	24	25	27
	7		1	3	5	6	8	10	12	14	16	18	20	22	24	26	28	30	32	34
n_1	8	0	2	4	6	8	10	13	15	17	19	22	24	26	29	31	34	36	38	41
	9	0	2	4	7	10	12	15	17	20	23	26	28	31	34	37	39	42	45	48
	10	0	3	5	8	11	14	17	20	23	26	29	33	36	39	42	45	48	52	55
	11	0	3	6	9	13	16	19	23	26	30	33	37	40	44	47	51	55	58	62
	12	1	4	7	11	14	18	22	26	29	33	37	41	45	49	53	57	61	65	69
	13	1	4	8	12	16	20	24	28	33	37	41	45	50	54	59	63	67	72	76
	14	1	5	9	13	17	22	26	31	36	40	45	50	55	59	64	67	74	78	83
	15	1	5	10	14	19	24	29	34	39	44	49	54	59	64	70	75	80	85	90
	16	1	6	11	15	21	26	31	37	42	47	53	59	64	70	75	81	86	92	98
	17	2	6	11	17	22	28	34	39	45	51	57	63	67	75	81	87	93	99	105
	18	2	7	12	18	24	30	36	42	48	55	61	67	74	80	86	93	99	106	112
	19	2	7	13	19	25	32	38	45	52	58	65	72	78	85	92	99	106	113	119
	20	2	8	13	20	27	34	41	48	55	62	69	76	83	90	98	105	112	119	127

TABLE A–5   *Critical values of U in the Mann-Whitney test for* $\alpha = .01$ *(two-tailed test). If the group sizes are unequal, n_1 is the smaller group.*

											n_2									
	1	2	3	4	5	6	7	8	9	10	11	12	13	14	15	16	17	18	19	20
1																				
2																			0	0
3									0	0	0	1	1	1	2	2	2	2	3	3
4					0	0	1	1	2	2	3	3	4	5	5	6	6	7	8
5				0	1	1	2	3	4	5	6	7	7	8	9	10	11	12	13
6			0	1	2	3	4	5	6	7	9	10	11	12	13	15	16	17	18
7			0	1	3	4	6	7	9	10	12	13	15	16	18	19	21	22	24
8			1	2	4	6	7	9	11	13	15	17	18	20	22	24	26	28	30
9		0	1	3	5	7	9	11	13	16	18	20	22	24	27	29	31	33	36
10		0	2	4	6	9	11	13	16	18	21	24	26	29	31	34	37	39	42
11		0	2	5	7	10	13	16	18	21	24	27	30	33	36	39	42	45	48
12		1	3	6	9	12	15	18	21	24	27	31	34	37	41	44	47	51	54
13		1	3	7	10	13	17	20	24	27	31	34	38	42	45	49	53	56	60
14		1	4	7	11	15	18	22	26	30	34	38	42	46	50	54	58	63	67
15		2	5	8	12	16	20	24	29	33	37	42	46	51	55	60	64	69	73
16		2	5	9	13	18	22	27	31	36	41	45	50	55	60	65	70	74	79
17		2	6	10	15	19	24	29	34	39	44	49	54	60	65	70	75	81	86
18		2	6	11	16	21	26	31	37	42	47	53	58	64	70	75	81	87	92
19	0	3	7	12	17	22	28	33	39	45	51	56	63	69	74	81	87	93	99
20	0	3	8	13	18	24	30	36	42	48	54	60	67	73	79	86	92	99	105

n_1 (row label, left side)

Reprinted with permission from Table X.4, Critical Values of *U* in the Wilcoxon (Mann-Whitney) Two-Sample Statistic, *CRC Handbook of Tables for Probability and Statistics* (2nd ed.). Copyright 1968, CRC Press, Inc., Boca Raton, Florida.

Selected critical values of the Kruskal-Wallis H statistic for three groups with n ≤ 5 in each group. Obtained values of H equal to or greater than the tabled value are significant at the .05 level. For group sizes not listed, no value of H is significant at .05.

Group sizes			
n_{A_1}	n_{A_2}	n_{A_3}	Value of H
3	2	2	4.714
3	3	1	5.143
3	3	2	5.361
3	3	3	5.600
4	2	2	5.333
4	3	1	5.208
4	3	2	5.444
4	3	3	5.727
4	4	1	4.967
4	4	2	5.455
4	4	3	5.599
4	4	4	5.692
5	2	1	5.000
5	2	2	5.160
5	3	1	4.960
5	3	2	5.251
5	3	3	5.649
5	4	1	4.986
5	4	2	5.273
5	4	3	5.631
5	4	4	5.618
5	5	1	5.127
5	5	2	5.339
5	5	3	5.706
5	5	4	5.643
5	5	5	5.780

TABLE A-7   *Critical values of T in the Wilcoxon Test for $\alpha = .05$ and $\alpha = .01$ (two-tailed test). A —*
indicates significance cannot be obtained at this level.

n	$\alpha = .05$	$\alpha = .01$	n	$\alpha = .05$	$\alpha = .01$
6	1	—	29	127	100
7	2	—	30	137	109
8	4	0	31	148	118
9	6	2	32	159	128
10	8	3	33	171	138
11	11	5	34	183	149
12	14	7	35	195	160
13	17	10	36	208	171
14	21	13	37	222	183
15	25	16	38	235	195
16	30	19	39	250	208
17	35	23	40	264	221
18	40	28	41	279	234
19	46	32	42	295	248
20	52	37	43	311	262
21	59	43	44	327	277
22	66	49	45	344	292
23	73	55	46	361	307
24	81	61	47	379	323
25	90	68	48	397	339
26	98	76	49	415	356
27	107	84	50	434	373
28	117	92			

Excerpted and adapted from Table X.2, Critical Values of T in the Wilcoxon Matched-Pairs Signed-Ranks Test. *CRC Handbook of Tables for Probability and Statistics* (2nd ed.). Copyright 1968, CRC Press, Inc., Boca Raton, Florida. Used by permission.

TABLE A-8   *Critical values of χ_r^2 for the Friedman Test for $a = 3$ with n between 3 and 9, and $a = 4$*
with n between 2 and 4. Obtained values of χ_r^2 equal to or greater than the tabled value
are significant at the .05 level.

$a = 3$		$a = 4$	
n	χ_r^2	n	χ_r^2
3	6.000	2	6.000
4	6.500	3	7.400
5	6.400	4	7.800
6	7.000		
7	7.143		
8	6.250		
9	6.222		

Excerpted from Table N in *Nonparametric Statistics* by S. Siegel. Copyright 1956 by McGraw-Hill, New York, New York. Used by permission.

Critical values of the chi square distribution for $\alpha = .05$ *and* $\alpha = .01$.   **TABLE A–9**

df	$\alpha = .05$	$\alpha = .01$
1	3.84	6.63
2	5.99	9.21
3	7.81	11.3
4	9.49	13.3
5	11.1	15.1
6	12.6	16.8
7	14.1	18.5
8	15.5	20.1
9	16.9	21.7
10	18.3	23.2
11	19.7	24.7
12	21.0	26.2
13	22.4	27.7
14	23.7	29.1
15	25.0	30.6
16	26.3	32.0
17	27.6	33.4
18	28.9	34.8
19	30.1	36.2
20	31.4	37.6
21	32.7	38.9
22	33.9	40.3
23	35.2	41.6
24	36.4	43.0
25	37.7	44.3
26	38.9	45.6
27	40.1	47.0
28	41.3	48.3
29	42.6	49.6
30	43.8	50.9

TABLE A-10   *Critical values of Spearman's rank-order correlation coefficient.*

N	$\alpha = .05$	$\alpha = .01$
5	——	——
6	0.886	——
7	0.786	0.929
8	0.738	0.881
9	0.700	0.833
10	0.648	0.794
11	0.618	0.818
12	0.591	0.780
13	0.566	0.745
14	0.545	0.716
15	0.525	0.689
16	0.507	0.666
17	0.490	0.645
18	0.476	0.625
19	0.462	0.608
20	0.450	0.591
21	0.438	0.576
22	0.428	0.562
23	0.418	0.549
24	0.409	0.537
25	0.400	0.526
26	0.392	0.515
27	0.385	0.505
28	0.377	0.496
29	0.370	0.487
30	0.364	0.478

Name Index

Subject Index*

*Page numbers for definitions are in italics.